NATIONAL CENTER FOR EDUCATION STATISTICS

THE **CONDITION**
OF **EDUCATION**
1996

D1450708

Thomas M. Smith
Beth Aronstamm Young
Susan P. Choy
Marianne Perie
Nabeel Alsalam
Mary R. Rollefson
Yupin Bae

with contributions by

Martha Naomi Alt
Lutz K. Berkner
Stephanie Cuccaro-Alamin
Paul T. Decker
Robert Fitzgerald
Mark C. Glander
Laura J. Horn
Phil Kaufman
Steven G. Klein
Alexander C. McCormick
Elliott A. Medrich
Sheau-Hue Shieh
Greg W. Steadman
Stephen R. Wenck

For sale by the U.S. Government Printing Office
Superintendent of Documents, Mail Stop: SSOP, Washington, DC 20402-9328
ISBN 0-16-048679-3

U.S. Department of Education
Office of Educational Research and Improvement   NCES 96-304

U.S. Department of Education
Richard W. Riley
Secretary

Office of Educational Research and Improvement
Sharon P. Robinson
Assistant Secretary

National Center for Education Statistics
Jeanne E. Griffith
Acting Commissioner

The National Center for Education Statistics (NCES) is the primary federal entity for collecting, analyzing, and reporting data related to education in the United States and other nations. It fulfills a congressional mandate to collect, collate, analyze, and report full and complete statistics on the condition of education in the United States; conduct and publish reports and specialized analyses of the meaning and significance of such statistics; assist state and local education agencies in improving their statistical systems; and review and report on education activities in foreign countries.

NCES activities are designed to address high priority education data needs; provide consistent, reliable, complete, and accurate indicators of education status and trends; and report timely, useful, and high quality data to the U.S. Department of Education, the Congress, the states, other education policymakers, practitioners, data users, and the general public.

We strive to make our products available in a variety of formats and in language that is appropriate to a variety of audiences. You, as our customer, are the best judge of our success in communicating information effectively. If you have any comments or suggestions about this or any other NCES product or report, we would like to hear from you. Please direct your comments to:

> National Center for Education Statistics
> Office of Educational Research and Improvement
> U.S. Department of Education
> 555 New Jersey Avenue NW
> Washington, DC 20208–5574

Suggested Citation

U.S. Department of Education. National Center for Education Statistics. *The Condition of Education 1996*, NCES 96–304, by Thomas M. Smith. Washington, D.C.: U.S. Government Printing Office, 1996.

June 1996

Editorial and Production Staff

Managing Editor:	Rebecca Pratt Mahoney, Pinkerton Computer Consultants, Inc.
Editors:	Ginger G. Rittenhouse, Pinkerton Computer Consultants, Inc.
	Andrea M. Livingston and Karyn Madden, MPR Associates, Inc.

The National Center for Education Statistics (NCES) gathers and publishes information on the status and progress of education in the United States. The congressional authorization for these activities (with antecedents to 1867) states that the purpose of the Center is to collect and report "...statistics and information showing the condition and progress of education in the United States and other nations in order to promote and accelerate the improvement of American education."—Section 402(b) of the National Education Statistics Act of 1994 (20 U.S.C. 9001). This law also mandates an annual statistical report on the subject from the Commissioner of Education Statistics. This 1996 edition of *The Condition of Education* responds to the requirements of that law.

This report contains 60 indicators that shed light on the condition of education in the United States. These indicators represent a consensus of professional thinking on the most significant national measures of the condition and progress of education to date, but tempered by the availability of current, valid information. In the text that follows, I will summarize some of the positive developments in American education and point out areas that continue to raise concern. In addition, I will discuss what we know about school quality and describe how the conditions facing the schools have changed.

For some issues of public concern, however, there are no data available that can provide a satisfactory national picture of recent educational developments. One such area where additional work remains is in developing measures of learner outcomes that go beyond the core content areas. These might include measures of integrative reasoning and curriculum exposure. A second area where work remains is in developing better measures of school quality and student learning opportunities.[1]

♦ *What are high school students studying and how are they performing?*

In the 13 years since *A Nation at Risk* advocated tougher course requirements for high school graduation, states and students have responded dramatically. **High school graduates are taking more courses overall, particularly academic courses.**[2] The proportion of students completing

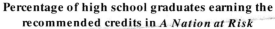

Percentage of high school graduates earning the recommended credits in *A Nation at Risk*

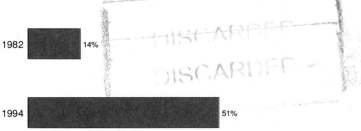

the "New Basics" curriculum in English, mathematics, science, and social studies has increased (*Indicator 28*), and a greater percentage of students are taking Advanced Placement (AP) courses.[3]

In addition, **more students are taking geometry, trigonometry, and calculus as well as advanced science courses, including chemistry and physics** (*Indicator 29*). Both college-bound and non-college-bound students are taking more foreign language courses than their counterparts did a decade before.[4] Furthermore, as of 1990, 42 of the 50 states had raised course requirements for high school graduation since the publication of *A Nation at Risk*, and 47 states had mandated student testing standards.[5] Of course, these increases can only be considered good news if the content of these courses is at least as rigorous as it was when the National Commission on Excellence in Education made their recommendations. There is some evidence that it is, but we have no national data on the content of courses.[6]

It is also encouraging to see these improvements in high school course taking reflected in **gains in mathematics and science achievement**. Between

Mathematics proficiency scores of students

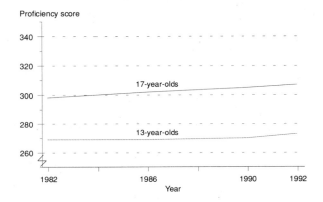

1982 and 1992, the mathematics and science proficiency scores of 17-year-olds on the National Assessment of Educational Progress (NAEP)

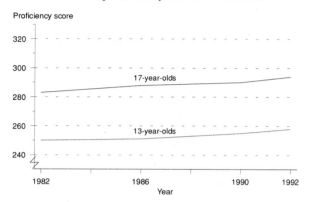

Science proficiency scores of students

increased (9 scale points on each assessment). One way to get an idea of how much improvement these gains represent is to compare them to variations in proficiencies between different-aged high school students. Using this comparison, the improvement for 17-year-olds from 1982 to 1992 was roughly equivalent to an additional year or more of learning in high school (*Indicators 15* and *16*). These gains in NAEP proficiency scores are one indication that 17-year-olds in 1992 had made substantial progress in mathematics and science relative to their peers in 1982.

Although proficiency scores in reading and writing have not shown similar increases,[7] **U.S. students compared favorably to their counterparts in other countries on an international assessment of basic reading literacy in 1991–92** (*Indicator 20*). In an international comparison of the literacy skills of adults in 1994, the United States had a large concentration of adults score at the highest levels on the prose literacy domain. The United States also had a greater concentration of adults score at the lowest levels of literacy than most of the other countries, however (*Indicator 21*).

Supporting this finding of generally favorable performance of the nation's students in reading literacy, low performing students have also progressed academically since the publication of *A Nation at Risk*. For example, **dropout rates have declined** (*Indicator 5*), and a greater percentage of dropouts are returning to earn a diploma or GED

within 2 years of their scheduled graduation (*Indicator 6*); **fewer high school students are taking remedial mathematics courses before graduating;**[8] and the **mathematics and science proficiencies of the lowest performing 17-year-olds have increased** (tables 15-3 and 16-3). However, between 1984 and 1992, the reading and writing proficiencies of the lowest performing students remained relatively stable,[9] and between 1992 and 1994, the reading performance of the poorest performing 12th-graders fell,[10] just as it did for all 12th-graders (*Indicator 15*).

At the same time that **more students are taking AP examinations** the **science proficiency scores of the highest performing 17-year-olds have increased** (table 16-3). In addition, since the early 1980s, the mathematics proficiency scores of the highest performing 17-year-olds have remained relatively stable (table 15-3).

It is significant that even though the number of Scholastic Assessment Test (SAT) test-takers as a percentage of high school graduates has increased almost 9 percentage points since 1983, the average mathematics score has increased 14 points, and the average verbal score has increased 3 points (*Indicator 22*). These findings are considered by many to be particularly positive because increasing participation tends to push down scores.

When examining differences in averages across NAEP scores, we should keep in mind that the

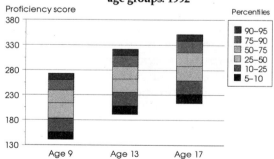

Distribution of reading proficiency within age groups: 1992

performance among students of the same age or in the same grade varies considerably. For example, in reading, mathematics, and science, many students score no higher at age 17 than many of their peers did at age 9, despite the fact that they differ by 8 years of schooling.[11] Schools must cope with this variation while trying to help each student learn as much as possible. It is not surprising, then, that there is also much variation across schools in the type of curriculum offered to students with different abilities and interests.[12]

As a nation, we put great value on mathematics and science. Recently, this has been expressed in Goal 5 of the National Education Goals: "U.S. students will be first in the world in science and mathematics achievement." **Although, as noted above, the mathematics and science scores of U.S. students have increased since the early 1980s, they remain low compared to their counterparts in many other countries** (*Indicators 23* and *24*). Moreover, considerable variation exists across states. On the one hand, 8th-grade students in some states perform as well as 13-year-old students from the best performing nations in an international comparison of mathematics achievement. On the other hand, students in other states are performing at levels similar to students in developing countries.[13]

♦ *How are minorities performing?*

Another area of continuing concern is the academic achievement of minority students in elementary and secondary school. For example, in 1994, the average reading proficiency scores of black 12th-graders were 29 scale points below those of white 12th-graders and were similar to the average proficiency scores of white 8th-

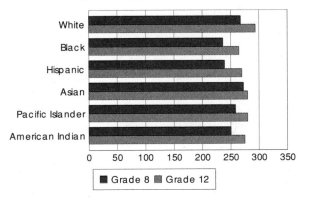

Average reading proficiency in 1994

graders. The white-Hispanic reading gap in 12th grade was a little narrower than white-black differences. White-black and white-Hispanic proficiency score differences were of similar

magnitudes in mathematics in 1992.[14] But, the white-black differences were greater than the white-Hispanic differences in science in 1990.[15] Whites and Asians also scored higher than blacks and Hispanics on history (*Indicator 18*) and geography (*Indicator 19*) assessments.

Many also are concerned that despite a **narrowing of the white-minority achievement gap during the 1980s, particularly in mathematics, recent data raise the possibility that the gap is no longer closing.** For instance, the most recent (1994) NAEP results in reading

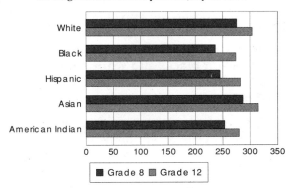

Average mathematics proficiency in 1994

suggest that minority groups may be beginning to lose some of the earlier gains they had made relative to whites.[16]

In addition to some narrowing in the white-minority achievement gap, there are other positive developments regarding the achievement and attainment of black and Hispanic students. The indicators in this volume contain far more information on different subpopulations than has been reviewed here. For example, an essay on minorities in higher education appears in the *Issues in Focus* section, and essays reviewing the educational progress of Hispanic students and of black students appear in the 1995 and 1994 editions of the *Condition*, respectively. A review of the considerable educational advances made by women over the past several decades can also be found in the 1995 edition.

Social scientists attribute much of the white-minority differences in achievement to the higher incidence of poverty in the families of minority children (*Indicator 44*) and the lower average educational levels of their parents. It is difficult for schools to compensate for such disadvantages. However, **there is evidence that extraordinary schools and teachers make a difference in how all students perform.** For example, research on early intervention and one-to-one tutoring demonstrates that at-risk students can achieve at far higher levels than they have in the past.[17] There is also some evidence, particularly in mathematics and science, that taking more challenging courses is related to higher performance and achievement.[18]

◆ *Are more young people finishing high school?*

Despite curricular changes that may have made school more difficult, students are persisting in their studies. Overall, **the percentage of students who leave high school before graduating has gradually declined, and differences between dropout rates for blacks and whites have also narrowed, although most of these changes occurred before the mid-1980s** (*Indicator 5*).

The decline in the dropout rate is encouraging because schools provide young people with the opportunity to explore their interests and develop their talents. It is also encouraging because staying in school is an important indication that a young person is learning to be a productive member of society and is less likely to suffer from poverty and unemployment (*Indicators 30, 32, 34,* and *36*).

High school completion rates have gradually risen, and for some subgroups are near or over the 90 percent recommended in the National Education Goal (*Indicator 25*). The rise is, in part, a result of greater student persistence in

Median earnings of wage and salary workers aged 25–34 (in 1995 constant dollars)

Males

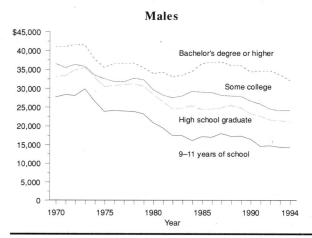

Median earnings of wage and salary workers aged 25–34 (in 1995 constant dollars)

Females

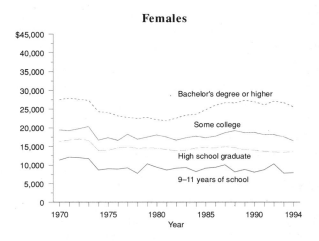

high school (as discussed above), but may also be a result of more dropouts returning to earn a GED credential or regular diploma (*Indicator 6*). Although the rise is a positive development, we must also be cautious because in today's economy a high school diploma or a GED credential may not be sufficient to avoid low earnings, unemployment, and, possibly, poverty.

Status of 1980 and 1990 sophomores who did not graduate on schedule 2 years after scheduled graduation

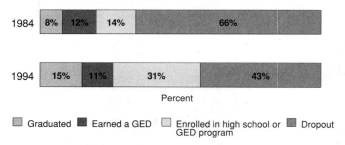

Since the early 1970s, the real wages of young adults with only a high school diploma or GED credential have declined (table 34-2), and the proportion of this group receiving AFDC or public assistance has increased (*Indicator 36*).

Generally, employment rates rise with education level (*Indicator 32*), and the likelihood of being involuntarily employed part time or part year declines (*Indicator 33*). The labor market opportunities for high school graduates are still better than for those who complete 9–11 years of education, however.

♦ *Are more young people going to college?*

In 1992, the rates of attainment in higher education for U.S. males and females were among the highest in the world (*Indicator 27*).[19] This is an indication that higher education is broadly accessible in the United States compared to other countries. It is also an indication of the rewards of college attendance. Even though some college graduates have faced a difficult labor market over the past few years, their job opportunities and earnings are much better than

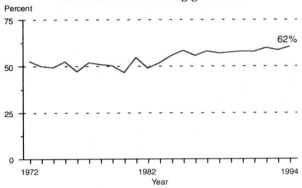

High school graduates who enrolled in college the October following graduation

Percent

those of high school graduates. In fact, throughout the 1980s, the earnings advantage for college graduates has grown stronger (*Indicator 34*).

It is not surprising that despite a rapid rise in tuition levels (*Indicator 12*) **more high school graduates are choosing to go immediately to college after high school graduation** (*Indicator 7*). It should be noted, however, that enrollments do not always translate into completions.

Although more students are entering college after high school, the data show that **it is very common for college students to enroll, leave, possibly return, and not finish within the expected period of time.** For example, among 1989–90 beginning postsecondary students seeking bachelor's degrees, fewer than half had graduated; 28 percent had neither completed nor were still working toward a bachelor's degree in spring 1994; and 8 percent had earned an associate's degree or a vocational certificate (*Indicator 10*). Among students who began their postsecondary education at a community college

in 1989–90, less than one-quarter had completed an associate's degree or vocational certificate there by 1994, although 37 percent had completed an award at some institution. Those who did not complete an award at their initial community college spent a substantial amount of time there, however, averaging 14 months of enrollment (*Indicator 9*).

Non-completion is not necessarily an indication of failure or a waste of resources. Often students, particularly those at 2-year institutions, enter and withdraw from college because of economic opportunities, or they may have begun a program with limited objectives that they were able to achieve. Also, many students attend part time, which can extend the time it takes them to complete a program (*Indicator 11*). Nevertheless, the high rates of non-completion and interrupted attendance may indicate that students do not have enough information about the actual skills in demand in the labor market before making decisions regarding their education. Moreover, they may have unrealistic views as to how much time, effort, and money will be needed to complete postsecondary education programs and acquire these skills.

High levels of participation in higher education are made possible by generally low tuition levels at public institutions and a financial aid system that primarily is based, particularly the federal component, on need. Average tuition and fees are also much lower at public institutions, where four out of five students are enrolled, than they are at private institutions (*Indicators 13* and *39*).

Costs incurred by dependent full-time undergraduates: 1992–93

Institution	Tuition and fees	Total cost	Net cost
Public 2-year	$1,072	$6,410	$5,717
Public 4-year	2,947	9,187	7,326
Private 4-year	11,004	17,301	11,552

SOURCE: Indicator 13.

But to attend postsecondary education on a full-time basis requires that the student not only pay the direct costs of education but also finance living expenses. For example, in 1992–93, the *total cost* a student had to finance, including both educational and living expenses, was about $9,200 for dependent full-time students attending public 4-year institutions. Total aid, including grants, loans, and work-study, reduced the amount that needed to be financed to $7,300. In addition, most financial aid is sensitive to family income, so this *net cost* was lowest ($5,070) for students from low income families and highest ($8,879) for those from high income families (*Indicator 13*).

Net cost incurred by and unmet need of dependent full-time undergraduates, by family income: 1992–93

| Family income | Net cost | | Unmet need | |
	Public 4-year	Private 4-year	Public 4-year	Private 4-year
All	$7,326	$11,552	$1,952	$4,171
Less than $27,000	5,070	5,872	3,132	4,425
27,000–44,999	6,426	8,590	2,429	4,980
45,000–59,999	7,598	10,407	1,784	4,204
60,000 or more	8,879	15,752	836	3,633

SOURCE: Indicator 13 and table 13-1.

Clearly, the increasing enrollment rates and rising tuition costs are profoundly affecting the nature of higher education. First, colleges are providing much remedial instruction to students who arrive with weak academic skills.[20] This may indicate that more students who once would not have considered continuing on to higher education are now enrolling, even though they must take courses for which they may not receive credit. Second, the percentage of full-time college students who report working more than 20 hours a week has increased since the early 1980s.[21]

Although working during the school year leaves less time for students to concentrate on their studies or to participate in extracurricular activities, some of the experience that students gain from working may benefit them after graduation. There is evidence, however, that working long hours while in college may reduce a student's likelihood of completing college or lengthen the time it takes for those who do complete it. Third, there is some evidence that college students are feeling increasingly stressed by the demands placed on them.[22]

♦ *What do we know about the quality of our schools?*

The information presented so far has focused on students and what they are or are not achieving. Because of the impact of family income and support on student performance, academic achievement is only a partial indicator of the quality of the schools that U.S. students attend. But what can be said directly about the quality of schools? Are schools providing a safe and supportive environment so that student energies can be devoted to learning? Are schools attracting people with enthusiasm, creativity, and commitment to teaching and supporting them with competitive salaries and sustained professional development? These are also important aspects of school quality.[23] Without question, much work remains to be done to produce reliable statistical measures of school quality.

Expenditures per student are often used as a proxy measure of the quality of education. But, this can only be considered a highly imprecise measure, because the results of hundreds of studies that examine the relationship between spending and outcomes, such as achievement test scores, dropout rates, and higher education enrollments, are mixed.[24] Neither a strong nor consistent relationship is found. However, no one can deny the importance of money to build schools, hire teachers, buy textbooks, and otherwise acquire the resources needed to create a safe, supportive learning environment. Among these resources are the intangible qualities of dedicated teachers, principals, and parents who create the learning environment.

At the elementary and secondary levels, **revenues per student have increased substantially** since the early 1980s, a sign that even with the strains of slower economic growth, our nation is willing to continue supporting its schools (*Indicator 50*). Yet, **revenues per student vary widely across states**: state governments, not the federal government, have responsibility for funding education, and they vary in their capacity and willingness to do so. In addition, there is considerable variation within states, because states delegate authority for operating and funding schools to local school districts. For instance, one estimate is that **the wealthiest districts have about 16 percent more cost-of-**

living adjusted revenue per student than the poorest districts. However, other factors such as students' educational needs require consideration

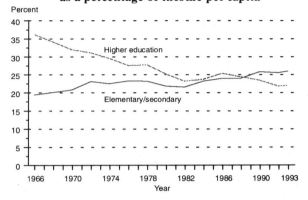

Revenues per student from public sources as a percentage of income per capita

before disparities in the allocation of education resources can be adequately measured. Districts with a large percentage of school-age children in poverty, however, do receive a much larger share of their revenue from federal and state sources than from local governments.[25]

An advantage of state and local funding of schools is that parents and citizens have more say in deciding how much education their children get and with what emphasis. A disadvantage is that wealth varies across school districts, leading to imbalances in the resources available to schools even when citizens are equally willing to fund them. This has resulted in complicated state formulas to assist poor school districts and in many court challenges to state education financing systems as insufficiently compensatory. In fact, the supreme courts of several states have declared the state education financing systems unconstitutional because of funding inequities, and more than half the states have cases pending. For example, as a result of a court challenge to its funding arrangements, Kentucky has completely overhauled its educational system from teacher certification requirements to governance structures. And a few years ago, Michigan decided to stop using the property tax to finance its schools, and instead to use a combination of income and sales taxes. Since poor school districts receive most of their revenue from the state, another disadvantage of state and local funding is that economic conditions may cause a state to change its support level at the very

moment poor school districts need the funds the most.

Although the level and distribution of education resources are very important, it is equally important that the resources be used effectively. Teachers' salaries are a major portion of the elementary and secondary budget, and good teachers are central to a high quality education system. Most of what we consider formal childhood education takes place in classrooms through interactions between teachers and students. And, teachers are one conduit through which education and societal values are passed.

Since the mid-1950s, the pupil-teacher ratio has declined steadily.[26] Average teacher salaries in public schools were also higher in 1995 than in 1960, although most of the gain since 1981 only recouped losses incurred during the 1970s (*Indicator 55*). Nevertheless, using a variety of measures, it appears that **teacher earnings are relatively low compared to those of many other professions that college students could pursue.**[27]

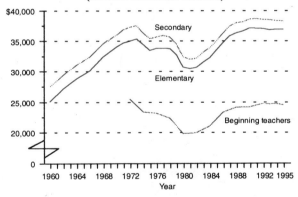

Average annual salaries of public school teachers (in 1995 constant dollars)

Policymakers have expressed some concern over whether this discourages the best and the brightest students from choosing teaching as a profession. However, evidence of this is mixed. For example, **some research indicates that those accepting teaching positions were more likely to have lower scores on the SAT and NTE** (National Teacher Examination) **than non-teaching college graduates,** and that those leaving teaching were more likely to have higher SAT and NTE scores than those remaining in the profession.[28] Evidence from the 1992 National Adult Literacy Survey (NALS) points in the opposite direction, however. In NALS, **the prose literacy scores of teachers are similar to the scores of many of their colleagues in other professions**, including private-sector executives and managers, engineers, physicians, writers and artists, social workers, sales representatives, education administrators, and registered nurses. Thus, with respect to at least prose literacy, there is little evidence that low salaries are attracting only the least able college graduates into teaching (*Indicator 58*).

Although many of the characteristics that determine the quality of a teacher are not easily measured, some teacher qualifications can be measured. Many analysts argue that one of the most important characteristics is training and preparation in the subject or field in which the teacher is teaching. Research has shown moderate but consistent support for the reasonable proposition that subject knowledge (knowing what you teach) and teaching skills (knowing how to teach) are important predictors of both teaching quality and student learning.[29] Knowledge of subject matter and of pedagogical methods does not, of course, guarantee quality teaching, but it is an important prerequisite.

Almost all teachers are certified to teach in their primary assignment field, and a large majority have majored or minored in this field. In fact, most teachers have graduate degrees. In school year 1993–94, the proportion of public secondary

Percentage of public secondary school students taught by teachers who majored or minored in the class subject: 1993–94

English	84%
Social sciences	92%
Mathematics	78%
Sciences	90%
Health and physical education	93%
Foreign languages	89%

school students taught by a teacher who either majored or minored in their class subject ranged from 78 percent in mathematics to 93 percent in health and physical education (*Indicator 57*).

There is considerable variation in teacher qualifications across states, however. For example, in 1991, the percentage of high school mathematics teachers who majored in mathematics or mathematics education ranged from 44 percent in California to about 90 percent in Alabama and Minnesota.[30] Although teacher qualifications and credentials may be an indication of minimal competency, these may be poor measures of subject matter and instructional competence.

To provide high quality education, schools must not only hire well qualified teachers but also must help current teachers improve their skills, stay current in their fields, and learn about new teaching methods. **In 1993–94, the vast majority of full-time public school teachers participated in school- and district-sponsored workshops or in-service training** (*Indicator 59*).

Considerable policy discussion has addressed the ability of schools to keep qualified teachers, both in general and in specific subject areas such as mathematics and science. **Overall, teacher attrition in public elementary and secondary schools seems to be low.** Only 1 in 20 full-time public school teachers left the teaching profession between the 1990–91 and 1991–92 school years. Furthermore, keeping mathematics and science teachers in the profession does not seem to be as big a problem as was once suggested. The percentage of full-time teachers in public secondary schools in 1990–91 who left teaching in the next year was no higher in mathematics and science than in other teaching fields.[31]

A high level of education and associated professional commitment among teachers benefits both students and the education system. These benefits come at a cost, however, because teachers must be paid enough to justify the investment they have made in their education. Nevertheless, education policymakers must address the more difficult issue of how to make the best use of available resources under changing conditions.

♦ *How have conditions facing the schools changed?*

Changing conditions that schools must confront are putting additional strains on revenues, even though revenues have increased. **First, schools are facing a period of rising enrollments after a**

long period of decline (*Indicator 38*). It is important to monitor these increases because they will affect school budgets as well as policies of teacher recruitment and retention.

Public school enrollment

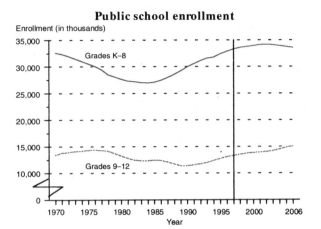

Second, many more disabled students, particularly those with learning disabilities, are receiving special services (*Indicator 43*). This has major financial implications for school districts. There is some evidence that the average cost of serving a special education student is as much as

Percentage of children served in federally supported programs for students with disabilities

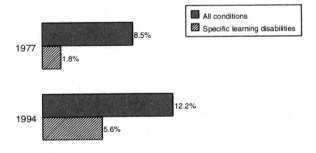

2.3 times the cost of serving a regular student (ranging from 1.9 times for students in resource programs to 10.6 times for students in residential programs).[32]

Third, many more students speak a language other than English at home and have difficulty speaking English, a likely indication that even more students may have difficulty reading and writing English.[33]

By law, school systems nationwide must provide services for children from non-English-language backgrounds. Because these students are

Percentage of children who have difficulty speaking English

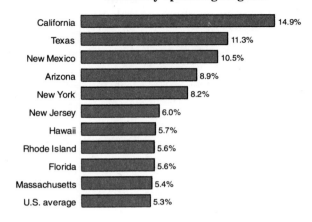

disproportionately concentrated in a few states (California, Texas, New Mexico, Arizona, and New York), the education systems in these states are under particular strain to respond to the special needs of these children.

Fourth, many children live in poverty (21 percent or 15.3 million), and these children typically live in neighborhoods and attend school together (*Indicator 44*). Thus, the schools in these neighborhoods are also facing heavy demands.

Percentage of children living in poverty in 1992

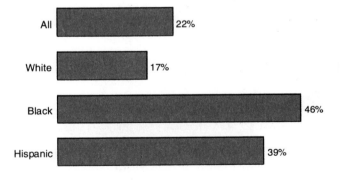

Fifth, an increasing percentage of public school teachers are reporting that physical conflicts and weapons possession are moderate or serious problems in their schools. Violence in and around schools directly affects educators and students by reducing school effectiveness and inhibiting students' learning. In 1993, more than one in five high school seniors reported being threatened at school.

Despite teachers' perceptions of growing safety problems in their schools,[34] victimization rates of high school seniors changed little between 1976

Percentages of public school teachers reporting physical conflicts among students and weapons possession as moderate or serious problems in their schools

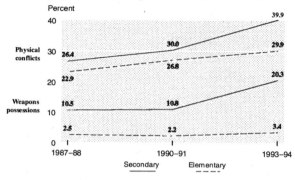

and 1993, except for a slight increase in the percentage of students who reported being threatened, both with and without a weapon. Although generally few differences were seen in school victimization rates among black and white high school seniors, black seniors were more likely than their white counterparts to have been threatened with a weapon at school (24 versus 14 percent).[35]

As this discussion indicates, there is not one answer to the complex question of whether the condition of education is improving. Some conditions are improving, while others are not. In a number of areas, research has not been able to disentangle the influences of several factors; therefore, we cannot be certain whether conditions are actually improving or not. However, this volume can help Americans interested in education policy to pose more sophisticated questions. In doing so, we can make progress toward understanding what produces high quality educational institutions, an educated citizenry, and a skilled work force.

Jeanne E. Griffith
Acting Commissioner of Education Statistics

NOTES:

[1] Special Study Panel on Education Indicators. *Education Counts: An Indicator System to Monitor the Nation's Educational Health.* Washington, D.C.: National Center for Education Statistics. September 1991.

[2] *The Condition of Education 1994, Indicator 23.*

[3] *The Condition of Education 1993, Indicator 27.*

[4] *The Condition of Education 1994, Indicator 26.*

[5] R. Coley and M. E. Goetz. *Educational Standards in the Fifty States: 1990.* Princeton, N.J.: Educational Testing Service; and Elliott A. Medrich, Robin R. Henke, and Cynthia L. Brown. *Overview and Inventory of State Requirements for School Coursework and Attendance* (NCES 92-663). Washington, D.C.: U.S. Department of Education, National Center for Education Statistics, 1992.

[6] Andrew C. Porter, Michael W. Kirst, Eric J. Osthoff, John L. Smithson, and Steven A. Schneider. *Reform Up Close: An Analysis of High School Mathematics and Science* Classrooms. Final report to the National Science Foundation on grant #SPA-8953-446 to the Consortium for Policy Research in Education, October 1993.

[7] *The Condition of Education 1995, Indicators 13 and 14.*

[8] *The Condition of Education 1995, Indicator 26.*

[9] *The Condition of Education 1995, tables 13-3 and 14-3.*

[10] U.S. Department of Education, National Center for Education Statistics. *NAEP 1994 Reading Report Card,* 1995.

[11] John Ralph, Dana Keller, and James Crouse. "How Effective Are American Schools?" *Phi Delta Kappan* (October 1994).

[12] Jennifer S. Manlove and David P. Baker. "Local Constraints on Opportunity to Learn Mathematics in High School." In M. Hallinan (ed.), *Making Schools Work: Promising Practices and Policies.* Plenum, 1995; and U.S. Department of Education, National Center for Education Statistics. *Curricular Differentiation in Public High Schools* (NCES 95-360). Washington, D.C.: December 1994.

[13] U.S. Department of Education, National Center for Education Statistics. *Education in States and Nations: Indicators Comparing U.S. States with the OECD Countries in 1988* (NCES 93-237). Washington, D.C.: October 1993, Indicator 16.

[14] U.S. Department of Education, National Center for Education Statistics. *NAEP 1992 Mathematics Report Card for the Nation and the States.* Washington, D.C.: April 1993.

[15] U.S. Department of Education, National Center for Education Statistics. *The 1990 Science Report Card.* Washington, D.C.: March 1992.

[16] U.S. Department of Education, National Center for Education Statistics. *1994 NAEP Reading: A First Look* (NCES 95-748). Washington, D.C.: May 1995.

[17] Robert E. Slavin, Nancy L. Karweit, and Barbara A. Wasik. "Preventing Early School Failure: What Works." *Educational Leadership* (December 1992/January 1993): 10–18; idem, eds., *Preventing Early School Failure.* Boston: Allyn and Bacon, 1994; and Barbara A. Wasik and Robert E. Slavin.

"Preventing Early Reading Failure with One-to-One Tutoring: A Review of Five Programs." *Educational Research Quarterly* 28 (1993): 178–200.

[18] Donald A. Rock and Judith M. Pollack. *Statistics in Brief: Mathematics Course-Taking and Gains in Mathematics Achievement* (NCES 95-714). U.S. Department of Education, National Center for Education Statistics. Washington, D.C.: 1995; and T. Hoffer, K. Rasinski, and W. Moore. *Social Background Differences in High School Mathematics and Science Coursetaking and Achievement* (NCES 95-206). U.S. Department of Education, National Center for Education Statistics. Washington, D.C.: 1995.

[19] For cross-country comparisons of net enrollment rates in higher education, see Organisation for Economic Co-operation and Development, Center for Educational Research and Innovation. *Education at a Glance: OECD Indicators*, 1995, table P06.

[20] U.S. Department of Education, National Center for Education Statistics. *College-Level Remedial Education in the Fall of 1989* (NCES 91-191). Washington, D.C.: May 1991.

[21] *The Condition of Education 1995, Indicator 51.*

[22] Alexander W. Astin, William S. Korn, Linda J. Sax, and Kathryn M. Mahoney. *The American Freshman: National Norms for 1994.* Cooperative Institutional Research Program, American Council on Education, and the University of California, Los Angeles, 1994.

[23] *Education Counts, 1991.*

[24] Eric Hanushek. "The Economics of School: Production and Efficiency in Public Schools." *Journal of Economic Literature* (March 1986); and Larry V. Hedges, Richard D. Laine, and Rob Greenwald. "Does Money Matter? A Meta-Analysis of Studies of the Effects of Differential School Inputs on Student Outcomes (An Exchange: Part I)." *Educational Researcher* (April 1994).

[25] *The Condition of Education 1995, Indicator 53.* Also see U.S. Department of Education, National Center for Education Statistics. *Disparities in Public School District Spending: 1989–90.*

[26] U.S. Department of Education, National Center for Education Statistics. *Digest of Education Statistics, 1995,* table 63.

[27] Mary Rollefson. *Issue Brief: Teacher Salaries—Are They Competitive?* (NCES 93-450). U.S. Department of Education, National Center for Education Statistics. Washington, D.C.: 1993, table 2; and F. H. Nelson and T. O'Brien. *How U.S. Teachers Measure Up Internationally: A Comparative Study of Teacher Pay, Training, and Conditions of Service.* American Federation of Teachers, Washington, D.C.: 1993, table II-1.

[28] Richard J. Murnane, Judith D. Singer, James J. Kemple, Randall J. Olson, and John B. Willet. *Who Will Teach?* Cambridge: Harvard University Press, 1991; and V.S. Vance and P.C. Schlechty. "The Distribution of Academic Ability in the Teaching Force: Policy Implications." *Phi Delta Kappan* 64: 22–27.

[29] R. Shavelson, L. McDonnell, and J. Oakes. *Indicators for Monitoring Mathematics and Science Education.* Santa Monica, CA: RAND, 1989; L. Darling-Hammond and L. Hudson. "Pre-college Science and Mathematics Teachers: Supply, Demand, and Quality." *Review of Research in Education.* Washington, D.C.: AERA, 1990; and R. Murnane and S. Raizen, eds. *Improving Indicators of the Quality of Science and Mathematics Education in Grades K–12.* Washington, D.C.: National Academy Press, 1989.

[30] Rolf Blank, Michael Matti, Iris Weiss, Stephen Broughman, and Mary Rollefson. *SASS by State.* (NCES 94-343). Washington, D.C.: U.S. Department of Education, National Center for Education Statistics, June 1994.

[31] *The Condition of Education 1995, Indicator 60.*

[32] M.T. Moore, E.W. Strang, M. Schwartz, and M. Braddock. *Patterns in Special Education Service Delivery and Cost.* Contract Number 300-84-0257. Washington, D.C.: Decision Research Corporation, 1988; and S. Chaikind, L.C. Danielson, and M.L. Brauen. "What Do We Know about the Costs of Special Education: A Selected Review." *Journal of Special Education* 26 (4) (1993): 344–370.

[33] *The Condition of Education 1994, Indicator 46.*

[34] U.S. Department of Education, National Center for Education Statistics. *How Safer Are the Public Schools: What Do Teachers Say?*, May 1996.

[35] *The Condition of Education 1995, Indicator 47.*

The Condition of Education 1996 was authored by a joint NCES/Pinkerton Computer Consultants, Inc./MPR Associates, Inc. team under the general direction of Thomas M. Smith, Director of the Condition of Education Project in the Data Development and Longitudinal Studies Group. Overall direction was provided by Thomas D. Snyder, Director of the Annual Reports Program. Rebecca Pratt Mahoney of Pinkerton Computer Consultants, Inc. coordinated the editing and production of this volume.

The authors wish to thank all those who contributed to the production of this report. Michelle Brown, Ginger Rittenhouse, Sharon Xu, Huong Huyen, and Caroline Magill of Pinkerton Computer Consultants, Inc. made significant contributions, for which we are especially grateful. Michelle Brown designed and edited all of the graphics for the indicators in the report and prepared them for printing. Ginger Rittenhouse carefully edited the manuscript and assisted in coordinating the production of the volume.

Sharon Xu and Caroline Magill produced tabulations from several data sets, including the October and March Current Population Surveys and the Schools and Staffing Survey. Huong Huyen produced tabulations from the Schools and Staffing Survey and the National Education Longitudinal Study of 1988. Other Pinkerton staff also made important contributions to the volume, including Agnes Alvarez, who produced tabulations from the National Survey of Postsecondary Faculty, and Tony Russo, who designed and formatted the index.

Among MPR Associates, Inc. staff, Andrea M. Livingston and Karyn Madden carefully edited the manuscript. Ellen Liebman provided programming assistance, and Connie Yin and Lynn Sally provided word processing assistance.

From outside the Department of Education, Eric Grodsky and Richard Phelps of Pelavin Research Institute calculated public expenditure data for countries other than the United States.

This volume has been reviewed by many people, often within tight time constraints and at the expense of their many other responsibilities. Their high professional standards, discerning eyes, and commitment to quality are crucial to the quality, utility, and relevance of the volume. Mary Frase painstakingly reviewed the entire manuscript through several drafts and made many important suggestions that improved the final result. Susan Ahmed, Samuel Barbett, Steve Broughman, Bob Burton, Kathryn Chandler, Mike Cohen, Claire Geddes, Elvie Hausken, Paula Knepper, Frank Morgan, Laurence Ogle, Peter Stowe, and Linda Zimbler of NCES all provided detailed and helpful reviews. Alan Ginsburg reviewed the document for the Office of the Undersecretary.

Several individuals served as invited external peer reviewers of the draft manuscript and made valuable contributions: Clifford Adelman of the National Institute on Postsecondary Education, Libraries, and Lifelong Learning; David Grissmer of RAND; and Thomas Kane of the President's Council of Economic Advisors.

Contents

List of NCES Publications
Information on NCES Online Library

"Why do we seek to know the condition of education? In the answer to this question will be found the reasons for the elaborate statistical record which forms a feature of all official school reports. We take an account of education so that we may know whether it is sufficient in amount and good in quality."

Henry Barnard
First Commissioner of Education

Introduction

During the 1980s, the country became increasingly aware of a range of critical national issues facing education. These issues included concerns about all children having an equal opportunity to receive a high quality education, general low academic performance, drug use and violence in the schools, unacceptably high dropout rates, the high cost of a college education, and the skills of workers lagging behind technological changes in the workplace. The 1990s have continued the emphasis expressed in the 1980s, with renewed concern over academic standards and school finance reform. These concerns continue to have serious implications, not only for schools and colleges but also for the future of individual citizens, U.S. economic competitiveness, and ultimately the structure and cohesiveness of American society and culture.

The Condition of Education provides a means to report where progress is being made in education and where it is not, to draw attention to emerging issues, and to inform the ongoing policy debate.

The structure of *The Condition of Education*

A quick tour of the volume may help readers make the best use of it. The core of the volume consists of 60 indicators. Each indicator is presented on two pages, with findings summarized in accompanying text, tables, and graphics. Also included in the back of the volume are supplemental tables providing additional details, and sometimes an explanatory note on a technical or data-related issue.

The 60 indicators are organized into six sections:

◆ Access, Participation, and Progress;

◆ Achievement, Attainment, and Curriculum;

◆ Economic and Other Outcomes of Education;

◆ Size, Growth, and Output of Educational Institutions;

◆ Climate, Classrooms, and Diversity in Educational Institutions; and

◆ Human and Financial Resources of Educational Institutions.

Instead of separating the indicators on elementary and secondary education from those on postsecondary education, the volume integrates issues ranging from early childhood education to postsecondary education into each of the six sections.

One can find information on an issue either by turning to the table of contents, which lists the 60 indicators, or by using the index, which references not only the indicators but also the supplemental tables. When an updated indicator is not available in this volume, the index lists the indicator number and edition of *The Condition of Education* that last published an indicator on that topic. Supplemental material also can be downloaded from the NCES World Wide Web (WWW) Site.

Preceding each section of indicators is a two-page overview that interprets and summarizes some of the findings in that section as they relate to an important issue.

At the bottom of each indicator page, readers can locate the data source for the indicator. The indicators presented in this report have been developed using data from studies carried out by NCES as well as from surveys conducted elsewhere, both within and outside of the federal government. A description of each source is provided in the *Sources of Data* section. Sometimes more knowledge about the type of survey used to gather the data can help readers interpret the indicator. Because some of the terms used may not be familiar to all readers, we also have included a glossary.

In the *Issues in Focus* section, we pull together evidence from both the 60 indicators and other sources on four important education issues:

♦ Education and worker productivity;

♦ Preparation for work;

♦ Minorities in higher education; and

♦ Teachers' working conditions.

These issues were selected, first because of their importance to current policy discussions, and second because a substantial amount of new information on these issues has been included in this volume and other recent NCES publications.

In the 1995 edition of *The Condition of Education*, essays were included on access to preschool education, trends in the achievement and attainment of Hispanic students relative to whites, progress in the achievement and attainment of women, and the cost of higher education.

References to indicators and tables contained in this volume appear in parentheses. The tables cited are in the *Supplemental Tables and Notes* section of the publication. Occasionally, there are references to indicators found in a previous edition of *The Condition of Education;* these can be recognized by the year following the reference. References to sources other than *The Condition of Education* are footnoted.

Issues in Focus

Education and worker productivity

by Paul Decker, Mathematica Policy Research, Inc.

The productivity of the U.S. work force is a primary determinant of the standard of living of the U.S. population. Worker productivity is typically measured as output per worker or per hour worked. It is affected by many factors, including the education and skills of the work force. Education and skills are important because they expand workers' capacity to perform tasks or to use productive technologies. In addition, better educated workers can adapt more easily to new tasks or to changes in old tasks. Education may also prepare workers to work more effectively in teams because it enhances their ability to communicate with and understand their co-workers.

Much of the recent concern about the productivity of U.S. workers has been prompted by uncertainty about the ability of domestic firms and workers to compete in an increasingly international marketplace. As growth in U.S. productivity has slowed over the past two decades and other countries achieve productivity levels similar to those in the United States, concern about U.S. competitiveness has increased. Some attribute the loss of the nation's productivity advantage to what they claim is the limited ability of the U.S. educational system to provide students with the skills necessary to succeed in the today's labor market. But, factors other than education also affect productivity, and these other factors must be considered when comparing productivity trends across countries.

Variation in the quality and quantity of education across countries is only one factor contributing to differences in worker productivity; capital investment, technical innovation, foreign trade, and government regulation can also affect productivity. But education remains an important contributor to productivity growth and therefore has a major influence on the standard of living. This essay highlights several measures of productivity and education, and addresses the link between these two sets of measures. A better understanding of the relationship between worker productivity and the condition of education is essential to understand how investment in education contributes to the U.S. economy.

Trends in worker productivity and the contribution of education

♦ *Worker productivity in the United States has increased continuously since the end of World War II, but growth has slowed since 1973.*

Worker productivity in the United States has grown almost continuously since the end of World War II, rising to a level in 1994 that is approximately three times that of 1947. Postwar growth in productivity was slower after 1973 than it was before 1973. Between 1947 and 1973, output per hour increased by nearly 3 percent per year, compared to slightly more than 1 percent per year between 1973 and 1993. It is unclear whether the slowdown in productivity growth since 1973 merely reflects fluctuation of the long-term growth rate, which is equal to about 2 percent, or whether it signals slower long-term growth.

Index of output per hour of all persons in the business sector: 1947–94

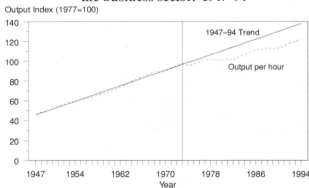

SOURCE: U.S. Department of Labor, Bureau of Labor Statistics, based on Data from the Current Employment Statistics, the Current Population Survey, and the national income and product accounts produced by the U.S. Department of Commerce, Bureau of Economic Analysis.

♦ *Since World War II, worker productivity has grown more slowly in the United States than in other industrialized countries.*

For several decades, productivity in other industrialized countries has been gradually catching up to that in the United States. However, the United States remained the leader as of 1990, with a Gross Domestic Product (GDP) per worker that was slightly higher than that in

Canada, and about 25 percent higher than that in Italy, the country with the third highest GDP.

Real GDP per worker in G-7 nations: 1950–90

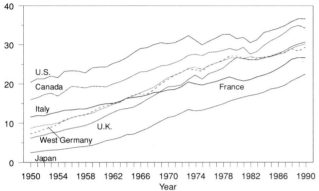

Real GDP per worker (in thousands of adjusted 1990 dollars)

SOURCE: Penn World Trade (Mark 5,6), distributed by the National Bureau of Economic Research.

According to one theory of productivity growth, referred to as the *convergence hypothesis*,[1] it is to be expected that productivity in lagging countries will converge on that of the United States because these countries can exploit technologies transferred from the United States, thereby closing the gap in worker productivity. This "catching-up" process suggests that the United States is inevitably at risk of losing its lead in worker productivity as long as other countries have the capabilities, such as an adequately educated work force, to exploit new productive technologies.

The ability of the United States to maintain a substantial lead in productivity for nearly a century is at least partly attributable to the two world wars, which destroyed the productive capacity of other countries while spurring technological innovation in U.S. manufacturing. However, the huge productivity advantage of the United States has dissipated under the more normal post-war economic conditions, which have allowed other countries to rebuild their productive capacities and expand their technological capabilities. It now appears that the other industrialized countries will eventually share the lead in productivity with the United States.

But insofar as the "catching-up" process involves the transfer of technology from the leader country to the lagging countries, the

process should eventually slow down as the lagging countries exhaust their opportunities to exploit new technologies from the leader. Eventually, the countries sharing the lead in productivity would presumably be in a position to exploit technological advances from each other.

◆   *Education is an important determinant of worker productivity.*

Increases in educational attainment are responsible for an estimated 10 to 20 percent of growth in worker productivity in the United States in recent decades.[2] These estimates also are similar to those for other industrialized countries.[3] The industrialized countries with the highest productivity levels generally have highly educated work forces. The convergence in productivity among these countries parallels that in educational attainment.

Factors other than education are also important to worker productivity. For example, increases in capital accounted for an estimated 40 percent of productivity growth in the United States between 1948 and 1990.[4] In the early 1960s, when the United States was the dominant economy in the world, the nation had a much higher ratio of capital to labor than other industrialized countries. Since then, the countries that are catching up to the United States in terms of productivity have accumulated capital at a faster rate than the United States. In addition to capital, such factors as technical innovation, foreign trade, and government regulation can also affect productivity.

The economic consequences of education for individuals

Ultimately, growth in a nation's productivity results from growth in the productivity of individual workers. The best available measure of a worker's productivity is typically that worker's wages, as employers generally pay wages equal to the marginal productivity of their workers. The impact of education on the productivity of workers can be determined by estimating the impact of education on wages.

Education may also improve workers' employment stability, enabling more educated workers to maintain their jobs or to quickly find new jobs in the face of changing economic conditions. The association between education and unemployment therefore can be a further indication of the effect of education on the productivity of workers.

Educational attainment

◆ *Workers with higher educational attainment are unemployed less and earn more than workers with lower educational attainment.*

Over the past 30 years, a substantial proportion of high school graduates and dropouts were

Percentage of recent school leavers who were unemployed, by educational attainment: 1960–94

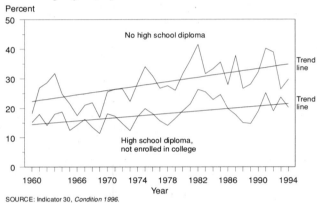

SOURCE: Indicator 30, *Condition 1996.*

unemployed shortly after leaving high school, with dropouts generally facing a higher unemployment rate than graduates. In 1994, 30 percent of recent dropouts were unemployed, compared to 20 percent of recent graduates not enrolled in college. The unemployment rates for

Earnings of wage and salary workers aged 25–34, by educational attainment and sex: 1994

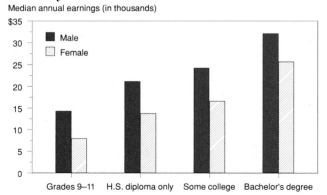

SOURCE: Indicator 34, *Condition 1996.*

both groups have increased since 1960.

Median earnings are positively associated with educational attainment. Among males aged 25–34 in 1994, median earnings of those with a college degree were equal to about $33,000 per year, which was more than 50 percent greater than the median earnings of high school graduates and nearly twice those of high school dropouts. The relationship between education and earnings for females is similar, although within each educational category, earnings are lower for females than for males.

◆ *Educational attainment in the United States has increased over the past 20 years.*

The proportion of 21- and 22-year-olds who have completed high school increased slowly, rising from approximately 82 percent in 1972 to about

High school completion, college enrollment, and college completion rates: 1972–95

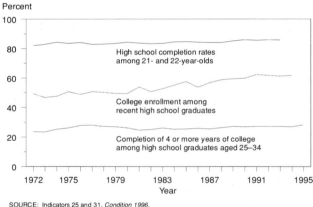

SOURCE: Indicators 25 and 31, *Condition 1996.*

86 percent in 1990. Subsequently, the rate remained relatively constant between 1990 and 1994. An increasing number of students who have completed high school also move on to college. Among recent high school graduates, the college enrollment rate increased from 49 percent in 1972 to 62 percent in 1994.

But many students who enroll in college do not complete 4 years there. The rate of completion of 4 years or more of college increased by about 4 percentage points between 1972 and 1976, but then declined for several years before starting to slowly rise again (table 25-3, *Condition 1996*). The completion rate of 28 percent in 1995 was similar to the rate of 20 years before.

♦ *Although the rate of college completion in the United States still far exceeds that in most other countries, educational attainment generally is increasing more slowly in the United States than in other industrialized countries.*

In each of the G-7 countries, the rate of secondary school completion is higher among 25- to 34-year-olds than among 25- to 64-year-olds, indicating that the rate of secondary school completion is

Secondary school completion: 1992

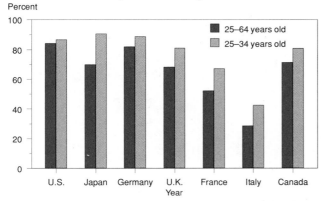

NOTE: In the United States, completing secondary school is defined as graduating from high school or earning a GED.

SOURCE: Indicator 27, *Condition 1996.*

increasing in these countries. Moreover, the gap between the completion rates of younger and older workers is larger in other G-7 countries than in the United States, suggesting that secondary school attainment is increasing at a faster rate in the other countries. The high school completion rates for young adults in Japan and Germany are now similar to those of young adults in the United States, while the rates for young adults in Canada and the United Kingdom are nearly equal to those of their counterparts in the United States.

Most G-7 countries still lag well behind the United States in higher education attainment. The proportion of the population aged 25–64 who have completed a college education is by far the highest in the United States. Even though the U.S. lead is smaller for adults aged 25–34, only Japan has a rate of higher education attainment among young adults comparable to that in the United States. The rate of college completion among young American adults has changed little during the past 20 years, while the rate for young adults in Japan has risen dramatically; thus,

Higher education completion: 1992

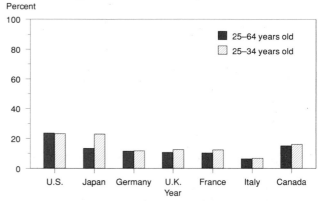

NOTE: In the United States, completing secondary school is defined as graduating from high school or earning a bachelor's degree.

SOURCE: Indicator 27, *Condition 1996.*

Japan has nearly caught up to the United States. The rate of higher education attainment in most other G-7 countries has increased more slowly than that in Japan, as indicated by the smaller attainment gaps between younger and older adults in those countries.

Academic achievement

♦ *Workers who have a record of high academic achievement, as measured by achievement test scores, are unemployed less and earn more than workers with lower scores.*

Workers who were 28 years old and who previously scored in the top quartile on the Armed Services Vocational Aptitude Battery (ASVAB) mathematics, science, or paragraph comprehension tests had a lower unemployment rate than other workers. For example, 2.5 percent

Percentage of workers aged 28 who were unemployed, by ASVAB score quartile: 1985–93

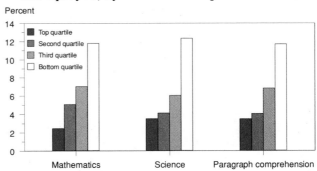

NOTE: ASVAB is the Armed Services Vocational Aptitude Battery. To control for differences in age at testing individuals were assigned to age-specific performance quartiles for each subject area based on their age testing.

SOURCE: National Longitudinal Survey of Youth.

of workers in the top quartile of the mathematics test were unemployed, compared to 7.7 percent of workers in the other three quartiles combined. Workers in the top quartile on the tests in each subject also earned more, on average, than other workers. For example, workers in the top quartile on the mathematics test earned an average of $13.52 per hour, compared to an average of $10.05 per hour for workers in the other three quartiles combined.

Mean hourly rate of pay for workers aged 28, by ASVAB score quartile: 1985–93

In 1992 constant dollars

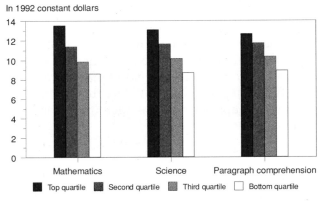

■ Top quartile ▨ Second quartile ▨ Third quartile ☐ Bottom quartile

SOURCE: National Longitudinal Survey of Youth.

◆ *Test scores of U.S. students generally increased in the 1980s and 1990s, offsetting declines that occurred during the 1970s.*

Among 17-year-old students, National Assessment of Educational Progress (NAEP) test scores increased between 1982 and 1992. Increases in mathematics and science scores reversed a trend of declining scores that existed throughout the 1970s. By 1992, the scores in these subjects had recovered to the 1973 levels. NAEP reading scores of 17-year-old students have increased slowly and steadily since the early 1970s.

◆ *U.S. students trail students from many other countries in mathematics and science achievement, but U.S. students tend to lead in reading achievement.*

Most of the countries included in a 1991 international study of mathematics and science achievement outperformed the United States in the mathematics achievement of both 9-year-old and 13-year-old students. With respect to science

achievement, 9-year-old U.S. students performed as well as those in most other countries, but 13-year-old U.S. students scored below their counterparts in half of the other countries. In a

Trends in average achievement of 17-year-olds in mathematics, reading, and science: 1969–92

Scale score

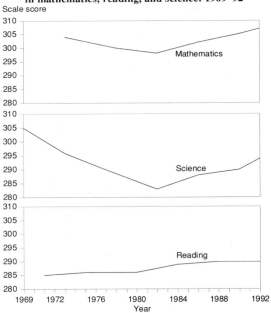

SOURCE: U.S. Department of Education, The National Assessment of Educational Progress *1992 Trends in Academic Progress.*

separate international study of reading achievement, the United States led 20 of 22 countries in reading scores for 9-year-olds and was equivalent to or led 21 of 22 countries for 14-year-olds.

International distribution of academic achievement relative to the United States: 1991–92

Subject and age	Number of countries performing:			
	Measurably higher than the U.S.	Not measurably different from the U.S.	Measurably lower than the U.S.	Number of countries in the study
Mathematics (1991)				
9-year-olds	7	2	0	10
13-year-olds	12	1	1	15
Science (1991)				
9-year-olds	0	7	2	10
13-year-olds	1	6	1	15
Reading (1991–92)				
9-year-olds	1	1	20	23
14-year-olds	3	15	6	23

SOURCE: Indicators 20, 23, and 24, *Condition 1993*.

Adult literacy

A 1992 study tested the performance of U.S. adults on three scales of literacy—prose, document, and quantitative—and categorized adults into five literacy levels according to their test scores, with level 1 being the lowest literacy level and level 5 being the highest.

♦ *Workers with higher literacy scores are unemployed less and earn more than workers with lower literacy scores.*

Unemployment rates are especially high for workers in the two lowest levels of literacy—levels 1 and 2—on each of the three literacy scales. For these workers, the unemployment rate

Unemployment rates of civilian noninstitutionalized adults, by proficiency level on three literacy scales: 1992

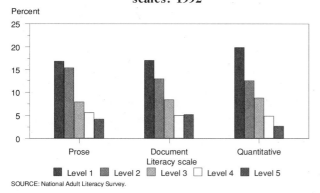

SOURCE: National Adult Literacy Survey.

ranges from 12 percent for workers with level 2 quantitative literacy to nearly 20 percent for those with level 1. Unemployment rates for individuals in the two highest literacy levels—levels 4 and

Mean weekly earnings of those employed full time, by proficiency level on three adult literacy scales: 1992

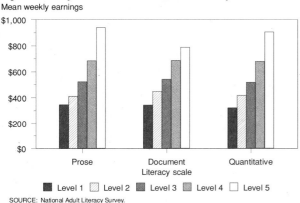

SOURCE: National Adult Literacy Survey.

5—are less than 6 percent.

Workers with high literacy scores earn more than other workers, on average. On the prose scale, for example, full-time workers in level 3 earn a mean weekly wage that is 51 percent higher than that of their counterparts in level 1. Those in level 5 earn a weekly wage that is nearly 80 percent higher than the wage of those in level 3.

♦ *The literacy proficiency of a substantial proportion of the U.S. labor force is limited, and only a small proportion of workers perform at a high literacy level.*

Forty percent or more of the adult labor force performed at the two lowest levels on each of the literacy scales, suggesting that many workers lacked the skills needed to interpret, integrate, and compare or contrast information using written materials common to the home or workplace. These workers appear to be unable to perform the types of tasks typical of certain occupations that demand high skills, such as professional, managerial, technical, high-level sales, skilled clerical, or craft and precision production occupations. Five percent or fewer of U.S. labor force participants scored in the highest proficiency levels, demonstrating an ability to perform well on a wide array of literacy tasks.

♦ *Literacy of the U.S. adult population is, on average, roughly similar to that of populations in other industrialized countries, but the United States has a greater proportion of adults at the lowest literacy levels.*

Percentage of the labor force in each proficiency level on the three literacy scales: 1992

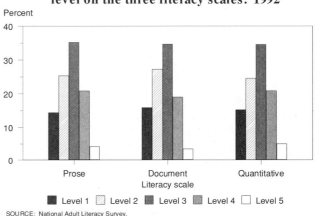

SOURCE: National Adult Literacy Survey.

On average, the proportion of the U.S. population in the highest literacy levels is similar to that in the other countries included in an international study of adult literacy. However, the United States has a higher concentration of adults in the lowest literacy level than nearly all of the other countries. More than 20 percent of the U.S. sample scored at the lowest literacy level on each of the three literacy scales, while the other

Estimated percentage of the population in each proficiency level on three adult literacy scales, by selected countries: 1994

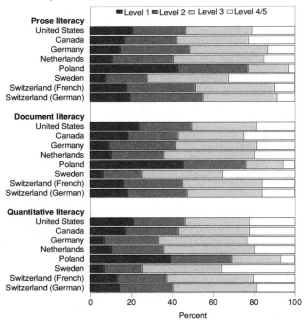

SOURCE: Organization for Economic Co-operation and Development and Statistics Canada, *Literacy, Economy and Society: Results of the First International Adult Literacy Survey: 1995.*

countries (except Poland) had less than 20 percent of the sampled population scoring at the lowest level on each scale.

Summary

Workers in the United States are still more productive, on average, than workers in any other country. However, worker productivity in several industrialized countries is gradually catching up to that in the United States, and eventually the United States is likely to share the lead in worker productivity. This convergence in

productivity is attributable, in part, to the rapid expansion of education in other countries. The education of the work force, according to at least some measures that contribute to economic success, is growing more rapidly in other countries than in the United States. But education is not the only determinant of worker productivity, and other factors no doubt have also played important roles in the rapid productivity growth in other countries.

Although the United States leads almost every other industrialized country in college attainment, and the academic achievement of U.S. students has been improving in recent years, U.S. students still tend to lag behind students in other countries with respect to some measures of achievement. In particular, the mathematics and science scores of U.S. students, especially older students, are lower than those of their counterparts in other industrialized countries. U.S. students do, however, perform relatively well on reading tests. But, adults in the United States may not be as skilled in some areas as their counterparts in other countries. Compared to other countries that have tested literacy, the United States has a higher concentration of adults who score at the lowest literacy levels.

NOTES:

[1] Moses Abramovitz. "Catching Up, Forging Ahead, and Falling Behind." *Journal of Economic History* 46 (June 1986): 385–406.

[2] U.S. Department of Labor, Bureau of Labor Statistics. *Labor Composition and U.S. Productivity Growth, 1948–90,* Bulletin 2426. Washington, D.C.: U.S. Government Printing Office, 1993; Dale W. Jorgensen. "The Contribution of Education to U.S. Economic Growth, 1948–73." In E. Dean ed., *Education and Economic Productivity.* Cambridge, MA: Ballinger, 1984; Edward F. Denison. *Accounting for Slower Economic Growth: The United States in the 1970s.* Washington, D.C.: Brookings Institute, 1979.

[3] Roland Sturm. "How Do Education and Training Affect a Country's Economic Performance? A Literature Survey." Santa Monica, CA: RAND, 1993.

[4] U.S. Department of Labor, Bureau of Labor Statistics. *Labor Composition and U.S. Productivity Growth, 1948–90,* Bulletin 2426. Washington, D.C.: U.S. Government Printing Office, 1993.

Preparation for work

by Elliott Medrich, MPR Associates, Inc.

Growing interest among policymakers, educators, and employers in the changing nature of work reflects two concerns: 1) today's workplace requires a range of capabilities that are quite different from the workplace of the past; and 2) schools could do more to teach students the skills that would be useful to them when they enter the labor force.

Ensuring that all students are ready for work, especially those who do not attend 4-year postsecondary institutions, requires a considerable reappraisal of the relationship between school and the workplace. What must be done to ensure that those entering the labor force have the training that is necessary for success in an increasingly competitive economic environment? What kinds of training and exposure—at school and in the workplace—will enable young people to achieve quality employment and high wages throughout their working life?

The equation is further complicated by the emergence of "high performance" work organizations. This new way of working reflects increasing attachment throughout the economy to new information technology. Success in the future work force will require flexible skills and learning capabilities, and making personal commitments to training and retraining throughout one's career.

Data below are presented on several issues that are central to the process of work preparation: course-taking patterns among high school and postsecondary students; student work experience as it relates to preparation for entry into the labor force; and adult involvement in education and training while employed.

Enrollment and course taking in preparation for work

High school

Since the 1970s, states have been tightening high school graduation requirements in "core subject" areas. Most states have increased the number of courses students seeking a diploma must complete in English, social studies, science, and mathematics.[1] To some extent, these changes have paralleled recommendations of the National Commission on Excellence in Education. The Commission's 1983 report, *A Nation at Risk*, which argued the case for strengthening course-taking requirements in these subject areas, became an anchor of the school reform movement.

Other research, more specifically concerned with workplace and employment skills, also recognized the importance of improving the basic academic capabilities of high school graduates. For example, in 1991, the Secretary's Commission on Achieving Necessary Skills (SCANS) identified the types of skills young people need in order to enter and succeed in the labor market.[2] The "foundation skills" described by SCANS, which were similar to those recommended in *A Nation at Risk*, closely followed the framework of course-taking requirements in academic areas that the states were adopting.[3]

The confluence of enhanced academic standards and workplace-readiness standards is no accident. A student who is well prepared for the challenges of the future workplace should have a strong academic background without regard to his or her specific job or career-related objectives.

♦ *High school graduates are taking more courses in academic core subjects.*

The range of curricula reforms and the number of standards introduced have been substantial. Between 1982 and 1994, the percentage of high school graduates earning the recommended units in core courses increased sharply. This was true both among states with more restrictive and those with less restrictive laws governing academic course-taking requirements for high school graduation. It was also true both for students enrolled in academic programs and those enrolled in vocational programs (Indicator 28, *Condition 1996*).

Students have also been earning fewer vocational units. Between 1982 and 1992, while academic units increased from 14.1 to 17.4, vocational units

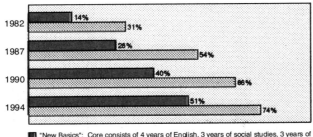

Percentage of high school graduates who earned recommended units in core courses

- ■ "New Basics": Core consists of 4 years of English, 3 years of social studies, 3 years of science, and 3 years of mathematics.
- ▨ Less restrictive curriculum: Core consists of 4 years of English, 3 years of social studies, 2 years of science, and 2 years of mathematics.

SOURCE: Indicator 28, *Condition 1996.*

declined from 4.6 to 3.8, a further indication of a trend toward focusing on academic coursework during high school (Indicator 23, *Condition 1994*).

♦ *High school graduates in 1992 were more likely than their counterparts in 1982 to have taken mathematics courses at the level of algebra 1 or higher, and science courses at the level of biology or higher.*

Changes in overall student course-taking patterns are further reflected in changes in student course-taking patterns in mathematics and

science. This is an important development, as these fields of study often require higher level thinking skills to solve complex problems—skills that are increasingly required in the workplace. Between 1982 and 1992, the proportions of students taking coursework in both subject areas have changed substantially, especially at advanced levels.

♦ *High school students' access to and use of computers increased substantially between 1984 and 1993.*

Computers are an important reality in the workplace, and computer literacy is becoming essential to functioning effectively in society. In this respect, the schools are a valuable venue for training and developing student computer skills. Further, there is evidence suggesting that the

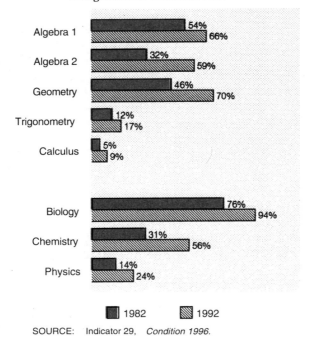

Percentage of high school graduates who took selected mathematics and science courses in high school: 1982 and 1992

■ 1982   ▨ 1992

SOURCE: Indicator 29, *Condition 1996.*

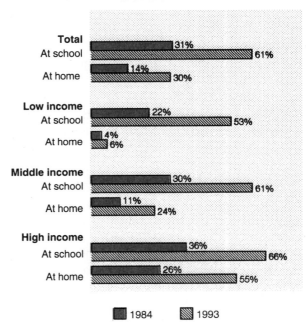

Percentage of students in grades 7–12 who used a computer at school or at home: 1984 and 1993

■ 1984   ▨ 1993

SOURCE: Indicator 5 *Condition 1995.*

infusion of technology in the classroom has implications for student learning as well. A recent study notes that using technology to support instruction improved student outcomes in language arts, mathematics, social studies, and science.[4]

The proportion of students with access to a computer at school or at home doubled between 1984 and 1993. Without regard to income, the majority of students in 1993 had access to a computer at school. However, a substantial gap in computer use exists outside school: students from higher income families were much more likely than students from middle or low income families to have a computer available to them at home.

♦ *Proficiency levels of 17-year-olds have improved in mathematics and science since the late 1970s.*

Proficiency in crucial subject areas is one way of measuring the capabilities of young adults as they enter the labor force. Between the late 1970s and 1992, proficiency scores among 17-year-olds in mathematics and science, as measured by NAEP, have improved, while reading proficiency

Average mathematics and science proficiency (scale scores) of 17-year-olds: 1977–92

Year	Mathematics	Science
1977	—	290
1978	300	—
1982	298	283
1986	302	288
1990	305	290
1992	307	294

— Not available.

SOURCE: Indicators 15 and 16, *Condition 1996*.

has remained stable. The 9 scale point increase in mathematics proficiency between 1982 and 1992, and the 11 scale point increase in science proficiency are particularly notable, as this is roughly the equivalent of the gain in proficiency with 1 year of age. These improvements in proficiency suggest that students are better prepared than they have been previously in fields of study that are key to success in advanced academics and for performance in an increasingly technical work environment.

Postsecondary education

Considerable evidence documents the lifelong employment and earnings advantage of advanced education and training.[5] While solid high school preparation may have some meaning in the labor force, advanced training through

postsecondary education provides additional, substantial benefits.

♦ *Increasing proportions of high school graduates are entering postsecondary education immediately after high school.*

High school graduates are considerably more likely to continue their education immediately after graduation than they were previously. In 1994, 62 percent of high school graduates enrolled in college the October following graduation, up

Percentage of high school graduates aged 16–24 who enrolled in college the October following graduation: 1973, 1983, and 1994

Characteristics	1973	1983	1994
Total	47	53	62
Male	50	52	61
Female	43	53	63
2-year college	15	19	21
4-year college	32	34	41
Males			
2-year college	15	20	23
4-year college	35	32	38
Females			
2-year college	15	18	19
4-year college	28	35	44

SOURCE: Indicator 7 and table 7-1, *Condition 1996*.

from 47 percent in 1973. Postsecondary enrollment patterns over time have differed for males and females, with college enrollment rates for females increasing more than for males, especially at 4-year colleges and institutions.

Differences in fields of concentration and course-taking patterns at subbaccalaureate and baccalaureate levels suggest substantial variation in work force preparation and employment opportunities following the completion of training.

♦ *Postsecondary subbaccalaureate degree majors vary considerably by sex and race/ethnicity.*

Students' focus in postsecondary education, as reflected in degree majors, provides insight into the depth, breadth, and direction of their training. While some graduates of subbaccalaureate programs go on to 4-year colleges and institutions, for many an associate's degree is the final degree that provides job-related training. Differences between the sexes in fields of study are substantial. Among white, black, and Hispanic recipients of associate's degrees in 1991, females were more likely than males to complete a degree in business or health, while males were more likely to complete a degree in technological fields (e.g., computer and information sciences, engineering, and science technologies) (Indicator 29, *Condition 1994*).

♦ *At the baccalaureate level, students are paying more attention to applied fields of study, as compared to a more general, liberal arts education.*

Changing opportunities within the job market can affect students' decisions about their coursework and their major field of study. At the baccalaureate level, data are limited to percentages of students who took one or more courses in selected subjects in 1985–86, but differences in course-taking patterns are evident.

Males were much more likely than females to have taken courses in physical sciences, mathematics, computer science, engineering, and

Percentage of bachelor's degree recipients who took one or more courses in different subjects: 1985–86

Field of study	Total	Male	Female
Computer science	42	48	38
Engineering	18	27	9
Mathematics	78	83	74
Life sciences	53	47	60
Physical sciences	67	72	62
Economics	53	60	46
Political science	41	43	37
Psychology	65	60	72
Sociology/ anthropology	61	56	66

SOURCE: Indicator 28, *Condition 1994*.

economics. Females were more likely than males to have taken life sciences, psychology, and sociology and less likely to have taken political science and economics.

The distribution of degrees conferred across fields suggest the kinds of skills and capabilities that students want, or believe they should have, before they enter the work force on a full-time basis. Five fields of study accounted for 72 percent

of all bachelor's degrees conferred in 1991. Business and management, social and behavioral sciences, humanities, education, and engineering—in that order—were the five fields of study in which most degrees were conferred in 1991. In 1971, these same five fields had represented 80 percent of bachelor's degrees conferred.

Working while enrolled

Bachelor's degrees conferred in selected fields of study: 1971, 1981, and 1991

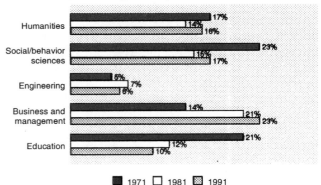

■ 1971   □ 1981   ▨ 1991

SOURCE: Indicator 41, *Condition 1994*.

Employment while in high school

♦ *Many high school students are exposed to the world of work—nearly 30 percent work at least part time.*

High school students work for many reasons. While employment may have some negative impact on students' school experience and their study time, especially if too much time is spent at work, workplace exposure can help students prepare for future, full-time employment.

Percentage of high school students aged 16–24 who were employed: 1970–92

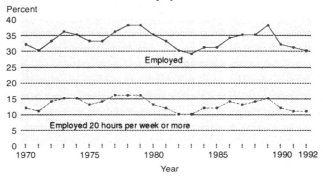

SOURCE: Indicator 49, *Condition 1994*.

Among all high school students aged 16–24 in 1992, 30 percent were employed. The total percent employed in 1992 was about the same as that in 1982, and less than that in 1972. In 1992, males were somewhat more likely to be employed than females, and whites were considerably more likely to be employed than were blacks or Hispanics.

Employment while in college

♦ *Among 16- to 24-year-old college students in 1993, almost half of full-time students and 85 percent of part-time students were employed.*

While work experience during college may or may not be associated with a student's major or career aspirations, work is now part of the postsecondary experience for many students. Employment while enrolled in college may, at the least, provide students with the resources they need to be able to continue their college education and may also give students a better idea of the needs and standards of the workplace. At the same time, it may reduce a student's prospects for completing college or may lengthen the time it takes for those who work to complete their education and training.

Percentage of 16- to 24-year old college students who were employed: 1973 and 1993

Characteristics	1973	1993
All students	36	46
Work 20 hours or more	17	25
Full-time students	36	46
Low income	42	51
Middle income	37	48
High income	34	42
Part-time students	85	85
Low income	82	68
Middle income	86	86
High income	84	91

SOURCE: Indicator 51 and tables 51-2 and 51-5, *Condition 1995*.

In 1993, nearly half (46 percent) of all 16- to 24-year-old full-time college students were employed, and about one-fourth worked at least 20 hours per week. Even more part-time students worked. About the same proportion of part-time

college students worked in 1993 as did in 1973. In 1993, full-time college students from high income families were less likely to be employed than were full-time students from middle or low income families. In contrast, part-time college students from high income families were more likely to be employed than were students from middle or low income families.

Enrollment and education while working

Some occupations require continuing education of varying amount and intensity, but in general, adult education provides an important opportunity for those who are already employed to keep pace with rapid changes in the workplace. Participation rates may indicate the importance of lifelong learning as a condition of employment in the future labor force. Fully 21 percent of all adults participated in adult education in 1995 for work-related purposes.

Percentage of adults who participated in adult education in the past 12 months for work-related purposes: 1995

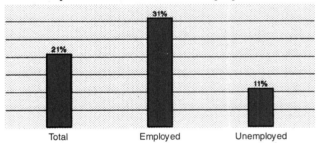

SOURCE: Indicator 14, *Condition 1996*.

Among those who participated in work-related courses, the majority took courses provided by businesses or professional associations. Others took work-related courses mostly provided by colleges or government agencies.

Ultimately, success in the workplace may require a lifelong commitment to training and personal skill building. In 1991, almost one-third of workers aged 16 and over had received some skill improvement training in their current job at some time during the 12 preceding months. Workers with higher levels of educational attainment were much more likely to receive training than were those with less education. Finally, workers in executive, professional, and technical occupations, followed by those in sales and administrative support, were most likely to receive such training on the job.

Percentage of workers aged 16 and over who received skill improvement training in the last 12 months, while in their current job

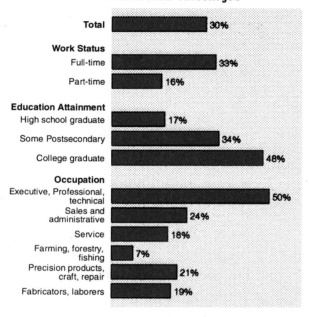

SOURCE: Indicator 12, *Condition 1995*.

Summary

In summary, course-taking patterns at the secondary level, and course-taking and degree major patterns at the postsecondary level, suggest that students are increasingly focused on preparing for the rigors of the labor market. In high school, students are taking more courses in academic core subjects and in higher level mathematics and science courses. They also have considerably more exposure to computers than they did a decade ago. In addition, more students are entering postsecondary education immediately after high school to pursue advanced education and training before entering the labor market.

At both the secondary and postsecondary levels, many students are employed while enrolled, which offers them some opportunity for exposure to the work environment. Once individuals enter the labor force, there is considerable opportunity for them to continue training. For example, many adults participate in adult education for work-related purposes, and many receive some skill improvement training in their jobs.

NOTES:
[1] U.S. Department of Education, National Center for Education Statistics. *Overview and Inventory of State Requirements for School Coursework and Attendance.* Washington, D.C.: 1992.
[2] Secretary's Commission on Achieving Necessary Skills (SCANS). *What Work Requires of Schools.* Washington, D.C.: 1991.
[3] Foundation competencies include *basic skills* (reading, writing, arithmetic and mathematics, speaking and listening); *thinking skills* (creativity, making decisions, solving problems, knowing how to learn, and reasoning); and *personal qualities* (individual responsibility, self-esteem, sociability, self-management, and integrity).
[4] Bailo, Ellen R., and Jay Sivin-Kachla. *Effectiveness of Technology in Schools, 1990–1994.* Washington, D.C.: Software Publishers Association, 1995.
[5] Kominski, Robert and Rebecca Sutterlin. *What's It Worth? Educational Background and Economic Status: Spring 1990.* Washington, D.C.: U.S. Bureau of the Census, 1992.

Minorities in higher education

by Thomas M. Smith, NCES

Minorities in the United States have long suffered lower economic prosperity and social status relative to the white majority. Higher education often serves as the best means of social mobility available to our nation's young people. For example, graduating from college is associated with more stable patterns of employment and higher earnings. As the gap in earnings between high school and college graduates continues to widen, attending college has become even more important for minorities who are trying to enter into a globally competitive labor market. This essay reviews the higher education aspirations and preparation, college enrollment, persistence, and completion rates of minorities in comparison with the majority white population. For the purpose of this essay, the Office of Management and Budget (OMB) standard classification scheme is used, and the categories of black, Hispanic, Asian/Pacific Islander, and American Indian/Alaskan Native are used to denote racial/ethnic minority groups. In the data used for many comparisons, however, the sample size of the two latter groups is too small for them to be reported separately and, therefore, they are not shown separately in these comparisons.

Plans and expectations

The proportion of all high school seniors in minority groups who planned to continue their education at 4-year colleges and institutions directly after high school increased between 1972 and 1992, although between-group differences have remained fairly constant.

Although many students decide whether or not to attend college early in their high school careers, students' plans as high school seniors are likely to reflect their previous academic performance, their financial means, and their educational and career goals. In both 1972 and 1992, similar proportions of black and white seniors planned to attend 4-year colleges and institutions. Hispanic seniors were less likely than white seniors to plan to attend a 4-year college in both 1972 and 1992, although the proportion of Hispanic seniors who planned to attend college increased by 9 percentage points

over this time period. In 1992, Asian/Pacific Islander seniors were more likely than white seniors to plan to attend a 4-year college immediately after high school graduation.

A larger proportion of black and Hispanic seniors planned to attend an academic program in a 2-year college in 1992 than in 1972: the proportion of black seniors increased from 5 percent to 11 percent, while the proportion of Hispanic seniors increased from 11 to 26 percent. However, no change occurred among white seniors over this time period. In 1992, Hispanic seniors were more likely than their white peers to plan to attend a 2-year academic program.

Percentage of high school seniors who planned to continue their education the next year at 4-year colleges or in 2-year academic programs

Race/ethnicity	4-year program		2-year academic program	
	1972	1992	1972	1992
Total	**34**	**54**	**11**	**13**
White	35	55	12	12
Black	32	52	5	11
Hispanic	11	20	11	26
Asian/Pacific Islander	47	65	18	12

SOURCE: National Longitudinal Study of 1972 and National Education Longitudinal Study of 1988, Second Follow-up.

Students consider many factors when selecting a college, including financial considerations, such as the cost of attendance and the availability of financial aid. The percentage of black, white, and Hispanic seniors who reported that tuition and expenses were very important considerations in selecting a college declined between 1972 and 1992. On the other hand, the proportions of Asian/Pacific Islander seniors who reported that tuition and fees were important factors did not differ significantly between the two time periods. Availability of financial aid, however, remained very important over this time period for black and Hispanic seniors. In 1992, black and Hispanic seniors were more likely to say that financial aid was a very important consideration in selecting a college (67 and 62 percent, respectively) than white seniors (40 percent).[1]

♦ *The proportion of high school students in all racial and ethnic groups expecting to complete only high school or less fell dramatically between 1972 and 1992, while the proportion expecting to graduate from college increased.*

Students' long-term expectations for education may differ substantially from their short-term plans. While not all high school seniors plan to attend college immediately after graduation, nearly all students expect to continue their education eventually. The proportion of seniors expecting to at least finish college ranged from 62 percent for Hispanics to 78 percent for Asian/Pacific Islanders in 1992. Since 1992, the proportions of white, black, and Hispanic seniors who expected to complete college increased by 20 percentage points, compared to an increase of 9 percentage points for Asian/Pacific Islander seniors.[2] Even though educational plans and expectations are generally high among white, black, Hispanic, and Asian/Pacific Islander high school seniors, wanting to go to college is only the first step in making the transition. Preparing to go to college is the second step.

Percentage of 1992 high school seniors expecting to complete various levels of education

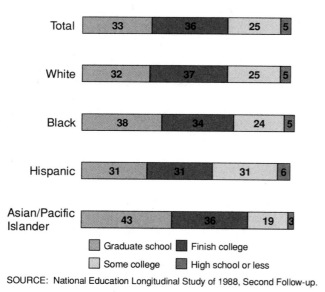

SOURCE: National Education Longitudinal Study of 1988, Second Follow-up.

Preparation and course-taking patterns

Success in higher education depends on good preparation in high school. Evidence from the Postsecondary Education Transcripts supports this statement. Of the students in the high school class of 1982 who participated significantly in higher education (as defined above), the percentage who completed a bachelor's degree was strongly related to the number of remedial courses the person took at postsecondary institutions. Among those who took no remedial courses, 57 percent completed a bachelor's degree. Among those who took 3 or more, roughly 25 percent completed their degree.

Bachelor's degree completion among participants in higher education for the high school class of 1982, by number of remedial courses taken: 1993

Number of remedial courses taken	Percent completing bachelor's degree
Total	46.1
None	57.4
1	48.7
2	37.2
3-4	26.2
More than 4	24.8

NOTE: Participants are defined as those who completed more than 10 credits. Remedial courses include remedial writing, remedial reading, remedial speech, development grammar, ESL, all pre-collegiate mathematics, and basic academic and developmental study skills.
SOURCE: U.S. Department of Education, National Center for Education Statistics, Postsecondary Education Transcript Studies of the High School and Beyond Study (HS&B) Sophomore Cohort, 1993.

♦ *Students from all minority groups are taking a more rigorous curriculum, although black, Hispanic, and American Indian/Alaskan Native students continue to trail their Asian/Pacific Islander and white counterparts in advanced mathematics and science course taking.*

Examining the transcripts of high school graduates shows if the academic rigor of the courses they take has changed over time. The average number of academic course units earned by public high school graduates increased between 1982 and 1992 for all racial and ethnic groups. In 1992, Asian/Pacific Islander graduates earned the most academic credits (18.5), while American Indian/Alaskan Native graduates earned the least (16.0); this range is equivalent to five semester courses. White graduates earned 17.6 credits, compared to Hispanic and black graduates who earned 16.9

and 16.7 credits, respectively (Indicator 23, *Condition 1994*).

This renewed emphasis on academic course taking also is reflected by the increase in the percentage of high school graduates taking the "New Basics" curriculum, a core curriculum composed of 4 units of English; 3 units each of science, social studies, and mathematics, recommended in *A Nation at Risk*.[3] The proportion of 1994 high school graduates who took this core curriculum ranged from about 44 percent for blacks, Hispanics, and American Indians/Alaskan Natives to about 54 percent for whites and 57 percent for Asians/Pacific Islanders. This represents a substantial increase from 1982, when only 14 percent of graduates took this stringent of a curriculum (Indicator 28, *Condition 1996*).

Percentage of high school graduates taking the "New Basics" curriculum

Race/ethnicity	1982	1994
Total	**14**	**51**
White	16	54
Black	12	45
Hispanic	7	44
Asian/Pacific Islander	21	57
American Indian/ Alaskan Native	7	44

SOURCE: Indicator 28, *Condition 1996*.

Students in all racial and ethnic groups are taking more advanced mathematics and science courses, although black, Hispanic, and American Indian/Alaskan Native graduates still trail their Asian/Pacific Islander and white counterparts in advanced mathematics and science course taking (table 29-2, *Condition 1996*). From a course-taking perspective at least, it appears that all racial and ethnic groups are better prepared for college today than they were in the early 1980s.

♦ *The reading skills of white seniors are better than those of their minority counterparts. Although the gap in white-black and white-Hispanic scores has narrowed somewhat, large differences still remain.*

Course taking is only one component of preparing for college; the skills that students gain from those classes is another important measure of their readiness to enter college. For example, a student's ability to comprehend and effectively use written language is a necessary skill to master prior to taking on a more advanced college curriculum. There is substantial variation in average reading proficiency among seniors from different racial and ethnic groups. In 1994, for instance, the reading proficiency of white seniors was higher than Asian/Pacific Islander seniors, who, in turn, scored higher than their black and Hispanic counterparts. However, the reading proficiency scores of American Indian/Alaskan Native seniors were are not statistically distinguishable from their Asian/Pacific Islander and Hispanic peers.

Average reading proficiency of seniors: 1994

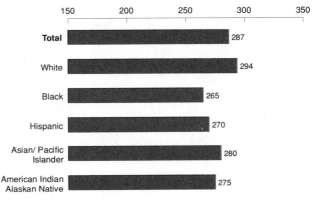

SOURCE: National Assessment of Educational Progress, 1994 Reading Assessment.

Reading proficiency scores for white, black, and Hispanic 17-year-olds are available for several years between 1975 and 1992. Although the reading gap between whites and their black and Hispanic counterparts remains wide, this gap has narrowed over time (Indicator 13, *Condition 1995*). In fact, the reading skills of white, black, and Hispanic 17-year-olds have all increased since the mid-1970s with the scores of black and Hispanic students increasing more than those of their white peers (Indicator 13, *Condition 1995*). There is some evidence, however, that the white-minority gap in reading is no longer narrowing.[4]

♦ *Among high school seniors, both Asian/Pacific Islanders and whites have higher mathematics proficiency than Hispanics, American Indians/Alaskan Natives, and blacks. Over the past 20 years, however, scores for whites have increased at a slower rate than those for blacks and Hispanics, thereby causing this gap to narrow.*

Proficiency in mathematics allows students to use higher level thinking skills to solve complex problems. If students do not have a firm grasp of mathematics upon leaving high school, they will be at a disadvantage when trying to master that material in college. Among the senior class of 1992, both Asian/Pacific Islanders and whites had higher mathematics proficiency scores than their Hispanic, American Indian/Alaskan Native, and black peers.[5]

Average mathematics proficiency of seniors: 1994

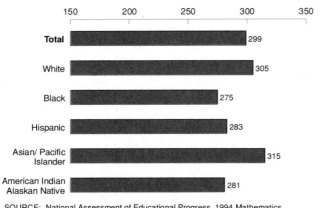

SOURCE: National Assessment of Educational Progress, 1994 Mathematics Assessment.

For the years 1973–92, mathematics trend data are available for white, black, and Hispanic 17-year-olds. These data suggest that although a large gap in mathematics proficiency exists at age 17 between whites and their black and Hispanic peers, the gap is narrowing (Indicator 16, *Condition 1996*). Among white 17-year-olds, the mathematics proficiency declined between 1973 and 1982, but has rebounded since. On the other hand, the mathematics scores of black and Hispanic 17-year-olds were level from 1973 to 1982, but have increased sizably between 1982 and 1992—narrowing the gap between the scores of blacks and Hispanics and their white counterparts.

◆ *With the exception of Asian/Pacific Islanders, large gaps in science proficiency exist between whites and other racial/ethnic groups. Science scores for most groups have increased since the early 1980s.*

The ability to apply scientific information, interpret data, and make inferences about scientific findings is a prerequisite for entry into most scientific fields. Adequate preparation in science in high school can influence success in college-level biology, chemistry, and physics— courses that often serve as gatekeepers for many scientific fields, including medicine and engineering. For the senior class of 1990, science proficiency scores are available for all racial/ethnic groups. Scores for white and Asian/Pacific Islander seniors were higher than those for black and Hispanic seniors. However, the average science proficiency of American Indian/Alaskan Native seniors was lower than that of white students, higher than the average science proficiency of black students, and not significantly different from the average science proficiency of Asian/Pacific Islander and Hispanic students.[6]

Average science proficiency of seniors: 1990

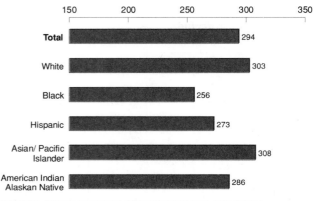

SOURCE: National Assessment of Educational Progress, 1994 Science Assessment.

Trend data on science proficiency are available for whites and blacks starting in 1970 and for Hispanics starting in 1977. These data demonstrate that between 1970 and 1982, the science proficiency of white and black 17-year-olds declined, but scores for both groups have risen since then. In 1992, the science proficiency of white 17-year-olds was still below their 1970 level, while black scores had fully regained ground. Moreover, between 1977 and 1982, scores for Hispanics declined, but have rebounded since (Indicator 16, *Condition 1996*).

♦ *Average SAT scores for minority test-takers have improved over the past 20 years, especially for college-bound blacks and American Indians/Alaskan Natives.*

The Scholastic Assessment Test (SAT) is designed to predict success in the freshman year of college. SAT scores are not just measures of the skills of those who could potentially go to college, but also of the skills of those who actually plan to go. Since 1976, the mean scores of black test-takers have risen 24 points on the verbal section and 34 points on the mathematics section, while the mean scores of whites have fallen 3 points on the verbal section and have risen 5 points on the mathematics section. American Indians/Alaskan Natives also had relatively large increases in SAT scores over this time period: 15 points on the verbal section and 27 points on the mathematics section (table 22-2, *Condition 1996*).

College enrollment rates

♦ *Blacks and Hispanics are less likely than whites to make an immediate transition from high school to college.*

Since most college students enroll in college immediately after completing high school, the percentage of high school graduates enrolled in college the October following graduation is an indicator of the total proportion who will ever enroll in college. College enrollment rates reflect both the accessibility of higher education to high school graduates, as well as their assessment of the relative value of attending college compared to working, entering the military, or other possible pursuits. Enrollment rates for white

high school graduates increased from 50 percent in the early 1970s to about 60 percent in the mid-1980s and have fluctuated between 60 and 65 percent since then. After a period of decline in the late 1970s and early 1980s, the percentage of blacks enrolling in college immediately after high school graduation rose again until the late 1980s, when it appeared to have leveled off at around 50 percent. Between 1972 and 1994, Hispanic enrollment rates have mostly fluctuated between 45 and 55 percent (Indicator 7, *Condition 1996*).

The type of institutions that high school graduates first attend can affect their likelihood of completing a bachelor's degree. Students who begin their higher education at a 2-year college are far less likely to earn a bachelor's degree than their counterparts who begin at a 4-year college (Indicators 10 and 26, *Condition 1996*). In 1994, white graduates were twice as likely to enroll in a 4-year college as a 2-year college after high school, while black graduates were about 1.5 times as likely and Hispanic graduates were equally likely to enroll in a 4-year college (table 7-2, *Condition 1996*).

♦ *Although the proportion of 1980 high school sophomores who made the immediate transition to college after high school varied by race/ethnicity, the proportion who delayed entry into college did not differ measurably by race/ethnicity.*

Although most college students first enrolled in college in the fall following their high school graduation, a sizable number delayed entry to college. Research has shown that delayed entry is negatively associated with earning a bachelor's degree (Indicators 10 and 26, *Condition 1996*). Although the proportion of 1980 high school sophomores who started college in the fall of 1982 varied by race/ethnicity, the proportion who delayed was similar for whites, blacks, Hispanics, and Asian/Pacific Islanders—about 14 percent each. A larger proportion of American Indians/Alaskan Natives (25 percent) were more likely to delay entry into college (table 26-1, *Condition 1996*).

♦ *Higher education enrollment rates of high school graduates aged 18–24 have risen substantially for whites and moderately for blacks, although whites are still more likely to enroll than blacks or Hispanics. Enrollment rates among older adults are similar for whites, blacks, and Hispanics.*

Percentage of high school graduates aged 16–24 who were enrolled in college the October following graduation: October 1972–94

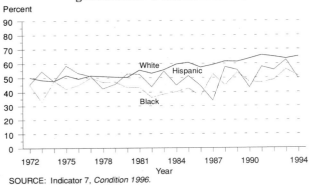

SOURCE: Indicator 7, *Condition 1996*.

Racial and ethnic differences in the college enrollment rates may reflect variations in access to and persistence in higher education. Between 1972 and 1994, white high school graduates aged 18–24 were more likely to be enrolled in college than were their black and Hispanic counterparts.

Percentage of 18- to 24-year-old high school graduates enrolled in college: October 1972–94

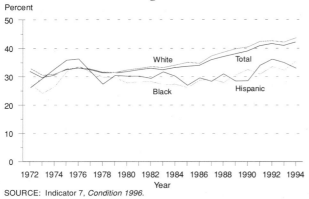

SOURCE: Indicator 7, *Condition 1996.*

Between 1992 and 1994, the average enrollment rate for whites was 9 percentage points higher than that of blacks and 8 percentage points higher than that of Hispanics. White enrollment rates for this age group have grown substantially since 1981, while enrollment growth for blacks and Hispanics grew moderately over this period (Indicator 8, *Condition 1996*).

Enrollment rates for older adults (high school graduates aged 25 or older) generally were much lower than those for their younger counterparts aged 18–24 regardless of racial/ethnic group. Between 1992 and 1994, the average college enrollment rates were similar for white, black, and Hispanic high school graduates aged 25–34 (Indicator 8, *Condition 1996*).

♦ *Hispanic college students are more likely to be enrolled part-time than their white or black peers.*

Students who initially enroll part-time in college are less likely to persist toward a bachelor's degree than those who enroll full time (Indicators 10 and 26, *Condition 1996*). Hispanic high school graduates aged 18–24 were far more likely to be enrolled in college part time, as opposed to full time, than were their white or black counterparts in 1994 (table 8-2, *Condition 1996*).

College persistence and completion

♦ *Among bachelor's degree seekers, whites and Asian/Pacific Islanders are more likely to persist toward a bachelor's degree than are their black and Hispanic counterparts.*

Half of all students beginning postsecondary education at 2- or 4-year colleges indicate that their initial degree goal is a bachelor's degree. Among beginning students seeking bachelor's degrees in 1989–90, 63 percent had either completed or were still working toward a bachelor's degree in spring 1994. An additional 8 percent had earned an associate's degree or a vocational certificate (Indicator 10, *Condition 1996*). Whites and Asians were more likely than blacks or Hispanics to have either earned a bachelor's degree or still to be working toward a bachelor's degree in spring 1994 (table 10-1, *Condition 1996*).

The proportion of bachelor's degree seekers who were no longer enrolled in spring 1994 but had earned associate's degrees or vocational certificates were similar for whites, blacks, Hispanics, and Asian/Pacific Islanders, although the latter were less likely to earn vocational certificates. Of 1989–90 bachelor's degree seekers who had not earned a degree and were no longer enrolled in spring 1994, blacks were more likely to have been enrolled for 18 months or less (57 percent) than were their white, Hispanic, or Asian/Pacific Islander counterparts (36, 40, and 37 percent, respectively).

♦ *Of those who began their postsecondary education at a community college in 1989–90, whites and blacks were less likely than Hispanics to have either earned a degree or certificate or still to be enrolled for one by spring 1994.*

About 44 percent of undergraduates attend public 2-year colleges. These institutions serve many purposes: they provide vocational training and skill development; they offer an inexpensive way to complete lower division requirements before entering a 4-year institution; and they meet purely avocational interests. Among students who began their postsecondary education at a community college in 1989–90, less than one-quarter had completed an associate's degree or vocational certificate there by spring 1994, although 37 percent had completed an award at

Proportion of 1989–90 first-time bachelor's degree seekers who had attained or were still enrolled toward a bachelor's degree in spring 1994

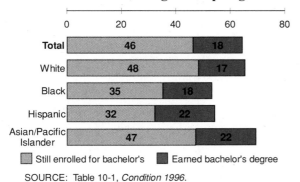

Still enrolled for bachelor's   Earned bachelor's degree

SOURCE: Table 10-1, *Condition 1996.*

Proportion of 1989-90 first-time community college students who transferred to another institution by spring 1994, by destination of first transfer

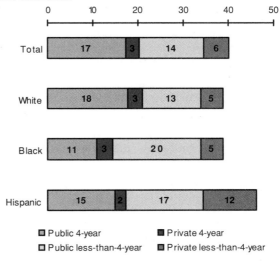

☐ Public 4-year   ■ Private 4-year
☐ Public less-than-4-year   ▧ Private less-than-4-year

SOURCE: Table 9-2, *Condition 1996*

some institution. Those who did not complete an award at this community college spent a substantial amount of time there, however, averaging 14 months of enrollment (Indicator 9, *Condition 1996*).

White community college students were more likely to earn an associate's degree at their first institution by spring 1994 than their black counterparts (18 and 9 percent, respectively) (table 9-1, *Condition 1996*). Hispanics completed associate's degrees at their first institution at a rate similar to whites, but were less likely to earn vocational certificates there. Both blacks and whites, however, were more likely to have neither earned an award nor still be enrolled for one by spring 1994 (55 and 50 percent, respectively) than were Hispanics (40 percent).

Four out of 10 first-time, beginning community college students transfer to another institution— half to a 4-year college or university and half to a less than 4-year institution. Transfer rates for whites and blacks were similar, both around 39 percent. Differences between white and Hispanic transfer rates were not statistically significant. Hispanics were more likely than whites, however, to transfer to a less-than-4-year institution as opposed to a 4-year institution (table 9-2, *Condition 1996*). In spring 1994, about 1 in 10 white, black, and Hispanic students who had started in a community college in 1989–90 had either earned a bachelor's degree or were enrolled in a 4-year college or institution (table 9-1, *Condition 1996*).

♦ *Compared to 1981 levels, the number of bachelor's degrees earned in 1993 was up for males and females in all racial/ethnic groups. The increase was greater for females than males in each racial/ethnic group.*

The ability of colleges and universities to attract and graduate minority students is important to the goal of equal opportunity. Changes in the number of degrees earned by minorities of both sexes, particularly in relation to the number earned by whites, provides a measure of higher education's progress toward this goal. Compared to 1981 levels, the number of bachelor's degrees earned in 1993 was up for males and females in all racial/ethnic groups, with the largest increases occurring for Asian/Pacific Islander and Hispanic males and females (two groups with large immigration rates). Between 1981 and 1993, Hispanic, Asian/Pacific Islander, and American Indian/Alaskan Native males and females showed higher percentage gains in the number of bachelor's degrees earned than did whites of the same sex.[7]

♦ *Black and American Indian/Alaskan Native college graduates were less likely than their white and Asian/Pacific Islander peers to have completed their bachelor's degree program in 4 years or less.*

Number of bachelor's degrees conferred (in thousands)

Race/ethnicity	Male			Female		
	1981	1993	Percent change	1981	1993	Percent change
White	406.2	435.1	7.1	401.1	512.2	27.7
Black	24.5	28.8	17.6	36.2	50.0	38.1
Hispanic	10.8	19.9	84.3	11.0	25.5	131.8
Asian/Pacific Islander	10.1	25.3	150.5	8.7	26.2	201.1
American Indian/ Alaskan/Native	1.7	2.4	41.2	1.9	3.2	68.4

SOURCE: Integrated Postsecondary Education Data System (IPEDS).

The traditional time to complete most bachelor's degree programs is 4 years. But, a number of circumstances such as changing schools or majors, stopping out for periods of time, attending on a part-time bases, or having difficulty enrolling in required classes may delay graduation. Taking longer to complete college not only causes students to incur additional

Percentage of college graduates completing the bachelor's degree within various years of starting college: 1993

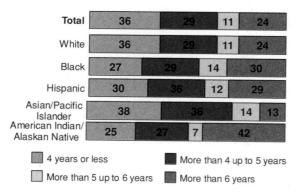

SOURCE: Table 11-2, *Condition 1996*.

tuition costs, but also delays them in starting their careers. Blacks and American Indian/Alaskan Native students are less likely than their white and Asian/Pacific Islander counterparts to complete college in 4 years or less. Among 1993

bachelor's degree recipients, 4 out of 10 American Indian/Alaskan Native graduates took longer than 6 years to complete college, while only 1 out of 10 Asian/Pacific Islander graduates took that long to complete college (Indicator 11 and table 11-1, *Condition 1996*).

♦ *Educational attainment rates for white, black, and Hispanic young adults have risen since the early 1970s, although young adult whites are still far more likely to have completed college than their black and Hispanic counterparts.*

Differences in college enrollment and persistence rates across racial/ethnic groups are reflected in

Percentage of 25- to 29-year-olds who earned a bachelor's degree: March 1971–95

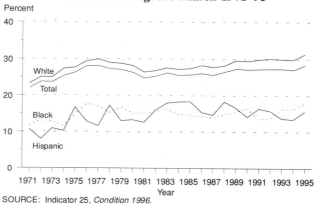

SOURCE: Indicator 25, *Condition 1996*.

educational attainment figures for young adults. The proportion of white, black, and Hispanic 25- to 29-year-olds with either some college or more or a bachelor's degree or more rose between 1971 and 1995 (Indicator 25, *Condition 1996*). Whites in this age group were still almost twice as likely as their black and Hispanic counterparts to have earned a bachelor's degree in 1995.

♦ *Asian/Pacific Islander college graduates were more likely than whites to have majored in engineering and computer science (a relatively high paying field). Black, Hispanic, and Asian/Pacific Islander graduates were less likely to major in education (a relatively low paying field).*

Career opportunities available to college students are affected by the fields they choose to study. For college graduates, both starting salary (Indicator 35, *Condition 1996*) and the degree to which job opportunities have career potential (Indicator 31, *Condition 1996*) are related to college major. In

1993, Asian/Pacific Islanders were far more likely than whites to major in biological/life sciences, computer and information sciences, or engineering, but were far less likely to major in education. Black bachelor's degree recipients were more likely than their white counterparts to major in business management, but were less

Percentage distribution of bachelor's degrees conferred, by field of study: 1993

Field of study	All	White	Black	Hispanic	Asian/ Pacific Islander	American Indian/ Alaskan Native
All fields	100.0	100.0	100.0	100.0	100.0	100.0
Biological/life sciences	4.1	3.8	3.6	4.1	10.1	3.8
Business management	22.1	21.6	24.6	21.1	22.9	18.5
Computer and information sciences	2.1	1.7	2.9	1.9	4.5	1.5
Education	9.3	10.2	7.2	6.6	2.1	11.4
Engineering	5.3	4.8	3.4	5.1	12.7	3.2
English language and literature	4.8	5.2	3.9	3.9	3.1	4.1
Health sciences	5.8	6.0	6.1	4.4	4.9	6.1
Humanities	2.9	2.8	3.5	4.2	2.0	4.5
Mathematics	1.3	1.3	1.3	1.0	1.8	1.0
Physical sciences	1.5	1.5	1.1	1.0	2.2	1.6
Psychology	5.8	5.8	6.1	7.0	5.0	6.1
Social sciences and history	11.7	11.6	12.8	13.4	11.1	13.6
Other	23.3	23.6	23.6	26.5	17.6	24.5

SOURCE: Integrated Postsecondary Education Data System (IPEDS).

likely to major in education. Hispanic bachelor's degree recipients were more likely than whites to major in the social sciences or history, but were less likely to major in education. American Indian/Alaskan Native bachelor's degree recipients were more likely than whites to major in the humanities or social sciences and history, but were less likely to major in business management.[8]

College access, participation, and completion: an alternative approach

An alternative approach to examining the experiences of minorities in postsecondary education is to look back at the experiences of two high school graduating classes at the point each reached age 30. The Postsecondary Education Transcript Studies (PETS) were conducted in 1984 for the high school class of 1972 and in 1993 for the high school class of 1982. Transcripts were requested from each member of the two graduating classes who reported attending a postsecondary institution. The transcripts provide information on courses taken, credits earned, and degrees completed and provides a rich source of information about the

experiences of these two groups in postsecondary education. The information in the table below was compiled on the basis of these two studies.

First, consider the proportion of each class for whom transcripts were received. This statistic can be interpreted as the proportion of the class who had access to postsecondary education. The percentage increased from 60 for the class of 1972 to 70 percent for the class of 1982. Note that this statistic includes both those who enroll in higher education immediately after high school graduation as well as those who delayed entry for up to 10 years. The increase is evident for whites, blacks, Hispanics and Asians.

Access, participation, and completion in postsecondary education for the high school class of 1972 as of 1984 and the high school class of 1982 as of 1993

	Total	White	Black	Hispanic	Asian
Percentage with 1 or more postsecondary transcripts					
1972	60	61	54	53	77
1982	70	73	62	58	92
Change	+10	+12	+8	+5	+14
Percentage with more than 10 completed postsecondary semester credits					
1972	51	53	42	43	70
1982	62	65	54	48	84
Change	+11	+12	+11	+5	+15
Percentage who attended a 4-year institution and completed more than 10 credits					
1972	37	38	30	24	54
1982	44	47	35	26	66
Change	+8	+9	+5	+2	+12
Percentage with a baccalaureate or higher degree					
1972	24	26	14	11	43
1982	29	32	15	13	52
Change	+4	+6	+2	+2	+9
Percentage with a bachelor's degree or higher degree among those who attended a 4-year institution and completed more than 10 credits.					
1972	66	68	49	44	81
1982	65	68	42	49	79
Change	-1	0	-7	+5	-2

NOTE: Transcripts were collected at approximately age 30 for each high school graduating class. American Indians and others are included in the total but are not shown separately.
SOURCE: U.S. Department of Education, National Center for Education Statistics, Postsecondary Education Transcript Studies of the National Longitudinal Study of the High School Class of 1972 and the High School and Beyond Study (HS&B) Sophomore Cohort, 1984 and 1993.

Second, consider the proportion of each class who completed more than 10 postsecondary credits. This statistic can be interpreted as the proportion who participated significantly in higher education. It corresponds roughly to those who completed the equivalent of at least one full-time semester. This percentage also increased between the two classes from 51 percent to 62 percent. Note that between 12 and 15 percent of those who attend a higher education institution do not complete more than 10 credits. Again, the increase is evident for whites, blacks, Hispanics, and Asians.

Third, consider the proportion of each class who completed more than 10 credits and attended a 4-year institution. This statistic can be interpreted as the proportion who have an opportunity to earn a bachelor's degree. This percentage is substantially lower than the percentage with significant participation as defined above—44 versus 62 percent in the class of 1982, for example. However, the percentage did increase between the two classes from 37 to 44 percent. While this increase was confined principally to whites and Asians, it should be noted that, in both generations, Hispanics attended community colleges at a higher rate than other groups.

Fourth, consider the proportion of each high school graduating class that completed a bachelor's degree or higher. Though associate's degrees are important credentials for many individuals, a bachelor's degree is associated with significant long-term economic advantages. This percentage increased moderately between the two classes from 24 to 29 percent. The increase was confined to whites. (Although it appears there was an increase for Asians as well, the small samples of Asians in the studies preclude a definitive conclusion).

Finally, among those who attended a 4-year institution and completed more than 10 credits, consider those who completed a bachelor's degree or higher degree. This is the proportion who had the opportunity to earn a bachelor's degree. Overall, there was no change in this proportion between the two generations: 66 percent for the class of 1972 and 65 percent for the class of 1982. Among racial/ethnic groups, however, there is evidence of a decline for blacks—from 49 to 42 percent. (Although it appears there was an increase in degree completions rates for Hispanics, the small sample sizes of Hispanics in the studies preclude a definitive conclusion).

Summary

As the gap in earnings between high school and college graduates continues to widen, access to a college education is becoming even more important for minorities wanting to share in the American dream. Almost all high school seniors expect to complete at least some college, although Hispanic seniors are less likely than their white, black, and Asian/Pacific Islander counterparts to plan to attend college right after high school. High school graduates from all racial and ethnic groups are taking a more rigorous high school curriculum, and mathematics and science test scores are generally up—although blacks, Hispanics, and American Indians/Alaskan Natives continue to trail their white and Asian/Pacific Islander counterparts in critical skill areas.

However, black and Hispanic high school graduates are less likely than their white peers to make the immediate transition to college and Hispanics are more likely to enroll in a 2-year college or as part-time students—two conditions that make it less likely they will persist toward a bachelor's degree. Among bachelor's degree seekers, whites and Asian/Pacific Islanders are more likely to persist towards a bachelor's degree than their black and Hispanic counterparts. Of those who earn a bachelor's degree, black and American Indian/Alaskan Native graduates are less likely than their white and Asian/Pacific Islander peers to finish in 4 years or less—a condition that delays their entrance into the full-time labor market.

Several minority groups do tend to major in fields that will help them recoup their college costs. Black, Hispanic, and Asian/Pacific Islander graduates were less likely than whites to major in education. Asian/Pacific Islander graduates were more likely than white graduates to major in computer science and engineering.

NOTES:

[1] U.S. Department of Education, National Center for Education Statistics. *Trends Among High School Seniors, 1972–1992*, table 3.3a.

[2] *Trends Among High School Seniors, 1972–1992*, table 4.1.

[3] The panel's recommendation of 0.5 units of computer science was not included here, because the use of computers has been integrated into many other courses.

[4] U.S. Department of Education, National Center for Education Statistics. *NAEP 1994 Reading: A First Look* (Revised edition), table 2.

[5] U.S. Department of Education, National Center for Education Statistics. *NAEP 1992 Mathematics Report Card for the Nation and the States*, table 2.1.

[6] U.S. Department of Education, National Center for Education Statistics. *The 1990 Science Report Card*, p. 10.

[7] U.S. Department of Education, National Center for Education Statistics. *Digest of Education Statistics, 1995*, table 256.

[8] *Digest of Education Statistics, 1995*, table 257.

Teachers' working conditions

by Susan P. Choy, MPR Associates, Inc.

To deliver high quality education, schools must attract, develop, and retain effective teachers. Working conditions play an important role in a school's ability to do so. Schools that are able to offer their teachers a safe, pleasant, and supportive working environment and adequate compensation are better able to attract and retain good teachers and motivate them to do their best. Teachers' working conditions are important to students as well as teachers because they affect how much individual attention teachers can give to students. Large class sizes or disruptive students, for example, can make both teaching and learning difficult.

Some aspects of teachers' working conditions go along with the job regardless of where a teacher works. For example, teacher salaries tend to be low relative to those earned by similarly qualified individuals in other professions regardless of the type or location of the school. Other aspects of teachers' working conditions, such as school safety, vary widely from school to school. Thus, in addition to being concerned about teachers' working conditions in general, we need to pay attention to the types of schools that tend to have desirable or difficult working conditions and, for equity reasons, to the characteristics of the students who attend them.

Data presented here describe a number of aspects of teachers' working conditions, including workload, compensation, school and district support for teachers' professional development, school decision making, school safety, student readiness to learn, and public respect for teachers.

Workload

Teaching workload has several dimensions, including the amount of time spent working, the number of classes taught, and the number of students in each class. The amount of time a teacher devotes to his or her job is partly self-determined, reflecting not only what the school requires or expects but also the teacher's efficiency, enthusiasm, and commitment.

♦ *The average amount of time a full-time teacher is required to spend at school is only about three-quarters of the teacher's work week.*

In school year 1993–94, full-time public school teachers were required to be at school for an average of 33 hours per week to conduct classes, prepare lessons, attend staff meetings, and fulfill a variety of other school-related responsibilities. The average was similar whether they worked at the elementary or secondary level (Indicator 48, *Condition 1996*).

In addition to the required time at school, a full-time public school teacher worked an average of 12 additional hours per week before and after school and on weekends. Teachers spent 3 of these hours in activities involving students and 9 hours in other school-related work, such as grading papers, preparing lessons, and meeting with parents.

Average hours full-time teachers worked per week before and after school and on weekends: School year 1993–94

School characteristics	Total school-related	With students	Other school-related
Public	12.1	3.3	8.7
School level			
Elementary	11.0	1.7	9.2
Secondary	13.2	5.0	8.2
Urbanicity			
Central city	11.6	3.0	8.6
Urban fringe/ large town	12.4	3.1	9.4
Rural/ small town	12.1	3.7	8.4
Percent low income students			
0–5	13.3	3.8	9.5
6–20	12.9	3.7	9.2
21–40	12.1	3.5	8.7
41–100	11.0	2.7	8.3
Private	12.9	3.6	9.3

SOURCE: Indicator 48 and table 48-1, *Condition 1996*.

Full-time public school teachers in rural/small town communities spent more time, on average, than those in other community types in activities involving students (table 48-1, *Condition 1996*). And, those in schools with relatively few low income students (5 percent or fewer students eligible for free or reduced-priced lunches) spent more time in activities involving students and also more time on other school-related activities than did those in schools with more than 40 percent low income students.

On average, full-time private school teachers were required to be at school about an hour longer per week and spent about an hour more outside of school than their public school counterparts.

In 1992, the average amount of time per year public school teachers at the primary level spent teaching (excluding other school responsibilities) in 15 countries (mostly European) ranged from a low of 624 hours in Sweden to a high of 1,093 hours in the United States, averaging 858 hours.[1]

♦ *Public school teachers tend to have larger classes than private school teachers.*

In school year 1993–94, public school teachers had an average class size of 23.2 and taught an average of 5.6 classes per day (excluding those in self-contained classrooms). The corresponding averages for private school teachers were 19.6 and 6.0, respectively (Indicator 48, *Condition 1996*).

Average class size and average number of classes per day for full-time teachers: School year 1993–94

School characteristics	Class size	Classes per day*
Public	23.2	5.6
Urbanicity		
Central city	24.1	5.5
Urban fringe/ large town	24.1	5.5
Rural/ small town	22.0	5.7
School size		
Less than 150	15.4	6.2
750 or more	24.5	5.4
Private	19.6	6.0

* Since elementary teachers do not tend to teach separate classes, only 8 percent of the teachers who responded to this question were elementary teachers, while 92 percent were secondary teachers.

SOURCE: Indicator 48 and table 48-1, *Condition 1996*.

Public school teachers in rural/small town areas had lower average class sizes than teachers in other community types, and those in the smallest schools (those with less than 150 students) had

lower average class sizes than those in the largest schools (those with 750 students or more) (table 48-1, *Condition 1996*).

♦ *Pupil-teacher ratios at the secondary level in the United States are high compared to those in other countries.*

Among 16 countries (primarily European, but also including Japan, Australia, and New Zealand), the ratio of students to teachers (full-time-equivalents) at the secondary level averaged 13.8 in public education. In the United States, the ratio averaged 16.7.[2]

Compensation

How much districts and schools pay their teachers and what criteria they use as a basis for salary increases are important aspects of teachers' working conditions. In recent years, many states and districts have been experimenting with new career paths and salary structures in an effort to attract and retain high quality teachers.

Salary schedules

♦ *In school year 1993–94, public school district salaries for teachers with a bachelor's degree but no experience averaged $21,900 (in current dollars).*

Scheduled salaries for teachers usually increase with education and experience. In school year 1993–94, public school districts paid an average of $40,500 at the top of their schedules (table 55-6, *Condition 1996*). Among private schools with salary schedules (about two-thirds of all private schools), salaries were considerably less, starting

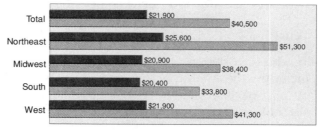

Average scheduled salaries (in 1995 constant dollars) in public school districts: School year 1993–94

■ Bachelor's degree, no experience ▨ Highest step

SOURCE: Table 55-6, *Condition 1996*.

at $16,200 and rising to $27,300. Regional differences in salary schedules were prominent, with public school districts in the Northeast paying the highest salaries, on average, and districts in the South generally paying the lowest salaries.

The smallest school districts (those with less than 1,000 students) tended to pay less, especially at the higher steps of the salary schedule. Their average salary rate at the highest step on the schedule was $36,500, compared to $43,800 in the next largest district size category (1,000 to 4,999 students) and even more in larger districts.

Adjusting for inflation, scheduled salary rates for teachers with a bachelor's degree but no experience declined by an average of about 4 percent in public school districts between 1987–88 and 1993–94, and rose by an average of about 2 percent in private schools.[3]

Average salaries

◆ *Adjusted for inflation, average salaries for public school teachers increased substantially between 1981 and 1995.*

Following a period of decline in the 1970s, public school teachers' salaries increased throughout the 1980s and into the early 1990s, reaching a peak in 1991 (Indicator 55, *Condition 1996*). In 1995, the average salary for public school teachers was $37,400, up 20 percent from $31,100 (in 1995 constant dollars) in 1981. At least some of this increase can be explained by the aging of the teacher work force. For example, between 1981 and 1991, the median number of years of teaching experience increased from 12 to 15 years. Adjusting for inflation, the average salary for beginning public school teachers increased 24 percent from 1980 to 1995 (table 55-1, *Condition 1996*).

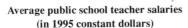

Average public school teacher salaries
(in 1995 constant dollars)

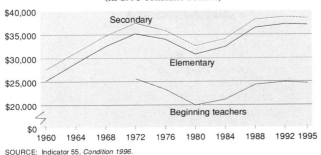

SOURCE: Indicator 55, *Condition 1996*.

◆ *Teachers earn less than many other college graduates with similar literacy skills; however, adjusting for inflation, education majors have fared better than other recent college graduates in terms of growth in earnings.*

In 1992, teachers had literacy skills similar to those of many other college graduates, including private-sector executives and managers, engineers, physicians, writers and artists, social workers, sales representatives, education administrators, and registered nurses. However, they often earned less. The average annual earnings for teachers (prekindergarten through secondary, public and private) employed full time were $26,000 in 1991, compared to $38,500 for all persons with a bachelor's degree who were employed full time (Indicator 58, *Condition 1996*).

Among recent college graduates who majored in education and who were working full time 1 year after earning their bachelor's degree and were not enrolled in school, the median salary (in 1995 constant dollars) increased by 5 percent between 1980 and 1993. In comparison, the increase for all recent college graduates was 1 percent (table 35-1, *Condition 1996*).

◆ *By some salary measures, teachers in the United States are better off than teachers in other countries.*

Comparing teacher salaries meaningfully across countries requires adjusting for differences in standards of living. One way to do this is to convert salaries to purchasing power parity (PPP) rates. Using this approach, the starting and maximum salaries for public school teachers at the primary level in the United States were higher than those in most European countries in 1992.[4]

Another way to assess the status of the teaching profession in a country is to compute the ratio of teacher salaries to the per capita Gross Domestic Product (GDP), an index of the economic well being of a country's population. Using this measure, starting salaries for public school teachers at the primary level in 25 countries (mostly European) were generally similar to or slightly above the country's per capita GDP (the average was 1.2); they were lowest in Sweden (0.8) and the United States (0.9).

Support for teachers' professional development

To provide high quality education, schools not only must hire well qualified teachers, but also must help them improve their skills, stay current in their fields, and learn about new teaching methods. District and school support for professional development is likely to contribute to higher teacher morale and lower attrition.

♦ *Most schools and districts provide support for teachers to develop professionally.*

In school year 1993–94, the vast majority of full-time public school teachers participated in school- and district-sponsored workshops or in-service training, regardless of school level or community type. However, participation was a little higher at the elementary level than at the secondary level for public school teachers (table 59-2, *Condition 1996*).

Percentage of full-time teachers who participated in district- and school-sponsored workshops or in-service training: School year 1993–94

School characteristics	Elementary Sponsored by:		Secondary Sponsored by:	
	District*	School	District*	School
Public	89.6	83.7	84.9	79.1
Central city	87.7	86.4	82.8	81.5
Urban fringe/ large town	91.0	83.2	84.7	78.7
Rural/ small town	89.9	82.1	86.3	78.0
Private	78.9	78.0	68.9	78.4

* For private schools refers to organizations with which the school was affiliated rather than districts.

SOURCE: Table 59-2, *Condition 1996*.

Full-time public school teachers were most commonly supported in their professional development through released time from teaching or scheduled time for professional development activities. Other types of support included professional growth credits and reimbursement of tuition, fees, or expenses. Private school teachers were less likely to receive professional growth credits and released time and scheduled time from teaching than were public school teachers, but they were more likely to receive tuition and/or fees than were their

public school counterparts (Indicator 59, *Condition 1996*).

Percentage of full-time public school teachers who received professional development support: School year 1993–94

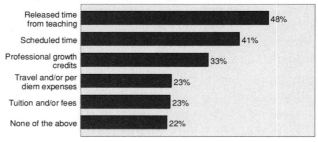

SOURCE: Indicator 59, *Condition 1996*.

School decision making

The extent to which teachers participate in decisions about school policies and issues and the autonomy that teachers have in the classroom have an important effect on school climate, a critical aspect of teachers' working conditions.

♦ *Teachers' perceptions of their influence over important policies in their schools vary by control of school.*

About one-third of all public school teachers thought that teachers in their school had a good deal of influence over important policies such as setting discipline policy, establishing curriculum,

Percentage of teachers who thought teachers had a good deal of influence over policies in their schools: 1993–94

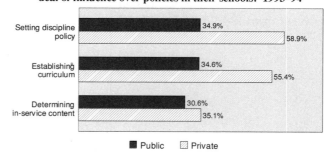

SOURCE: Indicator 47. *Condition 1996*.

and determining the content of in-service programs. In each of these areas, the proportions were higher for teachers in private schools (Indicator 47, *Condition 1996*).

At both the elementary and secondary levels, teachers in public schools with relatively few low income students (5 percent or fewer students eligible for free or reduced-price lunches) were generally more likely than teachers in schools with relatively large proportions of low income students (more than 40 percent of students eligible for free or reduced-price lunches) to report that teachers had a good deal of influence over their school's policies (tables 47-1 and 47-3, *Condition 1996*).

Teachers' perception of their influence over school policy appears to be related to school size as well. In school year 1993–94, teachers in the smallest public schools (those with less than 150 students) were more likely than teachers in the largest schools to think that teachers had a good deal of influence in these areas (tables 47-1, 2, and 3, *Condition 1996*).

Percentage of public school teachers who thought teachers had a good deal of influence over their school's policies: School year 1993–94

School characteristics	Discipline policy	In-service content	Establishing curriculum
Elementary	41.8	32.6	32.2
Low poverty rate			
5 percent or less	47.0	37.2	37.0
More than 40 percent	38.4	30.3	27.8
School size			
Less than 150	52.9	35.3	46.5
750 or more	34.4	32.3	27.7
Secondary	27.5	28.5	37.2
Low poverty rate			
5 percent or less	28.4	31.5	42.3
More than 40 percent	26.7	26.4	31.2
School size			
Less than 150	44.0	36.0	50.7
750 or more	23.8	27.4	33.9

SOURCE: Indicator 47 and tables 47-1 and 47-3, *Condition 1996*.

♦ *Teachers perceive that they have more control over some classroom practices than others.*

In school year 1993–94, the vast majority of teachers thought that they had a good deal of control in their own classroom over practices such as evaluating and grading students, selecting teaching techniques, and determining the amount of homework to be assigned. Relatively fewer felt that they had a good deal of control over disciplining students, deciding what was taught, and selecting textbooks and other instructional materials. Private school teachers

were more likely to think that they had a great deal of control in each of these areas, except for determining the amount of homework (Indicator 47, *Condition 1996*).

Percentage of public school teachers reporting they had a good deal of control over classroom practices: 1993–94

SOURCE: Indicator 47, *Condition 1996*.

School safety

Neither students nor teachers can perform at their best if they do not feel safe. Schools where teachers do not feel safe are likely to experience difficulty in attracting and retaining teachers. Perceptions of safety may be just as important as objective measures.

♦ *Some schools, especially those in central cities, find it necessary to implement security measures to protect students and staff.*

In 1993, 29 percent of children in grades 3–12 attended schools that employed security guards; 26 percent attended schools that locked the doors during the day; and 5 percent attended schools that had metal detectors. These precautions were far more common in central cities than in other types of communities (table 47-4, *Condition 1995*).

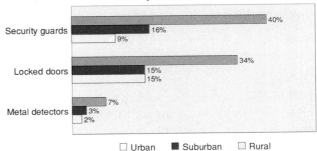

Percentage of students in schools with various security devices: 1993

□ Urban ■ Suburban □ Rural

SOURCE: Table 47-4, *Condition 1995*.

♦ *Increasing percentages of public school teachers are reporting that physical conflicts and weapons possession are moderate or serious problems in their schools.*

In school year 1993–94, 40 percent of public secondary teachers reported that physical conflicts among students were moderate or serious problems in their schools, up from about 30 percent just 3 years earlier. During the same period, the percentage who reported that weapons possession was a moderate or serious problem nearly doubled. Fewer elementary than secondary school teachers reported these problems as moderate or serious, but the percentage reporting physical conflicts as a moderate or serious problem grew steadily between 1987–88 and 1993–94.[5]

Percentage of public school teachers reporting physical conflicts among students and weapons possession as moderate or serious problems in their schools

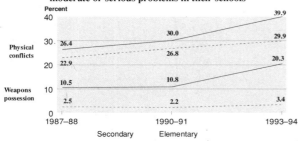
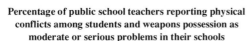

SOURCE: U.S. Department of Education, National Center for Education Statistics, "How Safe Are the Public Schools: What Do Teachers Say?" *Issue Brief*, 1996.

Overall, 15 percent of high school seniors in 1992 reported that they were threatened at school some time during the first semester. The percentages were about the same regardless of schools' urbanicity, but seniors attending schools with fewer than 400 students were less likely to have been threatened (11 percent) than seniors in larger schools, where 15 to 16 percent had been threatened (table 47-3, *Condition 1995*).

♦ *Victimization rates of high school seniors have not changed dramatically.*

Despite teachers' perceptions of growing safety problems in the schools, victimization rates of high school seniors changed little between 1976 and 1993, with the exception of a slight increase in the percentages of students who reported being threatened with or without a weapon. The most common type of victimization for high

school seniors was having something stolen (Indicator 47, *Condition 1995*).

Percentage of high school seniors who reported being victimized at school: 1976–93

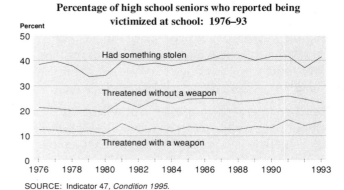

SOURCE: Indicator 47, *Condition 1995*.

♦ *About one in six high school seniors in 1992 had someone offer to sell them drugs at school during the first half of the school year.*

Because drug selling activity in a school is often accompanied by increased crime, the number of students reporting that they have been approached at school to buy drugs is indicative of the extent to which the school environment is affected by drug problems. Incidence in 1992 was greatest at public schools and least at private schools with a religious affiliation other than Catholic (Indicator 48, *Condition 1995*).

Percentage of high school seniors who reported someone offered to sell them drugs at school: 1992

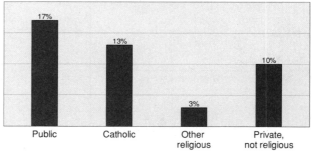

SOURCE: Indicator 48, *Condition 1995*.

Student readiness to learn

Classes full of students ready and eager to learn make a teacher's job much easier and more enjoyable. Students who disrupt classes by being late or frequently absent make their teachers' jobs more difficult. Students who use drugs or alcohol can contribute to disruption of class activities and crime in the schools. Also, students' readiness to learn in English is affected by their ability to speak English. Unless teachers are trained in teaching English as a second language or in bilingual education, having a large number of children with difficulty speaking English can make a teacher's job much more demanding.

♦ *The percentage of high school sophomores who came to school unprepared for class decreased between 1980 and 1990.*

The proportion of high school sophomores who reported that they usually or often came to school without completed homework dropped from 22 percent to 18 percent between 1980 and 1990. The percentages who came without books, paper, or pen and pencil also dropped. In both years, there was a relationship between poor performance on reading, vocabulary, and mathematics tests and coming to school unprepared. However, students in the lowest test quartile improved in all three areas (Indicator 44, *Condition 1994*).

Percentage of high school sophomores who came to school unprepared in 1980 and 1990

| Student behavior | | Test quartile | |
and year	Total	Lowest	Highest
Come to school without books			
1980	8.5	17.1	3.0
1990	6.3	12.8	2.5
Come to school without paper, pen, or pencil			
1980	15.1	21.9	10.8
1990	10.5	15.1	8.2
Come to school without homework completed			
1980	22.1	28.5	16.2
1990	18.1	23.8	14.3

SOURCE: Indicator 44, *Condition 1994*.

♦ *Teachers in many public high schools think that student absenteeism and tardiness are serious problems.*

At the high school level, 29 percent of public school teachers reported that student absenteeism was a serious problem in their school, and 19 percent reported that tardiness was a serious problem. Teachers in central city high schools with relatively large proportions of low income

students (more than 40 percent of students eligible for free or reduced-price lunches) were particularly likely to think that these were serious problems (Indicator 42, *Condition 1996*).

Percentage of teachers who thought absenteeism and tardiness were serious problems: 1992–93

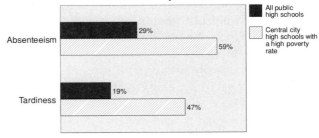

SOURCE: Indicator 42, *Condition 1996*.

♦ *Drug use by high school seniors declined dramatically in the 1980s and early 1990s, but marijuana use is on the increase again. Alcohol use has declined, but remains high.*

In 1978, one-half of all high school seniors reported using marijuana during the previous year. Reported marijuana use dropped to 26 percent by 1993, but rose to 31 percent in 1994. Use of alcohol also dropped in the 1980s and early 1990s, but not as dramatically as marijuana, and overall use remains high (Indicator 48, *Condition 1995*).

Percentage of high school seniors who reported using drugs or alcohol in the previous year

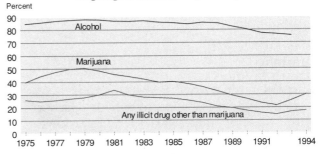

SOURCE: Indicator 48, *Condition 1995*.

Especially disturbing is the fact that 8 percent of high school seniors reported that they had been under the influence of alcohol while at school on at least 1 day during the previous month in 1993, and 9 percent reported that they had been under the influence of marijuana or other illegal drug at school (table 48-2, *Condition 1995*).

♦ *Increasing numbers of school-age children speak a language other than English at home and speak English with difficulty.*

In 1990, more than 5 percent of all school-age children spoke a language other than English at home and spoke English with difficulty, up from 4 percent in 1980. Thirty-three percent of these children lived in California. In five states (California, Texas, New Mexico, Arizona, and New York), more than 8 percent of school-age children spoke another language at home and had difficulty speaking English (Indicator 46, *Condition 1994*).

Respect for teachers

The public's level of respect for teachers is likely to affect the attractiveness of the teaching profession and the quality of new teachers. There is wide variation from country to country in the percentage who think that secondary teachers are "very respected" or "fairly well respected" as a profession.

♦ *Compared to secondary teachers in some other countries, secondary teachers in the United States are accorded a high degree of public respect.*

Among 10 European countries and the United States, an average of 9 percent of persons thought that secondary teachers were "very respected," and another 48 percent thought they were "fairly well respected." In the United States, 20 percent thought they were "very respected" and 48 percent thought they were "fairly well respected."[6]

Summary

Teachers put in more than a 40-hour week, on average, counting time spent outside of school hours. Their average salaries tend to be lower than many other professionals, but, adjusting for inflation, teachers' salaries increased substantially during the 1980s. Most teachers are supported in their professional development by their schools and districts. More than four out of five teachers reported that they had a good deal of control over how they taught and evaluated students. They were less likely to report that they had a great deal of control over selecting what they taught and what texts and materials they used, and over disciplining students. Public school teachers are increasingly worried about school safety at both the elementary and secondary levels, although victimization rates reported by high school seniors have not changed dramatically since the 1970s.

In some ways, public school teachers as a group appear to face more difficult working conditions than private school teachers. They have larger classes, on average, are less likely to think that teachers have a good deal of influence over important policies in their schools, and are less likely to think that they have a great deal of control over most classroom practices. They are also more likely to think that absenteeism and tardiness are serious problems in their schools, and public high school seniors are more likely to report that someone offered to sell them drugs at school. However, public school teachers earn substantially more than private school teachers, on average.

Working conditions vary considerably within the public school sector, depending on size, location, and percentage of low income students in the school. For example, central city public schools are more likely than those in other types of communities to have safety problems and higher absentee rates. Teachers in small public schools tend to have smaller classes than teachers in large schools and are more likely to think that teachers have a good deal of influence over school policies.

NOTES:

[1] Center for Educational Research and Innovation. *Education at a Glance: OECD Indicators*. Paris: Organization for Economic Co-operation and Development, 1995, 182.

[2] Center for Educational Research and Innovation. *Education at a Glance: OECD Indicators*, 1995, 179.

[3] U.S. Department of Education, National Center for Education Statistics. *Schools and Staffing in the United States: A Statistical Profile, 1993–94*, forthcoming.

[4] Center for Educational Research and Innovation. *Education at a Glance: OECD Indicators*, 1995, 187–88.

[5] U.S. Department of Education, National Center for Education Statistics. "How Safe Are the Public Schools: What Do Teachers Say?" *Issue Brief*, April 1996.

[6] Center for Educational Research and Innovation. *Education at a Glance: OECD Indicators*, 1995, 60.

Access, Participation, and Progress

Participation

Because of mandatory school attendance laws, enrollment rates among children aged 6–15 are close to 100 percent. Among younger children, however, enrollment rates have increased substantially over the past quarter century. In 1993, 27 percent of 3-year-olds and 54 percent of 4-year-olds were enrolled in school, up from 13 percent and 29 percent, respectively, in 1970. In 1994, almost all 5-year-olds (95 percent) were enrolled in school, compared to 81 percent in 1970 *(Indicator 1)*.

Enrollment rates (in schools and colleges) among 16- to 24-year-olds have also increased considerably. The enrollment rate among 20-year-olds, for example, was 47 percent in 1994, up from 39 percent in 1970 *(Indicator 1)*. This increase in enrollment among 16- to 24-year-olds reflects the increasing proportion of high school graduates going on to college *(Indicator 7)*, and to a lesser extent, it also reflects decreasing high school dropout rates *(Indicator 5)*.

Beyond traditional college age, enrollment rates taper off, with 15 percent of 25-year-olds and 6 percent of 34-year-olds enrolled in college in 1994. Enrollment rates for those aged 25–34 have remained relatively stable since 1970 *(Indicator 1)*.

Participation in adult education activities, an important avenue for acquiring new knowledge and upgrading skills, has been increasing. In 1995, 40 percent of all adults participated in adult education activities, up from 32 percent in 1991. Their reasons for participating varied, and some adults took more than one type of course. In 1995, 21 percent of all adults who participated in adult education took work-related courses; 20 percent took personal development courses; 6 percent took courses toward a credential (other than on a full-time basis); and 1 percent took basic skills courses *(Indicator 14)*.

The enrollment patterns described above varied by race/ethnicity. For example, at ages 3 and 4, similar percentages of white and black children were enrolled in school in 1995, while their Hispanic peers were much less likely to be enrolled. At age 5, however, children in all three racial/ethnic groups were about equally likely to be enrolled *(Indicator 2)*.

Racial/ethnic differences in participation rates exist in higher education as well. In 1994, the percentages of high school graduates aged 18–24 who were enrolled in college were lower for blacks and Hispanics (36 and 33 percent, respectively) than for whites (44 percent) *(Indicator 8)*. White adults were more likely than either their black or Hispanic peers to participate in adult education activities in 1995: 42 percent compared to 37 percent and 34 percent, respectively (table 14-1).

Access

Access to preschool for 3- and 4-year-olds is related to family income. In 1995, 61 percent of 3-year-olds and 81 percent of 4-year-olds from families with incomes of more than $50,000 were enrolled in school. For children from families in lower income groups, however, enrollment rates ranged from 26 to 38 percent for 3-year-olds and from 52 percent to 60 percent for 4-year-olds *(Indicator 2)*. This is not surprising because nursery schools are mostly private—representing 62 percent of prekindergarten enrollment in 1992 *(Indicator 37, Condition 1994)*—and charge tuition. The gap in enrollment rates closes by age 5 *(Indicator 2)*, because kindergartens are primarily public—representing 85 percent of enrollment in 1992 *(Indicator 37, Condition 1994)*.

Many children are attending schools over which their parents have exercised some choice. In 1993, more than half of all students in grades 3–12 were in this category. Twenty percent of students in grades 3–12 attended a school chosen by their parents. In addition, parents of 39 percent of students reported that their child attended an assigned public school, but their choice of residence was influenced by where the child would go to school. Children from families with incomes greater than $50,000 were more likely than children from families with incomes less than $15,000 to have parents who made both of these choices *(Indicator 4)*.

The percentage of high school graduates enrolling in college immediately after high school has increased—from 49 percent in 1972 to 62 percent in 1994. Access to college has increased for high school graduates from families at all income levels, but enrollment rates still vary with income. In 1994, 45 percent of high school graduates from low income families went directly to college, compared to 77 percent of high school graduates from high income families *(Indicator 7)*.

This increase in immediate college enrollment has occurred despite the fact that the cost of college attendance has increased much faster than family income. In 1980, average undergraduate tuition, room, and board at public institutions was equal to 10 percent of the median income for families with school-aged children. By 1994, it reached 14 percent. At private institutions, tuition, room, and board increased from 22 to 39 percent of the median income for families with school-aged children *(Indicator 12)*.

Student financial aid programs have helped reduce the cost of going to college, particularly for students from low income families. For example, grants covered an average of 29 percent of tuition and fees for all full-time dependent undergraduates at 4-year public institutions and 80 percent for students from low income families *(Indicator 13)*.

Progress

Historically, the majority of children in first grade have been 6 years old, but the percentage of first-graders who are 7 years or older has increased, rising from 13 percent in 1972 to 22 percent in 1994. The increase has been particularly striking among first-graders from high income families: 9 percent were 7 years or older in 1972, compared to 22 percent in 1994 *(Indicator 3)*. The increase is due to some combination of parents keeping children in preschool or at home longer, children repeating kindergarten or first grade, and states and districts changing the minimum age for starting school.

Since school attendance is usually mandatory for children 6 to 15 years old, persistence for this age group is not an issue. In the later years of high school, however, persistence becomes a matter of serious concern because of the negative economic and social consequences associated with dropping out. In October 1994, 5 percent of the students who had been in grades 10–12 the previous fall had dropped out of school during the year or had failed to return in the fall. Dropout rates were closely related to family income: 2 percent of students from high income

families dropped out, compared to 13 percent of students from low income families *(Indicator 5)*.

High school persistence has improved over the past decade: 88 percent of the sophomore class of 1990 completed high school on time, compared to 80 percent of the sophomore class of 1980. Moreover, dropouts from the sophomore class of 1990 were considerably more likely than their counterparts a decade earlier to return to school. Two years after their scheduled graduation, 58 percent of the 1990 sophomore dropouts either had completed or were re-enrolled in school, compared to 34 percent of the dropouts from the sophomore class of 1980 *(Indicator 6)*.

Persistence at the postsecondary level also is of concern because of the increased employment opportunities and income potential that accrue to bachelor's degree recipients. Among bachelor's degree seekers who enrolled in postsecondary education for the first time in 1989–90, 77 percent of those who began at a 4-year institution and 53 percent of those who began at a 2-year institution had completed some degree or were still working toward a bachelor's degree 5 years later *(Indicator 10)*.

Many students who start at a community college do not complete their education at the first institution in which they enroll. Among students who began their postsecondary education at a community college in 1989–90, 37 percent completed a degree at some institution by 1994; 22 percent of these students completed a certificate or associate's degree at their first institution. About one in five community college beginners later went to a 4-year institution as their first transfer (table 9-2).

The traditional time for completing a bachelor's degree is 4 years. In 1993, 31 percent of bachelor's degree recipients had completed their degree within 4 years of graduating from high school, and 70 percent completed their degree within 6 years. The proportion who completed within 4 years of high school graduation dropped from 45 percent to 31 percent between 1977 and 1990, but did not change between 1990 and 1993 *(Indicator 11)*.

School enrollment rates, by age

♦ Since 1970, almost all children between the ages of 6 and 15 have been enrolled in school.

♦ Enrollment rates for 3- to 5-year-olds were substantially higher in 1993 than in 1970. However, most of this increase had occurred by 1980.

> *Even though participation in formal education is generally only mandatory for those between ages 6 and 16, learning occurs throughout a person's life. School enrollment rates of younger and older persons are an indication of the importance of formal education in their lives.*

♦ Enrollment rates among 16- to 25-year-olds were higher in 1994 than in 1970. Enrollment rates among those over age 25 generally did not increase during this period.

Percentage of the population enrolled in school, by age: Selected Octobers 1970–94

October	Age																
	3	4	5	6	7	8	9	10	11	12	13	14	15	16	17	18
1970	13.2	28.7	80.6	98.9	99.7	99.8	99.9	100.0	99.9	99.9	99.7	99.0	98.1	94.1	87.2	57.8
1980	27.6	47.2	93.2	99.4	99.5	99.5	99.7	99.6	99.7	99.8	99.7	98.7	98.5	93.9	85.2	54.6
1990	(*)	(*)	93.2	99.8	99.5	99.9	99.6	99.6	99.6	99.7	99.6	99.6	98.4	95.6	89.5	64.4
1993	27.1	53.9	91.8	99.0	99.3	99.5	99.5	99.4	99.7	99.7	99.4	99.4	98.3	96.3	91.6	68.9
1994	(*)	(*)	95.1	98.4	99.6	99.1	99.2	99.3	99.2	99.6	99.4	99.0	98.6	96.3	92.4	67.7

October	Age															
	19	20	21	22	23	24	25	26	27	28	29	30	31	32	33	34
1970	45.8	39.1	30.7	20.2	16.3	14.7	12.6	10.8	9.6	7.7	7.6	6.4	7.0	5.4	5.2	5.4
1980	43.0	33.9	30.6	22.3	16.7	13.5	12.0	11.2	10.0	8.8	7.9	8.0	8.2	6.5	6.8	6.3
1990	50.6	42.9	36.4	28.1	19.2	16.2	11.8	11.7	9.7	8.7	6.9	6.5	7.6	5.5	4.2	5.4
1993	54.4	45.1	40.5	30.7	22.0	18.5	15.1	10.8	8.6	8.9	8.1	7.1	6.4	5.2	5.4	5.4
1994	52.8	46.8	43.1	30.3	23.9	18.9	15.2	12.8	10.8	8.5	7.2	8.2	6.2	6.5	6.3	6.3

Percentage of the population enrolled in school at selected ages: Selected Octobers 1970–94

October	Age												
	3	4	5	16	17	18	19	20	21	22	23	24	25
1970	13.2	28.7	80.6	94.1	87.2	57.8	45.8	39.1	30.7	20.2	16.3	14.7	12.6
1972	15.8	34.0	85.7	93.8	85.6	57.5	42.7	37.8	31.2	20.5	16.9	15.2	13.8
1974	20.0	38.3	89.9	93.7	82.9	53.2	39.4	33.4	31.6	20.1	15.9	13.8	14.0
1976	20.8	42.7	92.3	93.3	86.2	53.0	44.8	37.1	30.9	22.3	16.7	16.1	13.4
1978	25.7	44.7	92.1	94.7	85.0	52.4	42.7	33.7	28.6	21.9	16.2	14.7	11.8
1980	27.6	47.2	93.2	93.9	85.2	54.6	43.0	33.9	30.6	22.3	16.7	13.5	12.0
1982	27.6	46.1	91.5	94.6	88.1	57.1	43.4	38.9	32.7	22.2	17.2	13.8	12.6
1984	28.5	46.5	91.4	95.3	88.5	58.6	43.1	37.7	31.4	22.5	17.2	13.8	11.4
1986	29.3	49.5	91.8	95.5	89.6	61.0	49.6	36.8	30.6	25.4	16.4	13.8	11.3
1988	27.6	49.2	92.6	94.6	88.8	62.8	47.8	42.1	36.0	25.4	17.1	13.2	10.1
1990	(*)	(*)	93.2	95.6	89.5	64.4	50.6	42.9	36.4	28.1	19.2	16.2	11.8
1991	28.2	53.0	91.4	96.5	90.0	65.5	54.0	43.6	40.5	28.2	20.9	17.0	12.4
1992	27.7	52.1	92.4	96.3	91.9	68.1	54.6	46.6	41.5	29.0	21.9	17.6	13.3
1993	27.1	53.9	91.8	96.3	91.6	68.9	54.4	45.1	40.5	30.7	22.0	18.5	15.1
1994	(*)	(*)	95.1	96.3	92.4	67.7	52.8	46.8	43.1	30.3	23.9	18.9	15.2

Table reads: In 1994, 95.1 percent of 5-year-olds were enrolled in school.

* Comparable data were not available for children aged 3 and 4 due to changes in survey procedures.
NOTE: School includes nursery schools and kindergarten but excludes day care centers, and includes 2- and 4-year colleges and universities but excludes schools with programs of strictly less than 2 years. See the supplemental note to *Indicator 5* for a discussion on survey changes.

SOURCE: U.S. Department of Commerce, Bureau of the Census, October Current Population Surveys.

Percentage of the population enrolled in school, by age: Selected Octobers 1970–94

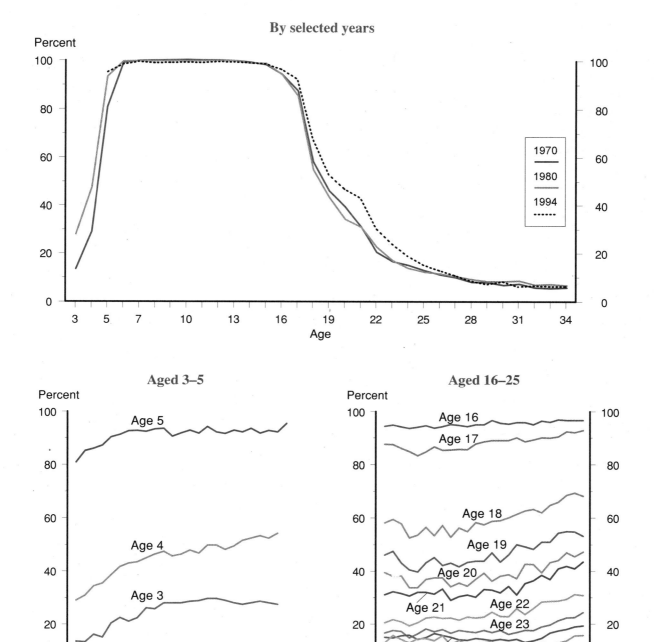

NOTE: For 1990 and 1994, comparable data were not available for children aged 3 and 4 due to changes in survey procedures.

SOURCE: U.S. Department of Commerce, Bureau of the Census, October Current Population Surveys.

Preprimary education enrollment

- In 1995, 37 percent of 3-year-olds, 61 percent of 4-year-olds, and 90 percent of 5-year-olds were enrolled in center-based programs or kindergarten. Among 5-year-olds from various family backgrounds, enrollment rates were similar.

- At ages 3 and 4, similar percentages of white and black children were enrolled in center-based programs and kindergarten in 1995, while their Hispanic peers were much less likely to be enrolled. At age 5, blacks and Hispanics were more likely than whites to be enrolled in kindergarten.

- In 1995, 3- and 4-year-olds from families with incomes of $50,000 or less were less likely to be enrolled than 3- and 4-year-olds from families with incomes of more than $50,000.

> *Participating in early childhood programs such as Head Start, nursery school, prekindergarten, and kindergarten provides children with valuable experience before entering first grade. Instruction received at the preprimary level may help prepare children to participate in elementary school. Many policymakers and educators believe that it is important to help children from disadvantaged backgrounds start elementary school on an equal footing with other children by involving them and their parents in preprimary programs beginning at earlier ages.*

- There was a positive relationship between parents' educational attainment and enrollment rates of 3- to 4-year-olds. As parental educational attainment increased, preprimary enrollment rates increased.

- At ages 3 and 4, enrollment rates for children who lived with one biological or adoptive parent were similar to those of children who lived with two biological or adoptive parents.

Percentage of 3-, 4-, and 5-year-olds enrolled in center-based programs and kindergarten, by race/ethnicity, family income, parents' highest education level, and family structure: 1995

Student characteristics	Enrollment rate								
	3-year-olds			4-year-olds			5-year-olds		
	Total	Center-based programs*	Kinder-garten	Total	Center-based programs*	Kinder-garten	Total	Center-based programs*	Kinder-garten
Total	**37.4**	**36.9**	**0.5**	**60.9**	**59.3**	**1.7**	**90.3**	**16.8**	**73.5**
Race/ethnicity									
White	40.2	40.0	0.3	60.8	59.5	1.3	88.6	17.8	70.8
Black	41.1	40.2	0.9	68.2	66.2	2.0	93.7	17.2	76.5
Hispanic	21.2	20.0	1.2	49.0	45.5	3.5	93.4	13.3	80.1
Family income									
$10,000 or less	26.2	25.8	0.4	54.3	53.6	0.7	90.9	16.7	74.2
10,001–20,000	27.0	27.0	0.0	52.3	50.1	2.3	89.7	12.7	77.0
20,001–35,000	27.7	27.3	0.4	49.7	48.5	1.2	90.7	15.4	75.4
35,001–50,000	38.1	36.8	1.3	59.5	56.5	2.9	88.5	16.6	71.9
50,001 or more	61.2	61.1	0.1	80.7	79.2	1.5	90.9	20.2	70.6
Parents' highest education level									
Less than high school diploma	16.0	14.6	1.3	42.4	41.6	0.8	92.5	11.8	80.7
High school diploma or GED	26.3	25.7	0.6	51.1	50.0	1.1	89.2	14.4	74.8
Some college/vocational/technical	35.6	35.4	0.3	63.3	61.4	1.9	90.2	16.2	74.0
Bachelor's degree	51.7	51.6	0.2	70.7	68.4	2.2	91.6	19.0	72.7
Graduate/professional school	60.8	60.4	0.4	77.9	75.6	2.3	89.8	24.4	65.3
Family structure									
Two biological or adoptive parents	38.6	38.0	0.6	61.3	59.5	1.7	88.8	17.6	71.2
One biological or adoptive parent	36.9	36.9	0.0	63.0	61.6	1.4	94.0	15.8	78.2
One biological and one step parent	23.1	20.4	2.7	46.9	43.9	3.0	89.4	12.2	77.2
Other relatives	20.8	20.8	0.0	61.3	61.3	0.0	88.0	20.8	67.3

Table reads: In 1995, 37.4 percent of 3-year-olds were enrolled in center-based programs or kindergarten.
* Center-based programs include nursery, prekindergarten, and Head Start programs.
NOTE: Details may not add to totals due to rounding.
SOURCE: U.S. Department of Education, National Center for Education Statistics, National Household Education Survey (NHES), 1995 (Early Childhood Program Participation File).

Percentage of 3-, 4-, and 5-year-olds enrolled in center-based programs and kindergarten, by race/ethnicity, family income, and parents' highest education level: 1995

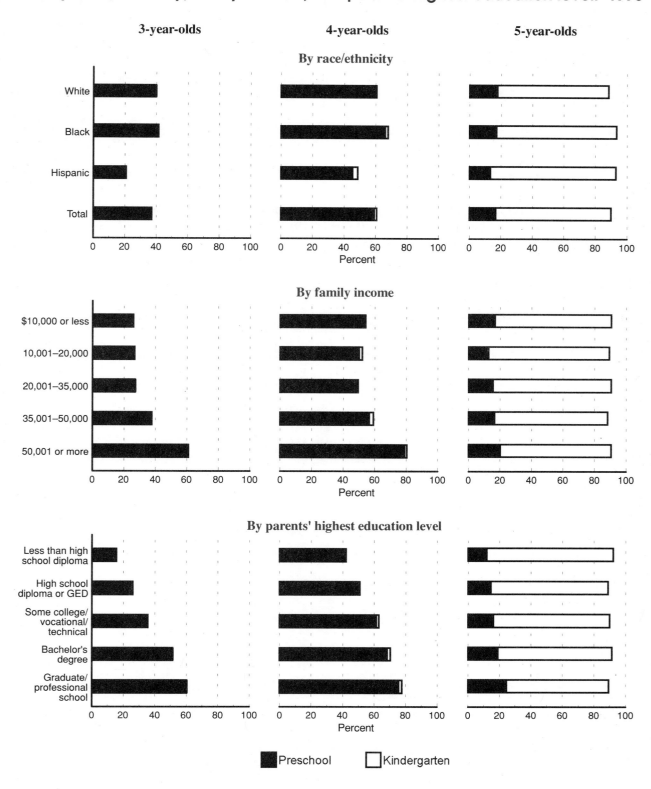

SOURCE: U.S. Department of Education, National Center for Education Statistics, National Household Education Survey (NHES), 1995 (Early Childhood Program Participation File).

Age of first-graders

♦ One in five first-graders was age 7 or older in 1994, compared to one in eight in 1972.

♦ In general, between 1972 and 1993, first-grade students from low income families were more likely to be age 7 or older than were first-grade students from high income families.

♦ Since 1972, a higher percentage of males than females in first grade have been age 7 or older.

♦ Between 1972 and the mid-1980s, the percentage of white first-graders who were age 7 or older increased faster than that of their black and Hispanic counterparts. Since the mid-1980s, similar percentages of white, black, and Hispanic first-graders were age 7 or older.

For generations, the majority of children in first grade have been 6 years old. Children age 7 or older are in first grade for a variety of reasons: their parents kept them in preschool or at home longer; they turned 6 after a state-mandated cut-off date; they were retained in kindergarten or first grade; or they missed school due to illness or other reasons. Changes in the age of first-graders could indicate the differences in the occurrences of these factors for various groups.

Percentage of first-grade students age 7 or older, by family income, sex, and race/ethnicity: October 1972–94

October	Total	Family income*			Sex		Race/ethnicity		
		Low	Middle	High	Male	Female	White	Black	Hispanic
1972	12.7	21.7	12.3	8.8	14.3	11.0	11.0	17.3	20.0
1973	12.9	20.9	12.8	9.2	14.6	11.1	12.0	14.7	20.7
1974	11.3	—	—	—	12.8	9.7	10.8	12.7	14.8
1975	12.3	21.4	11.8	8.9	14.1	10.5	11.3	14.8	17.6
1976	11.0	18.7	10.4	8.1	13.2	8.7	10.0	12.8	17.2
1977	12.2	16.9	12.1	9.6	15.1	9.2	12.0	13.5	12.3
1978	14.5	19.4	15.4	8.3	17.5	11.2	13.6	16.1	20.4
1979	14.8	19.1	16.0	7.7	17.0	12.2	—	—	—
1980	16.2	22.0	16.3	11.3	18.5	13.9	14.8	18.8	22.3
1981	15.6	22.9	15.0	11.3	18.8	12.0	15.5	17.0	15.7
1982	18.0	23.6	16.4	17.1	21.2	14.4	16.5	20.1	25.0
1983	16.3	22.0	16.1	11.7	17.5	15.0	14.9	17.6	23.8
1984	18.7	22.2	20.4	10.4	21.1	16.1	17.2	23.0	24.2
1985	19.0	23.8	17.8	18.2	22.0	15.8	18.5	20.3	21.4
1986	20.7	26.1	20.9	14.8	24.7	16.3	21.0	22.6	19.6
1987	21.2	30.6	19.5	17.3	23.9	18.3	21.5	20.6	20.5
1988	21.3	23.9	21.4	18.3	24.3	18.0	22.1	18.1	22.9
1989	22.3	25.8	21.9	20.8	26.1	18.3	23.8	19.3	21.3
1990	23.3	27.1	23.7	18.8	26.2	20.2	24.0	21.5	22.1
1991	21.2	27.1	20.3	18.4	23.9	18.3	21.6	22.3	17.8
1992	19.7	24.6	19.2	16.2	20.8	18.5	19.8	19.3	19.3
1993	19.4	24.8	19.4	15.4	21.9	16.9	19.1	18.4	23.6
1994	22.4	23.5	22.5	21.5	24.1	20.7	23.3	21.7	20.2

Table reads: In 1994, 22.4 percent of first-graders were age 7 or older.
— Not available.
* Low income is the bottom 20 percent of all family incomes; high income is the top 20 percent of all family incomes; and middle income is the 60 percent in-between.
NOTE: The percentage of first-graders age 7 or older in October can be affected by changes in the minimum age requirement for children starting school set by states and school districts. For example, between 1984 and 1991, seven states (with about 8.3 percent of elementary school enrollment) increased the minimum age requirement for children starting school by an average of 2 months, which could account for about a 1.3 percentage point increase in the percentage of first-grade students age 7 or older.

SOURCE: U.S. Department of Commerce, Bureau of the Census, October Current Population Surveys.

Percentage of first-grade students age 7 or older, by family income and sex: October 1972–94

By family income

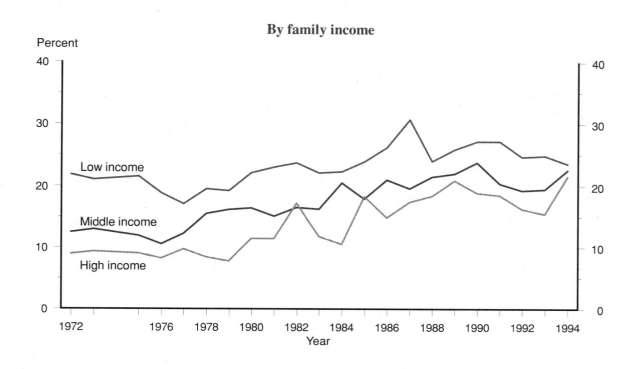

Percent

By sex

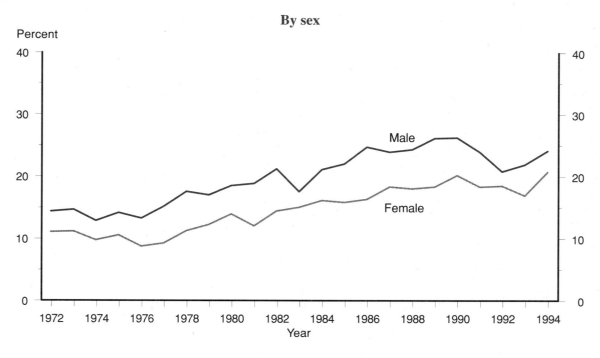

Percent

NOTE: Low income is the bottom 20 percent of all family incomes; high income is the top 20 percent of all family incomes; and middle income is the 60 percent in-between. Family income data were not available for 1974.

SOURCE: U.S. Department of Commerce, Bureau of the Census, October Current Population Surveys.

School choice

♦ In 1993, 20 percent of students in grades 3–12 attended a school chosen by their parents. Of these students, 11 percent attended a public school, and 9 percent attended a private school. In addition, parents of 39 percent of students reported that their child attended an assigned public school, but their choice of residence was influenced by where the child would go to school.

> *Since the late 1980s, school choice has become a popular education reform strategy. Parents who select which school their child attends do so for a variety of reasons, including academic, religious, or moral environment and convenience. Differences in the proportion of students who attend an assigned school and those who attend a school selected by their parents may reflect greater parental involvement and may increase competition among schools to attract and retain students.*

♦ Black students were more likely than white students to attend a school chosen by their parents (23 compared to 19 percent). Of those students who attended a school chosen by their parents, black students were more likely to attend a public school, while white students were more likely to attend a private school.

♦ Students from families with incomes over $50,000 were more likely than students from families with incomes less than $15,000 to attend a chosen school. In fact, 16 percent of students from families with incomes over $50,000 attended private schools, while 9 percent attended a chosen public school.

♦ Parents whose children were enrolled in a private school were more likely to be satisfied with certain aspects of the school than were parents whose children attended other types of schools. Parents whose children were enrolled in a chosen school were more likely than parents whose child attended an assigned public school to be satisfied with aspects of their child's school, such as the school itself, teachers, academic standards, and discipline policy (see supplemental table 4-4).

Percentage distribution of students in grades 3–12 who attended a chosen or assigned school, by race/ethnicity, urbanicity, parents' highest education level, and family income: 1993

| Student characteristics | Total | Chosen school | | | Assigned public school | | |
		Total	Public	Private	Total	Choice of residence influenced by school*	Other
Total	**100.0**	**19.7**	**10.9**	**8.8**	**80.2**	**39.1**	**41.1**
Race/ethnicity							
White	100.0	18.6	8.4	10.2	81.4	41.7	39.7
Black	100.0	22.6	18.9	3.7	77.5	33.2	44.3
Hispanic	100.0	20.3	13.6	6.7	79.8	32.3	47.5
Urbanicity							
Inside urban area	100.0	24.9	13.7	11.2	75.2	40.1	35.1
Outside urban area	100.0	12.4	7.3	5.1	87.6	35.2	52.4
Rural	100.0	12.0	6.5	5.5	88.1	39.2	48.9
Parents' highest education level							
Less than high school diploma	100.0	15.6	13.3	2.3	84.4	31.8	52.6
High school diploma or GED	100.0	16.4	11.2	5.2	83.5	36.1	47.4
Some college/vocational/technical	100.0	20.0	11.2	8.8	80.1	39.3	40.8
Bachelor's degree	100.0	23.1	8.8	14.3	77.0	45.2	31.8
Graduate/professional school	100.0	26.9	10.0	16.9	73.1	45.5	27.6
Family income							
Less than $15,000	100.0	17.1	13.9	3.2	82.9	33.9	49.0
15,001–30,000	100.0	18.7	12.2	6.5	81.2	34.9	46.3
30,001–50,000	100.0	18.8	9.4	9.4	81.3	39.6	41.7
50,001 or more	100.0	24.1	8.5	15.6	76.0	47.6	28.4

Table reads: In 1993, 19.7 percent of students in grades 3–12 attended a school chosen by their parents, of which 10.9 percent attended a public school, and 8.8 percent attended a private school.

* Students whose parents indicated that their choice of residence was influenced by where their child would go to school.

SOURCE: U.S. Department of Education, National Center for Education Statistics, National Household Education Survey (NHES), 1993 (School Safety and Discipline File).

Percentage distribution of students in grades 3–12 who attended a chosen or assigned school, by race/ethnicity and family income: 1993

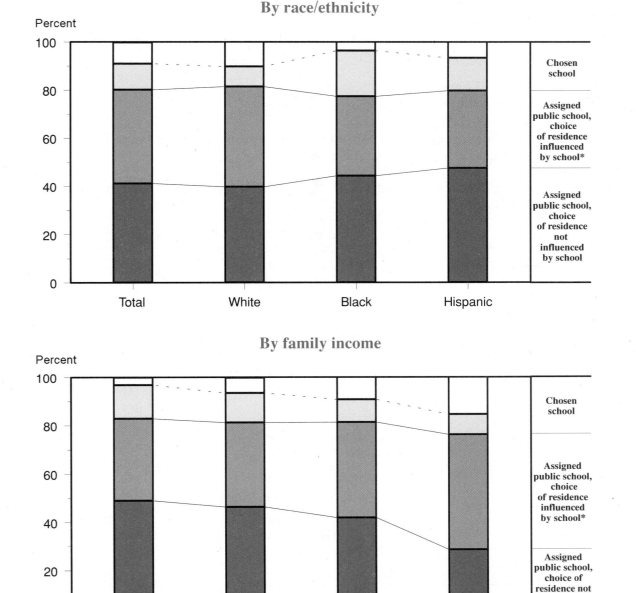

By race/ethnicity

By family income

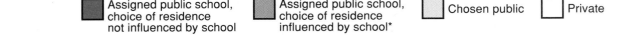

* Students whose parents indicated that their choice of residence was influenced by where their child would go to school.

SOURCE: U.S. Department of Education, National Center for Education Statistics, National Household Education Survey (NHES), 1993 (School Safety and Discipline File).

Dropout rates

♦ In October 1994, 5 percent of students who were in grades 10–12 the previous October were not enrolled again and had not graduated from high school—that is, they had dropped out of high school sometime during the year.

Students who drop out of school have fewer opportunities to succeed in the work force or to assume a fully functional place in society at large than those students who complete high school. The event dropout rate is one of several ways to define dropout rates. It is a measure of the proportion of students who drop out in a single year without completing high school.

♦ Generally, between 1972 and 1994, black and Hispanic high school students were more likely to drop out than whites. Also, students from low income families were more likely to drop out of high school than were their counterparts from middle and high income families.

Event dropout rates[1] for those in grades 10–12, aged 15–24, by sex, race/ethnicity, and family income: October 1972–94

October	Total	Sex		Race/ethnicity[2]			Family income[3]		
		Male	Female	White	Black	Hispanic	Low	Middle	High
1972	6.1	5.9	6.3	5.3	9.5	11.2	13.8	6.7	2.5
1973	6.3	6.8	5.7	5.5	9.9	10.0	17.1	6.8	1.8
1974	6.7	7.4	6.0	5.8	11.6	9.9	—	—	—
1975	5.8	5.4	6.1	5.0	8.7	10.9	15.3	5.9	2.6
1976	5.9	6.5	5.2	5.6	7.4	7.3	15.0	6.7	2.1
1977	6.5	6.9	6.1	6.1	8.6	7.8	15.1	7.5	2.2
1978	6.7	7.5	5.9	5.8	10.2	12.3	17.1	7.2	3.0
1979	6.7	6.8	6.7	6.0	9.9	9.8	16.7	6.8	3.6
1980	6.1	6.7	5.5	5.2	8.2	11.7	15.5	6.3	2.4
1981	5.9	6.0	5.8	4.8	9.7	10.7	14.0	6.0	2.8
1982	5.5	5.8	5.1	4.7	7.8	9.2	14.7	5.4	1.8
1983	5.2	5.8	4.7	4.4	7.0	10.1	10.1	5.9	2.2
1984	5.1	5.4	4.8	4.4	5.7	11.1	13.2	5.0	1.8
1985	5.2	5.4	5.0	4.3	7.8	9.8	13.7	5.1	2.1
1986	4.7	4.7	4.7	3.7	5.4	11.9	10.5	5.0	1.6
1987	4.1	4.3	3.8	3.5	6.4	5.4	9.9	4.5	0.9
1988	4.8	5.1	4.4	4.2	5.9	10.4	13.4	4.7	1.1
1989	4.5	4.5	4.5	3.5	7.8	7.8	10.0	5.0	1.1
1990	4.0	4.0	3.9	3.3	5.0	7.9	9.3	4.2	1.1
1991	4.0	3.8	4.2	3.2	6.0	7.3	10.6	4.0	1.0
1992	4.4	3.9	4.9	3.7	5.0	8.2	10.9	4.4	1.3
1993	4.5	4.6	4.3	3.9	5.8	6.7	12.3	4.3	1.3
1994[4]	5.3	5.2	5.4	4.2	6.6	10.0	13.0	5.2	2.1

Table reads: In October of 1994, 5.2 percent of male and 5.4 percent of female students in grades 10–12, aged 15–24, who were enrolled in October 1993 were not enrolled in school.

— Not available.

[1] The event dropout rate is the percentage of those in grades 10–12, aged 15–24, who were enrolled the previous October, but who were not enrolled and had not graduated the following October.

[2] Not shown separately but included in the total are non-Hispanics who are neither black nor white.

[3] Low income is the bottom 20 percent of all family incomes; high income is the top 20 percent of all family incomes; and middle income is the 60 percent in-between.

[4] In 1994, new survey collection techniques and population weighting were used. See the supplemental note to this indicator for further discussion.

NOTE: Beginning in 1992, the Current Population Survey (CPS) changed the questions used to obtain the educational attainment of respondents. See the supplemental note to *Indicator 25* for further discussion.

SOURCE: U.S. Department of Education, National Center for Education Statistics, *Dropout Rates in the United States: 1994* (based on the October Current Population Surveys).

Event dropout rates* for those in grades 10–12, aged 15–24: October 1972–94

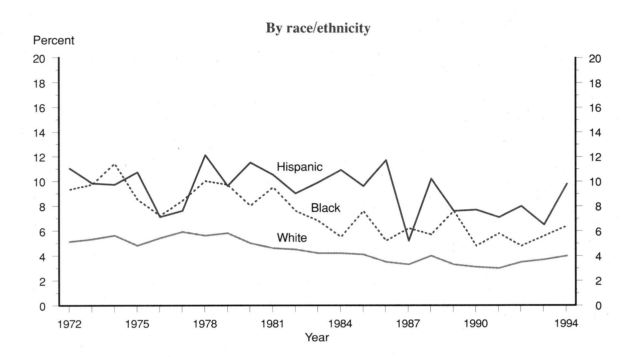

By race/ethnicity

Percent

By family income

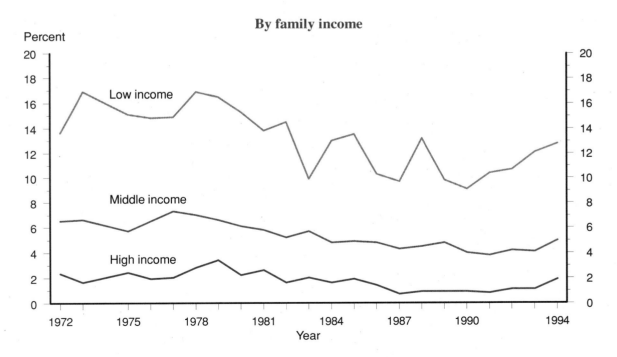

Percent

* The event dropout rate is the percentage of those in grades 10–12, aged 15–24, who were enrolled the previous October, but who who were not enrolled and had not graduated the following October.

NOTE: Low income is the bottom 20 percent of all family incomes; high income is the top 20 percent of all family incomes; and middle income is the 60 percent in-between.

SOURCE: U.S. Department of Education, National Center for Education Statistics, *Dropout Rates in the United States: 1994* (based on the October Current Population Surveys).

Dropouts who complete high school within 2 years of scheduled graduation

♦ Eighty-eight percent of the 1990 cohort had completed high school by August following their senior year of high school, compared to 80 percent of the sophomore class of 1980.

♦ Dropouts from the 1990 sophomore class were more likely to return to school than were their counterparts a decade earlier. Almost 58 percent of dropouts from the 1990 cohort either completed or were re-enrolled in school 2 years after their scheduled graduation, compared to 34 percent of dropouts from the 1980 cohort.

♦ Compared to their peers, dropouts who had poor basic skills in mathematics (test performance in the lowest quartile for their cohort) were less likely to receive an alternative credential such as a GED, and were more likely not to have completed high school 2 years later.

> *The decision to drop out of school does not always indicate the culmination of a young person's education. Many former students reconsider their decision to drop out and return to high school. Also, in the American educational system, alternative programs are available that give dropouts a "second chance" to complete their high school education. These programs include regular high school diploma programs as well as programs leading to a high school credential after passing the General Educational Development (GED) Tests.*

Percentage of 1980 and 1990 sophomore classes in August 1982 and 1992 and spring 1984 and 1994 according to educational status, by selected characteristics

Selected characteristics	Status in August following scheduled high school graduation			Status of August dropouts in the spring 2 years later				Total completed spring 2 years following scheduled graduation
	Completed high school[1]	Still enrolled[2]	Dropout	Graduated	Received alternative credential	Enrolled in high school[2]	Still dropouts	
				1990 Sophomore Cohort				
Total	**87.5**	**6.9**	**5.6**	**15.1**	**11.0**	**31.4**	**42.5**	**92.2**
Sex								
Male	87.2	7.6	5.2	12.0	11.1	30.6	46.3	92.2
Female	87.9	6.1	6.0	17.9	10.5	32.4	39.3	92.3
Race/ethnicity								
White	90.6	5.1	4.3	13.0	14.8	31.9	40.3	94.2
Black	78.9	13.5	7.6	22.4	6.7	33.2	37.8	87.1
Hispanic	77.5	11.6	10.9	9.5	6.0	33.8	50.6	85.0
Mathematics achievement in 10th grade								
Below lowest quartile	74.6	13.0	12.4	12.9	8.5	31.9	46.7	82.2
Above lowest quartile	93.2	4.2	2.6	19.9	16.1	30.4	33.6	96.6
				1980 Sophomore Cohort				
Total	**80.1**	**10.0**	**9.9**	**8.4**	**11.8**	**13.5**	**66.4**	**89.6**
Sex								
Male	76.7	12.4	11.0	8.8	11.9	11.9	67.3	88.4
Female	83.5	7.6	8.9	7.9	11.6	15.3	65.2	90.8
Race/ethnicity								
White	83.0	8.2	8.8	7.8	13.9	13.7	64.6	91.4
Black	71.7	17.0	11.3	11.8	7.0	18.7	62.5	85.0
Hispanic	68.8	14.4	16.8	8.4	9.9	6.5	75.3	82.2
Mathematics achievement in 10th grade								
Below lowest quartile	67.0	14.5	18.5	8.4	8.6	15.0	68.0	80.1
Above lowest quartile	89.1	6.9	4.1	8.4	20.8	9.2	61.6	95.8

[1] Includes those who graduated from high school and those who received an alternative credential.
[2] Enrolled in a regular high school or alternative program. For the 1990 cohort, 1.9 percent of the dropouts were enrolled in high school, while 29.5 percent were enrolled in an alternative program in the spring of 1994.

SOURCE: U.S. Department of Education, National Center for Education Statistics, High School and Beyond (HS&B) study, Sophomore Cohort, Base Year, First, and Second Follow-up Surveys, and National Education Longitudinal Study of 1988, First, Second, and Third Follow-up Surveys.

Status of 1980 and 1990 sophomores who did not graduate on schedule 2 years after scheduled high school graduation

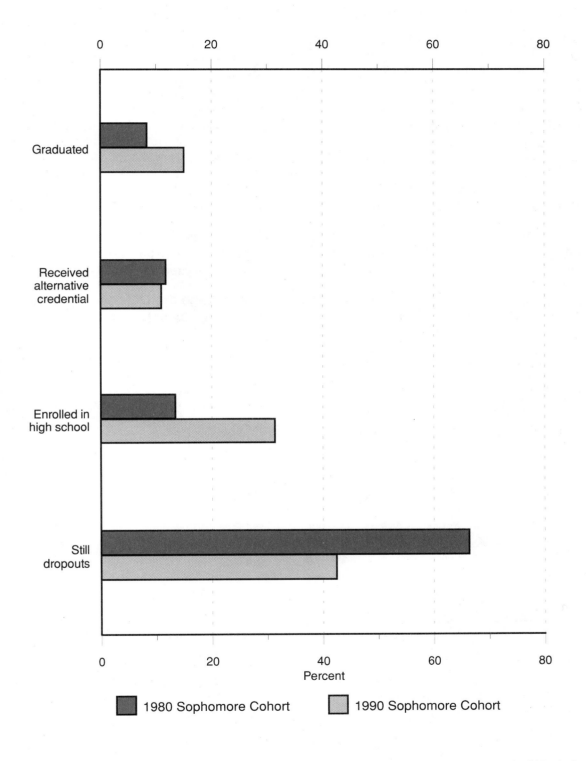

SOURCE: U.S. Department of Education, National Center for Education Statistics, High School and Beyond (HS&B) study, Sophomore Cohort, Base Year, First, and Second Follow-up Surveys, and National Education Longitudinal Study of 1988, First, Second, and Third Follow-up Surveys.

Immediate transition from high school to college

♦ Between 1973 and 1994, the proportion of high school graduates going directly to college increased from 47 to 62 percent.

♦ High school graduates from low income families were more likely to go directly to college in 1994 than in 1972. Still, in 1994, only 45 percent of high school graduates from low income families went directly to college, compared to 77 percent of those from high income families.

Since most college students enroll in college immediately after completing high school, the percentage of high school graduates enrolled in college the October following graduation is an indicator of the total proportion of that year's high school graduates who will ever enroll in college. The percentage enrolling not only reflects the accessibility of higher education to high school graduates, but also shows their assessment of the value of attending college compared to working, entering the military, traveling, or other possible pursuits.

♦ In 1994, 65 percent of white high school graduates enrolled in college, compared to 51 percent of their black counterparts.

♦ In 1994, high school graduates aged 16–24 who had at least one parent with a bachelor's degree were more likely to go directly to college than those graduates whose parents did not have a bachelor's degree (83 percent versus 43 to 65 percent) (see supplemental table 7-3).

Percentage of high school graduates aged 16–24 enrolled in college the October following graduation, by type of college, family income, and race/ethnicity: Selected Octobers 1972–94

October	Total	Type of college		Family income			Race/ethnicity		
		2-year	4-year	Low	Middle	High	White	Black	Hispanic
1972	49.2	—	—	26.1	45.2	63.8	49.7	44.6	45.0
1973	46.6	14.9	31.7	20.3	40.9	64.4	47.8	32.5	54.1
1975	50.7	18.2	32.6	31.2	46.2	64.5	51.1	41.7	58.0
1977	50.6	17.5	33.1	27.7	44.2	66.3	50.8	49.5	50.8
1979	49.3	17.5	31.8	30.5	43.2	63.2	49.9	46.7	45.0
1981	53.9	20.5	33.5	33.6	49.2	67.6	54.9	42.7	52.1
1983	52.7	19.2	33.5	34.6	45.2	70.3	55.0	38.2	54.2
1985	57.7	19.6	38.1	40.2	50.6	74.6	60.1	42.2	51.0
1987	56.8	18.9	37.9	36.9	50.0	73.8	58.6	52.2	33.5
1989	59.6	20.7	38.9	48.1	55.4	70.7	60.7	53.4	55.1
1990	60.1	20.1	40.0	46.7	54.4	76.6	63.0	46.8	42.7
1991	62.5	24.9	37.7	39.5	58.4	78.2	65.4	46.4	57.2
1992	61.9	23.0	38.9	40.9	57.0	79.0	64.3	48.2	55.0
1993	61.5	22.4	39.1	50.4	56.9	79.3	62.9	55.6	62.2
1994	61.9	21.0	40.9	44.7	57.9	77.1	64.5	50.8	49.1

Table reads: In 1994, 61.9 percent of high school graduates aged 16–24 were enrolled in college the October following their high school graduation.

— Not available. Data regarding type of college were not collected until 1973.

NOTE: Low income is the bottom 20 percent of all family incomes; high income is the top 20 percent of all family incomes; and middle income is the 60 percent in-between. Details may not add to totals due to rounding.

SOURCE: U.S. Department of Commerce, Bureau of the Census, October Current Population Surveys.

Percentage of high school graduates aged 16–24 enrolled in college the October following graduation: October 1972–94

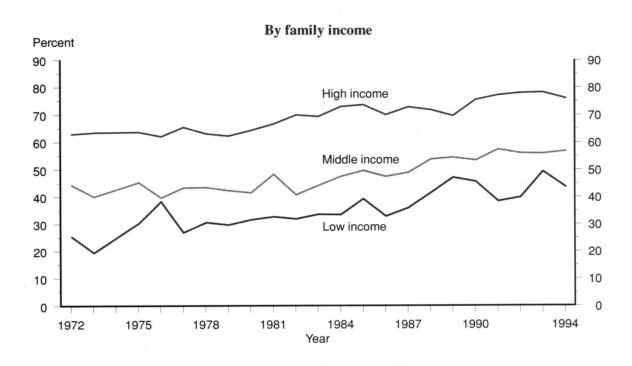

By family income

Percent

High income

Middle income

Low income

Year

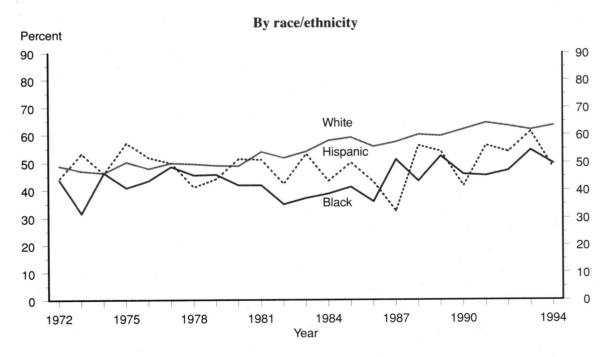

By race/ethnicity

Percent

White

Hispanic

Black

Year

NOTE: Low income is the bottom 20 percent of all family incomes; high income is the top 20 percent of all family incomes; and middle income is the 60 percent in-between.

SOURCE: U.S. Department of Commerce, Bureau of the Census, October Current Population Surveys.

Racial and ethnic differences in participation in higher education

♦ Between 1992 and 1994, white high school graduates aged 18–24 were more likely to be enrolled in college than were their black and Hispanic counterparts. For these years, the average enrollment rate for whites was 9 and 8 percentage points higher than that of blacks and Hispanics, respectively.

♦ The percentage of high school graduates aged 18–24 enrolled in college was higher in 1994 than in 1972 for whites and blacks. During this period, white high school enrollment rates grew substantially, rising from 33 to 44 percent, with most of the growth occurring after 1981. Enrollment rates for blacks of the same age grew moderately over this period.

> *Racial and ethnic differences in college enrollment rates may reflect differences in access to and persistence in higher education for groups with varying social and economic backgrounds. Differing enrollment rates are also a leading indicator of future differences in the earnings and productivity associated with postsecondary education. The college enrollment rate for 18- to 24-year-olds is influenced by the number who enroll immediately after graduating high school, the number who delay entry, and the number of years individuals in both of these groups stay in higher education.*

♦ Between 1992 and 1994, the average enrollment rates in 2-year colleges were similar for white and black high school graduates aged 18–24. Hispanic high school graduates of the same age were somewhat more likely than their white or black counterparts to be enrolled in 2-year institutions. However, both black and Hispanic high school graduates aged 18–24 were substantially less likely to be enrolled in 4-year institutions than were their white counterparts (see supplemental table 8-1).

♦ Enrollment rates for older adults, high school graduates aged 25 or older, generally were much lower than those for their younger counterparts aged 18–24 regardless of racial and ethnic group. Between 1992 and 1994, 3-year average college enrollment rates were similar for white, black, and Hispanic high school graduates aged 25–34.

Percentage of high school graduates enrolled in college, by age and race/ethnicity: October 1972–94

October	Aged 18–24				Aged 25–34				Aged 35 or older			
	Total	White	Black	Hispanic	Total	White	Black	Hispanic	Total	White	Black	Hispanic
1972	31.9	32.6	27.2	25.8	8.4	8.4	8.8	7.5	—	—	—	—
1973	29.7	30.2	23.8	29.1	8.2	8.1	7.7	10.7	—	—	—	—
1974	30.5	30.6	26.2	32.3	9.3	9.1	10.8	10.0	—	—	—	—
1975	32.5	32.3	31.5	35.5	9.9	9.6	11.5	11.3	—	—	—	—
1976	33.1	32.8	33.4	35.9	9.6	9.2	11.9	11.0	2.3	2.1	4.1	3.9
1977	32.5	32.3	31.3	31.5	10.3	9.8	13.9	12.4	—	—	—	—
1978	31.4	31.3	29.6	27.1	9.1	8.8	10.8	10.2	2.4	2.2	3.8	4.2
1979	31.2	31.3	29.4	30.2	9.1	8.9	9.2	11.6	2.4	2.3	3.3	2.9
1980	31.8	32.1	27.6	29.9	8.9	8.7	9.6	9.2	2.1	2.0	3.4	2.9
1981	32.4	32.7	28.0	29.9	9.0	8.5	10.2	10.8	2.3	2.1	3.7	4.0
1982	33.0	33.3	28.1	29.2	8.9	8.7	9.6	9.7	2.2	2.1	2.7	2.9
1983	32.5	33.0	27.0	31.5	9.1	8.7	8.8	9.8	2.3	2.2	2.7	3.1
1984	33.2	33.9	27.2	29.9	8.6	8.4	8.0	9.9	2.1	2.0	2.7	1.8
1985	33.7	34.9	26.0	26.8	8.7	8.6	7.5	9.7	2.3	2.2	2.9	3.4
1986	34.0	34.5	28.6	29.4	8.3	7.9	7.9	10.4	2.4	2.2	3.3	3.4
1987	36.0	37.2	29.1	28.2	8.1	7.9	7.9	8.9	2.3	2.3	2.6	2.5
1988	37.0	38.4	27.8	30.8	8.0	7.8	7.5	7.8	2.7	2.6	3.3	3.4
1989	38.0	39.7	30.5	28.3	8.2	8.3	6.2	7.1	2.5	2.5	2.1	3.7
1990	39.0	40.3	32.4	28.4	8.6	8.7	5.9	7.0	2.7	2.6	2.9	3.9
1991	40.8	42.3	30.8	33.9	9.0	8.7	8.1	8.6	2.7	2.6	3.4	2.9
1992	41.6	42.5	33.4	36.1	8.6	8.5	6.7	8.5	2.5	2.5	2.6	2.7
1993	41.0	42.0	32.2	34.9	8.5	8.2	8.1	9.5	2.6	2.4	3.3	3.1
1994	42.2	43.6	35.5	32.9	9.5	9.1	9.7	10.1	2.7	2.5	3.5	4.3

Table reads: In 1994, 42.2 percent of high school graduates aged 18–24 were enrolled in college.
— Not available.

SOURCE: U.S. Department of Commerce, Bureau of the Census, October Current Population Surveys.

Percentage of high school graduates enrolled in college, by age and race/ethnicity: October 1972–94

Aged 18–24

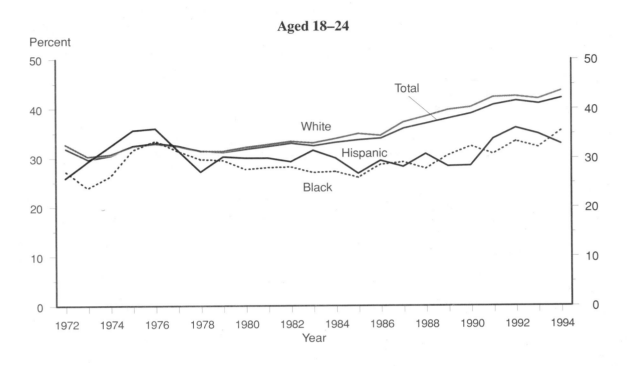

Aged 25–34

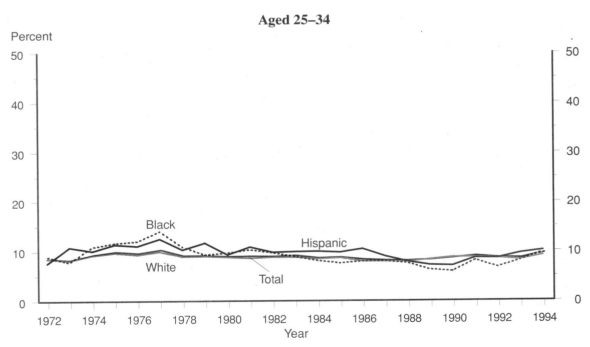

SOURCE: U.S. Department of Commerce, Bureau of the Census, October Current Population Surveys.

Community college outcomes

♦ Among students who began their postsecondary education at a community college in 1989–90, 37 percent completed a degree at some institution by 1994; 22 percent of these students completed a certificate or an associate's degree at their first institution. Those who did not complete an award at their first institution spent a substantial amount of time there—an average of 14 months of enrollment.

> About 45 percent of first-time undergraduates attend public 2-year colleges. These institutions serve many purposes: they provide vocational training and skill development; they offer an inexpensive way to complete lower division requirements before entering a 4-year institution; and they meet avocational interests. Examining outcomes for students who began their postsecondary education at public community colleges provides insight into how these diverse needs are being met.

♦ Nineteen percent of 1989–90 community college beginners transferred to a public 4-year institution, and 3 percent transferred to a private 4-year institution (see supplemental table 9-2). Of those who transferred to a 4-year institution, 38 percent completed an associate's degree before transferring.

♦ By 1994, 26 percent of those who transferred to 4-year institutions had completed a bachelor's degree, and 47 percent were still enrolled at a 4-year institution.

♦ The higher a student's socioeconomic status (SES), the more likely that student was to transfer to a 4-year institution; 35 percent of high SES students transferred, compared to 21 percent of middle SES and 7 percent of low SES students (see supplemental table 9-2).

Among 1989–90 beginning students at community colleges, percentage distribution and average number of months enrolled at first institution, by attainment at first institution and 1994 attainment/enrollment status

Selected characteristics	Attainment at first institution[1]			1994 attainment at any institution									
				Attained[2]						No degree			
					Certificate		Associate's			Enrolled			
	None	Certi-ficate	Asso-ciate's	Total	Not en-rolled at 4-year	Enrolled at 4-year	Not en-rolled at 4-year	Enrolled at 4-year	Bache-lor's	Total	Less-than-4-year	4-year	Not en-rolled
Total	77.8	5.0	17.2	36.7	12.3	0.6	13.5	4.0	6.3	14.7	9.6	5.1	48.6
Age as of 12/31/89													
18 years or younger	71.6	2.6	25.9	47.4	8.0	1.4	19.7	6.4	11.9	14.9	7.5	7.4	37.7
19 years	79.5	5.8	14.7	31.9	12.7	0.0	13.2	3.9	2.2	20.8	12.7	8.1	47.3
20–29 years	83.1	6.5	10.4	27.3	16.4	0.0	6.5	1.8	2.5	13.0	11.2	1.8	59.8
30 years or older	86.0	8.9	5.1	25.7	18.2	0.0	6.3	0.6	0.6	9.2	9.2	0.0	65.1
Enrollment status, first term													
Full-time	68.7	5.4	25.9	45.7	10.3	1.0	17.5	6.0	11.0	11.7	5.7	6.0	42.7
At least half, less than full-time	84.9	2.8	12.3	28.3	10.9	0.6	13.2	1.8	1.8	22.8	17.0	5.8	48.9
Less than half-time	87.7	6.6	5.8	27.1	16.9	0.0	6.7	0.6	2.2	13.0	9.3	3.7	59.9
First transfer													
Did not transfer	78.7	7.7	13.5	23.1	8.9	(3)	14.1	(3)	(3)	10.1	10.1	(3)	66.8
Transferred to less-than-4-year	93.8	2.2	4.0	47.2	32.8	0.0	13.8	0.0	0.6	16.3	16.3	0.0	36.6
Transferred to 4-year	61.2	0.7	38.1	59.5	0.6	2.8	12.3	18.3	25.6	25.9	2.8	23.2	14.5
Average number of months enrolled at first institution	14.2	15.5	28.3	20.4	11.9	(4)	25.6	26.2	22.5	24.8	27.3	20.2	11.4

[1] For students who earned more than one award at the first institution, the first award they earned.
[2] Highest degree attained at any institution. Students who have attained may also be enrolled.
[3] Not applicable.
[4] Too few sample observations for a reliable estimate.

SOURCE: U.S. Department of Education, National Center for Education Statistics, 1990 Beginning Postsecondary Students Longitudinal Study, Second Follow-up (BPS:90/94).

Attainment and enrollment among 1989–90 community college entrants: 1989–94

Percentage distribution of attainment outcomes

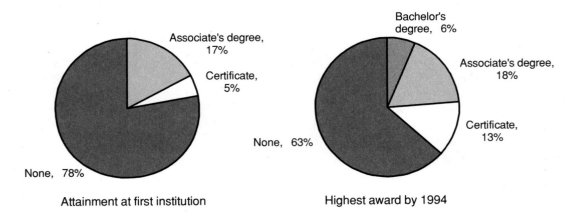

Attainment at first institution

Highest award by 1994

Average number of months enrolled at first institution, by award attained

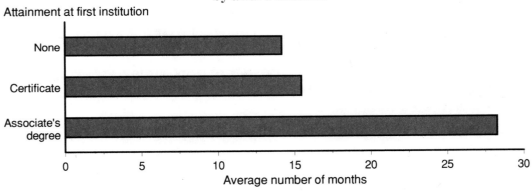

First transfer, by socioeconomic status

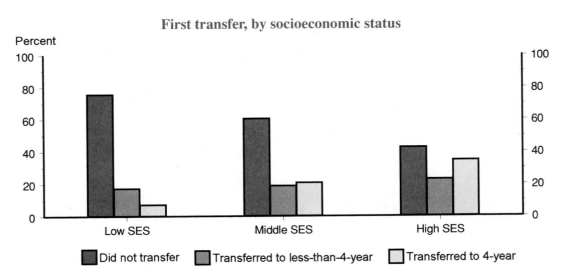

SOURCE: U.S. Department of Education, National Center for Education Statistics, 1990 Beginning Postsecondary Students Longitudinal Study, Second Follow-up (BPS:90/94).

Persistence toward a bachelor's degree

♦ Among beginning students seeking bachelor's degrees in 1989–90, three-quarters (77 percent) of those who began in 4-year institutions and more than half (54 percent) of those who began in 2-year institutions reported completing some degree or were still working toward a bachelor's degree 5 years later. Students who began in 4-year institutions were much more likely to have reported completing a bachelor's degree in 5 years than those who began in 2-year institutions (57 versus 8 percent).

> Personal, financial, and academic circumstances often interfere with the persistence required to complete bachelor's degree programs. Understanding the relationship between these circumstances and students' paths through postsecondary education is essential to help them succeed.

♦ Students who entered postsecondary education at age 18 or younger were more than twice (51 versus 19 percent) as likely as those who entered between the ages of 20 and 29 to have reported completing a bachelor's degree within 5 years, and five times more likely than students who entered at age 30 or later.

♦ Half of bachelor's degree seekers (52 percent) who first enrolled on a full-time basis reported having completed that degree within 5 years, compared to less than 15 percent of those who first enrolled less than full time.

♦ As socioeconomic status (SES) and parents' educational attainment levels increased, so did the likelihood of completing a bachelor's degree, or any degree, within 5 years. Bachelor's degree seekers of lower SES or whose parents had less education were more likely to have reported completing no degree (see supplemental table 10-1).

Percentage distribution of 1989–90 beginning postsecondary students seeking bachelor's degrees according to persistence toward and completion of bachelor's and other degrees as of spring 1994, by selected characteristics

Selected characteristics	Completed a degree				Still enrolled for bach-elor's[2]	No degree, no longer enrolled toward a bachelor's						
	Highest degree completed[1]			Total any degree		Total no degree	Number of months enrolled[3]					
	Bach-elor's	Asso-ciate's	Certi-ficate				Less than 9	9–18	19–27	28–36	37–45	More than 45
Total	**45.8**	**5.1**	**3.3**	**54.3**	**17.5**	**28.3**	**2.8**	**8.1**	**5.7**	**5.6**	**3.8**	**2.3**
Level of first institution												
4-year	57.1	2.5	2.1	61.7	15.3	23.1	1.9	5.5	5.3	4.9	3.3	2.1
2-year	7.9	13.9	7.2	29.0	25.3	45.8	5.4	16.8	7.0	8.2	5.3	3.0
Age as of 12/31/89												
18 years or younger	51.4	4.9	2.9	59.2	16.4	24.5	1.5	5.2	5.9	5.7	3.5	2.7
19 years	38.3	4.2	3.4	45.8	21.1	33.0	4.0	13.4	4.4	6.0	3.4	1.6
20–29 years	19.0	9.4	7.9	36.3	19.6	44.1	8.2	17.9	6.5	2.8	7.7	1.0
30 years or older	9.8	6.0	3.3	19.1	17.3	63.5	19.4	28.9	4.8	9.9	0.5	0.0
Enrollment status, first term												
Full-time	51.7	4.1	2.5	58.3	16.7	25.0	1.7	6.6	5.3	5.6	3.5	2.3
At least half, less than full-time	14.5	11.5	6.1	32.1	24.5	43.4	5.9	18.9	5.6	2.5	7.8	2.5
Less than half-time	10.5	4.9	11.4	26.8	26.8	46.4	17.3	8.0	9.1	8.0	0.3	3.7
Received aid in 1989–90												
No	36.9	7.0	4.5	48.4	21.0	30.7	3.0	8.7	6.2	6.3	3.9	2.7
Yes	55.1	3.2	2.2	60.4	13.8	25.8	2.7	7.5	5.2	4.9	3.7	1.9

[1] Includes students who were no longer working toward a bachelor's degree, but who had completed another type of degree.
[2] Includes students who had completed another type of degree or award (associate's degree: 11.8 percent, certificate: 2.7 percent), but who are still working toward a bachelor's degree.
[3] Enrollment can be full time or part time. Includes students who are still enrolled but who are no longer working toward a bachelor's.

SOURCE: U.S. Department of Education, National Center for Education Statistics, 1990 Beginning Postsecondary Students Longitudinal Study, Second Follow-up (BPS:90/94).

Percentage distribution of 1989–90 beginning postsecondary students seeking bachelor's degrees according to persistence toward and completion of bachelor's and other degrees as of spring 1994, by selected chararacteristics

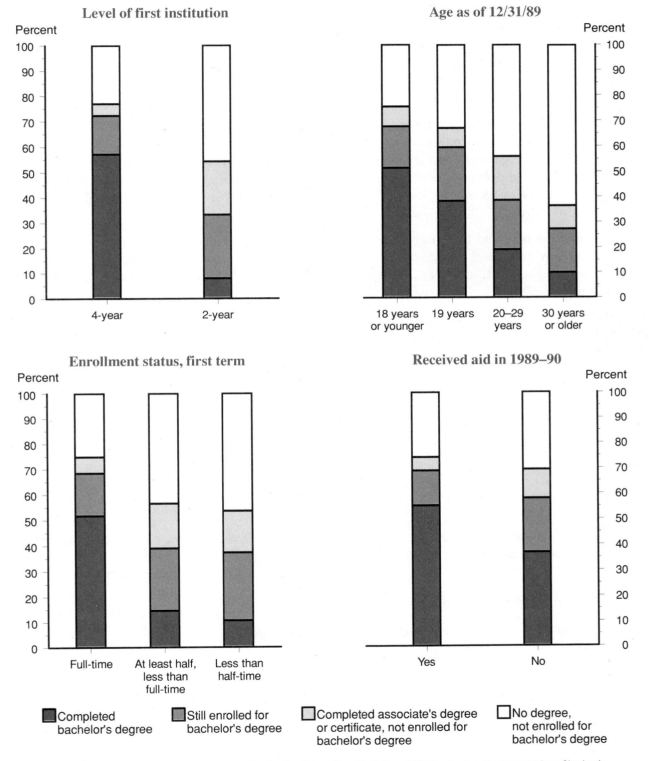

SOURCE: U.S. Department of Education, National Center for Education Statistics, 1990 Beginning Postsecondary Students Longitudinal Study, Second Follow-up (BPS:90/94).

Time to complete a bachelor's degree

♦ In 1993, about 31 percent of college graduates completed their bachelor's degree within 4 years after graduating from high school. The proportion who completed a bachelor's degree in 4 years after high school graduation dropped from 45 to 31 percent between 1977 and 1990, but did not change between 1990 and 1993. Females were more likely than males to complete their degree in 4 years.

> The traditional time to complete most bachelor's degrees is 4 years, but a number of circumstances such as changing schools or majors, stopping out for periods of time, attending school on a part-time basis, or having difficulty enrolling in required classes may delay graduation. Increased time to complete their degree can be costly to students who incur additional tuition and postponed entry into the labor market.

♦ About 36 percent of 1993 graduates completed a bachelor's degree within 4 years of beginning their postsecondary education, while 26 percent took more than 6 years to do so. Students who delayed their college enrollment or who began in a 2-year institution were more than twice as likely to take more than 6 years after starting college to complete their bachelor's degree.

♦ Students who received their bachelor's degree from a private 4-year institution were much more likely to complete their degree within 4 years of starting college than were students who graduated from a public 4-year institution; students in public 4-year institutions were more likely to completed their degree in 5 years.

Percentage of college graduates completing a bachelor's degree within various years following their high school graduation, by sex: Years of college graduation 1977, 1986, 1990, and 1993

Year of college graduation	Total				Male				Female			
	4 years or less	5 years or less	6 years or less	More than 6 years	4 years or less	5 years or less	6 years or less	More than 6 years	4 years or less	5 years or less	6 years or less	More than 6 years
1977	45.4	67.2	75.3	24.7	39.2	61.8	71.1	28.9	52.8	73.8	80.5	19.5
1986	34.5	60.2	70.8	29.2	30.8	57.4	69.8	30.2	38.2	62.9	71.8	28.2
1990	31.1	57.2	68.4	31.6	26.6	54.3	67.6	32.4	35.1	59.8	69.1	30.9
1993	31.1	58.7	69.9	30.1	26.5	55.9	69.4	30.6	34.8	61.0	70.3	29.7

SOURCE: U.S. Department of Education, National Center for Education Statistics, Recent College Graduates Survey for 1977–90 graduates and 1993 Baccalaureate and Beyond Longitudinal Study, First Follow-up (B&B:93/94).

Percentage of college graduates completing a bachelor's degree within various years of starting college, by selected student and institution characteristics: 1993

Student and institution characteristics	4 years or less	More than 4 up to 5 years	More than 5 up to 6 years	More than 6 years
Total	**35.5**	**27.9**	**11.0**	**25.6**
Years between high school graduation and beginning postsecondary education				
Less than 1 year	38.4	29.1	10.8	21.7
One year or more	10.8	17.5	12.4	59.3
First institution attended				
4-year	41.8	29.9	10.2	18.2
2-year	16.3	23.9	15.7	44.1
Institution granting bachelor's degree				
Public 4-year	28.2	33.0	13.6	25.2
Private 4-year	52.9	17.1	5.4	25.6

SOURCE: U.S. Department of Education, National Center for Education Statistics, 1993 Baccalaureate and Beyond Longitudinal Study, First Follow-up (B&B:93/94).

Time to complete a bachelor's degree

Percentage of college graduates completing a bachelor's degree within various years following their high school graduation, by sex: Years of college graduation 1977, 1986, 1990, and 1993

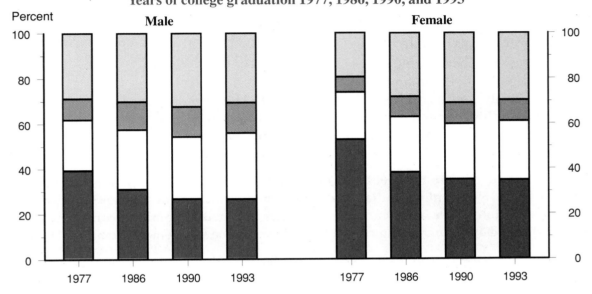

Percentage of college graduates completing a bachelor's degree within various years of starting college, by selected student and institution characteristics: 1993

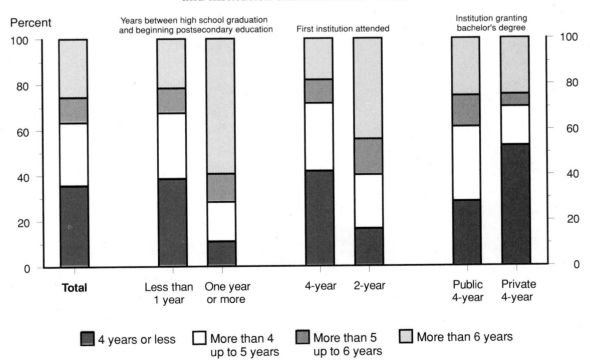

■ 4 years or less □ More than 4 up to 5 years ▨ More than 5 up to 6 years □ More than 6 years

SOURCE: U.S. Department of Education, National Center for Education Statistics, Recent College Graduates Survey for 1977–90 graduates and 1993 Baccalaureate and Beyond Longitudinal Study, First Follow-up (B&B:93/94).

College costs and family income

♦ Between 1980 and 1994, college costs (tuition, room, and board) rose rapidly in both public and private institutions, but increased more at private colleges than at public colleges (71 versus 45 percent in 1995 constant dollars).

A family's ability to afford college for its children depends on many factors, including tuition levels, availability of financial aid, family income and assets, and family size. Tuition, room, and board are a measure of the gross price of college. The average cost for tuition, room, and board as a percentage of family income is an indicator of the affordability of a college education.

♦ Between 1980 and 1994, tuition, room, and board at public institutions increased from 10 to 14 percent of median family income (for families with children 6 to 17 years old). This increase was larger for low income families than for high income families—it increased from 16 to 26 percent for families at the 25th percentile of family income, compared to an increase from 7 to 9 percent for those at the 75th percentile.

♦ After periods of decline in the 1960s and 1970s, tuition, room, and board at public institutions rose to a high of 15 percent of median family income (for all families) in 1993. At private institutions, tuition, room, and board as a percentage of median family income rose every year between 1979 and 1993, increasing from 23 to 41 percent (see supplemental table 12-1).

Average undergraduate tuition, room, and board (in 1995 constant dollars) as a percentage of income of families with children 6 to 17 years old,[1] by control of institution and selected family income percentiles: 1975–94

| | Public institutions | | | | | | Private institutions | | | | | |
| | Constant dollars | Family income percentile | | | | | Constant dollars | Family income percentile | | | | |
Year		10th	25th	50th	75th	90th		10th	25th	50th	75th	90th
1975	$4,587	31.1	16.4	10.2	7.3	5.4	$10,086	68.4	36.1	22.5	16.0	11.8
1976	4,654	30.9	16.3	10.0	7.1	5.3	10,162	67.4	35.6	21.8	15.6	11.5
1977	4,603	30.8	16.3	9.8	7.0	5.2	10,137	67.7	35.8	21.6	15.4	11.4
1978	4,445	30.2	15.6	9.4	6.8	5.0	10,063	68.4	35.2	21.3	15.4	11.3
1979	4,258	28.0	15.1	9.1	6.3	4.6	9,662	63.6	34.3	20.7	14.4	10.5
1980	4,183	32.3	16.3	9.6	6.6	4.8	9,642	74.6	37.6	22.1	15.1	11.1
1981	4,321	34.7	17.7	10.2	7.0	5.1	10,005	80.3	41.0	23.6	16.1	11.8
1982	4,582	41.5	19.5	11.0	7.4	5.4	10,766	97.5	45.8	25.9	17.5	12.6
1983	4,735	42.4	20.4	11.5	7.5	5.4	11,264	100.9	48.4	27.3	17.9	13.0
1984	4,920	43.7	20.5	11.7	7.7	5.5	11,842	105.2	49.3	28.1	18.5	13.2
1985	5,011	43.1	20.3	11.5	7.7	5.5	12,468	107.3	50.5	28.6	19.1	13.8
1986	5,223	46.4	21.3	11.9	7.8	5.6	13,283	118.0	54.1	30.2	19.8	14.2
1987	5,339	47.7	21.7	11.8	7.8	5.6	13,857	123.8	56.2	30.8	20.2	14.6
1988	5,385	[2]44.2	21.5	12.0	7.9	5.7	14,098	[2]115.8	56.2	31.3	20.6	14.8
1989	5,417	43.6	21.4	12.0	7.9	5.6	14,453	116.3	57.1	32.1	21.2	15.0
1990	5,424	46.3	22.2	12.6	8.2	5.7	14,721	125.7	60.2	34.2	22.2	15.6
1991	5,673	52.3	23.9	13.2	8.7	6.2	15,365	141.7	64.8	35.8	23.6	16.8
1992	5,763	51.5	24.8	13.6	8.8	6.2	15,679	140.1	67.5	37.0	24.0	17.0
1993[2]	5,946	58.0	26.6	14.3	9.1	6.3	16,183	157.8	72.3	38.8	24.7	17.1
1994[3]	6,053	55.0	26.2	14.2	9.1	6.3	16,470	149.6	71.3	38.7	24.8	17.2

[1] These families may have children aged 18 and older; however, they have at least one child between 6 and 17 years old, and none under 6. All families, not just married-couple families, are included. Supplemental table 12-1 provides data for a longer series of years, but is based on the incomes of all families.

[2] Revised from previously published figures.

[3] Preliminary data based on fall 1993 enrollment weights.

NOTE: Tuition data are for academic years beginning 1975–94, and family income data are for calendar years 1975–94. Both calendar and school year Consumer Price Indexes (CPIs) were used to calculate constant dollar figures. "Tuition, room, and board" includes those for 2-year and 4-year colleges and universities. In-state tuition and fees are used for public institutions.

SOURCE: U.S. Department of Education, National Center for Education Statistics, IPEDS "Fall Enrollment" and "Institutional Characteristics" surveys. U.S. Department of Commerce, Bureau of the Census, *Current Population Reports*, Series P-60, "Income, Poverty and Valuation of Non-cash Benefits," various years (based on the March supplement to the Current Population Survey).

Average undergraduate tuition, room, and board as a percentage of family income

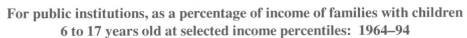

For public institutions, as a percentage of income of families with children 6 to 17 years old at selected income percentiles: 1964–94

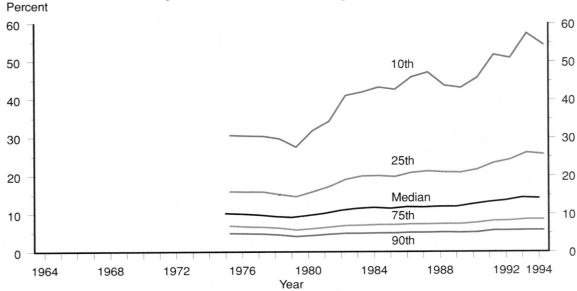

As a percentage of median income of all families, by control of institution: 1964–94

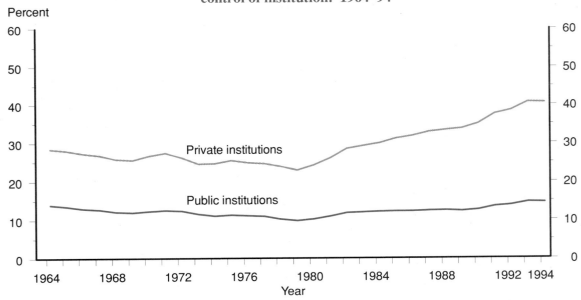

NOTE: Tuition data are for academic years beginning 1964–94, and family income data are for calendar years 1964–94. In-state tuition and fees are used for public institutions.

SOURCE: U.S. Department of Education, National Center for Education Statistics, IPEDS "Fall Enrollment" and "Institutional Characteristics" surveys. U.S. Department of Commerce, Bureau of the Census, *Current Population Reports,* Series P-60, "Income, Poverty and Valuation of Non-cash Benefits," various years (based on the March supplement to the Current Population Survey).

Net cost of attending postsecondary education

♦ Among all dependent, full-time undergraduate students attending public 4-year institutions, average grant aid received was 29 percent of the average tuition and fees charged during the 1992–93 academic year. This ratio varied from 80 percent for students from low income families to 10 percent for those from high income families. This ratio also varied from 16 percent for dependent, full-time students at private, for-profit institutions (calculated from supplemental table 13-1) to 37 percent for those at public 2-year institutions.

> *Cost may affect a student's access to a college education. The net cost of college attendance is total cost minus total aid—that is, tuition, fees, and living expenses minus grants, loans, and work study. Net cost as a percentage of total cost is a measure of the fraction of cost that remains to be financed by students and their families after student financial aid is used. However, living expenses arguably must be incurred whether or not a student attends college; loans must be repaid; and work study is payment for work. A second measure, grant aid as a percentage of tuition and fees paid, provides an indication of the discount received on educational expenses.*

♦ The average net cost (total cost minus total aid) was 80 percent of the average total cost ($7,326 versus $9,187) for dependent, full-time undergraduates attending public 4-year colleges. This ratio varied from 57 percent for students from low income families to 91 percent for those from high income families. This ratio also varied from 89 percent for students attending public 2-year colleges to 67 percent for students attending private, not-for-profit 4-year institutions.

♦ Among independent, full-time students at private, for-profit institutions, the average grant aid received ($1,346) was 28 percent of the average tuition and fees charged ($4,748). This ratio varied from 37 to 18 percent for students with low to high household income (calculated from supplemental table 13-1).

Cost of college attendance and student financial aid for dependent, full-time undergraduates, by type and control of institution and family income: Academic year 1992–93

Type and control of institution and family income of dependent students	Tuition and fees	Total cost	Grant aid	Total aid	Net cost	Ratios Grants to tuition and fees	Net cost to total cost
Public 4-year institutions							
Dependent, full-time students	$2,947	$9,187	$855	$1,864	$7,326	29	80
Low income	2,559	8,820	2,041	3,746	5,070	80	57
Lower middle	2,728	8,878	961	2,422	6,426	35	72
Upper middle	2,846	8,924	509	1,331	7,598	18	85
High income	3,382	9,758	354	890	8,879	10	91
Private, not-for-profit 4-year							
Dependent, full-time students	11,004	17,301	3,455	5,697	11,552	31	67
Low income	8,444	14,232	5,417	8,350	5,872	64	41
Lower middle	10,560	16,905	4,890	8,270	8,590	46	51
Upper middle	11,195	17,422	4,240	6,934	10,407	38	60
High income	12,399	18,958	1,736	3,150	15,752	14	83
Public 2-year							
Dependent, full-time students	1,072	6,410	395	600	5,717	37	89
Low income	948	6,199	1,027	1,322	4,848	108	78
Lower middle	1,052	5,995	312	588	5,348	30	89
Upper middle	1,134	7,060	122	247	6,686	11	95
High income	1,311	6,745	83	167	6,367	6	94

Table reads: In academic year 1992–93, the average grant for dependent, full-time students at public 4-year institutions was $855.

NOTE: Total cost includes budget allowances for student living expenses; total aid includes grants, loans, and work study; net cost is total cost minus total aid. See the supplemental note to this indicator for more detailed definitions of concepts.

SOURCE: U.S. Department of Education, National Center for Education Statistics, National Postsecondary Student Aid Study, 1993.

Cost of college attendance and student financial aid for dependent, full-time undergraduates, by type and control of institution and family income: Academic year 1992–93

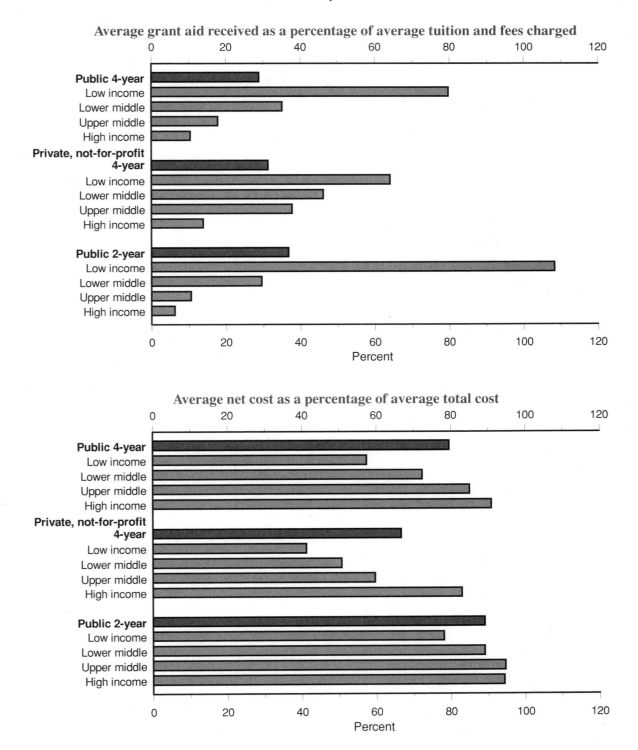

Average grant aid received as a percentage of average tuition and fees charged

Percent

Average net cost as a percentage of average total cost

Percent

SOURCE: U.S. Department of Education, National Center for Education Statistics, National Postsecondary Student Aid Study, 1993.

Participation in adult education

♦ Forty percent of adults participated in adult education activities in 1995, up from 32 percent in 1991. Of those adults who participated in 1995, about half (21 percent) took work-related courses, half (20 percent) took personal development courses, and 6 percent took courses related to a diploma, degree, or certification.

> In an age of rapid technological and economic change, lifelong learning is essential, both for individuals and for society as a whole. Adult education provides an avenue for acquiring new knowledge and upgrading workers' skills. Differences in participation rates among various groups may indicate the degree of access or the rewards of participation for these individuals.

♦ In both 1991 and 1995, adults with more education generally were more likely to participate in adult education activities than those with less education. In fact, almost 6 in 10 adults who had a bachelor's degree or higher participated in adult education, while in 1995, 3 in 10 adults who had a high school diploma did so.

♦ Employed adults were more likely to participate in adult education than those without jobs. In 1995, among those who were employed, participation rates of females were 9 percentage points higher than those of their male counterparts. Moreover, employed females were more likely than employed males to take work-related or personal development courses (see supplemental table 14-1).

♦ Among those who participated in work-related courses, the majority (60 percent) took courses provided by business or professional associations. About 20 percent took work-related courses provided by colleges, and 17 percent took work-related courses provided by government agencies (see supplemental table 14-2).

Adult education participation rates in the past 12 months, by type of adult education activity, educational attainment, and labor force status: 1991 and 1995

Educational attainment and labor force status	1991 total	1995				
			Type of adult education activity			
		Total[1]	Basic skills[2]	Credential[1]	Work-related	Personal
Total	**31.6**	**40.2**	**1.2**	**6.1**	**20.9**	**19.9**
Educational attainment						
Grade 8 or less	7.2	10.8	2.1	0.2	2.2	5.2
Grades 9–12[3]	14.3	22.9	5.6	1.6	6.9	10.4
High school diploma	22.5	30.9	0.8	3.5	14.2	15.7
Vocational/technical school	31.7	41.9	0.6	5.4	21.9	21.1
Some college	39.4	49.3	0.5	12.1	22.3	25.3
Associate's degree	49.1	56.1	0.4	10.9	32.1	27.4
Bachelor's degree or higher	52.2	58.2	(*)	7.7	37.9	27.9
Labor force status						
Employed	40.8	50.7	1.1	8.2	31.1	22.0
Unemployed	27.5	36.6	5.0	5.5	11.1	17.4
Not in labor force	14.5	21.3	0.9	2.2	3.4	16.2

Table reads: In 1995, 40.2 percent of adults participated in adult education; 20.9 percent of adults took work-related courses.

[1] The participation rate of adults aged 17 or older was determined by their involvement in one or more of six types of adult education activities in the 12 months prior to the interview; percentages may not add to totals because people participated in more than one type of activity (9 percent in 1995). Adults who participated in apprenticeship programs and English as a Second Language programs were included in the total, but are not shown separately. Adults who reported that they had participated only as full-time credential seekers were not included in the calculation of the participation rates.

[2] Only adults who had not received a high school diploma or equivalent, who had received a high school diploma in the past 12 months, or who had received a high school diploma in a foreign country were asked about their participation in the basic education/General Educational Development (GED) activities.

[3] In 1995, includes adults whose highest education level was grades 9–12 who had not received a high school diploma; in 1991, includes only adults whose highest education level was grades 9–11.

[4] Individuals with a bachelor's degree or higher were not asked about their participation in adult basic skills programs, GED preparation classes, adult high school, or high school equivalency programs.

SOURCE: U.S. Department of Education, National Center for Education Statistics, National Household Education Survey (NHES), 1991 and 1995 (Adult Education Component).

Adult education participation rates in the past 12 months, by educational attainment and labor force status: 1991 and 1995

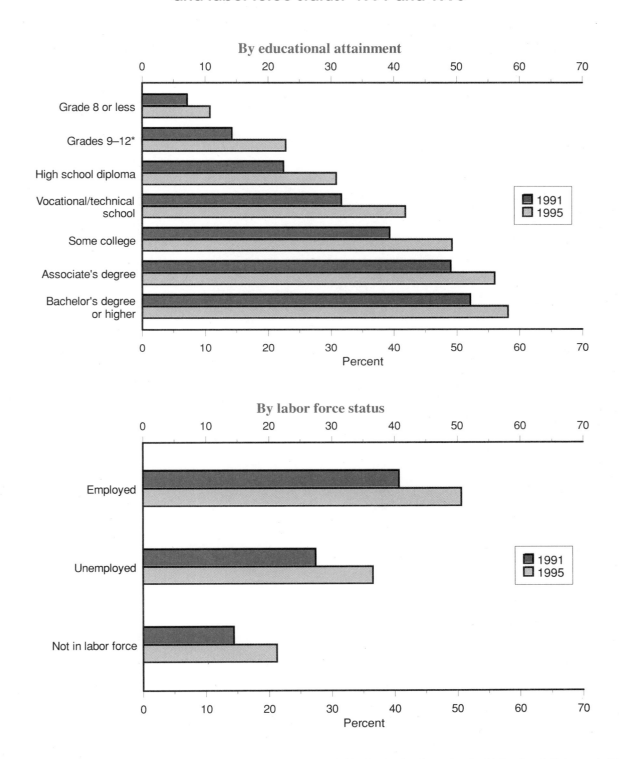

By educational attainment

| | 1991 |
| | 1995 |

Percent

By labor force status

| | 1991 |
| | 1995 |

Percent

* In 1995, includes adults whose highest education level was grades 9–12 who had not received a high school diploma; in 1991, includes only adults whose highest education level was grades 9–11.

SOURCE: U.S. Department of Education, National Center for Education Statistics, National Household Education Survey (NHES), 1991 and 1995 (Adult Education Component).

Achievement, Attainment, and Curriculum

Indicators of what students have learned in school are perhaps the most important measures of the outcomes of education. Although performance on examinations is one measure of what students have learned in school, examinations do not measure the wide array of skills and experiences that formal education provides. Educational attainment (e.g., finishing high school or college) is not only an indirect measure of how much subject matter students may have learned, but also of how much knowledge students potentially have gained in learning civic responsibilities, social skills, work ethics, and life skills. Furthermore, information about courses taken in high school and fields of study in college is an additional indirect indicator of the content of students' knowledge.

Achievement

The National Assessment of Educational Progress (NAEP) has assessed students' knowledge in reading, writing, science, mathematics, and other subjects for more than 20 years. NAEP analyzes both short- and long-term trends. One short-term trend indicates that reading proficiency remained relatively stable for 4th- and 8th-grade students between 1992 and 1994, while scores for 12th-graders decreased slightly (*Indicator 17*). A long-term trend shows that average science proficiency among 9-year-olds was higher in 1992 than in 1970; among 13-year-olds, it was about the same in 1992 as in 1970; and among 17-year-olds, it was lower (*Indicator 16*).

Mathematics achievement is assessed in three ways: through NAEP for 9-, 13-, and 17-year-olds; through the SAT and the ACT for college-bound high school seniors; and through the GRE for college graduates intending to continue their education. NAEP shows that average mathematics proficiency among 9- and 13-year-olds was slightly higher in 1992 than in 1973, and among 17-year-olds, it was about the same in 1992 as in 1973 after declining in the late 1970s (*Indicator 16*). Average scores on the mathematics section of the SAT fell somewhat during the 1970s, but rose during the early 1980s and early 1990s (*Indicator 22*). Unlike the case for 17-year-olds in NAEP, not all of the decline in SAT mathematics scores during the 1970s has been recouped.

Participation in the SAT exam has increased significantly, however. In 1995, 42 percent of high school seniors took the SAT, up from 32 percent in 1976 (table 22-1). During the same period, the percentage of minority test-takers has doubled—rising from 15 to 31 percent. The percentage of graduating seniors who took the ACT has risen, from 32 percent in 1991 to 37 percent in 1995. The ACT composite scores, however, have not changed during this time period (table 22-7). GRE test-takers as a percentage of college graduates rose from 29 percent in 1980 to 35 percent in 1993. Also, GRE quantitative scores increased 45 points between 1973 and 1993, mainly due to a sharp rise in scores during the 1980s (*Indicator 21, Condition 1995*).

Although overall scores have changed little over the last two decades, NAEP shows that the large gaps in achievement between whites and minorities have narrowed somewhat. Blacks have improved relative to whites in mathematics and science. For example, in 1973, average mathematics proficiency scores for 17-year-old blacks and Hispanics were well below those for 17-year-old whites (40 and 33 scale points, respectively). Although the gap was still large in 1992, the mathematics proficiency scores for 17-year-old white students increased only 2 scale points between 1973 and 1992, and the scores for 17-year-old blacks and Hispanics increased 16 and 15 scale points, respectively (*Indicator 16*). The same trend is evident in SAT mathematics scores between 1976 and 1995. Even though the mathematics scores of whites increased only 5 points over that period, those of blacks increased by 34 points and those of Hispanics by 10 to 16 points (*Indicator 22*).

In 1994, NAEP also assessed history and geography achievement (*Indicators 18 and 19*). U.S. history scores of whites and Asians were higher than those of blacks and Hispanics across all three grade levels, although the differences between the scores of blacks and whites and of Hispanics and whites were smaller in 8th and 12th grades than in 4th grade. In geography, at all three grade levels, males outperformed females; white and Asian students outperformed black and Hispanic students; and Hispanic students outperformed black students.

International comparisons

International comparisons of student achievement are available in basic reading literacy, mathematics, and science. Generally, U.S. students compare favorably to their counterparts in other large industrialized countries in reading, but unfavorably in mathematics and science; nevertheless, 9-year-olds from the United States are ranked higher in science than 9-year-olds from several other large industrialized countries (*Indicators 20, 23,* and *24*).

Adult literacy

In 1992, the literacy of adults aged 16 and older was assessed in three areas: prose, document, and quantitative. Approximately 20 percent of the adults in the United States performed at a low proficiency level. In each of the three areas, scores of whites averaged 67 to 75 points higher than those of Hispanics and 50 to 63 points higher than those of blacks. In addition, older Americans had lower literacy scores than younger Americans, and adults with more education had higher literacy scores than adults with less education (*Indicator 21* and tables 20-1 and 20-3, *Condition 1994*).

Adult literacy was assessed across seven countries in 1994. Relative to most other countries assessed, the United States had a large concentration of adults score at the highest literacy levels across the prose, document, and quantitative literacy domains. However, the United States also had a greater concentration of adults at the lowest levels of literacy (*Indicator 21*).

Attainment

High school completion

In 1995, 87 percent of all 25- to 29-year-olds had a high school diploma or an equivalency certificate, up from 78 percent in 1971. However, the completion rate varied among racial/ethnic groups. In 1995, 93 percent of whites had a high school diploma or the equivalent, compared to 87 percent of blacks and 57 percent of Hispanics. Blacks showed the most improvement: the percentage of blacks earning a high school diploma or equivalency certificate rose 28 percentage points between 1971 and 1995, compared to 11 and 9 percentage points for whites and Hispanics, respectively (*Indicator 25*). In terms of high school attainment, the United States compares favorably to other large industrialized countries. For instance, the United States has a similar or higher percentage of 25- to 64-year-olds who have completed high school than many other countries (*Indicator 27*). However, with respect to young adults aged 25–34, several other nations approach or surpass U.S. secondary education completion rates (table 27-1).

College attainment

In 1995, among 25- to 29-year-olds who had completed high school, 62 percent had completed at least some college, and 28 percent had earned a bachelor's degree or more (*Indicator 25*). In the United States, a larger proportion of young adults had earned college degrees compared to their counterparts in most other industrialized countries (*Indicator 27*). Two-thirds of all students who were high school sophomores in 1980 had attended some form of postsecondary education by 1992, and almost one-fourth had graduated from a 4-year institution. Both socioeconomic status and 10th-grade test scores were related to college attainment (*Indicator 26*).

Curriculum

The courses students take in high school and college are an indirect indication of the content of students' knowledge. A greater percentage of 1992 than 1982 high school graduates earned the number of units in the core courses—4 units in English, and 3 each in science, social studies, and mathematics—recommended in *A Nation at Risk* (*Indicator 28*). In 1994, 51 percent of high school graduates had earned at least this number of credits in the core subjects, compared to 14 percent in 1982. Graduates in 1994 took more mathematics and science courses in high school than 1982 graduates, particularly geometry, algebra II, biology, and chemistry (*Indicator 29*).

Business management is the most popular major in college: 22 percent of all bachelor's degree recipients in 1993 majored in this subject area (*Indicator 41*). At the graduate level, males were still twice as likely as females to earn degrees in business, although the gap has narrowed significantly since the early 1970s (*Indicator 27, Condition 1995*). At least 60 percent of undergraduate students take courses in the arts, English literature, psychology, sociology/anthropology, history, physical science, and mathematics (*Indicator 28, Condition 1994*).

Trends in the mathematics proficiency of 9-, 13-, and 17-year-olds

♦ **Average mathematics proficiency improved between 1978 and 1992 for all age groups.**

♦ **White, black, and Hispanic 9-year-olds showed large improvements in average mathematics proficiency between 1982 and 1992, after remaining stable between 1973 and 1982.**

Proficiency in mathematics is an important outcome of education. In an increasingly technological world, the mathematics skills of the nation's workers may be a crucial component of economic competitiveness. In addition, knowledge of mathematics is critical for success in science, computing, and a number of other related fields of study.

♦ **Although a large gap in mathematics proficiency exists between whites and their black and Hispanic peers for all age groups at ages 13 and 17, white scores increased at a slower rate than black and Hispanic scores, causing this gap to decrease over the last 20 years.**

♦ **The percentage of 17-year-olds scoring at or above level 250 increased from 92 to 97 percent; those scoring at or above level 300 increased from 52 to 59 percent; but those scoring at or above level 350 stayed at 7 percent (see supplemental table 15-2).**

♦ **There is much variation in the mathematics proficiency scores of students. In 1992, scores for all three age groups varied by about 100–110 scale points between the 5th percentile and the 95th percentile. The amount of variation has decreased since 1978, however, when the difference between the top and the bottom 5 percent ranged from 109 to 129 scale points (see supplemental table 15-3).**

Average mathematics proficiency (scale score), by sex and age: Selected years 1973–92

Year	Total			Male			Female		
	Age 9	Age 13	Age 17	Age 9	Age 13	Age 17	Age 9	Age 13	Age 17
1973	[1] 219	[1] 266	304	[1] 218	[1] 265	309	[1] 220	[1] 267	301
1978	[1] 219	[1] 264	[1] 300	[1] 217	[1] 264	[1,2] 304	[1] 220	[1] 265	[1] 297
1982	[1] 219	[1] 269	[1,2] 298	[1] 217	[1] 269	[1,2] 302	[1] 221	[1] 268	[1,2] 296
1986	[1] 222	[1] 269	[1] 302	[1,2] 222	[1,2] 270	[1,2] 305	[1] 222	268	[1] 299
1990	[2] 230	[2] 270	305	[2] 229	[2] 271	306	[2] 230	270	303
1992	[2] 230	[2] 273	307	[2] 231	[2] 274	309	[2] 228	[2] 272	304

Average mathematics proficiency (scale score), by race/ethnicity and age: Selected years 1973–92

Year	White			Black			Hispanic		
	Age 9	Age 13	Age 17	Age 9	Age 13	Age 17	Age 9	Age 13	Age 17
1973	[1] 225	[1] 274	310	[1] 190	[1] 228	[1] 270	[1] 202	[1] 239	[1] 277
1978	[1] 224	[1] 272	[1,2] 306	[1] 192	[1] 230	[1] 268	[1] 203	[1] 238	[1] 276
1982	[1] 224	[1] 274	[1,2] 304	[1] 195	[1,2] 240	[1] 272	[1] 204	[1,2] 252	[1] 277
1986	[1] 227	[1] 274	[1] 308	[2] 202	[2] 249	[2] 279	205	[2] 254	283
1990	[2] 235	276	310	[2] 208	[2] 249	[2] 288	[2] 214	[2] 255	284
1992	[2] 235	[2] 279	312	[2] 208	[2] 250	[2] 286	[2] 212	[2] 259	[2] 292

[1] Statistically significant difference from 1992.
[2] Statistically significant difference from 1973.
NOTE: **The mathematics proficiency scale ranges from 0 to 500.** (See supplemental table 15-1 for detailed explanations of levels.)

Level 150:	Simple arithmetic facts	Level 300:	Moderately complex procedures and reasoning
Level 200:	Beginning skills and understandings	Level 350:	Multi-step problem solving and algebra
Level 250:	Numerical operations and beginning problem solving		

SOURCE: U.S. Department of Education, National Center for Education Statistics, National Assessment of Educational Progress, *Trends in Academic Progress: Achievement of U.S. Students in Science, 1969 to 1992; Mathematics, 1973 to 1992; Reading, 1971 to 1992; and Writing, 1984 to 1992,* 1994.

Average mathematics proficiency (scale score): Selected years 1978–92

Average mathematics proficiency, by race/ethnicity and age

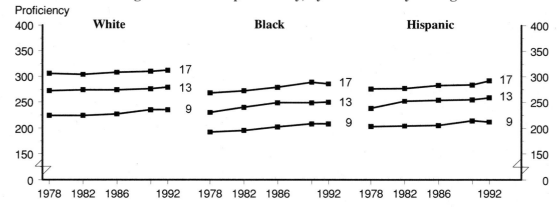

Percentile distribution of mathematics proficiency for 13-year-olds, by race/ethnicity

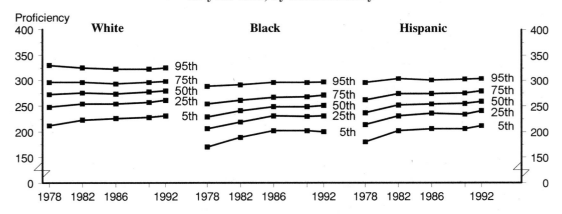

Percentile distribution of mathematics proficiency, by race/ethnicity and age: 1992

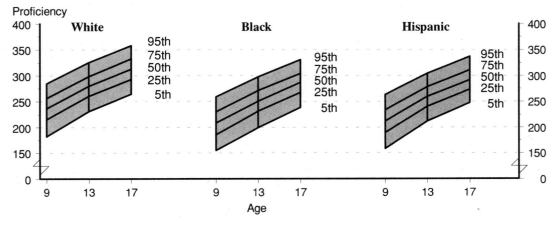

NOTE: The mathematics proficiency scale ranges from 0 to 500.

SOURCE: U.S. Department of Education, National Center For Education Statistics, National Assessment of Educational Progress, *Trends In Academic Progess: Achievement of U.S. Students in Science, 1969 to 1992; Mathematics, 1973 to 1992; Reading, 1971 to 1992; and Writing, 1984 to 1992,* 1994.

Trends in the science proficiency of 9-, 13-, and 17-year-olds

♦ In 1992, average science achievement was higher at all three age levels than in 1982. In addition, the gap between male and female scores at ages 13 and 17 decreased during that period, but the gap increased at age 9.

> *Competence in science is an important outcome of education. The ability to apply scientific information, interpret data, and make inferences about scientific findings is useful in a world that relies heavily on technological and scientific advances.*

♦ In 1992, the average science proficiency of blacks and Hispanics remained well below that of whites. However, between 1977 and 1992, the proficiency gap decreased between whites and blacks at age 9 and between whites and Hispanics at age 13.

♦ A higher percentage of 9-, 13-, and 17-year-olds demonstrated general science skills by reaching levels 200 and 250 in 1992 than did in 1982. In addition, more 17-year-olds reached levels 300 and 350 in 1992, exhibiting a greater understanding of science (see supplemental table 16-2).

♦ There is a great deal of variation in science proficiency scores within an age group. For example, the proficiency of white 9-year-olds varies by 120 scale points from the 5th percentile to the 95th percentile. By comparison, the difference in the median proficiency of white 9- and 17-year-olds is 66 scale points (see supplemental table 16-3).

Average science proficiency (scale score), by sex and age: Selected years 1970–92

	Total			Male			Female		
Year	Age 9	Age 13	Age 17	Age 9	Age 13	Age 17	Age 9	Age 13	Age 17
1970	[1] 225	255	[1] 305	[1] 228	257	[1] 314	223	253	[1] 297
1973	[1,2] 220	[1,2] 250	[1] 296	[1,2] 223	[1,2] 252	[2] 304	[1] 218	[1,2] 247	[2] 288
1977	[1,2] 220	[1,2] 247	[1,2] 290	[1,2] 222	[1,2] 251	[2] 297	[1,2] 218	[1,2] 244	[1,2] 282
1982	[1] 221	[1,2] 250	[1,2] 283	[1,2] 221	256	[1,2] 292	[1] 221	[1,2] 245	[1,2] 275
1986	[1] 224	[1] 251	[1,2] 288	[1] 227	256	[2] 295	[1] 221	[1,2] 247	[1,2] 282
1990	229	255	[2] 290	[1] 230	258	[2] 296	227	[1] 252	[2] 285
1992	[2] 231	258	[2] 294	[2] 235	260	[2] 299	227	256	[2] 289

Average science proficiency (scale score), by race/ethnicity and age: Selected years 1970–92

	White			Black			Hispanic		
Year	Age 9	Age 13	Age 17	Age 9	Age 13	Age 17	Age 9	Age 13	Age 17
1970	236	[1] 263	[1] 312	[1] 179	215	258	—	—	—
1973	[1,2] 231	[1,2] 259	[2] 304	[1] 177	[1,2] 205	[2] 250	—	—	—
1977	[1,2] 230	[1,2] 256	[1,2] 298	[1] 175	[1] 208	[1,2] 240	[1] 192	[1] 213	262
1982	[1,2] 229	[1,2] 257	[1,2] 293	[1] 187	217	[1,2] 235	[1] 189	[1,2] 226	[1,2] 249
1986	[1,2] 232	[1] 259	[1,2] 298	[2] 196	222	253	199	[1,2] 226	259
1990	238	264	[2] 301	[2] 196	[2] 226	253	[2] 206	[2] 232	262
1992	239	[2] 267	[2] 304	[2] 200	224	256	[2] 205	[2] 238	270

— Not available.

[1] Statistically significant difference from 1992.

[2] Statistically significant difference from 1970 for all groups except Hispanics. Statistically significant difference from 1977 for Hispanics.

NOTE: **The science proficiency scale ranges from 0 to 500.** (See supplemental table 16-1 for detailed explanations of levels.)

Level 150: Knows everyday science facts
Level 200: Understands simple scientific principles
Level 250: Applies general scientific information

Level 300: Analyzes scientific procedures and data
Level 350: Integrates specialized scientific information

SOURCE: U.S. Department of Education, National Center for Education Statistics, National Assessment of Educational Progress, *Trends in Academic Progress: Achievement of U.S. Students in Science, 1969 to 1992; Mathematics, 1973 to 1992; Reading, 1971 to 1992; and Writing, 1984 to 1992*, 1994.

Average science proficiency (scale score): Selected years 1977–92

Average science proficiency, by race/ethnicity and age

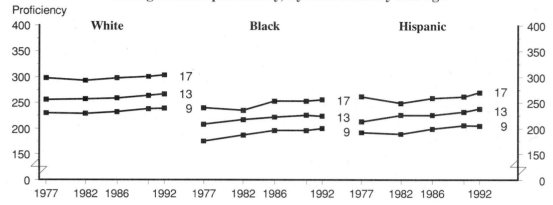

Percentile distribution of science proficiency for 17-year-olds, by race/ethnicity

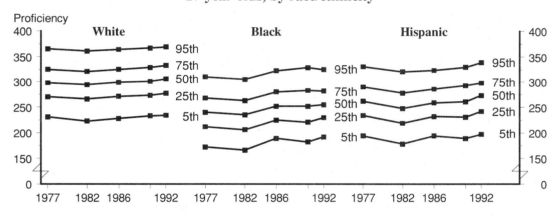

Percentile distribution of science proficiency, by race/ethnicity and age: 1992

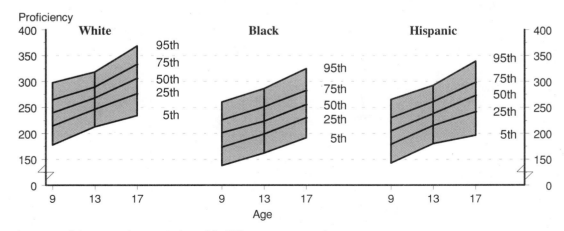

NOTE: The science proficiency scale ranges from 0 to 500.

SOURCE: U.S. Department of Education, National Center for Education Statistics, National Assessment of Educational Progress, *Trends In Academic Progress: Achievement of U.S. Students in Science, 1969 to 1992; Mathematics, 1973 to 1992; Reading, 1971 to 1992; and Writing, 1984 to 1992,* 1994.

Average reading proficiency of 4th-, 8th-, and 12th-graders

♦ Overall, average reading proficiency for 4th- and 8th-grade students was similar in 1992 and 1994. Average proficiency scores for 12th-grade students, however, decreased during this period.

♦ Average reading proficiency increased as the number of different types* of reading materials at home increased. More than one-third of 4th-graders and one-half of 8th- and 12th-graders reported having each of four types of reading materials (books, newspapers, magazines, and encyclopedias) at home in 1994.

> A student's ability to read is essential to the educational process and increases the likelihood that he or she will become a full participating member of society. Students' exposure to various types of reading materials at home, as well as students' habits outside of school, can play a critical role in their growth as readers.

♦ Generally, the more students read for fun on their own time, the higher their reading scores were. Between 1992 and 1994, the percentage of 12th-graders who reported that they never or hardly ever read for fun increased from 24 to 27 percent.

♦ Students who read 11 or more pages each day for school and homework had higher average reading proficiency scores than those who read less than 5 pages a day. Between 1992 and 1994, the percentage of 12th-graders who read 11 pages or more each day decreased as did 12th-grade reading scores.

♦ Students who watched 3 or fewer hours of television a day showed higher levels of reading proficiency than those who watched 6 or more hours each day. In 1994, 57 percent of 4th-graders and 59 percent of 8th-graders watched 3 or fewer hours daily, while 75 percent of 12th-graders did so.

Average reading proficiency (scale score), by grade and selected characteristics: 1992 and 1994

Selected characteristics	Grade 4				Grade 8				Grade 12			
	1992		1994		1992		1994		1992		1994	
	Percent	Score	Percent	Score	Percent	Score	Percent	Score	Percent	Score	Percent	Score
Total	**100**	**217**	**100**	**214**	**100**	**260**	**100**	**260**	**100**	**292**	**100**	**287**
Number of different types of reading materials at home*												
Four	37	226	38	227	51	268	50	270	60	298	55	295
Three	32	219	34	216	29	259	29	258	26	290	28	286
Two or fewer	31	204	29	197	20	241	21	239	14	274	17	269
Frequency of reading for fun on their own time												
Almost every day	44	223	45	223	22	277	21	277	23	304	24	302
Once or twice a week	32	218	32	213	28	263	26	264	28	296	24	294
Once or twice a month	12	210	12	208	25	258	25	257	26	290	24	285
Never or hardly ever	13	199	12	197	25	246	27	246	24	279	27	273
Amount read each day for school and homework												
11 or more pages	56	222	54	220	22	268	21	266	45	302	39	298
6 to 10 pages	23	217	23	214	16	266	16	269	24	290	24	288
5 or fewer pages	21	203	23	201	62	256	63	256	31	281	36	276
Time spent watching television each day												
6 hours or more	20	199	21	194	14	241	14	239	6	271	7	264
4 to 5 hours	22	216	22	216	27	258	27	257	20	284	18	280
2 to 3 hours	40	224	38	222	46	265	45	265	47	293	46	289
1 hour or less	19	221	19	220	13	270	14	270	27	301	29	297

Table reads: In 1994, 55 percent of students in grade 12 had four different types of reading materials at home and had an average reading proficiency scale score of 295.

* Types of reading materials at home include books, newspapers, magazines, and encyclopedias.

NOTE: The reading proficiency scale ranges from 0 to 500.

SOURCE: U.S. Department of Education, National Center for Education Statistics, National Assessment of Educational Progress, *1994 Reading Report Card for the Nation and the States*, 1996.

Average reading proficiency (scale score) and percentage of students with selected characteristics: 1992 and 1994

Percentage of students with different types* of reading materials at home: 1994

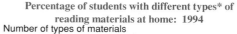
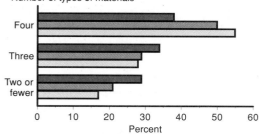

Proficiency scores of students with different types* of reading materials at home: 1994

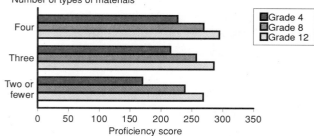

Percentage of students who read for fun on their own time: 1992 and 1994

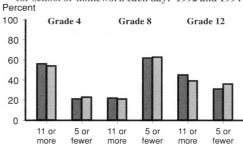

Proficiency scores of students, by extent of reading for fun on their own time: 1992 and 1994

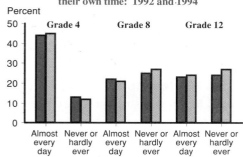

Percentage of students who read a number of pages for school or homework each day: 1992 and 1994

Proficiency scores of students who read a number of pages for school and homework each day: 1992 and 1994

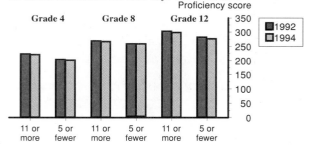

Percentage of students who watched a number of hours of television each day: 1994

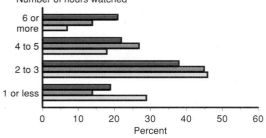

Proficiency scores of students who watched a number of hours of television each day: 1994

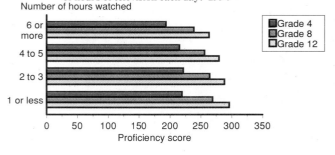

* Types of reading materials at home include books, newspapers, magazines, and encyclopedias.
SOURCE: U.S. Department of Education, National Center for Education Statistics, National Assessment of Educational Progress, *1994 Reading Report Card for the Nation and the States,* 1996.

Average U.S. history proficiency of 4th-, 8th-, and 12th-graders

♦ In 1994, average history proficiency scores of whites and Asians were higher than those of blacks and Hispanics in grades 4, 8, and 12. However, the difference between the average proficiency scores of white and black students and of white and Hispanic students was smaller in 8th and 12th grades than in 4th grade.

> *A working knowledge of U.S. history—the country's struggles, successes, and failings—allows citizens to make informed and intelligent decisions about contemporary issues. There has recently been a renewed interest in the role of history in education, prompting The National Education Goals Panel to include history on its list of key subjects.*

♦ In 1994, students at urban fringe schools had higher average history proficiencies than those in central city or rural schools at the 4th-grade and 8th-grade levels. However, in 12th grade, there were no measurable differences between the scores of students in urban fringe schools and those in central city schools—both outperformed students in rural schools (see supplemental table 17-2).

♦ Generally, students who spent more time watching television each day had lower average history proficiency scores. In both 4th and 8th grades, students who watched 3 or fewer hours of television per day scored higher than those who watched 4 or more hours of television per day. In 12th grade, even watching 1 hour of television per day was associated with lower average history proficiency scores, as those who watched 1 or less hour per day had higher average proficiency scores than did those who watched 2 or more hours per day (see supplemental table 17-3).

♦ There was a greater difference in the average history proficiencies between white students who scored in the top and bottom 10th percentile than between white students and black or Hispanic students who scored at the median. For example, in 1994, the difference between the 10th percentile and the 90th percentile of white 8th-graders was 73 points, while the difference between white and black 8th-graders who scored at the 50th percentile was 29 points, and the difference between white and Hispanic 8th-graders who scored at the 50th percentile was 24 points (see supplemental table 17-4).

Average U.S. history proficiency (scale score), by sex, race/ethnicity, and grade: 1994

Sex and race/ethnicity	Grade 4		Grade 8		Grade 12	
	Percentage distribution	Average proficiency	Percentage distribution	Average proficiency	Percentage distribution	Average proficiency
Total	100	205	100	259	100	286
Sex						
Male	50	203	50	259	50	288
Female	50	206	50	259	50	285
Race/ethnicity						
White	69	215	69	267	74	292
Black	15	177	15	239	12	265
Hispanic	11	180	11	243	9	267
Asian	2	209	2	270	3	287
Pacific Islander	1	200	1	252	1	280
American Indian	2	190	1	246	1	279

Table reads: In 1994, 4th-grade males had an average proficiency in U.S. history of 203 scale points.

NOTE: The history proficiency scale ranges from 0 to 500.

SOURCE: U.S. Department of Education, National Center for Education Statistics, National Assessment of Educational Progress, *1994 NAEP U.S. History Report Card*, 1996.

Average U.S. history proficiency (scale score): 1994

By grade and race/ethnicity

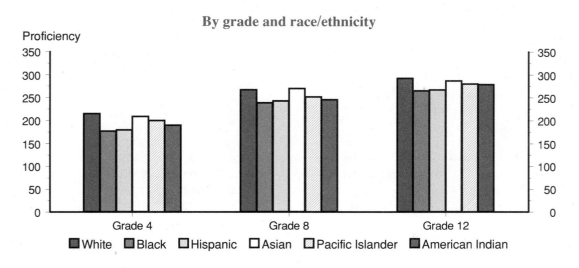

Proficiency

■ White ■ Black □ Hispanic □ Asian ▨ Pacific Islander ■ American Indian

By grade and urbanicity

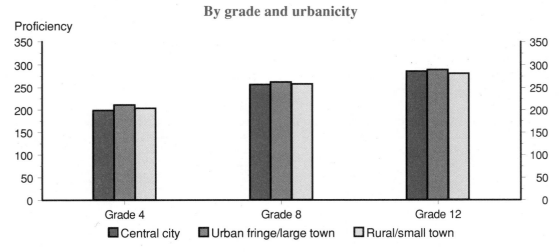

Proficiency

■ Central city ■ Urban fringe/large town □ Rural/small town

By grade and percentile

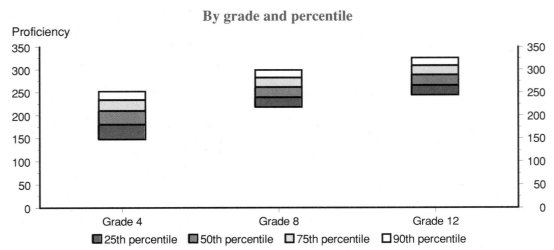

Proficiency

■ 25th percentile ■ 50th percentile □ 75th percentile □ 90th percentile

NOTE: The history proficiency scale ranges from 0 to 500.

SOURCE: U.S. Department of Education, National Center for Education Statistics, *National Assessment of Educational Progress, 1994 NAEP U.S. History Report Card,* 1996.

Average geography proficiency of 4th-, 8th-, and 12th-graders

♦ Overall, males had higher geography proficiency scores than females across all three grade levels.

♦ At all three grade levels, white and Asian students outscored black and Hispanic students, and Hispanic students outscored black students.

♦ In 1994, 4th-grade students in the Central region outperformed those in the other three regions. At the 8th-grade level, students in the Northeast and Central regions had higher scores than those in the Southeast and the West. At the 12th-grade level, students in the Southeast had lower average scores than did those in each of the other regions.

> In order to be able to compete in today's global economy, students require not just a familiarity with globes, atlases, and maps, but also the knowledge to fully understand these items and the skills necessary to put that knowledge into practice. The geography assessment focuses on particular places on Earth, spatial patterns on the Earth's surface, and physical and human processes that shape such patterns; interactions between environment and society; and spatial variations and connections among people and places.

♦ There is a strong positive relationship between average geography proficiency and parents' educational level. For example, 8th-grade students whose parents had a college degree scored an average of 7 scale points higher than those whose parents had some education after high school but did not graduate from college, 22 scale points higher than those whose parents had only a high school diploma and 34 scale points higher than those whose parents did not complete high school.

Average geography proficiency (scale score), by grade and selected characteristics: 1994

Selected characteristics	Grade 4		Grade 8		Grade 12	
	Percentage distribution	Average score	Percentage distribution	Average score	Percentage distribution	Average score
Total	**100**	**206**	**100**	**260**	**100**	**285**
Sex						
Male	51	208	51	262	50	288
Female	49	203	49	258	50	281
Race/ethnicity[1]						
White	69	218	69	270	74	291
Black	15	168	15	229	12	258
Hispanic	12	183	11	239	8	268
Asian	2	218	2	271	3	287
Region						
Northeast	22	203	20	266	21	284
Southeast	23	200	25	252	23	278
Central	25	215	24	268	28	289
West	30	205	31	255	29	286
Parents' education level[2]						
Did not finish high school	4	186	7	238	7	263
Graduated high school	12	197	22	250	22	274
Some education after high school	7	216	19	265	25	286
Graduated college	42	216	42	272	44	294

Table reads: In 1994, 4th-grade males had an average geography proficiency of 208 scale points.

[1] Included in the total but not shown separately are Pacific Islanders and American Indians.

[2] Thirty-four percent of 4th-graders, 10 percent of 8th-graders, and 3 percent of 12th-graders did not know their parents' education level.

NOTE: The geography proficiency scale ranges from 0 to 500.

SOURCE: U.S. Department of Education, National Center for Education Statistics, National Assessment of Educational Progress, *1994 Geography Report Card for the Nation and the States,* 1996.

Average geography proficiency (scale score), by grade: 1994

By race/ethnicity

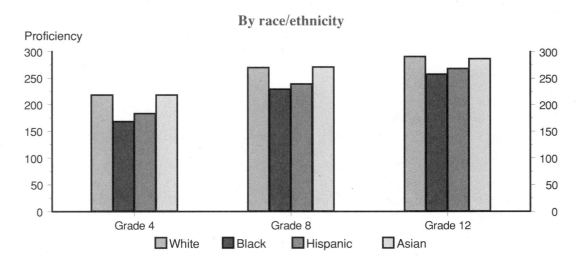

By region

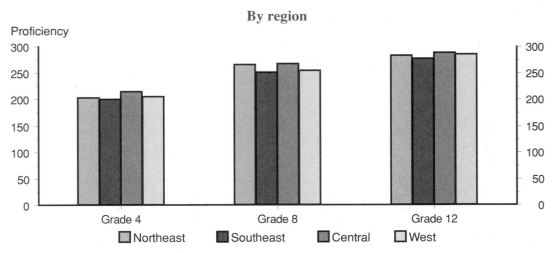

By parents' education level

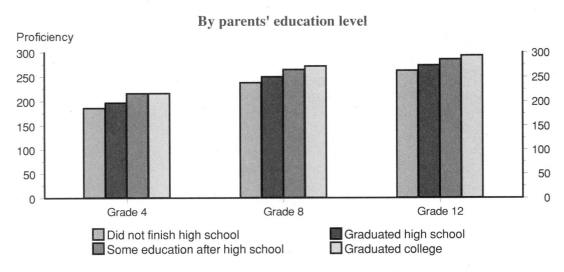

NOTE: The geography proficiency scale ranges from 0 to 500.
SOURCE: U.S. Department of Education, National Center for Education Statistics, National Assessment of Educational Progress, *1994 Geography Report Card for the Nation and the States*, 1996.

International comparisons of reading literacy

♦ In an international assessment of basic reading literacy, 9-year-olds from the United States performed better, on average, on the narrative domain than students from other large countries.

The ability to read is a minimum requirement to participate productively in a global economy and to fulfill basic civic responsibilities. Comprehending written language and effectively using written language are crucial for both future learning and the development of basic job skills.

♦ At age 14, students in the United States scored higher, on average, on the expository domain than students of similar ages in Italy, West Germany, and Spain.

♦ There is far greater variation in the basic reading literacy of students within each country than there are differences in averages among countries. For example, among 9-year-olds, the difference between the 10th and the 90th percentile on the narrative domain was 235 scale points in the United States, compared to a difference of 62 scale points between the United States and West Germany (see supplemental table 20-2).

♦ Children whose home language is different from the one spoken at school showed lower literacy levels in most of the larger countries, including the United States, at both ages 9 and 14 than did those children whose home language was the same as that spoken at school.

Average reading literacy (scale scores), by age and country: School year 1991–92

Larger countries	Average overall score			Average domain scale score			Non-school language spoken at home		School language spoken at home	
	Total	Male	Female	Narrative	Expository	Documents	Percentage of students	Average score	Percentage of students	Average score
Age 9										
United States	547	543	552	553	538	550	4	520	97	549
France	531	530	533	532	533	527	9	491	91	536
Italy	529	525	537	533	538	517	27	513	73	537
Spain	504	500	508	497	505	509	13	499	87	505
West Germany	503	501	508	491	497	520	11	461	90	509
Age 14										
France	549	553	549	556	546	544	4	516	96	552
United States	535	530	543	539	539	528	4	478	96	539
West Germany	522	522	526	514	521	532	8	455	92	530
Italy	515	511	520	520	524	501	26	488	74	525
Spain	490	488	492	500	495	475	11	481	89	491

Table reads: In the 1991–92 school year, 9-year-olds from the United States had an average reading literacy scale score of 547, while 9-year-olds from France had an average reading literacy scale score of 531.

NOTE: In the Study of Reading Literacy, 32 countries assessed the reading achievement of students in the grades where most 9- and 14-year-olds were enrolled. The countries above are the larger countries. The above scores were scaled using the Rasch procedure. The domain scores for each age group were scaled to a mean of 500 and a standard deviation of 100. The average overall score is the mean of the domain scale scores. Some student groups were excluded by the participating countries, such as those in private schools, in schools serving disabled children, or in schools where the language of instruction is different from the primary national language.

SOURCE: International Association for the Evaluation of Educational Achievement, Study of Reading Literacy, *How in the World Do Students Read?*, 1992.

Distribution of scale scores on reading literacy assessment, by country: School year 1991–92

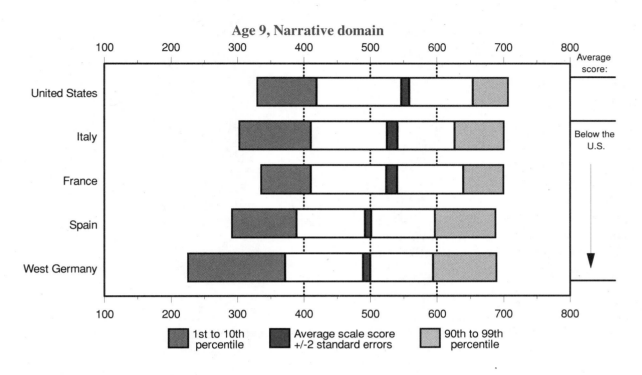

Age 9, Narrative domain

Age 14, Expository domain

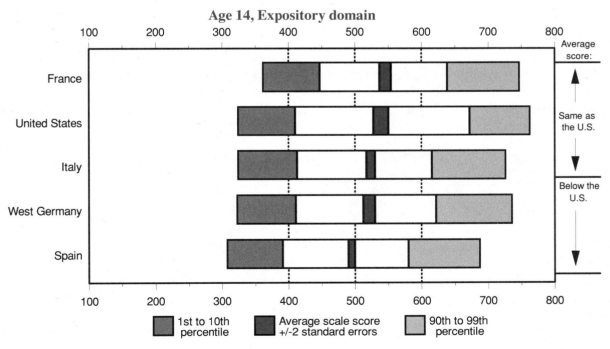

NOTE: The vertical lines at ability score 500 mark the average score for each age group for all participating countries. The standard deviation is 100.

SOURCE: International Association for the Evaluation of Educational Achievement, Study of Reading Literacy, *How In the World Do Students Read?*, 1992.

International comparisons of adult literacy

♦ Compared to most of the other countries assessed in 1994, the United States had a greater concentration of adults who scored at the lowest literacy levels across the prose, document, and quantitative literacy domains. However, the United States had one of the higher concentrations of adults who scored at or above level 4 on the prose scale.

♦ In 1994, the proportion of adults who scored at each literacy level was similar across the three scales in Canada and the United States. In Germany, the Netherlands, and Switzerland, on the other hand, the proportion of adults who scored at the highest literacy level (level 4/5) was greater on the quantitative scale than on the prose scale.

> *In recent years, literacy has been viewed as one of the fundamental tools necessary for successful economic performance in industrialized societies. Literacy is no longer defined merely as a basic threshold of reading ability, but rather as the ability to understand and use printed information in daily activities, at home, at work, and in the community. As society becomes more complex and low skill jobs continue to disappear, concern about adults' ability to use written information to function in society continues to increase. Within countries, literacy levels are affected by both the quality and quantity of the population's formal education, as well as their participation in informal learning activities.*

♦ The distribution of literacy proficiency across different age groups was fairly uniform in the United States, with the exception of the oldest age group, while in several other countries young adults had higher literacy levels than older adults. For example, the percentage of U.S. adults aged 26–35 who scored at or above level 4 on the prose scale was similar to the percentage of U.S. adults aged 46–55 scoring at that level (22 and 24 percent, respectively). Within Germany, the younger group was almost twice as likely to score at or above level 4 on the prose scale as the older group (20 and 11 percent, respectively). Differences by age in Switzerland, Sweden, and the Netherlands were similar to those in Germany (see supplemental table 21-2).

♦ Within particular occupations, the proportion of workers scoring at each literacy level varied across the assessed countries. For example, the proportion of skilled craft workers scoring at level 3 or above was lower in the United States than in other countries, particularly Germany (see supplemental table 21-3).

Percentage distribution of the population in selected countries scoring at each of the five literacy levels, by literacy scale: 1994

Country	Prose scale				Document scale				Quantitative scale			
	Level 1	Level 2	Level 3	Level 4/5	Level 1	Level 2	Level 3	Level 4/5	Level 1	Level 2	Level 3	Level 4/5
Canada	16.6	25.6	35.1	22.7	18.2	24.7	32.1	25.1	16.9	26.1	34.8	22.2
Germany	14.4	34.2	38.0	13.4	9.0	32.7	39.5	18.9	6.7	26.6	43.2	23.5
Netherlands	10.5	30.1	44.1	15.3	10.1	25.7	44.2	20.0	10.3	25.5	44.3	19.9
Poland	42.6	34.5	19.8	3.1	45.4	30.7	18.0	5.8	39.1	30.1	23.9	6.8
Sweden	7.5	20.3	39.7	32.4	6.2	18.9	39.4	35.5	6.6	18.6	39.0	35.8
Switzerland (French)	17.6	33.7	38.6	10.0	16.2	28.8	38.9	16.0	12.9	24.5	42.2	20.4
Switzerland (German)	19.3	35.7	36.1	8.9	18.1	29.1	36.6	16.1	14.2	26.2	40.7	19.0
United States	20.7	25.9	32.4	21.1	23.7	25.9	31.4	19.0	21.0	25.3	31.3	22.5

Table reads: In 1994, 21.1 percent of the population in the United States scored at or above level 4 on the prose literacy scale.
NOTE: The individuals who performed at level 1 demonstrated the lowest literacy proficiency, while those at level 5 displayed the highest literacy proficiency. See the supplemental note to this indicator for a description of the literacy scales and levels.

SOURCE: Organization for Economic Co-operation and Development and Statistics Canada, *Literacy, Economy and Society, Results of the International Adult Literacy Survey,* 1995.

Percentage distribution of the population in selected countries scoring at each of the five literacy levels, by literacy scale: 1994

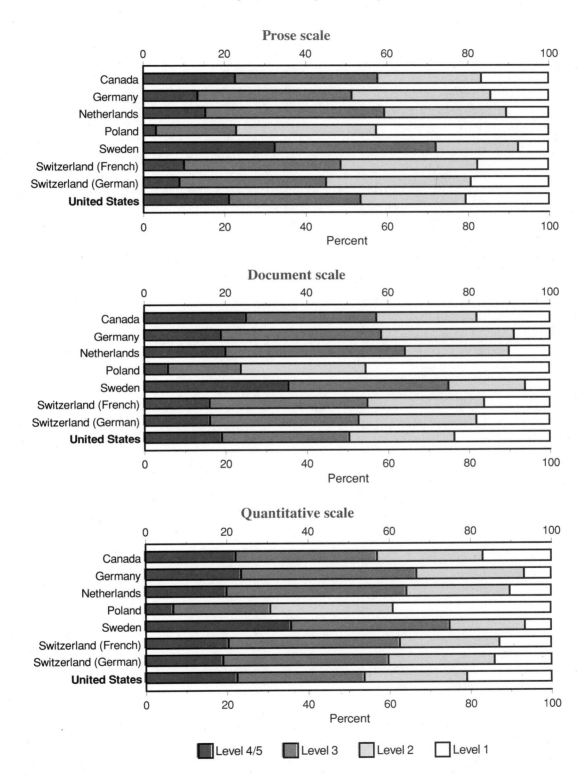

Prose scale

Document scale

Quantitative scale

Level 4/5   Level 3   Level 2   Level 1

NOTE: See the supplemental note to this indicator for a description of the literacy scales and levels.
SOURCE: Organization for Economic Co-operation and Development and Statistics Canada, *Literacy, Economy and Society, Results of the International Adult Literacy Survey,* 1995.

Scholastic Assessment Test (SAT) scores

♦ Average total SAT scores rose 8 points between 1994 and 1995. Verbal scores rose 4 points for male and 5 points for female test-takers, and mathematics scores rose 2 points for male and 3 points for female test-takers.

♦ The percentage of high school graduates who took the SAT remained at about 42 percent during the 1992–95 period, up from 35 percent in 1984. The proportion of minority SAT test-takers more than doubled between 1976 and 1995, rising from 15 to 31 percent (see supplemental table 22-1).

> *The Scholastic Assessment Test (SAT) is the test taken most frequently by college-bound students. It is designed to predict success in the freshman year of college, and to track the performance of groups of students who intend to enter college over time. When interpreting these scores, the reader should be aware that the proportion of high school graduates who take the exam changes over time.*

♦ Overall, average scores for minority test-takers have improved over the past 20 years. Between 1976 and 1995, the average scores of black test-takers rose 24 points on the verbal section and 34 points on the mathematics section, while the average scores of whites fell 3 points on the verbal section and rose 5 points on the mathematics section (see supplemental table 22-2).

♦ Between 1991 and 1995, the percentage of graduating seniors taking the American College Testing (ACT) program increased 5 percentage points, while the percentage taking the SAT remained the same. While scores on the ACT remained about the same over this time period, scores on the SAT rose 14 points (see supplemental tables 22-1 and 22-7).

Average SAT scores of college-bound seniors, by section and sex: 1972–95

Year	Verbal			Mathematics			Combined		
	Total	Male	Female	Total	Male	Female	Total	Male	Female
1972	453	454	452	484	505	461	937	959	913
1973	445	446	443	481	502	460	926	948	903
1974	444	447	442	480	501	459	924	948	901
1975	434	437	431	472	495	449	906	932	880
1976	431	433	430	472	497	446	903	930	876
1977	429	431	427	470	497	445	899	928	872
1978	429	433	425	468	494	444	897	927	869
1979	427	431	423	467	493	443	894	924	866
1980	424	428	420	466	491	443	890	919	863
1981	424	430	418	466	492	443	890	922	861
1982	426	431	421	467	493	443	893	924	864
1983	425	430	420	468	493	445	893	923	865
1984	426	433	420	471	495	449	897	928	869
1985	431	437	425	475	499	452	906	936	877
1986	431	437	426	475	501	451	906	938	877
1987	430	435	425	476	500	453	906	935	878
1988	428	435	422	476	498	455	904	933	877
1989	427	434	421	476	500	454	903	934	875
1990	424	429	419	476	499	455	900	928	874
1991	422	426	418	474	497	453	896	923	871
1992	423	428	419	476	499	456	899	927	875
1993	424	428	420	478	502	457	902	930	877
1994	423	425	421	479	501	460	902	926	881
1995	428	429	426	482	503	463	910	932	889

Table reads: The average verbal SAT score for college-bound males in 1995 was 429, down from 454 in 1972.

NOTE: The term "college-bound seniors" refers to those students from each high school graduating class who participated in the College Board Admissions Testing Program, and does not include all first-year college students, or all high school seniors, as about one-third of high school graduates participate in the American College Testing (ACT) Program. ACT scores can be found in supplemental table 22-7. See the supplemental note to this indicator for information on interpreting SAT scores.

SOURCE: College Entrance Examination Board, *National Report: College Bound Seniors, 1972–1995* (Copyright ©1995 by College Entrance Examination Board. All rights reserved.).

Percentage of high school graduates who took the SAT and average SAT scores of college-bound seniors, by section and sex: 1972–95

High school graduates

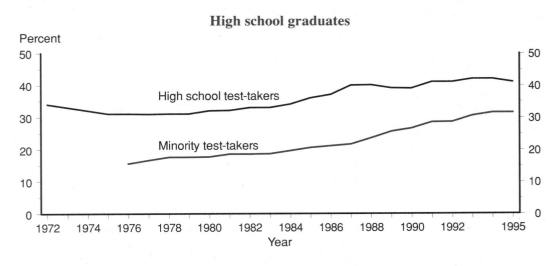

Verbal

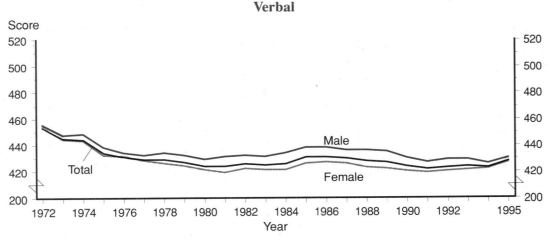

Mathematics

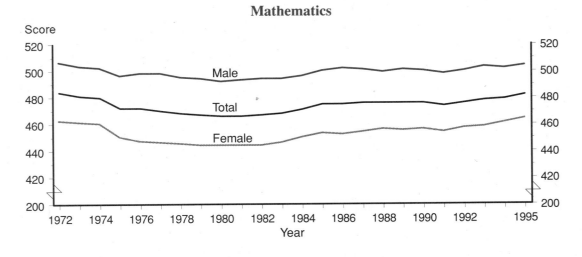

SOURCE: College Entrance Examination Board, *National Report: College Bound Seniors, 1972–1995* (Copyright © 1995 by College Entrance Examination Board. All rights reserved.).

International comparisons of mathematics performance

♦ **In the second International Assessment of Educational Progress (IAEP), 9-year-old students from the United States scored lower, on average, in mathematics performance than 9-year-olds from five other large countries.**

♦ **Thirteen-year-olds from the United States scored lower, on average, than students of the same age in the other large countries, except Spain.**

> *The technical skills of a nation's workers are a crucial component of its economic competitiveness. The youth of today will be tomorrow's workers and will be competing in the global marketplace. They will depend on the mathematics learned in this decade to succeed in the complex business and technological environments of the future.*

♦ **Average mathematics proficiency among 13-year-old students in the United States was 48 scale points below that of their South Korean counterparts. This was more than half of the difference between 9- and 13-year-olds in the United States, suggesting that United States students at age 13 may be performing at levels similar to Korean students 2 to 3 years younger.**

♦ **There is far greater variation in the mathematics proficiency of students within each country than there are differences in averages among countries. For example, among 13-year-olds, the difference between the 10th and 90th percentile was 124 scale points in the United States, compared to a difference in average proficiency between the United States and Taiwan of 51 scale points.**

Proficiency scores on mathematics assessment, by age and country: 1991

Larger countries[1]	Average proficiency score			Percentile score						
	Total	Male	Female	1st	5th	10th	Median	90th	95th	99th
Age 9										
South Korea	473	480	465	334	383	407	475	534	550	586
Taiwan	454	455	453	304	360	384	457	521	539	571
Soviet Union[2]	447	448	446	310	349	374	450	514	532	579
Spain[3]	432	432	432	287	330	353	437	499	518	551
Canada[4]	430	430	431	296	337	363	435	490	506	537
United States	420	422	419	278	305	333	427	492	513	549
Age 13										
Taiwan	545	546	544	368	424	454	550	631	659	694
South Korea	542	546	537	390	445	470	545	609	629	665
Soviet Union[2]	533	533	532	413	458	477	536	584	596	629
France	519	523	515	404	442	460	521	574	588	616
Canada[5]	513	515	512	400	443	462	515	564	580	608
Spain[3]	495	498	492	390	429	446	496	542	556	577
United States	494	494	494	366	407	430	495	554	574	616

Table reads: In 1991, 10 percent of 9-year-olds in the United States scored below 333 on the International Assessment of Educational Progress (IAEP) mathematics assessment.

[1] In the second IAEP, 14 countries assessed the mathematics achievement of 9-year-olds, and 20 countries assessed the mathematics achievement of 13-year-olds. The countries listed above are the larger countries that assessed virtually all age-eligible children, except as noted.

[2] Fourteen out of 15 republics in the former Soviet Union; Russian-speaking schools.

[3] Regions except Cataluña; Spanish-speaking schools.

[4] Four out of 10 provinces.

[5] Nine out of 10 provinces.

NOTE: Proficiency scores range from 0 to 1,000. The mean proficiency score for all participating populations, 9- and 13-year-olds together, is 500. The standard deviation is 100. See the supplemental note to this indicator for a discussion of proficiency scaling.

SOURCE: Educational Testing Service, International Assessment of Educational Progress, 1992.

Distribution of proficiency scores on mathematics assessment, by age and country: 1991

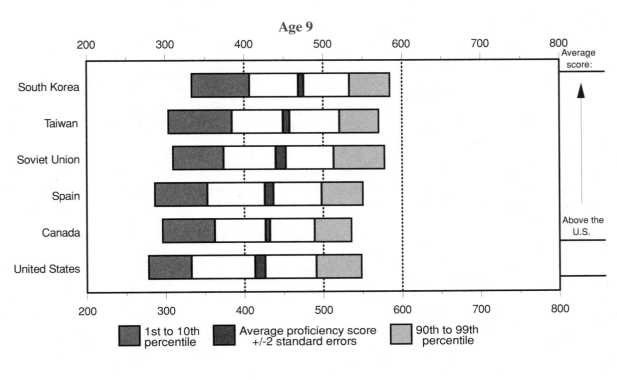

Age 9

1st to 10th percentile | Average proficiency score +/-2 standard errors | 90th to 99th percentile

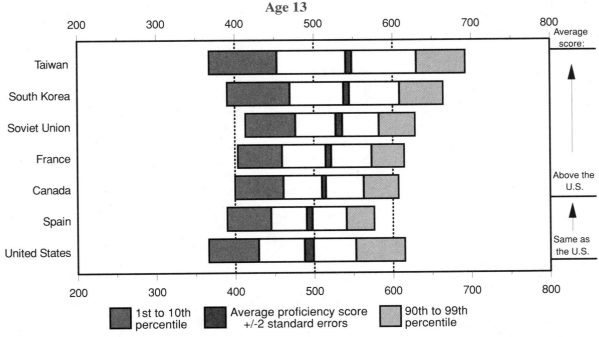

Age 13

1st to 10th percentile | Average proficiency score +/-2 standard errors | 90th to 99th percentile

NOTE: Proficiency scores range from 0 to 1,000. The mean proficiency score for all participating populations, 9- and 13-year-olds together, is 500. The standard deviation is 100.

SOURCE: Educational Testing Service, International Assessment of Educational Progress, 1992.

International comparisons of science performance

♦ **In the second International Assessment of Educational Progress (IAEP), 9-year-old students from South Korea scored higher, on average, in science performance than 9-year-olds from the United States. Students of the same age from Spain scored lower, on average.**

> *The scientific and technological skills of a nation's workers are a crucial component of its economic competitiveness. The youth of today will be tomorrow's workers and will be competing in the global marketplace. They will depend on the science learned in this decade to succeed in the complex business and technological environments of the future.*

♦ **Thirteen-year-olds from South Korea, Taiwan, the former Soviet Union, and Canada scored higher, on average, than U.S. students of the same age.**

♦ **The difference in average science proficiency scores between 9- and 13-year-olds in the United States (75 scale points) was less than the proficiency difference in other large countries (ranging from 95 to 111 scale points).**

♦ **Among 9-year-olds, boys performed better than girls in South Korea, Taiwan, and Spain. At age 13, this gender difference held across all large participating countries except Taiwan.**

Proficiency scores on science assessment, by age and country: 1991

Larger countries[1]	Average proficiency score			Percentile score						
	Total	Male	Female	1st	5th	10th	Median	90th	95th	99th
Age 9										
South Korea	460	474	446	303	357	383	460	541	563	609
Taiwan	456	466	445	254	321	359	458	553	576	627
United States	446	451	441	235	292	328	453	543	567	605
Canada[2]	437	439	434	257	316	346	443	517	538	582
Soviet Union[3]	434	441	428	284	328	356	433	515	547	588
Spain[4]	430	439	421	250	305	334	435	522	541	567
Age 13										
South Korea	571	580	559	395	457	490	575	649	670	710
Taiwan	563	567	560	339	420	463	572	655	673	715
Soviet Union[3]	541	546	535	383	438	465	545	612	629	661
Canada[5]	533	539	527	384	434	460	534	606	628	670
France	532	540	524	370	417	442	534	611	639	677
Spain[4]	525	531	519	380	428	453	534	611	639	677
United States	521	530	513	334	410	436	523	596	617	663
								601	627	665

Table reads: In 1991, 10 percent of 9-year-olds in the United States scored below 328 on the International Assessment of Educational Progress (IAEP) science assessment.

[1] In the second IAEP, 14 countries assessed the science achievement of 9-year-olds, and 20 countries assessed the science achievement of 13-year-olds. The countries listed above are the larger countries that assessed virtually all age-eligible children, except as noted.
[2] Four out of 10 provinces.
[3] Fourteen out of 15 republics in the former Soviet Union; Russian-speaking schools.
[4] Regions except Cataluña; Spanish-speaking schools.
[5] Nine out of 10 provinces.

NOTE: Proficiency scores range from 0 to 1,000. The mean proficiency score for all participating populations, 9- and 13-year-olds together, is 500. The standard deviation is 100. See the supplemental note to *Indicator 23* for a discussion of proficiency scaling.

SOURCE: Educational Testing Service, International Assessment of Educational Progress, 1992.

Distribution of proficiency scores on science assessment, by age and country: 1991

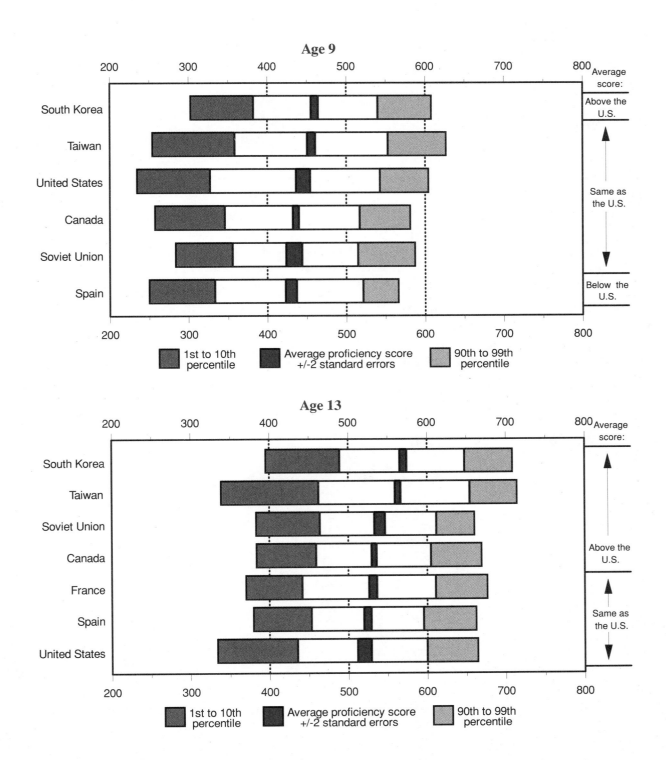

NOTE: Proficiency scores range from 0 to 1,000. The mean proficiency score for all participating populations, 9- and 13-year-olds together, is 500. The standard deviation is 100.

SOURCE: Educational Testing Service, International Assessment of Educational Progress, 1992.

Educational attainment

♦ Educational attainment of 25- to 29-year-olds increased between 1971 and 1995. The percentage of students completing high school rose 9 percentage points; the percentage of high school graduates completing at least some college rose 19 percentage points; and the percentage of high school graduates completing 4 or more years of college rose 6 percentage points.

> *Changes in educational attainment over time indicate changes in the demand for skills and knowledge in the work force. Also, changes in educational attainment can reflect the increasing emphasis society places on graduating from high school and college: completing high school and college is an important educational accomplishment that yields many benefits to those who achieve it. Better job opportunities and higher earnings are examples of those benefits.*

♦ While fewer black 25- to 29-year-olds had completed high school than their white counterparts in 1995, the gap between the percentage of blacks and whites completing high school narrowed considerably between 1971 and 1995, decreasing from 23 to 6 percentage points. Fifty-two percent of black high school graduates had completed at least some college in 1995, compared to 65 percent of white high school graduates, and a smaller percentage of black than white high school graduates had completed a bachelor's degree or higher (18 compared to 31 percent).

♦ In 1995, fewer Hispanic 25- to 29-year-olds had completed high school than their white counterparts. Fifty percent of Hispanic high school graduates had completed at least some college and 16 percent had completed a bachelor's degree or higher, compared to 65 and 31 percent, respectively, of their white counterparts. These gaps in educational attainment between Hispanics and whites did not closed between 1971 and 1995.

Percentage of 25- to 29-year-olds who have completed high school, and percentage of high school graduates who have completed 1 or more and 4 or more years of college, by race/ethnicity: Selected years March 1971–95

March	High school graduates*				High school graduates* completing:							
					1 or more years of college				4 or more years of college			
	Total	White	Black	Hispanic	Total	White	Black	Hispanic	Total	White	Black	Hispanic
1971	77.7	81.7	58.8	48.3	43.6	44.9	30.9	30.6	22.0	23.1	11.5	10.5
1973	80.2	84.0	64.1	52.3	45.3	46.6	33.5	31.6	23.6	24.8	12.7	10.8
1975	83.1	86.6	71.1	53.1	50.1	51.2	38.7	41.1	26.3	27.5	14.7	16.6
1977	85.4	88.6	74.5	58.0	53.2	54.8	41.7	41.1	28.1	29.8	16.9	11.5
1979	85.6	89.2	74.7	57.1	54.1	55.7	41.7	44.0	27.0	28.6	16.6	12.9
1981	86.3	89.8	77.6	59.8	50.1	51.2	42.5	39.6	24.7	26.3	14.9	12.5
1983	86.0	89.3	79.5	58.4	50.6	51.6	41.6	42.9	26.2	27.4	16.2	17.8
1985	86.2	89.5	80.5	61.0	50.8	51.8	42.7	44.2	25.7	27.3	14.4	18.2
1987	86.0	89.4	83.5	59.8	50.7	51.4	43.0	44.6	25.6	27.6	13.8	14.5
1989	85.5	89.3	82.3	61.0	51.3	52.8	42.1	44.3	27.3	29.5	15.4	16.5
1991	85.4	89.8	81.8	56.7	53.1	54.9	43.2	42.2	27.2	29.7	13.4	16.3
	Diploma or equivalency certificate				Some college or more				Bachelor's degree or higher			
1992	86.3	90.6	80.9	60.9	56.7	58.8	44.7	46.8	27.3	30.0	13.7	15.6
1993	86.7	91.2	82.7	60.9	58.9	61.0	48.4	48.8	27.3	29.8	16.1	13.6
1994	86.1	91.1	84.1	60.3	60.5	62.7	49.6	51.5	27.0	29.7	16.2	13.3
1995	86.9	92.5	86.8	57.2	62.2	64.6	52.0	50.3	28.4	31.2	17.8	15.5

Table reads: In 1995, 86.9 percent of those aged 25–29 had completed high school.
* 12 years of school completed for 1971–91, and high school diploma or equivalency certificate for 1992–95.
NOTE: Beginning in 1992, the Current Population Survey (CPS) changed the questions used to obtain the educational attainment of respondents. See the supplemental note to this indicator for further discussion.

SOURCE: U.S. Department of Commerce, Bureau of the Census, March Current Population Surveys.

Percentage of 25- to 29-year-olds who have completed high school and percentage of high school graduates who have completed 1 or more and 4 or more years of college, by race/ethnicity: March 1971–95

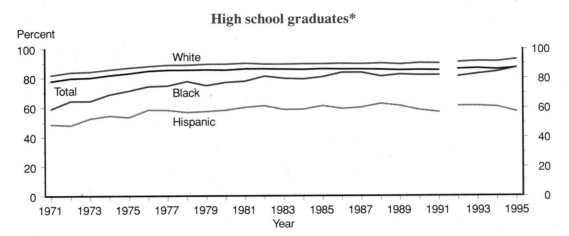

High school graduates*

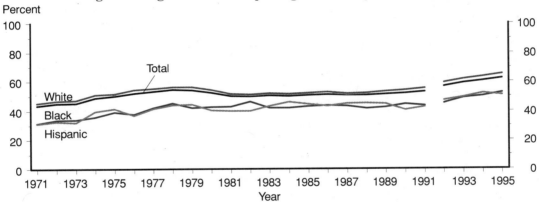

High school graduates* completing 1 or more years of college

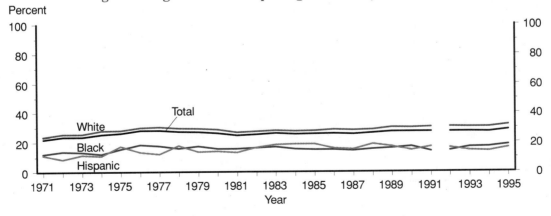

High school graduates* completing 4 or more years of college

* 12 years of school completed for 1971–91, and high school diploma or equivalency certificate for 1992–95.
NOTE: Beginning in 1992, the Current Population Survey (CPS) changed the questions used to obtain the educational attainment of respondents. See the supplemental note to this indicator for further discussion.
SOURCE: U.S. Department of Commerce, Bureau of the Census, March Current Population Surveys.

Postsecondary education enrollments and completions of the class of 1982

♦ Among 1980 sophomores who scored in the highest test quartile in 12th grade in 1982, high socioeconomic status (SES) students were much more likely than low SES students to enroll in a 4-year institution first (78 compared to 49 percent). Low SES students in the highest test quartile were more likely than high SES students to start at a public 2-year institution or not to enroll at all by 1992.

♦ Among the 1980 sophomore cohort in the highest test quartile in 12th grade, high SES students were much more likely than low SES students to have earned a bachelor's or advanced degree by 1992. Forty-three percent of low SES students who were in the highest test quartile in 12th grade in 1982 had not earned any postsecondary certificate or degree.

Many young people pursue postsecondary education in the first few years after high school. Postsecondary education is the key to many of the subsequent transitions and achievements these young people make, including entering the labor force, establishing careers and career goals, and forming a family. Higher levels of educational attainment are strongly correlated with more stable patterns of employment and higher earnings. The numbers of students enrolling in postsecondary education and completing a certificate or degree are indicators of access to these benefits.

♦ The way in which young people started their postsecondary education and their level of attainment 10 years later were highly related. Those who enrolled full time in 4-year institutions immediately after high school were much more likely to have completed a bachelor's degree than were students who enrolled part time immediately or who delayed their entry (see supplemental table 26-2).

Percentage distribution of 1980 high school sophomores according to type of postsecondary institution first attended, by 1982 test quartile and socioeconomic status: 1992

	Low test quartile				Middle test quartiles				High test quartile			
		Public		Never		Public		Never		Public		Never
Socioeconomic status	4-year	2-year	Other	attended	4-year	2-year	Other	attended	4-year	2-year	Other	attended
Total	**8.4**	**17.9**	**14.8**	**58.8**	**23.4**	**30.6**	**14.3**	**31.6**	**66.9**	**19.5**	**7.3**	**6.4**
Low quartile	6.8	13.5	14.9	64.8	13.7	24.4	16.1	45.8	48.5	27.5	9.1	14.9
Middle quartiles	10.2	23.1	13.0	53.7	22.1	32.6	14.9	30.5	59.0	23.9	8.5	8.6
High quartile	12.9	24.1	19.0	44.0	41.5	33.4	10.6	14.6	77.9	13.7	5.8	2.5

Table reads: Of 1980 high school sophomores in the low test quartile in 1982, 8.4 percent attended a 4-year institution first.

Percentage distribution of 1980 high school sophomores according to highest degree earned, by 1982 test quartile and socioeconomic status: 1992

	Low test quartile				Middle test quartiles				High test quartile			
	High school	Certif- icate/	Bach-	Ad-	High school	Certif- icate/	Bach-	Ad-	High school	Certif- icate/	Bach-	Ad-
Socioeconomic status	or less	assoc.	elor's	vanced	or less	assoc.	elor's	vanced	or less	assoc.	elor's	vanced
Total	**79.6**	**17.1**	**3.0**	**0.3**	**59.2**	**22.8**	**16.1**	**1.9**	**26.6**	**11.9**	**49.2**	**12.3**
Low quartile	82.4	15.1	2.1	0.4	70.4	21.9	7.1	0.6	43.1	25.3	25.6	6.1
Middle quartiles	78.6	17.7	3.5	0.2	58.6	24.3	15.4	1.7	33.9	14.3	44.0	7.8
High quartile	69.3	21.4	9.1	0.2	44.5	19.7	31.6	4.2	17.6	7.7	57.2	17.5

Table reads: Of 1980 high school sophomores in the low test quartile in 1982, 79.6 percent had attained no more than a high school diploma by 1992.

NOTE: Composite test scores are based on the average nonmissing scores on reading, vocabulary, and mathematics (part I) tests.

SOURCE: U.S. Department of Education, National Center for Education Statistics, High School and Beyond (HS&B) study 1980 Sophomore Cohort, Base Year, First, and Fourth Follow-up Surveys.

Postsecondary enrollment and attainment

Percentage distribution of 1980 high school sophomores according to type of postsecondary institution first attended, by 1982 test quartile: 1992

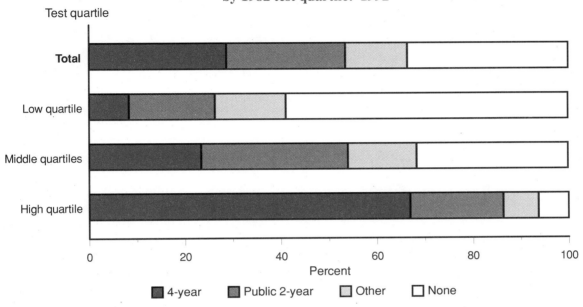

Percentage of 1980 high school sophomores who earned a bachelor's degree or higher by 1992, by 1982 test quartile and socioeconomic status (SES): 1992

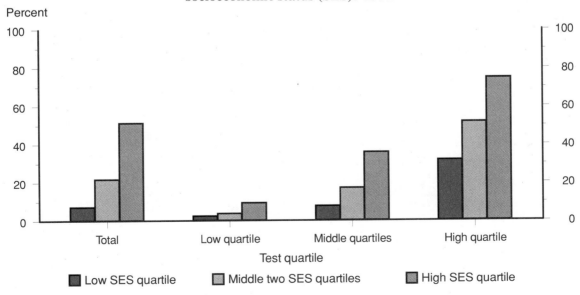

SOURCE: U.S. Department of Education, National Center for Education Statistics, High School and Beyond (HS&B) study 1980 Sophomore Cohort, Base Year, First, and Fourth Follow-up Surveys.

International comparisons of educational attainment, by age

♦ The educational attainment of the U.S. population in 1992 was high compared to other large industrialized countries. A similar or higher percentage of 25- to 64-year-olds in the United States had completed secondary and higher education than their counterparts in Japan, Germany, the United Kingdom, France, Italy, or Canada.

♦ In Japan, Germany, the United Kingdom, and Canada, 25- to 34-year-olds had completed secondary education at rates similar to their counterparts in the United States.

♦ Young males aged 25–34 in Japan were much more likely to complete higher education than males of the same age group in the other large industrialized countries. Young males in the United States ranked second.

♦ Young females aged 25–34 in the United States were much more likely to complete higher education than females and males of the same age in other large industrialized countries (with the exception of young males in Japan).

> *The percentage of the population completing secondary and higher education in the United States and other highly industrialized countries provides an indication of the skill level of the U.S. work force as compared to its economic competitors. Furthermore, contrasting the educational attainment of the general population to the attainment of younger age cohorts provides a means of comparing past and recent progress in the rate at which individuals complete high school or college.*

Percentage of the population in large industrialized countries who have completed secondary and higher education, by age, sex, and country: 1992

| Country | 25–64 years old | | 25–34 years old | | | | | |
| | Both sexes | | Both sexes | | Male | | Female | |
	Secondary education	Higher education	Secondary education	Higher education	Secondary education	Higher education	Secondary education	Higher education
Canada	71.3	15.0	80.8	16.1	79.0	16.0	82.5	16.2
France	52.2	10.2	67.1	12.3	68.4	12.4	65.7	12.1
Germany	81.9	11.6	88.6	11.8	90.9	13.0	86.3	10.5
Italy	28.4	6.4	42.4	6.8	41.5	6.8	43.3	6.7
Japan*	69.7	13.3	90.6	22.9	89.3	34.2	91.8	11.5
United Kingdom	68.1	10.7	80.9	12.5	82.2	14.3	79.6	10.7
United States	84.0	23.6	86.5	23.2	85.9	23.3	87.0	23.1

Table reads: In 1992, 84.0 percent of those aged 25–64 in the United States and 81.9 percent of those of similar age in Germany had completed secondary education.

* Data are for 1989.

NOTE: In the United States, completing secondary education is defined as graduating from high school or earning a GED; completing higher education is defined as earning a bachelor's degree or more.

SOURCE: Organization for Economic Co-operation and Development, Indicators of Education's Systems, *OECD Education Statistics 1985–1992.*

Percentage of the population in large industrialized countries who have completed secondary and higher education, by age, sex, and country: 1992

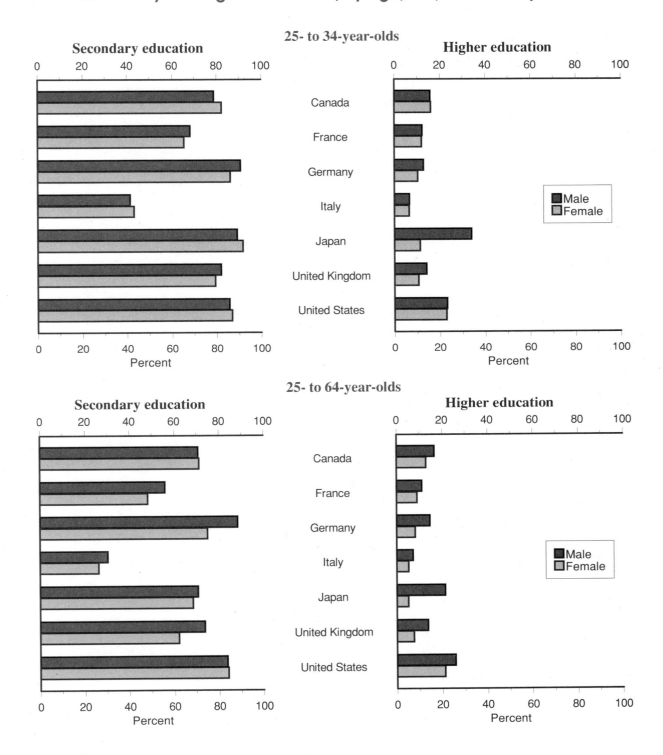

25- to 34-year-olds

Secondary education | Higher education

25- to 64-year-olds

Secondary education | Higher education

NOTE: In the United States, completing secondary education is defined as graduating from high school or earning a GED; completing higher education is defined as earning a bachelor's degree or more.

SOURCE: Organization for Economic Co-operation and Development, Indicators of Education's Systems, *OECD Education Statistics 1985–1992.*

High school course taking in the core subject areas

♦ Between 1982 and 1994, the percentage of high school graduates earning the less restrictive number of units in core courses more than doubled, while those earning the "New Basics" units more than tripled. These increases occurred for both sexes and all racial/ethnic groups.

> *In 1983, A Nation at Risk recommended that all students seeking a diploma be required to enroll in the "New Basics," a core curriculum composed of 4 years of English and 3 years each of social studies, science, and mathematics.[1] While several states have adopted this set of requirements, others have chosen a less restrictive set that requires 4 years of English, 3 years of social studies, and 2 years each of science and mathematics.*

♦ Students enrolled in both academic and vocational programs were just as likely as students enrolled solely in an academic program to fulfill the less restrictive requirements. However, students enrolled in an academic program only were more likely to meet the more restrictive "New Basics" requirements than those in both programs.

♦ For private school graduates, the percentage fulfilling the "New Basics" requirements increased 39 percentage points between 1982 and 1994, compared to an increase of 37 percentage points for public school graduates. While the increase was smaller for private school graduates (32 percentage points) than for public school graduates (44 percentage points), a greater proportion of private school students (80 percent) earned the less restrictive number of units in 1994 than public school students (73 percent) (see supplemental table 28-1).

Percentage of high school graduates earning the minimum number of units in core courses, by type of curriculum and selected characteristics: 1982, 1987, 1990, and 1994

Characteristics	"New Basics" curriculum				Less restrictive curriculum			
	1982	1987	1990	1994	1982	1987	1990	1994
Total	**14.0**	**28.3**	**39.6**	**50.6**	**31.4**	**53.6**	**66.2**	**73.8**
Sex								
Male	14.8	29.0	40.0	48.4	31.3	53.0	65.3	71.3
Female	13.3	27.6	39.2	52.6	31.5	54.2	67.1	76.3
Race/ethnicity								
White	15.5	29.3	40.6	53.6	32.4	53.0	65.6	75.0
Black	11.5	24.1	41.5	44.7	31.3	55.3	72.6	74.9
Hispanic	6.7	16.8	30.4	43.8	25.3	47.6	63.6	76.1
Asian/Pacific Islander	21.3	45.6	48.7	56.6	34.6	67.1	70.2	73.5
American Indian/Alaskan Native	6.5	24.6	21.6	43.6	35.3	62.1	49.9	73.0
Student program[2]								
Academic	30.6	47.6	56.3	63.3	56.3	72.8	81.3	83.1
Vocational	0.0	0.0	0.0	0.0	5.4	13.5	14.3	20.2
Both	18.6	26.2	35.6	47.3	56.9	71.0	78.2	82.4
Neither	0.0	0.0	0.0	0.0	5.3	12.7	14.5	14.7

Table reads: 14.8 percent of 1982 male high school graduates earned the minimum number of units in core courses under the "New Basics" curriculum, and 31.3 percent earned the minimum under the less restrictive curriculum.

[1] The "New Basics" curriculum also includes 0.5 units of computer science which was not included in this analysis.

[2] To be placed in the "Academic" category, a student must have earned at least 12 credits in the core courses and not have met the "Vocational" category requirements. To be placed in the "Vocational" category, a student must have earned at least three credits in a single occupationally specific vocational education area but not have met the course credit requirements for the academic category. "Both" means the student met the requirements for both the academic and vocational programs. "Neither" means the student did not meet the requirements for either the academic or the vocational programs.

NOTE: For a description of the sampling procedures and related issues for the High School and Beyond (HS&B) Transcript Study and the later transcript studies, see the supplemental note to this indicator.

SOURCE: U.S. Department of Education, National Center for Education Statistics, *The 1994 High School Transcript Study Tabulations: Comparative Data on Credits Earned and Demographics for 1994, 1990, 1987 and 1982 High School Graduates*, 1996.

Percentage of high school graduates earning a minimum number of units in core courses, by type of curriculum, sex, and race/ethnicity: 1982, 1987, 1990, 1994

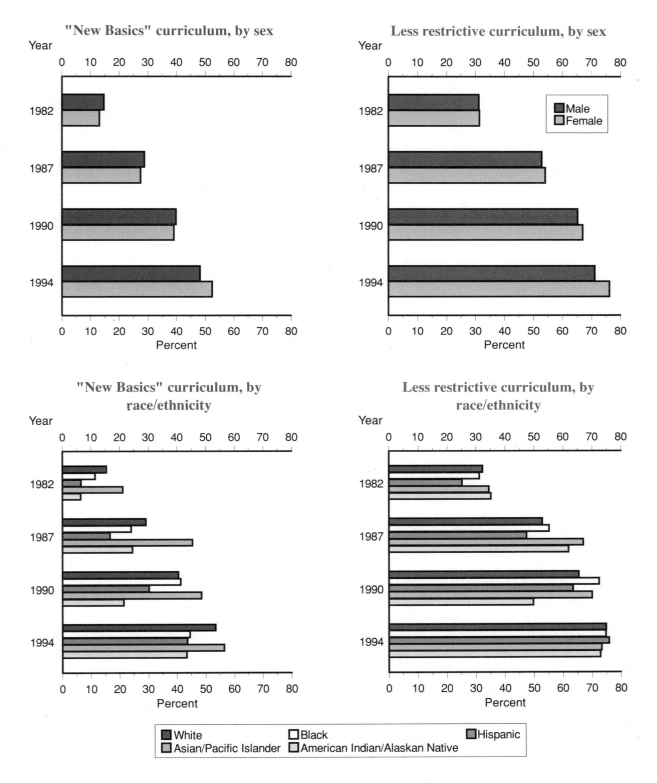

"New Basics" curriculum, by sex

Less restrictive curriculum, by sex

"New Basics" curriculum, by race/ethnicity

Less restrictive curriculum, by race/ethnicity

White Black Hispanic
Asian/Pacific Islander American Indian/Alaskan Native

SOURCE: U.S. Department of Education, National Center for Education Statistics, *The 1994 High School Transcript Study Tabulations: Comparative Data on Credits Earned and Demographics for 1994, 1990, 1987, and 1982 High School Graduates,* 1996.

High school mathematics and science course-taking patterns

♦ **High school graduates in 1994 were more likely to take mathematics courses at the level of algebra I or higher and science courses at the level of biology or higher than their counterparts in 1982.**

♦ **The proportion of high school graduates who took algebra II and the proportion who took chemistry increased 7 percentage points between 1990 and 1994 and increased over 25 percentage points between 1982 and 1994 (to 59 and 56 percent, respectively).**

> *Courses in mathematics and science can teach students to use higher level thinking skills to solve complex problems. These skills are considered valuable both in educational and marketplace settings. Analysis of course-taking patterns of high school graduates can indicate levels of exposure in these fields for individuals who are about to advance to higher education or to enter the work force.*

♦ **A larger percentage of 1994 graduates, both male and female, earned credit in biology, chemistry, and physics than their 1982 counterparts. Similar percentages of males and females earned credit in biology in both years. Females were more likely to earn credit in chemistry in 1994. Males were consistently more likely to earn credit in physics.**

♦ **The percentage of Hispanics and American Indians/Alaskan Natives taking algebra II more than doubled between 1982 and 1994, rising from 18 percent for Hispanics and from 11 percent for American Indians in 1982 to 51 percent for Hispanics and 39 percent for American Indians/Alaskan Natives in 1994 (see supplemental table 29-2).**

Percentage of high school graduates taking selected mathematics and science courses in high school, by sex: 1982, 1987, 1990, and 1994

Mathematics and science courses[1]	Total				Male				Female			
	1982[2]	1987[2]	1990[2]	1994	1982[2]	1987[2]	1990[2]	1994	1982[2]	1987[2]	1990[2]	1994
Mathematics[3]												
Algebra I	53.9	64.0	64.2	66.4	52.2	62.3	61.7	64.7	55.4	65.7	66.5	68.1
Geometry	45.5	59.7	63.4	70.4	45.0	58.8	62.4	68.3	45.9	60.4	64.4	72.4
Algebra II	32.2	48.1	51.7	58.6	32.4	47.3	50.0	55.4	32.0	48.9	53.3	61.6
Trigonometry	12.1	18.6	18.2	17.2	13.2	19.5	18.1	16.6	11.1	17.6	18.2	17.8
Analysis/pre-calculus	5.9	12.6	13.4	17.3	6.2	13.5	14.0	16.3	5.6	11.6	12.8	18.2
Calculus	4.6	6.0	6.5	9.2	5.1	7.4	7.5	9.4	4.1	4.6	5.6	9.1
Science												
Biology	76.4	87.8	91.3	93.5	74.2	86.3	90.0	92.3	78.4	89.4	92.5	94.7
Chemistry	30.9	43.7	49.0	56.0	31.9	44.3	47.9	53.2	30.0	43.2	50.0	58.7
Physics	14.2	19.2	21.5	24.4	18.8	24.0	25.4	26.9	10.0	14.6	18.0	22.0
Biology and chemistry	28.1	42.1	47.6	53.8	28.2	42.2	46.4	50.9	28.0	42.0	48.8	56.6
Biology, chemistry, and physics	10.6	16.4	18.8	21.3	13.4	20.1	21.8	23.1	7.9	12.8	16.1	19.6

Table reads: In 1994, 70.4 percent of high school graduates had taken geometry in high school.

[1] The minimum number of units used for inclusion in this indicator was 1.00 for individual courses except for algebra II, trigonometry, and analysis/pre-calculus where 0.5 was set as the minimum number of credits.

[2] Numbers have been revised from previously published figures. See the supplemental note to *Indicator 28* for further explanation.

[3] These data only report the percentage of students who earned credit in mathematics courses while in high school and do not count those students who took these courses prior to entering high school. In 1992, for example, approximately 93 percent of students had taken algebra I at any time prior to graduating from high school, and about 70 percent had taken geometry.

NOTE: See the supplemental note to *Indicator 28* for further explanation of courses and definitions.

SOURCE: U.S. Department of Education, National Center for Education Statistics, *The 1994 High School Transcript Study Tabulations: Comparative Data on Credits Earned and Demographics for 1994, 1990, 1987, and 1982 High School Graduates*, 1996.

Percentage of high school graduates taking selected mathematics and science courses in high school: 1982, 1987, 1990, and 1994

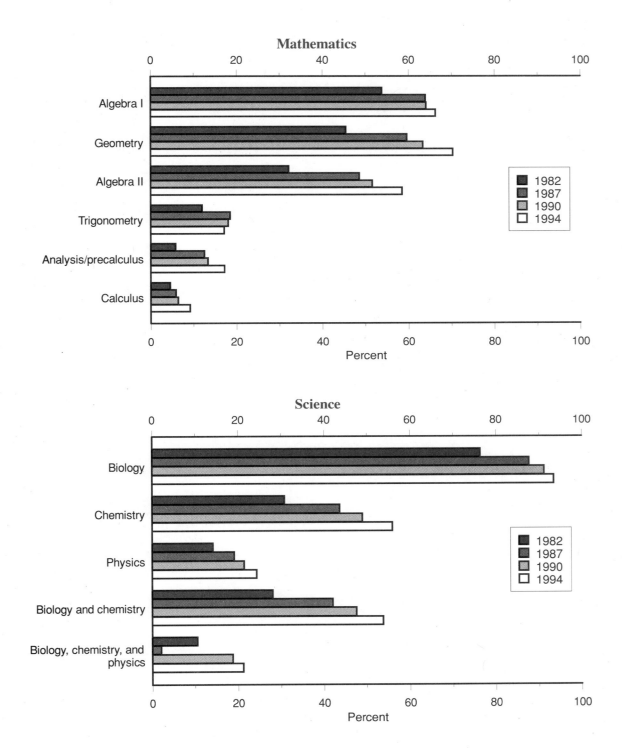

SOURCE: U.S. Department of Education, National Center for Education Statistics, *The 1994 High School Transcript Study Tabulations: Comparative Data on Credits Earned and Demographics for 1994, 1990, 1987, and 1982 High School Graduates*, 1996.

Economic and Other Outcomes of Education

Education is an investment in human skills. Like all investments, it involves both costs and returns. The cost of finishing high school to the student is quite low, because it consists mainly of the relatively low wages earned by a 16- to 19-year-old dropout. The cost to the student of attending college is higher, and principally includes tuition, books, fees, and the earnings given up by not working or by working part time in college. The returns come in many forms. Some are monetary, while others are personal, social, cultural, and economic. Some are directly related to the labor market, while others are not. Some accrue to the individual, others to society and the nation in general. Returns related to the labor market include better job opportunities, jobs that are less sensitive to general economic conditions, opportunities to participate in employer-provided training, and higher earnings. Other returns that are not related to the labor market but are often attributed to education include lower rates of welfare dependency *(Indicator 36)* and a greater interest and participation in civic affairs such as voting *(Indicator 37)*.

The costs and returns of investing in postsecondary education have changed over time, which affects the incentive for individuals to participate. Measures presented in this section illuminate changes in the rewards of finishing high school (or conversely, the penalties of not finishing) and changes in the rewards of investing in postsecondary education.

Penalties of not graduating from high school

These indicators suggest some general conclusions regarding the labor market penalties of not finishing high school. The immediate difficulty of making the transition from full-time school attendance to full-time work appears much greater for those who leave school before finishing high school. Without prior job experience or specialized training, school leavers may have difficulty finding jobs that they are willing to take. In October 1994, 64 percent of recent high school graduates not enrolled in college were employed, compared to 43 percent of recent school dropouts. The degree of advantage varied by race/ethnicity: 38 percent of recent black school graduates not enrolled in college and 34 percent of black school dropouts were employed in October 1994. Among whites, the corresponding percentages were 73 percent and 52 percent. White

school dropouts were more likely to be employed than black school graduates *(Indicator 30)*.

As individuals enter their 20s and early 30s, some of the problems of making the transition from school to the work force are solved, but the advantage of a high school diploma persists. For example, among males aged 25–34 in March 1995, the employment rate for those with 9–11 years of school was 72 percent, compared to 87 percent for high school graduates. Among females 25–34 years old, less than half (46 percent) of high school dropouts were employed, compared to 67 percent of those with a diploma *(Indicator 32)*.

Continuity of employment enables workers to become more productive as they gain specific job experience. This is an advantage both to the employer and the worker to the extent that this experience is reflected in wages. The employment advantages associated with finishing high school include a greater likelihood of full-time, year-round employment. While 74 percent of males and 57 percent of females aged 25–34 whose highest education level was high school worked full time, year round in 1994, 58 percent of males and 41 percent of females without a high school diploma did so *(Indicator 33)*.

Among workers aged 25–34, those with 9–11 years of school earned substantially less than those who had completed high school. In 1994, for example, the median annual salary of males with 9–11 years of school was 68 percent of the median salary of high school graduates. The median annual salary of female high school dropouts was 58 percent of that of female high school graduates *(Indicator 34)*.

Rewards of college attendance and graduation

The ratio of the median annual earnings of those who attend and graduate from college to the median annual earnings of high school graduates provides an indication of the financial returns of attending and graduating from college. In 1994, for males aged 25–34, the earnings premium for attending college and earning a bachelor's degree was 52 percent, and the earnings premium for attending college without attaining a bachelor's degree was 14 percent. For females in the same age group, the 1994 premium for attending and earning a bachelor's degree was even larger—86 percent, while the premium for attending without attaining a bachelor's degree was 20 percent *(Indicator 34)*.

While both males and females who persist in their education have substantial earnings advantages compared to school dropouts, there are persistent earnings differences between males and females with the same educational attainment. Among full-time, year-round workers, males at each education level earned more than females. For college graduates, the median male income in 1994 was $36,100 compared to $29,600 for females. The size of this gap in constant dollars has declined since 1970, when males who had a college degree and who worked full time, year round earned $43,900 and females earned $31,400 (table 34-4).

When students decide what to study in college, they often think about the possibilities of obtaining a job related to their major, and the earnings potential associated with these jobs. About three-fourths (78 percent) of 1992–93 graduates reported having a job related to their major in April 1994, and a similar proportion (76 percent) reported their jobs had career potential (Indicator 31). The median starting salary for 1992–93 graduates working full time and not enrolled in school was $23,000. Graduates who majored in computer sciences and engineering have higher starting salaries than graduates who majored in all other fields of study, while students who majored in the humanities, social sciences, and education have the lowest starting salaries (Indicator 35).

Some of the salary difference between male and female college graduates may be accounted for by different majors chosen by members of each sex, and also by differential involvement in the labor market. Females were more likely than males to major in education, and males were more likely to major in computer sciences and engineering. Nevertheless, among college graduates whose majors were business and management, social and behavioral sciences, and natural sciences, who were working full time and were not enrolled in school, females earned less than males (Indicator 35).

Welfare recipiency

The benefits of education to the individual include a higher income and a greater likelihood of employment. To the nation, these benefits correspond to a larger, more productive work force. Among those aged 25–34 who went beyond 8th grade, higher education levels also correspond to lower rates of welfare recipiency. For instance, in 1994, 14 percent of those in that age group with 9–11 years of school received income from AFDC or public assistance, while 6 percent of high school graduates received such income. Among black 25- to 34-year olds, the contrast is even more striking— 30 percent of those with 9–11 years of school received welfare income in 1994, compared to 13 percent of high school graduates (Indicator 36).

Voting

Education plays a vital role in preparing individuals for active participation in the political, economic, and social lives of their communities. One of the key civic activities associated with education is participation in elections.

There is a strong positive relationship between voting in congressional and presidential elections and education. As educational attainment increases, so does voting participation. About 13 percent of 25- to 44-year olds with 1–3 years of high school voted in the 1994 congressional elections, compared to 31 percent of those with 4 years of high school, 46 percent of those with 1–3 years of college, and 57 percent of those with 4 or more years of college. Reported participation in the presidential election of 1992 by educational attainment was higher. For example, while 27 percent of those with 1–3 years of high school voted, 79 percent of those with 4 or more years of college did so. Differences in voting behavior by educational attainment have generally widened over time (Indicator 37).

There are several factors that may influence this relationship. Persons with higher educational attainment may have a greater sense of the efficacy of their vote than persons with less education, and may better understand how to use their vote to influence the political process. In addition, since higher educational attainment is associated with higher earnings, the more educated may be more concerned with the outcomes of the political process as they affect their material well being. Regardless of the explanation, the differences among educational groups in voting participation have generally widened over time (Indicator 37).

NOTE:
* See Murphy, Kevin and Finis Welch. "Wage Premiums for College Graduates: Recent Growth and Possible Explanations," *Educational Researcher*, May 1989, for a more detailed description of changes between 1964 and 1986 in the relative earnings of workers with different levels of education and experience by sex and race.

Transition from high school to work

♦ In 1994, 64 percent of recent high school graduates not enrolled in college were employed, compared to 43 percent of recent school dropouts.

♦ During the period of economic recession between 1989 and 1992, the employment rates in both groups fell about 10 percentage points. However, in 1993, the employment rate for recent school dropouts increased markedly, rising more than 10 percentage points.

> *The transition from high school to work can be difficult. Without prior job experience or specialized training, school leavers may find it difficult to find jobs they are willing to take. The employment rate among school leavers, both those who have not finished high school and those who have finished but have not gone on to college, indicates the ease of making this transition.*

♦ Nearly every year between 1972 and 1994, white recent school dropouts were more likely to be employed than black recent high school graduates not enrolled in college. In fact, in 1994, the employment rate for white recent school dropouts was 52 percent, while the employment rate for black recent high school graduates not enrolled in college was 38 percent.

♦ Between 1960 and 1994, male recent high school graduates not enrolled in college and recent school dropouts were more likely than their female counterparts to be employed (see supplemental table 30-1).

Employment rates for recent high school graduates not enrolled in college and for recent school dropouts, by race/ethnicity: October 1972–94

October	Recent high school graduates not enrolled in college				Recent school dropouts			
	Total	White	Black	Hispanic	Total	White	Black	Hispanic
1972	70.1	73.5	48.3	(*)	46.8	47.0	42.8	(*)
1973	70.7	74.9	49.7	(*)	52.7	55.1	44.1	(*)
1974	69.1	72.9	46.0	(*)	49.3	53.9	36.2	(*)
1975	65.1	68.9	37.2	(*)	41.9	46.3	21.9	46.0
1976	68.8	73.1	38.6	(*)	44.8	49.6	20.9	(*)
1977	72.0	76.0	43.3	65.7	52.7	56.6	34.8	(*)
1978	74.9	79.0	45.8	68.9	51.2	54.2	22.3	(*)
1979	72.4	76.5	44.2	68.8	49.7	54.3	27.3	(*)
1980	68.9	74.6	34.7	(*)	44.6	51.2	20.9	47.8
1981	65.9	73.0	31.2	(*)	42.1	51.3	11.7	50.7
1982	60.4	68.4	29.3	43.5	38.0	44.6	16.2	(*)
1983	63.0	69.7	34.7	(*)	44.4	49.3	26.3	(*)
1984	64.0	70.7	44.8	49.4	44.0	51.4	24.2	35.7
1985	62.0	70.9	34.5	(*)	44.2	50.1	29.4	37.7
1986	65.2	71.5	41.1	64.6	48.0	50.4	31.5	46.5
1987	68.9	75.2	46.9	54.0	41.8	48.1	25.9	(*)
1988	71.9	78.2	55.8	57.3	43.6	47.6	17.6	56.1
1989	71.7	77.6	53.7	49.4	46.7	57.6	26.4	(*)
1990	67.8	75.0	45.2	(*)	46.3	56.3	30.9	(*)
1991	59.6	67.0	32.3	(*)	36.8	38.6	24.7	(*)
1992	62.7	71.9	37.0	54.2	36.2	43.1	(*)	28.3
1993	64.2	71.8	42.3	42.9	46.9	52.6	27.1	(*)
1994	64.2	73.1	38.0	46.0	42.9	51.7	34.1	28.6

Table reads: In 1994, 64.2 percent of recent high school graduates who were not enrolled in college were employed.

* Too few sample observations for a reliable estimate.

NOTE: Recent high school graduates are individuals aged 16–24 who graduated during the survey year. Recent school dropouts are individuals aged 16–24 who did not graduate and who were in school 12 months earlier, but who were not enrolled during the survey month. Due to a change in data sources for this analysis, some percentages are revised from previously published figures.

SOURCE: U.S. Department of Commerce, Bureau of the Census, October Current Population Surveys.

Employment rates for recent high school graduates not enrolled in college and for recent school dropouts, by graduation status and race/ethnicity: October 1972–94

By graduation status

Percent employed

Recent high school graduates not enrolled in college

Recent school dropouts

By race/ethnicity

Recent high school graduates not enrolled in college

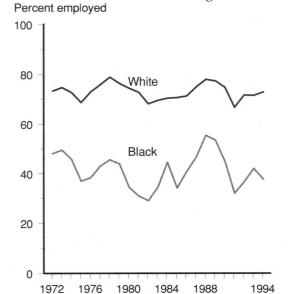

Percent employed

White

Black

Recent school dropouts

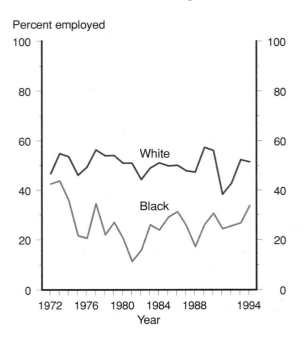

Percent employed

White

Black

NOTE: Recent high school graduates are individuals aged 16–24 who graduated during the survey year. Recent school dropouts are individuals aged 16–24 who did not graduate and who were in school 12 months earlier, but who were not enrolled during the survey month.
SOURCE: U.S. Department of Commerce, Bureau of the Census, October Current Population Surveys.

Transition from college to work

♦ In April 1994, two-thirds (67 percent) of recent college graduates were employed full time and were not enrolled in postsecondary education; 9 percent were employed part time and were not enrolled. About three-fourths (76 percent) of those who worked full time and who were not enrolled had jobs with career potential.

> The attainment of a bachelor's degree is one measure of the skills learned through college attendance. In recent years, concern about the difficulties encountered by recent graduates in making the transition from college to work has grown. Students, their families, and educational policymakers are interested in graduates' employment prospects and their relationship to fields of study.

♦ Although about three-fourths of recent graduates who were working full time and not enrolled reported their jobs were related to their field of study, only 60 percent reported a college degree was required to get their job.

♦ There were no measurable differences among the percentages of recent graduates who were unemployed by field of study (see supplemental table 31-1).

♦ Females who majored in seven fields of study (business and management, public affairs/social services, biological sciences, mathematics and science, social sciences, humanities, and "other" majors) were more likely than males to work in the traditionally female occupations of administrative and clerical support (see supplemental table 31-1).

Percentage of 1992–93 college graduates according to employment and enrollment status and relatedness of jobs to education, by selected characteristics: April 1994

Selected characteristics	Employment and enrollment status					Relatedness of job to education[1]		
	Employed full time, not enrolled	Employed part time, not enrolled	In labor force, enrolled[2]	Not in labor force, enrolled	Not employed, not enrolled[3]	Job related to field of study	Job required college degree	Job had career potential
Total	**67.1**	**8.7**	**12.4**	**5.5**	**6.3**	**77.6**	**59.9**	**75.7**
Field of study								
Business and management	80.0	5.3	7.9	1.9	4.9	87.1	54.1	79.6
Education	59.9	16.1	14.4	4.8	4.8	80.4	72.1	78.1
Engineering	69.2	3.4	13.7	7.2	6.5	90.0	83.0	85.8
Health professions	68.6	8.4	12.9	4.5	5.6	94.4	77.4	84.6
Public affairs/social services	70.3	9.0	9.2	5.0	6.5	73.5	53.0	71.6
Biological sciences	44.3	8.4	17.4	18.3	11.5	69.5	54.7	62.1
Mathematics and science	60.8	8.5	14.9	9.9	5.9	87.1	71.0	80.8
Social sciences	66.6	7.0	13.1	6.1	7.2	57.7	48.8	72.3
History	64.9	8.1	16.4	6.6	4.0	40.6	43.4	69.3
Humanities	59.2	12.8	13.5	5.9	8.5	58.2	50.1	69.1
Psychology	56.5	6.9	19.5	8.8	8.3	59.2	54.5	54.1
Other	69.4	9.0	11.4	3.6	6.6	75.2	55.0	70.5
Sex								
Male	69.2	6.8	11.9	6.3	5.7	76.6	59.1	78.0
Female	65.3	10.3	12.8	4.7	6.9	78.4	60.5	73.6
College grade point average								
Less than 3.0	71.7	8.9	11.1	2.2	6.1	73.2	54.6	74.2
3.0 to 3.49	68.2	7.9	12.7	5.0	6.3	78.7	63.0	74.7
3.5 and higher	61.1	9.3	14.1	9.4	6.0	81.5	61.6	79.2

Table reads: Of 1992–93 college graduates, 67.1 were employed full time and were not enrolled in postsecondary education in April 1994.

[1] Includes only those who worked full time and who were not enrolled in postsecondary education.

[2] Includes persons who worked full time or part time or who were unemployed.

[3] Includes persons who were not in the work force or who were unemployed.

SOURCE: U.S. Department of Education, National Center for Education Statistics, 1993 Baccalaureate and Beyond Longitudinal Study, First Follow-up (B&B:93/94).

Percentage of 1992–93 college graduates working full time and not enrolled in postsecondary education whose job was related to their field of study, and the percentage of those whose job required a college degree: April 1994

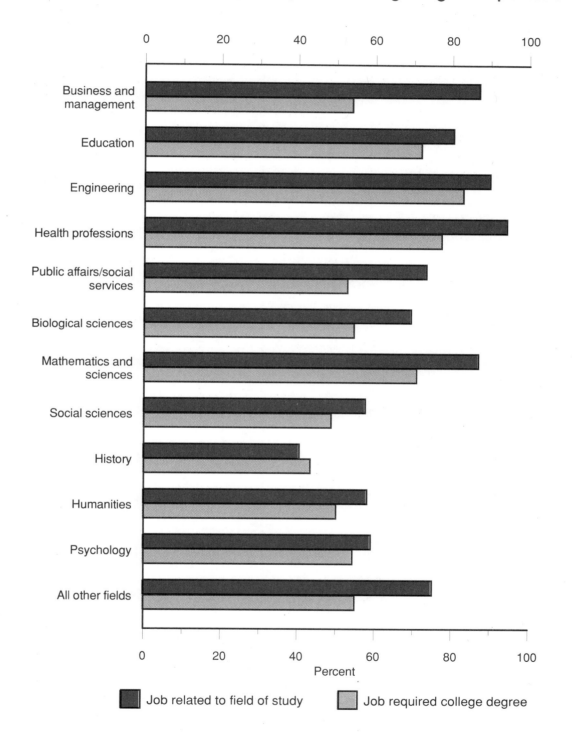

SOURCE: U.S. Department of Education, National Center for Education Statistics, 1993 Baccalaureate and Beyond Longitudinal Study, First Follow-up (B&B:93/94).

Employment of young adults

♦ Generally, the percentage of 25- to 34-year-olds who were employed was higher among those individuals with more education. In 1995, male and female college graduates aged 25–34 were much more likely to be employed than their counterparts who did not finish high school.

♦ The gap between the percentage of male and female college graduates aged 25–34 who were employed narrowed between 1971 and 1995, decreasing from 36 percentage points in 1971 to 10 percentage points in 1995.

The percentage of a population group with jobs is influenced by a variety of factors. Some factors influence the willingness of employers to offer jobs to individuals with different levels of education at the going wage rate, while others influence the willingness of these individuals to take jobs at the going wage rate. The higher the proportion of young adults who are employed, the better are their labor market opportunities relative to other things they could do, and vice versa.

♦ In 1995, the percentage of females aged 25–34 who were employed was higher than in 1971, regardless of their educational level. However, the percentage of females with a high school diploma or higher who were employed increased at a faster rate than did the percentage of females with only some high school.

Percentage of 25- to 34-year-olds who were employed, by sex and years of school completed: Selected years March 1971–95

| March | Male | | | | Female | | | |
	Grades 9–11	High school diploma	Some college	Bachelor's degree or higher	Grades 9–11	High school diploma	Some college	Bachelor's degree or higher
1971	87.9	93.6	89.9	92.5	35.4	43.1	44.9	56.9
1973	88.8	93.8	88.5	93.5	38.4	46.5	51.0	62.7
1975	78.0	88.4	87.7	93.5	35.4	48.1	53.6	66.3
1977	81.5	89.5	89.1	93.3	41.0	53.0	58.0	69.5
1979	80.5	91.3	90.9	94.1	43.2	58.0	64.2	74.0
1981	76.7	86.9	88.5	93.7	42.7	61.3	67.6	76.4
1983	69.3	78.6	83.8	91.1	37.1	58.8	68.3	79.2
1985	76.1	86.1	89.7	92.2	40.3	63.9	71.0	80.6
1987	75.0	86.8	89.0	92.1	44.0	65.6	72.2	81.4
1989	77.6	87.8	91.1	93.7	43.0	66.9	74.0	82.1
1991	69.9	84.9	88.6	91.8	42.3	67.0	73.5	82.6
1992	69.9	84.7	86.7	90.9	41.7	65.4	74.0	82.5
1993	71.0	83.6	87.2	92.3	42.2	66.0	73.0	81.6
1994	70.0	85.2	88.0	92.8	40.1	66.2	74.3	81.6
1995	71.8	86.6	89.6	92.9	45.8	67.2	73.0	83.4

Table reads: In 1995, 71.8 percent of males who had completed 9–11 years of school were employed.

NOTE: In 1992, the Current Population Survey (CPS) changed the questions used to obtain the educational attainment of respondents. The category "Grades 9–11" includes some who completed 12th grade but who have not received a high school diploma; "High school diploma" includes those who have an equivalency certificate; "Some college" includes those with an associate's degree or vocational certificate; and "Bachelor's degree or higher" includes those with an advanced degree. See the supplemental note to *Indicator 25* for further discussion. See the supplemental note to this indicator for a discussion of labor force statistics.

SOURCE: U.S. Department of Commerce, Bureau of the Census, March Current Population Surveys.

Percentage of 25- to 34-year-olds who were employed, by sex and years of school completed: March 1971–95

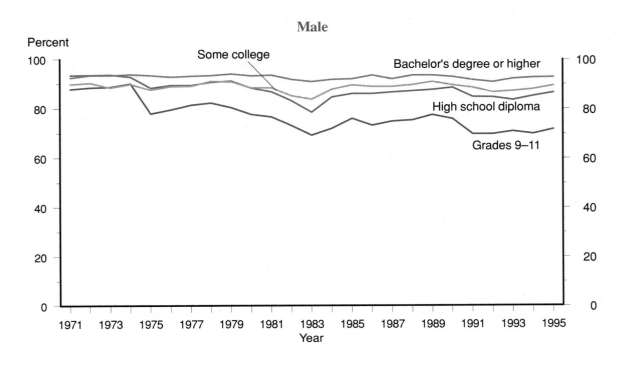

Male

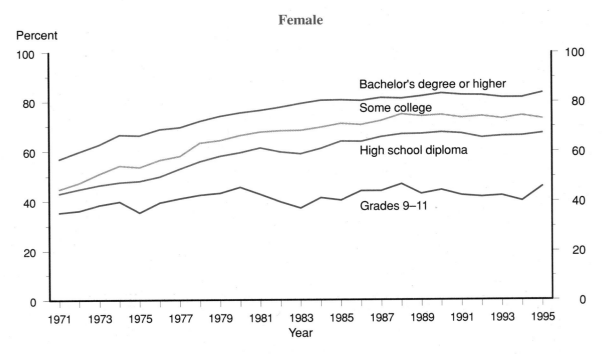

Female

NOTE: In 1992, the Current Population Survey (CPS) changed the questions used to obtain the educational attainment of respondents. The category "Grades 9–11" includes some who completed 12th grade but who have not received a high school diploma; "High school diploma" includes those who have an equivalency certificate; "Some college" includes those with an associate's degree or vocational certificate; and "Bachelor's degree or higher" includes those with an advanced degree. See the supplemental note to *Indicator 25* for further discussion. See the supplemental note to this indicator for a discussion of labor force statistics.

SOURCE: U.S. Department of Commerce, Bureau of the Census, March Current Population Surveys.

Weeks and hours worked, by educational attainment

♦ In 1994, 82 percent of males and 66 percent of females aged 25–34 in the work force with bachelor's degrees worked full time, year round, compared to 58 percent of males and 41 percent of females who had not completed high school.

> Individuals who complete higher levels of education, on average, have higher earnings, better benefits, and more satisfying work. One important determinant of these outcomes is steady work. Steady work generally brings valuable job experience and skills and, ultimately, more rewarding work. Without steady work, an individual's labor market opportunities are likely to worsen over time.

♦ Males who had not completed high school were more likely to work part year (fewer than 50 weeks) than those who had a bachelor's degree (35 compared to 15 percent) and to do so involuntarily (72 compared to 43 percent). Females who had not completed high school were also more likely to work part year than those who had a bachelor's degree (44 compared to 25 percent), but not more likely to do so involuntarily (35 and 29 percent, respectively).

Percentage distribution of 25- to 34-year-olds in the work force and, of those not employed full time and year round, the percentage for whom that status was involuntary,[1] by work status, sex, and educational attainment: 1994

Sex and educational attainment	Work status				Status involuntary[1]		
	Year-round, primarily full-time worker	Primarily part-time worker	Part-year worker	Non-worker[2]	Of part-time workers	Of part-year workers	Of non-workers
Total	67.1	14.1	24.9	2.1	26.3	48.7	64.4
Sex							
Male	74.5	7.4	20.8	1.6	42.1	65.9	85.5
Female	58.4	21.9	29.8	2.7	20.0	34.5	49.2
Educational attainment, by sex							
Male							
Less than high school completion	57.6	10.9	34.7	4.2	58.1	71.6	88.5
High school completion	73.8	5.6	22.3	1.8	62.1	79.4	90.2
Some college, no degree	76.4	8.8	18.1	1.1	34.1	64.8	—
Associate's degree	80.5	8.1	14.4	0.8	19.0	56.8	—
Bachelor's degree	82.1	6.0	14.8	0.8	26.8	42.5	—
Advanced degree	76.7	9.6	19.8	0.6	15.8	28.1	—
Female							
Less than high school completion	40.6	26.5	44.4	8.2	37.0	35.4	55.2
High school completion	57.1	22.6	30.1	3.5	20.9	39.0	53.6
Some college, no degree	55.7	26.1	31.5	1.9	17.6	32.1	43.5
Associate's degree	63.3	20.1	24.3	1.8	19.1	38.1	—
Bachelor's degree	65.9	18.1	25.0	1.0	13.2	28.9	—
Advanced degree	64.4	14.4	30.3	0.7	17.1	29.6	—

— Too few sample observations for a reliable estimate.

[1] "Involuntary" includes as the main reason for not working either full time or year round: the inability to find full-time work, a shortage of work/materials, illness, or disability. Those whose reasons were "other" are not included in this analysis.

[2] Includes those who did not work but who looked for work at least 1 week during the calendar year.

NOTE: The first four columns of the table do not add to 100 percent because part-time and part-year workers may overlap.

SOURCE: U.S. Department of Commerce, Bureau of the Census, March Current Population Survey, 1995.

Percentage distribution of 25- to 34-year-olds in the work force, by educational attainment: 1994

Percentage who worked full time and year round, by sex

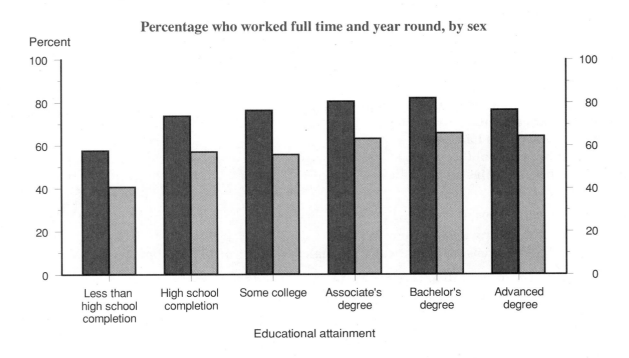

Percentage whose status of working only part of the year was involuntary, by sex

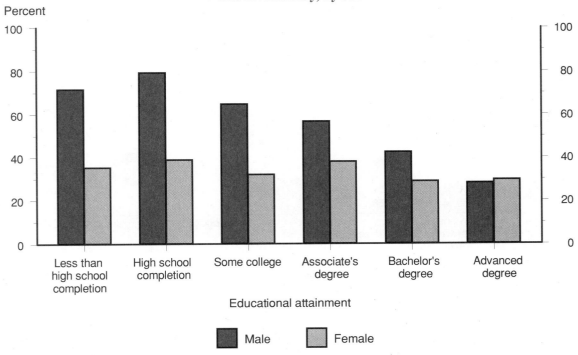

SOURCE: U.S. Department of Commerce, Bureau of the Census, March Current Population Survey, 1995.

Annual earnings of young adults

♦ **In 1994, the median annual earnings of young adults aged 25–34 who had not completed high school were substantially lower than those of their counterparts who had completed high school (32 and 42 percent* lower for males and females, respectively). Young adults who had completed a bachelor's degree or higher earned substantially more than those who had only completed high school (52 and 86 percent* more for males and females, respectively).**

Wages and salaries are influenced by many factors, including the employer's perception of the productivity and availability of workers with different levels of education and the economic conditions in the industries that typically employ workers with different levels of education. Annual earnings are influenced by the number of weeks worked in a year and the usual hours worked each week. The ratio of annual earnings of high school dropouts or college graduates to those of high school graduates is affected by all of these factors; it is a measure of the earnings disadvantage of not finishing high school and the earnings advantage of completing college.

♦ **Between 1974 and 1994, the earnings advantage of obtaining a bachelor's degree or higher increased dramatically for males (rising from 14 to 52 percent).**

♦ **Since 1970, the earnings advantage for 25- to 34-year-olds with some college or a bachelor's degree or higher was generally greater for females than for males.**

Ratio* of median annual earnings of wage and salary workers aged 25–34 whose highest education level was grades 9–11, some college, or a bachelor's degree or higher to those with a high school diploma, by sex: Selected years 1970–94

Year	Grades 9–11		Some college		Bachelor's degree or higher	
	Male	Female	Male	Female	Male	Female
1970	0.84	0.69	1.10	1.19	1.24	1.68
1972	0.80	0.70	1.04	1.16	1.19	1.63
1974	0.81	0.62	1.02	1.19	1.14	1.74
1976	0.78	0.61	1.03	1.14	1.19	1.58
1978	0.77	0.54	1.05	1.17	1.18	1.55
1980	0.73	0.65	1.04	1.24	1.19	1.52
1982	0.71	0.66	1.12	1.21	1.34	1.63
1984	0.63	0.56	1.15	1.21	1.36	1.61
1986	0.69	0.65	1.18	1.21	1.50	1.78
1988	0.68	0.56	1.10	1.31	1.42	1.81
1990	0.71	0.58	1.14	1.34	1.48	1.92
1991	0.64	0.64	1.14	1.32	1.53	1.90
1992	0.68	0.76	1.13	1.34	1.60	2.00
1993	0.67	0.59	1.12	1.31	1.57	1.99
1994	0.68	0.58	1.14	1.20	1.52	1.86

Table reads: In 1994, the median annual earnings for males whose highest education level was grades 9–11 were 68 percent of the median annual earnings of males who had a high school diploma.

* This ratio is most useful when compared to 1.0. For example, the ratio of 1.52 in 1994 for males whose highest education level was a bachelor's degree or higher means that they earned 52 percent more than males who had a high school diploma. The ratio of 0.68 in 1994 for males whose highest education level was grades 9–11 means that they earned 32 percent less than males who had a high school diploma.

NOTE: In 1992, the Current Population Survey (CPS), which collected earnings for calendar year 1991, changed the questions used to obtain educational attainment of respondents. The category "Grades 9–11" now includes some who completed 12th grade but who have not received a high school diploma; "High school diploma" includes those who have an equivalency certificate; "Some college" includes those with an associate's degree or vocational certificate; and "Bachelor's degree or higher" includes those with an advanced degree. See the supplemental note to *Indicator 25* for further discussion.

SOURCE: U.S. Department of Commerce, Bureau of the Census, March Current Population Surveys.

Ratio* of median annual earnings of wage and salary workers aged 25–34 whose highest education level was grades 9–11, some college, or a bachelor's degree or higher to those with a high school diploma, by sex: 1970–94

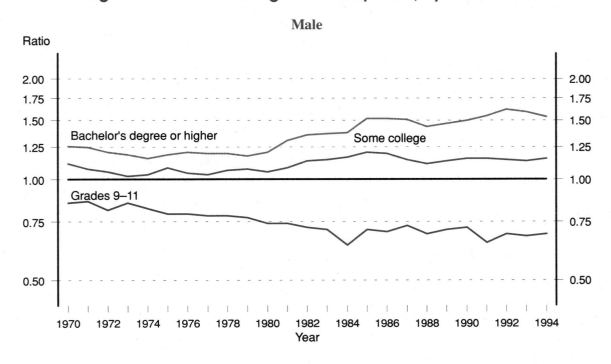

Male

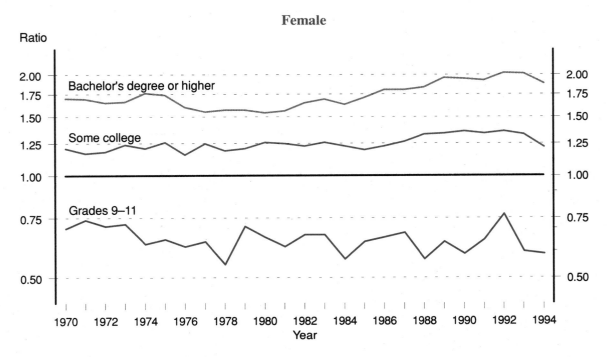

Female

* This ratio is most useful when compared to 1.0. For example, the ratio of 1.52 in 1994 for males whose highest education level was a bachelor's degree or higher means that they earned 52 percent more than males who had a high school diploma. The ratio of 0.68 in 1994 for males whose highest education level was grades 9–11 means that they earned 32 percent less than males who had a high school diploma.

SOURCE: U.S. Department of Commerce, Bureau of the Census, March Current Population Surveys.

Starting salaries of college graduates

♦ Between 1977 and 1993, college graduates who majored in computer sciences and engineering had much higher starting salaries than did graduates in all other fields of study; while the salary benefit of majoring in such fields was high, it declined between 1980 and 1993.

♦ Starting salaries among graduates who majored in the humanities or education have fluctuated over time, but in general, they were considerably lower than the starting salaries for all graduates. Salaries in both fields, however, rose relative to those of all graduates between 1984 and 1993.

> *One of the values that students place on the field of study they choose for their bachelor's degree is the earning potential associated with occupations in that field. Starting salaries offered by employers are related not only to the value of the skills learned by college graduates but also to the supply of qualified individuals. Thus, differences in starting salaries shed light on the changing demands of the labor market and the response of students and the education system to those changes.*

♦ Among 1993 graduates, females were much more likely than males to major in education, and males were more likely than females to major in computer sciences and engineering; the most common field of study for both males and females was business. The starting salary benefits for those who majored in business increased between 1986 and 1993.

♦ Median starting salaries for 1993 male graduates were substantially higher than those for female graduates, both overall and within certain fields of study including business, social and behavioral sciences, and natural sciences.

Percentage difference between median starting salaries for all college graduates and college graduates in particular major fields of study: Selected years of graduation 1977–93

Major field of study	Year of graduation					
	1977	1980	1984	1986	1990	1993
	Percent above or (below) median for all college graduates					
Humanities	(20.3)	(15.4)	(18.6)	(17.1)	(13.6)	(11.1)
Social and behavioral sciences	(10.6)	(11.4)	(12.6)	(8.8)	(9.4)	(9.0)
Natural sciences	(1.8)	(0.8)	(5.0)	(6.2)	(1.8)	(7.5)
Computer sciences and engineering	46.4	61.0	44.8	34.3	41.0	35.8
Education	(14.1)	(18.6)	(20.1)	(18.6)	(11.7)	(15.3)
Business and management	14.4	13.2	4.8	2.6	4.6	10.4
Other professional or technical	2.8	6.8	(1.3)	(2.9)	2.2	3.3

Annual median starting salaries (in 1995 constant dollars) of 1993 college graduates, by sex and major field of study, and the percentage difference between male and female starting salaries

Major field of study	All graduates	Male		Female		Percent female/male difference
		Percent in field	Median salary	Percent in field	Median salary	
Total	$22,968	100	$25,423	100	$21,401	*(15.8)
Humanities	20,413	9	21,210	12	20,062	(5.4)
Social and behavioral sciences	20,903	13	22,710	15	20,025	*(11.8)
Natural sciences	21,248	7	23,578	6	19,959	*(15.3)
Computer sciences and engineering	31,187	16	31,518	3	29,348	(6.9)
Education	19,450	6	20,668	17	19,125	(7.5)
Business and management	25,347	32	26,986	23	23,165	*(14.2)
Other professional or technical	23,731	17	23,711	23	23,746	0.1

* Male salaries greater than female salaries (p<0.05).
NOTE: Data presented pertain to bachelor's degree recipients who were working full time and who were not enrolled in postsecondary education 1 year after graduation.
SOURCE: U.S. Department of Education, National Center for Education Statistics, Recent College Graduates Surveys (1977–90) and 1993 Baccalaureate and Beyond Longitudinal Study, First Follow-up (B&B:93/94).

Starting salaries of college graduates

Percentage difference between median starting salaries for college graduates in all fields and college graduates in particular major fields of study: Selected years of graduation 1977–93

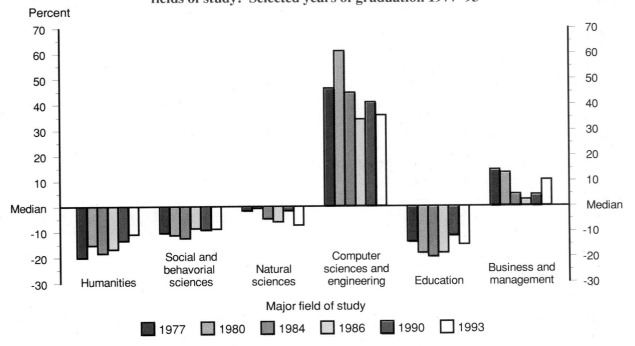

Median annual starting salaries (in 1995 constant dollars) of 1993 college graduates with measurable starting salary differences between males and females, by fields of study

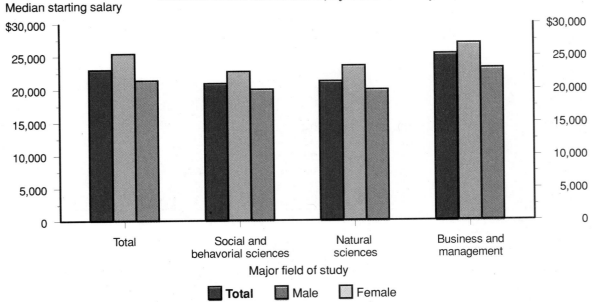

NOTE: Data presented pertain to bachelor's degree recipients who were working full time and who were not enrolled in postsecondary education 1 year after graduation.
SOURCE: U.S. Department of Education, National Center for Education Statistics, Recent College Graduates Surveys (1977–90) and 1993 Baccalaureate and Beyond Longitudinal Study, First Follow-up (B&B:93/94).

Welfare participation, by educational attainment

♦ In 1994, high school dropouts were more than twice as likely to receive income from Aid to Families with Dependent Children (AFDC) or public assistance as high school graduates who did not go on to college (14 compared to 6 percent).

♦ Between 1972 and 1994, high school dropouts, graduates who did not go on to college, and individuals with 13–15 years of school became more likely to receive AFDC or public assistance income.

> *Public investment in education has many potential benefits for the nation, including reduced reliance on welfare and public assistance programs among those who attain higher levels of education. The extent to which individuals with more education rely less on such income may be viewed, at least partly, as a return on the social cost of providing public education.*

Percentage of persons aged 25–34 who received income from AFDC or public assistance, by years of education completed: 1972–94

| | Years of school completed | | | | | | | | | | | |
| | All persons | | | | | | White | | Black | | Hispanic | |
Year*	All levels	Less than 9 years	9–11 years	12 years	13–15 years	16 years or more	9–11 years	12 years	9–11 years	12 years	9–11 years	12 years
1972	4.0	11.5	9.7	3.2	1.5	0.4	6.0	2.2	23.2	12.2	9.6	3.4
1973	3.9	11.7	10.3	3.3	1.7	0.6	5.6	2.1	25.9	12.1	16.2	5.5
1974	4.3	15.0	11.7	3.3	2.0	0.8	8.0	2.4	25.0	10.7	14.2	3.8
1975	3.6	11.3	11.0	3.3	1.5	0.3	7.0	2.4	27.8	10.0	10.6	3.4
1976	3.8	10.9	12.2	3.5	2.1	0.4	7.5	2.3	27.0	11.4	15.0	4.7
1977	3.9	11.7	12.0	3.9	2.1	0.3	8.0	2.6	26.4	12.4	13.1	6.6
1978	3.9	10.8	12.7	3.6	2.5	0.4	7.7	2.3	28.1	12.4	13.7	6.9
1979	3.9	12.4	12.8	3.8	2.1	0.6	7.9	2.5	26.8	12.0	15.1	5.4
1980	4.2	11.8	12.7	4.4	2.5	0.4	8.5	3.2	25.3	12.9	14.2	4.5
1981	4.4	11.5	13.6	4.6	2.7	0.5	9.5	2.9	29.1	14.9	13.3	5.0
1982	4.0	9.6	14.1	4.3	2.1	0.3	10.3	2.6	25.8	13.6	14.2	5.4
1983	4.2	11.4	14.7	4.3	2.5	0.3	10.7	2.6	26.8	13.4	15.5	5.2
1984	4.3	13.2	14.9	4.2	2.4	0.8	10.6	2.7	30.3	12.6	10.6	5.7
1985	4.2	11.8	14.0	4.4	2.6	0.4	9.5	3.1	30.7	11.7	13.2	5.2
1986	4.2	11.8	14.1	4.5	2.4	0.3	11.2	2.9	25.7	11.8	10.6	6.8
1987	4.2	13.2	12.5	4.5	2.5	0.3	7.8	2.9	28.5	12.4	10.7	5.9
1988	4.0	11.5	13.8	4.2	2.1	0.2	9.2	2.8	28.9	11.6	14.0	4.8
1989	3.9	8.8	13.4	4.1	2.4	0.4	8.5	2.9	30.3	10.9	12.0	4.4
1990	4.4	8.9	15.1	4.7	2.5	0.5	10.6	3.2	30.9	13.0	13.2	5.3
1991	5.0	11.4	16.0	5.5	3.1	0.5	11.9	4.0	28.6	13.1	15.1	6.0
1992	5.1	9.9	17.1	5.6	3.7	0.5	11.3	4.0	35.6	13.2	15.0	7.2
1993	5.3	9.6	16.2	6.3	3.7	0.4	11.5	3.8	31.3	15.9	14.6	8.2
1994	4.9	8.3	14.3	5.8	4.4	0.4	10.0	4.2	29.9	12.9	10.6	5.4

Table reads: In 1994, among persons aged 25–34 with 9–11 years of school, 14.3 percent received income from AFDC or public assistance. Among persons with 12 years of school, 5.8 percent received such income.

* Respondents were asked how much AFDC or public assistance income they received during the previous calendar year. In this table, the "Year" column reflects that calendar year, rather than the survey year.

NOTE: Beginning in 1992, the Current Population Survey (CPS) changed the questions used to determine the educational attainment of respondents. See the supplemental note to *Indicator 25* for further discussion.

SOURCE: U.S. Department of Commerce, Bureau of the Census, March Current Population Surveys.

Percentage of persons aged 25–34 who received income from AFDC or public assistance, by years of education completed: 1974, 1984, and 1994

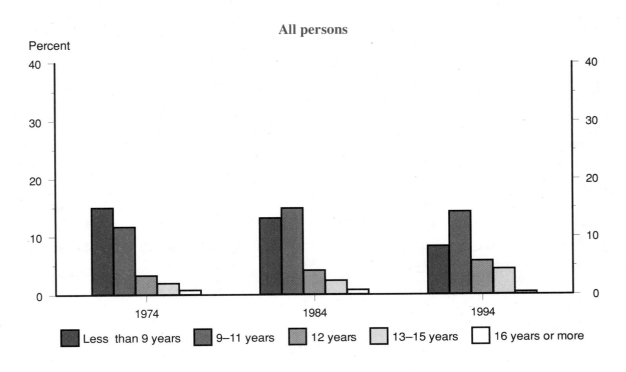

All persons

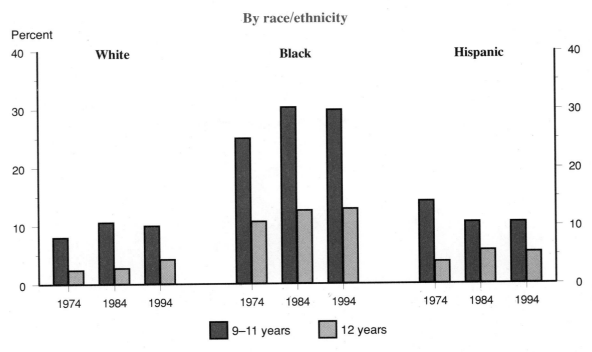

By race/ethnicity

SOURCE: U.S. Department of Commerce, Bureau of the Census, March Current Population Surveys.

Voting behavior, by educational attainment

♦ There is a strong positive relationship between voting behavior and educational attainment. As educational attainment increases, so does voting participation.

♦ In the 1994 congressional elections, college graduates aged 25–44 were 86 percent more likely than high school graduates to vote, while high school dropouts of the same age were 58 percent less likely than high school graduates to do so.

Education plays a vital role in preparing individuals to actively participate in the political, economic, and social lives of their communities. Voting rates for groups with differing amounts of education are one indication of the relationship between educational attainment and exercising civic responsibility, such as voting.

♦ Differences in voting behavior by educational attainment have generally widened over time among 25- to 44-year-olds.

♦ Young adults aged 18–24 who were enrolled in college were more likely to have voted in the 1994 congressional elections than their peers who were not enrolled in school (27 and 17 percent, respectively) (see supplemental table 37-1).

Voting rates and ratios of voting rates for the population aged 25–44, by type of election and educational attainment: Selected years 1964–94

Type of election and year	Total[1]	1–3 years of high school	4 years of high school	1–3 years of college	4 or more years of college
		Voting rates			
Congressional elections					
1974	42.2	24.7	41.9	49.7	59.3
1982	40.4	19.2	35.6	46.7	56.8
1990	40.7	17.8	34.4	47.9	57.4
1994[2]	39.1	12.9	30.6	45.7	57.0
Presidential elections					
1964	69.0	60.5	75.5	82.9	86.2
1976	58.7	38.5	57.8	67.4	78.5
1984	54.5	29.0	49.1	62.1	74.7
1988	54.0	26.3	47.4	61.7	75.0
1992[2]	58.3	27.0	49.8	66.9	78.5
		Ratio of voting rates to those of high school graduates			
Congressional elections					
1974	—	0.59	1.00	1.19	1.41
1982	—	0.54	1.00	1.31	1.59
1990	—	0.52	1.00	1.39	1.67
1994[2]	—	0.42	1.00	1.49	1.86
Presidential elections					
1964	—	0.80	1.00	1.10	1.14
1976	—	0.67	1.00	1.17	1.36
1984	—	0.59	1.00	1.27	1.52
1988	—	0.56	1.00	1.30	1.58
1992[2]	—	0.54	1.00	1.34	1.58

Table reads: In 1994, 57.0 percent of those aged 25–44 who had completed 4 or more years of college voted in the congressional election, 86 percent more than high school graduates.
— Not applicable.
[1] Includes those with less than 9 years of school.
[2] Beginning in 1992, the Current Population Survey (CPS) changed the questions used to obtain the educational attainment of respondents. See the supplemental note to *Indicator 25* for further discussion.
NOTE: To minimize the impact of age on voting trends, this table is confined to individuals aged 25–44. The voting rate is calculated as the number of voters aged 25–44 divided by the total number of individuals, both non-U.S. and U.S. citizens, in the age group.
SOURCE: U.S. Department of Commerce, Bureau of the Census, *Current Population Reports*, "Voting and Registration in the Election of November....," Series P-20, Nos. 143, 293, 322, 383, 440, 453, 466, and PPL-25.

Voting rates for the population aged 25–44, by type of election and educational attainment: Selected years 1964–94

Congressional elections

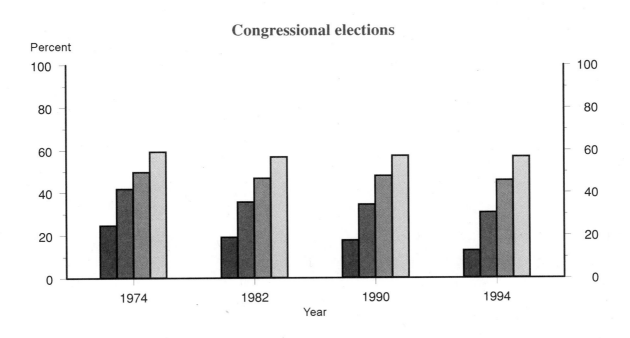

Presidential elections

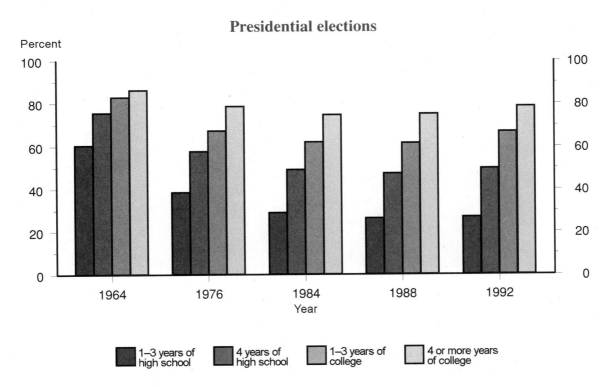

NOTE: Beginning in 1992, the Current Population Survey (CPS) changed the questions used to obtain the educational attainment of respondents. See the supplemental note to *Indicator 25* for further discussion.

SOURCE: U.S. Department of Commerce, Bureau of the Census, *Current Population Reports*, "Voting and Registration in the Election of November...," Series P-20, Nos. 143, 293, 322, 383, 440, 453, 466, and PPL-25.

The education system must adapt to demographic changes in the population, as well as respond to changing social and economic conditions. In turn, these changes in the education system influence major support industries, future entries to the labor force, and future economic activity. The indicators in this section provide some evidence of changes in the size, growth, and output of educational institutions.

Enrollment

In 1994, approximately 64 million people in the United States, almost one in four, were enrolled in elementary and secondary schools, colleges, and universities.[1] This figure included 36 million students in kindergarten through grade 8; 13.6 million in grades 9–12; 5.5 million in 2-year colleges; and 8.7 million in 4-year colleges and universities (tables 38-1 and 39-1).

Although most students are enrolled in public educational institutions, a considerable number are enrolled in private institutions. In 1995, private schools enrolled 12 percent of all students in grades K–8 and 9 percent of all students in grades 9–12 (*Indicator 38*). For postsecondary education, the split between public and private institutions depended strongly on the type of institution; private institutions enrolled 4 percent of all 2-year college students, but 33 percent of all 4-year college and university students in 1994 (table 39-1). Institutions with less-than-2-year programs are predominately private and for-profit.[2]

The amount of time students in kindergarten and higher education spent in school changed substantially between 1970 and 1992. For example, the percentage of kindergartners who attend full day has more than tripled between 1970 and 1992. Forty-four percent of kindergarten students attended full day in 1992, compared to 13 percent in 1970 (*Indicator 37, Condition 1994*). Moreover part-time undergraduates in colleges and universities were more prevalent in recent years (an average of 41.8 percent between 1989 and 1991) than they were two decades earlier (an average of 28.2 percent between 1969 and 1971).[3] However, most of this increase occurred between 1972 and 1982. Since then, the percentage of undergraduates attending college part time has remained fairly stable.

Growth of enrollment

After the end of World War II, the number of births per year reached a peak of 4.3 million in 1957. The baby boom period between 1946 and 1964 was followed by a period of declining births, which reached a low of 3.1 million in 1973. Since then, the number of births has gradually risen, peaking at 4.2 million in 1990.[4] These trends are reflected, with lags, in the growth and decline of enrollments. For example, between 1970 and 1985, total public school enrollment fell about 14 percent, whereas between 1985 and 1995, it rose 14 percent. Private school enrollment remained relatively stable between 1970 and 1995, rising about 6 percent (*Indicator 38*).

Changes in enrollment trends appear first in elementary schools, and later in secondary schools. Enrollment in public schools in kindergarten through grade 8 declined throughout the 1970s, reaching a low point in 1984, but has risen since then. Enrollment in public schools in grades 9–12 declined between 1976 and 1990, fluctuating slightly in the mid-1980s. It then increased between 1990 and 1995, and is projected to continue increasing into the 21st century (table 38-1).

In higher education, the level of enrollment is not as closely tied to the number of births as it is in elementary and secondary schools, where enrollment is nearly universal. Total enrollment in higher education rose throughout almost all of the 1970s, as would be expected, given the increasing number of high school graduates. In the first half of the 1980s, enrollment remained relatively stable with a small drop in 1984. It rose each year between 1985 and 1992, despite the falling number of high school graduates after 1988 (*Indicator 40*), but then dropped slightly between 1992 and 1994 (*Indicator 39*). Two of the factors that account for the continued growth in enrollment are increasing enrollment rates among new high school graduates (*Indicator 7*) and an increasing number of college-age people (as a result of the children of baby boomers entering college).

The distribution of total enrollment between public and private institutions has changed little over the last two decades. Public institutions continue to enroll nearly 8 out of every 10 students. Within the public sector, enrollment in 2-year institutions grew faster than it did in 4-

year institutions during the late 1980s and early 1990s. As a result, between 1985 and 1994, 2-year institutions increased their share of public enrollment from 35 to 37 percent, while 4-year institutions decreased their share from 43 to 41 percent (*Indicator 39*).

Diplomas and degrees

Whereas enrollment indicates the size of the education system, degree completions are one measure of the quantity of education the system is delivering. Each diploma or degree awarded indicates that the education system has made more knowledge and skill available in society. In 1994, public and private high schools awarded 2.5 million diplomas, and GED programs awarded half a million equivalency credentials.[5]

At the undergraduate level, the two most common credentials are the associate's and bachelor's degrees. The number of associate's degrees awarded, many of which are in occupationally specific fields, declined slightly during the late 1980s, following a period of rapid growth during the 1970s. The number of associate's degrees awarded increased in the early 1990s, and by 1993, more than half a million associate's degrees were awarded—representing an increase of 18 percent since 1988. The number of bachelor's degrees awarded grew throughout the 1980s and early 1990s. In 1993, colleges and universities awarded 1.2 million bachelor's degrees—25 percent more than in 1980 (table 40-1).

At the graduate level, more master's degrees were awarded than any other type of degree. In 1993, there were almost 370,000 master's degrees awarded, in contrast to 75,000 first-professional degrees and 42,000 doctor's degrees. The distribution of the type of degrees awarded changed somewhat during the last half of the 1980s. Following years of negative or little growth, the number of doctor's degrees awarded rose 28 percent between 1985 and 1993. Conversely, after a long period of growth, the number of first-professional degrees awarded decreased between 1985 and 1988, was stable through 1990, and then rose 6 percent between 1990 and 1993, returning to the 1985 level (table 40-1). The number of master's degrees awarded was 24 percent greater in 1993 than in 1980; this

number declined 5 percent between 1980 and 1984, and then increased annually after 1984.

Fields of study

In 1993, about one-third of the bachelor's degrees awarded were in the fields of the humanities and the social/behavioral sciences, and more than one-fifth were awarded in business management. Sixteen percent of bachelor's degrees awarded that year were in the fields of science and engineering (9 percent in computer sciences and engineering, and 7 percent in natural sciences) (table 41-3).

The distribution of bachelor's degrees across fields of study has shifted several times over the last two decades (table 41-3). The proportion of degrees awarded in the humanities and social/behavioral sciences decreased in the 1970s and early 1980s, but has increased every year since 1986. Between 1977 and 1989, bachelor's degrees awarded in the natural sciences declined as a percentage of all bachelor's degrees awarded, but remained fairly stable in the early 1990s. The proportion of degrees awarded in computer sciences and engineering grew in the late 1970s and early 1980s but has declined since 1986. The proportion of bachelor's degrees awarded in business management grew during the late 1970s and early 1980s, but declined slightly in the early 1990s. The percentage of bachelor's degrees awarded in education in 1993 (9 percent) was less than half of what it was in the early 1970s (21 percent).

NOTES:

[1] U.S. Department of Education, National Center for Education Statistcs, *Digest of Education Statistics, 1995*, table 3.

[2] U.S. Department of Education, National Center for Education Statistics. Integrated Postsecondary Education Data System (IPEDS), "Institutional Characteristics" survey.

[3] U.S. Department of Education, National Center for Education Statistics. *Digest of Education Statistics, 1995*, table 181.

[4] U.S. Department of Commerce, Bureau of the Census. *Statistical Abstract of the United States, 1995*, table 87.

[5] U.S. Department of Education, National Center for Education Statistics. *Digest of Education Statistics, 1995*, tables 98 and 100.

Elementary and secondary school enrollment

♦ From 1980 to 1995, total public school enrollment rose 14 percent, after falling 14 percent between 1970 and 1985; public schools continue to enroll almost 9 out of 10 children (see supplemental table 38-2).

♦ Total private school enrollment increased 4 percent between 1970 and 1985, but rose only 3 percent between 1985 and 1995.

♦ Total public school enrollment is projected to rise from 45.9 million in 1996 to 48.5 million by 2006, an increase of almost 6 percent. During this same period, total private school enrollment is expected to increase 5 percent, rising from 5.8 million to 6.1 million.

> School enrollment is one measure of the size of the education system and of the demand for teachers, buildings, and other resources. Past trends and projected future changes in the composition of enrollment across levels of education and regions of the country, as well as between public and private schools, indicate the types of teachers and other resources required. Demographics, such as birth rates and immigration, are a primary factor in determining elementary and secondary school enrollment.

♦ Between 1970 and 1994, the share of total public school enrollment increased in the South and West, while it declined in the Northeast and the Midwest.

Elementary and secondary school enrollment in thousands, by control and level of school, with projections: Selected years, fall 1970–2006

Year/period	Public schools			Private schools		
	Grades K–12[1]	Grades K–8[1]	Grades 9–12	Grades K–12[1]	Grades K–8[1]	Grades 9–12
1970	45,894	32,558	13,336	5,363	4,052	1,311
1985	39,422	27,034	12,388	5,557	4,195	1,362
1995[2]	45,076	32,383	12,693	5,700	4,431	1,269
	Projected			Projected		
1996	45,885	32,837	13,049	5,798	4,493	1,304
2006	48,528	33,507	15,021	6,086	4,585	1,501
	Percentage change			Percentage change		
1970–85	-14.1	-17.0	-7.1	3.6	3.5	3.9
1985–95[2]	14.3	19.8	2.5	2.6	5.6	-6.8
	Projected percentage change			Projected percentage change		
1996–2006	5.8	2.0	15.1	5.0	2.0	15.1

Table reads: Public school enrollment in grades K–12 declined from 45,894,000 in 1970 to 39,422,000 in 1985, a percentage change of -14.1.
[1] Includes kindergarten and some nursery school students.
[2] Estimates based on preliminary data.

Percentage distribution of public elementary and secondary school enrollment, by region: Selected years, fall 1970–94

Fall of year	Northeast	Midwest	South	West
1970	21.5	28.2	32.2	18.2
1975	21.6	27.4	32.7	18.3
1980	20.1	26.2	34.6	19.2
1985	18.6	25.0	35.8	20.6
1992[1]	17.6	23.8	35.9	22.7
1993[1]	17.6	23.7	35.9	22.8
1994[2]	17.7	23.6	35.8	22.9

Table reads: In 1970, 21.5 percent of the nation's public elementary and secondary school students were enrolled in schools in the Northeast.
[1] Revised from previously published figures.
[2] Estimated.
NOTE: See the note in supplemental table 38-3 for a definition of regions. Enrollment includes a relatively small number of nursery school students.
SOURCE: U.S. Department of Education, National Center for Education Statistics, *Digest of Education Statistics, 1995* (based on Common Core of Data) and *Projections of Education Statistics to 2006*, 1996.

Elementary and secondary school enrollment, by control and level of school and region

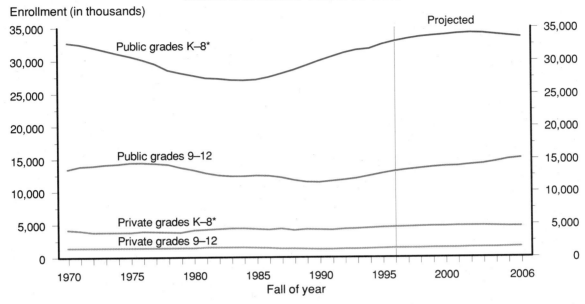

Elementary and secondary enrollment, by control and level of school: Fall 1970–2006

Enrollment (in thousands)

Projected

Public grades K–8*

Public grades 9–12

Private grades K–8*

Private grades 9–12

Fall of year

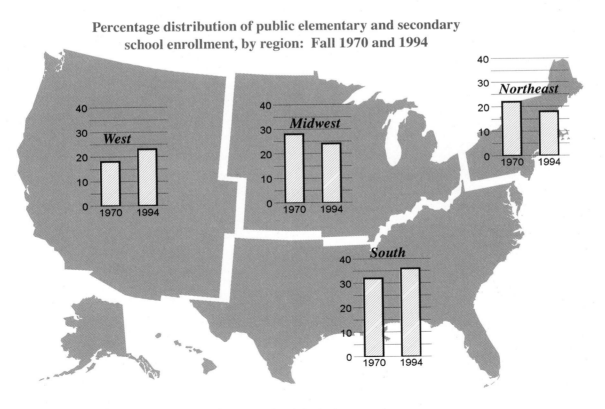

Percentage distribution of public elementary and secondary school enrollment, by region: Fall 1970 and 1994

West
1970 1994

Midwest
1970 1994

Northeast
1970 1994

South
1970 1994

* Enrollment includes a relatively small number of nursery school students.
SOURCE: U.S. Department of Education, National Center for Education Statistics, *Digest of Education Statistics, 1995* (based on Common Core of Data) and *Projections of Education Statistics to 2006,* 1996.

College and university enrollment, by type and control of institution

◆ After rising fairly steadily between 1972 and 1991, total enrollment in public 4-year institutions decreased slightly between 1991 and 1994. Total enrollment in private 4-year institutions grew during the 1970s, fluctuated between 1981 and 1985, and has grown steadily since then.

◆ Enrollment in public 2-year institutions fell between 1982 and 1985. However, between 1985 and 1992, it increased annually, with the largest growth occurring between 1990 and 1991. Enrollment fell slightly again between 1992 and 1994.

Colleges and universities offering 2- and 4-year programs under public and private control address somewhat different student needs. Fluctuations in enrollments may indicate, among other things, changes in student interest in the various kinds of services offered, the cost of attendance, and the availability of student financial aid.

◆ The distribution of total enrollment between public and private institutions has changed little over the last two decades. Public institutions continue to enroll nearly 8 out of every 10 students.

◆ Within the public sector, enrollment in 2-year institutions grew faster than it did in 4-year institutions during the late 1980s and early 1990s. As a result, 2-year public institutions increased their share of enrollment from 35 to 37 percent between 1985 and 1994.

Index and percentage of total enrollment in higher education, by control and type of institution: Fall 1972–94

Fall of year	Index of total enrollment (1981=100)					Percentage of total enrollment			
	All institutions	Public 4-year	Public 2-year	Private 4-year	Private 2-year	Public 4-year	Public 2-year	Private 4-year	Private 2-year
1972	74.5	85.7	58.9	81.5	48.9	48.1	28.7	22.0	1.3
1973	77.6	87.7	64.5	82.8	[1]52.0	47.2	30.1	21.5	1.3
1974	82.6	91.0	73.3	85.0	50.3	46.0	32.1	20.7	1.2
1975	90.4	96.7	85.6	89.1	56.8	44.7	34.3	19.8	1.2
1976	89.0	94.9	83.7	89.5	55.9	44.5	34.1	20.2	1.2
1977	91.2	95.7	87.1	92.3	59.9	43.8	34.6	20.4	1.3
1978	91.0	95.1	86.5	93.2	[1]65.7	43.6	34.4	20.6	1.4
1979	93.5	96.4	90.5	95.3	67.9	43.0	35.1	20.5	1.4
1980	97.8	99.3	96.6	98.1	83.9	42.4	35.8	20.2	1.6
1981	100.0	100.0	100.0	100.0	100.0	41.8	36.2	20.1	1.9
1982	100.4	100.2	100.9	99.5	100.4	41.7	36.4	19.9	2.0
1983	100.8	101.1	99.5	101.2	100.8	41.9	35.8	20.2	2.1
1984	99.0	100.6	95.5	101.0	99.0	42.5	35.0	20.5	2.1
1985	99.0	100.8	95.3	100.7	99.0	42.5	34.9	20.5	2.1
1986	101.1	102.6	98.5	101.4	101.1	42.4	35.3	20.2	2.1
1987	103.2	105.1	101.3	102.8	103.2	42.5	35.6	20.0	1.8
1988	105.5	107.3	103.0	105.8	105.5	42.5	35.4	20.2	2.0
1989	109.4	110.2	109.0	108.2	109.4	42.1	36.1	19.9	2.0
1990	111.7	113.2	111.5	109.7	111.7	42.3	36.2	19.8	1.8
1991	116.1	114.3	120.6	112.6	116.1	41.1	37.6	19.5	1.7
1992	117.1	114.2	122.4	115.1	117.1	40.7	37.9	19.8	1.6
1993	115.6	113.3	119.1	116.0	115.6	40.9	37.3	20.2	1.6
1994[2]	115.4	112.8	118.5	117.5	115.4	40.8	37.2	20.5	1.5

Table reads: In 1994, there were 15.4 percent more students enrolled in all institutions of higher education than there were in 1981; 40.8 percent of those students were enrolled in public 4-year institutions.
[1] Revised from previously published figures.
[2] Preliminary data.
SOURCE: U.S. Department of Education, National Center for Education Statistics, *Digest of Education Statistics, 1996* (based on IPEDS/HEGIS "Fall Enrollment" surveys), forthcoming.

Index and percentage of total enrollment in higher education, by control and type of institution: Fall 1972–94

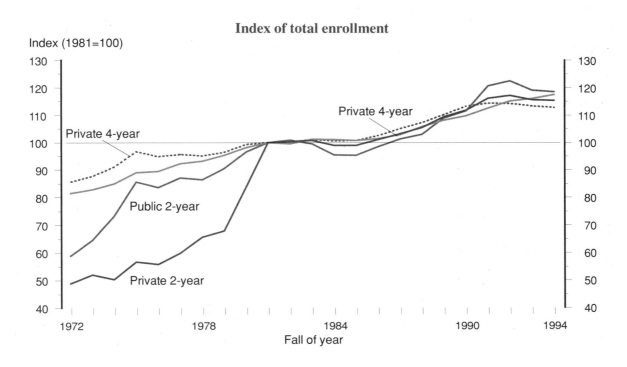

Index of total enrollment

Index (1981=100)

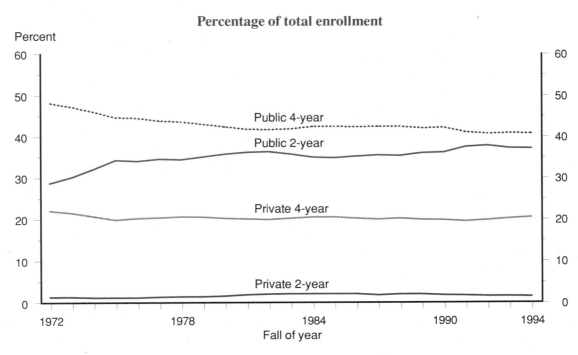

Percentage of total enrollment

SOURCE: U.S. Department of Education, National Center for Education Statistics, *Digest of Education Statistics, 1996* (based on IPEDS/HEGIS "Fall Enrollment" surveys), forthcoming.

Degrees conferred, by level

♦ In 1993, the number of associate's, bachelor's, master's, doctor's, and first-professional degrees awarded all reached their highest levels to date, despite a decline in the number of high school diplomas and GED credentials awarded during most of the 1980s and early 1990s.

♦ Following years of decline or little growth, the number of doctor's degrees conferred rose 28 percent between 1985 and 1993.

♦ The number of master's degrees conferred fell between 1977 and 1984, but increased each year after that, rising 30 percent between 1984 and 1993.

> Trends in the number of degrees conferred, by degree level, can indicate changes in the productivity of the nation's higher education system, the allocation of resources within the system, and the level of newly trained individuals within society. Viewed in relation to the eligible population—for example, the number of high school graduates—the data show whether degrees conferred have lagged behind or have exceeded growth in that population.

♦ After a period of decline in the mid-1980s, the number of both associate's and first-professional degrees conferred grew between 1988 and 1993 (18 and 7 percent, respectively).

Index of the number of degrees conferred (1981=100), by degree level, and the number of high school completions: Academic years ending 1971–93

Academic year ending	Associate's degrees	Bachelor's degrees	Master's degrees	Doctor's degrees	First-professional degrees[1]	High school diploma and GED recipients[2,3]
1971	[3]60.6	89.8	77.9	97.4	52.7	89.9
1972	[3]70.1	94.9	85.1	101.2	60.3	92.2
1973	75.9	98.6	89.1	105.5	69.5	93.3
1974	82.6	101.1	93.7	102.6	74.8	95.7
1975	86.5	98.7	98.9	103.4	77.7	98.7
1976	94.0	99.0	105.4	103.4	87.1	99.0
1977	97.6	98.3	107.2	100.8	89.4	98.9
1978	99.0	98.5	105.4	97.5	92.5	99.7
1979	96.7	98.5	101.8	99.3	95.7	100.5
1980	96.3	99.4	100.8	99.0	97.5	100.3
1981	100.0	100.0	100.0	100.0	100.0	100.0
1982	104.4	101.9	99.9	99.2	100.1	99.1
1983	[3]108.0	103.7	98.0	99.4	[3]101.5	95.6
1984	[3]108.6	104.2	96.1	100.8	[3]103.5	91.0
1985	109.2	104.7	96.8	100.0	104.3	88.2
1986	107.1	105.6	97.6	102.1	102.7	87.6
1987	104.8	106.0	97.8	103.3	99.5	89.5
1988	104.5	106.4	101.2	105.8	98.3	90.7
1989	104.9	108.9	105.0	108.4	98.5	87.8
1990	109.3	112.4	109.7	116.4	98.7	85.4
1991	115.7	117.0	114.0	119.2	100.0	84.5
1992	121.1	121.5	119.3	123.4	103.0	83.7
1993	123.6	124.6	125.0	127.8	104.8	84.3

Table reads: The number of associate's degrees conferred in 1993 was 23.6 percent greater than the number awarded in 1981.

[1] Includes degrees in chiropractic, dentistry, law, medicine, optometry, osteopathy, pharmacy, podiatry, theology, and veterinary medicine.

[2] "High school diploma and GED recipients" are graduates of regular public and private day school programs or recipients of GED credentials.

[3] Revised from previously published figures.

SOURCE: U.S. Department of Education, National Center for Education Statistics, *Digest of Education Statistics, 1995* (based on IPEDS/HEGIS "Degrees Conferred" surveys and Common Core of Data; American Council on Education, annual GED surveys).

Index of the number of degrees conferred (1981=100), by degree level, and the number of high school completions: Academic years ending 1971–93

Associate's and bachelor's degrees conferred and high school completions

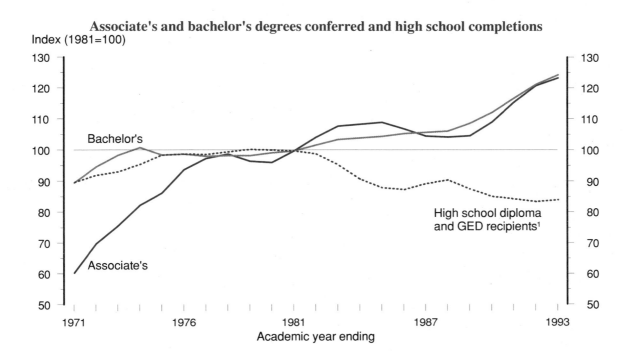

Advanced degrees

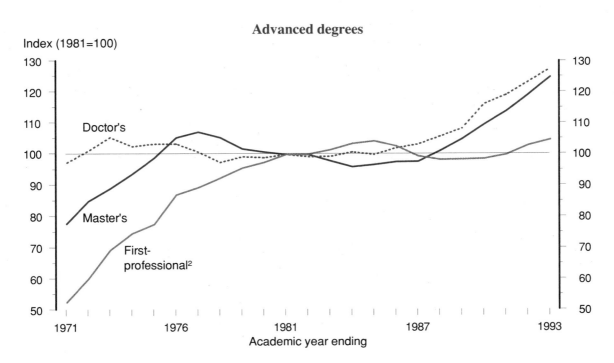

[1] "High school diploma and GED recipients" are graduates of regular public and private day school programs or recipients of GED credentials.
[2] Includes degrees in chiropractic, dentistry, law, medicine, optometry, osteopathy, pharmacy, podiatry, theology, and veterinary medicine.
SOURCE: U.S. Department of Education, National Center for Education Statistics, *Digest of Education Statistics, 1995* (based on IPEDS/HEGIS "Degrees Conferred" surveys and Common Core of Data; American Council on Education, annual GED surveys).

Bachelor's degrees conferred, by field of study

♦ After declining for several years, the number of degrees conferred in the humanities and the social and behavioral sciences has grown since the mid-1980s. Combined with business degrees, these three types of degrees have constituted half or more of all degrees conferred since 1971.

♦ After a sharp decline between 1986 and 1991, the number of degrees conferred in computer sciences and engineering leveled off between 1991 and 1993.

Changing opportunities within the job market affect the fields in which students choose to major. In turn, students' choices of major affect the demand for courses and faculty, as well as the supply of new graduates in different fields. Trends in the number and proportion of bachelor's degrees conferred in different fields help to identify these changing conditions.

♦ Natural science degrees as a percentage of all degrees conferred dropped from 10 percent in 1971 to less than 7 percent in 1993; a major factor in this decrease was the sharp decline in the percentage of degrees conferred in mathematics between 1971 and 1981 (see supplemental table 41-3).

♦ Business degrees grew as a percentage of all bachelor's degrees conferred between 1971 and 1988, when they reached a peak of 24 percent. Between 1988 and 1993, their share of total degrees fell to 22 percent (see supplemental table 41-3).

Index of the number of bachelor's degrees conferred and the percentage of total bachelor's degrees conferred, by field of study: Selected academic years ending 1971–93

Field of study	1971	1976	1981	1986	1991	1992	1993
	Index of the number of degrees (1981=100)						
All fields	**89.8**	**99.0**	**100.0**	**105.6**	**117.0**	**121.5**	**124.6**
Humanities	107.1	112.4	100.0	99.0	128.6	138.7	145.1
Social/behavioral sciences	136.7	124.8	100.0	95.0	129.8	139.5	143.0
Life sciences	82.7	125.6	100.0	89.1	91.5	99.4	108.8
Physical sciences	89.4	89.6	100.0	90.7	68.2	70.8	73.3
Mathematics	218.1	142.8	100.0	150.0	133.9	129.3	129.6
Computer and information sciences	15.8	37.4	100.0	277.0	165.9	162.4	160.0
Engineering	70.9	60.7	100.0	120.4	97.2	96.7	97.9
Engineering technologies	44.0	67.8	100.0	165.9	146.2	139.5	137.3
Education	163.1	142.9	100.0	80.6	102.5	99.9	99.7
Business management	57.7	71.4	100.0	119.3	125.3	129.0	129.1
Health sciences	39.6	84.8	100.0	101.2	92.8	97.0	105.4
Other technical/professional	43.2	86.6	100.0	97.3	109.2	119.4	124.7
	Percentage of total degrees						
All fields	**100.0**	**100.0**	**100.0**	**100.0**	**100.0**	**100.0**	**100.0**
Humanities	17.1	16.3	14.3	13.4	15.7	16.3	16.7
Social/behavioral sciences	23.0	19.1	15.1	13.6	16.8	17.4	17.4
Life sciences	4.3	5.9	4.6	3.9	3.6	3.8	4.0
Physical sciences	2.5	2.3	2.6	2.2	1.5	1.5	1.5
Mathematics	3.0	1.8	1.2	1.7	1.4	1.3	1.3
Computer and information sciences	0.3	0.6	1.6	4.2	2.3	2.2	2.1
Engineering	5.3	4.1	6.8	7.7	5.6	5.4	5.3
Engineering technologies	0.6	0.9	1.3	2.0	1.6	1.4	1.4
Education	21.0	16.7	11.6	8.8	10.1	9.5	9.3
Business management	13.7	15.3	21.3	24.0	22.8	22.6	22.0
Health sciences	3.0	5.9	6.8	6.5	5.4	5.4	5.8
Other technical/professional	6.2	11.2	12.8	11.8	12.0	12.6	12.9

Table reads: The number of degrees conferred in the humanities in 1993 was 45.1 percentage points higher than the number conferred in 1981. In 1993, the percentage of humanities degrees conferred was 16.7 percent of all degrees conferred.

SOURCE: U.S. Department of Education, National Center for Education Statistics, *Digest of Education Statistics, 1995* (based on IPEDS/HEGIS "Degrees Conferred" surveys).

Index of the number of bachelor's degrees conferred (1981=100), by selected fields of study: Academic years ending 1971–93

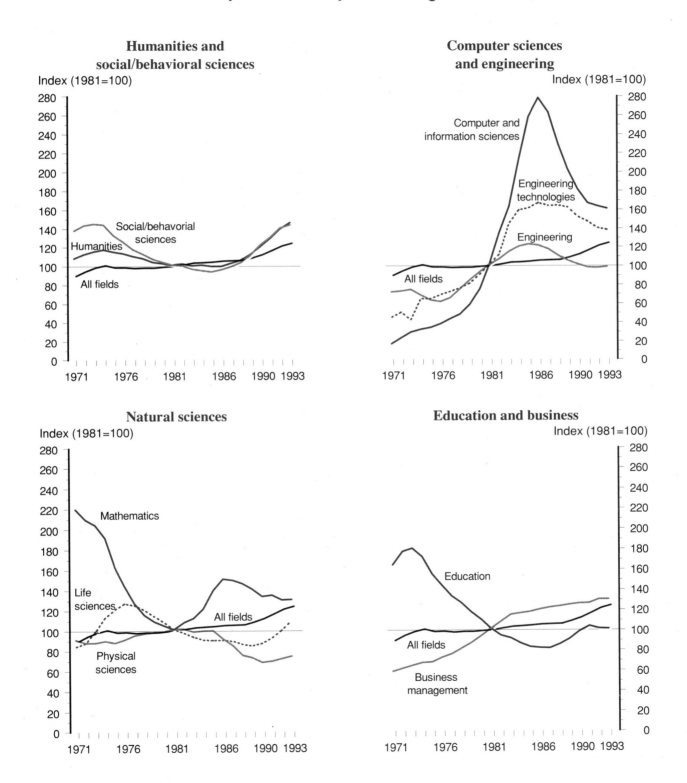

Humanities and social/behavioral sciences

Index (1981=100)

Computer sciences and engineering

Index (1981=100)

Natural sciences

Index (1981=100)

Education and business

Index (1981=100)

SOURCE: U.S. Department of Education, National Center for Education Statistics, *Digest of Education Statistics, 1995* (based on IPEDS/HEGIS "Degrees Conferred" surveys).

Climate, Classrooms, and Diversity in Educational Institutions

Education quality is reflected not only in the subjects taught and student achievement levels, but also in the learning environment in schools. A school's learning environment is enhanced by the diversity of its students, opportunities they have for community involvement, and their access to teachers. Teachers, in turn, affect school climate by their involvement in policy decisions, autonomy in their classrooms, and use of professional time.

Diversity of students

The characteristics and needs children bring to school based on their family backgrounds, economic well being, disabilities, and race/ethnicity influence the environment in which learning occurs.

Race/ethnicity

The racial/ethnic composition of the student population contributes to the increasing linguistic and cultural diversity of our nation's elementary and secondary schools. Along with the rich opportunities for learning that diversity brings, come challenges and risks associated with poverty, which is more concentrated among minority than nonminority students. Growth in the Hispanic population over the past decades has increased their representation in schools of all types. Like black students, Hispanic students are more concentrated in central city public schools than in other areas. In 1993, black and Hispanic students together made up over 50 percent of students in central city public schools (*Indicator 40, Condition 1995*).

There is less student racial/ethnic diversity at the postsecondary level than at the elementary and secondary levels. In 1992, one out of five postsecondary students was a member of a minority group, compared to one out of three public elementary/secondary students (*Indicator 45*). This difference is due both to lower college enrollment rates of minorities, with the exception of Asian/Pacific Islanders, and to their smaller representation in the college-aged population. Colleges and universities have sought to increase the racial/ethnic diversity of their student bodies, and since the mid-1970s, minority enrollment has increased from 15 to 23 percent. This increase is due primarily to increased enrollment of Hispanic and Asian/Pacific Islander students, whereas the enrollment of black students has remained fairly steady at 9 to 10 percent of all students. Minority students were more concentrated in 2-year than in

4-year institutions, with the difference due mostly to the higher proportion of Hispanic students in 2-year institutions. At 4-year institutions, the proportion of black students was twice that of Hispanic students.

Poverty

After declining in the 1960s, the percentage of children in poverty rose to nearly 22 percent in 1983, and has fluctuated between 19 and 22 percent since then. Black and Hispanic children were more than twice as likely as white children to be poor (*Indicator 44*). Both the increased incidence of poverty among black and Hispanic children and their concentration in central city public schools have implications for those schools.

Students with disabilities

The number of students participating in federal programs for children with disabilities has been increasing at a faster rate then total public school enrollment. Between 1977 and 1994, the number of students who participated in federal programs for children with disabilities increased 46 percent, while total public school enrollment decreased 2 percent (table 43-1). This increase was also characterized by a shift in the classification of students by type of disability: the percentage of students with specific learning disabilities doubled, and those with speech and language impairments and with mental retardation decreased (*Indicator 43*).

Climate

Student absenteeism and tardiness

Exposure to classroom learning is limited by the amount of time students spend there. When students are absent or tardy, they not only forgo their own learning opportunities, but also may interfere with the learning opportunities of their classmates. On a typical school day in 1994, nearly 6 percent of students in the nation were absent from school (*Indicator 42*). In general, more students were absent in public than private schools, and in central city than suburban schools. In public schools, absenteeism increased with the grade level of the school, ranging from 5 percent in elementary to 8 percent in high schools. Teachers' perceptions of the seriousness of absenteeism, tardiness, and cutting class follow similar patterns: in central city high schools, between 25 and 50 percent of teachers consider these problems to be serious.

Drugs and alcohol are detrimental to individual users. When they are used in and around schools, they also are detrimental to learning and may create other problems. The same is true of school crime. Although in-school drug and alcohol use has fallen dramatically over the past decade, it appears again to be rising. Students still encounter people trying to sell drugs at school, and this is more likely to occur in public than in private schools, and in urban rather than rural schools (*Indicator 48, Condition 1995*). While drug use has declined, student crime and victimization rates have leveled off (*Indicator 47, Condition 1995*). However, the percentage of teachers who reported physical conflict among students and possession of weapons as problems in their schools has increased (NCES, "How Safe Are the Public Schools: What do Teachers Say?", *SASS Issue Brief, 1995*).

Participation in community service

Student participation in community service is seen as beneficial to both students and the projects and people they serve, and is required in many high schools for graduation. Forty-four percent of 1992 high school seniors had performed some type of community service in the previous 2 years, most of it on a strictly voluntary basis (*Indicator 46*). Overall, 8 percent of seniors participated because it was required for a class, but this varied from 34 percent of students in Catholic schools to 6 percent of students in public schools.

Classrooms

Teachers' authority to set school policy; their autonomy to determine what and how subjects are taught in their classrooms; and the amount of time they spend teaching and interacting with students are all conditions that vary by school, and may influence the quality of the educational enterprise.

Participation in school and classroom decision making

In general, both public and private school teachers believe that individually they have more control over decisions affecting their own classrooms than they do as a group over decisions affecting the school as a whole (*Indicator 47*). Perceived influence, both at the school level and within the classroom, is more widespread among private than public school teachers, and among secondary than elementary teachers, with the exception of disciplining students, in which case more elementary than secondary teachers perceive they have considerable control.

Teacher workload and use of time

On average, both public and private school teachers, elementary and secondary, new and experienced, worked well beyond a 40 hour week in school year 1993–94 (*Indicator 48*). Although, on average, public and private school teachers were required to be at school 33 to 35 hours per week, they spent an additional 11 to 15 hours after school and on weekends in school-related activities. About one-fourth of these extra hours were spent interacting with students in activities such as coaching, tutoring, field trips, and transporting students. The remaining time was spent on activities such as preparing for classes, grading papers, and attending parent conferences and meetings. Less experienced teachers (those with less than 4 years of classroom experience) tended to spend more extra time (ranging from a half to two hours per week) than did more experienced teachers, but this time was allocated in the same proportions to student-related activities versus other types of activities.

As college costs have continued to rise, students and parents have joined in the debate on how faculty balance their time, focusing on how much time students are taught by professors versus lecturers and instructors. Between 1987 and 1992, a shift occurred among full-time faculty in how they allocated their time to these activities, as faculty in general tended to spend less of their time teaching (from 61 to 58 percent) and more on service and other duties (from 3 to 5 percent) (*Indicator 49*). And although instructors and lecturers were still likely to spend a greater portion of their time teaching than were professors, there was an increase across almost all levels of faculty in the number of student contact hours. Allocation of faculty time varies by type of institution; however, faculty at 2-year institutions spend more of their time teaching (almost 70 percent) and have many more student contact hours than faculty at 4-year institutions. In the progression from liberal arts and comprehensive colleges to doctoral and research universities, faculty spent proportionately less time teaching and more time conducting research. Overall, however, faculty in 1992 spent relatively less time teaching and more time on service and other duties than they did 5 years earlier.

Student absenteeism and tardiness

♦ Overall, an average of 6 percent of all students were absent on a typical school day in 1993–94. In each urbanicity type, students in public schools were more likely than those in private schools to be absent.

♦ In public schools, the absentee rate was highest in central city and lowest in rural schools. In public central city schools, the absentee rate increased with school level and the percentage of students who were eligible for free or reduced-price lunch.

> *An important aspect of students' access to education is the amount of time they actually spend in the classroom. When students are absent from school, arrive late, or cut class, they forgo opportunities to learn. Furthermore, when students disrupt classes by being late or absent, they interfere with lessons in progress and with other students' opportunities to learn.*

♦ In public elementary, middle, and combined schools, absentee rates generally increased with rates of student poverty, as measured by the percentage of students eligible for free or reduced-price lunch (see supplemental table 42-1).

♦ In central city public high schools with a high poverty level (schools where more than 40 percent of students were eligible for free or reduced-price lunch), the average absentee rate was 12 percent (see supplemental table 42-1). In these high schools, 59 percent of teachers considered absenteeism, 47 percent considered tardiness, and 40 percent considered cutting class to be a serious problem (see supplemental table 42-2).

♦ Public school teachers' perceptions of the seriousness of absenteeism, tardiness, and cutting class rose sharply from elementary to middle school, and from middle to high school (see supplemental table 42-2).

Average percentage of students absent on a typical school day, by urbanicity and other selected school characteristics: School year 1993–94

| Urbanicity | Total | Control | | Public school level | | | | Percentage of students eligible for free or reduced-price lunch in public high schools | | | |
		Public	Private	Elemen-tary	Middle	High	Com-bined	0–5	6–20	21–40	41–100
Total	**5.5**	**5.9**	**4.1**	**5.2**	**6.3**	**8.0**	**7.1**	**8.7**	**7.4**	**7.9**	**8.6**
Central city	5.7	6.4	4.2	5.5	7.0	9.7	9.8	7.6	9.0	10.5	12.0
Urban fringe/ large town	5.3	6.0	3.7	5.0	6.3	8.8	8.6	8.7	7.9	10.5	8.6
Rural/small town	5.3	5.6	4.1	4.9	5.7	7.2	5.8	9.7	6.6	6.5	7.5

Percentage of teachers who reported that absenteeism or tardiness was a serious problem in their school, by urbanicity and other selected school characteristics: School year 1993–94

| Urbanicity | Total | Control | | Public school level | | | | Percentage of students eligible for free or reduced-price lunch in public high schools | | | |
		Public	Private	Elemen-tary	Middle	High	Com-bined	0–5	6–20	21–40	41–100
						Absenteeism					
Total	**12.9**	**14.4**	**2.2**	**6.8**	**10.9**	**29.0**	**26.3**	**18.0**	**25.9**	**34.8**	**38.8**
Central city	18.2	21.9	2.1	11.9	18.1	45.5	44.5	25.8	33.9	51.6	58.6
Urban fringe/ large town	12.1	13.9	2.2	5.8	8.6	30.6	29.2	18.5	30.7	43.5	52.9
Rural/small town	9.3	9.8	2.4	3.8	7.8	19.6	15.7	14.3	18.7	22.1	20.6
						Tardiness					
Total	**9.5**	**10.6**	**2.5**	**5.7**	**9.7**	**19.4**	**16.5**	**13.4**	**18.0**	**19.6**	**27.5**
Central city	14.8	17.6	2.8	10.7	18.0	33.0	28.5	23.5	22.1	31.8	47.2
Urban fringe/ large town	9.4	10.5	2.7	5.8	7.8	20.0	19.5	13.1	21.9	23.3	30.0
Rural/small town	5.5	5.8	1.7	1.8	5.5	12.1	9.1	10.0	13.2	11.6	12.1

SOURCE: U.S. Department of Education, National Center for Education Statistics, Schools and Staffing Survey, 1993–94 (Teacher and School Questionnaires).

Student absenteeism and tardiness, by selected school characteristics: School year 1993–94

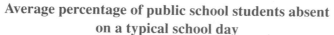

Average percentage of public school students absent on a typical school day

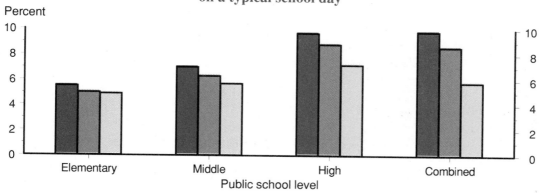

Percentage of public high school teachers who reported that absenteeism was a serious problem in their school

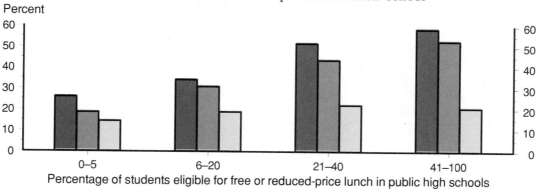

Percentage of public high school teachers who reported that tardiness was a serious problem in their school

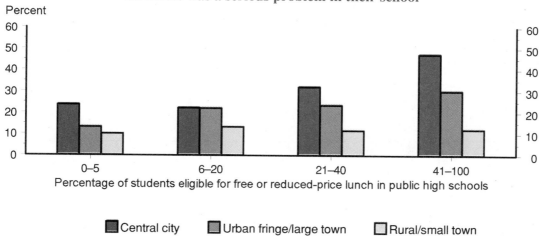

SOURCE: U.S. Department of Education, National Center for Education Statistics, Schools and Staffing Survey, 1993–94 (Teacher and School Questionnaires).

Education of students with disabilities

◆ The number of students participating in federal programs for children with disabilities has been increasing at a faster rate than total public school enrollment. Between 1977 and 1994, the number of students who participated in federal programs for children with disabilities increased 46 percent, while total public school enrollment decreased 2 percent (see supplemental table 43-1).

> *The Individuals with Disabilities Education Act (IDEA) mandates that all children have available to them a free and appropriate education designed to meet their unique needs. Changes in the number and distribution of students with disabilities affect the level of effort required of educators and policymakers to comply with the current law and help them to forecast the need for future resources.*

◆ In 1992, males with specific learning disabilities represented 7 percent of total public school enrollment, while females with this type of disability accounted for only 3 percent (see supplemental table 43-4).

◆ The percentage of disabled students identified as having specific learning disabilities rose 24 percentage points (from 22 to 46 percent) between 1977 and 1994, while the proportion identified as mentally retarded or with speech or language impairments each fell 16 percentage points (from 26 to 10 percent and from 35 to 19 percent of the total, respectively).

◆ The ratio of the number of students with specific learning disabilities per special education teacher serving them increased from 18 to 24 between 1977 and 1993. However, the ratio for all students with disabilities decreased over the same period; in 1977, there were 21 students per teacher, and in 1993, 16 students per teacher (see supplemental table 43-6).

Children from birth to age 21 who were served by federally supported programs for students with disabilities, by type of disability: Selected school years ending 1977–94

Type of disability	1977	1979	1981	1983	1985	1987	1989	1991	1993[1]	1994
	Percentage distribution									
All disabilities	100.0	100.0	100.0	100.0	100.0	100.0	100.0	100.0	100.0	100.0
Specific learning disabilities	21.6	29.1	35.3	40.9	42.5	43.8	43.7	44.7	45.9	45.5
Speech or language impairments	35.3	31.2	28.2	26.6	26.1	26.0	21.3	20.7	19.4	18.8
Mental retardation	26.0	23.2	20.0	17.8	16.1	14.7	12.4	11.2	10.1	10.3
Serious emotional disturbance	7.7	7.7	8.4	8.3	8.6	8.8	8.3	8.2	7.8	7.7
Preschool disabled[2]	(²)	(²)	(²)	(²)	(²)	(²)	8.7	9.3	10.4	10.9
	As a percentage of total public K–12 enrollment[1]									
All disabilities	8.3	9.1	10.1	10.8	11.0	11.0	11.3	11.6	12.0	12.4
Specific learning disabilities	1.8	2.7	3.6	4.4	4.7	4.8	4.9	5.2	5.5	5.6
Speech or language impairments	2.9	2.9	2.9	2.9	2.9	2.9	2.4	2.4	2.3	2.3
Mental retardation	2.2	2.1	2.0	1.9	1.8	1.6	1.4	1.3	1.2	1.3
Serious emotional disturbance	0.6	0.7	0.8	0.9	0.9	1.0	0.9	0.9	0.9	1.0
Preschool disabled[2]	(²)	(²)	(²)	(²)	(²)	(²)	1.0	1.1	1.2	1.4

Table reads: In 1994, the number of children served by federally supported programs for students with disabilities equaled 12.4 percent of public K–12 enrollment.

[1] Revised from previously published figures.

[2] Prior to the 1987–88 school year, preschool disabled students were included in the counts by disabling condition. Beginning in the 1987–88 school year, states were no longer required to report preschool students (0–5 years) with disabilities by disabling condition.

NOTE: This analysis includes students who were served under Chapter 1 of the Education Consolidation and Improvement Act (ECIA) and Part B of IDEA.

SOURCE: U.S. Department of Education, Office of Special Education and Rehabilitative Services, *Annual Report to Congress on the Implementation of the Individuals with Disabilities Education Act*, various years; and National Center for Education Statistics, *Digest of Education Statistics, 1995.*

Children from birth to age 21 who were served by federally supported programs for students with disabilities, by type of disability: School years ending 1977–94

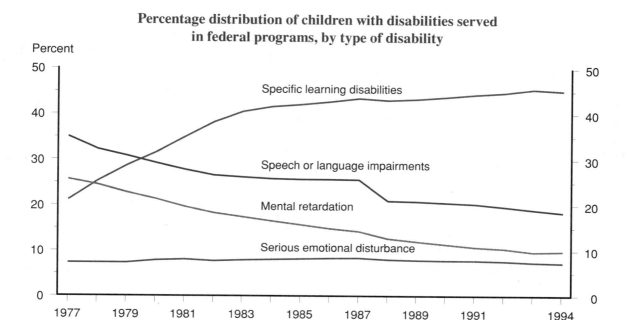

Percentage distribution of children with disabilities served in federal programs, by type of disability

Percent

- Specific learning disabilities
- Speech or language impairments
- Mental retardation
- Serious emotional disturbance

Year

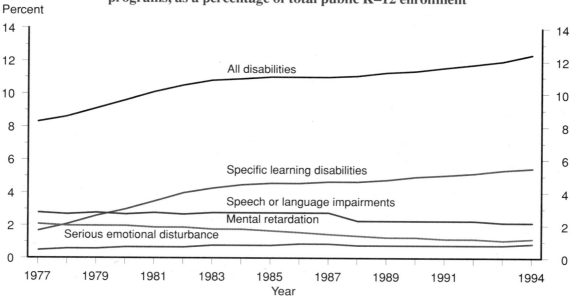

Number of children with disabilities who were served by federal programs, as a percentage of total public K–12 enrollment

Percent

- All disabilities
- Specific learning disabilities
- Speech or language impairments
- Mental retardation
- Serious emotional disturbance

Year

NOTE: Includes students who were served under Chapter 1 of ECIA and Part B of IDEA. Prior to the 1987–88 school year, preschool students were included in the counts by disabling condition. Beginning in the 1987–88 school year, states were no longer required to report preschool students (0–5 years) with disabilities by disabling condition.
SOURCE: U.S. Department of Education, Office of Special Education and Rehabilitative Services, *Annual Report to Congress on the Implementation of the Individuals with Disabilities Education Act*, various years; and National Center for Education Statistics, *Digest of Education Statistics, 1995.*

Children in poverty

♦ Of all children, the proportion who live in families with incomes below the poverty level decreased substantially during the 1960s to 15 percent in 1970, then rose to 22 percent in 1983. Between 1983 and 1994, the poverty rate for children has fluctuated between 19 and 22 percent.

♦ In 1994, both black and Hispanic children were more than twice as likely as white children to live in poverty.

♦ Since 1975, at least half the children in poverty lived in a female-headed household. The percentage of children in poverty who lived in a female-headed household increased to a high of 59 percent in 1988 and has fluctuated between 55 and 59 percent from 1988 to 1994.

> *The effects of poverty on children's education are well documented. Children from poor families have lower than average achievement and higher than average dropout rates. These children may not come to school ready to learn, and therefore may need additional services.*

♦ Between 1960 and 1994, the percentage of black children in poverty who lived in a female-headed household was consistently higher than the percentage of white or Hispanic children who did so. In 1994, 82 percent of black children in poverty lived in a female-headed household, compared to 46 percent of white and Hispanic children.

Percentage of children less than 18 years old who live in families with incomes below the poverty level: Selected years 1960–94

Year	Percent of children who live in poverty				Percent of children in poverty who live with a female householder[1]			
	Total	White	Black	Hispanic[2]	Total	White	Black	Hispanic[2]
1960[3]	26.5	20.0	65.6	—	23.8	21.0	29.4	—
1965[4]	20.7	14.4	47.4	—	31.7	27.0	49.7	—
1970	14.9	10.5	41.5	—	45.8	36.6	60.8	—
1975	16.8	12.5	41.4	[5]33.1	51.4	41.7	70.1	41.0
1980	17.9	13.4	42.1	33.0	52.8	41.3	75.4	47.1
1981	19.5	14.7	[5]44.9	35.4	52.2	42.0	74.3	48.5
1982	21.3	16.5	47.3	38.9	—	—	—	—
1983	21.8	17.0	46.2	37.7	50.0	39.3	74.5	42.5
1984	21.0	16.1	46.2	38.7	52.4	41.8	74.9	47.2
1985	20.1	15.6	43.1	39.6	53.8	43.0	78.4	49.6
1986	19.8	15.3	[5]42.7	37.1	56.6	45.7	80.5	49.5
1987[5]	19.7	14.7	44.4	38.9	57.4	47.0	80.2	47.6
1988[5]	19.0	14.0	42.8	37.3	59.3	50.0	79.6	49.1
1989	19.0	14.1	43.2	35.5	56.7	46.3	78.1	46.4
1990	19.9	15.1	44.2	37.7	57.9	46.9	80.3	47.8
1991	21.1	16.1	45.6	39.8	59.0	47.4	83.1	47.0
1992[5]	21.6	16.5	46.3	39.0	55.3	43.2	79.1	37.5
1993	22.0	17.0	45.9	39.9	56.8	45.0	81.6	45.6
1994	21.2	16.3	43.3	41.1	57.7	46.4	82.2	45.6

Table reads: In 1994, 21.2 percent of all children less than 18 years old lived in families with incomes below the poverty level.
— Not available.
[1] No husband is present in the household. The householder is the person who owns or rents the housing unit.
[2] Hispanics may be of any race.
[3] Data presented for 1960 include 1959 data for blacks and 1960 data for whites and total.
[4] Data presented for 1965 include 1967 data for blacks and 1965 data for whites and total.
[5] Revised from previously published figures.

SOURCE: U.S. Department of Commerce, Bureau of the Census, *Current Population Reports*, Series P-60, "Income, Poverty, and Valuation of Non-cash Benefits: 1994" (based on March Current Population Surveys).

Percentage of children less than 18 years old who live in families with incomes below the poverty level: Selected years 1960–94

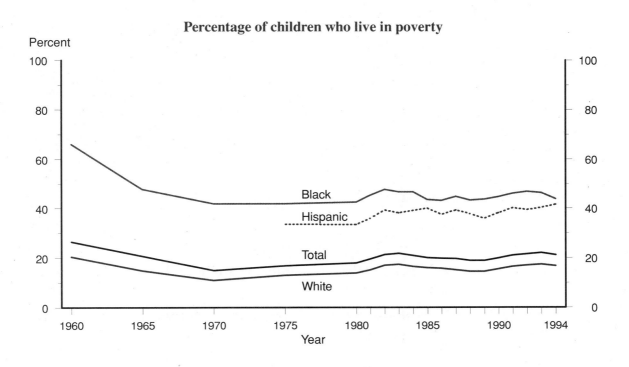

Percentage of children who live in poverty

Percent

Black

Hispanic

Total

White

Year

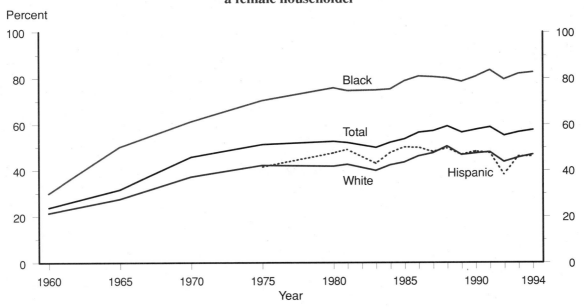

Percentage of children in poverty who live with a female householder

Percent

Black

Total

White

Hispanic

Year

NOTE: Hispanics may be of any race. Data presented for 1960 include 1959 data for blacks and 1960 data for whites and total. Data presented for 1965 include 1967 data for blacks and 1965 data for whites and total.

SOURCE: U.S. Department of Commerce, Bureau of the Census, *Current Population Reports*, Series P-60, "Income, Poverty, and Valuation of Non-cash Benefits: 1994" (based on March Current Population Surveys).

Racial and ethnic distribution of college students

♦ The student body at the nation's colleges and universities has become increasingly heterogeneous since the mid-1970s. Minority students increased from 15 percent of all students in 1976 to 23 percent in 1993. This increase was primarily due to the increased enrollment of Hispanic and Asian/Pacific Islander students, who, as a percentage of all college students, increased over 3 percentage points each.

> *Colleges and universities seek diversity in their student bodies; variety in the backgrounds and interests of students enhances the learning environment. The racial/ethnic mix of college students is one aspect of student diversity. Variations in the racial/ethnic composition of college enrollment suggest differences in the needs, interests, and backgrounds of the student body.*

♦ Black students accounted for 10 percent of the total enrollment at colleges and universities in 1993. Hispanics made up 7 percent, Asian/Pacific Islanders 5 percent, and American Indian/Alaskan Natives 1 percent of enrolled students.

♦ In 1993, minority students made up a greater proportion of the student body at 2-year than at 4-year institutions (27 compared to 20 percent, respectively).

♦ About equal proportions of black and Hispanic students enrolled in 2-year public colleges; however, about twice as many blacks as Hispanics enrolled in 4-year institutions in 1993.

Percentage of total enrollment in higher education institutions, by race/ethnicity and control and type of institution: Selected years, fall 1976–93

| Fall of year and control and type of institution | White | Minority | | | | | Nonresident alien |
		Total minority	Black	Hispanic	Asian/ Pacific Islander	American Indian/ Alaskan Native	
All institutions							
1976	82.6	15.4	9.4	3.5	1.8	0.7	2.0
1978[1]	81.9	15.9	9.4	3.7	2.1	0.7	2.3
1980	81.4	16.1	9.2	3.9	2.4	0.7	2.5
1982	80.7	16.6	8.9	4.2	2.8	0.7	2.7
1984	80.2	17.0	8.8	4.4	3.2	0.7	2.7
1986	79.3	17.9	8.7	4.9	3.6	0.7	2.8
1988	78.8	18.4	8.7	5.2	3.8	0.7	2.8
1990[1]	77.6	19.6	9.0	5.7	4.1	0.7	2.8
1992[1]	75.1	21.8	9.6	6.6	4.8	0.8	3.1
1993[2]	74.1	22.7	9.9	6.9	5.1	0.9	3.2
By control and type of institution: Fall 1993[2]							
Public	73.5	23.8	10.0	7.6	5.2	1.0	2.7
Private	76.2	18.9	9.6	4.4	4.4	0.5	4.9
4-year	76.0	19.8	9.3	4.9	4.9	0.7	4.2
Public	75.8	20.5	9.4	5.3	5.1	0.8	3.7
Private	76.4	18.4	9.2	4.2	4.6	0.4	5.2
2-year public[3]	71.1	27.3	10.6	10.1	5.4	1.1	1.6

Table reads: In the fall of 1993, minority students made up 18.8 percent of all students at private institutions, of which 4.2 percent were Hispanic.

[1] Revised from previously published figures.
[2] Estimates based on preliminary data.
[3] Ninety-seven percent of 2-year students are enrolled in public institutions.
NOTE: Details may not add to totals due to rounding.

SOURCE: U.S. Department of Education, National Center for Education Statistics, *Digest of Education Statistics, 1995* (based on the IPEDS/HEGIS "Fall Enrollment" surveys).

Percentage of minority enrollment in higher education institutions

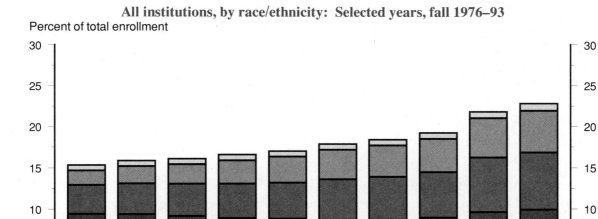

All institutions, by race/ethnicity: Selected years, fall 1976–93

Percent of total enrollment

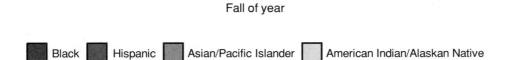

■ Black ■ Hispanic ■ Asian/Pacific Islander □ American Indian/Alaskan Native

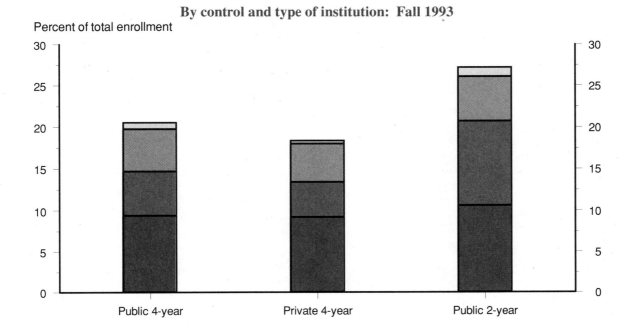

By control and type of institution: Fall 1993

Percent of total enrollment

SOURCE: U.S. Department of Education, National Center for Education Statistics, *Digest of Education Statistics, 1995* (based on the IPEDS/HEGIS "Fall Enrollment" surveys).

Community service performed by high school seniors

♦ In 1992, 44 percent of high school seniors reported that they performed some type of community service during the previous 2 years. Thirty-eight percent of seniors reported that some or all of their community service was voluntary, and 15 percent reported that some or all of their service was required.

♦ Eight percent of high school seniors reported, in 1992, performing community service during the previous 2 years that was required for class; 2 percent reported performing court ordered service and 8 percent reported that service; was required for other reasons.

Currently, there is considerable interest in involving a greater number of students in community service. Having students perform community service is seen as beneficial for both society and the individual. Community service provides staffing for community projects, prepares students for future roles in the community, and may provide students with experience they can use in their future careers. Data on community service performed by high school seniors show who participates and to what extent.

♦ Approximately 51 percent of high school seniors in schools with a low poverty level (5 percent or less receiving free or reduced-price lunch) reported that they performed some type of community service during the previous 2 years, compared to 36 percent of high school seniors in schools with a high level of poverty (40 percent or more receiving free or reduced-price lunch).

♦ High school seniors who attended Catholic and other private schools were more likely to perform community service during the previous 2 years than were high school seniors who attended public schools. In fact, 34 percent of those high school seniors who attended Catholic schools performed community service that was required for a class.

Percentage of high school seniors who reported performing community service during the previous 2 years, and the percentage of community service that was voluntary or required, by selected school characteristics and achievement test quartile: 1992

School characteristics and achievement test quartile	Total*	Strictly voluntary*	Some or all of community service was:			
			Required			
			Total*	For class	Court ordered	For other reasons
Total	**44.0**	**37.5**	**15.1**	**7.6**	**1.5**	**8.4**
Control of school						
Public	42.0	36.3	13.2	5.9	1.5	7.7
Catholic	66.7	49.6	45.1	33.7	1.8	17.4
Private, other	56.7	49.6	21.1	10.0	1.1	12.9
Percentage of students receiving free or reduced-price lunch						
0–5	50.5	43.8	18.8	10.3	1.6	9.6
6–20	45.1	38.9	16.0	7.4	1.8	9.5
21–40	39.3	33.3	11.8	4.8	1.1	7.2
41–100	35.6	27.6	12.3	5.5	1.1	8.1
Achievement test quartile						
First (low)	29.4	22.2	10.3	5.3	1.2	5.7
Second	33.0	28.1	9.9	5.4	0.9	5.4
Third	41.8	35.7	14.3	6.9	1.7	7.7
Fourth (high)	59.5	52.4	21.7	11.3	1.7	11.9

Table reads: In 1992, 44.0 percent of high school seniors reported performing community service during the previous 2 years, and 37.5 percent of seniors reported that all or some of the community service they performed was strictly voluntary.

* Seniors were asked to give as many responses as were applicable when reporting whether any of the community service they performed was voluntary or required; therefore, "total," "strictly voluntary," and "required total" counts seniors only once, and details may not add to totals.

SOURCE: U.S. Department of Education, National Center for Education Statistics, National Education Longitudinal Study of 1988, Second Follow-up (1992).

Percentage of high school seniors who reported performing community service during the previous 2 years, and the percentage of community service that was voluntary or required: 1992

By control of school

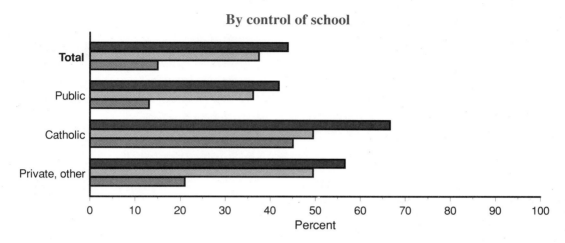

By percentage of students receiving free or reduced-price lunch

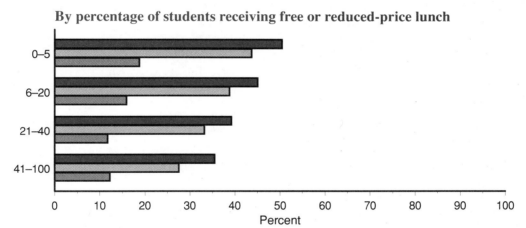

By achievement test quartile

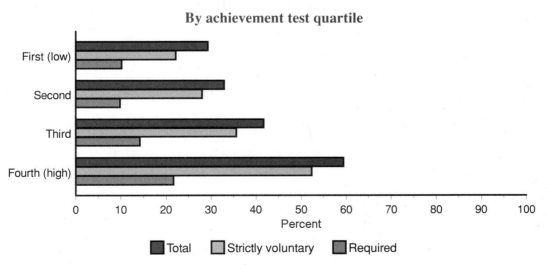

■ Total   ■ Strictly voluntary   ■ Required

NOTE: Seniors were asked to give as many responses as were applicable when reporting whether any of the community service they performed was voluntary or required; therefore, "total" counts seniors only once, and details may not add to totals.
SOURCE: U.S. Department of Education, National Center for Education Statistics, National Education Longitudinal Study of 1988, Second Follow-up (1992).

Teachers' participation in school decision making

◆ In 1994, a higher percentage of teachers perceived having a good deal* of control over their classroom decisions than they perceived teachers having a good deal of influence over their school's policies (ranging from 57 to 88 percent and 31 to 38 percent, respectively).

◆ Private school teachers were more likely than public school teachers to perceive having influence over their school policies and control over most of their classroom decisions in 1994.

> *Two aspects that can affect school climate and responsiveness are the extent to which teachers participate in making decisions about important school policies and issues, and the autonomy teachers have in the classroom. Data on teachers' influence over school policies and control of their classrooms can contribute to current debates on teacher professionalism.*

◆ Public and private secondary teachers were more likely than elementary teachers to perceive having a good deal* of control over classroom decisions, except for the decision to discipline students over which elementary teachers perceived having more control.

◆ Private school principals were more likely than public school principals to attribute a good deal of influence to teachers on setting discipline policy and establishing curriculum.

Teachers' and principals' perceptions of the amount of influence or control teachers had over selected school and classroom decisions in their schools, by control and level of school: 1994

Decisions	All schools	Public			Private		
		Total	Elementary	Secondary	Total	Elementary	Secondary
Percentage of teachers reporting that teachers had a good deal* of influence in their school over:							
Setting discipline policy	37.9	34.9	41.8	27.5	58.9	64.6	50.9
Determining the content of in-service programs	31.2	30.6	32.6	28.5	35.1	36.1	33.7
Establishing curriculum	37.2	34.6	32.2	37.2	55.4	54.5	56.6
Percentage of teachers reporting a good deal* of control in their classroom over:							
Selecting textbooks and other instructional materials	57.0	55.5	49.1	62.4	67.9	62.4	75.7
Selecting content, topics, and skills to be taught	62.3	60.5	54.2	67.4	74.6	69.3	82.3
Selecting teaching techniques	87.1	86.4	83.8	89.2	91.6	90.0	93.9
Evaluating and grading students	87.5	86.9	84.0	90.0	91.6	90.3	93.5
Disciplining students	70.9	69.0	73.4	64.2	84.3	86.3	81.5
Determining the amount of homework to be assigned	86.8	86.7	83.7	89.9	87.4	85.7	89.8
Percentage of principals reporting that teachers had a good deal* of influence over:							
Setting discipline policy	75.7	74.7	75.5	72.5	80.2	82.2	68.9
Determining the content of in-service programs	70.0	70.7	70.3	71.6	67.1	66.6	70.1
Establishing curriculum	63.7	61.4	59.7	66.2	74.4	74.0	76.9

Table reads: In 1994, 34.9 percent of public school teachers and 58.9 percent of private school teachers reported that teachers had a good deal of influence over setting discipline policies in their schools.

* Respondents were asked about influence and control on a scale of 0–5, with 0 meaning "no influence" or "no control," and 5 meaning a "great deal of influence" or "complete control." Responses 4 and 5 were combined in this analysis.

NOTE: Excludes a small number of teachers whose schools did not respond to the questionnaire.

SOURCE: U.S. Department of Education, National Center for Education Statistics, Schools and Staffing Survey, 1993–94 (Teacher and Administrator Questionnaires).

Teachers' and principals' perceptions of the amount of influence or control teachers had over school and classroom decisions, by control of school: 1994

Percentage of teachers reporting that teachers had a good deal* of influence in their school over:

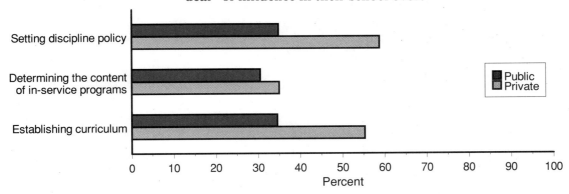

Percentage of teachers reporting a good deal* of control in their classroom over:

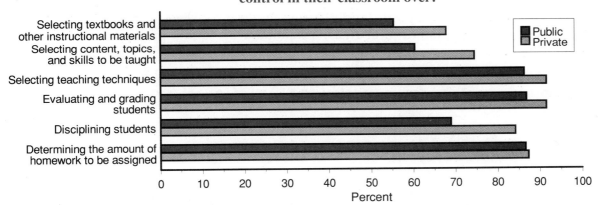

Percentage of principals reporting teachers had a good deal* of influence over:

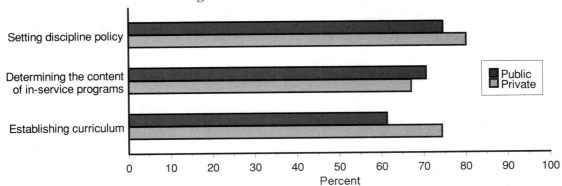

* Respondents were asked about influence and control on a scale of 0–5, with 0 meaning "no influence" or "no control," and 5 meaning "a great deal of influence" or "complete control." Responses 4 and 5 were combined in this analysis.

SOURCE: U.S. Department of Education, National Center for Education Statistics, Schools and Staffing Survey, 1993–94 (Teacher and Administrator Questionnaires).

Teaching workload of full-time teachers

♦ While full-time public school teachers were required to be at school 33 hours per week on average in 1994, they reported working 45 hours per week; private school teachers were required to be at school an average of 34 hours per week, but reported working 47 hours per week. Public and private full-time teachers reported spending extra hours (12 and 13 hours, respectively) before and after school and on weekends; of these extra hours, about one-fourth were spent in activities involving students.

Ongoing debates about teachers' salaries, professional status, and instructional time spark interest in the amount of time teachers spend working, the number of classes they teach per day, and the number of students in each class. A teacher's work day does not end when classes are over. They are likely to spend additional time outside of school hours on work-related activities.

♦ In 1994, public school teachers' classes were larger than those of their private school counterparts (23 students compared to 20 students per class).

♦ In 1994, less experienced teachers (those with less than 4 years of teaching experience) worked more total hours per week than did more experienced teachers (those with 4 or more years of teaching experience).

♦ Teachers' average class sizes varied by school urbanicity, percentage of minority students enrolled, and school size. In both public and private schools, class sizes were larger in central cities and urban fringe areas than in rural areas, in schools with higher proportions of minority students, and in larger versus smaller schools (see supplemental tables 48-1 and 48-2).

Average hours per week full-time teachers spent at school and in school-related activities, class size, and classes taught per day, by control and level of school and years of teaching experience: 1994

Control and level of school and teacher characteristics	Average hours worked per week	Average hours required at school	Average hours spent before and after school and on weekends			Average class size	Average number of classes taught per day*
			Total	Activities involving students	Other related activities		
Public	**45.2**	**33.2**	**12.1**	**3.3**	**8.7**	**23.2**	**5.6**
Level of school							
Elementary	44.0	33.0	11.0	1.7	9.2	22.7	6.4
Secondary	46.5	33.3	13.2	5.0	8.2	23.2	5.5
Years of teaching experience							
Less than 4 years	48.3	34.4	14.0	4.2	9.8	23.2	5.5
4 years or more	44.8	33.0	11.8	3.2	8.6	23.2	5.6
Private	**47.1**	**34.2**	**12.9**	**3.6**	**9.3**	**19.6**	**6.0**
Level of school							
Elementary	45.8	34.4	11.4	2.3	9.1	20.0	7.5
Secondary	49.1	34.0	15.2	5.7	9.5	19.5	5.7
Years of teaching experience							
Less than 4 years	48.6	35.1	13.5	4.0	9.6	18.6	6.0
4 years or more	46.8	34.0	12.8	3.6	9.2	19.8	6.0

Table reads: In 1994, public school teachers were required to be at school an average of 33.2 hours per week, and their average class size was 23.2 students.

* Since elementary teachers do not tend to teach separate classes, only 8 percent of the teachers who responded to this question were elementary teachers, while 92 percent were secondary teachers.

NOTE: Excludes a small number of teachers whose schools did not respond to the questionnaire. Details may not add to totals due to rounding.

SOURCE: U.S. Department of Education, National Center for Education Statistics, Schools and Staffing Survey, 1993–94 (Teacher Questionnaire).

Average hours per week full time teachers spent before and after school and on weekends, by control and level of school and years of teaching experience: 1994

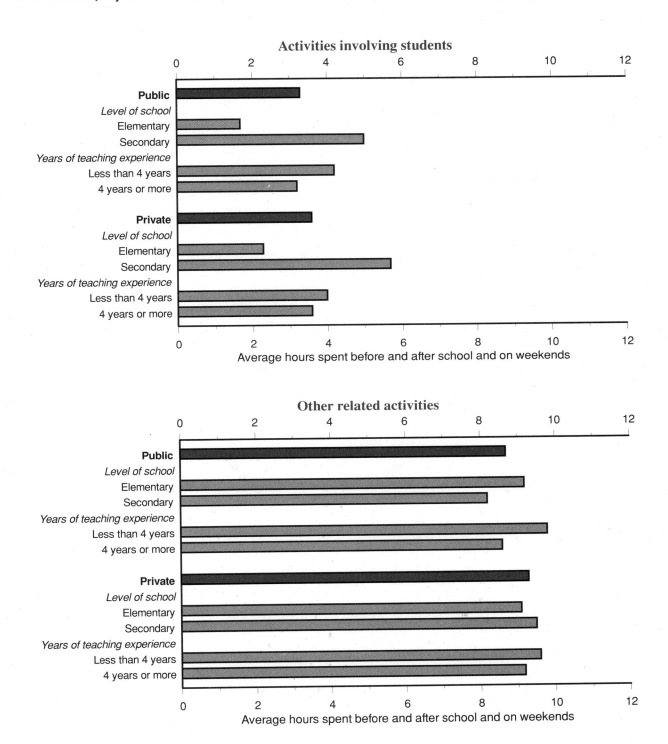

Activities involving students

Average hours spent before and after school and on weekends

Other related activities

Average hours spent before and after school and on weekends

SOURCE: U.S. Department of Education, National Center for Education Statistics, Schools and Staffing Survey, 1993–94 (Teacher Questionnaire).

Teaching workload of full-time postsecondary faculty

♦ In 1992, faculty members spent 59 percent of their work hours teaching, 16 percent conducting research, and 12 percent performing administrative tasks.

♦ Between 1987 and 1992, the percentage of time full-time postsecondary faculty members spent teaching decreased (from 61 to 59 percent), while the percentage of time they spent on service and other duties increased (from 3 to 5 percent).

Teaching students is only one aspect of a postsecondary faculty member's job. Faculty members also spend time on other activities such as research, freelance work, administrative tasks, and professional growth activities. Debates about tenure, instructional time, and the overall quality of a college education raise questions about the actual time postsecondary faculty spend teaching relative to the time they spend doing these other activities.

♦ Generally, full professors tended to spend a higher percentage of their time conducting research than other professors in 1992. Assistant professors, instructors, and lecturers spent a higher proportion of time teaching than full or associate professors.

♦ Full-time postsecondary faculty members at 2-year institutions had more student contact hours per week in 1992 than did faculty at other institutions (over 75 percent more than those at research and liberal arts institutions and 40 percent more than those at doctoral and comprehensive institutions) (see supplemental table 49-1).

Percentage of time full-time postsecondary faculty spent on various activities, by academic rank and type of institution: Fall 1987 and fall 1992

| Activity | Total* | Academic rank | | | | | Type of institution | | | | |
		Full professor	Associate professor	Assistant professor	Instructor	Lecturer	Research	Doctoral	Comprehensive	Liberal arts	2-year
					Fall 1992						
Total*	100.0	100.0	100.0	100.0	100.0	100.0	100.0	100.0	100.0	100.0	100.0
Teaching	58.8	53.8	56.5	60.6	70.7	63.6	45.2	53.2	61.1	64.8	70.1
Research/scholarship	16.4	20.0	18.1	19.0	5.7	10.3	31.0	23.3	13.6	9.6	4.7
Professional growth	4.5	4.0	4.5	4.2	5.5	5.1	3.3	3.6	4.8	4.5	5.6
Administration	12.1	14.1	12.4	8.6	9.4	13.0	12.2	11.9	12.1	13.8	11.1
Outside consulting/ freelance work	2.8	3.0	3.1	2.1	2.9	2.6	2.9	2.6	2.8	2.4	2.8
Service and other	5.4	5.0	5.3	5.3	5.8	5.4	5.3	5.2	5.6	4.7	5.7
					Fall 1987						
Total*	100.0	100.0	100.0	100.0	100.0	100.0	100.0	100.0	100.0	100.0	100.0
Teaching	61.2	55.1	58.3	63.2	73.4	69.8	46.9	55.2	64.9	67.7	73.3
Research/scholarship	16.3	20.0	19.2	18.3	4.8	9.2	31.1	22.2	12.2	10.3	4.4
Professional growth	4.1	3.2	3.8	3.9	6.2	5.4	3.2	3.5	4.2	4.3	5.0
Administration	12.8	15.6	13.1	10.1	9.6	8.6	13.7	13.6	12.7	13.3	10.9
Outside consulting/ freelance work	2.6	2.8	2.6	2.0	2.9	3.9	2.8	2.8	2.6	1.7	2.7
Service and other	3.2	3.2	3.0	2.7	3.2	3.2	2.6	2.6	3.3	2.9	3.9

Table reads: In the fall semester of 1992, full-time postsecondary faculty spent 58.8 percent of their work time in teaching activities.
* Included in the total but not shown separately are other types of academic ranks and postsecondary institutions.
NOTE: Totals may not add to 100.0 due to rounding. Includes only those faculty who taught at least one class for credit. Medical faculty are not included in this analysis. See the supplemental note to this indicator for further definitions of time spent by faculty.

SOURCE: U.S. Department of Education, National Center for Education Statistics, National Survey of Postsecondary Faculty, 1988 and 1993.

Percentage of time full time postsecondary faculty spent on various activities: Fall 1987 and fall 1992

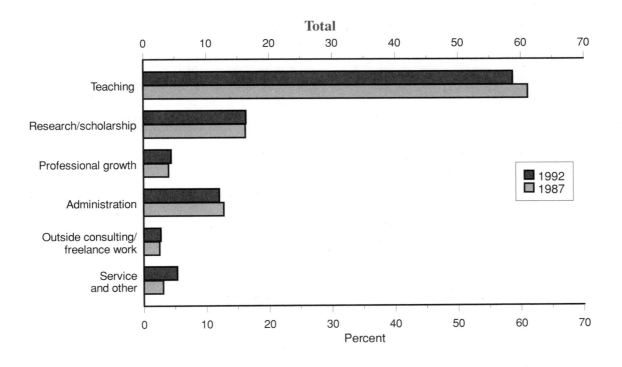

Total

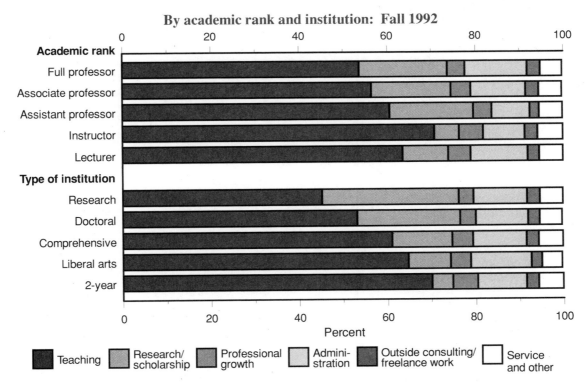

By academic rank and institution: Fall 1992

NOTE: Medical faculty are not included in this analysis.

SOURCE: U.S. Department of Education, National Center for Education Statistics, National Survey of Postsecondary Faculty, 1988 and 1993.

Student exposure to faculty at institutions of higher education

♦ At research, doctoral, and comprehensive institutions in both 1987 and 1992, the majority of classroom exposure to faculty for students in undergraduate upper division courses and graduate courses was with senior faculty—full professors and associate professors.

> *An institution's most experienced faculty are its senior faculty. They have more teaching, research, and administrative experience. More contact with these faculty may enhance the quality of the learning environment for students at colleges and universities. One measure of a student's contact with senior faculty is the percentage of a student's classroom time spent with full or associate professors.*

♦ At comprehensive institutions in 1992, undergraduate students in lower division courses had less classroom exposure to senior faculty than did students in upper division courses.

♦ Students in undergraduate courses at research institutions had about the same classroom exposure to senior-level faculty as did students in undergraduate courses at comprehensive and liberal arts institutions. However, for undergraduate students in classes taught by senior-level faculty, those at research institutions were more likely to be in classes of more than 50 students than those at comprehensive and liberal arts institutions (see supplemental table 50-1).

Percentage of classroom hours 4-year college and university students were exposed to faculty of different ranks, by type of institution, level of classes, and course division: Fall 1987 and fall 1992

Academic rank	Fall 1987					Fall 1992[1]				
	Type of institution and course division					Type of institution and course division				
	Total	Re-search	Doctoral	Compre-hensive	Liberal arts	Total	Re-search	Doctoral	Compre-hensive	Liberal arts
Undergraduate, lower division courses						**Undergraduate, lower division courses**				
Full professor	30.4	33.6	28.5	30.1	27.3	27.8	30.4	25.1	27.9	26.4
Associate professor	26.3	34.5	28.6	22.4	20.6	23.6	31.9	23.8	20.6	20.9
Assistant professor	20.5	16.7	19.7	20.6	29.0	23.1	17.3	26.5	24.2	24.4
Instructor	12.8	4.1	17.0	16.6	12.8	16.2	10.4	16.3	18.4	17.7
Lecturer	8.1	10.6	4.9	8.7	4.5	7.0	9.6	6.8	6.7	3.7
Other	1.9	0.5	1.3	1.7	5.8	2.4	(²)	1.5	2.2	7.0
Undergraduate, upper division courses						**Undergraduate, upper division courses**				
Full professor	31.1	36.2	31.4	29.4	24.6	33.5	36.9	30.7	33.5	29.0
Associate professor	25.5	30.6	27.7	22.9	19.7	25.8	27.8	24.7	25.6	23.6
Assistant professor	25.7	18.9	24.5	27.5	38.8	23.5	22.8	25.9	22.8	25.2
Instructor	8.8	7.0	9.3	9.0	12.6	9.6	4.2	11.2	11.1	14.4
Lecturer	7.4	6.1	6.6	9.9	0.6	5.3	7.6	4.8	4.4	4.4
Other	1.4	1.3	0.6	1.3	3.7	2.2	(²)	2.8	2.7	3.4
Graduate courses						**Graduate courses**				
Full professor	41.8	44.0	39.2	38.3	(²)	40.7	44.3	48.0	33.7	11.1
Associate professor	28.5	27.2	35.7	26.6	(²)	27.1	31.3	17.2	27.8	24.0
Assistant professor	19.3	19.9	20.7	17.5	(²)	17.7	12.6	27.0	19.2	17.6
Instructor	4.3	1.7	3.2	10.1	(²)	8.7	6.2	4.4	12.5	32.7
Lecturer	3.8	3.2	0.8	7.2	(²)	3.5	2.9	(²)	4.8	(²)
Other	2.4	4.0	0.3	0.3	(²)	2.3	(²)	(²)	2.0	(²)

[1] Revised from previously published figures.

[2] Too few sample observations for a reliable estimate.

NOTE: Total student classroom hours were calculated as the number of classroom hours per week multiplied by the number of students in each course summed over all classes, as reported by faculty members. The percentages were calculated as the sum of the classroom hours spent with faculty of a particular rank divided by total student classroom hours. See the supplemental note to *Indicator 49* for definitions of faculty, institutions, and course divisions used in this analysis.

SOURCE: U.S. Department of Education, National Center for Education Statistics, National Survey of Postsecondary Faculty, 1988 and 1993.

Percentage of classroom hours 4-year college and university students were exposed to senior faculty, by type of institution, level of classes, and course division: Fall 1987 and 1992

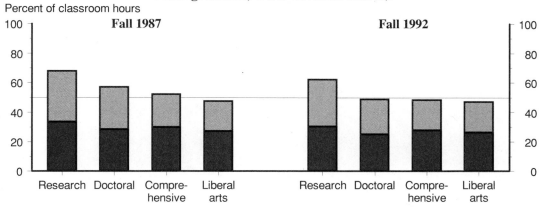

Undergraduate, lower division courses

Percent of classroom hours

Fall 1987   **Fall 1992**

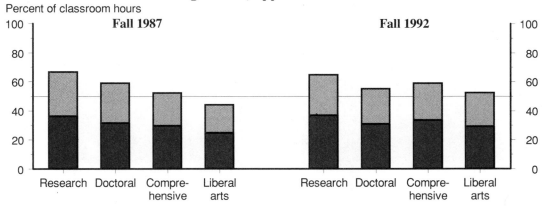

Undergraduate, upper division courses

Percent of classroom hours

Fall 1987   **Fall 1992**

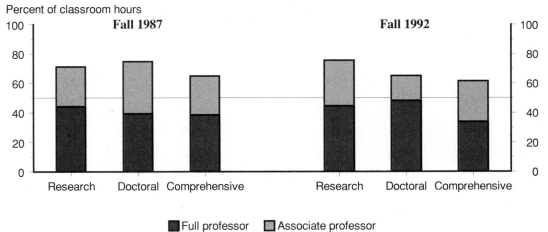

Graduate courses

Percent of classroom hours

Fall 1987   **Fall 1992**

■ Full professor   ▨ Associate professor

SOURCE: U.S. Department of Education, National Center for Education Statistics, National Survey of Postsecondary Faculty, 1988 and 1993.

Human and Financial Resources of Educational Institutions

During the 1980s and early 1990s, education officials at our nation's schools, colleges, and universities faced challenges in providing students with a quality education, in light of constraints in the human and financial resources available to them. Nationwide the qualifications and training of teachers continue to be of concern. The percentage of limited-English-proficient and disabled students continues to rise. Also, postsecondary education institutions are confronting declining support from government appropriations and an increasing reliance on other financial sources, such as tuition. Furthermore, calls to raise the quality of education have grown as Americans feel increasing competitive pressure from the global marketplace.

Financial resources

The United States invests a substantial amount of its financial resources in education. Two ways of measuring this investment are 1) revenues from public sources for a particular level of education, divided by the number of students enrolled at that level; and 2) the national index of public effort to fund education, which is the ratio of the first measure to income per capita.

Elementary/secondary education

During the post-World War II era, per-pupil revenues from public sources for students in elementary and secondary schools increased substantially every decade. Between 1950 and 1993, these revenues increased about four and a half times, rising from $1,230 to $5,526 per student (adjusted for inflation) (*Indicator 51*). This trend may have been driven by many factors. For example, the education system has assumed greater responsibility in many areas, such as the education of disabled students. In addition, public policy has increased spending on children from poor families and has sought to increase the quality of education of minorities to a level comparable to that of the majority. Furthermore, the number of teachers and other school staff more than doubled between 1960 and 1993.[*][1]

The ability of taxpayers to finance a larger education budget has increased over time, but public revenue has risen at a much faster rate than the ability of the taxpayer to pay for public education. Between 1950 and 1993, personal income per capita increased about 140 percent, whereas public revenues per student rose almost 350 percent. This change is captured in the national effort index (per-student revenues for elementary and secondary education from public sources as a percentage of personal income per capita). Revenues per student comprised 14 percent of personal income per capita in 1950, and 26 percent in 1993 (*Indicator 51*).

Some school districts receive more revenue per student than others. For instance, the wealthiest districts, in terms of median household income, had 16 percent more cost-of-living adjusted revenue per student than the poorest districts (*Indicator 53, Condition 1995*).

Among G-7 countries, the United States has one of the highest levels of public education expenditures per student as a percentage of Gross Domestic Product (GDP) (*Indicator 52*).

Higher education

Public revenues for higher education (adjusted for inflation) in 1993 were about $4,665 per student compared to $2,613 in 1950. The public education revenue per student raised for higher education increased between 1930 and the mid-1960s, and has remained fairly stable since then (*Indicator 51*).

Between 1980 and 1993, average revenue per student rose at public 4-year colleges and universities. While revenue from tuition and fees rose, revenue from government sources fell. Expenditures for administration and research rose more than expenditures for instruction. Although only a small part of the total, scholarship and fellowship expenditures also rose a great deal over this period (*Indicators 53* and *54*). At private 4-year colleges and universities, both revenue per student and expenditures per student rose more than at public institutions between 1980 and 1993. Not surprisingly, revenue from tuition and fees also increased dramatically at private institutions over this period.

Generally, among G-7 countries, only Canada showed a higher level of public education expenditures as a percentage of GDP for higher education than the United States (*Indicator 52*).

Human resources

The most important resource in education is personnel. In 1991, in elementary and secondary education, there were 11 full-time-equivalent (FTE) staff per 100 students. Of these, six were classroom teachers; three were support staff, such as secretaries and bus drivers; and the remaining two were principals, assistant principals, school district administrators, librarians, guidance counselors, and teacher aides (*Indicator 57, Condition 1993*).

Supply of teachers

Over the last two decades, as fewer college graduates enter the teaching profession and student enrollments increase, policymakers have become concerned about the source of supply of new teachers. Schools depend on new college graduates, transfers, and reentering teachers to fill positions. Even though reentrants offer more teaching experience they demand higher salaries than first-time teachers. However, first-time teachers have higher rates of attrition. Between 1988 and 1991, the sources of supply of newly hired teachers shifted, as both public and private schools hired a larger proportion of first-time teachers (*Indicator 56*).

Teacher qualifications and training

Although it is very difficult to assess the quality of a teacher, many think that the education of teachers is an important measure of a teacher's qualifications. In public schools, in the 1993–94 school year, 9 out of 10 secondary students in science and social studies classes were taught by a teacher who either majored or minored in science or social studies, respectively. However, just over 8 out of 10 of students in English classes were taught by a teacher who majored or minored in English, and less than 8 out of 10 students in mathematics classes were taught by a teacher who majored or minored in math (*Indicator 57*).

While teachers' initial education and training are important, ongoing professional development throughout teachers' careers also contributes significantly to their teaching qualifications. In the 1993–94 school year, a majority of public school teachers received in-service education or professional development in topics such as the use of educational technology, methods of teaching, student assessment, and cooperative learning. Teachers received support for professional development in the form of time away from teaching, travel expenses, tuition and fees, and professional growth credits. However, 22 percent of public school teachers received none of this support for professional development (*Indicator 59*).

Teacher salaries

The cost of staff resources is determined not only by the number of staff employed but also by their salaries. In 1995, the average annual salary of public elementary school teachers was $36,874 and for $38,249 secondary school teachers. Between 1960 and 1972, teachers' salaries (adjusted for inflation) in public schools rose, fell until 1980, but then rose again throughout the 1980s, reaching their peak in 1991. Average beginning teacher salaries did not rise as rapidly as average teacher salaries during the 1980s. In fact, the average beginning teacher salary was $24,463 in 1995, about the same level as two decades earlier (*Indicator 55*).

Teacher salaries are relatively low when compared to salaries of other professions that college students could pursue. Policymakers are concerned whether this discourages the best and brightest from choosing teaching as a profession. However, in 1992, elementary and secondary school teachers had prose literacy skills similar to those of physicians, engineers, social workers, writers and artists, private sector executives and managers, registered nurses, and sales representatives in the business and financial fields (*Indicator 58*).

Higher education faculty

In 1992, almost 80 percent of full-time faculty had earnings in addition to their basic faculty salaries, ranging from 64 percent of agriculture faculty to 87 percent of fine arts faculty. That year faculty members' basic salary was 84 percent of their total earned income. The proportion of earnings derived from other sources varied by field, from almost 13 percent among the humanities faculty to 20 percent among business faculty. Despite gains in the 1980s and early 1990s, the salaries of faculty (adjusted for inflation) were lower in 1994 than they had been two decades earlier (*Indicator 60*).

NOTE:

* U.S. Department of Education, National Center for Education Statistics, *Digest of Education Statistics, 1995,* table 81.

National index of public effort to fund education

♦ **After a 10 point increase between 1930 and 1970 (from 10.6 to 20.7), the national index of public effort to fund elementary and secondary education increased, with slight fluctuations, to 25.9 in 1993. Public education revenues per elementary and secondary student (in 1995 constant dollars) have risen from $658 in 1930 to $5,526 in 1993.**

The national index of public effort to fund education is a measure of money raised for the education of students relative to the wealth of the taxpayers. The numerator is revenues per student, a measure of average financial resources available for the education of each student. The denominator is personal income per capita, a measure of the taxpayer's average ability to pay.

♦ **The national index of public effort to fund higher education was 21.9 in 1993, one of the lowest levels since 1930. However, higher education public revenues per student (in 1995 constant dollars) have been relatively stable since 1970, with the exception of a drop in the early 1980s.**

♦ **After declining during the 1970s to mid-1980s, elementary and secondary public education revenues as a percentage of Gross Domestic Product (GDP) rose between 1988 and 1993, but have not rebounded to the levels in the early to mid-1970s. Higher education revenues as a percentage of GDP have remained about 1 percent since the mid-1960s.**

National index of public effort to fund education (public revenues per student in relation to per capita personal income), by level: Selected school years ending 1930–93

| School year ending | National index[1] | | Public education revenues | | | | Per capita personal income[2,3] |
| | Elementary/ secondary | Higher education | Per student[2] | | As a percentage of GDP | | |
			Elementary/ secondary	Higher education	Elementary/ secondary	Higher education	
1930[4]	10.6	22.5	$658	$1,391	2.0	0.2	$6,192
1940[4]	14.6	26.0	881	1,568	2.5	0.2	6,041
1950	13.9	29.4	1,230	2,613	2.1	0.4	8,873
1960	17.2	33.5	1,876	3,660	3.0	0.5	10,922
1966	19.3	36.1	2,503	4,677	3.6	0.8	12,940
1970	20.7	31.9	3,189	4,903	4.2	1.0	15,377
1972	23.0	31.0	3,619	4,881	4.6	1.1	15,739
1974	22.4	29.5	3,781	4,987	4.3	1.1	16,896
1976	23.2	27.5	4,016	4,749	4.5	1.2	17,289
1978	23.1	27.7	4,076	4,883	4.1	1.1	17,621
1980	21.7	25.1	4,085	4,716	3.9	1.1	18,804
1982	21.5	23.1	3,926	4,211	3.6	1.1	18,254
1984	23.1	23.6	4,206	4,295	3.7	1.0	18,173
1986	23.9	25.3	4,653	4,918	3.7	1.1	19,445
1988	23.9	24.3	4,914	4,997	3.7	1.1	20,601
1990	25.7	23.4	5,464	4,975	4.0	1.1	21,278
1992	25.4	21.7	5,486	4,688	4.1	1.1	21,620
1993	25.9	21.9	5,526	4,665	4.1	1.0	21,335

Table reads: In 1993, $26 of revenue per elementary/secondary student was raised for each $100 of income received by members of the population.

[1] Revised from previously published figures.

[2] In constant 1995 dollars.

[3] For the calendar year in which the school year began.

[4] Income and population are for the calendar year in which the school year ended.

NOTE: Public funds for education may be used at many types of institutions, both publicly and privately controlled. For comparability across levels of education, enrollment in both publicly and privately controlled institutions is included. For more information about the calculation of this indicator, see the supplemental note.

SOURCE: U.S. Department of Education, National Center for Education Statistics, *Digest of Education Statistics, 1995* (based on Common Core of Data and IPEDS/HEGIS "Fall Enrollment" surveys). U.S. Department of Commerce, Bureau of Economic Analysis, *Economic Report to the President*, various years.

National index of public effort to fund education (public revenues per student relation to per capita personal income), by level: Selected school years ending 1930–93

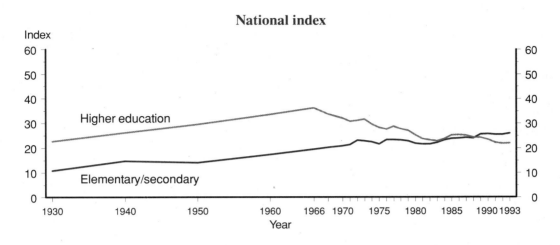

National index

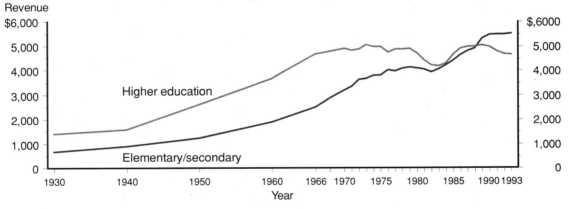

Public education revenues per student (in 1995 constant dollars)

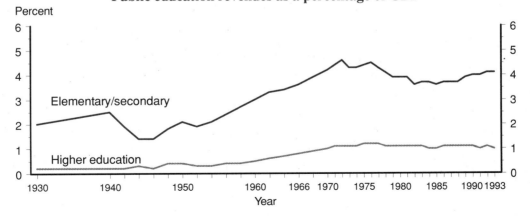

Public education revenues as a percentage of GDP

SOURCE: U.S. Department of Education, National Center for Education Statistics, *Digest of Education Statistics, 1995* (based on Common Core of Data and IPEDS/HEGIS "Fall Enrollment" surveys). U.S. Department of Commerce, Bureau of Economic Analysis, *Economic Report to the President,* various years.

International comparisons of public expenditures for education

♦ Across most measures of public education expenditures, Canada, the United States, and the United Kingdom spent more than other G-7 countries in the 1991–92 school year.

♦ Public expenditures in the United States were 0.2 percent of the Gross Domestic Product (GDP) for preprimary education, 3.5 percent for the primary-secondary grade levels, and 1.2 percent for higher education. France spent a larger fraction for preprimary education, while the former West Germany spent the same fraction as the United States. Only Canada and the United Kingdom expended a larger fraction than the United States for primary-secondary education, and only Canada expended a larger proportion for higher education.

> *Public education expenditures are an indication of public investment in education. In the United States and other countries, there are additional private expenditures for education. Three alternative measures allow examination of the magnitude of public investment in education. The first provides a measure of the fraction of a country's resources that are allocated to public education. The second provides a measure of the public investment in each child in the education system. The third provides a measure of public educational investment in each child compared to available resources per person in the country.*

♦ In the primary-secondary grades, public expenditures per student in the G-7 countries ranged from about $2,700 in Japan to $4,800 in Canada and $5,000 in the United States. In higher education, public expenditures ranged from about $2,100 in Japan to $10,700 in Canada and $7,100 in the United States.

Public expenditures for education, by level of education and country: School year 1991–92

| | As a percent of GDP[2] | | | Per student[1] | | | | | |
| | | | | Constant 1991–92 U.S. dollars[3] | | | As a percentage of GDP per capita | | |
G-7 countries	Pre-primary	Primary-secondary	Higher education	Pre-primary	Primary-secondary	Higher education	Pre-primary	Primary-secondary	Higher education
Canada[4]	—	4.4	2.6	—	$4,752	$10,715	—	23.9	53.8
France	0.6	3.4	0.8	$2,302	3,636	4,701	12.4	19.6	25.4
Former West Germany[5]	0.2	2.0	0.8	1,180	3,048	5,749	5.8	15.0	28.3
Italy	—	3.3	0.6	—	3,978	3,676	—	22.9	21.2
Japan	0.1	2.3	0.3	1,300	2,698	2,103	6.6	13.6	10.6
United Kingdom[6]	—	3.9	1.0	—	3,473	9,154	—	21.3	56.2
United States	0.2	3.5	1.2	2,286	4,950	7,097	9.7	21.1	30.2

— Not available.

[1] Enrollment is in all institutions, public and private, and is based on headcount estimates for preprimary through 12th grade. For higher education, it is full-time-equivalent enrollment.

[2] Gross Domestic Product (GDP) is Gross National Product (GNP) less net property income from abroad.

[3] Purchasing Power Parity (PPP) indices were used to convert other currencies to U.S. dollars. Because the fiscal year has a different starting date in different countries, within-country Consumer Price Indices (CPIs) were used to adjust the PPP indices to account for inflation.

[4] Canada did not report separate figures for expenditures on preprimary education; preprimary expenditures are included in the primary-secondary expenditure figures. If one were to apportion Canada's expenditures across the preprimary and primary-secondary education levels according to their relative enrollments, and then remove the preprimary expenditures, it would reduce Canada's expenditures per student as a percentage of GDP by 0.2 percentage points, and its expenditures per student as a percentage of GDP per capita by 1.0 percentage point, while increasing its expenditures by $181.

[5] Includes contributions to the pension funds of teachers who are civil servants. Expenditure data for publicly supported private schools include capital expenditures.

[6] Excludes expenditures on nursing and paramedical education.

NOTE: The fiscal year begins in different months in the above countries. See the supplemental note to *Indicator 51* for an explanation of how expenditures were adjusted. See the supplemental note to this indicator for an explanation of how expenditures were adjusted and for further discussion on higher education and private expenditures.

SOURCE: Organization for Economic Co-operation and Development, Center for Educational Research and Innovation, International Indicators Project, 1995.

Public expenditures for education, by level of education and country: School year 1991–92

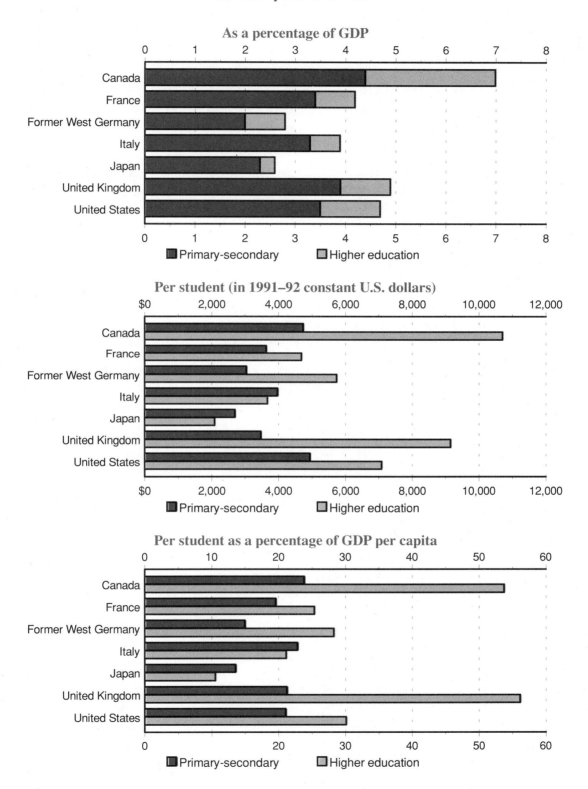

As a percentage of GDP

■ Primary-secondary ■ Higher education

Per student (in 1991–92 constant U.S. dollars)

■ Primary-secondary ■ Higher education

Per student as a percentage of GDP per capita

■ Primary-secondary ■ Higher education

SOURCE: Organization for Economic Co-operation and Development, Center for Educational Research and Innovation, International Indicators Project, 1995.

Higher education expenditures per student

♦ Overall spending per full-time-equivalent (FTE) student increased at all types of higher education institutions between 1983 and 1993. In 1995 constant dollars, increases ranged from 10 percent at public 2-year colleges (from $5,378 to $5,937 per FTE student) to 44 percent at private universities (from $23,610 to $34,039 per FTE student).

> *Faculty and staff salaries and institutionally supported research account for a large share of higher education expenditures. Since differences in institutional spending can affect the quality of instruction and learning experiences, understanding variations in expenditure categories can provide some insight into the organization and operation of higher education institutions.*

♦ Although instructional expenditures per FTE student increased between 1983 and 1993, instructional spending as a percentage of total expenditures fell at all types of institutions. Decreases were greater in public universities, public 4-year colleges, and private 4-year colleges than in private universities and public 2-year colleges (see supplemental table 53-2).

♦ Research expenditures have climbed by 44 percent in private universities (from $4,219 to $6,077) and by 43 percent in public universities (from $2,841 to $4,051) between 1983 and 1993. Over the decade, research spending accounted for roughly 18 percent of total institutional expenditures in private universities, and climbed from 19 to 22 percent of total spending in public universities (see supplemental table 53-2).

Educational and general expenditures of institutions of higher education per full-time-equivalent (FTE) student (in 1995 constant dollars), by selected expenditure categories and type of institution: Academic years ending 1977–93

| Academic year ending | Universities* | | | | | | Colleges | | | | | |
| | Private | | | Public | | | Private 4-year | | Public 4-year | | Public 2-year | |
	Total	Instruc-tion	Re-search	Total	Instruc-tion	Re-search	Total	Instruc-tion	Total	Instruc-tion	Total	Instruc-tion
1977	$22,807	$8,672	$4,803	$14,732	$5,744	$2,704	$11,243	$4,199	$10,743	$4,983	$5,790	$2,957
1978	22,576	8,568	4,691	14,889	5,842	2,763	11,212	4,204	10,854	5,017	5,831	2,951
1979	22,865	8,544	4,736	15,432	6,028	2,921	11,351	4,220	11,202	5,112	6,030	3,026
1980	23,228	8,795	4,768	15,289	5,926	2,980	11,561	4,239	11,343	5,089	5,938	2,986
1981	23,485	8,952	4,653	15,035	5,792	2,956	11,602	4,184	11,217	5,029	5,683	2,877
1982	23,396	9,137	4,429	14,823	5,754	2,854	11,751	4,242	11,162	5,095	5,678	2,889
1983	23,610	9,296	4,219	14,806	5,749	2,841	12,010	4,351	10,903	4,979	5,378	2,736
1984	25,365	9,782	4,497	15,180	5,854	2,902	12,426	4,468	11,028	4,977	5,459	2,774
1985	26,444	10,051	4,797	15,922	6,095	3,093	12,899	4,592	11,662	5,223	5,993	3,013
1986	27,535	10,399	5,090	16,597	6,255	3,266	13,387	4,694	12,086	5,443	6,191	3,090
1987	29,997	11,522	5,532	16,855	6,404	3,367	14,151	4,859	12,058	5,391	6,279	3,116
1988	30,326	11,384	5,677	17,282	6,452	3,560	14,478	4,933	12,281	5,476	6,185	3,043
1989	30,846	11,714	5,683	17,527	6,453	3,673	14,555	4,919	12,037	5,369	6,225	3,086
1990	31,259	11,822	5,823	17,522	6,408	3,743	14,834	4,974	12,173	5,404	6,070	3,022
1991	32,200	12,331	5,726	17,825	6,464	3,874	15,069	5,036	11,828	5,246	6,134	3,058
1992	33,243	12,686	5,793	17,781	6,407	3,908	15,495	5,128	12,016	5,191	5,872	2,954
1993	34,039	13,067	6,077	18,146	6,470	4,051	15,584	5,111	12,411	5,211	5,937	2,975

* Includes doctoral-granting institutions with and without medical schools.
NOTE: The Higher Education Price Index (HEPI) was used to calculate constant dollars. Data for academic years 1976–77 through 1985–86 include only institutions that provided both enrollment and finance data.

SOURCE: U.S. Department of Education, National Center for Education Statistics, Financial Statistics of Institutions of Higher Education Survey and Integrated Postsecondary Education Data System (IPEDS), "Finance" survey.

Educational and general expenditures of institutions of higher education per full-time-equivalent (FTE) student (in 1995 constant dollars), by selected expenditure categories and type of institution: Academic years ending 1977–93

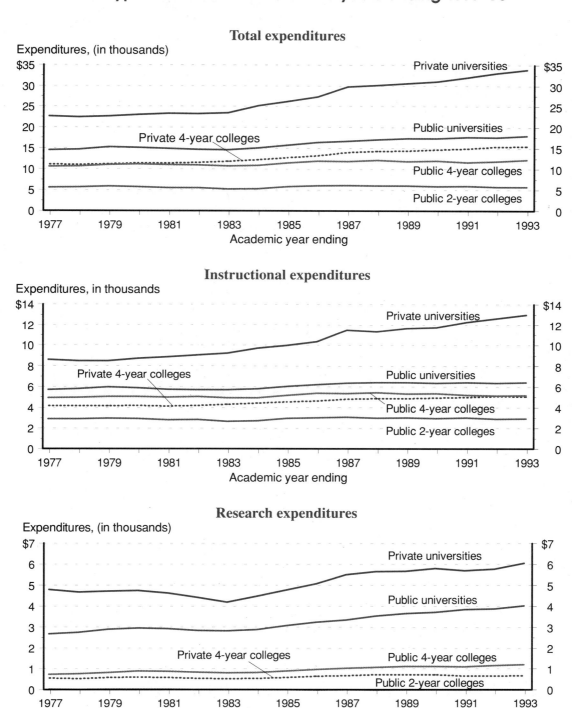

Total expenditures

Expenditures, (in thousands)

Private universities
Public universities
Private 4-year colleges
Public 4-year colleges
Public 2-year colleges

Academic year ending

Instructional expenditures

Expenditures, in thousands

Private universities
Private 4-year colleges
Public universities
Public 4-year colleges
Public 2-year colleges

Academic year ending

Research expenditures

Expenditures, (in thousands)

Private universities
Public universities
Private 4-year colleges
Public 4-year colleges
Public 2-year colleges

Academic year ending

SOURCE: U.S. Department of Education, National Center for Education Statistics, Financial Statistics of Institutions of Higher Education Survey and Integrated Postsecondary Education Data System (IPEDS), "Finance" survey.

Higher education revenues per student

♦ The primary source of revenue for public institutions is from federal, state, and local government appropriations. Between 1983 and 1993, government appropriations per full-time-equivalent (FTE) student fell both in constant dollars and as a share of all revenue at public institutions. At public universities, for example, government appropriations per FTE

> *A substantial proportion of higher education revenues is made up of student tuition and fees, government appropriations, and private gifts and endowment. Since access to higher education is partially determined by its cost to students, changes in the relative importance of these revenue sources can influence a student's decision to pursue a higher education degree.*

student fell from $7,760 to $7,386 in constant dollars and from 52 to 43 percent as a share of revenue between 1983 and 1993 (see supplemental table 54-2).

♦ A second important source of revenue for public institutions is tuition and fees. Between 1983 and 1993, tuition and fees per FTE student increased both in constant dollars and as a share of all revenue at all public institutions. At public universities, for example, tuition and fees rose from $2,814 to $3,941 in constant dollars and from 19 to 23 percent as a share of revenue between 1983 and 1993 (see supplemental table 54-2).

♦ Between 1983 and 1993, average tuition and fee revenue per FTE student increased at private universities, rising from $10,306 to $14,491 in constant dollars. In addition, revenue from private gifts and endowment income per FTE student climbed by 51 percent (from $4,729 to $7,130), compared to 2 percent at private 4-year colleges (from $2,545 to $2,587).

Current fund revenues of institutions of higher education per full-time-equivalent (FTE) student (in 1995 constant dollars), by selected revenue sources and type of institution: Academic years ending 1977–93

| | Universities[1] | | | | Colleges | | | | | |
| | Private | | Public | | Private 4-year | | Public 4-year | | Public 2-year | |
Academic year ending	Tuition and fees[2]	Gifts and endow-ment	Tuition and fees[2]	Government appro-priations	Tuition and fees[2]	Gifts and endow-ment	Tuition and fees[2]	Government appro-priations	Tuition and fees[2]	Government appro-priations
1977	$8,941	$4,658	$2,424	$8,176	$6,770	$2,356	$1,818	$7,279	$992	$4,400
1978	8,927	4,620	2,456	8,357	6,814	2,288	1,795	7,442	954	4,448
1979	9,017	4,668	2,496	8,623	6,857	2,303	1,763	7,713	956	4,512
1980	9,064	4,677	2,469	8,456	6,931	2,400	1,746	7,801	962	4,412
1981	9,292	4,823	2,484	8,109	6,973	2,409	1,767	7,615	957	4,150
1982	9,639	4,857	2,598	7,924	7,184	2,487	1,848	7,580	1,011	4,093
1983	10,306	4,729	2,814	7,760	7,504	2,545	1,900	7,363	1,016	3,806
1984	10,983	5,416	2,934	8,066	7,752	2,574	2,059	7,296	1,055	3,887
1985	11,377	5,697	2,954	8,609	8,012	2,696	2,120	7,860	1,124	4,225
1986	11,807	5,918	3,135	8,836	8,267	2,749	2,207	8,038	1,146	4,438
1987	12,618	6,203	3,270	8,602	8,787	2,872	2,205	7,731	1,155	4,447
1988	12,939	6,444	3,423	8,667	9,013	2,852	2,290	7,796	1,139	4,336
1989	13,176	6,547	3,498	8,608	9,156	2,832	2,343	7,432	1,191	4,329
1990	13,329	6,672	3,589	8,508	9,451	2,782	2,389	7,272	1,193	4,162
1991	13,772	6,763	3,709	8,268	9,743	2,742	2,403	6,701	1,244	4,137
1992	14,155	6,781	3,874	7,722	10,103	2,633	2,719	6,663	1,309	3,909
1993	14,491	7,130	3,941	7,386	10,281	2,587	3,102	6,659	1,637	3,851

[1] Includes doctoral-granting institutions with and without medical schools.

[2] Federally supported student aid received through students (e.g., Pell grants) is included under tuition and auxiliary enterprises.

SOURCE: U.S. Department of Education, National Center for Education Statistics, Financial Statistics of Institutions of Higher Education Survey and Integrated Postsecondary Education Data System (IPEDS), "Finance" survey.

Current fund revenues of institutions of higher education per full-time-equivalent (FTE) student (in 1995 constant dollars), by selected revenue sources and type of institution: Academic years ending 1977–93

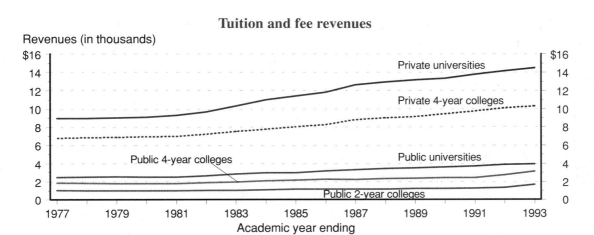

Tuition and fee revenues

Revenues (in thousands)

Private universities

Private 4-year colleges

Public 4-year colleges

Public universities

Public 2-year colleges

Academic year ending

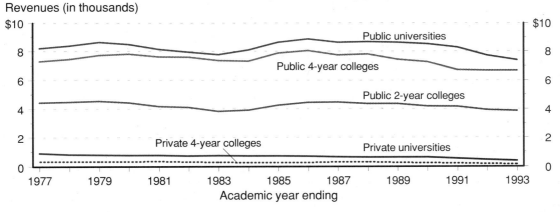

Federal, state, and local government appropriations

Revenues (in thousands)

Public universities

Public 4-year colleges

Public 2-year colleges

Private 4-year colleges

Private universities

Academic year ending

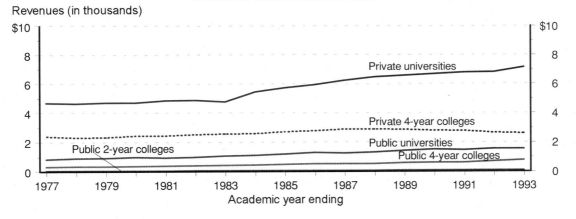

Gifts and endowment revenue

Revenues (in thousands)

Private universities

Private 4-year colleges

Public universities

Public 2-year colleges

Public 4-year colleges

Academic year ending

SOURCE: U.S. Department of Education, National Center for Education Statistics, Financial Statistics of Institutions of Higher Education Survey and Integrated Postsecondary Education Data System (IPEDS), "Finance" survey.

Salaries of teachers

♦ Between 1980 and 1995, the average salary of all public school teachers, adjusted for inflation, increased 19 percent, rising from $31,412 to $37,436.

♦ Following a period of decline in the 1970s, public school teachers' salaries increased continuously throughout the 1980s and into the early 1990s, reaching a peak of $37,725 in 1991. Since then, salaries have fluctuated slightly (see supplemental table 55-1).

How to attract and retain quality teachers has long been discussed among education officials. Concerns about such issues have led to reforms designed to increase teacher benefits. These measures include creating new career steps or paths; establishing teaching positions with greater authority and responsibility; instituting merit pay schemes; and experimenting with teachers' salary structures. These measures have been associated with increases in teachers' salaries.

♦ The average beginning salary of public school teachers increased 24 percent between 1980 and 1995, rising from $19,749 to $24,463.

♦ Public and private school teachers in rural schools had lower average base salaries than teachers in urban fringe or central city schools. Central city public school teachers had lower average base salaries than urban fringe public school teachers.

Average annual salaries (in 1995 constant dollars) of public elementary and secondary school teachers: Selected school years ending 1960–95

School year ending	All teachers	Elementary teachers	Secondary teachers	Beginning teachers*
1960	$25,959	$25,023	$27,419	(*)
1964	29,682	28,740	31,024	(*)
1968	33,330	32,365	34,538	(*)
1972	36,014	34,971	37,223	$25,462
1976	34,694	33,813	35,622	23,109
1980	31,412	30,624	32,374	19,749
1984	32,908	32,236	33,837	20,984
1988	36,954	36,274	37,961	24,082
1992	37,635	36,989	38,476	24,717
1994	37,407	36,863	38,297	24,670
1995	37,436	36,874	38,249	24,463

* Salary for beginning teachers is for the calendar year and is not available for 1960, 1964, and 1968.

Average compensation received by full-time public school teachers, by urbanicity and percentage of minority students in school: School year 1993–94

Percentage of minority students within urbanicity	School earnings*				Non-school compensation
	Total school earnings	Base salary	Summer supplemental	Other school compensation	
Total	**$35,464**	**$34,153**	**$2,070**	**$2,170**	**$5,114**
Central city	35,851	34,448	2,324	2,214	5,495
Less than 20 percent	34,588	33,430	1,756	2,014	4,885
20 percent or more	36,139	34,697	2,417	2,236	5,624
Urban fringe/large town	39,631	38,293	2,077	2,266	5,078
Less than 20 percent	40,304	39,001	1,833	2,313	4,636
20 percent or more	38,747	37,373	2,246	2,213	5,384
Rural/small town	32,025	30,800	1,817	2,073	4,890
Less than 20 percent	32,873	31,611	1,761	2,103	5,024
20 percent or more	30,150	28,962	1,933	2,074	4,608

* Detailed school earnings were computed using only teachers who reported those earnings; therefore, details do not add to total. Included in "total" and "other school compensation" are other sources of income reported after excluding outside income. Data were calculated from the SASS School and Teacher Questionnaires. Therefore, salaries shown here may not match other published figures.

SOURCE: U.S. Department of Education, National Center for Education Statistics, *Digest of Education Statistics, 1995* and Schools and Staffing Survey, 1993–94 (School, Administrator, and Teacher Questionnaires). American Federation of Teachers, *Survey and Analysis of Salary Trends 1995*, December 1995.

Average annual salaries of public school teachers

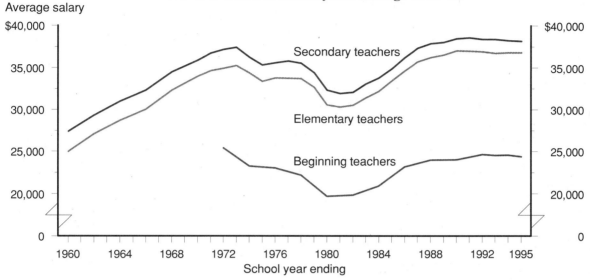

Average annual salaries (in 1995 constant dollars) of public school teachers: Selected school years ending: 1960–95*

Average salary

Secondary teachers

Elementary teachers

Beginning teachers

School year ending

* Plotted points for average annual salaries for public school teachers are even years 1960–68 and all years 1970–95. Plotted points for average beginning salaries for public school teachers are even years 1972–88 and all years 1990–95.

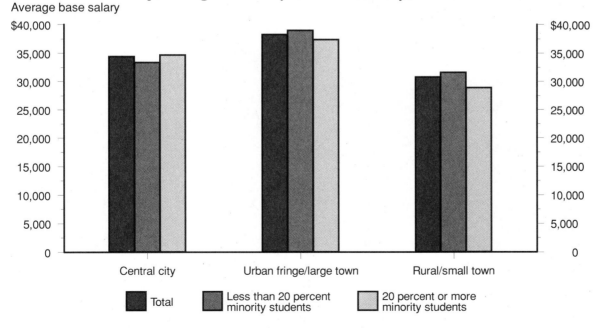

Average base salaries of full-time public school teachers, by urbancity and percentage of minority students: School year 1993–94

Average base salary

Central city   Urban fringe/large town   Rural/small town

| ■ Total | ■ Less than 20 percent minority students | □ 20 percent or more minority students |

SOURCE: U.S. Department of Education, National Center for Education Statistics, *Digest of Education Statistics, 1995* and Schools and Staffing Survey, 1993–94 (School, Administrator, and Teacher Questionnaires). American Federation of Teachers, *Survey and Analysis of Salary Trends 1995*, December 1995.

Sources of supply of newly hired teachers

♦ **Between 1988 and 1994, there was a shift in the sources of supply of newly hired teachers as both public and private schools hired larger proportions of first-time teachers and smaller proportions of transfers and reentrants.**

♦ **Transfers from other teaching positions comprised about one-third of new hires in 1994. In the public sector, the majority of these teachers came from other public schools in the same state.**

♦ **In 1994, 57 percent of public and 43 percent of private first-time teachers came directly from college, representing a decrease of about 10 percentage points since 1988.**

♦ **In 1994, substitute teaching was an entry route into teaching for substantial proportions of both first-time and reentrant teachers.**

> *In the last two decades, as fewer college graduates have entered the teaching profession and student enrollments have increased, policymakers have become concerned about the supply of new teachers needed to meet the demand. Our school systems depend on first-time, transfer, and reentering teachers to meet demand. Reentrants offer more teaching experience and training but at higher salaries than first-time teachers. First-time teachers have higher attrition rates from the profession than transfer and reentrant teachers. The extent of dependence on these alternative sources has implications for school budgets and teacher recruitment and retention.*

Percentage distribution of newly hired teachers, by control of school, supply source, and main activity in the previous year: School years ending 1988, 1991, and 1994

Supply source and main activity in the previous year	Public schools			Private schools		
	1988	1991	1994	1988	1991	1994
Total	**100.0**	**100.0**	**100.0**	**100.0**	**100.0**	**100.0**
First-time teachers	**30.6**	**41.7**	**45.8**	**25.2**	**34.0**	**42.4**
Transfers	**36.6**	**34.3**	**31.4**	**38.1**	**36.1**	**34.3**
Within state and sector	20.8	21.6	20.2	19.0	18.1	14.6
Across state	8.3	7.1	7.1	8.3	7.0	11.5
Across sector	7.5	5.6	4.1	10.9	11.0	8.1
Reentrants	**32.8**	**24.0**	**22.9**	**36.7**	**30.0**	**23.3**
Main previous year activity						
First-time teachers	**100.0**	**100.0**	**100.0**	**100.0**	**100.0**	**100.0**
Work in education (non-teaching)	5.7	5.2	10.7	4.8	7.5	13.6
Work outside education	11.0	10.0	11.6	24.5	20.6	19.9
College	66.5	58.4	56.7	51.8	48.7	43.1
Homemaking/childrearing	3.6	4.4	2.1	7.7	5.8	5.8
Other	13.3	22.0	18.9	11.3	17.4	17.6
Substitute teaching	—	18.0	17.2	—	12.0	15.2
Reentrants	**100.0**	**100.0**	**100.0**	**100.0**	**100.0**	**100.0**
Work in education (non-teaching)	10.3	19.1	15.0	8.9	11.7	19.9
Work outside education	17.4	17.9	19.2	21.2	26.1	26.0
College	18.0	10.4	18.1	20.0	5.6	11.9
Homemaking/childrearing	27.8	19.3	14.6	28.6	23.1	21.4
Other	26.5	33.3	33.1	21.3	33.6	20.9
Substitute teaching	—	23.8	29.6	—	18.7	18.1

Table reads: In 1994, 45.8 percent of all newly hired teachers in public schools were first-time teachers.

— Substitute teaching was not a response option in the 1988 SASS questionnaire.

NOTE: Newly hired teachers are defined as regular teachers who teach half time or more, and who did not hold regular teaching positions in that public school district or private school in the previous year. Excludes a small number of teachers whose schools did not respond to the questionnaire.

SOURCE: U.S. Department of Education, National Center for Education Statistics, Schools and Staffing Survey, 1987–88, 1990–91, and 1993–94 (Teacher Questionnaire).

Percentage distribution of newly hired teachers, by control of school, supply source, and main activity in the previous year

Supply source: School years ending 1988, 1991, and 1994

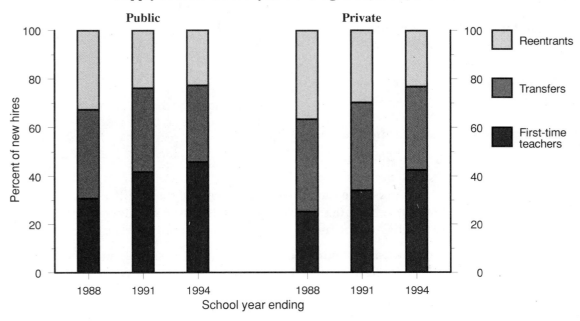

Main activity in the previous year: School year ending 1994

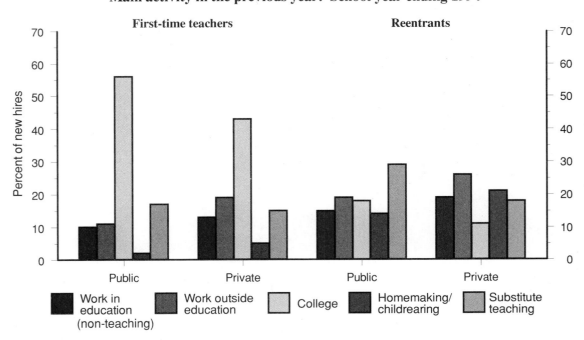

SOURCE: U.S. Department of Education, National Center for Education Statistics, Schools and Staffing Survey, 1987–88, 1990–91, and 1993–94 (Teacher Questionnaire).

Education and certification of secondary teachers

♦ In school year 1993–94, about three-quarters or more of public and private secondary students in all the core subjects, except mathematics, were taught by teachers who majored in that subject at the undergraduate or graduate level. Students in mathematics classes were less likely than students in any other core subject to be taught by a teacher who majored in that field.

♦ Private secondary students were more likely to be taught science* by teachers who majored in a science than were public school students. In both public and private schools, biology students were more likely than chemistry or physics students to have teachers who majored in that specific science.

Concern about the quality of education in the United States has focused interest on teacher qualifications and student exposure to well qualified teachers, especially in the core subject areas: English, mathematics, natural sciences, and social sciences. Educational background is one measure of teachers' qualifications. Whether teachers either majored or minored or are certified in the fields they teach is an indication of their substantive and academic qualifications in those subjects.

♦ Students at public secondary schools with a high poverty level (more than 40 percent of students eligible for free or reduced-price lunch) were less likely to be taught any of the core subjects by a teacher who majored in that subject than were students at public secondary schools with a low poverty level (5 percent or less eligible for free or reduced-price lunch) (see supplemental table 57-2).

♦ In public secondary schools, mathematics students were generally less likely to be taught by teachers who were certified, majored, majored or minored, or who held a graduate degree in their class subject than were students taking any other main subject.

Percentage of secondary students in selected subjects taught by teachers with selected qualifications, by control of school and class subject: School year 1993–94

Control of school and class subject	Majored in class subject	Majored or minored in class subject	Graduate degree in class subject	Certified in class subject
Public				
English	75.6	83.7	24.4	90.4
Social sciences	85.4	91.8	29.8	88.8
Mathematics	68.3	78.3	19.8	85.8
Science*	81.1	90.3	28.4	91.1
Biology	67.4	75.6	13.7	86.8
Chemistry	54.7	69.6	20.2	87.4
Physics	31.8	43.8	9.6	80.1
Foreign languages	81.3	89.5	26.5	88.7
Visual and performing arts	86.3	87.6	32.0	87.6
Health and physical education	91.3	93.3	23.2	91.7
Vocational education	80.8	82.8	23.5	88.5
Private				
English	74.2	79.1	27.9	65.0
Social sciences	89.0	91.2	29.8	68.3
Mathematics	63.8	71.4	18.0	53.6
Science*	85.4	91.8	30.2	70.1
Biology	71.7	78.9	19.2	76.6
Chemistry	46.5	67.7	15.1	56.4
Physics	38.0	46.6	6.8	40.8
Foreign languages	69.3	76.3	27.1	53.3
Visual and performing arts	83.0	86.2	38.3	61.3
Health and physical education	76.1	84.5	23.6	63.0
Vocational education	54.2	56.2	18.3	50.0

Table reads: In school year 1993–94, 68.3 percent of public secondary students in mathematics classes were taught by a teacher who majored in mathematics at the undergraduate or graduate level.

* It is easier to have majored, minored, or become certified in "science" than in a specific discipline, such as biology, because a teacher from any scientific field may qualify in science, whereas a discipline requires a specific match.

SOURCE: U.S. Department of Education, National Center for Education Statistics, Schools and Staffing Survey, 1993–94 (Teacher Questionnaire).

Percentage of secondary students in selected subjects taught by teachers who majored in the class subject at the undergraduate level: School year 1993–94

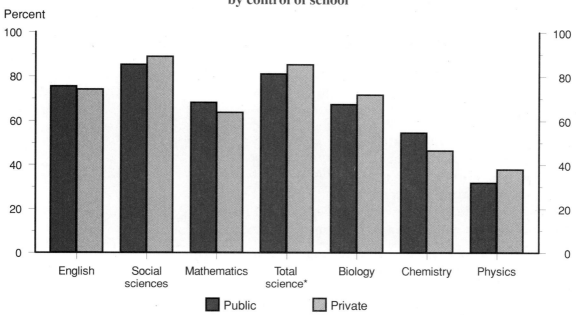

Students taught by teachers who majored in the class subject, by control of school

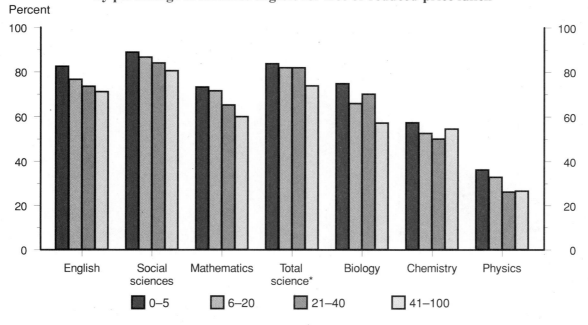

Public school students taught by teachers who majored in the class subject, by percentage of students eligible for free or reduced-price lunch

* It is easier to have majored, minored, or become certified in "science" than in a specific discipline, such as biology, because a teacher from any scientific field may qualify in science whereas a discipline requires a specific match.
SOURCE: U.S. Department of Education, National Center for Education Statistics, Schools and Staffing Survey, 1993–94 (Teacher Questionnaire).

Literacy of teachers

♦ **In 1992, teachers had literacy skills that were similar to private-sector executives and managers, engineers, physicians, writers and artists, social workers, sales representatives, education administrators, and registered nurses. Scientists were the only professionals who had measurably higher prose literacy skills than teachers.**

An important issue in the education reform debate is the effect of comparatively low salaries on teacher quality. Prose literacy scores are one of the best available measures of verbal ability, a factor identified by research as being associated with teacher quality. If teachers have lower prose literacy scores relative to college graduates in other occupations, this could indicate that relatively low salaries may not be attracting the most skilled college graduates to the teaching profession and keeping them in it. If, however, the literacy levels of teachers are no lower than those of their counterparts in other occupations, other benefits (e.g., job security, a shorter work year, the opportunity to work with children, good retirement benefits, etc.) may be more important for attracting quality teachers than salary alone.

♦ **Although teachers had literacy skills that were similar to college graduates in many other occupations, their earnings were often substantially less. However, the average total number of weeks worked in 1991 was lower for teachers than for college graduates in many other occupations.**

Prose literacy scores, labor market outcomes, and other characteristics of full-time employed bachelor's degree recipients, by selected occupations: 1992

Selected occupations	Average prose literacy scores	Average annual earnings in 1991	Average weekly wage last week	Average weeks worked in 1991	Average age	Percentage with graduate degrees	Percentage female
All bachelor's degree recipients	334	[1]$38,530	[1] $805	[1]49	[1]40	[1]35	[1]38
Scientists	[1]354	[1]39,320	[1] 805	[1]49	[1]36	43	[1]21
Lawyers and judges	352	[1]71,223	1,871	[1]49	41	[1]94	[1]17
Accountants and auditors	344	[1]38,463	[1] 832	[1]50	[1]37	[1]28	[1]38
Private-sector executives and managers	341	[1]56,044	[1]1,052	[1]51	41	[1]33	[1]26
Postsecondary teachers	340	47,867	924	48	45	[1]90	[1]29
Engineers	339	[1]48,408	[1]952	[1]50	41	[1]32	[1]8
Physicians	335	[1]121,120	[1]2,454	49	44	[1]100	[1]16
Teachers[2]	333	25,983	568	45	42	48	71
Writers and artists	332	29,507	589	46	39	33	47
Social workers	332	26,739	551	[1]50	40	38	60
Sales representatives	328	[1]39,872	[1]900	[1]49	42	[1]10	[1]23
Education administrators	326	[1]44,130	[1]888	[1]50	[1]49	[1]79	57
Registered nurses	326	[1]33,981	[1]741	49	38	[1]16	[1]88
Sales supervisors and proprietors	316	32,720	669	[1]51	41	[1]21	[1]20

Table reads: In 1992, the average prose literacy score for all bachelor's degree recipients was 334, and it was 333 for teachers.

[1] Statistically significant difference from teachers.

[2] Includes prekindergarten and kindergarten teachers, elementary and secondary school teachers, teachers in special education, and teachers not elsewhere categorized.

NOTE: Individuals scoring between 326 and 375 were able to integrate or synthesize information from complex or lengthy passages. For example, at proficiency level 328, test-takers were able to state in writing an argument made in a lengthy newspaper article. See the supplemental note to *Indicator 21* for a further description of literacy levels.

SOURCE: U.S. Department of Education, National Center for Education Statistics, National Adult Literacy Survey, 1992.

Prose literacy scores, labor market outcomes, and other characteristics of full-time employed bachelor's degree recipients, by selected occupations: 1992

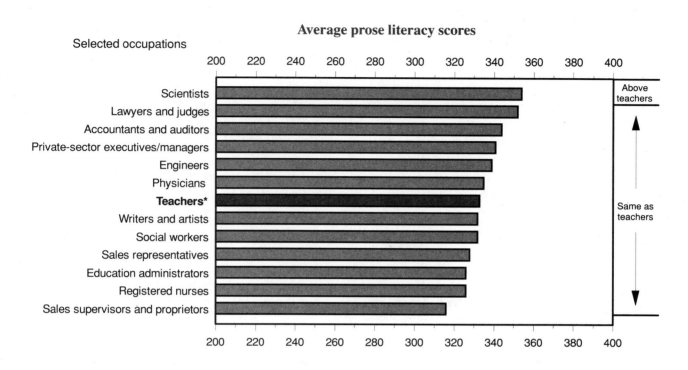

Average prose literacy scores

Selected occupations

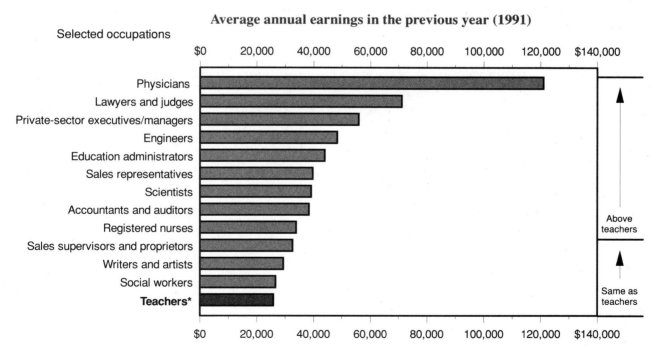

Average annual earnings in the previous year (1991)

Selected occupations

* Includes prekindergarten and kindergarten teachers, elementary and secondary school teachers, teachers in special education, and teachers not elsewhere categorized.
SOURCE: U.S. Department of Education, National Center for Education Statistics, National Adult Literacy Survey, 1992.

Teachers' participation in professional development

♦ In school year 1993–94, 50 percent or more of full-time public school teachers participated in professional development on topics including uses of educational technology for instruction, methods of teaching in their subject field, student assessment, and cooperative learning in the classroom.

> *Professional development for current teachers includes both seminars offered by schools or school districts and courses affiliated with institutions of higher education. The extent to which teachers pursue professional development while continuing to teach may indicate either the commitment of the teaching profession to improve teaching practice, or salary structures that reward participation in professional development.*

♦ Full-time public school teachers were more likely to participate in activities on all types of professional development topics than were full-time private school teachers. Full-time public elementary school teachers were more likely to participate in activities on four of the five types of professional development topics than were their secondary school counterparts.

♦ In school year 1993–94, 48 percent of full-time public school teachers received released time from teaching, and 41 percent received scheduled time for professional development. Twenty-two percent received none of the available types of support.

♦ Full-time public school teachers were more likely to receive professional growth credits and released and scheduled time from teaching than were their private school counterparts. However, private school teachers were more likely to receive tuition and/or fees than were public school teachers.

♦ Public elementary and secondary teachers in their first 3 years of teaching were more likely to have participated in a formal teacher induction program than were teachers with 4 or more years of experience (see supplemental table 59-1).

Percentage of full-time teachers who participated in professional development during the 1993–94 school year, by topic, type of support they received, and control and level of school

Professional development topic and type of support received	Public			Private		
	Total	Elementary	Secondary	Total	Elementary	Secondary
In-service education or professional development topic						
Uses of educational technology for instruction	50.1	49.7	50.7	34.3	32.8	38.5
Methods of teaching in specific subject field	64.4	69.7	55.0	59.8	63.1	50.8
In-depth study in specific field	30.1	31.6	27.5	25.9	24.7	29.2
Student assessment	52.0	55.4	45.8	40.4	42.5	34.7
Cooperative learning in the classroom	51.5	52.7	49.2	43.6	45.5	38.5
Type of support received during the 1993–94 school year for in-service education or professional development						
Released time from teaching	48.1	50.7	43.5	41.7	42.6	39.2
Scheduled time	40.7	43.6	35.4	36.3	37.1	34.3
Travel and/or per diem expenses	23.3	21.2	26.9	21.1	19.8	24.6
Tuition and/or fees	23.0	24.3	20.7	35.3	36.0	33.3
Professional growth credits	32.7	34.8	28.9	26.0	27.7	21.3
None of the above	22.2	19.4	27.1	26.0	25.1	28.4

Table reads: In school year 1993–94, 50.1 percent of public school teachers and 34.3 percent of private school teachers participated in professional development activities on the topic "the use of educational technology for instruction."

NOTE: Excludes a small number of teachers whose schools did not respond to the questionnaire.

SOURCE: U.S. Department of Education, National Center for Education Statistics, Schools and Staffing Survey, 1993–94 (Teacher Questionnaire).

Percentage of full-time teachers who participated in professional development during the 1993–94 school year, by control and level of school

In-service education or professional development topic

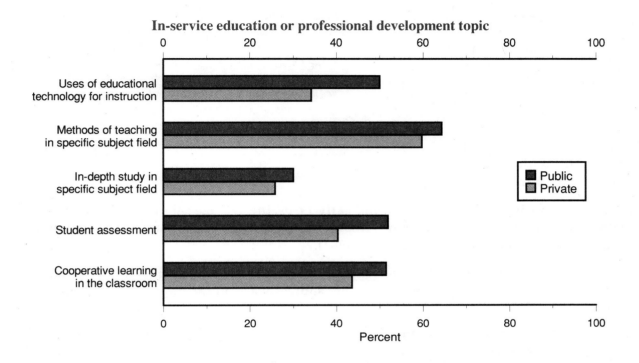

Type of support received for in-service education or professional development

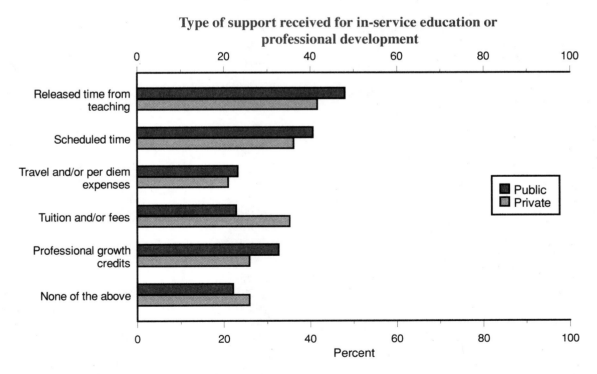

SOURCE: U.S. Department of Education, National Center for Education Statistics, Schools and Stafffing Survey, 1993–94 (Teacher Questionnaire).

Salaries and total earnings of full-time postsecondary faculty

♦ In 1992, 79 percent of full-time faculty received earnings in addition to their basic faculty salary. The mean basic faculty salary was $45,401, while the mean total earned income was $56,597.

♦ The proportion of total earnings derived from sources other than basic faculty salaries ranged from almost 13 percent among the humanities faculty to 20 percent among business faculty.

♦ Business and engineering faculty had higher basic salaries than humanities and education faculty.

Faculty salaries are an important component in attracting and retaining qualified instructional personnel. When evaluating the adequacy of full-time faculty salaries, it is essential to examine the earnings faculty members receive from other sources along with their total earned income and base salary amount. It is also important to note that salaries are a significant component of college and university expenditures.

♦ Despite gains during most of the 1980s and early 1990s, the average salaries (adjusted for inflation) of faculty across all academic ranks were lower in 1994 than they had been more than two decades earlier (see supplemental table 60-1).

♦ While faculty members tended to have a higher basic salary the higher their academic rank, the proportion of total earnings derived from other sources was similar among faculty from all academic ranks.

Earnings of full-time postsecondary faculty (in 1995 constant dollars), by control of institution, academic discipline, and academic rank: Fall 1992

Control of institution, academic discipline, and academic rank	Percent of faculty with earnings in addition to basic faculty salary (BFS)	Mean basic faculty salary (BFS)	Mean total earned income (TEI)	BFS as a percentage of TEI (mean)
Total*	**78.9**	**$45,401**	**$56,597**	**84.4**
Control of institution				
Public	78.4	45,611	56,626	84.7
Private	80.2	44,888	56,527	83.7
Academic discipline				
Agriculture	64.2	48,175	59,295	86.9
Business	80.6	49,391	65,423	80.3
Education	81.1	42,127	52,142	84.2
Engineering	80.8	55,634	71,417	81.1
Fine arts	87.4	40,714	50,758	83.7
Humanities	74.6	41,059	50,758	87.5
Natural sciences	76.7	47,414	48,775	86.0
Social sciences	83.5	46,089	58,155	83.9
Academic rank				
Full professor	81.2	56,919	71,788	84.1
Associate professor	81.0	46,296	56,856	84.7
Assistant professor	76.9	36,940	45,488	85.0
Instructor	76.1	33,507	42,919	82.8
Lecturer	69.8	34,707	42,829	85.0

Table reads: In the fall semester of 1992, 78.9 percent of full-time postsecondary faculty had earnings in addition to their basic faculty salary.

* Included in the total but not shown separately are other academic disciplines and ranks.

NOTE: Medical faculty are not included in this analysis. See the supplemental note to this indicator for additional information on sources of earned income.

SOURCE: U.S. Department of Education, National Center for Education Statistics, National Survey of Postsecondary Faculty, 1993.

Earnings of full-time postsecondary faculty (in 1995 constant dollars)

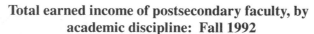

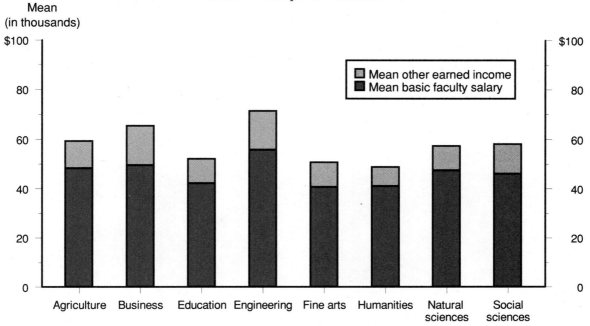

Total earned income of postsecondary faculty, by academic discipline: Fall 1992

Mean
(in thousands)

☐ Mean other earned income
■ Mean basic faculty salary

Agriculture Business Education Engineering Fine arts Humanities Natural sciences Social sciences

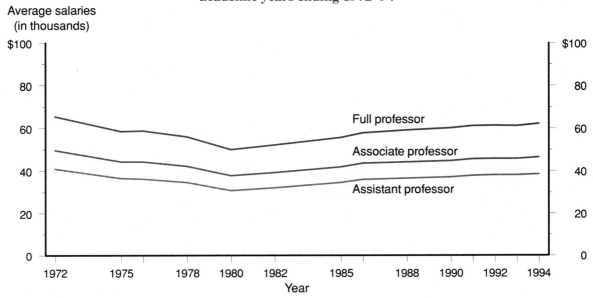

Average salaries (in 1995 constant dollars) of full-time faculty in all institutions of higher education, by academic rank: Selected academic years ending 1972–94

Average salaries
(in thousands)

Full professor

Associate professor

Assistant professor

Year

NOTE: Medical faculty are not included in this analysis.

SOURCE: U.S. Department of Education, National Center for Education Statistics, National Survey of Postsecondary Faculty, 1993, and *Digest of Education Statistics* (based on IPEDS/HEGIS "Salaries of Full-time Instructional Faculty" surveys), various years.

Supplemental Tables and Notes

Below are listed all of the supplemental tables and notes prepared for *The Condition of Education 1996*. Due to space limitations, all of the tables listed are not included in the printed volume; only those shown in bold are included here. To receive the complete set of tables (and any associated standard error tables), please fill out the reader's survey card and return it to the address shown.

Indicator 1

Table 1-1   Percentage of the population enrolled in school, by age: October 1970–94

Indicator 2

Table 2-1   Percentage of 3-year-olds enrolled in center-based programs and kindergarten, by selected student characteristics: 1995

Table 2-2   Percentage of 4-year-olds enrolled in center-based programs and kindergarten, by selected student characteristics: 1995

Table 2-3   Percentage of 5-year-olds enrolled in center-based programs and kindergarten, by selected student characteristics: 1995

Note   Preprimary enrollment rates

Indicator 3

Table 3-1   Percentage of second-grade students age 8 or older, by family income, sex, and race/ethnicity: October 1972–94

Table 3-2   Percentage of fourth-grade students age 10 or older, by family income, sex, and race/ethnicity: October 1972–94

Table 3-3   Percentage of seventh-grade students age 13 or older, by family income, sex, and race/ethnicity: October 1972–94

Note   Family income

Indicator 4

Table 4-1   Students in grades 3–6 who attended a chosen or assigned school, by race/ethnicity, urbanicity, parents' highest education level, and family income: 1993

Table 4-2   Students in grades 7–8 who attended a chosen or assigned school, by race/ethnicity, urbanicity, parents' highest education level, and family income: 1993

Table 4-3   Students in grades 9–12 who attended a chosen or assigned school, by race/ethnicity, urbanicity, parents' highest education level, and family income: 1993

Table 4-4   Percentage of parents of students in grades 3–12 who were very satisfied with aspects of their child's school, by type of school attended and grade level: 1993

Table 4-5   Parents' perceptions of their child's school, for children in grades 3–12, by type of school attended and grade level: 1993

Note   School choice

Indicator 5

Table 5-1   Status dropout rates for persons aged 16–24, by sex, race/ethnicity, and family income: October 1972–94

Table 5-2   Tenth- to 12th-grade cohort dropout rates, by sex and race/ethnicity: 1982 and 1992

Note   Dropout rates

Indicator 6

Table 6-1   Percentage of the sophomore class of 1980 in August 1982 and spring 1984 according to educational status, by selected characteristics

Table 6-2   Percentage of the sophomore class of 1990 in August 1992 and spring 1994 according to educational status, by selected characteristics

Table 6-3   Status of the sophomore classes of 1980 and 1990 in August 1982 and 1992 and spring 1984 and 1994, by educational status

Indicator 7

Indicator 8

Indicator 9

Indicator 10

Indicator 11

Indicator 12

Indicator 13

Indicator 21

    Table 21-1   Percentage distribution of the five literacy levels within selected income quintiles, by literacy scale and country: 1994

    Table 21-2   **Percentage distribution of the population in selected age groups scoring at each of the five literacy levels, by literacy scale and country: 1994**

    Table 21-3   **Percentage distribution of the population in selected occupations scoring at each of the five literacy levels, by literacy scale and country: 1994**

    Table 21-4   Percentage distribution of the population with selected educational attainment levels scoring at each of the five literacy levels, by literacy scale and country: 1994

    Note   Definitions of literacy scales and levels

Indicator 22

    Table 22-1   **SAT test-takers as a percentage of high school graduates, percentage of test-takers who are minorities, SAT mean scores, standard deviations, and percentage scoring 600 or higher: 1972–95**

    Table 22-2   **Average SAT scores of college-bound seniors, by race/ethnicity: 1976–95**

    Table 22-3   Percentage of college-bound seniors taking the SAT who scored in various ranges on the verbal and mathematics sections of the SAT, by sex: 1995

    Table 22-4   Distribution of college-bound seniors and average verbal and mathematics SAT scores, by selected characteristics: 1988, 1991, and 1995

    Table 22-5   Average verbal and mathematics SAT scores of college-bound seniors, by class rank expressed in quintiles: 1977–95

    Table 22-6   Percentage of students intending to major in selected fields and their average verbal and mathematics SAT scores: 1995

    Table 22-7   **Percentage of graduating seniors taking the ACT and ACT composite scores, by race/ethnicity and type of program: 1991–95**

    Note   Interpreting SAT test scores and the new version of the SAT

Indicator 23

    Table 23-1   Distribution of proficiency scores of 9-year-olds on mathematics assessment, by country: 1991

    Table 23-2   Distribution of proficiency scores of 13-year-olds on mathematics assessment, by country: 1991

    Note   Proficiency scores for IAEP mathematics and science

Indicator 24

    Table 24-1   Distribution of proficiency scores of 9-year-olds on science assessment, by sex, percentile and country: 1991

    Table 24-2   Distribution of proficiency scores of 13-year-olds on science assessment, by country: 1991

Indicator 25

    Table 25-1   Percentage of 25- to 29-year olds who have completed high school, by race/ethnicity and sex: March 1971–95

    Table 25-2   Percentage of 25- to 29-years-old high school graduates who have completed 1 or more years of college, by race/ethnicity and sex: March 1971–95

    Table 25-3   Percentage of 25- to 29-years-old high school graduates who have completed 4 or more years of college, by race/ethnicity and sex: March 1971–95

    Note   Educational attainment

Indicator 26

Table 26-1   Percentage distribution of 1980 high school sophomores according to the timing, enrollment status, and institution type of their initial enrollment in postsecondary education, by student characteristics: 1982 and 1992

Table 26-2   Percentage distribution of 1980 high school sophomores according to highest degree earned through 1992, by selected characteristics

Indicator 27

Table 27-1   Percentage of the population who have completed secondary and higher education, by sex, country, and age: 1992

Indicator 28

Table 28-1   Percentage of high school graduates earning a minimum number of units in core courses, by curriculum type and school characteristics: 1982, 1987, 1990, and 1994

Table 28-2   Percentage of high school graduates earning the minimum number of units in core courses, by sex: 1982, 1987, 1990, and 1994

Indicator 29

Table 29-1   Percentage of high school graduates taking selected mathematics and science courses in high school, by sex: 1982, 1987, 1990, and 1994

Table 29-2   Percentage of high school graduates taking selected mathematics and science courses in high school, by race/ethnicity: 1982, 1987, 1990, and 1994

Table 29-3   Percentage of high school graduates taking selected mathematics and science courses in high school, by control of school: 1982, 1987, 1990, and 1994

Table 29-4   Percentage of high school graduates taking selected mathematics and science courses in high school, by urbanicity: 1987 and 1994

Table 29-5   Percentage of high school graduates taking selected mathematics and science courses, by geographic region: 1982 and 1994

Table 29-6   Percentage of high school graduates taking selected mathematics and science courses, by school program: 1982 and 1994

Indicator 30

Table 30-1   Employment rates for recent high school graduates not enrolled in college and for recent school dropouts, by sex: October 1960–94

Table 30-2   Employment rates for recent high school graduates not enrolled in college and for recent school dropouts, by family income: October 1972–94

Table 30-3   Employment rates for recent high school graduates not enrolled in college and for recent school dropouts, by parents' highest education level: October 1994

Indicator 31

Table 31-1   Percentage of 1992–93 college graduates who were working in administrative or clerical support occupations and the percentage who were unemployed, by sex and field of study: April 1994

Indicator 32

Table 32–1   Percentage of 25- to 34-year-olds who were employed, by sex and years of school completed: March 1971–95

Table 32–2   Percentage of 25- to 34-year-olds who were unemployed, by sex and years of school completed: March 1971–95

Note   Labor force statistics

Indicator 33

Table 33-1 Percentage distribution of 25- to 34-year-olds in the work force and of those not employed full-time and year-round, the percentage for whom that status was involuntary, by work status, sex, educational attainment, and race/ethnicity: Calendar year 1994

Table 33-2 Percentage of workers aged 25–34 who usually worked full-time or part-time during the year, and the percentage of part-time workers for whom that status was involuntary, according to hours worked, by sex, educational attainment, and race/ethnicity: Calendar year 1994

Table 33-3 Percentage distribution of 25- to 34-year-olds in the work force, by work status, sex, educational attainment, sex, and race/ethnicity: Calendar year 1994

Indicator 34

Table 34-1 Median annual earnings (in 1995 constant dollars) of wage and salary workers aged 25–34 whose highest education level was grades 9–11, by sex and race/ethnicity: 1970–94

Table 34-2 Median annual earnings (in 1995 constant dollars) of wage and salary workers aged 25–34 whose highest education level was a high school diploma, by sex and race/ethnicity: 1970–94

Table 34-3 Median annual earnings (in 1995 constant dollars) of wage and salary workers aged 25–34 whose highest education level was some college, by sex and race/ethnicity: 1970–94

Table 34-4 Median annual earnings (in 1995 constant dollars) of wage and salary workers aged 25–34 whose highest education level was a bachelor's degree or higher, by sex and race/ethnicity: 1970–94

Table 34-5 Ratio of median annual earnings of wage and salary workers aged 25–34 whose highest education level was grades 9–11, some college, or a bachelor's degree or higher to those with a high school diploma, by sex: 1970–94

Indicator 35

Table 35-1 Median salaries (in 1995 constant dollars) of college graduates who were working full time and who were not enrolled in college 1 year after graduation, by field of study, sex, and race/ethnicity: Selected years of graduation 1977–93

Table 35-2 Percentage distribution of college graduates who were working full time and who were not enrolled in college 1 year after graduation, by field of study, sex, and race/ethnicity: Selected years of graduation 1977–93

Indicator 36

Table 36-1 Percentage of 25- to 34-year-olds who received income from AFDC or public assistance, according to years of school completed, by sex, race/ethnicity, and region of the United States: 1972–94

Indicator 37

Table 37-1 Percentage of 18- to 24-year-olds who reported voting and being registered to vote, by sex, race/ethnicity, and enrollment status: November 1994

Indicator 38

Table 38-1 Elementary and secondary school enrollment in thousands, by control and level of school, with projections: Fall 1970–2006

Table 38-2 Percentage of total elementary and secondary school enrollment, by control and level of school, with projections: Fall 1970–2006

Table 38-3 Enrollment in public elementary and secondary schools in thousands, by region: Fall 1970–94

Indicator 39

Indicator 40

Indicator 41

Indicator 42

Indicator 43

Indicator 45

Indicator 46

Indicator 47

Indicator 48

Indicator 54

Table 54-1   Current fund revenues (in 1995 constant dollars) of institutions of higher education per full-time-equivalent (FTE) student, by type of revenue sources and institution: Academic years ending 1977–93

Table 54-2   Percentage distribution of current fund revenues of institutions of higher education per full-time-equivalent (FTE) student according to revenue source, by type of institution: Academic years ending 1977–93

Indicator 55

Table 55-1   **Average annual salaries (in 1995 constant dollars) of public elementary and secondary teachers: Selected school years ending 1960–95**

Table 55-2   Ratio of average annual salary of public elementary and secondary teachers to per capita Gross Domestic Product (GDP): Selected school years ending 1960–95

Table 55-3   Average annual salaries (in 1995 constant dollars) of all teachers: School years ending 1981 and 1995, percentage change in salaries between 1981 and 1995, and 1994 per capita personal income, by region and state

Table 55-4   Average compensation (in current dollars) received by full-time public school teachers, by selected school characteristics: Summer 1993 and school year 1993–94

Table 55-5   Average compensation (in current dollars) received by full-time private school teachers, by selected school characteristics: Summer 1993 and school year 1993–94

Table 55-6   **Percentage of public school districts and private schools with salary schedules, average scheduled salary (in current dollars) of full-time teachers, by highest degree earned and years of teaching experience, percentage of schools without salary schedules, and average lowest and highest schedules: School year 1993–94**

Indicator 56

Table 56-1   Percentage distribution of newly hired teachers in public schools, by region and school characteristics: School year ending 1994

Table 56-2   Percentage distribution of newly hired teachers in private schools, by region and school characteristics: School year ending 1994

Indicator 57

Table 57-1   Percentage of secondary students in selected subjects taught by teachers with selected qualifications, by control of school, urbanicity, and class subject: School year 1993–94

Table 57-2   **Percentage of public secondary students in selected subjects taught by teachers with selected qualifications, by percentage of students eligible for free or reduced-price lunch and class subject: School year 1993–94**

Table 57-3   Percentage of public secondary students in selected subjects taught by teachers with selected qualifications, by urbanicity, percentage of students eligible for free or reduced price-lunch, and class subject: School year 1993–94

Table 57-4   Percentage of secondary students in selected subjects taught by teachers with selected qualifications, by control of school, percentage of minority students enrolled in school, and class subject: School year 1993–94

Table 57-5   Percentage of secondary students in selected subjects taught by teachers with selected qualifications, by control of school, school size, and class subject: School year 1993–94

Note   Definition of student percentages, certification in class subject, and major/minor in class subject

Indicator 59

Table 59-1 **Percentage of teachers who participated in a formal teacher induction or a master or mentor program, by years of teaching experience and control and level of school: 1994**

Table 59-2 **Percentage of full-time teachers who participated in professional development activities during the 1993–94 school year, by topic, type of support and activity, outcomes, and level, control and urbanicity of school**

Table 59-3 Percentage of public full-time teachers who participated in professional development activities during the 1993–94 school year, by topic, type of support and activity, outcomes, level and control of school, and percentage of students eligible for free or reduced-price lunch

Table 59-4 Percentage of full-time teachers who participated in professional development activities during the 1993–94 school year, by topic, type of support and activity, outcomes, level and control of school, and school size

Table 59-5 Percentage of full-time public school teachers who participated in professional development activities during the 1993–94 school year, by topic, type of support and activity, outcomes, and percentage of students eligible for free or reduced-priced lunch within urbanicity

Table 59-6 Percentage of all full-time teachers who participated in professional development activities, by professional development topic and state: 1994

Indicator 60

Table 60-1 **Average salaries (in constant 1995 dollars) of full-time faculty in institutions of higher education, by academic rank and type and control of institution: Selected academic years ending 1972–94**

Table 60-2 Earnings of full-time postsecondary faculty (in constant 1995 dollars) by control of institution, academic discipline, academic rank, and type of institution: Fall 1987 and fall 1992

Note Salaries of full-time postsecondary faculty

Note on preprimary enrollment rates

Age of the child

For this analysis, the age of the child was calculated as of December 31, 1994.

Enrollment rates

The numerator of the enrollment rate used in this analysis is the number of children aged 3, 4, or 5 years old who, as of December 31, 1994, were enrolled in center-based programs or kindergarten. The denominator is the total number of children aged 3, 4, and 5 as of December 31, 1994. Children who were enrolled in first grade or higher, or who were in the "ungraded" category, were excluded from this analysis.

Race/ethnicity

A child's race/ethnicity is the composite of the National Household Education Survey (NHES) variables "race" and "Hispanic." If the child's ethnicity was Hispanic, he or she was classified as Hispanic, regardless of whether his or her race was classified as white, black, or other. Children of "other" race/ethnicity were included in the totals but not shown separately in this analysis.

Parents' highest education level

"Parents' highest education level" is the highest level of education of the child's parents or nonparent guardians who resided in the household. It is based on the highest education level of the mother or female guardian and the highest education level of the father or male guardian. If only one parent resided in the household, that parent's highest education level was used.

Poverty measure

The poverty measure used in this analysis was developed by combining information about household composition and household income. Household composition is the count of family members based on the relationship among the household members. The number of family members is the number of persons in the immediate family of the child (e.g., parents, siblings, and the child him/herself). If the child had no parents in the household, the total number of household members was used.

Household income is the second part of the poverty measure. NHES collects data on household income in increments of $5,000 up to $75,000. Information on the actual household income, which was available for about 7 percent of the population, was also used. Because exact household income was not available in most cases, the measure is an approximation. The household was categorized as poor if:

- The number of family was 2 and the household income is $5,000 or less;

- The number of family was 2 and the actual household income is less than $10,000;

- The number of family was 3 and the household income is $10,000 or less;

- The number of family was 3 and the actual household income is less than $12,000;

- The number of family was 4 or 5 and the household income is $15,000 or less;

- The number of family was 5 and the actual household income is less than $18,000;

- The number of family was 6 or 7 and the household income is $20,000 or less;

- The number of family was 7 and actual household income is less than $23,000;

- The number of family was 8 and the household income is $25,000 or less; or

- The number of family was 9 or higher and the household income is $30,000 or less.

SOURCE: U.S. Department of Education, National Center for Education Statistics, National Household Education Survey (NHES), 1995.

Note on family income

The Current Population Survey (CPS) includes a family income variable that is used as a measure of a student's economic standing in many indicators in this publication. The three family income categories used in this publication are low, middle, and high income. Low income is the bottom 20 percent of all family incomes; high income is the top 20 percent of all family incomes; and middle income is the 60 percent in-between. The table that follows shows the real dollar amounts, rounded to the nearest $100, of the breakpoints between low and middle income and between middle and high income. For example, in 1994, low income was defined as the range between $0–11,800; middle income was defined as the range between $11,801–55,600; and high income was defined as the range between $55,601 and over. Therefore, the breakpoints between low and middle income and between middle and high income are $11,800 and $55,600, respectively.

Dollar value (in current dollars)at the breakpoint between low and middle and between middle and high income categories of family income: October 1970–94

October	Breakpoints between:	
	Low and middle	Middle and high
1970	$3,300	$11,900
1971	—	—
1972	3,500	13,600
1973	3,900	14,800
1974	—	—
1975	4,300	17,000
1976	4,600	18,300
1977	4,900	20,000
1978	5,300	21,600
1979	5,800	23,700
1980	6,000	25,300
1981	6,500	27,100
1982	7,100	31,300
1983	7,300	32,400
1984	7,400	34,200
1985	7,800	36,400
1986	8,400	38,200
1987	8,800	39,700
1988	9,300	42,100
1989	9,500	44,000
1990	9,600	46,300
1991	10,500	48,400
1992	10,700	49,700
1993	10,800	50,700
1994	11,800	55,600

— Not available.

NOTE: Amounts are rounded to the nearest $100.

Table 4-4 **Percentage of parents of students in grades 3–12 who were very satisfied[1] with aspects of their child's school, by type of school attended and grade level: 1993**

Child's grade and aspects of child's school	Total	Chosen school			Assigned public school		
		Total	Public	Private	Total	Choice of residence influenced by school[2]	Other
Grades 3–12							
School	55.9	70.7	61.2	82.5	52.3	56.0	48.7
Teachers	58.3	67.6	61.5	75.2	56.0	58.9	53.1
Academic standards	58.4	72.1	63.0	83.4	55.0	59.3	51.0
Discipline policy	58.5	72.6	63.0	84.4	55.1	58.2	52.2
Grades 3–6							
School	62.1	75.1	67.4	84.2	58.7	62.1	55.3
Teachers	67.0	72.8	69.6	76.7	65.4	68.0	62.9
Academic standards	62.3	74.6	65.6	85.5	59.0	62.6	55.6
Discipline policy	64.5	77.1	70.0	85.6	61.2	63.1	59.3
Grades 7–8							
School	49.9	69.1	58.1	81.2	45.8	49.5	42.2
Teachers	52.2	66.0	59.0	73.8	49.2	51.9	46.7
Academic standards	53.9	70.9	62.0	80.7	50.2	54.0	46.6
Discipline policy	53.9	73.1	61.9	85.5	49.7	52.9	46.7
Grades 9–12							
School	52.1	66.6	55.9	81.0	48.6	52.3	45.2
Teachers	51.5	62.3	53.9	73.7	48.9	52.2	45.8
Academic standards	56.4	70.0	60.9	82.3	53.1	58.2	48.4
Discipline policy	54.1	66.9	55.6	82.2	51.1	55.2	47.3

[1] Includes those who responded "very satisfied," from a scale of "very satisfied," "somewhat satisfied," " somewhat dissatisfied," and "very dissatisfied."

[2] Students whose parents indicated that their choice of residence was influenced by where their child would go to school.

SOURCE: U.S. Department of Education, National Center for Education Statistics, National Household Education Survey (NHES), 1993 (School Safety and Discipline File).

Note on school choice

Race/ethnicity

A child's race/ethnicity is the composite of the National Household Education Survey (NHES) variables "race" and "Hispanic." If the child's ethnicity was Hispanic, he or she was classified as Hispanic, regardless of whether his or her race was classified as white, black, or other. Children of "other" race/ethnicity were included in the totals but not shown separately in this analysis.

Parents' highest education level

"Parents' highest education level" is the highest level of education of the child's parents or non-parent guardians who resided in the household. It is based on the highest education level of the mother or female guardian and the highest education level of the father or male guardian. If only one parent resided in the household, that parent's highest education level was used.

Private school enrollment data from two different surveys

According to data from the Schools and Staffing Survey (SASS), 9.8 percent of students in grades 3–12 were enrolled in private schools. Data from NHES show that 8.8 percent of students in grades 3–12 were enrolled in private schools. These differences in enrollment rates may be due to differences in survey methodology.

The SASS collects information on enrollment from a sample of schools, which is selected from a universe of schools. The schools in the sample were asked to report how many students were enrolled in their schools. The NHES is a household survey that asks parents to report the type of school in which their child was enrolled. Population estimates in the NHES were controlled to population totals developed by the Census Bureau.

Urbanicity

The NHES urbanicity variable is a linked-derived variable that categorizes the respondent's ZIP code as "urban" or "rural." The variable was created using the respondent's ZIP code to extract data from the 1990 Census of Population Summary Tape File 3B. "Urban" is further broken down into inside "urbanized area" (UA) and "outside UA." Definitions for these categories were taken directly from the 1990 Census of Population. A UA comprises a place and the adjacent densely settled surrounding territory that together have a minimum population of 50,000. The term "place" in the UA definition includes both incorporated places, such as cities and villages, and census-designated places, which are unincorporated areas designated by the Census Bureau in cooperation with state and local agencies in order to permit tabulation of data for Census Bureau products. The "densely settled surrounding territory" adjacent to places consists of contiguous and non-contiguous territories of relative high population density within short distances. "Urban outside of UA" generally includes incorporated or unincorporated places outside of the UA with a minimum population of 2,500.

SOURCE: U.S. Department of Education, National Center for Education Statistics, National Household Education Survey (NHES), 1993.

Note on dropout rates

There are several ways to define and calculate dropout rates. Each type of dropout rate measures a different facet of dropping out. Three types of dropout rates are presented in this indicator: event rates, status rates, and cohort rates.

Event dropout rates

The event dropout rate is the percentage of students enrolled in grades 10–12 in October of a given year who are dropouts 1 year later. The high school persistence rate is 100 minus the event dropout rate.

Calculating this rate requires estimating 1) the number of students who left high school before graduating (recent dropouts), and 2) the number of students who were enrolled in grades 10, 11, and 12 the previous October. Using data from the October Current Population Survey (CPS), the first is estimated as the number of persons aged 15–24 who were not enrolled during the month of the survey, who were enrolled 1 year earlier, and who have not completed 12 years of school. The second is estimated by the sum of three groups of 15- to 24-year-olds who were enrolled the previous October: 1) recent dropouts, 2) those enrolled in grades 11 and 12 during the survey month, and 3) those who have completed 12 (or more) years of school and who indicated that they graduated during the survey year. Those enrolled in special schools are counted as "not enrolled in regular school" and may be classified as recent dropouts if they had been enrolled in a regular school the previous October.

Status dropout rates

The status dropout rate is the total number of those who, at any given time, are not enrolled in school and who have not completed high school.

CPS data are used to calculate the number or proportion of individuals who, as of October of any given year, have not completed high school and are not currently enrolled in school. The numerator of this rate is the number of individuals aged 16–24 who, as of October of any given year, have not completed high school and who are not currently enrolled in school. The denominator is the number of persons in that age group in October of that year.

Those persons who are still in school and those who have completed high school after dropping out are not counted as dropouts.

Cohort dropout rates

The cohort dropout rate is the percentage of students who were not enrolled in high school and who had not graduated based on repeated measures of a group of individuals with a set of shared experiences. In this analysis, that set of shared experiences is enrollment in 10th grade in a given year.

The initial experience used to define the cohort group can be date of birth, age at a particular point in time, entry into school, grade level in school, or any one of a number of other specific events. These analyses can be done in one of two ways. Consecutive ages or grades taken from existing cross-sectional data across a series of years can be linked to portray the experiences of an age or grade cohort. Alternatively, a prospective study can be used, where particular grades in school have been selected as the starting points for longitudinal studies of educational process and experiences.

Change in questions used to report educational attainment

From 1972 to 1991, educational attainment in the CPS was reported as "years of school completed." Individuals with 12 years of school completed were regarded as high school graduates, and those with 16 years completed as college graduates. Years of schooling completed were based on responses to two questions: 1) "What is the highest grade . . . ever attended?" and 2) "Did . . . complete it?" For example, an individual who responded that the highest grade he or she ever attended was the first year of college and that he or she did not complete it was regarded as having completed 12 years of school.

Beginning in 1992, these two questions were changed to a single question: "What is the highest level of school ... has completed or the highest degree ... has received?" The earlier high school levels are listed as single summary categories such as "9th grade, 10th grade, or 11th grade." Then, several new categories were added, including "12th grade, no diploma;" "H.S. graduate—diploma or equivalent;" and "Some college—no degree." Finally, college degrees were listed by type, allowing for a more exact understanding of educational attainment. See the supplemental note to *Indicator 25* for further discussion of the effects of this change in the measurement of educational attainment.*

Procedural changes

In 1994, the Bureau of the Census introduced several changes to procedures used in the CPS that may affect the comparability of statistics to those derived from earlier surveys. First, in 1994, the sample weights were calculated using information from both the 1980 and the 1990 Decennial Census. In earlier surveys, 1990 population figures were based on the 1980 Decennial Census and information collected during the 1980s on births, deaths, and migration. If, for some groups, the latter produces different estimates of their population than the former, the sample weights would change, as would statistics used to calculate them.

Second, the Bureau began using Computer-Aided Personal (and Telephone) Interviews (CAPI and CATI) to administer the survey in 1994. For earlier surveys, printed questionnaires were given to interviewers to complete. It is well known that the method in which a survey is administered can have effects on the responses. Although substantial testing was done to minimize or predict these effects, all questions were not tested. Therefore, some statistics, such as dropout rates, may be affected by the change in survey procedures

---

NOTE:

* U.S. Department of Education, National Center for Education Statistics, *Dropout Rates in the United States: 1994.*

Table 7-2   **Percentage of high school graduates aged 16–24 who were enrolled in college the October following graduation, by race/ethnicity and type of college: October 1972–94**

October	White			Black			Hispanic		
	Total	2-year	4-year	Total	2-year	4-year	Total	2-year	4-year
1972	49.7	—	—	44.6	—	—	45.0	—	—
1973	47.8	14.6	33.2	32.5	11.4	21.1	54.1	30.1	24.0
1974	47.2	13.9	33.3	47.2	16.4	30.8	46.9	30.0	16.8
1975	51.1	18.0	33.1	41.7	13.1	28.7	58.0	30.6	27.5
1976	48.8	14.9	33.9	44.4	11.3	33.1	52.7	36.5	16.2
1977	50.8	16.7	34.1	49.5	16.6	32.8	50.8	32.3	18.5
1978	50.5	16.4	34.1	46.4	17.5	28.9	42.0	20.4	21.6
1979	49.9	16.8	33.1	46.7	21.0	25.7	45.0	21.3	23.6
1980	49.8	18.8	31.0	42.7	18.8	23.9	52.3	30.9	21.4
1981	54.9	20.2	34.3	42.7	15.5	27.3	52.1	29.7	22.4
1982	52.7	19.5	33.2	35.8	12.7	23.2	43.2	23.4	19.8
1983	55.0	19.5	35.5	38.2	15.7	22.5	54.2	16.9	37.3
1984	59.0	18.7	40.3	39.8	19.8	20.0	44.3	23.9	20.4
1985	60.1	20.1	40.0	42.2	13.2	29.0	51.0	26.8	24.2
1986	56.8	19.9	36.9	36.9	12.7	24.3	44.0	28.5	15.5
1987	58.6	19.2	39.4	52.2	15.8	36.4	33.5	13.4	20.1
1988	61.1	22.2	38.9	44.4	16.7	27.6	57.1	25.9	31.2
1989	60.7	19.6	41.2	53.4	20.8	32.6	55.1	37.2	17.9
1990	63.0	19.7	43.3	46.8	19.6	27.2	42.7	27.0	15.7
1991	65.4	25.8	39.6	46.4	18.7	27.7	57.2	25.2	32.0
1992	64.3	23.0	41.3	48.2	17.4	30.8	55.0	29.4	25.6
1993	62.9	21.9	41.0	55.6	18.9	36.7	62.2	37.8	24.4
1994	64.5	20.7	43.8	50.8	19.8	31.0	49.1	25.9	23.2

— Not available. Data regarding type of college were not collected until 1973.

NOTE: Details may not add to totals due to rounding.

SOURCE: U.S. Department of Commerce, Bureau of the Census, October Current Population Surveys.

Table 7-3   Percentage of high school graduates aged 16–24 who were enrolled in college the October following graduation, by type of college, college enrollment status, and parents' highest education level:[1] October 1994

Parents' highest education level	Total	Type of college		Enrollment status	
		2-year	4-year	Full-time	Part-time
Less than high school graduate	43.0	24.5	18.5	36.1	6.9
High school graduate	49.9	18.1	31.8	44.7	5.2
Some college	65.0	24.8	40.1	59.5	5.5
Bachelor's degree or higher	82.5	20.2	62.3	78.7	3.8
Not available[2]	43.1	18.5	24.6	36.2	6.9

[1] Parents' highest education level is defined as 1) either the highest educational attainment of the two parents who reside with the student, or if only one parent is in the residence, the highest educational attainment of that parent; or 2) when neither parent resides with the student (5 percent of the cases reported), the highest educational attainment of the head of the household and his or her spouse.

[2] Parents' highest education level is not available 1) for those who do not live with their parents and who are classified as the head of the household (not including those who live in college dormitories); and 2) for those whose parents' educational attainment was not reported. In 1994, 29 percent of respondents aged 16–24 were in this category.

SOURCE: U.S. Department of Commerce, Bureau of the Census, October Current Population Surveys.

Table 8-1   Percentage of high school graduates enrolled in college, by age, race/ethnicity, and type of institution: October 1973–94

October	Aged 18–24				Aged 25–34				Aged 35 or older			
	Total	White	Black	Hispanic	Total	White	Black	Hispanic	Total	White	Black	Hispanic
2-year institutions												
1973	6.3	6.3	4.6	9.8	2.1	2.0	2.3	3.6	—	—	—	—
1974	7.0	6.4	7.2	14.6	2.4	2.2	3.6	3.3	—	—	—	—
1975	8.1	7.7	9.3	13.6	3.0	2.7	5.2	5.5	—	—	—	—
1976	7.8	7.3	8.6	14.4	3.1	2.7	4.8	6.5	0.9	0.9	1.4	2.1
1977	8.0	7.5	9.8	13.9	3.1	2.8	5.5	4.6	—	—	—	—
1978	8.0	7.6	7.9	11.9	2.7	2.5	4.1	4.6	1.0	0.9	1.7	1.9
1979	7.6	7.1	8.4	13.3	2.6	2.4	3.2	4.4	1.0	0.9	1.1	1.6
1980	8.5	8.1	9.0	11.9	2.8	2.6	3.4	3.8	0.8	0.8	1.4	1.1
1981	9.0	8.6	7.9	14.3	2.7	2.5	3.2	4.2	0.9	0.8	1.5	2.6
1982	9.3	9.0	7.4	14.6	2.8	2.6	3.5	4.0	0.9	0.8	1.0	1.4
1983	8.9	8.8	7.4	12.1	2.8	2.6	3.5	5.3	0.9	0.9	0.7	1.2
1984	8.6	8.2	9.2	10.8	2.7	2.6	2.8	3.5	0.8	0.7	1.0	0.8
1985	8.6	8.3	8.4	10.5	2.8	2.7	2.7	4.1	0.9	0.8	1.1	1.1
1986	9.0	9.0	6.9	12.3	2.7	2.6	2.5	4.1	0.9	0.9	1.3	0.9
1987	9.8	9.5	8.7	12.0	2.5	2.3	2.6	3.8	0.9	0.8	1.0	1.0
1988	10.6	10.6	7.8	13.4	2.5	2.3	3.5	3.3	0.9	0.9	1.4	1.5
1989	9.9	9.5	9.1	13.2	2.5	2.4	2.4	3.3	0.9	0.9	0.9	2.0
1990	10.5	10.2	10.6	13.2	2.8	2.7	2.7	3.5	1.0	0.9	1.1	1.9
1991	11.8	11.3	11.3	14.9	3.2	3.0	3.6	3.8	1.0	1.0	1.3	1.3
1992	12.0	11.2	10.7	17.6	2.9	2.8	2.3	3.8	0.9	0.9	0.9	1.4
1993	11.7	11.5	9.4	16.2	2.7	2.4	3.4	4.2	1.0	0.9	1.4	1.5
1994	11.1	10.8	10.5	13.1	3.1	2.7	3.9	4.4	1.0	0.9	1.2	2.0
4-year institutions												
1973	15.6	15.9	12.5	13.3	1.9	1.8	2.4	2.5	—	—	—	—
1974	15.6	15.9	13.6	11.8	1.8	1.6	3.2	1.8	—	—	—	—
1975	15.7	15.8	15.1	15.9	2.0	1.9	2.6	2.5	—	—	—	—
1976	24.4	24.6	23.9	19.4	6.3	6.2	6.8	3.8	1.3	1.2	2.7	1.8
1977	23.1	23.4	19.9	16.8	6.6	6.4	7.6	7.2	—	—	—	—
1978	22.6	22.9	20.8	14.5	6.1	6.0	6.0	5.4	1.4	1.3	2.0	2.4
1979	22.8	23.5	19.6	15.7	6.2	6.2	5.3	6.6	1.4	1.4	2.1	1.2
1980	22.2	23.0	17.0	16.9	5.6	5.7	5.5	4.6	1.2	1.1	1.7	1.7
1981	22.4	23.1	18.8	15.0	5.8	5.6	6.2	5.7	1.4	1.3	2.2	1.3
1982	22.7	23.4	19.5	13.6	5.8	5.8	5.6	4.5	1.3	1.2	1.7	1.5
1983	22.6	23.4	18.4	17.9	5.9	5.8	4.9	4.4	1.4	1.3	1.9	1.9
1984	23.4	24.5	16.9	17.4	5.6	5.5	4.7	6.2	1.2	1.2	1.6	0.9
1985	23.8	25.3	16.4	14.8	5.6	5.7	4.1	5.3	1.4	1.3	1.8	2.1
1986	24.2	24.7	20.7	16.3	5.3	5.1	5.0	6.0	1.4	1.3	1.9	2.3
1987	26.2	27.7	20.3	16.1	5.6	5.5	5.3	5.0	1.5	1.4	1.6	1.5
1988	26.4	27.8	20.0	17.4	5.4	5.5	3.9	4.5	1.8	1.7	1.9	1.9
1989	28.1	30.1	21.4	15.1	5.8	5.9	3.8	3.8	1.6	1.6	1.2	1.7
1990	28.4	30.2	21.8	15.1	5.8	6.1	3.3	3.5	1.7	1.7	1.8	2.0
1991	29.1	30.9	19.5	19.1	5.8	5.7	4.5	4.8	1.7	1.7	2.1	1.6
1992	29.6	31.3	22.7	18.5	5.7	5.6	4.4	4.7	1.6	1.6	1.7	1.3
1993	29.3	30.6	22.8	18.7	5.8	5.8	4.7	5.2	1.6	1.5	2.0	1.6
1994	31.1	32.8	25.1	19.8	6.5	6.4	5.8	5.7	1.7	1.6	2.3	2.3

— Not available.

SOURCE: U.S. Department of Commerce, Bureau of the Census, October Current Population Surveys.

Table 8-2 Percentage of high school graduates enrolled in college, by age, race/ethnicity, and enrollment status: October 1972–94

October	Age 18–24				Age 25–34				Age 35 or older			
	Total	White	Black	Hispanic	Total	White	Black	Hispanic	Total	White	Black	Hispanic
					Full-time							
1972	27.3	28.0	22.0	20.7	3.2	3.2	3.4	3.2	—	—	—	—
1973	25.4	25.8	20.4	23.8	2.9	2.7	4.1	3.1	—	—	—	—
1974	25.4	25.4	22.0	25.1	3.5	3.3	4.3	3.7	—	—	—	—
1975	27.2	27.0	26.7	28.1	4.2	3.8	6.8	4.6	—	—	—	—
1976	27.7	27.3	29.3	29.0	3.5	3.2	5.5	4.2	0.4	0.4	1.2	0.8
1977	26.8	26.7	25.8	25.7	3.9	3.4	7.1	4.8	—	—	—	—
1978	25.9	25.8	25.8	18.9	3.3	3.1	4.2	3.8	0.4	0.3	0.8	0.6
1979	25.9	25.8	25.2	24.3	3.1	2.9	3.7	5.7	0.4	0.3	0.9	0.7
1980	26.5	26.9	23.6	22.3	3.0	2.8	3.6	4.0	0.3	0.3	0.8	0.7
1981	27.0	27.2	23.6	24.6	3.2	2.9	4.4	3.9	0.4	0.3	1.3	1.4
1982	27.1	27.6	23.1	20.4	3.5	3.3	4.2	4.3	0.4	0.4	0.9	0.0
1983	25.0	25.1	22.8	22.7	3.7	3.2	4.3	4.2	0.4	0.4	0.8	0.4
1984	27.8	28.7	21.6	23.7	3.5	3.2	3.7	4.1	0.4	0.4	0.5	0.3
1985	28.3	29.6	21.4	21.1	3.3	3.0	3.7	3.7	0.4	0.4	0.7	0.8
1986	28.3	29.0	24.3	21.2	3.2	2.8	4.0	4.2	0.5	0.5	1.0	1.0
1987	29.7	30.9	23.9	20.1	2.9	2.6	3.7	3.6	0.5	0.5	0.8	0.4
1988	30.7	31.9	24.1	22.7	3.1	2.9	2.8	2.8	0.5	0.5	0.7	0.5
1989	31.9	33.6	25.9	21.0	3.2	3.1	2.2	2.8	0.7	0.6	0.6	1.2
1990	32.6	34.3	25.6	20.9	3.6	3.5	3.0	2.2	0.6	0.6	0.7	1.0
1991	34.6	35.9	26.5	25.7	3.9	3.6	3.5	3.7	0.6	0.6	1.0	0.4
1992	34.9	36.2	27.6	26.0	3.6	3.5	3.1	2.4	0.7	0.7	0.9	0.8
1993	31.9	31.9	27.3	26.4	3.9	3.7	3.3	4.1	0.7	0.6	1.2	0.8
1994	34.6	36.2	29.6	21.4	4.3	4.0	3.8	4.4	0.8	0.7	1.0	1.5
					Part-time							
1972	4.6	4.5	5.2	5.1	5.2	5.2	5.4	4.3	—	—	—	—
1973	4.3	4.4	3.5	5.3	5.3	5.4	3.6	8.5	—	—	—	—
1974	5.1	5.1	4.2	7.2	5.8	5.8	6.5	6.3	—	—	—	—
1975	5.3	5.3	4.8	7.4	5.7	5.8	4.7	6.7	—	—	—	—
1976	5.4	5.5	4.2	7.0	6.1	6.0	6.4	6.8	1.9	1.7	2.9	3.1
1977	5.6	5.6	5.5	5.3	6.4	6.3	6.9	7.5	—	—	—	—
1978	5.4	5.5	3.8	8.2	5.8	5.7	6.6	6.4	2.0	1.9	3.0	3.6
1979	5.3	5.4	4.1	5.8	6.0	6.0	5.6	5.9	2.0	2.0	2.4	2.3
1980	5.3	5.3	4.1	7.6	5.9	5.9	6.0	5.3	1.8	1.7	2.6	2.2
1981	5.5	5.5	4.5	5.3	5.7	5.5	5.8	6.9	1.9	1.8	2.4	2.6
1982	5.8	5.6	5.0	8.8	5.4	5.5	5.4	5.4	1.8	1.7	1.8	2.9
1983	5.4	5.3	4.2	8.8	5.4	5.5	4.5	5.5	1.9	1.8	1.9	2.7
1984	5.4	5.2	5.6	6.2	5.1	5.2	4.2	5.8	1.7	1.6	2.2	1.5
1985	5.4	5.4	4.6	5.8	5.4	5.6	3.7	6.0	1.8	1.8	2.2	2.6
1986	5.7	5.6	4.3	8.3	5.1	5.1	3.9	6.2	1.8	1.8	2.3	2.3
1987	6.4	6.3	5.1	8.1	5.2	5.3	4.2	5.3	1.8	1.8	1.9	2.2
1988	6.3	6.6	3.7	8.1	4.9	5.0	4.6	5.0	2.2	2.1	2.6	2.8
1989	6.0	6.1	4.6	7.3	5.1	5.2	4.0	4.4	1.9	1.9	1.5	2.5
1990	6.4	6.0	6.8	7.4	4.8	5.1	3.0	4.8	2.0	2.0	2.2	2.9
1991	6.2	6.3	4.3	8.3	5.2	5.2	4.6	4.9	2.1	2.0	2.4	2.4
1992	6.7	6.4	5.8	10.2	5.0	5.0	3.5	5.9	1.8	1.8	1.7	1.9
1993	6.9	7.1	4.9	8.5	4.7	4.6	4.8	5.3	1.8	1.8	2.2	2.3
1994	7.6	7.3	5.9	11.6	5.3	5.1	5.9	5.7	2.0	1.9	2.4	2.9

— Not available.

SOURCE: U.S. Department of Commerce, Bureau of the Census, October Current Population Surveys.

Table 9-1 Among 1989–90 beginning students at community colleges, percentage distribution according to attainment at first institution and 1994 attainment at any institution, by selected characteristics

Selected characteristics	Attainment at first institution[1]			1994 attainment at any institution									
				Attained[2]						No degree			
					Certificate		Associate's				Enrolled		
	None	Certi-ficate	Asso-ciate's	Total	Not en-rolled at 4-year	En-rolled at 4-year	Not en-rolled at 4-year	En-rolled at 4-year	Bache-lor's	Total	Less-than-4-year[3]	4-year	Not en-rolled
Total	**77.8**	**5.0**	**17.2**	**36.7**	**12.3**	**0.6**	**13.5**	**4.0**	**6.3**	**14.7**	**9.6**	**5.1**	**48.6**
Sex													
Male	81.2	4.7	14.1	33.8	12.1	0.6	11.9	3.6	5.6	17.1	10.5	6.7	49.1
Female	74.5	5.3	20.2	39.6	12.6	0.6	15.0	4.5	7.0	12.4	8.7	3.7	48.1
Race/ethnicity													
White	76.7	5.2	18.1	37.3	11.5	0.8	14.3	4.1	6.6	13.0	7.8	5.3	49.7
Black	80.9	7.9	11.2	31.8	16.1	0.0	8.1	4.4	3.1	13.2	9.5	3.6	55.1
Hispanic	82.7	1.0	16.3	38.0	15.2	0.0	12.0	3.6	7.2	22.2	18.5	3.8	39.8
Asian/Pacific Islander	—	—	—	—	—	—	—	—	—	—	—	—	—
American Indian/Alaskan Native	—	—	—	—	—	—	—	—	—	—	—	—	—
Parents' educational attainment													
Less than high school graduate	85.8	6.9	7.3	27.7	19.4	0.0	6.2	0.0	2.2	11.4	11.4	0.0	60.9
High school graduate	74.8	6.8	18.4	38.1	12.2	0.8	15.1	3.2	6.9	10.6	7.3	3.3	51.3
Some postsecondary	72.7	5.1	22.3	36.8	10.0	0.7	13.1	6.2	6.9	17.5	12.0	5.6	45.7
Bachelor's degree	81.2	1.3	17.5	39.2	12.9	0.0	13.0	8.3	5.1	21.6	12.8	8.7	39.2
Advanced degree	74.8	0.0	25.2	47.6	1.5	2.2	27.2	3.2	13.6	23.3	8.2	15.1	29.1
Socioeconomic status													
Lowest quartile	80.1	10.1	9.9	30.2	17.7	0.0	9.8	0.8	1.9	10.3	9.7	0.6	59.5
Middle two quartiles	79.0	5.3	15.7	34.3	13.4	0.3	10.2	4.8	5.7	16.4	11.1	5.3	49.3
Highest quartile	74.4	1.4	24.2	44.8	7.2	1.5	21.3	4.8	10.1	14.5	6.9	7.6	40.7
Family income[4]													
Less than $20,000	75.7	4.8	19.5	39.4	12.0	0.0	17.8	3.6	5.9	15.5	10.4	5.1	45.2
20,000–39,999	75.3	3.5	21.2	43.4	11.7	1.1	12.8	7.7	10.0	13.8	6.4	7.4	42.9
40,000–59,999	70.8	2.7	26.5	42.4	10.3	0.9	17.8	4.1	9.3	13.1	8.4	4.7	44.6
60,000 or more	76.5	1.4	22.1	46.9	3.3	2.1	26.7	4.8	10.0	24.6	9.2	15.5	28.5
Age as of 12/31/89													
18 years or younger	71.6	2.6	25.9	47.4	8.0	1.4	19.7	6.4	11.9	14.9	7.5	7.4	37.7
19 years	79.5	5.8	14.7	31.9	12.7	0.0	13.2	3.9	2.2	20.8	12.7	8.1	47.3
20–29 years	83.1	6.5	10.4	27.3	16.4	0.0	6.5	1.8	2.5	13.0	11.2	1.8	59.8
30 years or older	86.0	8.9	5.1	25.7	18.2	0.0	6.3	0.6	0.6	9.2	9.2	0.0	65.1
Expected educational attainment													
Less than 2 years of postsecondary education	80.2	16.2	3.6	23.9	19.8	0.0	4.1	0.0	0.0	12.3	8.5	3.9	63.8
2 to 3 years of postsecondary education	82.2	6.6	11.2	30.2	18.3	0.0	9.5	1.0	1.4	11.8	11.1	0.7	58.0
Bachelor's degree or higher	76.4	2.4	21.2	40.6	9.0	0.9	16.0	5.7	9.0	16.1	9.4	6.7	43.3
High school credential													
High school diploma	77.2	4.6	18.2	38.0	12.2	0.7	14.1	4.4	6.7	15.5	10.2	5.4	46.5
Equivalency certificate	86.4	10.1	3.5	21.2	15.1	0.0	4.3	0.0	1.9	2.7	2.7	0.0	76.2
None	—	—	—	—	—	—	—	—	—	—	—	—	—
Diploma/delayed entry status													
Diploma, did not delay	73.1	2.8	24.1	45.5	9.5	1.1	18.8	6.1	10.0	16.3	8.4	7.8	38.3
Diploma, delayed entry	83.4	7.5	9.1	26.4	16.3	0.0	6.8	1.8	1.5	14.5	12.8	1.6	59.1
No diploma	85.3	9.5	5.1	21.8	14.2	0.0	5.9	0.0	1.7	4.5	2.5	2.0	73.7

Table 9-1 Among 1989–90 beginning students at community colleges, percentage distribution according to attainment at first institution and 1994 attainment at any institution, by selected characteristics—Continued

	Attainment at first institution[1]			1994 attainment at any institution									
				Attained[2]						No degree			
					Certificate		Associate's				Enrolled		
Selected characteristics	None	Certificate	Associate's	Total	Not enrolled at 4-year	Enrolled at 4-year	Not enrolled at 4-year	Enrolled at 4-year	Bachelor's	Total	Less-than-4-year[3]	4-year	Not enrolled
Self-rating of academic ability													
Above average	69.9	6.7	23.5	47.3	12.8	1.3	14.9	6.8	11.4	16.7	9.8	6.9	36.1
Average or below	80.4	4.5	15.2	33.1	11.7	0.4	12.9	3.3	4.8	14.2	9.8	4.4	52.7
Marital status in 1989–90													
Never married	75.8	3.6	20.7	41.1	11.0	0.8	16.3	4.8	8.1	16.2	10.2	6.1	42.7
Married	81.1	9.3	9.6	26.3	15.4	0.0	6.5	2.2	2.2	9.2	9.2	0.0	64.5
Divorced/separated/widowed	88.5	9.4	2.2	29.9	25.6	0.0	3.3	0.0	1.0	8.8	5.9	3.0	61.2
Number of children in 1989–90													
None	76.7	3.6	19.7	38.3	9.8	0.8	15.0	4.8	7.8	16.2	10.2	6.1	45.4
One	81.6	11.6	6.8	32.2	23.9	0.0	6.2	2.1	0.0	7.0	6.2	0.8	60.8
Two	84.3	10.5	5.2	26.5	21.0	0.0	4.4	1.1	0.0	11.9	9.7	2.1	61.7
Three or more	83.9	6.8	9.3	33.7	18.7	0.0	11.1	0.0	4.0	9.1	9.1	0.0	57.2
Enrollment status in 1989–90													
Exclusively full-time	70.7	4.6	24.8	47.1	10.8	0.9	17.7	6.6	11.1	14.3	7.8	6.4	38.6
Mixed	70.4	6.0	23.6	51.3	16.3	0.0	21.5	6.3	7.3	13.6	6.5	7.1	35.1
Exclusively part-time	88.6	4.0	7.4	22.5	12.7	0.6	6.8	1.5	1.0	16.8	13.2	3.6	60.7
Enrollment status, first term													
Full-time	68.7	5.4	25.9	45.7	10.3	1.0	17.5	6.0	11.0	11.7	5.7	6.0	42.7
At least half, less than full-time	84.9	2.8	12.3	28.3	10.9	0.6	13.2	1.8	1.8	22.8	17.0	5.8	48.9
Less than half-time	87.7	6.6	5.8	27.1	16.9	0.0	6.7	1.4	2.2	13.0	9.3	3.7	59.9
Grade point average in 1989–90													
Below 2.75	80.6	4.4	15.0	34.2	11.6	0.7	11.8	2.9	7.3	17.5	9.5	8.0	48.2
2.75–3.24	73.4	3.8	22.8	40.3	6.8	1.3	18.9	6.5	6.8	11.4	5.5	5.9	48.3
3.25 or higher	69.8	7.9	22.3	41.5	14.8	0.7	15.7	4.0	6.3	14.6	12.3	2.3	43.9
Academic integration in 1989–90[5]													
Low	90.1	9.9	0.0	15.4	13.7	0.0	0.0	0.0	1.7	16.7	10.4	6.3	67.8
Moderate	77.5	2.8	19.7	39.1	13.1	0.0	12.0	4.7	9.3	13.0	8.6	4.4	47.9
High	78.4	6.1	15.5	35.3	10.4	0.0	13.3	4.4	7.2	23.8	17.1	6.7	40.9
Social integration in 1989–90[6]													
Low	85.4	6.4	8.2	21.5	10.2	0.0	7.7	0.5	3.1	15.7	13.3	2.4	62.8
Moderate	79.0	3.0	18.0	47.8	13.7	1.2	19.7	4.3	8.9	14.2	7.5	6.8	38.0
High	—	—	—	—	—	—	—	—	—	—	—	—	—
Degree goal in 1989–90[7]													
Not working toward degree	98.9	1.1	0.0	12.7	5.8	0.0	3.7	0.0	3.2	13.9	10.0	3.8	73.4
Certificate/license	71.0	24.1	4.9	39.5	34.1	0.0	5.4	0.0	0.0	6.4	4.7	1.7	54.2
Associate's degree	73.9	3.1	23.0	41.5	11.1	0.8	17.2	4.7	7.8	13.1	8.8	4.3	45.4
Bachelor's degree	80.6	1.1	18.4	36.6	6.9	0.8	14.3	6.5	8.1	23.2	13.5	9.7	40.2

Table 9-1 Among 1989–90 beginning students at community colleges, percentage distribution according to attainment at first institution and 1994 attainment at any institution, by selected characteristics—Continued

Selected characteristics	Attainment at first institution[1]			1994 attainment at any institution									
				Attained[2]						No degree			
					Certificate		Associate's				Enrolled		
	None	Certificate	Associate's	Total	Not enrolled at 4-year	Enrolled at 4-year	Not enrolled at 4-year	Enrolled at 4-year	Bachelor's	Total	Less-than-4-year[3]	4-year	Not enrolled
Degree program in 1989–90[8]													
Undergraduate certificate	80.2	10.1	9.7	36.1	21.4	0.9	8.3	3.0	2.4	14.7	10.9	3.7	49.3
Associate's degree	76.2	3.4	20.5	37.5	9.6	0.5	16.1	4.3	7.0	15.9	10.3	5.6	46.6
Bachelor's degree	—	—	—	—	—	—	—	—	—	—	—	—	—
Other undergraduate	80.6	7.7	11.7	35.0	16.1	0.7	9.1	4.1	5.0	9.9	5.6	4.3	55.2
Months enrolled in 1989–90													
1–6 months	88.7	5.0	6.3	24.1	14.1	1.0	8.4	0.0	0.7	11.6	9.6	2.0	64.3
7–9 months	76.6	5.6	17.8	38.2	12.4	0.5	12.9	4.5	7.9	12.9	7.0	5.9	49.0
10–12 months	69.0	4.6	26.4	46.9	10.7	0.4	18.3	7.3	10.2	18.5	11.1	7.4	34.6
Received aid in 1989–90													
No	79.6	4.7	15.7	35.5	12.2	0.7	13.8	3.8	5.0	17.0	11.7	5.3	47.5
Yes	73.2	5.8	21.0	39.9	12.7	0.4	12.6	4.7	9.6	8.6	4.0	4.6	51.5
Received grant in 1989–90													
No	79.2	4.6	16.2	35.7	12.0	0.7	13.7	4.0	5.4	16.4	11.2	5.3	47.9
Yes	73.5	6.2	20.3	39.9	13.4	0.5	12.7	4.3	9.0	9.3	4.5	4.7	50.9
Received loan in 1989–90													
No	77.8	5.0	17.2	36.6	12.4	0.6	13.5	4.0	6.2	15.2	10.0	5.2	48.2
Yes	77.2	5.3	17.5	38.8	11.8	0.0	12.9	5.0	9.1	4.6	0.0	4.6	56.6
Employed while enrolled[9]													
None	75.7	15.7	8.7	33.1	23.1	0.0	7.2	0.0	2.8	9.7	6.0	3.6	57.3
1–50 percent	69.5	6.6	23.9	54.8	20.3	0.0	18.8	6.4	9.4	15.3	11.3	4.0	29.9
More than 50 percent	79.3	3.4	17.2	34.4	9.8	0.8	13.3	4.2	6.3	14.9	9.7	5.2	50.7
Hours worked per week while enrolled													
None	77.4	9.8	12.8	40.5	21.2	0.0	10.8	3.0	5.6	11.1	6.4	4.8	48.4
1–20 hours	73.3	3.9	22.8	45.4	11.3	0.9	16.4	7.3	9.6	14.6	7.6	7.0	40.0
More than 20 hours	79.2	4.0	16.9	33.3	10.2	0.7	13.4	3.4	5.6	15.7	11.0	4.7	51.0
First transfer													
Did not transfer	78.7	7.7	13.5	23.1	8.9	(10)	14.1	(10)	(10)	10.1	10.1	(10)	66.8
Transferred to less-than-4-year	93.8	2.2	4.0	47.2	32.8	0.0	13.8	0.0	0.6	16.3	16.3	0.0	36.6
Transferred to 4-year	61.2	0.7	38.1	59.5	0.6	2.8	12.3	18.3	25.6	25.9	2.8	23.2	14.5

— Too few sample observations for a reliable estimate.

[1] For students who earned more than one award at the first institution, the first award they earned.

[2] Highest degree attained at any institution. Students who have attained may also be enrolled.

[3] Almost all of those enrolled at less-than-4-year institutions were enrolled at 2-year institutions.

[4] Limited to dependent students.

[5] Examines whether the student attended career-related lectures, participated in study groups with other students, talked about academic matters with faculty, or met with advisor concerning academic plans.

[6] Examines whether the student had contact with faculty outside the class, went places with friends from school, or participated in student assistance center/programs or school clubs.

[7] Student-reported degree goal.

[8] Institution-reported degree program.

[9] Percent of months enrolled in which a student was also employed (1989–94).

[10] Not applicable.

SOURCE: U.S. Department of Education, National Center for Education Statistics, 1990 Beginning Postsecondary Students Longitudinal Study, Second Follow-up (BPS:90/94).

Table 9-2   Among 1989–90 beginning students at community colleges, percentage distribution according to transfer status, by selected characteristics

Selected characteristics	Did not transfer	First transfer, by destination[1]				
		Total	Public 4-year	Private 4-year	Public less-than-4-year	Private less-than-4-year
Total	**57.8**	**42.2**	**19.2**	**3.2**	**14.2**	**5.6**
Sex						
Male	57.4	42.6	20.3	2.8	12.7	6.8
Female	58.2	41.8	18.1	3.6	15.6	4.5
Race/ethnicity						
White	59.2	40.8	19.4	3.5	13.0	4.9
Black	60.9	39.1	11.4	3.4	19.4	5.0
Hispanic	48.6	51.4	20.1	2.4	17.2	11.7
Asian/Pacific Islander	—	—	—	—	—	—
American Indian/Alaskan Native	—	—	—	—	—	—
Parents' educational attainment						
Less than high school graduate	68.0	32.0	5.7	0.2	14.9	11.1
High school graduate	64.1	35.9	17.8	3.4	10.5	4.3
Some postsecondary	55.1	44.9	20.7	3.3	14.7	6.3
Bachelor's degree	48.0	52.0	26.3	1.5	17.3	6.9
Advanced degree	26.7	73.3	39.1	10.8	22.5	1.1
Socioeconomic status						
Lowest quartile	75.6	24.4	5.8	1.4	13.4	3.9
Middle two quartiles	60.4	39.6	17.6	3.1	12.6	6.3
Highest quartile	42.5	57.5	30.1	4.6	17.2	5.6
Family income[2]						
Less than $20,000	55.5	44.5	18.5	3.1	15.4	7.5
20,000–39,999	48.1	51.9	28.8	3.7	12.3	7.1
40,000–59,999	48.3	51.7	27.3	4.5	14.9	4.9
60,000 or more	41.1	58.9	29.7	6.8	20.8	1.6
Age as of 12/31/89						
18 years or younger	42.3	57.7	29.6	5.3	17.3	5.5
19 years	60.1	39.9	20.4	1.9	14.9	2.8
20–29 years	72.3	27.7	9.0	1.8	9.4	7.7
30 years or older	78.8	21.2	2.5	1.0	11.7	6.1
Expected educational attainment						
Less than 2 years of postsecondary education	88.6	11.4	3.9	0.0	7.3	0.3
2 to 3 years of postsecondary education	76.2	23.8	3.2	0.0	12.2	8.4
Bachelor's degree or higher	47.0	53.1	27.1	4.8	15.9	5.4
High school credential						
High school diploma	56.5	43.5	20.4	3.5	13.8	5.8
Equivalency certificate	73.9	26.1	2.7	0.0	19.1	4.3
None	—	—	—	—	—	—
Diploma/delayed entry status						
Diploma, did not delay	46.0	54.0	28.5	4.5	15.4	5.5
Diploma, delayed entry	72.6	27.4	7.9	1.9	11.3	6.2
No diploma	73.5	26.5	4.5	0.0	18.0	4.1

Table 9-2   Among 1989–90 beginning students at community colleges, percentage distribution according to transfer status, by selected characteristics— Continued

Selected characteristics	Did not transfer	First transfer, by destination[1]				
		Total	Public 4-year	Private 4-year	Public less-than-4-year	Private less-than-4-year
Self-rating of academic ability						
Above average	50.4	49.7	26.9	5.6	11.7	5.5
Average or below	60.5	39.5	16.7	2.6	14.8	5.4
Marital status in 1989–90						
Never married	51.3	48.8	23.7	4.0	14.6	6.4
Married	82.8	17.3	5.4	0.1	9.0	2.7
Divorced/separated/widowed	71.9	28.1	5.3	2.2	12.7	7.9
Number of children in 1989–90						
None	52.8	47.2	23.2	3.9	14.2	5.9
One	81.1	18.9	2.8	2.3	10.8	3.0
Two	78.6	21.4	5.7	0.3	9.0	6.4
Three or more	—	—	—	—	—	—
Enrollment status in 1989–90						
Exclusively full-time	48.0	52.0	28.2	3.3	14.5	6.1
Mixed	43.6	56.4	22.1	9.3	16.3	8.7
Exclusively part-time	70.4	29.6	9.0	2.8	12.5	5.3
Enrollment status, first term						
Full-time	48.2	51.8	29.2	4.0	13.5	5.2
At least half, less than full-time	59.4	40.6	12.8	3.1	18.9	5.8
Less than half-time	75.5	24.5	7.3	1.6	10.1	5.5
Grade point average in 1989–90						
Below 2.75	53.0	47.0	22.7	2.8	15.3	6.2
2.75–3.24	52.9	47.1	26.3	0.9	15.6	4.3
3.25 or higher	63.3	36.8	15.7	5.7	12.5	2.9
Academic integration in 1989–90[3]						
Low	70.6	29.4	11.2	0.0	10.5	7.7
Moderate	56.5	43.5	20.0	4.9	12.5	6.1
High	55.7	44.3	14.4	7.9	19.6	2.4
Social integration in 1989–90[4]						
Low	81.3	18.7	6.8	2.2	7.8	1.9
Moderate	48.9	51.1	25.6	4.5	13.0	8.0
High	—	—	—	—	—	—
Degree goal in 1989–90[5]						
Not working toward degree	65.6	34.4	4.9	3.8	14.9	10.8
Certificate/license	87.3	12.7	0.5	1.9	4.5	5.9
Associate's degree	56.1	43.9	18.7	4.2	15.5	5.6
Bachelor's degree	40.3	59.7	36.5	2.2	16.2	4.8
Degree program in 1989–90[6]						
Undergraduate certificate	57.0	43.0	13.1	3.7	0.0	0.0
Associate's degree	56.5	43.6	21.5	3.3	13.8	4.9
Bachelor's degree	—	—	—	—	—	—
Other undergraduate	63.3	36.8	14.3	3.0	14.8	4.7

Table 9-2   Among 1989–90 beginning students at community colleges, percentage distribution according to transfer status, by selected characteristics—Continued

Selected characteristics	Did not transfer	First transfer, by destination[1]				
		Total	Public 4-year	Private 4-year	Public less-than-4-year	Private less-than-4-year
Months enrolled in 1989–90						
1–6 months	66.6	33.4	7.0	1.6	17.3	7.6
7–9 months	63.1	36.9	20.8	1.6	9.1	5.4
10–12 months	47.0	53.1	28.9	5.7	14.5	4.0
Received aid in 1989–90						
No	58.1	41.9	17.7	2.9	15.6	5.7
Yes	57.3	42.7	22.9	4.0	10.4	5.6
Received grant in 1989–90						
No	58.1	41.9	17.9	3.3	15.3	5.4
Yes	57.0	43.0	22.9	3.1	10.7	6.3
Received loan in 1989–90						
No	57.5	42.5	19.2	3.3	14.4	5.6
Yes	64.4	35.6	17.7	2.4	9.8	5.8
Employed while enrolled[7]						
None	78.5	21.5	6.4	0.3	13.0	1.8
1–50 percent	40.6	59.4	26.6	3.6	21.1	8.1
More than 50 percent	58.9	41.1	19.2	3.4	12.7	5.7
Hours worked per week while enrolled						
None	55.3	44.7	15.6	2.5	21.7	4.8
1–20 hours	46.8	53.2	32.2	3.3	11.9	5.7
More than 20 hours	61.6	38.4	16.5	3.4	12.7	5.8
Attainment before transfer						
Did not transfer	100.0	(8)	(8)	(8)	(8)	(8)
Transferred without award	(8)	100.0	37.1	6.9	39.3	16.7
Transferred with certificate	(8)	—	—	—	—	—
Transferred with Associate's degree	(8)	100.0	79.8	10.8	8.2	1.2

— Too few sample observations for a reliable estimate.

[1] Destination of first transfer. See the supplemental note to this indicator for a definition of "transferred."

[2] Limited to dependent students.

[3] Examines whether the student attended career-related lectures, participated in study groups with other students, talked about academic matters with faculty, or met with advisor concerning academic plans.

[4] Examines whether the student had contact with faculty outside the class, went places with friends from school, or participated in student assistance center/programs or school clubs.

[5] Student-reported degree goal.

[6] Institution-reported degree program.

[7] Percent of months enrolled in which a student was also employed (1989–94).

[8] Not applicable.

SOURCE: U.S. Department of Education, National Center for Education Statistics, 1990 Beginning Postsecondary Students Longitudinal Study, Second Follow-up (BPS:90/94).

Note on community college outcomes

The tables and figures presented in this indicator describe outcomes for first-time beginning students in postsecondary education who were enrolled in community colleges in academic year 1989–90. While this represents nearly half of all first-time beginners (45 percent), it represents a minority of the community college student body (22 percent) because it excludes continuing and returning students.

1994 attainment at any institution

The columns in the text table and table 9-1 that describe students' attainment and enrollment status as of 1994 characterize students with respect to highest postsecondary award attained and current enrollment status. Some students who attained an associate's degree also had attained a certificate, and some students who had attained a bachelor's degree also had attained a certificate or an associate's degree. Those who completed a certificate and an associate's degree were broken out with respect to enrollment at a 4-year institution. For these students, the "not enrolled at 4-year" column includes students who were enrolled at less-than-4-year institutions and students who were not enrolled.

Definition of transfer

Since the Beginning Postsecondary Student Longitudinal Study (BPS:90/94) does not include information on the transfer of credit between institutions, transfer as defined for this indicator does not imply transfer of credit. Rather, it simply characterizes observed transitions between institutions. For transfer to a less-than-4-year institution, any transition that was not followed by a return to the first institution constitutes a transfer. For transfer to a 4-year institution, any entry into a 4-year institution constitutes a transfer, regardless of subsequent enrollment, at the institution of origin.

It is also important to note that the transfer measures refer to the *first* transfer. Students may transfer more than once. For example, some students classified as having transferred to a less-than-4-year institution may have subsequently entered a 4-year institution.

SOURCE: U.S. Department of Education, National Center for Education Statistics, 1990 Beginning Postsecondary Students Longitudinal Study, Second Follow-up (BPS:90/94).

Table 10-1   Percentage distribution of 1989–90 beginning postsecondary students seeking bachelor's degrees according to persistence toward and completion of bachelor's and other degrees as of spring 1994, by selected characteristics

Selected characteristics	Completed a degree				Still enrolled for bachelor's[2]	No degree, no longer enrolled toward a bachelor's						
	Highest degree completed[1]			Total any degree		Total no degree	Number of months enrolled[3]					
	Bachelor's	Associate's	Certificate				Less than 9	9–18	19–27	28–36	37–45	More than 45
Total	**45.8**	**5.1**	**3.3**	**54.3**	**17.5**	**28.3**	**2.8**	**8.1**	**5.7**	**5.6**	**3.8**	**2.3**
Sex												
Male	41.3	4.8	2.7	48.8	20.3	30.9	2.9	9.6	6.7	5.9	3.9	1.9
Female	50.3	5.4	4.0	59.7	14.6	25.7	2.8	6.6	4.7	5.3	3.6	2.7
Age as of 12/31/89												
18 years or younger	51.4	4.9	2.9	59.2	16.4	24.5	1.5	5.2	5.9	5.7	3.5	2.7
19 years	38.3	4.2	3.4	45.8	21.1	33.0	4.0	13.4	4.4	6.0	3.4	1.6
20–29 years	19.0	9.4	7.9	36.3	19.6	44.1	8.2	17.9	6.5	2.8	7.7	0.9
30 years or older	9.8	6.0	3.3	19.1	17.3	63.5	19.4	28.9	4.8	9.9	0.5	0.0
Race/ethnicity												
White	48.1	4.9	3.3	56.4	16.6	27.0	3.0	6.8	5.9	5.3	3.7	2.2
Black	34.3	7.3	3.6	45.2	18.0	36.8	5.4	15.5	5.1	6.1	2.0	2.6
Hispanic	32.4	3.5	5.4	41.3	22.1	36.6	0.5	14.0	6.4	4.6	7.8	3.3
Asian/Pacific Islander	46.8	5.3	0.6	52.8	21.8	25.5	0.0	9.4	2.1	10.2	1.2	2.5
American Indian/Alaskan Native	—	—	—	—	—	—	—	—	—	—	—	—
Marital status in 1989–90												
Never married	48.1	5.3	3.4	56.8	17.4	25.8	1.7	6.9	5.7	5.1	3.8	2.4
Married	20.1	2.4	4.2	26.7	17.8	55.5	13.7	27.6	5.9	7.9	0.4	0.0
Divorced/widowed/separated	11.6	9.5	0.6	21.7	18.4	59.9	28.8	22.8	7.5	0.0	0.9	0.0
Number of children in 1989–90												
None	47.2	5.2	3.2	55.6	17.3	27.1	2.4	7.2	5.7	5.6	3.8	2.4
One	12.8	9.5	2.7	25.0	13.1	61.9	22.4	25.6	9.4	2.8	1.7	0.0
Two	0.0	—	—	—	—	—	—	—	—	—	—	—
Three or more	—	—	—	—	—	—	—	—	—	—	—	—
Socioeconomic status												
Lowest quartile	22.1	5.7	3.8	31.7	16.5	51.8	8.2	25.0	7.6	5.7	3.4	1.9
Middle two quartiles	38.9	4.8	3.5	47.1	19.4	33.5	3.0	9.5	7.3	7.3	3.4	2.9
Highest quartile	52.9	5.3	3.2	61.5	16.3	22.3	2.1	5.2	4.4	4.5	4.0	2.0
Family income[4]												
Less than $20,000	36.9	4.9	1.4	43.2	19.2	37.6	3.2	10.7	6.8	7.4	6.1	3.4
20,000–39,999	43.2	5.3	4.1	52.6	18.2	29.2	2.9	8.9	5.5	6.3	3.0	2.5
40,000–59,999	48.5	4.1	4.4	57.0	16.1	26.9	1.8	7.2	6.5	5.9	3.4	2.0
60,000 or more	60.6	6.0	1.5	68.1	16.0	15.9	0.4	2.5	3.9	3.6	4.0	1.6
Parents' educational attainment												
Less than high school graduate	33.6	3.6	6.1	43.4	7.8	48.8	10.9	11.1	6.4	11.2	5.7	3.6
High school graduate	35.0	7.3	4.6	46.9	18.4	34.7	6.4	11.6	6.6	5.2	3.3	1.6
Some postsecondary	45.1	4.8	3.0	52.9	17.5	29.6	1.2	9.7	7.7	4.5	3.5	2.9
Bachelor's degree	48.8	5.4	3.6	57.7	19.2	23.1	0.8	4.8	4.6	5.6	4.3	3.0
Advanced degree	61.2	2.9	0.7	64.8	16.4	18.9	1.0	3.0	3.8	5.9	3.7	1.5
High school credential												
High school diploma	46.5	5.2	3.4	54.4	17.3	28.3	2.8	8.1	5.7	5.6	3.7	2.3
Equivalency certificate	—	—	—	—	—	—	—	—	—	—	—	—
None	—	—	—	—	—	—	—	—	—	—	—	—
Diploma/delayed entry status[5]												
Diploma, did not delay	50.3	4.9	2.9	58.2	17.0	24.8	1.8	6.3	5.4	5.5	3.5	2.3
Diploma, delayed entry	17.3	7.1	6.6	30.9	21.5	47.6	8.9	18.9	7.1	4.3	6.1	2.2
No diploma	15.0	2.4	3.7	21.0	14.1	64.8	13.4	22.7	8.1	18.3	0.8	1.5
Level of first institution												
4-year	57.1	2.5	2.1	61.7	15.3	23.1	1.9	5.5	5.3	4.9	3.3	2.1
2-year	7.9	13.9	7.2	29.0	25.3	45.8	5.4	16.8	7.0	8.2	5.3	3.0
Less-than-2-year	—	—	—	—	—	—	—	—	—	—	—	—
Received aid in 1989–90												
No	36.9	7.0	4.5	48.4	21.0	30.7	3.0	8.7	6.2	6.3	3.8	2.7
Yes	55.1	3.2	2.2	60.4	13.8	25.8	2.7	7.5	5.2	4.9	3.7	1.9
Received loan in 1989–90												
No	42.4	6.1	3.3	51.8	18.9	29.4	2.8	8.7	5.4	6.1	3.9	2.3
Yes	57.7	1.9	3.5	63.1	12.6	24.4	2.8	5.8	6.6	3.9	3.1	2.1
Received grant in 1989–90												
No	39.3	6.9	4.3	50.6	19.6	29.8	3.1	8.6	5.8	6.1	3.9	2.4
Yes	55.1	2.6	1.9	59.6	14.4	26.0	2.4	7.3	5.6	5.0	3.5	2.2

Table 10-1   Percentage distribution of 1989–90 beginning postsecondary students seeking bachelor's degrees according to persistence toward and completion of bachelor's and other degrees as of spring 1994, by selected characteristics—Continued

Selected characteristics	Completed a degree — Highest degree completed[1] Bachelor's	Associate's	Certificate	Total any degree	Still enrolled for bachelor's[2]	No degree, no longer enrolled toward a bachelor's — Total no degree	Number of months enrolled[3] Less than 9	9–18	19–27	28–36	37–45	More than 45
Employed while enrolled[6]												
None	35.0	0.9	1.4	37.3	13.5	49.2	9.3	26.5	5.0	4.3	2.4	1.7
1–50 percent	54.9	4.8	3.1	62.8	17.7	19.5	1.2	4.2	3.7	6.2	2.8	1.4
More than 50 percent	42.9	5.8	3.5	52.1	17.4	30.4	2.8	8.6	6.9	5.2	4.1	2.8
Enrollment status in 1989–90												
Exclusively full-time	51.1	5.7	2.6	59.5	15.9	24.6	1.7	6.0	5.7	6.0	3.2	2.1
Mixed	46.4	2.8	6.0	55.1	22.4	22.4	0.3	5.1	4.0	5.4	5.3	2.3
Exclusively part-time	4.1	7.8	6.5	18.3	21.6	60.1	14.0	24.0	5.6	3.9	6.2	6.5
Enrollment status, first term												
Full-time	51.7	4.1	2.5	58.3	16.7	25.0	1.7	6.6	5.3	5.6	3.5	2.3
At least half, less than full-time	14.5	11.5	6.1	32.1	24.5	43.4	5.9	18.9	5.9	2.5	7.8	2.5
Less than half-time	10.5	4.9	11.4	26.8	26.8	46.4	17.3	8.0	9.1	8.0	0.3	3.7
Hours worked per week while enrolled												
None	49.8	4.4	2.0	56.2	17.8	26.0	2.3	8.4	3.8	5.8	3.2	2.5
1–20 hours	51.3	5.2	2.5	59.0	16.4	24.5	0.7	5.7	5.7	6.8	4.4	1.3
More than 20 hours	40.4	5.4	4.5	50.3	17.9	31.7	4.5	9.5	6.5	4.8	3.6	2.9
Grade point average in 1989–90												
Below 2.75	37.4	5.2	3.5	46.2	20.0	33.8	3.3	7.9	7.3	7.5	5.8	2.0
2.75 to 3.24	55.1	4.7	2.2	62.0	19.2	18.8	1.0	6.9	2.9	4.4	2.4	1.2
3.25 or higher	63.5	4.3	2.3	70.1	12.3	17.6	1.5	4.5	2.3	4.2	1.6	3.5
Months enrolled in 1989–90												
1–6 months	7.2	11.9	6.5	25.6	16.3	58.1	22.4	14.6	8.6	7.7	4.5	0.3
7–9 months	50.2	4.2	3.2	57.6	15.4	27.0	1.2	9.6	5.8	5.5	3.2	1.7
10–12 months	50.7	4.3	2.8	57.9	18.9	23.2	0.0	5.9	5.1	5.3	3.9	3.0
Academic integration in 1989–90[7]												
Low	24.1	9.9	5.4	39.5	18.0	42.5	8.5	18.0	10.1	2.3	1.7	1.9
Moderate	36.8	5.5	3.6	45.8	19.1	35.1	4.8	11.0	7.2	5.5	3.3	3.2
High	52.0	4.5	3.0	59.5	16.5	24.0	1.3	6.0	4.7	5.9	4.2	2.0
Social integration in 1989–90[8]												
Low	19.1	6.2	6.1	31.4	22.3	46.4	8.9	25.2	6.6	2.4	0.4	3.0
Moderate	39.1	6.8	3.4	49.4	18.5	32.1	3.5	9.3	6.5	5.7	4.5	2.7
High	56.9	3.1	2.7	62.7	15.5	21.8	1.0	4.6	4.8	6.1	3.5	1.9
Self-rating of academic ability												
Above average	61.6	2.7	1.5	65.8	15.0	19.2	0.7	5.4	4.1	4.0	3.1	1.9
Average or below	34.3	6.8	4.6	45.7	19.1	35.2	4.3	10.0	7.0	6.9	4.3	2.6

[1] Includes students who are no longer working toward a bachelor's degree, but who had completed another type of degree or award.

[2] Includes students who had completed another type of degree or award (associate's degree: 11.8 percent, certificate: 2.7 percent), but are still working toward a bachelor's degree.

[3] Enrollment can be full time or part time. Includes students who are still enrolled but are no longer working toward a bachelor's degree.

[4] Limited to dependent students.

[5] Students were considered to have a diploma only if they had a regular high school diploma. Students with a GED or other high school credentials were considered to have no diploma.

[6] Percent of months enrolled in which a student was also employed in 1989–94.

[7] Examines whether the student attended career-related lectures, participated in study groups with other students, talked about academic matters with faculty, or met with advisor concerning academic plans.

[8] Examines whether the student had contact with faculty outside of class, went places with friends from school, or participated in student assistance centers/programs or school clubs.

SOURCE: U.S. Department of Education, National Center for Education Statistics, 1990 Beginning Postsecondary Students Longitudinal Study, Second Follow-up (BPS:90/94).

Note on postsecondary persistence and degree completion

This indicator was constructed using data from the Beginning Postsecondary Students Longitudinal Study (BPS). BPS is based on a subsample of the 1990 National Postsecondary Student Aid Study (NPSAS), which consists of students beginning their postsecondary education for the first time at community colleges, vocational schools, and institutions granting bachelor's degrees during the 1989–90 academic year. The first BPS follow-up survey was conducted in the spring of 1992, 2 years after the student's entry into postsecondary education, and the second follow-up was conducted during the spring of 1994. BPS provides detailed information regarding individual student's attendance patterns for 5 years following his or her first enrollment into postsecondary education. (For more information on BPS, please see the *Sources of Data* section.)

The indicator examines persistence toward and completion of bachelor's and other types of degrees for students whose initial postsecondary degree objective when they first began postsecondary education in 1989–90 was a bachelor's degree, without regard to the type of institution in which they first enrolled. Using the student's reported degree objective rather than the type of program offered by the particular institution permits comparison of rates of persistence and degree completion between students with the same degree objective but with different demographic, institutional, and attendance characteristics.

Initial degree objective

Whether the student was seeking a bachelor's degree was determined by his or her response to the question "Toward which degree or other award are the courses you are taking leading?" Students could therefore be attending a 2-year institution but their degree objective was a bachelor's degree. Half of all beginning postsecondary students were working toward a bachelor's degree in 1989–90, and 25 percent of these students began at 2-year institutions that did not offer bachelor's degrees.

Persistence and degree completion

As this indicator was constructed, students were first divided into two broad categories: those who completed a bachelor's degree, and those who did not. Without regard to completion of other degrees, students who had not attained a bachelor's degree were then classified according to whether or not they were still enrolled toward a bachelor's degree. Students who were still enrolled toward a bachelor's degree were classified as such, while those who were no longer enrolled toward a bachelor's degree but had completed an associate's degree or certificate were categorized according their highest degree completed. The remaining students who had not completed a degree after 5 years (bachelor's degree, associate's degree, or certificate) or who were still enrolled but not working toward a bachelor's degree, were categorized according to the number of months they were enrolled in postsecondary education. It is important to note that the number of months enrolled are not necessarily continuous months, so they cannot be used as an indicator of when the student left postsecondary education or stopped working toward a bachelor's degree. Rather, presenting the data in this manner is designed to give the an indication of the time spent in postsecondary attendance, although no degree was completed.

Table 11-1   Percentage of college graduates completing a bachelor's degree within various years of starting college, by selected student characteristics: 1993

Student characteristics	4 years or less	More than 4 up to 5 years	More than 5 up to 6 years	More than 6 years
Total	**35.5**	**27.9**	**11.0**	**25.6**
Sex				
Male	30.7	30.3	13.4	25.6
Female	39.4	25.9	9.1	25.7
Race/ethnicity				
White	36.9	27.5	10.5	25.0
Black	24.8	27.8	15.2	32.2
Hispanic	23.3	28.7	13.1	34.9
Asian/Pacific Islander	35.6	34.4	12.9	17.1
American Indian/Alaskan Native	27.4	22.1	7.5	43.0
Ever taken remedial instruction				
Yes	21.2	26.5	16.3	36.0
No	36.4	27.9	10.3	25.3
Cumulative undergraduate GPA				
Less than 3.0	26.2	33.9	16.0	23.9
3.0–3.49	39.1	29.5	9.8	21.7
3.5 or higher	39.9	18.5	7.5	24.2
Major field of study				
Humanities and social/behavioral sciences	43.2	24.8	11.3	20.7
Humanities	40.7	24.4	12.5	22.4
Social and behavioral sciences	44.9	25.1	10.4	19.5
Natural sciences, computer sciences, and engineering	36.9	27.8	12.7	22.6
Natural sciences	45.4	23.5	11.0	20.2
Computer sciences and engineering	27.0	32.9	14.8	25.4
Technical/professional	31.2	29.4	10.4	29.1
Education	32.5	30.5	11.3	25.7
Business management	31.6	27.9	8.8	31.6
Other technical/professional	29.7	30.6	11.9	27.7

SOURCE: U.S. Department of Education, National Center for Education Statistics, 1993 Baccalaureate and Beyond Longitudinal Study, First Follow-up (B&B: 93/94).

Table 12-1   Average undergraduate tuition, room, and board (in 1995 constant dollars) as a percentage of income of all families, by selected family income percentiles and control of institution: 1964–94

Year	Public institutions				Private institutions			
	Constant dollars	Family income percentiles			Constant dollars	Family income percentiles		
		20th	50th	80th		20th	50th	80th
1964	$4,645	29.0	14.4	9.2	$9,323	58.3	28.8	18.6
1965	4,704	27.7	14.0	9.0	9,595	56.6	28.5	18.3
1966	4,760	25.6	13.4	8.7	9,853	53.1	27.7	17.9
1967	4,777	25.5	13.2	8.5	9,901	52.8	27.3	17.6
1968	4,782	24.0	12.6	8.1	9,937	49.8	26.2	16.9
1969	4,863	23.4	12.4	7.9	10,227	49.1	26.0	16.7
1970	4,947	24.7	12.7	8.1	10,525	52.5	27.1	17.2
1971	5,036	25.6	13.0	8.2	10,824	55.1	27.9	17.7
1972	5,201	25.4	12.8	8.0	10,837	52.9	26.7	16.7
1973	4,968	23.8	12.0	7.5	10,362	49.5	25.0	15.6
1974	4,608	22.5	11.5	7.2	10,033	48.9	25.1	15.7
1975	4,587	23.4	11.8	7.3	10,086	51.4	25.9	16.1
1976	4,654	23.3	11.6	7.3	10,162	50.9	25.3	15.8
1977	4,603	23.1	11.4	7.0	10,137	50.9	25.1	15.5
1978	4,445	21.8	10.8	6.6	10,063	49.3	24.4	15.0
1979	4,258	20.7	10.3	6.4	9,662	46.9	23.4	14.6
1980	4,183	21.9	10.7	6.5	9,642	50.6	24.7	15.1
1981	4,321	23.6	11.5	6.9	10,005	54.6	26.6	15.9
1982	4,582	25.9	12.4	7.2	10,766	60.7	29.0	17.0
1983	4,735	26.4	12.5	7.4	11,264	62.9	29.8	17.5
1984	4,920	26.8	12.7	7.4	11,842	64.5	30.5	17.8
1985	5,011	26.8	12.7	7.4	12,468	66.6	31.7	18.3
1986	5,223	27.0	12.7	7.4	13,283	68.7	32.4	18.9
1987	5,339	27.5	12.9	7.5	13,857	71.4	33.4	19.5
1988	5,385	27.6	13.0	7.5	14,098	72.3	33.9	19.5
1989	5,417	27.5	12.9	7.4	14,453	73.3	34.3	19.7
1990	5,424	27.6	13.1	7.5	14,721	74.8	35.6	20.5
1991	5,673	29.8	14.1	8.0	15,365	80.6	38.1	21.8
1992	5,763	31.2	14.4	8.2	15,679	84.9	39.1	22.4
1993[1]	5,946	33.0	15.1	8.4	16,183	89.8	41.2	22.8
1994[2]	6,053	32.6	15.1	8.4	16,470	88.8	41.1	22.8

[1] Revised from previously published figures.

[2] Preliminary data based on fall 1993 enrollment weights.

NOTE: Tuition data are for academic years beginning 1964–94, and family income data are for calendar years 1964–94. Both calendar and school year Consumer Price Indexes (CPIs) were used to calculate constant dollar figures. "Tuition, room, and board" includes those for 2-year and 4-year colleges and universities. In-state tuition and fees are used for public institutions.

SOURCE: U.S. Department of Education, National Center for Education Statistics, *Digest of Education Statistics*, 1995, tables 37 and 306. U.S. Department of Commerce, Bureau of the Census, *Current Population Reports*, Series P-60, "Income, Poverty, and Valuation of Non-cash Benefits," various years (based on the March supplement to the Current Population Survey).

Table 13-1 Cost of college attendance and student financial aid for undergraduate students, by type and control of institution, dependency and attendance status, and family or household income of student: 1992–93

Type and control of institution, dependency and attendance status, and family or household income of student[1]	Estimated population (thousands)	Tuition and fees	Total cost[2]	Grant aid	Total aid[3]	Net cost[4]	Expected family contribution[5]	Additional family contribution[6]
Public 4-year institutions								
Dependent, full-time, full-year, 1 institution	2,151	$3,111	$9,816	$963	$2,038	$7,778	$9,253	$2,156
Low income	434	2,686	9,356	2,288	4,073	5,283	2,485	3,337
Lower middle	434	2,893	9,498	1,081	2,671	6,827	5,158	2,777
Upper middle	485	2,995	9,699	636	1,587	8,113	7,735	2,018
High income	627	3,512	10,285	388	949	9,336	18,110	982
Dependent, full-time	2,999	2,947	9,187	855	1,864	7,326	9,347	1,952
Low income	607	2,559	8,820	2,041	3,746	5,070	2,505	3,132
Lower middle	601	2,728	8,878	961	2,422	6,426	5,255	2,429
Upper middle	719	2,846	8,924	509	1,331	7,598	7,840	1,784
High income	831	3,382	9,758	354	890	8,879	18,727	836
Private, not-for-profit 4-year								
Dependent, full-time, full-year, 1 institution	1,110	11,872	18,537	3,787	6,127	12,409	11,264	4,485
Low income	218	9,768	16,097	6,274	9,548	6,549	2,490	5,056
Lower middle	191	11,238	17,925	5,399	9,024	8,914	4,928	5,296
Upper middle	184	12,037	18,642	4,901	7,756	10,886	8,117	4,475
High income	451	12,948	19,781	1,886	3,331	16,449	19,550	3,856
Dependent, full-time	1,427	11,004	17,301	3,455	5,697	11,552	10,927	4,171
Low income	302	8,444	14,232	5,417	8,350	5,872	2,343	4,425
Lower middle	253	10,560	16,905	4,890	8,270	8,590	4,989	4,980
Upper middle	244	11,195	17,422	4,240	6,934	10,407	7,988	4,204
High income	548	12,399	18,958	1,736	3,150	15,752	19,755	3,633
Private, for-profit								
Dependent, full-time	352	5,223	10,510	810	3,154	7,350	5,026	4,330
Low income	145	4,921	9,684	1,498	3,754	5,888	1,865	4,711
Lower middle	111	5,321	10,420	384	3,040	7,353	4,717	4,481
Upper middle	51	6,017	12,324	131	2,436	9,911	7,046	4,542
High income	30	5,689	12,785	184	2,607	10,200	19,409	1,719
Independent, full-time	726	4,748	10,248	1,346	3,395	6,840	2,534	5,467
Low income	337	4,616	9,855	1,712	3,610	6,225	1,112	5,690
Lower middle	186	4,783	10,240	1,198	3,507	6,722	2,375	5,378
Upper middle	115	4,778	10,432	836	2,967	7,449	3,280	5,770
High income	87	5,137	11,530	931	2,923	8,625	7,367	4,403
Public 2-year								
Dependent, full-time	1,413	1,072	6,410	395	600	5,717	7,119	1,886
Low income	336	948	6,199	1,027	1,322	4,848	2,418	2,852
Lower middle	460	1,052	5,995	312	588	5,348	4,685	1,857
Upper middle	308	1,134	7,060	122	247	6,686	6,701	1,992
High income	215	1,311	6,745	83	167	6,367	20,693	199
Independent, part-time	3,894	347	2,661	204	344	2,301	4,921	1,188
Low income	547	467	4,166	653	1,036	3,122	1,533	2,225
Lower middle	859	393	3,152	233	440	2,694	3,975	1,449
Upper middle	1,192	315	2,435	115	209	2,220	5,491	1,100
High income	1,293	294	1,897	78	112	1,759	6,457	657
Private 2-year								
Dependent, full-time	77	3,857	9,122	1,023	2,286	6,779	6,104	2,375
Low income	22	3,620	8,350	2,246	4,087	4,181	2,016	2,906
Lower middle	17	3,841	8,568	662	2,541	6,027	5,740	1,666
Upper middle	20	3,843	9,307	250	891	8,416	6,812	2,609
High income	—	—	—	—	—	—	—	—

— Not available.

[1] The four categories of family income correspond to the four quartiles of family income calculated separately for dependent and independent students. For dependent students, the dividing points between income categories are $27,000, $45,000, and $60,000. For independent students, the dividing points are $10,000, $21,000, and about $36,000.
[2] Includes budget allowances for student living expenses and is adjusted for less than full-time or full-year attendance.
[3] Includes grants, loans, work-study earnings, and other forms of aid such as PLUS loans to parents.
[4] Total cost minus total aid.
[5] Expected Family Contribution (EFC) is calculated using the Congressional Methodology (CM) and is dependent on family income and assets and on the number of siblings in college. The student is also expected to contribute from summer job earnings. However, there are exceptions, and EFC can be zero.
[6] Total cost minus total aid (excluding certain aid such as PLUS loans to parents that can be used to finance EFC) minus EFC. However, EFC is greater than net cost for many students, particularly those from high income families. Additional Family Contribution (AFC) is set to zero for those students. Thus, the average AFC is greater than the difference between average net cost and average expected family contribution in the previous two columns.

NOTE: See the supplemental note to this indicator for further discussion of financial aid concepts and their calculation.

SOURCE: U.S. Department of Education, National Center for Education Statistics, National Postsecondary Student Aid Study, 1993 (Data Analysis System).

Note on postsecondary costs and student financial aid

The following definitions are used in the tables of *Indicator 13* and may clarify who or what is included or excluded in the various statistics.

Family income: For dependent students, the four family income categories ("low income," "lower middle," "upper middle," and "high income") were calculated on the basis of the income of their parents and correspond to the four quartiles of the distribution of parental family income. For independent students, the calculation was the same but was based on the income of the student and his or her spouse. It was the sum of adjusted gross income for the 1991 calendar year and any untaxed income.

Dependency status: Students were considered independent of their parents for financial aid purposes if the institutional records indicated they were independent, or if one of the following seven criteria were met: 1) the student was 24 years old on 12/31/92; 2) the student was a veteran; 3) the student was an orphan or a ward of the court; 4) the student had legal dependents other than a spouse; 5) the student was married and not claimed as a dependent on a parent's 1992 tax return; 6) the student was a graduate student and not claimed as a dependent on a parent's 1992 tax return; or 7) the student was single, an undergraduate, had not been claimed as a dependent on a parent's tax return for the previous 2 years, and was self-sufficient for 2 years before receiving any federal aid.

Tuition and fees: The actual amount of tuition charged the student for all terms he or she attended at all institutions during the 1992–93 academic year.

Total cost: The sum of tuition, fees, and the student budget for non-tuition expenses. The latter includes the cost of books and supplies, room and board, and commuting and other costs. The latter is also adjusted for students who attended less than full time for the full 1992–93 academic year. If the student was enrolled less than full time, full year, the student budget allowance for non-tuition expenses was set equal to 75 percent of the allowance for full time, full year students during the months that the student attended at least half time but less than full time,

and to 25 percent during months the student attended less than half time.

Grants: Total amount of all grants from federal, state, institutional, or other sources such as employer-paid tuition and National Merit Scholarships.

Net cost: Total cost (total student budget allowance, tuition and non-tuition combined, adjusted for actual attendance status) minus total aid. Total aid is comprehensive and includes, for example, SLS loans (federal supplemental loans for students), PLUS loans to parents (federal loans to parents with at least half-time dependent students), and aid received from the Department of Veterans Affairs and Department of Defense.

Expected family contribution (EFC): Used to calculate a student's need for financial aid. The most widely used methodology during the 1992–93 academic year was the Congressional Methodology (CM). The CM EFC is the sum of two components: a student contribution, and a parent contribution. The student is expected to contribute from savings and from summer jobs. The amount the parents are expected to contribute depends on their income and assets and whether they have other children in college. The EFC variable used in this indicator was taken from the student's financial aid records if available, computed using the CM if all the necessary information was available, and imputed using regression methods otherwise. This variable can be interpreted as what is a reasonable amount for the student and family to contribute from currently available resources toward the student's postsecondary education.

Additional family contribution or unmet need: Equal to total cost (see above) minus total aid subject to EFC limitations minus EFC. Negative values were set to zero. Total aid subject to EFC limitations includes Pell grants, Stafford loans, federal campus-based aid, and any other grant aid. It does not include SLS and PLUS loans that may be used to finance EFC. This variable can be interpreted as the amount students and their families must finance in addition to the EFC to meet estimated costs of attendance and student living.

Table 14-1 Adult education participation rates for the past 12 months, by type of adult education activity, educational attainment, labor force status, race/ethnicity, age, and sex: 1995

| Characteristics | Total[1] | Type of adult education activity | | | |
		Basic skills[2]	Credential[1]	Work-related	Personal
		Total			
Total	**40.2**	**1.2**	**6.1**	**20.9**	**19.9**
Educational attainment					
Grade 8 or less	10.8	2.1	0.2	2.2	5.2
Grades 9–12[3]	22.9	5.6	1.6	6.9	10.4
High school diploma	30.9	0.8	3.5	14.2	15.7
Vocational/technical school	41.9	0.6	5.4	21.9	21.1
Some college	49.3	0.5	12.1	22.3	25.3
Associate's degree	56.1	0.4	10.9	32.1	27.4
Bachelor's degree or higher	58.2	(4)	7.7	37.9	27.9
Labor force status					
Employed	50.7	1.1	8.2	31.1	22.0
Unemployed	36.6	5.0	5.5	11.1	17.4
Not in labor force	21.3	0.9	2.2	3.4	16.2
Race/ethnicity					
White	41.5	0.7	6.0	22.8	20.8
Black	37.0	2.3	7.3	16.2	18.9
Hispanic	33.7	3.6	4.8	11.8	13.8
Age					
17–24	47.0	4.6	12.6	14.7	21.5
25–34	48.4	1.2	9.4	25.8	22.2
35–44	49.2	1.1	7.3	30.1	22.8
45–54	45.9	0.6	4.9	29.7	20.5
55–64	28.0	0.2	1.1	14.2	16.3
65 and older	15.2	50.0	0.2	2.3	13.5
		Male			
Total	**38.2**	**1.2**	**5.6**	**21.8**	**15.8**
Educational attainment					
Grade 8 or less	10.7	2.2	50.0	2.9	4.2
Grades 9–12[3]	25.0	5.9	2.4	7.9	9.6
High school diploma	27.4	0.8	3.7	14.4	11.2
Vocational/technical school	39.8	1.1	5.3	22.2	14.6
Some college	44.8	0.5	10.2	22.2	19.8
Associate's degree	52.3	0.4	11.5	31.7	21.5
Bachelor's degree or higher	54.7	(4)	6.4	37.6	22.6
Labor force status					
Employed	46.5	1.1	7.0	29.0	17.9
Unemployed	33.3	4.7	3.9	11.3	14.6
Not in labor force	16.3	0.8	2.1	3.7	10.5
Race/ethnicity					
White	39.1	0.7	5.4	23.8	16.2
Black	34.9	1.6	7.6	15.4	17.1
Hispanic	34.5	4.5	4.1	13.0	11.5
Age					
17–24	46.1	5.2	10.9	14.9	18.9
25–34	46.1	1.1	9.0	26.7	17.4
35–44	47.1	0.9	6.5	30.7	18.3
45–54	41.8	0.5	3.9	29.0	15.8
55–64	24.7	50.0	1.2	14.3	12.7
65 and older	11.9	50.0	0.2	2.9	9.4

Table 14-1 Adult education participation rates for the past 12 months, by type of adult education activity, educational attainment, labor force status, race/ethnicity, age, and sex: 1995—Continued

Characteristics	Total[1]	Type of adult education activity			
		Basic skills[2]	Credential[1]	Work-related	Personal
		Female			
Total	**42.1**	**1.2**	**6.5**	**20.2**	**23.5**
Educational attainment					
Grade 8 or less	10.9	1.9	0.3	1.4	6.3
Grades 9–12[3]	21.2	5.4	1.1	6.0	11.1
High school diploma	33.7	0.7	3.4	13.9	19.4
Vocational/technical school	43.0	0.3	5.5	21.6	24.8
Some college	53.2	0.5	13.7	22.4	30.0
Associate's degree	59.7	0.3	10.4	32.4	32.8
Bachelor's degree or higher	62.4	(4)	9.3	38.3	34.1
Labor force status					
Employed	55.6	1.1	9.7	33.4	26.8
Unemployed	39.9	5.2	7.0	10.9	20.1
Not in labor force	24.2	0.9	2.3	3.2	19.4
Race/ethnicity					
White	43.8	0.7	6.6	21.9	25.1
Black	38.4	2.7	7.1	16.7	20.1
Hispanic	32.8	2.8	5.4	10.6	15.9
Age					
17–24	48.0	4.1	14.3	14.4	24.0
25–34	50.4	1.3	9.7	25.1	26.5
35–44	51.3	1.3	8.1	29.4	27.3
45–54	49.9	0.6	5.9	30.4	25.1
55–64	31.1	0.4	1.1	14.2	19.5
65 and older	17.6	[5]0.0	0.1	1.8	16.4

[1] The participation rate of adults aged 17 or older was determined by their involvement in one or more of six types of adult education activities in the 12 months prior to the interview; therefore, percentages may not add to totals because people participated in more than one type of activity (9 percent). Adults who participated in apprenticeship programs and English as a Second Language programs were included in the total, but are not shown separately. Adults who reported that they had participated only as full-time credential seekers are not included in the calculation of the participation rates.

[2] Only adults who had not received a high school diploma or equivalent, who had received a high school diploma in the past 12 months, or who had received a high school diploma in a foreign country were asked about their participation in the basic education/General Educational Development (GED) activities.

[3] Includes adults whose highest education level was grades 9–12 who had not received a high school diploma.

[4] Individuals with a bachelor's degree or higher were not asked about their participation in adult basic skills programs, GED preparation classes, adult high school, or high school equivalency programs.

[5] Percentages less than 0.05 are rounded to 0.0.

SOURCE: U.S. Department of Education, National Center for Education Statistics, National Household Education Survey (NHES), 1995 (Adult Education Component).

Table 14-2   Percentage of work-related adult education activities, by type of provider, educational attainment, labor force status, race/ethnicity, and age: 1995

Characteristics	Type of provider for work-related adult education activities						
	Elementary/ secondary	Post-secondary	Trade organization	Private	Business	Govern-ment	Other
Total	**4.3**	**20.4**	**11.1**	**6.6**	**59.6**	**17.3**	**2.5**
Educational attainment							
Grade 8 or less	5.3	6.9	11.4	0.0	67.9	12.3	10.7
Grades 9–12*	5.1	15.8	8.0	4.4	61.8	13.3	1.8
High school diploma	3.6	13.5	9.0	6.0	62.4	17.2	2.5
Vocational/technical school	1.0	19.0	13.4	4.1	67.5	9.5	2.8
Some college	2.1	18.6	10.9	7.1	58.2	18.9	2.3
Associate's degree	1.3	18.4	18.8	5.0	57.7	17.7	1.2
Bachelor's degree or higher	6.3	25.4	10.8	7.4	58.4	17.7	2.6
Labor force status							
Employed	4.4	20.1	10.9	6.4	60.7	17.4	2.4
Unemployed	2.4	29.6	13.2	6.1	47.5	16.2	5.9
Not in labor force	3.1	22.4	14.2	10.0	46.3	17.3	2.1
Race/ethnicity							
White	4.4	20.2	10.8	6.5	61.3	16.7	2.4
Black	3.2	20.8	12.9	6.3	47.8	23.1	2.5
Hispanic	5.6	22.0	10.7	7.7	57.3	15.5	2.9
Age							
17–24	3.1	24.1	7.8	6.2	54.7	13.4	1.4
25–34	2.8	17.1	12.2	6.9	63.2	14.7	2.9
35–44	4.3	19.9	11.4	6.2	61.1	18.1	2.2
45–54	6.2	23.5	10.5	6.9	57.9	18.7	3.1
55–64	4.5	21.3	10.7	5.6	54.4	22.5	1.7
65 and older	3.9	16.8	14.1	10.9	49.9	21.5	0.0

* Includes adults whose highest education level was grades 9–12 who had not received a high school diploma.

NOTE: Information on the type of provider of work-related adult education activities was aggregated as follows: Elementary/ secondary: elementary, junior high school, or high school; Postsecondary: 2-year community or junior college, 2-year vocational school, or 4-year college or university; Trade organization: private vocational, trade, business, hospital, or flight school, and adult learning center; Private: private community organization, church or religious organization, tutor, or private instructor; Business: business or industry or professional association; and Government: federal, state, county, or local government, or public library. Percentages were based on individuals who participated in work-related activities only. Because individuals may take more than one work-related adult education course, details may add to more than 100 percent.

SOURCE: U.S. Department of Education, National Center for Education Statistics, National Household Education Survey (NHES), 1995 (Adult Education Component).

Table 15-1   Explanations of levels of mathematics proficiency

Level 350: Multi-step problem solving and algebra

Students at this level can apply a range of reasoning skills to solve multi-step problems. They can solve routine problems involving fractions and percents, recognize properties of basic geometric figures, and work with exponents and square roots. They can solve a variety of two-step problems using variables, identify equivalent algebraic expressions, and solve linear equations and inequalities. They are developing an understanding of functions and coordinate systems.

Level 300: Moderately complex procedures and reasoning

Students at this level are developing an understanding of number systems. They can compute with decimals, simple fractions, and commonly encountered percents. They can identify geometric figures, measure lengths and angles, and calculate areas of rectangles. These students are also able to interpret simple inequalities, evaluate formulas, and solve simple linear equations. They can find averages, make decisions on information drawn from graphs, and use logical reasoning to solve problems. They are developing the skills to operate with signed numbers, exponents, and square roots.

Level 250: Numerical operations and beginning problem solving

Students at this level have an initial understanding of the four basic operations. They are able to apply whole number addition and subtraction skills to one-step word problems and money situations. In multiplication, they can find the product of a two-digit and a one-digit number. They can also compare information from graphs and charts, and are developing an ability to analyze simple logical relations.

Level 200: Beginning skills and understandings

Students at this level have considerable understanding of two-digit numbers. They can add two-digit numbers, but are still developing an ability to regroup in subtraction. They know some basic multiplication and division facts, can recognize relations among coins, read information from charts and graphs, and use simple measurement instruments. They are developing some reasoning skills.

Level 150: Simple arithmetic facts

Students at this level know some basic addition and subtraction facts, and most can add two-digit numbers without regrouping. They recognize simple situations in which addition and subtraction apply. They also are developing rudimentary classification skills.

SOURCE: U.S. Department of Education, National Center for Education Statistics, National Assessment of Educational Progress, *Trends in Academic Progress: Achievement of U.S. Students in Science, 1969 to 1992; Mathematics, 1973 to 1992; Reading, 1971 to 1992; and Writing, 1984 to 1992, 1994.*

Table 15-2   Percentage of students scoring at or above five levels of mathematics proficiency: 1978, 1982, 1986, 1990, and 1992

Proficiency levels	Age	Year				
		1978	1982	1986	1990	1992
Level 350:	9	0	0	0	0	0
Multi-step problem	13	1	0	[2]0	[2]0	0
solving and algebra	17	7	[2]6	6	7	7
Level 300:	9	1	1	1	1	1
Moderately complex	13	18	17	16	17	19
procedures and reasoning	17	[1]52	[1]48	[1]52	[2]56	[2]59
Level 250:	9	[1]20	[1]19	[1]21	[2]28	[2]28
Numerical operations and	13	[1]65	[1,2]71	[2]73	[2]75	[2]78
beginning problem solving	17	[1]92	[1]93	[2]96	[2]96	[2]97
Level 200:	9	[1]70	[1]71	[1]74	[2]82	[2]81
Beginning skills and	13	[1]95	[2]98	[2]99	[2]98	[2]99
understandings	17	100	100	100	100	100
Level 150:	9	[1]97	[1]97	[1,2]98	[2]99	[2]99
Simple arithmetic	13	100	100	100	100	100
facts	17	100	100	100	100	100

[1] Statistically significant difference from 1992.
[2] Statistically significant difference from 1978.

SOURCE: U.S. Department of Education, National Center for Education Statistics, National Assessment of Educational Progress, *Trends in Academic Progress: Achievement of U.S. Students in Science, 1969 to 1992; Mathematics, 1973 to 1992; Reading, 1971 to 1992; and Writing, 1984 to 1992*, 1994.

Table 15-3   Percentile distribution of mathematics proficiency scores, by age and race/ethnicity: 1978, 1982, 1986, 1990, and 1992

Percentile	Age 9					Age 13					Age 17				
	1978	1982	1986	1990	1992	1978	1982	1986	1990	1992	1978	1982	1986	1990	1992
All students															
5th	157	159	163	173	172	198	212	218	218	221	241	245	252	253	256
10th	171	173	177	186	185	213	225	230	230	233	254	256	263	264	267
25th	195	196	199	208	208	238	246	248	250	253	276	276	281	283	286
50th	220	220	223	231	231	265	270	269	271	274	301	299	301	305	308
75th	244	243	246	252	253	291	292	290	292	294	325	322	323	327	328
90th	264	263	264	271	271	313	311	309	310	312	345	341	343	345	345
95th	276	274	276	282	282	327	322	321	320	323	356	351	354	356	355
White															
5th	166	168	171	182	182	212	223	226	228	231	252	253	261	260	264
10th	179	181	184	194	194	226	234	236	239	242	263	264	270	270	274
25th	201	202	205	215	215	248	254	254	257	260	284	282	287	289	293
50th	225	225	228	236	236	272	275	273	277	279	307	304	307	310	313
75th	248	247	250	256	256	296	296	293	296	298	329	325	328	330	332
90th	267	265	267	274	274	317	314	312	313	315	347	343	346	347	348
95th	278	276	278	285	284	330	325	323	323	325	358	353	356	357	357
Black															
5th	134	137	146	156	155	170	189	202	202	200	217	225	237	245	238
10th	147	150	158	167	166	184	200	213	212	212	228	234	244	254	249
25th	169	172	180	186	186	206	219	231	230	231	246	251	260	269	267
50th	193	197	203	208	209	229	241	249	249	251	268	271	279	287	287
75th	216	218	224	231	230	254	261	267	268	271	290	291	296	307	304
90th	236	237	241	249	249	276	280	284	285	286	310	311	312	326	321
95th	248	248	251	259	259	288	291	296	296	297	321	321	325	338	331
Hispanic															
5th	144	148	155	162	159	180	202	206	206	212	224	232	236	229	248
10th	156	161	164	173	169	192	214	216	216	224	234	241	248	242	258
25th	179	181	185	193	190	214	231	236	234	241	253	255	265	264	273
50th	204	205	206	216	212	237	252	254	255	259	275	275	283	282	292
75th	227	226	226	235	234	262	274	274	275	279	298	297	301	304	311
90th	250	246	245	252	253	284	293	292	292	295	320	315	319	325	328
95th	260	257	254	262	263	296	304	301	303	304	332	327	329	336	336

SOURCE: U.S. Department of Education, National Center for Education Statistics, National Assessment of Educational Progress, *Trends in Academic Progress: Achievement of U.S. Students in Science, 1969 to 1992; Mathematics, 1973 to 1992; Reading, 1971 to 1992; and Writing, 1984 to 1992*, 1994.

Note on NAEP cohorts

The NAEP mathematics and science trend assessments included in this volume report trends in the progress of students by age. Proficiencies are reported for ages 9, 13, and 17. The modal grades for these age groups are 4th, 8th, and 11th grades, respectively. In both subjects, it would appear that the time span between the youngest and middle age group is greater than that between the middle and oldest age group. However, the way age is defined (on a calendar or fiscal year basis) and the time at which each age is assessed (fall, winter, or spring) results in the same length of time (or years of school) between the three age groups. A discussion of this methodology follows.

Age is determined on a calendar year basis for 9- and 13-year-olds, but on a fiscal year basis for 17-year-olds. In other words, the mathematics and science scores in 1992 represent students born in 1982 (9-year-olds), students born in 1978 (13-year-olds), and students born between October 1, 1974 and September 30, 1975 (17-year-olds).

In addition to different age definitions, the time of the school year in which the assessment is administered varies across age levels: 9-year-olds are tested in the winter; 13-year-olds are tested in the fall; and 17-year-olds are tested in the spring for both assessments. Since 9-year-olds are tested between January and February of the year in which they turn 10, and 13-year-olds are tested between October and December of the year in which they turn 13, the 13-year-olds have had almost 3 3/4 years more of school than the 9-year-olds.

Likewise, since 17-year-olds are tested between March and May, they will be between 16 1/2 and 17 1/2 at the time of the assessment (the difference is due to age being determined on a fiscal year basis); thus, they have had about 3 3/4 more years of school than the 13-year-olds.

These various methods of determining a student's age and the various testing times have been adopted in order to measure a uniform period of growth among the three age/grade groups. Comparing age cohorts over time can be more problematic, however. Nine-year-olds in 1988 generally represent the same age cohort as 13-year-olds in 1992, two points in time not quite 4 years apart. However, the 17-year-olds tested in 1992 were generally younger than the 1988 13-year-old age cohort was in 1992. Therefore, care must be taken when examining student cohorts across assessments in different years.

Table 16-1   Explanations of levels of science proficiency

Level 350: Integrates specialized scientific information

Students at this level can infer relationships and draw conclusions using detailed scientific knowledge from the physical sciences, particularly chemistry. They also can apply basic principles of genetics and interpret the societal implications of research in this field.

Level 300: Analyzes scientific procedures and data

Students at this level can evaluate the appropriateness of the design of an experiment. They have more detailed scientific knowledge, and the skill to apply their knowledge in interpreting information from text and graphs. These students also exhibit a growing understanding of principles from the physical sciences.

Level 250: Applies general scientific information

Students at this level can interpret data from simple tables and make inferences about the outcomes of experimental procedures. They exhibit knowledge and understanding of the life sciences, including a familiarity with some aspects of animal behavior and of ecological relationships. These students also demonstrate some knowledge of basic information from the physical sciences.

Level 200: Understands simple scientific principles

Students at this level are developing some understanding of simple scientific principles, particularly in the life sciences. For example, they exhibit some rudimentary knowledge of the structure and function of plants and animals.

Level 150: Knows everyday science facts

Students at this level know some general scientific facts of the type that could be learned from everyday experiences. They can read simple graphs, match the distinguishing characteristics of animals, and predict the operation of familiar apparatus that work according to mechanical principles.

SOURCE: U.S. Deparment of Education, National Center for Education Statistics, National Assessment of Education Progress, *Trends in Academic Progress: Achievement of U.S. Students in Science, 1969 to 1992; Mathematics, 1973 to 1992; Reading, 1971 to 1992; and Writing, 1984 to 1992,* 1994.

Table 16-2   Percentage of students scoring at or above five levels of science proficiency: 1977, 1982, 1986, 1990, and 1992

Proficiency level	Age	Year				
		1977	1982	1986	1990	1992
Level 350:	9	0	0	0	0	0
Integrates specialized	13	[1]1	0	[2]0	0	[2]0
scientific information	17	8	[1]7	8	9	10
Level 300:	9	3	2	3	3	3
Analyzes scientific	13	11	10	9	11	12
procedures and data	17	[1]42	[1,2]37	[1]41	43	[2]47
Level 250:	9	[1]26	[1]24	[1]28	[2]31	[2]33
Applies general	13	[1]49	[1]51	[1]52	[1,2]56	[2]61
scientific information	17	82	[1,2]77	81	81	83
Level 200:	9	[1]68	[1]71	[1,2]72	[2]76	[2]78
Understands simple	13	[1]86	[1,2]90	[2]92	[2]92	[2]93
scientific principles	17	97	[1,2]96	97	97	98
Level 150:	9	[1]94	[1]95	[1,2]96	[2]97	[2]97
Knows everyday	13	[1]98	[2]100	[2]100	[2]100	[2]100
science facts	17	100	100	100	100	100

[1] Statistically significant difference from 1992.
[2] Statistically significant difference from 1977.

SOURCE: U.S. Department of Education, National Center for Education Statistics, National Assessment of Educational Progress, *Trends in Academic Progress: Achievement of U.S. Students in Science, 1969 to 1992; Mathematics, 1973 to 1992; Reading, 1971 to 1992; and Writing, 1984 to1992,* 1994.

Table 16-3 **Percentile distribution of science proficiency scores, by age and race/ethnicity: 1977, 1982, 1986, 1990, and 1992**

Percentile	Age 9					Age 13					Age 17				
	1977	1982	1986	1990	1992	1977	1982	1986	1990	1992	1977	1982	1986	1990	1992
All students															
5th	144	151	155	160	163	174	185	189	191	193	213	203	212	210	218
10th	161	167	170	176	178	191	200	203	206	209	231	222	230	229	234
25th	190	194	196	202	204	218	224	227	230	235	261	252	260	260	264
50th	222	221	225	230	232	249	251	252	256	260	291	285	290	292	296
75th	251	249	253	257	258	278	277	276	281	284	320	315	319	323	327
90th	276	272	277	279	281	302	299	298	302	303	346	342	344	348	350
95th	291	286	291	292	294	317	313	310	315	315	362	357	360	363	364
White															
5th	163	167	166	177	178	191	198	204	209	213	231	223	228	233	234
10th	178	182	181	190	192	205	211	216	220	226	246	239	245	249	251
25th	202	204	206	213	214	229	233	237	241	246	270	266	271	273	277
50th	230	229	233	238	240	256	258	259	264	268	298	294	299	301	306
75th	257	255	259	262	264	283	282	282	287	289	325	321	325	329	333
90th	281	278	282	284	285	307	303	302	307	307	350	346	349	352	355
95th	295	291	295	296	298	321	316	314	319	318	365	361	364	367	368
Black															
5th	107	124	133	131	138	144	160	168	170	162	172	166	189	182	192
10th	123	137	147	145	152	158	173	180	182	177	187	181	202	197	207
25th	147	159	170	170	174	181	194	198	202	199	212	206	225	220	230
50th	174	188	196	196	201	207	217	221	226	224	240	235	252	252	255
75th	203	214	223	224	226	235	241	244	249	251	268	263	280	283	282
90th	229	236	246	247	284	260	262	264	269	272	293	289	306	314	308
95th	244	246	260	260	260	275	275	277	283	286	310	305	323	329	325
Hispanic															
5th	125	127	134	146	143	147	166	171	174	180	194	178	194	189	197
10th	140	142	148	159	157	161	179	181	185	193	208	194	209	204	215
25th	164	162	173	181	179	186	201	202	206	215	234	219	232	231	242
50th	191	191	200	206	205	213	226	226	231	238	262	248	259	260	273
75th	219	216	226	233	230	240	249	250	256	261	290	278	286	293	298
90th	246	236	252	253	254	266	271	270	280	282	317	302	310	317	323
95th	261	246	265	267	265	282	285	283	294	292	331	321	324	330	339

SOURCE: U.S. Department of Education, National Center for Education Statistics, National Assessment of Educational Progress, *Trends in Academic Progress: Achievement of U.S. Students in Science, 1969 to 1992; Mathematics, 1973 to 1992; Reading, 1971 to 1992; and Writing, 1984 to 1992, 1994.*

Table 18-2 Average U.S. history proficiency, by grade, control of school, urbanicity, and geographic region: 1994

Control of school, urbanicity, and geographic region	Grade 4		Grade 8		Grade 12	
	Percentage distribution	Average proficiency	Percentage distribution	Average proficiency	Percentage distribution	Average proficiency
Total	**100**	**205**	**100**	**259**	**100**	**286**
Control of school						
Public	90	203	90	257	89	284
Nonpublic	10	222	10	278	11	299
Catholic	6	221	6	279	6	298
Other nonpublic	4	224	4	277	5	299
Urbanicity						
Central city	35	198	36	257	31	286
Urban fringe/large town	43	211	38	262	43	289
Rural/small town	22	203	26	258	26	281
Geographic region						
Northeast	22	204	20	266	20	289
Southeast	23	201	25	251	23	282
Central	25	212	24	266	27	288
West	30	202	31	256	30	286

SOURCE: U.S. Department of Education, National Center for Education Statistics, National Assessment of Educational Progress, *1994 NAEP U.S. History Report Card*, 1996.

Table 18-3 Average U.S. history proficiency and time spent doing homework and watching television each day, by grade: 1994

Time spent doing homework and watching television each day	Grade 4		Grade 8		Grade 12	
	Percentage distribution	Average proficiency	Percentage distribution	Average proficiency	Percentage distribution	Average proficiency
Total	**100**	**205**	**100**	**259**	**100**	**286**
Time spent doing homework each day						
Usually don't have any	13	209	7	245	13	272
Usually don't do it	3	180	8	244	8	279
1/2 hour or less	39	204	22	279	23	287
1 hour	30	209	36	262	29	287
More than 1 hour	16	200	27	266	26	295
Time spent doing *history* homework each day*						
None	—	—	14	253	—	—
1/2 hour	—	—	34	258	—	—
1 hour	—	—	26	263	—	—
2 hours	—	—	15	269	—	—
More than 2 hours	—	—	12	264	—	—
Time spent watching television each day						
1 hour or less	20	210	13	266	27	293
2–3 hours	38	212	45	264	47	288
4–5 hours	21	205	27	257	18	280
6 hours or more	21	185	15	245	7	267

— Not available.

* Amount of time spent on history homework was reported only for those 8th-graders who were taking a U.S. history course.

SOURCE: U.S. Department of Education, National Center for Education Statistics, National Assessment of Educational Progress, *1994 NAEP U.S. History Report Card*, 1996.

Table 18-4   Percentiles of average U.S. history proficiency, by grade: 1994

Percentile	Grade 4	Grade 8	Grade 12
All students			
10th	147	217	243
25th	180	239	265
50th	210	261	288
75th	234	282	309
90th	253	299	326
White			
10th	168	229	253
25th	194	248	273
50th	219	268	294
75th	240	287	313
90th	257	302	328
Black			
10th	122	198	226
25th	149	218	244
50th	179	239	265
75th	207	259	286
90th	228	278	304
Hispanic			
10th	120	202	222
25th	148	222	242
50th	183	244	266
75th	212	264	291
90th	235	283	312

SOURCE: U.S. Department of Education, National Center for Education Statistics, National Assessment of Educational Progress, *1994 NAEP U.S. History Report Card,* 1996.

Table 20-2   Average scores across narrative, expository, and documents domains for 9-year-olds on reading literacy assessment, by country: School year 1991–92

Country	Average score			Percentile score, narrative domain					
	Narrative	Expository	Documents	1st	5th	10th	90th	95th	99th
Belgium[1]	510	505	506	293	361	385	612	643	695
British Columbia, Canada[2]	502	499	500	186	345	389	619	644	697
Cyprus	492	475	476	283	351	373	601	626	686
Denmark	463	467	496	186	186	299	592	628	682
East Germany[3]	482	493	522	219	324	361	590	626	686
Finland[4]	568	569	569	353	420	466	649	681	708
France[5]	532	533	527	335	381	411	640	672	701
Greece	514	511	488	303	367	400	622	647	699
Hong Kong[6]	494	503	554	273	350	383	601	618	677
Hungary[7]	496	493	509	299	362	390	588	617	661
Iceland[8]	518	517	519	297	361	390	627	647	700
Indonesia[9]	402	411	369	205	280	316	489	528	566
Ireland[10]	518	514	495	301	363	390	631	649	701
Italy[11]	533	538	517	303	379	411	627	650	701
Netherlands	494	480	481	311	359	382	591	625	688
New Zealand	534	531	521	299	365	403	647	679	707
Norway[12]	525	528	519	186	342	390	629	654	702
Portugal	483	480	471	300	356	386	587	617	670
Singapore	521	519	504	306	364	395	623	653	701
Slovenia	502	489	503	296	355	389	648	650	700
Spain[13]	497	505	509	291	357	389	597	641	687
Sweden	536	542	539	239	364	406	644	673	706
Switzerland	506	507	522	237	362	391	602	642	696
Trinidad/Tobago	455	458	440	232	312	343	567	605	676
United States[14]	553	538	550	330	389	420	655	685	708
Venezuela[15]	378	396	374	186	186	220	474	500	554
West Germany[16]	491	497	520	226	340	372	594	629	690

[1] Schools in French-speaking Belgium only; students instructed in Flemish or German were excluded.

[2] Students in government Native Indian schools were excluded.

[3] Students in special schools for disabled students and institutions for specially talented students were excluded.

[4] Swedish-speaking, special education, and laboratory schools were excluded.

[5] Private schools were excluded (16 percent).

[6] International schools, ESF Foundation schools, schools not participating in Secondary School Places Allocation System (SSPA), and schools with class size of less than 20 were excluded.

[7] Very small schools in remote areas and non-graded schools were excluded.

[8] Schools where there were fewer than 5 students were excluded.

[9] Schools outside of Java, Riau (Sumatra), and East Nusa Tenggara were excluded (30 percent of target population).

[10] Private schools and schools with fewer than 5 students were excluded.

[11] Non-government schools were excluded.

[12] Schools for Lapps were excluded.

[13] Students from schools with fewer than 10 students in the defined grade and from schools where the medium of instruction was not Castilian Spanish were excluded.

[14] Students in eligible schools not capable of taking the test (5 percent) were excluded.

[15] Students attending private rural schools were excluded.

[16] Students in special schools for disabled students and non-graded private schools were excluded.

SOURCE: International Association for the Evaluation of Educational Achievement, Study of Reading Literacy, *How in the World Do Students Read?*, 1992.

Table 21-2 Percentage distribution of the population in selected age groups scoring at each of the five literacy levels, by literacy scale and country: 1994

Country and age	Prose scale					Document scale					Quantitative scale				
	Total	Level 1	Level 2	Level 3	Level 4/5	Total	Level 1	Level 2	Level 3	Level 4/5	Total	Level 1	Level 2	Level 3	Level 4/5
Canada															
16–25	100.0	10.7	25.7	43.7	19.9	100.0	10.4	22.3	36.4	31.0	100.0	10.1	28.6	44.6	16.7
26–35	100.0	12.3	28.5	33.1	26.1	100.0	13.5	25.3	33.8	27.5	100.0	12.0	25.5	35.1	27.5
36–45	100.0	13.3	18.6	36.8	31.3	100.0	13.8	22.0	36.8	27.4	100.0	11.9	22.4	35.6	30.1
46–55	100.0	20.6	30.2	30.9	18.4	100.0	23.0	31.0	23.6	22.4	100.0	23.9	32.2	24.8	19.0
56–65	100.0	37.6	26.4	28.0	8.1	100.0	43.8	23.7	23.8	8.7	100.0	39.7	21.5	31.4	7.4
Germany															
16–25	100.0	8.9	29.5	46.2	15.4	100.0	5.2	29.0	43.0	22.8	100.0	4.4	26.4	47.1	22.0
26–35	100.0	12.4	30.6	37.3	19.7	100.0	5.9	29.2	40.0	24.9	100.0	4.9	23.3	42.9	28.9
36–45	100.0	14.5	31.5	39.4	14.5	100.0	9.5	30.6	38.5	21.4	100.0	6.5	22.9	44.3	26.3
46–55	100.0	14.2	37.4	37.5	10.9	100.0	7.4	35.0	43.1	14.5	100.0	7.0	27.1	41.2	24.7
56–65	100.0	22.1	43.2	30.1	4.7	100.0	17.7	40.9	32.6	8.8	100.0	10.8	34.9	40.8	13.5
Netherlands															
16–25	100.0	8.3	22.1	50.1	19.5	100.0	6.1	16.8	51.1	26.0	100.0	7.7	21.0	50.1	21.1
26–35	100.0	6.4	20.5	50.6	22.5	100.0	5.9	19.2	45.7	29.3	100.0	6.7	19.9	45.3	28.2
36–45	100.0	8.6	30.4	46.6	14.3	100.0	9.2	24.2	49.5	17.1	100.0	10.1	25.0	46.0	18.9
46–55	100.0	13.9	38.8	37.5	9.8	100.0	12.6	35.7	38.0	13.7	100.0	12.8	31.0	39.8	16.4
56–65	100.0	20.1	47.5	27.7	4.7	100.0	22.6	40.5	30.1	6.8	100.0	17.6	36.2	36.9	9.3
Poland															
16–25	100.0	26.7	38.3	29.1	5.9	100.0	32.2	33.1	26.2	8.5	100.0	29.6	32.6	31.0	6.7
26–35	100.0	35.0	39.0	22.2	3.7	100.0	39.2	33.8	19.7	7.4	100.0	32.7	33.0	25.6	8.7
36–45	100.0	42.0	38.0	17.2	2.8	100.0	42.6	33.6	18.1	5.7	100.0	36.1	32.1	23.4	8.4
46–55	100.0	53.5	29.6	16.0	1.0	100.0	55.6	27.0	13.3	4.1	100.0	47.7	26.9	19.5	5.9
56–65	100.0	69.5	20.5	9.8	0.2	100.0	70.1	20.9	7.6	1.4	100.0	60.8	21.4	15.6	2.2
Sweden															
16–25	100.0	3.8	16.7	39.8	39.7	100.0	3.1	16.6	39.6	40.7	100.0	4.9	17.6	39.0	38.4
26–35	100.0	4.9	14.2	39.2	41.7	100.0	3.9	10.4	38.1	47.6	100.0	4.0	14.3	36.3	45.4
36–45	100.0	7.1	19.7	41.5	31.7	100.0	6.6	18.2	39.8	35.4	100.0	7.0	16.5	41.2	35.2
46–55	100.0	8.2	21.8	41.8	28.2	100.0	6.8	19.7	43.1	30.3	100.0	5.8	19.7	40.5	34.0
56–65	100.0	15.9	32.7	35.3	16.2	100.0	12.2	33.3	36.0	18.5	100.0	12.9	27.0	37.5	22.6
Switzerland (French)															
16–25	100.0	10.5	31.0	43.1	15.4	100.0	8.7	24.9	40.4	26.0	100.0	6.2	21.4	47.0	25.4
26–35	100.0	11.1	29.4	46.5	13.0	100.0	11.5	22.4	44.5	21.6	100.0	8.8	20.6	47.8	22.9
36–45	100.0	22.1	33.5	35.5	8.9	100.0	19.2	32.9	34.2	13.7	100.0	16.6	25.2	36.4	21.8
46–55	100.0	20.9	35.1	36.1	7.9	100.0	18.0	29.8	42.4	9.7	100.0	16.1	22.7	43.2	18.0
56–65	100.0	27.7	43.3	26.8	2.3	100.0	27.5	38.1	29.8	4.6	100.0	19.2	36.0	33.8	11.0
Switzerland (German)															
16–25	100.0	7.3	35.5	43.4	13.8	100.0	7.1	25.7	41.0	26.3	100.0	6.9	21.9	48.2	22.9
26–35	100.0	16.6	26.8	44.6	12.0	100.0	17.4	20.7	38.8	23.1	100.0	13.1	20.7	40.8	25.4
36–45	100.0	24.2	34.3	32.4	9.1	100.0	21.5	30.3	36.3	12.0	100.0	19.0	26.3	37.9	16.9
46–55	100.0	19.4	41.7	34.7	4.2	100.0	21.0	33.8	35.0	10.2	100.0	14.8	28.5	41.2	15.5
56–65	100.0	30.4	46.0	19.5	4.1	100.0	22.8	39.9	30.6	6.7	100.0	15.8	37.6	35.7	10.8
United States															
16–25	100.0	—	—	—	—	100.0	—	—	—	—	100.0	—	—	—	—
26–35	100.0	19.6	23.2	35.7	21.6	100.0	21.6	22.9	34.5	21.0	100.0	20.1	20.9	35.6	23.5
36–45	100.0	19.5	21.4	30.0	29.2	100.0	23.5	19.7	31.4	25.4	100.0	18.2	23.2	26.9	31.6
46–55	100.0	18.3	25.7	32.2	23.8	100.0	21.4	28.2	33.2	17.3	100.0	19.0	25.2	32.3	23.6
56–65	100.0	23.6	30.7	31.1	14.7	100.0	29.3	32.9	26.0	11.7	100.0	22.4	29.6	32.0	16.0

— Data for this age group are inaccurate due to sampling and non-response problems.

SOURCE: Organization for Economic Co-operation and Development and Statistics Canada, *Literacy, Economy and Society, Results of the International Adult Literacy Survey*, 1995.

Table 21-3 Percentage distribution of the population in selected occupations scoring at each of the five literacy levels, by literacy scale and country: 1994

Country and occupation	Prose scale					Document scale					Quantitative scale				
	Total	Level 1	Level 2	Level 3	Level 4/5	Total	Level 1	Level 2	Level 3	Level 4/5	Total	Level 1	Level 2	Level 3	Level 4/5
Canada															
Manager/professional	100.0	3.2	17.4	36.5	42.9	100.0	2.6	14.9	32.4	50.1	100.0	2.2	15.0	36.4	46.4
Technician	100.0	4.3	26.4	26.3	43.0	100.0	3.5	12.1	58.6	25.9	100.0	3.9	17.7	33.4	45.0
Clerk	100.0	6.0	27.8	51.2	15.1	100.0	8.2	26.8	36.7	28.3	100.0	4.9	34.6	40.7	19.7
Sales/service	100.0	10.9	29.2	34.5	25.4	100.0	16.4	29.7	29.0	24.8	100.0	15.2	30.7	40.8	13.4
Skilled crafts workers	100.0	29.7	23.1	33.4	13.8	100.0	24.7	30.5	28.8	16.1	100.0	22.2	34.5	29.3	13.9
Machine operator/assembler	100.0	29.1	19.6	39.9	11.4	100.0	27.7	31.3	26.4	14.6	100.0	29.0	28.6	33.7	8.8
Agriculture/primary	100.0	18.6	27.9	39.6	13.8	100.0	17.5	31.4	32.7	18.4	100.0	21.2	25.0	36.1	17.7
Germany															
Manager/professional	100.0	4.5	19.1	44.4	32.0	100.0	1.5	20.0	36.4	42.1	100.0	1.9	14.1	37.3	46.7
Technician	100.0	3.9	22.9	49.0	24.2	100.0	2.3	14.0	54.2	29.6	100.0	1.7	15.4	51.6	31.3
Clerk	100.0	9.6	39.0	38.9	12.5	100.0	5.4	31.1	44.2	19.3	100.0	5.2	26.1	45.6	23.1
Sales/service	100.0	10.4	36.9	36.3	16.5	100.0	5.5	37.3	39.3	17.9	100.0	5.0	25.2	44.5	25.3
Skilled crafts workers	100.0	14.4	35.6	42.9	7.1	100.0	6.7	33.0	46.5	13.7	100.0	3.2	23.8	48.2	24.8
Machine operator/assembler	100.0	21.6	52.8	20.0	5.7	100.0	11.7	48.3	32.1	7.8	100.0	11.2	40.6	36.0	12.3
Agriculture/primary	100.0	36.8	31.3	28.0	3.9	100.0	19.0	39.1	28.7	13.2	100.0	17.6	27.2	38.5	16.7
Netherlands															
Manager/professional	100.0	3.2	20.0	52.1	24.7	100.0	2.3	17.1	52.5	28.0	100.0	1.9	15.1	48.9	34.2
Technician	100.0	2.7	19.6	54.4	23.3	100.0	2.6	15.1	49.6	32.7	100.0	2.9	17.4	50.7	29.0
Clerk	100.0	6.0	24.2	53.2	16.5	100.0	5.0	20.3	55.1	19.5	100.0	4.5	26.7	51.9	16.8
Sales/service	100.0	8.5	29.5	44.2	17.8	100.0	7.1	24.1	49.0	19.8	100.0	7.8	24.1	47.1	21.0
Skilled crafts workers	100.0	10.4	44.6	37.8	7.1	100.0	9.1	36.2	39.1	15.6	100.0	10.1	31.9	44.4	13.6
Machine operator/assembler	100.0	19.1	36.5	36.8	7.6	100.0	12.8	33.4	36.2	17.5	100.0	13.4	24.8	41.5	20.3
Agriculture/primary	100.0	16.9	31.6	43.1	8.4	100.0	16.4	24.2	43.7	15.7	100.0	18.3	27.2	44.0	10.4
Poland															
Manager/professional	100.0	13.1	31.2	40.9	14.8	100.0	19.2	28.4	33.9	18.4	100.0	11.5	26.3	37.5	24.7
Technician	100.0	23.4	45.1	28.0	3.6	100.0	22.2	39.2	29.8	8.8	100.0	18.5	32.7	36.1	12.7
Clerk	100.0	25.1	43.3	28.5	3.1	100.0	33.1	31.7	28.1	7.1	100.0	27.5	31.7	29.5	11.3
Sales/service	100.0	30.5	43.4	22.0	4.2	100.0	34.3	32.9	25.8	6.9	100.0	28.2	36.8	28.1	6.8
Skilled crafts workers	100.0	47.2	38.6	14.0	0.3	100.0	47.1	30.4	16.6	5.9	100.0	41.8	29.3	24.2	4.6
Machine operator/assembler	100.0	48.7	35.0	15.7	0.5	100.0	57.7	27.3	12.7	2.3	100.0	42.7	31.0	19.8	6.5
Agriculture/primary	100.0	62.9	27.8	8.5	0.7	100.0	60.5	29.3	8.9	1.3	100.0	54.3	28.5	15.2	2.0
Sweden															
Manager/professional	100.0	2.4	12.1	38.4	47.0	100.0	1.6	13.7	38.2	46.4	100.0	1.5	15.4	37.0	46.1
Technician	100.0	3.3	16.5	43.1	37.1	100.0	2.8	14.8	41.7	40.8	100.0	3.5	15.0	41.5	40.0
Clerk	100.0	3.4	18.5	43.2	35.0	100.0	2.2	15.8	41.1	40.9	100.0	3.9	14.7	42.1	39.4
Sales/service	100.0	6.6	22.4	38.8	32.1	100.0	5.9	21.5	41.3	31.3	100.0	7.3	21.4	39.8	31.5
Skilled crafts workers	100.0	10.0	26.4	42.5	21.1	100.0	8.4	17.3	44.5	29.8	100.0	6.4	19.5	44.0	30.0
Machine operator/assembler	100.0	7.7	27.5	41.4	23.4	100.0	7.3	19.3	45.3	28.1	100.0	7.9	16.1	42.0	34.0
Agriculture/primary	100.0	11.6	30.0	39.4	19.0	100.0	11.0	25.5	37.8	25.8	100.0	8.0	26.5	39.1	26.4
Switzerland (French)															
Manager/professional	100.0	7.0	17.3	53.3	22.4	100.0	5.4	15.9	49.0	29.7	100.0	4.0	10.8	44.8	40.5
Technician	100.0	8.4	29.5	48.5	13.5	100.0	6.9	30.4	47.9	14.8	100.0	3.7	18.7	57.6	20.0
Clerk	100.0	3.5	39.1	45.7	11.6	100.0	6.3	31.2	46.1	16.4	100.0	3.2	25.1	52.0	19.6
Sales/service	100.0	27.0	45.7	24.6	2.6	100.0	16.7	39.5	34.9	8.9	100.0	19.7	36.3	34.4	9.6
Skilled crafts workers	100.0	25.2	35.7	37.7	1.4	100.0	21.8	28.8	32.0	17.3	100.0	12.2	28.4	40.3	19.0
Machine operator/assembler	100.0	28.0	30.4	31.9	9.7	100.0	27.9	34.7	23.3	14.1	100.0	27.4	31.5	33.0	8.2
Agriculture/primary	100.0	24.8	48.2	24.2	2.8	100.0	19.6	45.1	28.5	6.7	100.0	18.6	39.0	36.7	5.7

Table 21-3   **Percentage distribution of the population in selected occupations scoring at each of the five literacy levels, by literacy scale and country: 1994— Continued**

Country and occupation	Prose scale					Document scale					Quantitative scale				
	Total	Level 1	Level 2	Level 3	Level 4/5	Total	Level 1	Level 2	Level 3	Level 4/5	Total	Level 1	Level 2	Level 3	Level 4/5
Switzerland (German)															
Manager/professional	100.0	5.1	31.4	50.4	13.0	100.0	5.0	28.6	44.0	22.4	100.0	3.6	16.5	49.8	30.1
Technician	100.0	3.5	29.9	52.6	14.0	100.0	4.4	22.4	47.7	25.4	100.0	2.6	20.5	49.4	27.5
Clerk	100.0	6.3	38.0	40.4	15.3	100.0	7.1	32.0	42.4	18.5	100.0	8.5	26.4	45.4	19.7
Sales/service	100.0	15.9	44.3	34.7	5.0	100.0	20.1	38.1	36.0	5.8	100.0	12.1	38.8	38.2	10.9
Skilled crafts workers	100.0	24.8	46.5	26.2	2.4	100.0	22.0	36.8	32.7	8.5	100.0	11.5	36.5	39.5	12.5
Machine operator/assembler	100.0	40.1	35.9	24.0	0.0	100.0	30.6	27.3	31.0	11.1	100.0	27.9	24.5	39.6	8.1
Agriculture/primary	100.0	33.3	43.9	20.5	2.3	100.0	31.3	31.9	24.6	12.2	100.0	26.2	32.7	27.0	14.0
United States															
Manager/professional	100.0	3.9	15.6	37.0	43.4	100.0	5.1	14.9	41.0	39.1	100.0	3.7	14.1	36.6	45.6
Technician	100.0	2.4	16.3	47.3	34.0	100.0	4.2	17.0	48.7	30.1	100.0	2.3	10.8	44.4	42.5
Clerk	100.0	7.3	29.8	41.7	21.2	100.0	11.1	34.0	33.1	21.8	100.0	10.6	31.7	35.5	22.1
Sales/service	100.0	24.2	26.1	32.3	17.4	100.0	26.6	25.4	32.8	15.2	100.0	25.1	28.5	29.3	17.2
Skilled crafts workers	100.0	29.4	38.0	25.5	7.1	100.0	29.9	37.6	25.0	7.4	100.0	28.7	31.5	28.9	10.9
Machine operator/assembler	100.0	28.9	36.9	27.8	6.3	100.0	35.4	32.2	25.8	6.6	100.0	30.4	30.9	27.5	11.2
Agriculture/primary	100.0	31.7	21.2	24.5	22.7	100.0	36.4	12.2	27.3	24.1	100.0	33.6	9.5	42.5	14.4

SOURCE: Organization for Economic Co-operation and Development and Statistics Canada, *Literacy, Economy and Society, Results of the International Adult Literacy Survey*, 1995.

Note on definitions of literacy scales and levels

This indicator reports the results of a wide-ranging test of literacy skills given to a large sample of adults (ranging from 1,500 to 1,800 per country) in Europe and North America in fall 1994. The International Adult Literacy Survey (IALS) was a collaborative effort among seven governments and three intergovernmental organizations. Each country was required to draw a probability sample that could be representative of the civilian, non-institutionalized population aged 16–65. In six countries, the survey was conducted in the national language; in Canada, respondents were given a choice of taking the survey in either English or French; in Switzerland, respondents in French-speaking and German-speaking cantons responded to survey questions in their respective languages.

As literacy cannot be narrowed down to a single skill suited for dealing with all types of text, nor defined as an infinite set of skills, the IALS defined literacy in terms of three scales, each encompassing a common set of skills relevant for diverse tasks:

Prose literacy: The knowledge and skills required to understand and use information from texts, including editorials, news stories, poems, and fiction;

Document literacy: The knowledge and skills required to locate and use information contained in various formats, including job applications, payroll forms, transportation schedules, maps, tables, and graphics; and

Quantitative literacy: The knowledge and skills required to apply arithmetic operations, either alone or sequentially, to numbers embedded in printed materials, such as balancing a checkbook, figuring a tip, completing an order form, or determining the amount of interest on a loan from an advertisement.

In each of these three scales, rather than expressing a threshold for achieving literacy, a scale from 0–500 was constructed, upon which tasks of varying difficulty were placed. These scales were developed through the item response theory (IRT) scaling procedures. First, the difficulty of tasks was ranked on a scale

according to how well respondents actually performed. Then, each scale was divided into five levels, reflecting the empirically determined progression of information-processing skills and strategies. Next, individuals were assigned scores between 0 and 500 according to how well they performed on a variety of tasks at different levels. Finally, the percentage of readers falling into each skill level was calculated.

A person's ability in each literacy scale can be expressed by a score, defined as the point at which he or she has an 80 percent chance of successfully performing a given task. If a person scores at level 2, it means that this individual has an 80 percent chance of successfully performing level 2 tasks and a greater than 80 percent chance of performing level 1 tasks. It does not mean, however, that individuals with low proficiency cannot succeed at tasks that are rated at higher skill levels—only that the probability of their success is relatively low. Below is a description of the three literacy scales and the tasks required at each proficiency level:

Prose literacy includes text from newspapers, magazines, and brochures accompanied by one or more questions or directives asking the reader to perform specific tasks. These tasks represent three major aspects of information processing: locating, integrating, and generating. Locating tasks require the reader to find information in the text based on conditions or features specified in the question or directive. Integrating tasks ask the reader to pull together two or more pieces of information in the text. Generating tasks ask the reader to produce a written response by processing information from the text, making text-based references, and drawing on back-ground knowledge.

Prose Level 1 (Difficulty values 0–225). Most of the tasks at this level require the reader to locate and match a single piece of information in the text that is identical to or synonymous with the information given in the directive. If a plausible incorrect answer is present in the text, it tends not to be near the correct information.

Prose Level 2 (Difficulty values 226–275). Tasks at this level tend to require the reader to locate one or more pieces of information in the text; however, several distracters may be present and the reader may need to make low-level inferences. Tasks at this level also begin to ask readers to integrate two or more pieces of information, or to compare and contrast information.

Prose Level 3 (Difficulty values 276–325). Tasks at this level tend to direct readers to search the text to match information, requiring the reader to make low-level inferences or to locate text that meets specified conditions. Sometimes the reader is required to identify several pieces of information that are located in different sentences or paragraphs rather than search for information located in a single sentence. Readers may also be asked to integrate or to compare and contrast information across paragraphs or sections of text.

Prose Level 4 (Difficulty values 326–375). These tasks require readers to perform multiple-feature matching or to provide several responses where the requested information must be identified through text-based inferences. Tasks at this level may also require the reader to integrate or contrast pieces of information that are sometimes presented in relatively lengthy texts. Typically, these texts contain more distracting information, and the information that is requested is more abstract.

Prose Level 5 (Difficulty values 376–500). Some tasks at this level require the reader to search for information in dense text that contains a number of plausible distracters. Some tasks require readers to make high-level inferences or use specialized knowledge.

Document literacy involves using materials such as tables, schedules, charts, graphs, maps, and forms. Questions or directives associated with the various document tasks are categorized into four basic types: locating, cycling, integrating, and generating. Locating, integrating, and generating refer to the same skills as those in prose literacy. Cycling tasks require the reader to locate and match one or more features of information, but differ from locating tasks in that they require the reader to engage in a series of feature matches to satisfy conditions given in the question.

Document Level 1 (Difficulty values 0–225). Most of the tasks at this level require the reader to locate a piece of information based on a literal match. Distracting information, if present, is typically located away from the correct answer. Some tasks may direct the reader to enter personal information onto a form.

Document Level 2 (Difficulty values 226–275). Document tasks at this level are more varied. While some still require the reader to match a single feature, more distracting information may be present, and the match may require a low-level inference. Some tasks at this level may require the reader to enter information onto a form or to cycle through information in a document.

Document Level 3 (Difficulty values 276–325). Tasks at this level appear to be the most varied. Some require the reader to make identical or synonymous matches; however, these matches usually require the reader to take conditional information into account or to match multiple features of information.

Document Level 4 (Difficulty values 326–375). Tasks at this level, like those in the previous levels, ask the reader to match multiple features of information, to cycle through documents, and to integrate information; frequently, these tasks require the reader to make higher order inferences to arrive at the correct answer. Sometimes the reader must take conditional information into account.

Document Level 5 (Difficulty values 376–500). Tasks at this level require the reader to search through complex displays of information that contain multiple distracters, make high-level inferences, process conditional information, or use specialized knowledge.

Quantitative literacy involves using numbers and arithmetic operations to complete a task. These tasks require the reader to locate and extract numbers from different types of documents that contain similar but irrelevant information, infer numbers from printed directions, or calculate numbers using multiple operations.

Quantitative Level 1 (Difficulty values 0–225). Although no quantitative tasks used in the IALS fall below the score of 225, experience suggests that such tasks would require the reader to perform a single, relatively simple operation (usually addition) for which either the numbers are already entered into the given document and the operation is stipulated, or the numbers are provided and the operation does not require the reader to borrow.

Quantitative Level 2 (Difficulty values 226–275). Tasks at this level typically require readers to perform a single arithmetic operation (frequently addition or subtraction) using numbers that are easily located in the text or document. The operation to be performed may be easily inferred from the wording of the question or the format of the material (for example, a bank deposit form or an order form).

Quantitative Level 3 (Difficulty values 276–325). Tasks at this level typically require the reader to perform a single operation. However, the operations are more varied—some multiplication and division tasks are found at this level. Sometimes two or more numbers are needed to solve the problem, and the numbers are frequently embedded in more complex displays. While semantic relation terms such as "how many" or "calculate the difference" are often used, some of the tasks require the reader to make higher order inferences to determine the appropriate operation.

Quantitative Level 4 (Difficulty values 326–375). With one exception, the tasks at this level require the reader to perform a single arithmetic operation in which the quantities or the operations are not easily determined. That is, for most of the tasks at this level, the question or directive does not provide a semantic relation term such as "how many" or "calculate the difference" to help the reader.

Quantitative Level 5 (Difficulty values 376–500). Tasks at this level require readers to perform multiple operations sequentially; the reader must pull out the features of the problem from the material provided or rely on background knowledge to determine the quantities or operations needed.

SOURCE: Organization for Economic Co-operation and Development and Statistics Canada, *Literacy, Economy and Society, Results of the International Adult Literacy Survey,* 1995.

Table 22-1   SAT test-takers as a percentage of high school graduates, percentage of test-takers who are minorities, SAT mean scores, standard deviations, and percentage scoring 600 or higher: 1972–95

Year	Number of high school graduates[1]	SAT test-takers Number[1]	As a percent of high school graduates[2]	Percent minority	Total mean	Verbal Mean	Verbal Standard deviation	Verbal Percentage scoring 600 or higher	Mathematics Mean	Mathematics Standard deviation	Mathematics Percentage scoring 600 or higher
	(in thousands)										
1972	3,001	1,023	34.1	—	937	453	111	11	484	115	17
1973	3,036	1,015	33.4	—	926	445	108	10	481	113	16
1974	3,073	985	32.1	—	924	444	110	10	480	116	17
1975	3,133	996	31.8	—	906	434	109	8	472	115	15
1976	3,148	1,000	31.8	15.0	903	431	110	8	472	120	17
1977	3,155	979	31.0	16.1	899	429	110	8	470	119	16
1978	3,127	989	31.6	17.0	897	429	110	8	468	118	15
1979	3,117	992	31.8	17.1	894	427	110	7	467	117	15
1980	3,043	992	32.6	17.9	890	424	110	7	466	117	15
1981	3,020	994	32.9	18.1	890	424	110	7	466	117	14
1982	2,995	989	33.0	18.3	893	426	110	7	467	117	15
1983	2,888	963	33.3	18.9	893	425	109	7	468	119	16
1984	2,767	965	34.9	19.7	897	426	110	7	471	119	17
1985	2,677	977	36.5	20.0	906	431	111	7	475	119	17
1986	2,643	1,001	37.9	—	906	431	110	8	475	121	17
1987	2,694	1,080	40.1	21.8	906	430	111	8	476	122	18
1988	2,773	1,134	40.9	23.0	904	428	109	7	476	120	17
1989	2,727	1,088	39.9	25.3	903	427	111	8	476	121	18
1990	2,588	1,026	39.7	26.6	900	424	111	7	476	123	18
1991	[3]2,493	1,033	[3]41.4	28.0	896	422	111	7	474	123	17
1992	[3]2,483	1,034	[3]41.6	28.5	899	423	112	7	476	123	18
1993	[3]2,481	1,044	[3]42.1	30.0	902	424	113	7	478	125	19
1994	[3,4]2,479	1,050	42.4	31.0	902	423	113	7	479	124	18
1995	[4]2,553	1,068	41.8	31.0	910	428	113	8	482	127	21

— Not available.

[1] Includes those in public and private schools.

[2] This figure represents high school graduates who took the SAT at any time while they were in high school as a percentage of all high school graduates.

[3] Data have been revised from previously published figures.

[4] Number of public high school graduates is based on state estimates.

SOURCE: College Entrance Examination Board, *National Report: College Bound Seniors, 1972–1995* (Copyright ©1995 by College Entrance Examination Board. All rights reserved.). U.S. Department of Education, National Center for Education Statistics, *Digest of Education Statistics, 1995*, table 99.

Table 22-2   Average SAT scores of college-bound seniors, by race/ethnicity: 1976–95

Year	White Verbal	White Math	Black Verbal	Black Math	Mexican American Verbal	Mexican American Math	Puerto Rican Verbal	Puerto Rican Math	Other Hispanic Verbal	Other Hispanic Math	Asian American Verbal	Asian American Math	American Indian Verbal	American Indian Math
1976	451	493	332	354	371	410	364	401	—	—	414	518	388	420
1977	448	489	330	357	370	408	355	397	—	—	405	514	390	421
1978	446	485	332	354	370	402	349	388	—	—	401	510	387	419
1979	444	483	330	358	370	410	345	388	—	—	396	511	386	421
1980	442	482	330	360	372	413	350	394	—	—	396	509	390	426
1981	442	483	332	362	373	415	353	398	—	—	397	513	391	425
1982	444	483	341	366	377	416	360	403	—	—	398	513	388	424
1983	443	484	339	369	375	417	358	403	—	—	395	514	388	425
1984	445	487	342	373	376	420	358	405	—	—	398	519	390	427
1985	449	490	346	376	382	426	368	409	—	—	404	518	392	428
1986	—	—	—	—	—	—	—	—	—	—	—	—	—	—
1987	447	489	351	377	379	424	360	400	387	432	405	521	393	432
1988	445	490	353	384	382	428	355	402	387	433	408	522	393	435
1989	446	491	351	386	381	430	360	406	389	436	409	525	384	428
1990	442	491	352	385	380	429	359	405	383	434	410	528	388	437
1991	441	489	351	385	377	427	361	406	382	431	411	530	393	437
1992	442	491	352	385	372	425	366	406	383	433	413	532	395	442
1993	444	494	353	388	374	428	367	409	384	433	415	535	400	447
1994	443	495	352	388	372	427	367	411	383	435	416	535	396	441
1995	448	498	356	388	376	426	372	411	389	438	418	538	403	447

— Not available.

NOTE: The first year for which SAT scores by racial/ethnic group are available is 1976. Data were not collected by racial/ethnic group in 1986. The term "college-bound seniors" refers to those students from each high school graduating class who participated in the College Board Admissions Testing Program, and does not include all first-year college students, or all high school seniors. See the supplemental note to this indicator for information on interpreting SAT scores.

SOURCE: College Entrance Examination Board, *National Report: College Bound Seniors, 1972–1995* (Copyright ©1995 by College Entrance Examination Board. All rights reserved.).

Table 22-7 **Percentage of graduating seniors taking the ACT[1] and ACT composite scores, by race/ethnicity and type of program: 1991–95**

Percentage of graduating seniors taking the ACT and ACT composite scores	Year				
	1991	1992	1993	1994	1995
Percentage of graduating seniors taking the ACT	32.0	33.5	35.3	36.0	37.0
ACT composite score[2] Total	20.6	20.6	20.7	20.8	20.8
Race/ethnicity					
White	21.3	21.3	21.4	21.4	21.5
Black	17.0	17.0	17.1	17.0	17.1
Asian/Pacific Islander	21.6	21.6	21.7	21.7	21.6
Mexican/Chicano	18.4	18.4	18.5	18.4	18.6
Other Hispanic	19.3	19.3	19.3	19.3	18.7
American Indian	18.2	18.1	18.4	18.5	18.6
Type of program[3]					
College preparatory	22.1	22.0	22.0	22.0	22.0
Non-college preparatory	19.1	19.1	19.1	19.1	19.1

[1] The American College Testing (ACT) Program Assessment is used for college admissions, placement, scholarship programs, recruitment and retention, and academic advising.
[2] The ACT composite score ranges from 1 to 36 and reflects the scores of the 4 tests: English, Mathematics, Reading, and Science Reasoning.
[3] A college preparatory program is defined as one that includes the basic core curriculum of 4 years of English and 3 years each of mathematics, social studies, and science.
SOURCE: American College Testing Program, *1995 ACT Assessment Results: Summary Report.*

Note on interpreting SAT test scores and the new version of the SAT

Interpreting test scores

According to the College Board, the new version of the Scholastic Assessment Test (SAT) is designed to measure verbal and quantitative reasoning skills related to academic performance in college. SAT scores are statistically controlled to maintain the same meaning from year to year, and therefore useful comparisons over time can be made.[1]

Since 1941, SAT scores have been expressed relative to the performance of a group of approximately 11,000 candidates who took the test in 1941.[2] The mean raw score of that group was given the scaled score of 500, with a standard deviation of 100. In order for scores to be compared to this reference group, a short set of common items is included in each year's forms. Each new form is then linked with a previous form through these common items, allowing the forms to be equated back to the 1941 form. Therefore, a score of 500 on any form of the SAT corresponds to the mean of the 1941 group. Likewise, a score of 600 falls one standard deviation above the mean of the 1941 group, and a score of 400 falls one standard deviation below the mean of the 1941 group.[3]

The decline or rise of test scores depends on many factors. Changes can involve variations in the composition of the test-takers. For example, between 1963 and 1970, there was a significant decline in SAT scores. Because of a continuing increase in the proportion of high school graduates going to college over this period, the group of test-takers became progressively less selective, and this was likely a major factor in the decline in scores.[4] The College Board notes that the relationship between SAT test scores and students' characteristics are "complex and interdependent."[5] For example, educational, demographic, and socioeconomic factors might influence test scores. However, while these factors may be related, they are not necessarily causal. Moreover, changes in test scores can also be related to variations in performance among similar types of test-takers.

Standard deviation units

Performance on the SAT can be measured in a number of ways. Changes in standard deviation units is one useful metric. Standard deviation units indicate how scores, on average, deviated from the mean. Since the standard deviation is measured on a *common scale* across different tests, it can also be used to compare score changes on a variety of measures.[6]

Once changes in scores across measures have been noted, the significance of these changes should be considered. Some have considered a decline of one standard deviation to be significant. This designation, however, is arbitrary.[7] In *Investment in Learning*, Howard Bowen provides some guidelines for describing changes in standard deviation units (SDUs).[8]

Estimated changes as expressed in SDUs	Descriptive judgment
+.75 or above	Extreme increase
+.40 to .74	Large increase
+.20 to .39	Moderate increase
+.10 to .19	Small increase
-.09 to +.09	No change
-.10 to -.19	Small decline
-.20 to -.39	Moderate decline
-.40 to -.74	Large decline
-.75 or below	Extreme decline

Changes in standard deviation units are calculated using the following formula:

$$\frac{\mu_1 - \mu_2}{\sqrt{\frac{1}{2}(\sigma_1^2 + \sigma_2^2)}}$$

where μ_1 and μ_2 are the mean scores in years 1 and 2, respectively, and σ_1 and σ_2 are the standard deviations of scores in years 1 and 2, respectively. For example, table 22-1 indicates that between 1980 and 1985, mean verbal scores increased 7 points, and between 1980 and 1987, mean mathematics scores increased 10 points.

Applying the above formula, the following standard deviation units are produced:

Verbal: 431-424/110.5 = +.063

Math: 476-466/119.5 = +.084

According to Bowen's template, the changes in standard deviation units suggest no significant change in scores during this period. Using the same calculation, the declines in verbal and mathematics scores from 1972 to 1993 were -.259 and -.050, respectively—moderate and not significant declines.

The new version of the SAT

A new version of the SAT was introduced in March 1994. The new SAT is divided into two sections—the SAT I: Reasoning Tests and the SAT II: Subject Tests. The SAT I is organized into verbal and mathematics sections similar to the previous version of the SAT, while the SAT II replaces the achievement tests for assessing knowledge in specific subject areas. Using psychometric methods of equating, the Educational Testing Service (ETS) made the scores from the SAT I comparable to the scores from the former SAT, thus allowing comparisons of scores from 1972 through 1995.

The mathematics section on the new SAT I is very similar to the mathematics section on the original SAT, except that it contains some grid-in (or fill-in-the-blank) items, and test-takers can now use calculators. The verbal section of the new SAT I has changed more significantly, however. In the original SAT, students were asked to complete four types of items: reading comprehension, sentence completion, analogies, and antonyms. On the new version, students must complete only three types of verbal items: critical reading, sentence completion, and analogies. As a result of these changes, the new SAT I does not provide verbal subscores comparable to the subscores of the original SAT; however, the overall verbal scores are comparable between the two versions of the test.

NOTES:

[1] College Entrance Examination Board. *National Report: College Bound Seniors*, 1995.

[2] Anne Anastasi. *Psychological Testing*. MacMillan, Fifth edition, 1982, p. 90.

[3] College Entrance Examination Board. *National Report: College Bound Seniors*, 1995.

[4] College Entrance Examination Board. *On Further Examination: Report of the Advisory Panel on the Scholastic Aptitude Test Score Decline*, 1977.

[5] College Entrance Examination Board, *National Report: College Bound Seniors*, 1995.

[6] The Congress of the United States, Congressional Budget Office. *Trends in Educational Achievement*, April 1986.

[7] Clifford Adelman. *The Standardized Test Scores of College Graduates, 1964–1982*. National Institute of Education, 1985, p.11.

[8] Howard Bowen. *Investment in Learning*. Jossey-Bass, 1977.

Note on proficiency scores for IAEP mathematics and science

Indicators 23 and *24* contain mean proficiency scores and standard errors for each population participating in the second International Assessment of Educational Progress (IAEP). Proficiency scores allow the comparison of average proficiency across age groups within and between countries. Mean proficiency scores and standard errors were obtained following a series of different statistical analyses: item parameters estimation using item response theory (IRT), vertical equating of scales for 9- and 13-year-olds, and plausible values technology for estimation of proficiency distributions.

First, for each age group in mathematics and science, a random sample of 200 students was drawn from each participating population to build a reference population. Then, a three-parameter logistic item response model was fitted using this reference population. Following examinations of goodness of fit statistics and consultation with content specialists, no items were excluded from the item parameter estimation.

Since there were some common items for 9- and 13-year-olds, it was possible to equate item parameter estimates to put proficiency scores for these two age groups on the same proficiency scale. This was done with a linear transformation of the 9-year-olds' item parameters estimates using the 13-year-olds' item parameters estimates as the target scale. Finally, five draws from each

student's proficiency distribution were obtained using plausible values technology developed for the National Assessment of Educational Progress (NAEP). This technology used three different sets of values as input: item parameters estimates from the reference population, students' item mathematics or science responses, and students' answers to the background questions.

The proficiency scores were rescaled to give a mean of 500 and a standard deviation of 100. To do so, the proficiency scores for all the participating populations were merged, 9- and 13-year-olds together. An overall mean and an overall standard deviation were then calculated using the individual students' weights. These values were used to transform linearly the five proficiency scores of each student on the targeted scale with mean and standard deviation as previously fixed (500 and 100, respectively).

Population mean proficiency scores were computed as the average of the five proficiency score means. Computation of standard errors of these means included contribution from two sources. A first contribution made use of the sampling plan and consisted of the jackknifed standard error of the first proficiency score. A second contribution was linked to the variation implicit in the presence of five possible proficiency scores. These two quantities were combined to give information concerning the variability of the results.

Note on educational attainment

The Current Population Survey (CPS), which is used for *Indicators 25, 32, 34,* and others, changed the questions used to determine a respondent's educational attainment beginning in 1992. Before 1992, the educational attainment questions were 1) "What is the highest grade or year of regular school...has ever attended?" and 2) "Did ...complete the grade?" There were 19 response categories for grades 1–8, 1st–4th year of high school, and 1st–6th year of college.

If respondents attended, for example, grade 12 but did not complete it, it was assumed that they had completed grade 11. If the highest grade respondents had completed was 9, 10, or 11, they were classified as high school dropouts. If the highest grade completed was 12 or greater, they were considered to have completed high school. If they had completed the 4th year of college or greater, they were considered to have completed college.

Beginning in 1992, the two questions were changed to a single question: "What is the highest level of school...has completed or the highest degree...has received?" In the new response categories, several of the lower levels were collapsed into a single summary category such as "1st, 2nd, 3rd, or 4th grades." At the high school level, a new category "12th grade, no diploma" was added. The biggest change was in the categories for high school completion and beyond, which are as follows:

♦ High school graduate, high school diploma or equivalent (e.g., GED)

♦ Some college but no degree

♦ Associate's degree in college, academic program

♦ Associate's degree in college, occupational or vocational program

♦ Bachelor's degree (e.g., B.A., A.B., B.S.)

♦ Master's degree (e.g., M.A., M.S., M.Eng., M.Ed., M.S.W., M.B.A.)

♦ Professional school degree (e.g., M.D., D.D.S., D.V.M., L.L.B., J.D.)

♦ Doctoral degree (e.g., Ph.D., Ed.D.)

The new question puts more emphasis on credentials received beginning at the high school level, and it puts less emphasis on the level attended or completed in college if that attendance did not lead to a credential.

This change created some uncertainty about the comparability of measures, such as high school completion rates and college completion rates over time. Below is a discussion of the possible effects the new question may have on high school and college completion rates.

High school completion: The earlier educational attainment question did not explicitly address high school equivalency certificates. Therefore, it is possible that an individual who attended grade 10, dropped out without completing it, and later took the GED test and received a high school equivalency credential would not have been counted as completing high school. The new question, however, explicitly treats these individuals as high school graduates. Since 1988, an additional question has been added to the October CPS to explicitly ask respondents whether they had taken the GED. The vast majority of those who responded "yes" were classified as high school graduates using the attainment question.

The earlier educational attainment question treated individuals who completed grade 12 as high school graduates. However, the new question added a new response category called "12th grade, no diploma," and these respondents were not treated as graduates. However, the number of individuals in this category historically has been very small. In summary, it appears that the question change has had minor effects on measured high school completion rates.

College completion: With the increasing prevalence of individuals taking more than 4 years to earn a bachelor's degree, some researchers are concerned that the college completion rate based on the category "4th year or higher of college completed" would overstate the bachelor's degree (or higher) completion rate. However, the college completion rates among those aged 25–29 in 1992 and 1993 using the new CPS question were very similar to the completion rates for those in 1990 and 1991 using the old questions.

In summary, it appears that the question change has had a very small effect on measured college completion rates.

Some college: With the new question, someone who attends college for only a few months should respond "Some college," but with the old question they should have responded "Attended first year of college and did not complete it." In the past, the calculation of the percentage of the population with 1–3 years of college excluded these individuals. However, with the new question, the information to exclude them is not available, and those with only a few months of college are included in the category "Some college." So, in principle, the percentage of individuals with "Some college" or an associate's degree would be expected to be larger than the percentage with 1–3 years of college. Therefore, it does not appear useful to compare the percentage of those with "Some college or an associate's degree" using the new item, to the percentage of those who completed "1–3 years of college" using the old item.

Indicators 32 and *34* use labor force statistics for the civilian population and annual median earnings for wage and salary workers with

different levels of educational attainment. The discussion above suggests that the "high school graduate with no further education" category based on the new item is larger than before, because it includes all those with an equivalency certificate; however, it is actually smaller than before because it excludes those who completed "12th grade, no diploma" and those with only a few months of college. The latter group is now included in the "1–3 years of college" category.

Nevertheless, the employment and earnings of the respondents who have been added and dropped from each category are similar; therefore, the net effect of the misclassification on employment rates and average annual earnings is likely to be minor. For this reason, it was decided that it would be useful to continue to compare the employment rates and median annual earnings of recent cohorts with "Some college or an associate's degree" to older cohorts who completed "1–3 years of college."

For further information on this issue, see Robert Kominski and Paul M. Siegel, "Measuring Education in the Current Population Survey," *Monthly Labor Review*, September 1993.

Table 26-1 Percentage distribution of 1980 high school sophomores according to the timing, enrollment status, and institution type of their initial enrollment in postsecondary education, by selected characteristics: 1982 and 1992

Selected characteristics	Fall 1982					Delayed entry[1]			Other enroll-ment[3]	No enroll-ment
	Full-time 4-year	Full-time public 2-year	Part-time 4-year	Part-time public 2-year	Other[2]	4-year	Public 2-year	Other[2]		
Total	**23.4**	**10.5**	**1.1**	**4.1**	**5.0**	**4.2**	**10.3**	**5.9**	**1.9**	**33.6**
Sex										
Male	22.0	9.3	1.0	3.4	4.3	4.7	10.3	5.0	1.9	38.1
Female	24.8	11.6	1.2	4.8	5.8	3.8	10.2	6.8	1.9	29.3
Grades in high school										
Mostly As (90–100)	69.7	7.2	1.3	3.0	3.7	3.8	2.2	0.6	0.6	7.9
Half As/Bs (85–89)	52.3	13.1	2.2	3.9	5.0	3.7	5.8	2.4	0.9	10.8
Mostly Bs (80–84)	35.8	14.1	1.3	5.4	6.1	5.0	8.7	3.7	1.4	18.7
Half Bs/Cs (75–79)	18.8	12.3	1.0	4.5	6.1	4.7	12.7	6.8	1.5	31.6
Mostly Cs (70–74)	7.7	8.7	0.9	4.0	4.8	4.5	13.4	7.6	2.4	46.0
Half Cs/Ds (65–69)	3.7	4.0	0.3	2.8	2.6	2.5	8.8	9.3	3.4	62.6
Mostly Ds (60–64)	4.9	2.3	0.1	0.7	3.5	3.5	5.3	10.6	2.7	66.5
Program in high school										
General	11.5	9.2	0.9	4.1	4.5	4.0	12.8	7.3	2.1	43.8
Academic	44.4	13.0	1.6	4.6	5.6	5.1	7.4	3.9	1.1	13.2
Vocational	5.8	8.6	0.6	3.6	5.0	3.4	11.7	7.4	2.6	51.5
Location (census region) of high school										
Northeast	30.1	9.0	0.7	1.8	5.9	4.6	7.6	6.6	2.0	31.7
Central	25.5	9.3	1.3	4.2	6.3	3.6	10.7	5.0	1.7	32.6
South	19.8	10.1	1.5	3.8	3.9	4.7	9.5	6.4	1.9	38.4
West	18.1	15.0	0.5	7.4	3.9	3.8	14.6	5.7	2.1	28.8
Socioeconomic status										
Low quartile	8.7	7.9	0.6	2.3	4.3	4.0	9.3	8.3	2.7	52.0
Middle two quartiles	21.5	11.9	1.4	5.2	6.1	4.1	11.8	5.7	1.4	31.0
High quartile	48.4	12.3	1.3	4.9	5.1	5.4	6.6	3.0	1.4	11.7
Test score composite 1982[4]										
Low quartile	5.2	5.6	0.2	2.8	3.9	3.1	9.5	8.1	2.8	58.8
Middle two quartiles	17.7	13.6	1.4	5.1	6.2	4.4	11.9	6.4	1.8	31.6
High quartile	60.4	10.0	1.8	3.2	4.3	4.7	6.2	2.5	0.5	6.4
All courses[5]										
No	20.3	10.6	1.1	4.3	5.4	4.1	10.6	6.2	2.0	35.4
Yes	80.3	6.7	2.2	0.5	1.0	2.8	3.4	1.4	0.0	1.6
Race/ethnicity										
White	25.6	11.0	1.1	4.4	5.3	4.1	10.1	5.5	1.7	31.2
Black	18.9	8.8	0.7	2.8	4.3	5.1	9.7	8.6	2.5	38.7
Hispanic	11.1	9.5	1.4	3.8	4.6	3.8	10.7	6.1	2.1	46.9
Asian/Pacific Islander	40.6	16.1	2.1	7.0	2.8	3.7	11.1	3.3	0.8	12.5
American Indian/Alaskan Native	8.4	6.1	0.2	2.8	3.0	9.2	16.6	5.2	2.5	46.0
Parents' educational attainment 1980[6]										
No high school diploma	8.0	7.4	0.8	2.8	4.1	3.6	9.2	6.1	1.9	56.1
High school graduate	13.4	9.7	1.1	3.2	5.5	4.0	11.6	7.2	2.3	42.0
Vocational/technical	18.9	11.1	1.0	4.7	5.6	3.9	12.7	9.0	1.2	31.9
Some college	27.3	14.2	1.5	4.4	5.7	5.0	11.0	5.4	2.2	23.2
Bachelor's degree	43.4	12.7	1.1	7.8	4.7	5.1	7.7	3.0	0.8	13.5
Advanced degree	52.3	13.7	1.6	3.9	3.6	3.6	6.7	2.5	1.7	10.4

[1] Student first enrolled in postsecondary education after October 1982.
[2] Includes less-than-4-year institutions other than public 2-year.
[3] Includes students who could not be placed in one of the other categories, usually because information on timing of enrollment was missing.
[4] Composite score based on the average nonmissing scores on reading, vocabulary, and mathematics (part 1) tests administered in 1982.
[5] Whether student took 4 English credits, 3 social studies credits, 3 mathematics credits, 2 foreign language credits, and 0.5 computer science credits.
[6] Mother's or father's educational attainment, whichever was higher.

SOURCE: U.S. Department of Education, National Center for Education Statistics, High School and Beyond (HS&B) study 1980 Sophomore Cohort, Base Year, First, and Fourth Follow-up surveys.

Table 26-2 Percentage distribution of 1980 high school sophomores according to highest degree earned through 1992, by selected characteristics

Selected characteristics	Less than high school	High school	Certif-icate	Assoc-iate's	Bach-elor's	Master's	First-profess-ional	Doctor-ate
Total	**5.8**	**51.5**	**11.0**	**7.9**	**20.0**	**2.7**	**0.9**	**0.2**
Sex								
Male	6.5	53.5	9.7	6.7	19.5	2.6	1.3	0.2
Female	5.0	49.5	12.4	9.1	20.5	2.8	0.5	0.1
Grades in high school								
Mostly As (90–100)	0.5	17.8	2.4	3.9	54.7	13.8	6.3	0.6
Half As/Bs (85–89)	0.6	30.0	6.2	7.7	44.1	8.1	2.6	0.7
Mostly Bs (80–84)	0.7	42.8	9.7	10.6	31.2	3.7	1.1	0.2
Half Bs/Cs (75–79)	2.7	58.3	11.8	9.5	16.1	1.3	0.3	0.0
Mostly Cs (70–74)	8.5	63.9	13.5	6.7	7.0	0.4	0.1	0.0
Half Cs/Ds (65–69)	18.9	59.8	14.3	4.4	2.4	0.1	0.1	0.2
Mostly Ds (60–64)	32.0	48.7	11.4	1.1	5.3	1.4	0.0	0.0
Program in high school								
General	8.8	59.6	13.8	7.4	9.5	0.7	0.2	0.1
Academic	1.0	36.4	8.4	7.9	38.1	5.8	2.0	0.3
Vocational	9.7	64.9	12.1	8.1	4.7	0.4	0.1	0.1
Location (census region) of high school								
Northeast	3.1	46.2	10.2	9.1	25.4	4.6	1.2	0.3
Central	5.4	50.7	10.1	9.4	20.5	2.6	1.2	0.2
South	6.7	56.4	11.6	6.2	16.4	2.2	0.5	0.1
West	8.2	50.2	12.7	7.2	19.4	1.5	0.8	0.1
Socioeconomic status								
Low quartile	9.0	64.6	12.3	6.9	6.4	0.7	0.1	0.0
Middle two quartiles	3.9	53.8	11.5	9.1	19.0	2.0	0.5	0.1
High quartile	1.4	32.7	7.0	7.6	41.2	6.9	2.7	0.5
Test score composite in 1982[1]								
Low quartile	15.6	64.0	13.0	4.1	3.0	0.2	0.0	0.1
Middle two quartiles	3.1	56.2	12.8	10.1	16.1	1.5	0.3	0.0
High quartile	0.1	26.5	4.8	7.2	49.2	8.7	3.0	0.6
All courses[2]								
No	6.0	53.6	11.5	8.1	17.8	2.2	0.7	0.1
Yes	0.0	12.9	3.2	8.5	60.9	12.5	1.6	0.5
Race/ethnicity								
White	4.9	49.1	10.1	8.4	23.1	3.2	1.0	0.2
Black	6.9	59.6	16.3	5.2	10.0	1.5	0.5	0.2
Hispanic	11.9	59.6	11.2	7.3	9.0	0.6	0.3	0.0
Asian/Pacific Islander	0.6	40.9	6.9	6.2	32.7	4.7	7.5	0.7
American Indian/Alaskan Native	17.8	58.2	11.8	5.0	6.7	0.5	0.0	0.0

Table 26-2   Percentage distribution of 1980 high school sophomores according to highest degree earned through 1992, by selected characteristics—Continued

Selected characteristics	Less than high school	High school	Certif-icate	Assoc-iate's	Bach-elor's	Master's	First-profess-ional	Doctor-ate
Parents' educational attainment in 1980[3]								
No high school diploma	13.4	63.3	11.0	5.7	5.7	0.7	0.2	0.1
High school graduate	6.1	59.5	13.0	8.3	11.5	1.2	0.3	0.1
Vocational/technical	4.2	55.1	13.3	8.0	17.1	1.7	0.6	0.0
Some college	2.7	48.7	12.6	10.6	22.6	2.3	0.4	0.2
Bachelor's degree	1.6	36.3	7.3	7.7	39.5	5.9	1.4	0.4
Advanced degree	1.1	31.2	5.0	7.9	43.4	7.4	3.5	0.5
Type of start in postsecondary education								
Fall 1982 full-time 4-year	0.0	21.2	3.5	4.6	57.8	9.0	3.4	0.5
Fall 1982 full-time public 2-year	0.3	36.5	11.9	24.4	24.6	2.1	0.2	0.0
Fall 1982 part-time 4-year	0.0	52.2	6.7	10.0	27.2	3.5	0.1	0.4
Fall 1982 part-time public 2-year	1.6	59.5	13.4	9.4	14.4	0.9	0.8	0.0
Fall 1982 other	0.2	23.0	34.3	24.5	15.7	1.9	0.4	0.0
Delay 4-year[4]	0.4	55.6	8.1	7.4	24.0	3.7	0.4	0.4
Delay public 2-year	1.7	63.0	16.9	12.0	6.2	0.2	0.0	0.0
Delay other[4]	1.9	31.4	48.4	14.4	3.8	0.1	0.1	0.0
Other enrollment[5]	0.0	0.0	86.5	5.1	6.0	1.1	0.4	0.8
No enrollment	16.1	83.9	0.0	0.0	0.0	0.0	0.0	0.0

[1] Composite score based on the average nonmissing scores on reading, vocabulary, and mathematics (part 1) tests administered in 1982.

[2] Whether student took 4 English credits, 3 social studies credits, 3 mathematics credits, 2 foreign language credits, and 0.5 computer science credits.

[3] Mother's or father's educational attainment, whichever was higher.

[4] Includes less-than-4-year institutions other than public 2-year.

[5] Includes students who could not be placed in one of the other categories, usually because information on timing of enrollment was missing.

SOURCE: U.S. Department of Education, National Center for Education Statistics, High School and Beyond (HS&B) study 1980 Sophomore Cohort, Base Year, First, and Fourth Follow-up surveys.

Table 27-1   Percentage of the population who have completed secondary and higher education, by sex, country, and age: 1992

Country	Both sexes		Male		Female	
	Secondary education	Higher education	Secondary education	Higher education	Secondary education	Higher education
25–64 years old						
Large countries						
Canada	71.3	15.0	71.0	16.8	71.5	13.2
France	52.2	10.2	56.2	11.3	48.4	9.2
Germany	81.9	11.6	88.6	14.8	75.1	8.3
Italy	28.4	6.4	30.5	7.3	26.4	5.4
Japan[1]	69.7	13.3	70.9	21.5	68.5	5.2
United Kingdom	68.1	10.7	73.9	13.8	62.2	7.7
United States[2]	84.0	23.6	83.8	26.0	84.3	21.3
Other countries						
Australia[3]	52.8	11.8	62.9	12.9	42.6	10.7
Austria	68.0	6.9	77.7	7.9	58.3	6.0
Belgium	45.3	8.8	47.0	11.6	43.6	6.1
Denmark	58.9	13.3	63.4	14.0	54.4	12.7
Finland	61.5	10.4	61.1	12.1	61.9	8.8
Ireland	42.2	8.3	38.9	9.8	45.5	6.9
Netherlands	57.9	20.9	63.8	23.8	51.9	17.8
New Zealand	56.4	11.1	62.2	13.5	50.8	8.7
Norway	79.0	12.4	79.9	14.8	78.1	10.0
Portugal[4]	14.2	5.0	14.7	5.4	13.7	4.6
Spain	22.9	10.0	25.7	10.7	20.3	9.4
Sweden	69.9	11.7	68.3	12.2	71.4	11.2
Switzerland	80.8	8.0	87.0	11.0	74.6	5.1
25–34 years old						
Large countries						
Canada	80.8	16.1	79.0	16.0	82.5	16.2
France	67.1	12.3	68.4	12.4	65.7	12.1
Germany	88.6	11.8	90.9	13.0	86.3	10.5
Italy	42.4	6.8	41.5	6.8	43.3	6.7
Japan[1]	90.6	22.9	89.3	34.2	91.8	11.5
United Kingdom	80.9	12.5	82.2	14.3	79.6	10.7
United States[2]	86.5	23.2	85.9	23.3	87.0	23.1
Other countries						
Australia[3]	56.6	13.1	65.2	13.1	47.8	13.1
Austria	78.9	7.9	85.0	7.6	72.7	8.3
Belgium	59.9	11.5	57.7	13.2	62.2	9.6
Denmark	66.9	[5]13.3	67.7	[5]12.9	66.0	[5]13.7
Finland	81.7	11.1	79.8	12.2	83.7	9.9
Ireland	55.8	9.8	50.3	10.1	61.1	9.6
Netherlands	67.9	23.6	68.6	24.3	67.1	22.8
New Zealand	59.6	12.6	64.1	14.3	55.4	10.9
Norway	88.1	12.7	86.5	12.9	89.7	12.4
Portugal[4]	20.6	6.9	18.7	6.1	22.5	7.7
Spain	41.3	16.3	41.2	14.5	41.3	18.1
Sweden	[5]83.0	9.3	81.4	9.4	84.7	9.3
Switzerland	87.2	8.7	89.7	11.4	84.7	6.1

Table 27-1   Percentage of the population who have completed secondary and higher education, by sex, country, and age: 1992—Continued

Country	Both sexes		Male		Female	
	Secondary education	Higher education	Secondary education	Higher education	Secondary education	Higher education
35–44 years old						
Large countries						
Canada	77.5	17.4	77.1	19.1	77.9	15.8
France	57.0	11.2	60.9	11.7	53.2	10.7
Germany	86.9	15.4	91.3	18.8	82.5	11.9
Italy	34.5	9.2	37.0	10.2	31.9	8.1
Japan[1]	77.0	14.5	77.0	23.6	77.0	5.4
United Kingdom	71.1	13.0	77.4	16.6	64.9	9.3
United States[2]	88.2	26.8	88.0	28.6	88.3	25.1
Other countries						
Australia[3]	56.3	14.7	67.1	16.3	45.5	13.1
Austria	70.4	9.4	78.2	10.0	62.7	8.7
Belgium	51.5	10.7	53.2	13.7	49.7	7.6
Denmark	60.9	16.2	65.4	16.2	56.1	16.1
Finland	69.1	13.0	67.9	14.5	70.3	11.5
Ireland[3]	43.6	8.9	41.0	10.6	46.3	7.2
Netherlands	61.0	24.2	66.8	27.7	54.7	20.5
New Zealand	58.3	12.9	63.7	15.1	53.1	10.6
Norway	83.2	15.5	83.7	18.5	82.6	12.2
Portugal[4]	16.7	6.4	17.7	7.1	15.6	5.7
Spain	24.3	10.9	28.0	12.0	20.8	9.9
Sweden	76.1	14.4	73.1	14.9	79.2	13.8
Switzerland	83.9	9.5	88.2	12.6	79.4	6.2
45–54 years old						
Large countries						
Canada	65.4	14.9	66.1	18.6	64.7	11.1
France	47.3	10.4	52.6	12.2	41.9	8.6
Germany	80.6	11.4	87.8	16.0	73.1	6.7
Italy	20.5	5.6	24.4	7.0	16.8	4.3
Japan[1]	59.6	9.1	62.4	15.8	56.9	2.5
United Kingdom	62.0	9.1	70.6	12.9	53.5	5.3
United States[2]	82.7	24.1	82.8	29.0	82.6	19.6
Other countries						
Australia[3]	50.7	10.9	61.8	12.8	39.1	8.9
Austria	64.9	5.9	77.3	8.5	52.7	3.3
Belgium	38.2	7.4	41.6	11.1	34.8	3.6
Denmark	58.0	13.2	63.3	14.9	52.6	11.5
Finland	52.1	10.4	52.0	12.6	52.2	8.1
Ireland	34.7	7.8	32.5	10.1	37.1	5.5
Netherlands	52.2	18.4	61.2	22.5	42.9	14.1
New Zealand	54.6	10.1	62.4	13.7	46.8	6.4
Norway	75.4	12.6	77.0	15.9	73.7	9.3
Portugal[4]	10.4	3.7	12.2	4.7	[5]8.8	2.8
Spain	13.8	7.1	17.9	9.0	9.8	5.3
Sweden	65.4	13.6	63.4	14.1	67.5	13.1
Switzerland	77.5	7.8	85.8	10.9	68.9	4.6

[1] 1989 data.

[2] In the United States, completing secondary education is defined as graduating from high school or earning a GED; completing higher education is defined as earning a bachelor's degree or more.

[3] 1993 data.

[4] 1991 data.

[5] Revised from previously published figures.

SOURCE: Organization for Economic Cooperation and Development, Indicators of Education's Systems, *OECD Education Statistics 1985–1992.*

Table 28-1 **Percentage of high school graduates earning a minimum number of units in core courses, by curriculum type and school characteristics: 1982, 1987, 1990, and 1994**

School characteristics	"New Basics" curriculum				Less restrictive curriculum			
	1982	1987	1990	1994	1982	1987	1990	1994
Total	**14.0**	**28.3**	**39.6**	**50.6**	**31.4**	**53.6**	**66.2**	**73.8**
Control of school								
Public	12.7	28.0	38.0	49.5	29.4	53.2	65.0	73.4
Private	24.6	33.0	56.3	63.3	47.9	58.4	79.1	79.5
Urbanicity								
Big city	—	33.0	39.5	53.1	—	60.0	69.1	75.2
Urban fringe	—	27.6	41.7	49.7	—	54.0	67.8	72.6
Medium city	—	27.9	44.0	50.2	—	50.2	70.6	71.4
Small place	—	27.2	37.5	50.2	—	52.1	63.5	74.9
Geographic region								
Northeast	24.7	39.8	45.2	57.5	45.8	61.6	64.7	74.9
South	14.0	31.5	53.2	58.0	36.5	61.5	82.7	83.9
Midwest	9.5	20.6	27.5	42.4	20.7	37.2	46.7	59.9
West	6.9	21.5	27.4	41.7	20.8	55.1	66.9	73.5

— Not available.

* The "New Basics" curriculum requires 4 years of English and 3 years each of social studies, science, and mathematics. The less restrictive curriculum requires 4 years of English, 3 years of social studies, and 2 years each of science and mathematics.

SOURCE: U.S. Department of Education, National Center for Education Statistics, *The 1994 High School Transcript Study Tabulations: Comparative Data on Credits Earned and Demographics for 1994, 1990, 1987, and 1982 High School Graduates*, 1996.

Note on high school transcript studies

Indicators 28 and *29* contain data from high school transcript studies conducted by the National Center for Education Statistics (NCES). Data on average course credits, or Carnegie units, for high school graduates come from the following studies: 1987, 1990, and 1994 data are from the 1987, 1990, and 1994 National Assessment of Educational Progress (NAEP) High School Transcript Studies; and 1982 data are from the High School and Beyond (HS&B) Transcript Study. A brief description of these studies, including descriptions of the sampled populations, follows.

The 1987, 1990, and 1994 NAEP High School Transcript Studies were conducted using nearly identical methodology and techniques. The sample of schools was a nationally representative, and included schools having grade 12 or 17-year-old students. The sample was also representative of graduating seniors from each school.

Since the focus of the transcript studies was high school graduates, schools with 17-year-olds, but without 12th grade were not included in the subsample used in these analyses. Of the remaining schools, only those students who graduated were selected.

Between May and November of 1994, high school transcripts were collected from 25,573 students who graduated in 1994. To be consistent with the 1982 study, students with an Individualized Education Program (IEP) were omitted from all estimates in the tables. Also, students with incomplete transcripts were dropped, bringing the number of transcripts analyzed to 24,374. These students attended 340 schools that had previously been sampled by the NAEP.

In spring 1991, transcripts were collected from 21,607 students who graduated from high school in 1990. These students attended 330 schools that had previously been sampled for the NAEP.

The sample of schools for the 1987 High School Transcript Study consisted of a nationally representative sample of 497 secondary schools selected for the 1986 NAEP for grade 11, 17-year-old students, of which 433 schools participated. The 1987 study was restricted to students who were in grade 11 during the 1985–86 school year. There are 27,732 graduates from 1987 represented in the tables. Data for 1987, 1990, and 1994 in *Indicators 28* and *29* are from the NCES publication *The 1994 High School Transcript Study Tabulations*.

High School and Beyond (HS&B) is a survey of high school sophomores and seniors. In 1982, high school transcripts were collected for members of the sophomore cohort who were selected to be in the second follow-up survey (about 12,000 transcripts). As in the 1987, 1990, and 1994 NAEP High School Transcript Studies, records were obtained from all types of high schools. However, because the 1982 HS&B used a different method of identifying disabled students than the NAEP High School Transcript Studies, students who had participated in a special education program were excluded from the tabulations in order to make the figures consistent.

Each of the transcript studies used the taxonomy of Classification of Secondary School Courses (CSSC), which contains approximately 2,200 course codes used to define course content and level. These studies also included additional course and student information, such as grade and credit received, grade level, graduation status, age, gender, and race/ethnicity.

The numbers in all the tables differ from previous editions of *The Condition of Education* for two reasons. First, a new exclusionary rule was applied to the transcripts this year. Each year the transcripts must be examined for validity and completeness. Incomplete transcripts, those of students receiving special education diplomas, or those from schools which have unique definitions of credit hours were excluded. In previous years, transcripts showing that a student had taken more than 32 credit hours were excluded based on the supposition that their schools must be using shorter class periods than other schools, and thus one credit hour would not mean the same thing in these schools as in the average school. A case-by-case analysis of these schools showed that their class periods were no shorter than the average school; instead, these schools had particularly stringent graduation requirements. Therefore, the data for all years were recalculated to include these transcripts.

Second, in previous editions of *the Condition*, students who had taken algebra II or beyond in high school but had not taken algebra I or geometry were assumed to have taken these courses prior to entering high school and were included in the percentage of students who had taken these courses. This year, the numbers reflect only those students who took these courses *while in high school*. The numbers for these two subjects appear to have dropped from previous years, but in actuality, only the number of students who were included in the analysis has dropped.

SOURCE: U.S. Department of Education, National Center for Education Statistics, *The 1994 High School Transcript Study Tabulations*, 1996.

Table 29-2 Percentage of high school graduates taking selected mathematics and science courses in high school, by race/ethnicity: 1982, 1987, 1990, and 1994

Mathematics and science courses (credits)	1982[1]					1987[1]				
	White	Black	Hispanic	Asian/ Pacific Islander	American Indian/ Alaskan Native	White	Black	Hispanic	Asian/ Pacific Islander	American Indian/ Alaskan Native
Mathematics[2]										
Any mathematics (1.00)	98.7	99.2	97.2	100.0	99.6	98.9	98.2	99.1	99.8	98.7
Algebra I (1.00)	57.8	42.4	42.4	55.5	33.2	66.1	54.6	53.6	63.6	60.9
Geometry (1.00)	51.0	28.8	25.6	64.9	33.2	63.0	42.2	39.6	81.1	43.2
Algebra II (0.50)	36.0	22.0	18.0	45.6	10.8	51.6	30.8	29.2	66.4	27.6
Trigonometry (0.50)	13.7	6.0	6.4	26.8	3.0	20.4	10.6	9.8	41.3	4.2
Analysis/pre-calculus (0.50)	6.8	2.2	2.8	14.5	1.8	13.2	5.1	7.3	39.4	5.4
Statistics/probability (0.50)	1.2	0.5	0.1	1.7	30.0	1.4	0.3	0.2	1.5	0.0
Calculus (1.00)	5.4	1.3	1.7	12.8	4.0	5.6	2.2	3.6	29.4	0.4
AP calculus (1.00)	1.8	0.3	0.4	5.5	0.1	2.7	1.4	2.6	23.5	0.4
Science										
Any science (1.00)	96.9	97.4	93.8	96.2	92.1	98.8	98.1	98.6	99.3	99.8
Biology (1.00)	78.3	73.0	68.2	83.7	66.7	88.7	84.7	85.4	91.5	90.2
AP/honors biology (1.00)	7.4	4.6	3.1	11.9	0.6	2.7	1.4	1.6	4.2	0.3
Chemistry (1.00)	34.1	21.9	15.5	52.8	25.9	46.6	28.4	29.1	69.8	26.4
AP/honors chemistry (1.00)	3.3	1.6	1.3	5.8	0.9	3.4	1.1	2.2	15.3	0.6
Physics (1.00)	16.3	7.3	5.7	34.8	8.1	20.6	9.7	9.9	46.5	8.3
AP/honors physics (1.00)	1.2	0.9	0.4	3.4	30.0	1.6	0.4	0.8	5.6	1.4
Engineering (1.00)	0.2	0.1	0.1	30.0	30.0	0.1	0.4	0.1	0.4	30.0
Astronomy (0.50)	1.3	0.4	0.7	30.0	30.0	0.9	0.3	0.7	0.7	0.5
Geology/earth science (0.50)	14.0	10.0	11.2	9.6	18.8	14.0	18.1	11.6	12.4	12.3
Biology and chemistry (2.00)	31.3	19.7	14.2	48.5	21.9	45.1	27.2	27.9	66.3	24.8
Biology, chemistry, and physics (3.00)	12.2	4.8	3.9	28.4	7.8	17.6	8.3	8.2	41.8	6.2

Mathematics and science courses (credits)	1990[1]					1994				
	White	Black	Hispanic	Asian/ Pacific Islander	American Indian/ Alaskan Native	White	Black	Hispanic	Asian/ Pacific Islander	American Indian/ Alaskan Native
Mathematics[2]										
Any mathematics (1.00)	99.5	99.5	99.9	99.9	100.0	99.6	99.3	99.2	100.0	98.9
Algebra I (1.00)	64.2	65.1	64.8	63.2	61.7	67.5	65.0	70.7	61.7	58.7
Geometry (1.00)	65.6	56.2	53.6	70.6	55.7	72.7	58.1	69.4	75.8	60.0
Algebra II (0.50)	55.0	41.4	35.7	59.9	47.1	61.6	43.7	51.0	66.6	39.2
Trigonometry (0.50)	19.3	14.0	10.8	35.1	14.7	18.6	13.6	9.8	25.3	6.7
Analysis/pre-calculus (0.50)	14.8	6.2	7.2	25.3	7.6	18.2	9.8	13.9	33.9	8.7
Statistics/probability (0.50)	1.0	1.1	0.9	1.5	0.3	2.3	1.7	1.0	1.1	1.2
Calculus (1.00)	6.9	2.8	3.8	18.5	4.2	9.6	3.8	6.0	23.4	3.8
AP calculus (1.00)	4.2	1.2	3.0	15.6	3.0	7.3	2.0	4.6	21.0	2.2
Science										
Any science (1.00)	99.3	99.6	99.3	99.8	100.0	99.7	99.5	99.3	99.3	99.7
Biology (1.00)	91.5	91.3	90.3	90.4	90.5	94.4	91.3	94.0	90.9	91.2
AP/honors biology (1.00)	5.0	3.8	2.4	6.3	1.9	4.6	2.7	3.3	8.3	1.7
Chemistry (1.00)	51.5	40.3	38.4	63.6	35.5	58.5	43.8	46.5	69.3	41.3
AP/honors chemistry (1.00)	3.7	2.5	1.1	7.7	4.5	4.3	2.1	2.5	7.7	0.6
Physics (1.00)	23.1	14.6	13.3	38.4	14.7	26.1	14.7	16.0	42.3	10.3
AP/honors physics (1.00)	2.1	0.7	1.0	5.9	0.5	2.5	1.4	1.8	6.0	0.3
Engineering (1.00)	0.1	0.1	30.0	30.0	30.0	0.2	0.4	0.1	1.0	30.0
Astronomy (0.50)	1.4	0.4	1.1	0.7	1.7	2.0	0.6	0.4	0.8	2.2
Geology/earth science (0.50)	27.6	15.9	14.0	15.7	31.0	23.8	23.3	15.3	16.7	23.2
Biology and chemistry (2.00)	50.2	39.5	36.5	60.1	34.2	56.4	42.2	45.1	64.8	39.6
Biology, chemistry, and physics (3.00)	20.6	12.0	10.2	33.7	10.8	22.7	13.0	13.4	37.2	8.0

[1] Numbers were revised from previously published figures.

[2] These data only report the percentage of students who earned credit in each mathematics course while in high school and does not count those students who took these courses prior to entering high school. In 1992, for example, approximately 93 percent of students had taken algebra I at some point before graduating high school, either before or during high school, and about 70 percent had taken geometry.

[3] Percent is less than 0.05 and is rounded to 0.0.

SOURCE: U.S. Department of Education, National Center for Education Statistics, *The 1994 High School Transcript Study Tabulations: Comparative Data on Credits Earned and Demographics for 1994, 1990, 1987, and 1982 High School Graduates*, 1996.

Table 30-1   Employment rates for recent high school graduates not enrolled in college and for recent school dropouts, by sex: October 1960–94

October	Recent high school graduates not enrolled in college			Recent school dropouts		
	Total	Male	Female	Total	Male	Female
1960	65.0	75.3	58.8	50.9	61.8	40.8
1961	65.4	70.1	62.5	49.4	60.3	38.3
1962	68.3	77.8	61.5	40.4	61.9	23.3
1963	64.7	72.6	59.5	45.1	64.4	27.0
1964	63.4	79.2	53.5	41.6	63.0	24.0
1965	71.9	84.3	63.2	48.0	66.8	26.8
1966	64.9	79.7	55.8	51.4	69.4	33.6
1967	65.9	78.3	57.7	50.3	65.0	34.4
1968	67.3	79.1	60.2	50.0	65.5	34.0
1969	70.1	83.2	61.1	51.0	69.8	30.9
1970	63.2	76.1	52.6	44.7	56.5	31.9
1971	65.2	77.5	55.6	46.8	59.3	31.7
1972	70.1	79.9	62.3	46.8	64.7	28.3
1973	70.7	81.7	61.9	52.7	62.5	40.0
1974	69.1	76.0	63.2	49.3	63.8	32.2
1975	65.1	74.1	57.5	41.9	54.8	29.5
1976	68.8	75.9	61.7	44.8	58.0	28.2
1977	72.0	77.7	67.2	52.7	64.0	39.3
1978	74.9	81.6	67.5	51.2	63.7	34.8
1979	72.4	79.2	66.7	49.7	65.3	34.3
1980	68.9	72.7	65.0	44.6	51.9	34.8
1981	65.9	70.0	62.1	42.1	54.2	29.3
1982	60.5	64.9	56.0	38.0	44.4	30.5
1983	63.0	66.1	60.1	44.4	51.6	35.8
1984	64.0	69.1	59.7	44.0	53.1	33.7
1985	62.0	65.0	59.3	44.2	51.9	35.8
1986	65.2	69.4	61.6	48.0	57.9	36.9
1987	68.9	76.9	61.9	41.8	46.0	36.6
1988	71.9	74.2	69.5	43.6	53.7	30.6
1989	71.7	77.4	65.6	46.7	52.2	40.1
1990	67.8	73.1	61.9	46.3	51.3	40.6
1991	59.6	62.3	56.1	36.8	48.8	25.0
1992	62.7	68.8	55.8	36.2	44.8	28.7
1993	64.2	67.6	60.6	46.9	61.6	30.1
1994	64.2	70.4	57.7	42.9	58.2	27.1

NOTE: Recent high school graduates are individuals aged 16–24 who graduated during the survey year. Recent school dropouts are individuals aged 16–24 who did not graduate and who were in school 12 months earlier, but who were not enrolled during the survey month. Due to a change in data sources, some percentages are revised from previously published figures.

SOURCE: U.S. Department of Labor, Bureau of Labor Statistics, *Labor Force Statistics Derived from the Current Population Survey: 1940–87.* U.S. Department of Commerce, Bureau of the Census, October Current Population Surveys.

Table 31-1   Percentage of 1992–93 college graduates who were working in administrative or clerical support occupations, and the percentage who were unemployed, by sex and field of study: April 1994

Field of study	Percentage in administrative or clerical occupations		Percentage unemployed	
	Male	Female	Male	Female
Total	**13.0**	**21.8**	**4.8**	**4.3**
Business and management	17.1	31.4	3.8	3.4
Education	12.9	13.5	2.9	3.5
Engineering	4.7	7.3	6.0	7.6
Health professions	7.0	7.6	4.3	4.6
Public affairs/social services	6.8	21.4	4.2	4.8
Biological sciences	12.1	21.5	6.5	8.3
Mathematics and science	12.5	22.1	5.6	3.8
Social sciences	19.5	33.5	4.6	4.9
History	15.3	22.3	6.5	3.6
Humanities	13.4	26.8	7.3	3.3
Psychology	22.6	22.0	5.2	5.0
Other	9.0	21.4	3.5	5.2

SOURCE: U.S. Department of Education, National Center for Education Statistics, 1993 Baccalaureate and Beyond Longitudinal Study, First Follow-up (B&B:93/94).

Note on labor force statistics

The Bureau of Labor Statistics (BLS) uses three categories to classify the labor force status of an individual: employed, unemployed, and not in the labor force.

An *employed* individual is someone with a job and who is working. Also included are those individuals who are not working, but who have jobs from which they are temporarily absent due to illness, vacation, labor-management disputes, bad weather, and personal reasons. Those who are in the military are also counted as employed.

An *unemployed* individual is someone who has no job, but who is available for work, and who has made specific efforts to find employment some time during the prior 4 weeks. Also included are those persons waiting to be recalled to a job from which they had been laid off, or who are waiting to report to a new job within 30 days. Individuals who are neither employed nor unemployed are *not in the labor force*.

The *labor force* is made up of all persons classified as employed or unemployed. The *unemployment rate* represents the number of unemployed individuals as a percentage of those in the labor force. The *labor force participation rate* is the ratio of those in the labor force to the population. The *employment-population ratio* is the percentage of employed individuals in the population. *Indicator 32* refers to this last statistic as the *employment rate*.

Each of these statistics is typically reported in two forms: one that includes those in the military and one that excludes them. For instance, the *civilian employment-population ratio* is the percentage of all employed civilians in the civilian non-institutional population. The *civilian labor force participation rate* is the ratio of the civilian labor force to the civilian non-institutional population. The labor force statistics reported in *Indicator 32* and its associated supplemental tables are for the civilian non-institutional population. *Indicator 32* reports the form that excludes those in the military.

Each of these measures can be computed for groups classified by age, sex, race/ethnicity, etc.

When classifying the labor force status of an individual, it is necessary to define: full-time, part-time, year-round, involuntary, and voluntary workers.

Full-time workers are those who reported being employed for 35 or more hours per week (including self-employment); this number may either be hours worked during the survey reference week or during the usual hours worked in the previous calendar year (*Indicator 33*). Included in this minimum 35 hours per week are paid leave for illness, vacation, holidays, and other paid time off. *Part-time workers*, in contrast, are those who are employed 1–34 hours per week.

Year-round workers are those who worked 50 or more weeks during the previous calendar year, while *part-year workers* are those who worked 1–49 weeks. Paid vacation time and sick leave count as time worked.

The distinction between whether an individual's employment status was *involuntary* or *voluntary*, as shown in *Indicator 33*, is made based on the main reason the individual gave for that status. For example, individuals who worked part time and who gave as the reason for working part time "could find only part-time job" or "slack work/materials shortage" were considered to have not chosen to work part time and therefore, were placed in the involuntary category. Those who worked less than year round were designated as involuntary status if their main reason for working part year was "no work available" or "ill or disabled," while others were categorized as voluntary if their main reason was "taking care of home or family," "going to school," or being "retired." Those who didn't work at all during the previous calendar year were categorized as involuntary if their main reason for not working was "ill or disabled" or "could not find work."

Additional details on these labor force statistics are available in the explanatory notes of *Employment and Earnings*, published monthly by the U.S. Department of Labor, Bureau of Labor Statistics.

Table 34-2   Median annual earnings (in 1995 constant dollars) of wage and salary workers aged 25–34 whose highest education level was a high school diploma, by sex and race/ethnicity: 1970–94

Year	Male				Female			
	All	White	Black	Hispanic	All	White	Black	Hispanic
All wage and salary workers								
1970	$33,039	$33,627	$24,521	$29,309	$16,395	$13,220	$14,305	$14,195
1971	33,424	33,835	25,125	27,947	16,772	13,904	13,405	13,394
1972	34,877	35,479	26,830	31,389	17,057	14,411	14,138	14,720
1973	35,498	35,823	28,702	29,206	16,683	13,857	14,749	15,364
1974	32,919	33,648	28,093	31,056	14,024	13,652	15,360	16,546
1975	30,432	31,267	25,598	27,569	14,019	13,559	15,839	14,915
1976	30,806	31,754	23,307	28,000	14,671	14,206	16,847	14,257
1977	31,008	32,567	23,587	26,432	14,915	14,650	16,301	14,772
1978	31,211	32,720	24,030	27,956	14,564	14,153	16,827	14,596
1979	30,622	32,192	23,175	25,090	14,707	14,588	15,483	14,784
1980	28,465	29,602	20,946	23,016	14,604	14,665	14,633	14,154
1981	26,512	27,579	20,712	22,265	14,237	14,091	14,508	14,918
1982	24,638	25,720	18,965	21,780	13,904	13,763	14,319	14,043
1983	24,781	26,069	18,040	22,562	14,061	13,881	15,241	13,387
1984	25,381	27,361	16,972	23,076	14,688	14,680	14,507	14,811
1985	24,418	26,253	19,277	20,011	14,736	14,979	13,544	14,458
1986	24,528	26,309	17,020	20,791	14,662	14,856	13,134	15,018
1987	24,902	26,915	17,121	21,643	15,015	15,230	14,176	14,785
1988	25,502	26,830	19,955	21,722	14,755	15,123	13,771	14,578
1989	24,865	26,109	18,935	20,167	14,206	14,524	12,817	14,087
1990	23,286	24,876	18,084	18,826	14,075	14,424	12,918	12,786
1991	22,668	24,188	17,195	18,102	13,779	14,181	12,164	13,835
1992	21,627	23,145	15,883	18,669	13,602	14,101	12,152	13,177
1993	21,474	22,769	16,767	17,598	13,454	14,380	10,704	13,096
1994	21,150	22,236	16,057	17,655	13,756	14,293	12,897	12,643
Year-round, full-time wage and salary workers								
1970	$34,536	$35,377	$27,574	$30,810	$21,682	$22,090	$19,183	(*)
1971	34,904	35,617	28,040	31,516	21,409	21,464	20,947	(*)
1972	36,170	37,110	28,472	32,293	22,012	22,247	20,802	$22,373
1973	36,650	37,335	31,251	32,495	21,466	21,550	21,274	22,011
1974	34,863	35,353	31,708	33,695	21,159	21,143	21,143	21,591
1975	33,486	34,009	30,427	30,248	21,236	21,156	21,725	20,542
1976	33,375	34,118	28,484	30,783	21,480	21,666	20,992	20,712
1977	34,292	30,198	27,017	26,859	21,819	18,785	19,291	18,240
1978	35,243	35,788	30,012	32,962	21,549	21,820	20,897	20,707
1979	33,752	34,765	27,342	28,946	20,871	21,183	19,487	19,463
1980	31,337	32,110	25,451	26,794	20,588	20,831	19,583	19,829
1981	30,019	31,003	25,957	25,791	19,741	19,945	19,396	18,540
1982	28,984	30,188	24,005	25,818	19,373	19,535	18,522	19,242
1983	29,199	30,618	21,708	25,745	19,567	19,893	18,654	18,856
1984	30,037	31,218	20,884	27,370	19,970	20,556	17,880	19,322
1985	28,478	30,019	22,644	23,320	20,240	20,801	17,374	19,704
1986	28,530	29,751	22,492	25,509	20,178	20,531	17,237	21,699
1987	28,592	29,796	21,399	26,119	20,421	20,823	18,265	19,967
1988	28,162	29,273	21,853	25,449	19,953	20,557	17,321	19,289
1989	27,015	28,273	22,435	23,401	19,825	20,048	18,345	19,279
1990	25,847	27,872	20,054	21,748	19,144	19,587	16,728	17,107
1991	25,222	26,963	19,385	22,123	19,569	20,025	17,733	18,908
1992	24,756	26,237	18,728	21,734	19,283	19,807	18,062	19,215
1993	23,747	25,398	19,624	20,788	18,954	20,025	15,493	17,555
1994	23,757	24,807	20,146	20,698	17,903	18,450	16,034	17,232

* Too few sample observations for a reliable estimate.

NOTE: Beginning with the March 1992 survey, which collected earnings for calendar year 1991, new questions were used to obtain the educational attainment of respondents. See the supplemental note to *Indicator 25* for further discussion.

SOURCE: U.S. Department of Commerce, Bureau of the Census, March Current Population Surveys.

Table 34-4   Median annual earnings (in 1995 constant dollars) of wage and salary workers aged 25–34 whose highest education level was a bachelor's degree or higher, by sex and race/ethnicity: 1970–94

Year	Male				Female			
	All	White	Black	Hispanic	All	White	Black	Hispanic
All wage and salary workers								
1970	$41,045	$40,841	(*)	(*)	$27,608	$23,980	$29,822	(*)
1971	41,026	40,628	$36,492	(*)	27,951	25,530	28,507	(*)
1972	41,628	41,306	38,376	(*)	27,721	25,107	28,640	(*)
1973	41,413	40,801	35,917	(*)	27,416	24,940	27,149	(*)
1974	37,679	38,340	31,292	(*)	24,353	24,202	25,894	(*)
1975	35,549	35,913	31,756	(*)	24,163	23,738	26,790	(*)
1976	36,605	36,913	34,197	(*)	23,206	22,839	26,763	(*)
1977	36,512	36,874	32,789	(*)	22,841	22,428	26,587	(*)
1978	36,731	36,844	34,983	$35,112	22,577	22,371	23,421	(*)
1979	35,500	35,705	31,108	30,749	22,852	22,839	23,294	(*)
1980	33,912	34,477	28,349	29,597	22,207	22,068	23,953	(*)
1981	34,309	34,745	29,054	27,472	21,971	21,814	22,790	$22,899
1982	33,035	33,385	28,590	31,753	22,658	22,487	23,622	21,570
1983	33,527	34,011	26,628	29,944	23,445	23,345	24,175	23,035
1984	34,463	35,541	27,780	29,533	23,678	23,586	24,494	23,303
1985	36,602	37,001	33,793	36,363	24,876	24,875	24,141	24,801
1986	36,896	37,547	28,795	37,161	26,103	25,983	25,794	25,045
1987	37,016	38,599	25,569	33,982	26,749	26,547	27,281	27,492
1988	36,109	38,149	27,321	28,250	26,719	26,930	26,555	24,853
1989	36,052	37,574	26,675	26,091	27,391	27,378	26,313	28,572
1990	34,380	35,231	30,106	31,371	27,049	27,292	27,013	24,307
1991	34,600	35,292	26,386	28,837	26,173	26,726	24,014	22,238
1992	34,646	35,807	29,093	28,885	27,209	27,327	25,930	26,091
1993	33,656	34,542	27,921	28,179	26,798	27,229	23,848	23,852
1994	32,116	33,636	24,116	27,845	25,655	26,035	23,249	23,288
Year-round, full-time wage and salary workers								
1970	$43,947	$44,160	(*)	(*)	$31,412	$31,184	(*)	(*)
1971	43,483	43,898	(*)	(*)	30,645	30,793	$30,188	(*)
1972	44,194	44,484	$40,069	(*)	31,266	31,325	30,141	(*)
1973	44,370	44,942	38,668	(*)	31,112	31,025	31,999	(*)
1974	41,825	42,303	36,064	(*)	29,129	29,366	27,067	(*)
1975	39,907	40,205	33,606	(*)	29,085	29,267	27,595	(*)
1976	40,384	40,463	37,182	(*)	29,276	29,206	29,663	(*)
1977	40,016	35,700	29,840	(*)	28,389	25,988	24,503	(*)
1978	40,036	40,148	37,918	(*)	27,710	27,744	25,891	(*)
1979	38,925	38,914	37,448	(*)	27,443	27,617	25,431	(*)
1980	37,436	37,760	30,747	$33,121	27,591	27,729	26,767	(*)
1981	37,594	37,819	33,388	35,106	27,603	27,779	25,638	(*)
1982	36,154	36,664	32,132	34,699	27,291	27,541	25,378	(*)
1983	37,789	38,230	32,503	32,826	27,283	27,587	25,321	$25,743
1984	38,206	38,547	31,099	34,494	28,613	28,756	27,453	28,848
1985	39,005	39,766	36,514	39,184	29,842	30,286	25,940	29,251
1986	40,667	41,495	32,788	40,691	30,580	30,856	28,012	28,281
1987	40,925	41,650	31,552	37,617	29,978	30,473	28,080	29,869
1988	40,062	40,692	28,591	33,093	31,014	31,682	28,230	29,881
1989	39,383	40,729	28,802	32,345	31,811	31,928	29,413	31,581
1990	37,189	37,680	31,718	36,422	31,341	31,590	30,073	28,421
1991	39,435	40,117	30,733	35,541	30,469	30,811	26,362	27,248
1992	38,838	39,642	32,891	31,262	30,707	30,829	29,400	28,948
1993	38,139	38,872	29,035	32,036	31,670	32,079	27,319	27,276
1994	36,072	36,674	25,543	31,857	29,614	30,197	25,683	26,028

* Too few sample observations for a reliable estimate.

NOTE: Beginning with the March 1992 survey, which collected earnings for calendar year 1991, new questions were used to obtain the educational attainment of respondents. See the supplemental note to *Indicator 25* for further discussion.

SOURCE: U.S. Department of Commerce, Bureau of the Census, March Current Population Surveys.

Table 37-1   Percentage of 18- to 24-year-olds who reported voting and being registered to vote, by sex, race/ethnicity, and enrollment status: November 1994

Enrollment status	Total	Sex		Race/ethnicity		
		Male	Female	White	Black	Hispanic*
Reported voting						
Total	**20.0**	**18.5**	**21.4**	**21.1**	**17.4**	**9.8**
Enrolled in high school	13.4	12.3	15.3	14.3	11.7	9.4
Enrolled in college	26.7	26.0	27.4	28.3	23.6	24.0
Full time	26.5	26.4	26.5	28.1	23.1	22.2
Part time	28.1	23.4	31.6	29.6	26.3	27.0
Not enrolled in school	16.7	15.2	18.3	17.4	15.5	6.2
18 to 20 years old	10.6	9.0	12.0	10.6	12.7	6.7
21 to 24 years old	19.3	17.7	20.8	20.2	16.8	5.9
Reported being registered to vote						
Total	**42.2**	**40.7**	**43.6**	**43.8**	**41.8**	**19.5**
Enrolled in high school	25.6	26.9	23.5	26.4	25.2	21.1
Enrolled in college	54.6	53.2	55.8	58.0	50.4	37.8
Full time	55.4	54.5	56.3	59.1	50.8	36.8
Part time	50.4	46.2	53.6	52.9	47.5	39.4
Not enrolled in school	36.7	35.5	37.8	37.1	40.3	14.6
18 to 20 years old	27.9	27.0	28.7	28.2	31.4	14.6
21 to 24 years old	40.2	38.9	41.6	40.7	44.3	14.6

* Persons of Hispanic origin may be of any race.

SOURCE: U.S. Department of Commerce, Bureau of the Census, *Current Population Reports*, "Voting and Registration in the Election of November 1994," PPL-25, table 6.

Table 38-1   Elementary and secondary school enrollment in thousands, by control and level of school, with projections: Fall 1970–2006

Fall of year	Total	Public schools Grades K–12[2]	Grades K–8[2]	Grades 9–12	Private schools[1] Grades K–12[2]	Grades K–8[2]	Grades 9–12
1970	51,257	45,894	32,558	13,336	5,363	4,052	1,311
1971	51,271	46,071	32,318	13,753	5,200	3,900	1,300
1972	50,726	45,726	31,879	13,848	5,000	3,700	1,300
1973	[3]50,445	[3]45,445	31,401	14,044	5,000	3,700	1,300
1974	50,073	45,073	30,971	14,103	5,000	3,700	1,300
1975	49,819	44,819	30,515	14,304	5,000	3,700	1,300
1976	[3]49,478	[3]44,311	29,997	14,314	5,167	3,825	1,342
1977	48,717	43,577	29,375	14,203	5,140	3,797	1,343
1978	[3]47,637	[3]42,551	28,463	14,088	5,086	3,732	1,353
1979	[3]46,651	[3]41,651	28,034	13,616	5,000	3,700	1,300
1980	46,208	40,877	27,647	13,231	5,331	3,992	1,339
1981	45,544	40,044	27,280	12,764	5,500	4,100	1,400
1982	[3]45,166	[3]39,566	27,161	12,405	5,600	4,200	1,400
1983	44,967	39,252	26,981	12,271	5,715	4,315	1,400
1984	44,908	39,208	26,905	12,304	5,700	4,300	1,400
1985	[3]44,979	[3]39,422	27,034	12,388	5,557	4,195	1,362
1986	45,205	39,753	27,420	12,333	5,452	4,116	1,336
1987	[3]45,488	40,008	27,933	12,076	5,479	4,232	1,247
1988	[3]45,430	[3]40,189	28,501	11,687	5,241	4,036	1,206
1989	[3]45,898	[3]40,543	29,152	11,390	5,355	4,162	1,193
1990	[3]46,448	41,217	29,878	11,338	5,232	4,095	1,137
1991	47,246	42,047	30,506	11,541	5,199	4,074	1,125
1992[3]	48,190	42,816	31,081	11,735	5,375	4,212	1,163
1993[4]	48,947	43,476	31,515	11,961	5,471	4,280	1,191
1994[4]	49,610	44,034	31,703	12,331	5,576	4,345	1,232
1995[4]	50,776	45,076	32,383	12,693	5,700	4,431	1,269
Projected							
1996	51,683	45,885	32,837	13,049	5,798	4,493	1,304
1997	52,400	46,524	33,226	13,299	5,876	4,547	1,329
1998	52,921	46,988	33,522	13,466	5,933	4,587	1,346
1999	53,342	47,365	33,692	13,673	5,977	4,610	1,367
2000	53,668	47,656	33,852	13,804	6,012	4,632	1,380
2001	53,933	47,891	34,029	13,862	6,042	4,656	1,386
2002	54,168	48,102	34,098	14,004	6,066	4,666	1,400
2003	54,312	48,234	34,065	14,169	6,078	4,661	1,416
2004	54,449	48,365	33,882	14,483	6,084	4,636	1,448
2005	54,587	48,497	33,680	14,818	6,090	4,609	1,481
2006	54,615	48,528	33,507	15,021	6,086	4,585	1,501

[1] Beginning in fall 1980, data include estimates for the expanded universe of private schools.
[2] Includes most kindergarten and some nursery school students.
[3] Revised from previously published figures.
[4] Estimates based on preliminary data.

NOTE: The private school enrollment figures for years 1971–75, 1979, 1981–82, 1984, and 1986 are estimated. The 1987 private school enrollment numbers are taken from the Private School Survey. Private school enrollment figures for grades K–8 and 9–12 for the years 1988–93 are estimated from the K–12 totals. Projections are based on data through 1993. Enrollment figures may not add to totals due to rounding.

SOURCE: U.S. Department of Education, National Center for Education Statistics, *Digest of Education Statistics, 1995*, table 3 and *Projections of Education Statistics to 2006*, 1996, table 1.

Table 38-2   Percentage of total elementary and secondary school enrollment, by control and level of school, with projections: Fall 1970–2006

Fall of year	Total	Public schools			Private schools[1]		
		Grades K–12[2]	Grades K–8[2]	Grades 9–12	Grades K–12[2]	Grades K–8[2]	Grades 9–12
1970	100.0	89.5	63.5	26.0	10.5	7.9	2.6
1971	100.0	89.9	63.0	26.8	10.1	7.6	2.5
1972	100.0	90.1	62.8	27.3	9.9	7.3	2.6
1973	100.0	90.1	62.2	27.8	9.9	7.3	2.6
1974	100.0	90.0	61.9	28.2	10.0	7.4	2.6
1975	100.0	90.0	61.3	28.7	10.0	7.4	2.6
1976	100.0	89.6	60.6	28.9	10.4	7.7	2.7
1977	100.0	89.4	60.3	29.2	10.6	7.8	2.8
1978	100.0	89.3	59.8	29.6	10.7	7.8	2.8
1979	100.0	89.3	60.1	29.2	10.7	7.9	2.8
1980	100.0	88.5	59.8	28.6	11.5	8.6	2.9
1981	100.0	87.9	59.9	28.0	12.1	9.0	3.1
1982	100.0	87.6	60.1	27.5	12.4	9.3	3.1
1983	100.0	87.3	60.0	27.3	12.7	9.6	3.1
1984	100.0	87.3	59.9	27.4	12.7	9.6	3.1
1985	100.0	87.6	60.1	27.5	12.4	9.3	3.0
1986	100.0	87.9	60.7	27.3	12.1	9.1	3.0
1987	100.0	88.0	61.4	26.5	12.0	9.3	2.7
1988	100.0	88.5	62.7	25.7	11.5	8.9	2.7
1989	100.0	88.3	63.5	24.8	11.7	9.1	2.6
1990	100.0	[3]88.7	[3]64.3	24.4	11.3	8.8	[3]2.4
1991	100.0	89.0	64.6	24.4	11.0	8.6	2.4
1992	100.0	88.8	[3]64.5	24.4	11.2	[3]8.7	2.4
1993[4]	100.0	88.8	64.4	24.4	11.2	8.7	2.4
1994[4]	100.0	88.8	63.9	24.9	11.2	8.8	2.5
1995[4]	100.0	88.8	63.8	25.0	11.2	8.7	2.5
				Projected			
1996	100.0	88.8	63.5	25.2	11.2	8.7	2.5
1997	100.0	88.8	63.4	25.4	11.2	8.7	2.5
1998	100.0	88.8	63.3	25.4	11.2	8.7	2.5
1999	100.0	88.8	63.2	25.6	11.2	8.6	2.6
2000	100.0	88.8	63.1	25.7	11.2	8.6	2.6
2001	100.0	88.8	63.1	25.7	11.2	8.6	2.6
2002	100.0	88.8	62.9	25.9	11.2	8.6	2.6
2003	100.0	88.8	62.7	26.1	11.2	8.6	2.6
2004	100.0	88.8	62.2	26.6	11.2	8.5	2.7
2005	100.0	88.8	61.7	27.1	11.2	8.4	2.7
2006	100.0	88.9	61.4	27.5	11.1	8.4	2.7

[1] Beginning in fall 1980, data include estimates for the expanded universe of private schools.

[2] Includes kindergarten and some nursery school students.

[3] Revised from previously published figures.

[4] Estimates based on preliminary data.

NOTE: The private school enrollment figures for years 1971–75, 1979, 1981–82, 1984, and 1986 are estimated. The 1987 private school enrollment numbers are taken from the Private School Survey. Private school enrollment figures for grades K–8 and 9–12 for the years 1988–93 are estimated from the K–12 totals. Projections are based on data through 1993. Enrollment figures may not add to totals due to rounding.

SOURCE: U.S. Department of Education, National Center for Education Statistics, *Digest of Education Statistics, 1995*, table 3 and *Projections of Education Statistics to 2006*, 1996, table 1.

Table 39-1   Total and full-time equivalent (FTE) enrollment in higher education, by control and type of institution: Fall 1972–94

Fall of year	All institutions	Public 4-year	Public 2-year	Private 4-year	Private 2-year
Total enrollment					
1972	[1]9,214,820	4,429,696	2,640,939	[1]2,028,938	115,247
1973	9,602,123	4,529,895	2,889,621	[1]2,060,128	[1]122,479
1974	10,223,729	4,703,018	3,285,482	2,116,717	118,512
1975	11,184,859	4,998,142	3,836,366	2,216,598	133,753
1976	11,012,137	4,901,691	3,751,786	2,227,125	131,535
1977	11,285,787	4,945,224	3,901,769	2,297,621	141,173
1978	11,260,092	4,912,203	3,873,690	[1]2,319,422	[1]154,777
1979	11,569,899	4,980,012	4,056,810	2,373,221	159,856
1980	12,096,895	5,128,612	4,328,782	2,441,996	197,505
1981	12,371,672	5,166,324	4,480,708	2,489,137	235,503
1982	12,425,780	5,176,434	4,519,653	2,477,640	252,053
1983	12,464,661	5,223,404	4,459,330	2,517,791	264,136
1984	12,241,940	5,198,273	4,279,097	2,512,894	251,676
1985	12,247,055	5,209,540	4,269,733	2,506,438	261,344
1986	12,503,511	5,300,202	4,413,691	2,523,761	265,857
1987	12,766,642	5,432,200	4,541,054	2,558,220	235,168
1988	13,055,337	5,545,901	4,615,487	2,634,281	259,668
1989	13,538,560	5,694,303	4,883,660	2,693,368	267,229
1990	[1]13,818,637	5,848,242	4,996,475	2,730,312	243,608
1991	14,358,953	5,904,748	5,404,815	2,802,305	247,085
1992	14,486,315	5,900,012	5,484,555	2,863,913	237,835
1993	[1]14,304,803	5,851,760	5,337,328	[1]2,887,176	228,539
1994[2]	14,278,790	5,825,213	5,308,467	2,923,867	221,243
Full-time equivalent (FTE) enrollment					
1972[1]	7,253,712	3,706,238	1,746,613	1,700,554	100,308
1973[1]	7,453,467	3,721,035	1,908,533	1,718,191	105,708
1974[1]	7,805,454	3,847,542	2,097,257	1,758,706	101,949
1975	[1]8,479,688	4,056,500	2,465,810	[1]1,843,903	[1]113,475
1976	8,312,502	3,998,450	2,351,453	1,849,551	113,048
1977	8,415,339	4,039,071	2,357,405	1,896,005	122,858
1978	8,348,482	3,996,126	2,283,073	[1]1,936,231	[1]133,052
1979	8,487,317	4,059,304	2,333,313	1,956,768	137,932
1980	8,819,013	4,158,267	2,484,027	2,003,105	173,614
1981	9,014,521	4,208,506	2,572,794	2,041,341	191,880
1982	9,091,648	4,220,648	2,629,941	2,028,275	212,784
1983	[1]9,166,398	[1]4,265,807	2,615,672	2,059,415	225,504
1984	8,951,695	4,237,895	2,446,769	2,054,816	212,215
1985	8,943,433	4,239,622	2,428,159	2,054,717	220,935
1986[1]	9,064,165	4,295,494	2,482,551	2,064,831	221,291
1987[1]	9,229,736	4,395,728	2,541,961	2,090,776	201,269
1988[1]	9,464,271	4,505,774	2,591,131	2,158,372	208,994
1989	9,780,881	4,619,828	2,751,762	2,193,774	215,517
1990[1]	9,983,436	4,740,049	2,817,933	2,227,959	197,495
1991	10,360,606	4,795,704	3,067,141	2,285,750	212,011
1992	10,435,759	4,797,884	3,113,817	2,330,478	193,580
1993	[1]10,351,415	4,765,983	3,046,411	[1]2,354,938	184,083
1994[2]	10,348,072	4,749,524	3,034,872	2,387,817	175,859

[1] Revised from previously published figures.
[2] Preliminary data.

NOTE: Increases in enrollments in private 2-year institutions during 1980 and 1981 reflect the addition of schools accredited by the National Association of Trade and Technical Schools. Because of a revision in data compilation procedures, FTE figures for 1986 and later years are not directly comparable with data for earlier years.

SOURCE: U.S. Department of Education, National Center for Education Statistics, *Digest of Education Statistics, 1996*, tables 168 and 194 (based on the IPEDS/HEGIS "Fall Enrollment" survey), forthcoming.

Table 40-1   Number of degrees conferred, by level of degree, and number of high school completions: Academic years ending 1971–93

Academic year ending	Associate's	Bachelor's	Master's	Doctor's	First-professional[1]	High school diploma and GED recipients[2,3]
1971	[3]252,311	839,730	230,509	32,107	37,946	3,165,000
1972	[3]292,014	887,273	251,633	33,363	43,411	3,247,000
1973	316,174	922,362	263,371	34,777	50,018	3,284,000
1974	343,924	945,776	277,033	33,816	53,816	3,368,000
1975	360,171	922,933	292,450	34,083	55,916	3,475,000
1976	391,454	925,746	311,771	34,064	62,649	3,485,000
1977	406,377	919,549	317,164	33,232	64,359	3,483,000
1978	412,246	921,204	311,620	32,131	66,581	3,508,000
1979	402,702	921,390	301,079	32,730	68,848	3,536,000
1980	400,910	929,417	298,081	32,615	70,131	3,531,000
1981	416,377	935,140	295,739	32,958	71,956	3,520,000
1982	[3]434,526	952,998	295,546	32,707	72,032	3,489,000
1983	[3]449,620	969,510	289,921	32,775	[3]73,054	3,365,000
1984	[3]452,240	974,309	284,263	33,209	[3]74,468	3,204,000
1985	454,712	979,477	286,251	32,943	75,063	3,104,000
1986	446,047	987,823	288,567	33,653	73,910	3,082,000
1987	[3]436,304	991,264	289,349	34,041	71,617	3,152,000
1988	435,085	994,829	299,317	34,870	70,735	3,194,000
1989	436,764	1,018,755	310,621	35,720	70,856	3,091,000
1990	455,102	1,051,344	324,301	38,371	70,988	3,007,000
1991	481,720	1,094,538	337,168	39,294	71,948	2,974,000
1992	504,231	1,136,553	352,838	40,659	74,146	2,947,000
1993	514,756	1,165,178	369,585	42,132	75,387	2,966,000

[1] Includes degrees in chiropractic, dentistry, law, medicine, optometry, osteopathy, pharmacy, podiatry, theology, and veterinary medicine.

[2] "High school diploma and GED recipients" are graduates of regular public and private day school programs or recipients of GED credentials.

[3] Revised from previously published figures.

SOURCE: U.S. Department of Education, National Center for Education Statistics, *Digest of Education Statistics, 1995*, tables 98, 100, and 236 (based on IPEDS/HEGIS "Degrees Conferred" surveys and Common Core of Data; American Council on Education, annual GED surveys).

Table 41-3   Percentage distribution of bachelor's degrees conferred, by field of study: Academic years ending 1971–93

Field of study	1971	1972	1973	1974	1975	1976	1977	1978
Total	**100.0**	**100.0**	**100.0**	**100.0**	**100.0**	**100.0**	**100.0**	**100.0**
Humanities and social and behavioral sciences	40.1	39.5	38.7	37.9	36.7	35.4	33.9	32.7
Humanities	17.1	16.8	16.6	16.5	16.5	16.3	15.9	15.5
Social and behavioral sciences	23.0	22.7	22.1	21.4	20.2	19.1	18.0	17.1
Natural sciences	9.8	9.2	9.3	9.7	9.9	9.9	9.9	9.5
Life sciences	4.3	4.2	4.6	5.1	5.6	5.9	5.8	5.6
Physical sciences	2.5	2.3	2.2	2.2	2.3	2.3	2.5	2.5
Mathematics	3.0	2.7	2.5	2.3	2.0	1.8	1.6	1.4
Computer sciences and engineering	6.2	6.1	6.0	5.8	5.6	5.6	6.1	6.8
Computer and information sciences	0.3	0.4	0.5	0.5	0.5	0.6	0.7	0.8
Engineering and engineering technologies	6.0	5.8	5.6	5.3	5.1	5.0	5.4	6.0
Engineering	5.3	5.1	5.0	4.5	4.3	4.1	4.5	5.1
Engineering technologies	0.6	0.7	0.5	0.8	0.8	0.9	0.9	1.0
Technical/professional	43.8	45.1	45.9	46.6	47.8	49.1	50.2	51.0
Education	21.0	21.5	21.0	19.6	18.1	16.7	15.6	14.7
Business management	13.7	13.7	13.7	13.9	14.4	15.3	16.2	17.3
Health sciences	3.0	3.2	3.6	4.4	5.3	5.8	6.2	6.5
Other technical/professional	6.2	6.7	7.6	8.7	10.0	11.2	12.1	12.5
Not classified in a field of study	0.0	0.0	0.0	0.0	0.0	0.0	0.0	0.0

Field of study	1979	1980	1981	1982	1983	1984	1985	1986
Total	**100.0**	**100.0**	**100.0**	**100.0**	**100.0**	**100.0**	**100.0**	**100.0**
Humanities and social and behavioral sciences	31.3	30.3	29.5	29.0	27.8	27.4	26.9	27.0
Humanities	15.0	14.6	14.3	14.2	13.8	13.8	13.5	13.4
Social and behavioral sciences	16.4	15.7	15.1	14.8	14.0	13.7	13.4	13.6
Natural sciences	9.2	8.8	8.4	8.2	7.8	7.8	8.0	7.8
Life sciences	5.3	5.0	4.6	4.4	4.1	4.0	3.9	3.9
Physical sciences	2.5	2.5	2.6	2.5	2.4	2.4	2.4	2.2
Mathematics	1.3	1.3	1.2	1.3	1.3	1.4	1.6	1.7
Computer sciences and engineering	7.7	8.6	9.6	10.5	11.7	13.0	13.8	13.9
Computer and information sciences	0.9	1.2	1.6	2.1	2.6	3.3	4.0	4.2
Engineering and engineering technologies	6.8	7.4	8.0	8.4	9.2	9.7	9.8	9.7
Engineering	5.8	6.3	6.8	7.0	7.4	7.8	7.9	7.7
Engineering technologies	1.0	1.1	1.3	1.4	1.7	1.9	1.9	2.0
Technical/professional	51.8	52.3	52.5	52.3	52.7	51.8	50.3	51.2
Education	13.7	12.7	11.6	10.6	10.1	9.5	9.0	8.8
Business management	18.6	19.9	21.3	22.4	23.4	23.6	23.8	24.0
Health sciences	6.7	6.9	6.8	6.7	6.7	6.6	6.6	6.5
Other technical/professional	12.8	12.8	12.8	12.6	12.5	12.2	11.0	11.8
Not classified in a field of study	0.0	0.0	0.0	0.0	0.0	0.0	0.0	0.0

Table 41-3 Percentage distribution of bachelor's degrees conferred, by field of study: Academic years ending 1971–93—Continued

Field of study	1977	1978	1979	1990	1991	1992	1993
Total	**100.0**	**100.0**	**100.0**	**100.0**	100.0	100.0	100.0
Humanities and social and behavioral sciences	27.8	28.8	30.1	31.7	32.5	33.7	34.1
Humanities	13.8	14.1	14.7	15.3	15.7	16.3	16.7
Social and behavioral sciences	14.1	14.6	15.4	16.4	16.8	17.4	17.4
Natural sciences	7.6	7.2	6.8	6.5	6.5	6.6	6.8
Life sciences	3.8	3.7	3.5	3.5	3.6	3.8	4.0
Physical sciences	2.0	1.8	1.7	1.5	1.5	1.5	1.5
Mathematics	1.7	1.7	1.6	1.4	1.4	1.3	1.3
Computer sciences and engineering	13.4	12.4	11.3	10.3	9.5	9.0	8.8
Computer and information sciences	4.0	3.5	3.0	2.6	2.3	2.2	2.1
Engineering and engineering technologies	9.4	8.9	8.3	7.7	7.2	6.8	6.7
Engineering	7.4	7.0	6.5	6.1	5.6	5.4	5.3
Engineering technologies	1.9	1.9	1.9	1.7	1.6	1.4	1.4
Technical/professional	51.2	51.5	51.5	51.2	50.3	50.1	49.9
Education	8.8	9.2	9.5	10.0	10.1	9.5	9.3
Business management	24.3	24.4	24.2	23.7	22.8	22.6	22.0
Health sciences	6.4	6.1	5.8	5.5	5.4	5.4	5.8
Other technical/professional	11.8	11.8	12.0	12.1	12.0	12.6	12.9
Not classified in a field of study	0.0	0.2	0.2	0.3	1.2	0.6	0.5

SOURCE: U.S. Department of Education, National Center for Education Statistics, *Digest of Education Statistics, 1995*, table 243 (based on IPEDS/HEGIS "Degrees Conferred" surveys).

Table 42-1   Average percentage of students absent on a typical school day, by urbanicity and other selected school characteristics: School year 1993–94

School characteristics	Total	Central city	Urban fringe/ large town	Rural/ small town
Total	**5.5**	**5.7**	**5.3**	**5.3**
Control and level of school				
Public	5.9	6.4	6.0	5.6
Elementary	5.2	5.5	5.0	4.9
Middle	6.3	7.0	6.3	5.7
High	8.0	9.7	8.8	7.2
Combined	7.1	9.8	8.6	5.8
Private	4.1	4.2	3.7	4.1
Elementary	4.1	4.1	3.5	4.4
Middle	—	—	—	—
High	3.8	4.1	4.8	2.2
Combined	4.2	4.6	3.7	3.9
Public school size within level				
Elementary				
Less than 300	4.9	5.5	5.6	4.6
300–499	5.1	5.3	4.7	5.0
500 or more	5.4	5.7	5.0	5.2
Middle				
Less than 400	5.4	—	—	5.4
400–699	6.2	7.2	5.3	5.5
700 or more	7.2	7.3	7.2	6.9
High				
Less than 500	7.8	10.3	10.5	7.2
500–999	7.3	8.2	7.9	6.9
1,000 or more	9.1	9.9	8.3	7.9
Combined				
Less than 300	7.0	11.2	—	5.7
300–499	6.2	—	—	5.6
500 or more	7.5	9.2	8.4	6.1
Public school percent minority within level				
Elementary				
Less than 20 percent	4.6	4.6	4.6	4.5
20 percent or more	5.9	6.0	5.7	5.7
Middle				
Less than 20 percent	5.7	5.7	6.3	5.5
20 percent or more	7.0	7.7	6.3	6.2
High				
Less than 20 percent	7.1	7.7	8.1	6.8
20 percent or more	9.6	10.8	9.7	8.3
Combined				
Less than 20 percent	5.9	7.7	7.2	5.5
20 percent or more	8.1	10.5	9.7	6.2
Percentage of students eligible for free or reduced-price lunch within level				
Elementary				
0–5	4.4	4.6	—	3.8
6–20	4.6	4.8	4.5	4.3
21–40	4.7	4.8	4.8	4.7
41–100	5.8	6.3	5.5	5.3

Table 42-1   Average percentage of students absent on a typical school day, by urbanicity and other selected school characteristics: School year 1993–94— Continued

School characteristics	Total	Central city	Urban fringe/ large town	Rural/ small town
Middle				
0–5	4.9	4.8	—	—
6–20	5.2	5.4	5.4	5.0
21–40	6.5	6.8	7.2	6.2
41–100	7.2	8.6	6.8	5.8
High				
0–5	8.7	7.6	8.7	9.7
6–20	7.4	9.0	7.9	6.6
21–40	7.9	10.5	10.5	6.5
41–100	8.6	12.0	8.6	7.5
Combined				
0–5	6.3	—	—	6.0
6–20	6.8	9.1	—	5.6
21–40	7.3	9.3	—	5.9
41–100	7.5	12.7	—	5.9

— Too few sample observations for a reliable estimate.

SOURCE: U.S. Department of Education, National Center for Education Statistics, Schools and Staffing Survey, 1993–94 (Teacher and School Questionnaires).

Table 42-2 **Percentage of teachers who reported that student absenteeism, tardiness, or cutting class was a serious problem in their school, by urbanicity and other selected school characteristics: School year 1993–94**

School characteristics	Absenteeism				Tardiness				Cutting class			
	Total	Central city	Urban fringe/ large town	Rural/ small town	Total	Central city	Urban fringe/ large town	Rural/ small town	Total	Central city	Urban fringe/ large town	Rural/ small town
Total	**12.9**	**18.2**	**12.1**	**9.3**	**9.5**	**14.8**	**9.4**	**5.5**	**4.5**	**7.6**	**4.2**	**2.4**
Control and level of school												
Public	14.4	21.9	13.9	9.8	10.6	17.6	10.5	5.8	5.1	9.3	4.8	2.5
Elementary	6.8	11.9	5.8	3.8	5.7	10.7	5.8	1.8	0.9	1.8	0.6	0.4
Middle	10.9	18.1	8.6	7.8	9.7	18.0	7.8	5.5	3.2	7.6	1.8	1.4
High	29.0	45.5	30.6	19.6	19.4	33.0	20.0	12.1	13.1	25.7	14.1	6.0
Combined	26.3	44.5	29.2	15.7	16.5	28.5	19.5	9.1	11.9	27.9	11.0	3.9
Private	2.2	2.1	2.2	2.4	2.5	2.8	2.7	1.7	0.7	0.3	0.9	1.0
Elementary	1.0	1.2	0.9	0.8	1.9	2.5	1.5	1.1	0.3	0.1	0.5	0.2
Middle	3.5	—	—	—	0.4	—	—	—	0.0	—	—	—
High	5.1	4.2	4.8	9.2	4.3	3.6	5.0	4.5	2.6	1.5	2.6	5.1
Combined	2.5	1.8	3.9	2.2	2.6	2.6	3.4	1.6	0.5	0.1	0.8	0.7
Public school size within level												
Elementary												
Less than 300	4.1	8.5	5.3	2.6	2.9	6.1	5.0	1.4	0.4	0.6	0.5	0.3
300–499	5.8	10.1	4.7	3.8	4.3	8.0	3.7	2.4	0.5	1.0	0.2	0.5
500 or more	8.3	13.3	6.5	4.6	7.3	12.7	7.0	1.5	1.2	2.3	0.8	0.4
Middle												
Less than 400	8.0	26.4	5.8	6.6	6.1	17.6	8.9	4.5	1.3	2.1	0.0	1.4
400–699	8.5	15.1	7.1	6.3	7.7	13.3	6.6	5.5	2.8	7.0	1.3	1.8
700 or more	13.4	18.9	9.9	10.8	12.2	20.1	8.4	6.5	4.1	8.2	2.3	0.9
High												
Less than 500	16.6	29.5	23.5	14.6	9.6	23.3	15.6	7.5	5.3	15.4	10.5	3.7
500–999	23.7	37.1	23.7	21.6	15.8	32.3	15.3	13.5	8.0	17.0	8.9	6.2
1,000 or more	36.8	48.1	33.3	24.5	25.2	33.9	21.9	16.9	18.8	27.8	16.0	9.4
Combined												
Less than 300	15.7	30.4	21.7	11.3	7.3	10.1	8.1	6.5	5.1	12.1	1.6	4.0
300–499	16.9	35.7	33.8	13.5	7.6	3.4	17.6	6.6	5.9	5.4	12.1	5.2
500 or more	30.2	46.4	29.5	18.0	20.0	31.4	20.7	10.9	14.3	30.4	11.7	3.5
Public school percent minority within level												
Elementary												
Less than 20 percent	2.5	4.7	2.1	2.2	1.9	4.5	1.8	1.3	0.2	0.2	0.1	0.4
20 percent or more	11.3	14.1	10.3	7.2	9.5	12.6	10.5	2.9	1.5	2.3	1.2	0.6
Middle												
Less than 20 percent	5.5	8.3	4.3	5.8	3.7	3.6	3.5	3.9	0.8	1.5	0.5	0.9
20 percent or more	16.7	21.3	14.5	11.8	16.2	22.6	13.7	8.9	5.8	9.6	3.5	2.4
High												
Less than 20 percent	19.3	28.4	21.3	16.6	12.3	19.1	14.3	10.0	6.5	10.5	8.6	4.7
20 percent or more	41.7	51.7	41.6	27.9	28.7	38.1	26.8	17.7	21.7	31.3	20.6	9.7
Combined												
Less than 20 percent	18.0	18.5	26.5	15.3	11.2	16.1	17.1	8.5	4.8	10.3	7.3	3.0
20 percent or more	33.4	50.6	31.6	16.3	21.2	31.5	21.7	10.0	18.1	32.1	14.3	5.3

Table 42-2   Percentage of teachers who reported that student absenteeism, tardiness, or cutting class was a serious problem in their school, by urbanicity and other selected school characteristics: School year 1993–94—Continued

School characteristics	Absenteeism				Tardiness				Cutting class			
	Total	Central city	Urban fringe/ large town	Rural/ small town	Total	Central city	Urban fringe/ large town	Rural/ small town	Total	Central city	Urban fringe/ large town	Rural/ small town
Percentage of students eligible for free or reduced-price lunch within level												
Elementary												
0–5	1.1	2.7	0.5	1.4	1.3	4.5	0.4	0.9	0.0	0.0	0.0	0.0
6–20	1.8	4.0	1.0	1.8	1.3	1.9	1.3	0.9	0.4	0.3	0.1	0.8
21–40	4.1	6.2	4.4	2.8	3.7	5.2	5.2	2.0	0.2	0.2	0.1	0.3
41–100	11.1	15.4	14.1	5.3	9.3	14.4	13.4	2.1	1.5	2.7	1.7	0.4
Middle												
0–5	1.4	2.7	1.2	1.4	2.6	3.4	3.0	0.6	0.4	2.6	0.2	0.1
6–20	4.4	5.4	4.0	4.1	4.2	4.4	4.0	4.4	0.8	0.6	0.4	1.5
21–40	10.0	12.8	11.5	8.2	6.9	10.0	8.1	5.1	1.9	2.3	3.5	0.9
41–100	19.4	25.6	20.1	10.5	18.5	26.3	17.7	8.3	7.3	12.4	4.0	2.5
High												
0–5	18.0	25.8	18.5	14.3	13.4	23.5	13.1	10.0	7.7	10.7	8.8	4.7
6–20	25.9	33.9	30.7	18.7	18.0	22.1	21.9	13.2	10.5	15.6	13.4	6.0
21–40	34.8	51.6	43.5	22.1	19.6	31.8	23.3	11.6	14.4	25.6	19.6	6.3
41–100	38.8	58.6	52.9	20.6	27.5	47.2	30.0	12.1	21.6	40.2	28.7	6.0
Combined												
0–5	19.7	30.8	18.5	18.5	11.9	6.5	15.6	5.0	8.4	8.6	10.8	2.4
6–20	25.0	33.5	22.6	21.4	18.0	25.3	19.3	13.5	9.6	19.3	9.6	4.3
21–40	28.8	41.2	45.5	14.8	16.6	28.3	23.3	7.0	10.8	21.3	15.2	2.9
41–100	26.8	52.8	30.6	13.5	16.6	31.0	19.5	9.1	15.6	39.1	11.4	4.5

— Too few sample observations for a reliable estimate.

SOURCE: U.S. Department of Education, National Center for Education Statistics, Schools and Staffing Survey, 1993–94 (Teacher and School Questionnaires).

Table 43-1 Number of children who were served by federally supported programs for students with disabilities, by type of disability: School years ending 1977–94

Type of disability	1977	1978	1979	1980	1981	1982	1983	1984	1985
	Number served (in thousands)[1]								
All disabilities	**3,692**	**3,751**	**3,889**	**4,005**	**4,142**	**4,198**	**4,255**	**4,298**	**4,315**
Specific learning disabilities	796	964	1,130	1,276	1,462	1,622	1,741	1,806	1,832
Speech or language impairments	1,302	1,223	1,214	1,186	1,168	1,135	1,131	1,128	1,126
Mental retardation	959	933	901	869	829	786	757	727	694
Serious emotional disturbance	283	288	300	329	346	339	352	361	372
Hearing impairments	87	85	85	80	79	75	73	72	69
Orthopedic impairments	87	87	70	66	58	58	57	56	56
Other health impairments	141	135	105	106	98	79	50	53	68
Visual impairments	38	35	32	31	31	29	28	29	28
Multiple disabilities	—	—	50	60	68	71	63	65	69
Deaf-blindness	—	—	2	2	3	2	2	2	2
Preschool disabled[2]	(3)	(3)	(3)	(3)	(3)	(3)	(3)	(3)	(3)

Type of disability	1986	1987	1988	1989	1990	1991	1992	1993[4]	1994
	Number served (in thousands)[1]								
All disabilities	**4,317**	**4,374**	**4,447**	**4,544**	**4,641**	**4,762**	**4,949**	**5,125**	**5,373**
Specific learning disabilities	1,862	1,914	1,928	1,987	2,050	2,130	2,234	2,354	2,444
Speech or language impairments	1,125	1,136	953	967	973	985	997	996	1,009
Mental retardation	660	643	582	564	548	534	538	519	554
Serious emotional disturbance	375	383	373	376	381	390	399	401	414
Hearing impairments	66	65	56	56	57	58	60	60	64
Orthopedic impairments	57	57	47	47	48	49	51	52	57
Other health impairments	57	52	45	43	52	55	58	65	83
Visual impairments	27	26	22	23	22	23	24	23	25
Multiple disabilities	86	97	77	85	86	96	97	102	110
Deaf-blindness	2	2	1	2	2	1	1	1	1
Preschool disabled[2]	(3)	(3)	363	394	422	441	484	531	587

— Not available.

[1] Includes students who were served under Chapter 1 of the Elementary Consolidation and Improvement Act (ECIA) and Part B of Individuals with Disabilities Education Act (IDEA).

[2] Includes preschool children aged 3–5 years and 0–5 years who were served under Chapter 1 and Part B of the IDEA, respectively.

[3] Prior to the 1987–88 school year, preschool disabled students were included in the counts by disabling condition. Beginning in the 1987–88 school year, states were no longer required to report preschool students (aged 0–5) with disabilities by disabling condition.

[4] Revised from previously published figures.

NOTE: Counts are based on reports from the 50 states and the District of Columbia only (i.e., figures from the U.S. territories are not included). Increases since 1987–88 are due in part to new legislation enacted in fall 1986, which mandates public school education services appropriate for all disabled children aged 3–5. Details may not add to totals due to rounding.

SOURCE: U.S. Department of Education, Office of Special Education and Rehabilitative Services, *Annual Report to Congress on the Implementation of the Individuals with Disabilities Education Act*, various years; and National Center for Education Statistics, *Digest of Education Statistics, 1995*, table 51.

Table 43-4 **Participation in special education programs as a percentage of total public school enrollment, by selected types of disability, sex, and race/ethnicity of student: School years ending 1986, 1988, 1990, and 1992**

Type of disability, sex, and race/ethnicity	1986	1988	1990	1992
Total				
All disabilities listed	6.2	6.3	6.8	7.3
Specific learning disabilities	4.3	4.4	4.8	5.3
Mental retardation*	1.3	1.3	1.3	1.3
Serious emotional disturbance	0.6	0.6	0.7	0.7
Male				
All disabilities listed	8.2	8.6	9.2	9.7
Specific learning disabilities	5.8	6.2	6.6	7.2
Mental retardation*	1.4	1.6	1.6	1.5
Serious emotional disturbance	0.9	0.9	1.0	1.1
Female				
All disabilities listed	4.0	4.1	4.4	4.7
Specific learning disabilities	2.6	2.7	3.0	3.3
Mental retardation*	1.1	1.1	1.1	1.1
Serious emotional disturbance	0.3	0.2	0.3	0.3
White				
All disabilities listed	5.9	6.1	6.7	7.2
Specific learning disabilities	4.3	4.5	5.0	5.3
Mental retardation*	1.1	1.0	1.1	1.1
Serious emotional disturbance	0.6	0.6	0.7	0.7
Black				
All disabilities listed	8.2	8.3	8.7	9.3
Specific learning disabilities	4.4	4.5	5.0	5.8
Mental retardation*	2.7	3.0	2.8	2.5
Serious emotional disturbance	1.0	0.8	0.9	1.0
Hispanic				
All disabilities listed	5.5	6.2	6.3	6.5
Specific learning disabilities	4.3	4.5	4.7	5.3
Mental retardation*	0.8	1.4	1.3	0.8
Serious emotional disturbance	0.5	0.3	0.3	0.4

* Includes all students classified with any level of mental retardation.

NOTE: The *National Summaries from the Elementary and Secondary School Civil Rights Survey* report includes data for the three disability categories shown. Therefore, the "All disabilties listed" category shown in this table includes only the following three categories: specific learning disabilities, mental retardation, and serious emotional disturbance. Prior to the 1987–88 school year, preschool disabled students were included in the counts by disabling condition. Beginning in the 1987–88 school year, states were no longer required to report preschool students (aged 0–5) with disabilities by disabling condition.

SOURCE: U.S. Department of Education, Office for Civil Rights, *National Summaries from the Elementary and Secondary School Civil Rights Survey*, various years.

Table 43-6   Ratio of the number of students with disabilities per special education teacher serving them, by type of disability: Selected school years ending 1977–93

Type of disability	1977	1978	1979	1980	1981	1982	1983	1990	1991	1992	1993
All disabilities	**21**	**19**	**19**	**18**	**18**	**18**	**18**	**16**	**16**	**16**	**16**
Specific learning disabilities	18	18	18	17	17	19	21	23	22	23	24
Speech or language impairments	71	62	64	49	48	56	58	25	25	23	24
Mental retardation	14	12	13	13	12	12	13	13	12	12	12
Serious emotional disturbance	13	14	13	12	13	14	13	14	13	14	14
Hearing impairments	10	10	9	9	10	9	9	9	9	9	9
Orthopedic impairments	16	18	12	14	13	12	13	15	15	14	15
Other health impairments	28	26	21	21	31	22	16	19	19	27	30
Visual impairments	11	10	8	9	9	10	9	8	8	8	8
Multiple disabilities	—	—	—	15	13	13	12	11	13	13	13
Deaf-blindness	—	—	—	3	8	5	2	14	4	7	6

— Not available.

SOURCE: U.S. Department of Education, Office of Special Education and Rehabilitative Services, *Annual Report to Congress on the Implementation of the Individuals with Disabilities Education Act*, various years.

Table 47-1   Public elementary teachers' perceptions of the amount of influence or control teachers had over selected school and classroom decisions in their school, by percentage of students eligible for free or reduced-price lunch and school size: 1993–94

| Decisions | Total | Percentage of students eligible for free or reduced-price lunch | | | | School size | | | |
		0–5	6–20	21–40	41–100	Less than 150	150–499	500–749	750 and more
Percentage of teachers reporting that teachers had a good deal* of influence in their school over:									
Setting discipline policy	41.8	47.0	42.6	46.1	38.4	52.9	43.1	42.4	34.4
Determining the content of in-service programs	32.6	37.2	34.1	35.0	30.3	35.3	31.8	33.5	32.3
Establishing curriculum	32.2	37.0	35.7	36.4	27.8	46.5	34.6	29.6	27.7
Percentage of teachers reporting a good deal* of control in their classroom over:									
Selecting textbooks and other instructional materials	49.1	51.2	49.4	53.6	46.7	69.9	52.9	46.3	39.9
Selecting content, topics, and skills to be taught	54.2	48.5	50.7	58.1	54.8	73.5	56.6	50.1	51.9
Selecting teaching techniques	83.8	85.3	83.6	87.3	81.9	90.3	84.0	83.5	82.6
Evaluating and grading students	84.0	85.9	83.2	86.4	83.1	86.7	84.8	83.3	83.0
Disciplining students	73.4	75.7	77.1	75.8	70.2	79.2	74.2	73.6	69.9
Determining the amount of homework to be assigned	83.7	79.7	82.6	84.8	84.8	88.6	84.1	83.5	81.8

* Respondents were asked about influence and control on a scale of 0–5, with 0 meaning "no influence" or "no control" and 5 meaning a "great deal of influence" or "complete control." Responses 4 and 5 were combined in this analysis.

NOTE: Excludes a small number of teachers whose schools did not respond to the questionnaire.

SOURCE: U.S. Department of Education, National Center for Education Statistics, Schools and Staffing Survey, 1993–94 (Teacher Questionnaire).

Table 47-2   Public elementary principals' perceptions of the amount of influence groups had over selected school and classroom decisions, by percentage of students eligible for free or reduced-price lunch and school size: 1993–94

Decisions	Total	Percentage of students eligible for free or reduced-price lunch				School size			
		0–5	6–20	21–40	41–100	Less than 150	150–499	500–749	750 and more
Percentage of principals reporting that a group had a good deal* of influence over:									
Setting discipline policy									
State Department of Education	18.4	11.3	15.3	15.0	22.6	19.7	17.6	18.5	21.0
School district staff	55.4	58.4	56.6	53.7	55.5	58.7	53.1	57.4	58.1
School board	61.5	56.7	60.7	63.3	61.9	67.7	60.6	60.4	63.9
Principal	85.5	90.4	86.7	88.3	82.9	89.3	84.7	86.1	85.1
Teachers	75.5	80.7	79.8	79.1	71.3	83.3	74.6	75.8	·73.2
Parent association	19.4	25.0	20.2	20.5	18.2	11.0	18.1	22.1	24.1
Determining content of in-service programs									
State Department of Education	22.0	12.9	16.9	20.2	27.0	20.3	23.4	18.5	24.0
School district staff	67.8	65.5	67.9	68.7	67.3	53.4	69.4	67.7	70.8
School board	20.8	20.1	18.8	19.1	22.6	14.8	21.2	20.2	24.6
Principal	72.5	76.2	74.4	71.0	71.3	75.7	70.8	75.0	71.8
Teachers	70.3	75.0	73.6	73.6	66.3	73.7	68.3	74.0	68.9
Parent association	5.3	3.5	4.1	5.7	6.1	3.3	4.9	5.3	8.3
Establishing curriculum									
State Department of Education	65.8	52.7	62.3	65.7	70.0	59.4	64.2	68.1	71.8
School district staff	64.6	73.6	70.5	62.2	62.1	64.3	64.5	64.8	64.9
School board	39.3	41.4	44.4	35.2	39.2	28.7	40.3	38.2	45.0
Principal	52.2	66.2	54.5	48.8	50.5	63.1	52.0	49.0	52.8
Teachers	59.7	75.1	65.2	60.2	54.1	72.1	59.6	57.6	56.3
Parent association	10.0	14.7	12.0	7.6	9.9	9.0	9.0	11.7	10.8
Deciding how the school budget will be spent									
State Department of Education	30.0	23.4	28.4	31.7	31.3	33.8	30.8	29.4	25.4
School district staff	48.9	42.5	46.2	51.7	49.7	34.4	47.3	52.3	58.6
School board	64.6	62.7	66.0	66.0	63.1	76.3	67.7	57.7	58.6
Principal	64.5	72.2	67.3	65.3	61.9	63.5	62.3	67.6	68.0
Teachers	41.9	44.2	42.9	43.1	40.5	36.1	39.3	47.1	45.2
Parent association	9.0	9.7	7.6	8.8	9.9	5.8	7.4	11.4	13.2

* Respondents were asked about influence on a scale of 0–5, with 0 meaning "no influence" and 5 meaning a "great deal of influence." Responses 4 and 5 were combined in this analysis.

NOTE: Excludes a small number of principals whose schools did not respond to the questionnaire.

SOURCE: U.S. Department of Education, National Center for Education Statistics, Schools and Staffing Survey, 1993–94 (Administrator Questionnaire).

Table 47-3 Public secondary teachers' perceptions of the amount of influence or control teachers had over selected school and classroom decisions in their school, by percentage of students eligible for free or reduced-price lunch and school size: 1993–94

Decisions	Total	Percentage of students eligible for free or reduced-price lunch				School size			
		0–5	6–20	21–40	41–100	Less than 150	150–499	500–749	750 and more
Percentage of teachers reporting that teachers had a good deal* of influence in their school over:									
Setting discipline policy	27.5	28.4	26.7	28.7	26.7	44.0	33.1	29.6	23.8
Determining the content of in-service programs	28.5	31.5	29.3	28.4	26.4	36.0	30.2	28.9	27.4
Establishing curriculum	37.2	42.3	39.6	37.8	31.2	50.7	43.9	38.1	33.9
Percentage of teachers reporting a good deal* of control in their classroom over:									
Selecting textbooks and other instructional materials	62.4	66.1	64.8	62.2	57.4	82.3	73.4	64.3	56.7
Selecting content, topics, and skills to be taught	67.4	68.8	68.5	67.8	64.6	84.5	76.1	69.0	62.9
Selecting teaching techniques	89.2	89.1	90.2	89.9	88.0	93.2	91.1	89.9	88.1
Evaluating and grading students	90.0	90.0	90.5	90.7	89.0	91.7	91.4	90.5	89.3
Disciplining students	64.2	70.0	65.0	64.6	59.1	73.1	68.2	66.6	61.4
Determining the amount of homework to be assigned	89.9	90.0	89.9	90.5	89.4	90.8	91.6	89.1	89.6

* Respondents were asked about influence and control on a scale of 0-5, with 0 meaning "no influence" or "no control" and 5 meaning a "great deal of influence" or "complete control." Responses 4 and 5 were combined in this analysis.

NOTE: Excludes a small number of teachers whose schools did not respond to the questionnaire.

SOURCE: U.S. Department of Education, National Center for Education Statistics, Schools and Staffing Survey, 1993–94 (Teacher Questionnaire).

Table 47-4 **Public secondary principals' perceptions of the amount of influence groups had over selected school and classroom decisions, by percentage of students eligible for free or reduced-price lunch and school size: 1993–94**

Decisions	Total	Percentage of students eligible for free or reduced-price lunch				School size			
		0–5	6–20	21–40	41–100	Less than 150	150–499	500–749	750 and more
Percentage of principals reporting that a group had a good deal* of influence over:									
Setting discipline policy									
State Department of Education	14.5	14.1	13.0	14.3	17.8	13.4	12.7	17.7	14.8
School district staff	50.1	44.8	48.1	51.3	56.3	47.1	48.6	49.9	52.7
School board	64.8	57.6	62.0	68.9	68.7	62.4	64.2	65.5	66.0
Principal	89.9	91.8	91.5	88.1	89.2	90.3	91.6	91.9	87.4
Teachers	72.5	76.8	75.8	67.6	70.9	70.3	75.2	77.4	68.7
Parent association	15.0	18.4	14.2	13.1	17.3	14.6	12.3	16.6	16.6
Determining content of in-service programs									
State Department of Education	20.1	11.3	14.8	23.7	28.0	22.6	20.6	18.6	19.3
School district staff	62.9	62.5	59.5	66.8	62.5	55.2	59.0	65.0	68.5
School board	18.8	14.1	14.5	21.9	23.5	18.6	18.4	19.0	19.1
Principal	72.0	74.7	71.3	72.2	72.6	73.4	73.9	70.8	70.4
Teachers	71.6	77.4	73.2	70.4	68.1	71.1	71.6	69.7	72.9
Parent association	4.7	6.4	3.4	5.5	5.2	7.7	4.7	4.4	3.5
Establishing curriculum									
State Department of Education	62.4	52.1	60.4	66.8	67.2	54.3	63.2	65.0	63.9
School district staff	61.4	64.6	63.2	60.2	58.9	56.4	60.2	61.3	64.5
School board	39.8	39.0	38.8	38.9	42.5	36.0	38.4	41.9	41.5
Principal	58.3	59.1	61.0	57.3	54.7	61.8	62.6	58.4	53.1
Teachers	66.2	74.1	71.1	63.8	57.4	68.4	70.2	64.0	62.9
Parent association	7.9	11.4	6.3	7.9	7.9	6.5	8.1	8.6	7.9
Deciding how the school budget will be spent									
State Department of Education	28.8	19.9	23.7	31.7	37.5	32.7	34.7	27.5	22.9
School district staff	45.6	45.1	43.9	48.8	45.7	29.6	43.2	48.5	52.9
School board	67.8	63.9	66.3	69.7	68.9	72.5	75.0	66.7	60.3
Principal	60.1	65.9	61.9	60.5	54.6	55.2	54.3	61.7	66.3
Teachers	38.6	48.1	38.8	39.4	32.0	38.5	33.1	39.8	42.5
Parent association	4.3	7.0	3.6	3.6	4.7	5.1	3.4	4.1	4.8

* Respondents were asked about influence on a scale of 0–5, with 0 meaning "no influence" and 5 meaning a "great deal of influence." Responses 4 and 5 were combined in this analysis.

NOTE: Excludes a small number of principals whose schools did not respond to the questionnaire.

SOURCE: U.S. Department of Education, National Center for Education Statistics, Schools and Staffing Survey, 1993–94 (Administrator Questionnaire).

Table 48-1   Average hours per week full-time public school teachers spent at school and in school-related activities, class size, and classes taught per day, by selected school characteristics: 1994

| School characteristics | Average hours worked per week | Average hours required at school | Average hours spent before and after school and on weekends | | | Average class size | Average number of classes taught per day* |
			Total	Activities involving students	Other related activities		
Total	**45.2**	**33.2**	**12.1**	**3.3**	**8.7**	**23.2**	**5.6**
Urbanicity							
Central city	44.2	32.6	11.6	3.0	8.6	24.1	5.5
Urban fringe/large town	45.3	32.9	12.4	3.1	9.4	24.1	5.5
Rural/small town	45.8	33.7	12.1	3.7	8.4	22.0	5.7
Percent of students eligible for free or reduced-price lunch							
0–5	45.8	32.6	13.3	3.8	9.5	23.4	5.5
6–20	46.1	33.1	12.9	3.7	9.2	23.2	5.5
21–40	45.9	33.7	12.1	3.5	8.7	23.2	5.6
41–100	44.0	33.0	11.0	2.7	8.3	23.1	5.7
Percent of students eligible for free or reduced-price lunch within urbanicity							
Central city							
0–5	45.1	33.1	12.1	2.9	9.2	23.6	5.6
6–20	45.0	32.7	12.3	3.3	9.0	24.7	5.3
21–40	45.6	33.2	12.4	3.4	9.1	24.4	5.4
41–100	43.2	32.4	10.9	2.6	8.2	23.7	5.7
Urban fringe/large town							
0–5	45.5	32.1	13.3	3.8	9.5	24.0	5.4
6–20	46.0	33.0	13.0	3.4	9.6	23.9	5.5
21–40	45.5	33.3	12.2	2.9	9.3	24.2	5.6
41–100	44.3	32.9	11.5	2.3	9.2	25.1	5.5
Rural/small town							
0–5	47.0	33.2	13.9	4.3	9.5	22.3	5.6
6–20	46.6	33.5	13.2	4.3	8.8	21.9	5.7
21–40	46.2	34.2	12.0	3.8	8.1	22.2	5.8
41–100	44.7	33.7	11.0	3.1	8.0	21.8	5.7
School size							
Less than 150	46.4	34.5	11.9	4.3	7.5	15.4	6.2
150–499	44.2	32.8	11.4	2.7	8.6	20.7	6.0
500–749	45.3	33.4	12.0	2.8	9.2	23.3	5.7
750 or more	45.9	33.2	12.7	4.1	8.6	24.5	5.4
Percentage of minority students							
Less than 20 percent	45.7	33.4	12.3	3.5	8.9	22.6	5.7
20 percent or more	44.7	32.9	11.8	3.2	8.6	23.8	5.5

* Since elementary teachers do not tend to teach separate classes, only 8 percent of the teachers who responded to this question were elementary teachers, while 92 percent were secondary teachers.

NOTE: Excludes a small number of teachers whose schools did not respond to the questionnaire. Details may not add to totals due to rounding.

SOURCE: U.S. Department of Education, National Center for Education Statistics, Schools and Staffing Survey, 1993–94 (Teacher Questionnaire).

Table 48-2 Average hours per week full-time private school teachers spent at school and in school-related activities, class size, and classes taught per day, by selected school characteristics: 1994

School characteristics	Average hours worked per week	Average hours required at school	Average hours spent before and after school and on weekends			Average class size	Average number of classes taught per day*
			Total	Activities involving students	Other related activities		
Total	**47.1**	**34.2**	**12.9**	**3.6**	**9.3**	**19.6**	**6.0**
Urbanicity							
Central city	47.0	34.2	12.8	3.7	9.1	20.3	6.0
Urban fringe/large town	47.0	34.2	12.8	3.5	9.3	20.1	6.1
Rural/small town	47.6	34.3	13.3	3.6	9.7	16.6	6.0
School size							
Less than 150	45.5	34.2	11.3	2.2	9.0	11.6	6.3
150–499	47.1	34.3	12.9	3.5	9.3	19.1	6.3
500–749	47.3	34.0	13.3	4.1	9.3	21.4	5.7
750 or more	50.1	34.4	15.7	6.2	9.5	22.9	5.7
Percentage of minority students							
Less than 20 percent	47.1	34.3	12.8	3.5	9.3	19.3	6.1
20 percent or more	47.2	34.0	13.1	4.0	9.2	20.1	5.8

* Since elementary teachers do not tend to teach separate classes, only 8 percent of the teachers who responded to this question were elementary teachers, while 92 percent were secondary teachers.

NOTE: Excludes a small number of teachers whose schools did not respond to the questionnaire. Details may not add to totals due to rounding.

SOURCE: U.S. Department of Education, National Center for Education Statistics, Schools and Staffing Survey, 1993–94 (Teacher Questionnaire).

Table 49-1 Mean classroom hours per week, mean student contact hours per week, and average class size for full-time postsecondary faculty, by academic rank, type and control of institution, and academic discipline of class taught: Fall 1987 and fall 1992

Characteristics	Mean classroom hours per week	Mean student contact hours per week	Average class size
	Fall 1992		
Total*	**10.9**	**320.8**	**29.5**
Academic rank			
Full professor	9.5	303.4	31.8
Associate professor	10.0	308.4	30.5
Assistant professor	10.2	293.0	28.4
Instructor	16.0	422.7	25.8
Lecturer	8.6	301.8	35.7
Type of institution			
Research	6.6	249.6	37.9
Doctoral	8.5	295.7	34.9
Comprehensive	10.7	316.2	29.1
Liberal arts	10.9	239.0	21.2
2-year	16.1	444.1	27.1
Control of institution			
Public	11.3	345.6	30.9
Private	9.9	260.1	25.8
Academic discipline of class taught			
Agriculture	10.9	310.3	28.4
Business	11.0	317.4	29.3
Education	10.2	277.5	25.8
Engineering	9.5	243.6	25.4
Fine arts	12.3	270.0	21.6
Humanities	10.9	297.0	26.8
Natural sciences	10.2	366.5	35.8
Social sciences	9.5	357.8	36.0
	Fall 1987		
Total*	**10.2**	**306.3**	**29.5**
Academic rank			
Full professor	8.9	275.6	31.4
Associate professor	9.3	302.3	31.9
Assistant professor	9.8	280.8	27.3
Instructor	14.1	394.8	26.1
Lecturer	9.5	443.5	42.4
Type of institution			
Research	6.3	251.0	39.2
Doctoral	8.5	274.1	33.4
Comprehensive	10.5	305.2	28.5
Liberal arts	10.7	235.6	21.3
2-year	15.1	425.2	26.6
Control of institution			
Public	10.6	331.0	30.7
Private	9.2	250.1	26.6
Academic discipline of class taught			
Agriculture	8.8	247.0	29.6
Business	10.6	327.5	29.9
Education	9.8	261.4	24.4
Engineering	9.5	256.4	27.2
Fine arts	12.1	279.5	22.1
Humanities	10.1	276.9	26.6
Natural sciences	9.6	353.7	35.3
Social sciences	8.8	330.9	37.0

* Included in the total but not shown separately are other types of academic ranks, institutions, and academic disciplines.

NOTE: See the supplemental note to this indicator for definitions of classroom and student contact hours.

SOURCE: U.S. Department of Education, National Center for Education Statistics, National Survey of Postsecondary Faculty, 1988 and 1993.

Note on teaching workload of full-time postsecondary faculty

The 1988 National Survey of Postsecondary Faculty (NSOPF) was a survey of faculty who had at least some instructional duties (such as teaching one or more courses) in for-credit, higher education courses during the fall 1987 term.

Unlike NSOPF-88, which was limited to faculty whose regular assignments included instruction, the faculty universe for NSOPF-93 was expanded to include anyone who was designated as faculty, whether or not their responsibilities included instruction, as well as other (non-faculty) personnel with instructional responsibilities.

For the purposes of *Indicator 49*, analysis was restricted to full-time faculty who taught at least one class for credit. *Indicator 50*, however, uses classes taught by both full-time and part-time faculty who taught at least one class for credit. Teaching assistants were excluded from both analyses.

These analyses includes all those who had any instructional duties in the fall of 1987 and 1992. Therefore, it includes those faculty whose principal activity that semester was research, technical, clinical, service, or administration, as long as the faculty member taught at least one class for credit. In fact, in fall 1992, 15 percent of all faculty who taught at least one class for credit had a principal activity other than teaching.

The analysis for this indicator categorizes institutions of higher education into five types, as shown below. Remaining institutions, such as religious or specialized institutions, were included in the totals but are not shown separately.

Types of institutions

Research university: Institution among the 100 leading universities that receives federal research funds. Each of these universities awards substantial numbers of doctorates across many fields.

Doctoral university: Institution that offers a full range of baccalaureate programs and Ph.D. degrees in at least three disciplines, but tends to be less focused on research and receives fewer federal research dollars than the research universities.

Comprehensive institution: Institution that offers liberal arts and professional programs. The master's degree is the highest degree offered.

Liberal arts institution: Institution that is smaller and generally more selective than comprehensive colleges and universities. A liberal arts institution primarily offers bachelor's degrees, although some offer master's degrees.

2-year institution: Institution that offers certificate or degree programs through the Associate of Arts level. Two-year institutions, with few exceptions, offer no bachelor's degrees, although some offer master's degrees.

Time allocation

NSOPF survey respondents were asked to estimate the percentage of total working hours they spent on each of the activities below:

Teaching: Includes teaching; grading papers; preparing courses; developing new curricula; advising or supervising students; or working with student organizations or intramural sports.

Research/scholarship: Includes conducting research; reviewing or preparing articles or books; attending or preparing for professional meetings or conferences; reviewing proposals; seeking outside funding; giving performances or exhibitions in the fine or applied arts; or giving speeches.

Professional growth: Includes taking courses or pursuing an advanced degree or other professional development activities to remain current in their field of practice.

Administration: Performing administrative activities.

Outside consulting or freelance work: Conducting outside consulting or other employment.

Service/other: Includes providing legal or medical service or psychological counseling to clients or patients; providing paid or unpaid community or public service, or service to professional societies/associations, or participating in other activities or work not listed above.

Classroom and student contact hours

Classroom hours: The number of hours per week faculty members spent teaching.

Student contact hours: The sum of the number of hours per week faculty members spent teaching over all classes, multiplied by the number of students in each class.

Class size: The total number of student contact hours divided by the mean number of classroom hours faculty spent per week.

Course divisions

Undergraduate, lower division courses: Courses designed for students in the first or second year of a 4-year bachelor's degree program.

Undergraduate, upper division courses: Courses designed for students in the third or fourth year of a 4-year bachelor's degree program.

Graduate courses: Courses designed for students in a post-baccalaureate degree program, including a master's or doctor's program.

Medical faculty

For the purposes of this indicator, medical institutions and their faculty, as well as medical faculty at other institutions, were excluded from the analysis.

SOURCE: U.S. Department of Education, National Center for Education Statistics, *Profiles of Faculty in Higher Education Institutions*, 1988 and 1993.

Table 50-1   Percentage of classes in 4-year colleges and universities where class size is above 25 and above 50 students, by type of institution, level of class, and academic rank: Fall 1987 and fall 1992

Academic rank	Research Class size:		Doctoral Class size:		Comprehensive Class size:		Liberal arts Class size:	
	above 25	above 50	above 25	above 50	above 25	above 50	above 25	above 50
Fall 1992[1]								
Undergraduate, lower division courses								
Total	**55.4**	**30.7**	**57.0**	**21.9**	**51.4**	**10.2**	**31.8**	**4.3**
Full professor	65.3	38.5	61.8	28.6	59.2	14.7	38.4	7.3
Associate professor	62.9	38.8	64.5	29.6	51.6	10.6	34.2	4.2
Assistant professor	54.2	30.8	64.4	23.2	51.4	9.5	32.8	4.8
Instructor	51.3	17.4	44.2	11.4	44.8	5.9	22.8	0.6
Lecturer	29.7	13.5	43.1	12.5	46.9	9.9	40.9	1.8
Other	16.1	5.9	41.7	10.2	39.7	3.7	13.6	4.8
Undergraduate, upper division courses								
Total	**48.3**	**15.6**	**45.5**	**8.7**	**40.9**	**4.9**	**16.3**	**1.2**
Full professor	48.8	15.7	45.4	9.7	43.9	6.3	19.3	1.3
Associate professor	49.7	18.2	47.9	6.8	43.9	5.0	18.1	1.3
Assistant professor	52.5	14.5	49.3	10.1	37.5	3.6	13.6	0.5
Instructor	37.0	3.2	39.0	5.4	38.0	5.6	11.6	1.0
Lecturer	36.9	16.7	35.0	10.4	40.7	3.4	28.2	4.4
Other	64.1	24.6	42.2	13.0	22.9	0.8	9.9	3.0
Graduate courses								
Total	**28.0**	**10.8**	**24.7**	**8.4**	**24.4**	**3.4**	**15.8**	**1.0**
Full professor	26.4	12.7	28.0	11.5	26.0	5.1	11.6	2.1
Associate professor	34.6	14.2	22.3	4.9	24.4	2.8	17.2	2.8
Assistant professor	22.0	2.5	21.4	9.0	26.6	4.3	11.7	0.0
Instructor	20.1	8.0	23.9	2.3	19.3	0.0	28.8	0.0
Lecturer	34.5	3.2	32.6	0.0	22.8	0.0	11.8	0.0
Other	38.5	23.2	17.6	4.1	11.0	0.0	(2)	(2)
Fall 1987								
Undergraduate, lower division courses								
Total	**57.0**	**31.9**	**55.9**	**19.7**	**50.2**	**8.6**	**30.4**	**3.8**
Full professor	73.0	48.0	62.0	25.9	56.7	12.9	32.7	6.3
Associate professor	71.4	44.3	61.7	30.8	50.2	8.3	33.9	3.1
Assistant professor	43.1	21.8	49.7	19.1	53.1	6.6	29.5	5.0
Instructor	37.2	3.1	59.0	10.0	38.3	7.3	21.3	2.4
Lecturer	38.2	15.7	(2)	(2)	47.8	4.7	(2)	(2)
Other	(2)	(2)	(2)	(2)	(2)	(2)	40.5	0.0
Undergraduate, upper division courses								
Total	**48.6**	**15.9**	**40.9**	**7.8**	**34.1**	**4.1**	**16.8**	**1.6**
Full professor	49.1	17.7	37.6	10.6	34.4	2.2	21.2	3.8
Associate professor	50.2	17.0	47.1	6.3	28.7	4.2	16.6	0.8
Assistant professor	52.0	10.4	42.9	11.8	39.0	4.2	17.4	1.0
Instructor	38.4	12.3	32.2	2.2	29.0	2.0	11.7	1.0
Lecturer	43.7	19.9	(2)	(2)	43.3	13.9	(2)	(2)
Other	(2)	(2)	(2)	(2)	(2)	(2)	(2)	(2)
Graduate courses								
Total	**20.7**	**6.7**	**17.6**	**4.1**	**21.6**	**1.9**	**(2)**	**(2)**
Full professor	18.2	5.7	19.6	7.2	22.1	2.0	(2)	(2)
Associate professor	27.6	10.3	17.1	2.8	21.5	3.7	(2)	(2)
Assistant professor	23.1	7.2	15.3	1.5	17.1	0.0	(2)	(2)
Instructor	(2)	(2)	(2)	(2)	(2)	(2)	(2)	(2)
Lecturer	(2)	(2)	(2)	(2)	(2)	(2)	(2)	(2)
Other	(2)	(2)	(2)	(2)	(2)	(2)	(2)	(2)

[1] Revised from previously published figures.
[2] Too few sample observations for a reliable estimate.

SOURCE: U.S. Department of Education, National Center for Education Statistics, National Survey of Postsecondary Faculty, 1988 and 1993.

Note on calculation of the national index of public effort to fund education

There are many indices of public investment in education available. Choosing the most appropriate measure has been an issue among international comparisons as well as national trends. The national index of public effort provides a measure of public investment for each student, compared to available societal resources.

Public education revenues per student are the ratio of total public education revenues to public and private enrollment. Per capita income is the ratio of total personal income to total population; personal income is for the calendar year in which the school year began; and total population is as of July 1, the year in which the school year began. The index can be expressed algebraically, therefore, as a function of four variables:

$$National\ effort\ index = \frac{Public\ education\ revenues\ per\ student}{Per\ capita\ income}\ x\ 100$$

or

$$National\ effort\ index = \frac{Public\ education\ revenues\ /\ Total\ personal\ income}{Total\ enrollment\ /\ Total\ population}\ x\ 100$$

Revenue data from elementary/secondary and higher education are based on different accounting systems and are not entirely comparable. For example, elementary and secondary public revenues represent additions to assets (cash) from taxes, appropriations, and other funds, which do not incur an obligation that must be met at some future date (loans) in all public schools. These include revenues that are spent on construction of buildings and other investments in the physical plant. Because of the difficulty in constructing a comparable time series, public funds going to private schools (for Head Start, disabled children, etc.) have been excluded. For higher education, educational and general public revenues are those available from public sources at both public and private institutions for the *regular or customary activities* of an institution that are a part of, contributory to, or necessary to its instructional or research programs. These include salaries and travel funds for faculty and administrative or other employees; purchase of supplies or materials for *current* use in classrooms, libraries, laboratories, or offices; and operation and maintenance of the educational plant. In contrast to elementary/secondary public revenues, higher education public revenues, as defined in this indicator, do not include public funds that would be used for expansion of the physical plant. As a result, the reader should focus on the changes over time in the elementary/secondary and the higher education measures rather than on comparisons across all levels.

Enrollment includes all institutions, regardless of control. No adjustments were made for part-time enrollment.

Total education revenues were adjusted from current school dollars, using the Consumer Price Index (CPI), prepared by the U.S. Department of Labor, Bureau of Labor Statistics. Personal income was adjusted from current calendar year dollars into 1995 constant dollars.

Alternative approaches to calculating adjusted costs and expenditures can be found in the following publications:

Halstead, Kent. *Inflation Measures for Schools, Colleges, and Libraries: 1995 Update.* Washington, D.C.: Research Associates of Washington, September, 1995.

Rothstein, Richard, with Karen Hawley Miles (1995). *Where's the Money Gone?* Washington, D.C.: Economic Policy Institute, (1995).

Note on international comparisons of current public education expenditures

The purpose of this indicator is to compare *public* support for education, relative to Gross Domestic Product (GDP), population, and school enrollment, across the developed countries for which data are available.

Definitions

Public education expenditures include funds provided to both public and private schools by federal, state, and local governments either directly or through students. This includes expenditures at public schools funded by public sources and subsidies to students at private schools from government agencies.

Private education expenditures are expenditures financed by private sources—households, private nonprofit institutions, businesses, and corporations. For example, this includes expenditures supported by public and private school tuition and fees, and expenses for books and materials that must be purchased by the students themselves.

Current expenditures are expenditures for educational goods and services whose life span should not in principle exceed the current year (salaries of personnel, school books and other teaching materials, scholarships, minor repairs and maintenance to school buildings, administration, and so on). Current expenditures exclude both capital expenditures (construction of buildings, major repairs, major items of equipment, vehicles) and the service debt.

This indicator focuses on the portion of current education expenditures at both public and private schools funded by public sources.

Expenditures in the United States

Elementary and secondary education

For the United States, *current public expenditures for elementary and secondary education* include current expenditures in local public school districts funded by state and local taxes, federal programs administered by the U.S. Department of Education (ED), and federal programs operated outside of ED that are not administered by state or local education agencies, e.g., Head Start,

Department of Defense Schools, and schools operated by the Bureau of Indian Affairs.

Also included are federal expenditures to operate ED and other activities, such as research, statistics, assessment, and school improvement, and state expenditures to operate state departments of education and other direct state expenditures, including state schools for the deaf and blind and reform schools.

Some expenditures, such as those for federal or state agency administration and those for non-graded special education programs, cannot be assigned to particular grade levels by any obviously universally superior method. These expenditures defy strict grade-level categorizations. Like some other countries, the United States has chosen to prorate these expenditures over the grade levels based on the relative size of enrollments, staffing, and salaries. Other countries, however, have chosen not to allocate such expenditures, classifying them, instead, as "undistributed."

Higher education

Current public expenditures for higher education in the United States include expenditures at both public and private colleges and universities funded by federal, state, and local governments. The Integrated Postsecondary Education Data System (IPEDS), the core postsecondary education data collection program for NCES, gathers institutional reports for revenue received by both public and private institutions from both public and private sources. Current expenditures by public and private nonprofit institutions are separated into public and private expenditures based on the share of current fund revenues from federal, state, and local sources.

Most federal aid goes to students who then spend it on education (e.g., tuition) and non-education (room and board) services. It was assumed that 60 percent of federally administered Pell grants were spent on education by students.

With the exception of Pell grant money, public expenditures for less-than-2-year public and private institutions were not available; therefore, *current public expenditures for higher education* in the United States are biased downward.

However, since the students participating in these institutions are also excluded from higher education enrollments, the estimate of *public expenditures per student* would be biased upward if the per-student public expenditures in less-than-2-year institutions were less than those in other higher education institutions.

Per student expenditures are calculated as current public expenditures divided by enrollment in both public and private schools. This is a measure of the average public investment per student in the education system, rather than a measure of the total resources each student receives, which would include private expenditures. For Germany, Japan, and the United States, private education expenditures are a significant portion of the GDP.

Total expenditures for education in 1992

| | Percentage of GDP | | |
Country	Total	Public sources	Private sources
Canada	7.4	7.2	0.2
France	5.9	5.5	0.4
Former West Germany*	5.6	4.1	1.5
Italy	—	5.1	—
Japan	4.7	3.6	1.1
Spain	5.3	4.6	0.7
United Kingdom	—	5.2	—
United States	7.0	5.4	1.6

— Not available.
* Data for private sources from 1991.
NOTE: Data revised from previously published figures. *Total expenditures* include current expenditures, capital expenditures, and interest on debt service.

SOURCE: Organization for Economic Co-operation and Development, *Education at a Glance: OECD Indicators*, 1995, table F1 (B3).

How students are classified

The International Standard Classification of Education (ISCED) was designed as an instrument for presenting statistics of education internationally. Many countries report education statistics to UNESCO and the Organization for Economic Co-operation and Development (OECD) using the ISCED. In this classification system, education is divided into several levels.

The following are summary definitions used in this indicator:

♦ *Education preceding the first level (preprimary education)* where it is provided, usually begins at age 3, 4, or 5 (sometimes earlier) and lasts from 1–3 years. For the United States, this would be mostly nursery schools and kindergarten classes.

♦ *Education at the first level (primary education)* usually begins at age 5, 6, or 7 and lasts for about 5 or 6 years. For the United States, the first level starts with grade 1 and ends with grade 6.

♦ *Education at the second level (lower secondary education)* begins at about age 11 or 12 and lasts for about 3 years. For the United States, second level starts with grade 7 and ends with grade 9.

♦ *Education at the third level (upper secondary education)* begins at about age 14 or 15 and lasts about 3 years. For the United States, the third level starts with grade 10 and ends with grade 12.

♦ *Education at the fifth level (non-university higher education)* is provided at community colleges, vocational-technical colleges, and other degree-granting institutes whose programs typically take 2 years or more, but less than 4 years, to complete.

♦ *Education at the sixth level (university higher education)* is provided in undergraduate programs at 4-year colleges and universities in the United States and, generally, at universities in other countries. Completion of education at the third level (upper secondary education) is usually required as a minimum condition of admission, and admission is, in many cases, competitive.

♦ *Education at the seventh level (graduate and professional higher education)* is provided in graduate and professional schools that generally require a university diploma as a minimum condition for admission.

♦ *Education at the ninth level (undistributed)* is a classification reserved for enrollments, expenditures, or programs that cannot be unambiguously assigned to one of the aforementioned levels. Some countries, for example, assign non-graded special education or recreational non-degree adult education programs to this level. Other countries assign nothing to this level, preferring instead to allocate enrollments, expenditures, and programs to levels as best they can.

"Undistributed" expenditures are reported separately from other expenditures in tables 52-2 through 52-5. They are not included or allocated in any way in table 52-1. France, Germany, and Japan, among the G-7 countries, report some amount of expenditure as undistributed.

How expenditures are compared across countries

To compare public expenditures per student in the United States to expenditures per student in other countries, expenditures must be denominated in a common currency. Conversion of other countries' expenditures to U.S. dollars facilitates comparison with expenditures in the United States. There are at least two methods of conversion: 1) market exchange rates, and 2) Purchasing Power Parity Indices (PPPIs).

The market exchange rate is the rate at which an individual can exchange the currencies of two countries. It is determined by relative confidence in the governments, their monetary systems, and the economies of the two countries and by the relative demand for the goods and services that the two countries trade. Market exchange rates can be highly volatile.[1]

PPPIs are calculated by comparing the cost of a fixed market basket of goods in each country. Changes over time in a PPPI are determined by the rates of inflation in each country. Since PPPIs are not volatile, they were used here to adjust expenditure and GDP figures.[2]

Because the fiscal year has a different starting month in different countries, within-country Consumer Price Indices (CPIs), calculated by the International Monetary Fund, were used to adjust educational expenditure data to allow for inflation between the starting month of the fiscal year and July 1, 1992. See supplemental table 51-5 for both the PPPIs used in this indicator and the CPI adjustment ratios.

Problems in comparing education expenditures across countries

The coverage and character of the education expenditure data that countries submit to the OECD vary somewhat. Sometimes an individual expenditure item may be included in the

expenditure data from one country, but may not be included in those from another.

Discrepancies arise because one country may collect certain kinds of data that another country either does not collect, or does not collect in its "education" data collections. Or, one country may define what constitutes an "education" expenditure differently than another country does. Discrepancies between which expenditure items are included in one country's expenditure figures and not in another's tend to arise in three general domains:

Non-instructional (ancillary) services: Some countries provide fewer ancillary services in their schools and, thus, include fewer expenditures for such services in their education expenditure figures. Examples of ancillary services are school cafeterias; dormitories; intramural school sports programs; school health clinics or visiting school nurse services; attendance (i.e., truancy) services; and speech or psychological therapy services. U.S. schools tend to subsidize relatively more ancillary services through their education budgets than do schools in most other countries. In some countries (e.g., Germany), *none* of the aforementioned services are provided at the primary and lower secondary levels by many schools.

Private expenditures: Some countries' education systems receive large private contributions. The most common forms of private contributions to education are student tuition or fees; organizational subsidies, such as those provided by religious denominations to their own schools; and corporate in-kind contributions, such as those provided by German and Austrian firms to find vocational courses on the shop floor for participating youth apprentices. Private expenditures have not been included in the indicators used in this report, in part because precise figures for private education expenditures are not available for the United States or for several other countries.

The boundaries of education: Fewer (though, still some) inconsistencies arise when comparing just the *instructional* expenditures for *primary* and *secondary* public education in the *academic* track. But, the "borderlands" of education, in particular, tend to cause comparability problems. These borderlands include preprimary education and day care, special education, adult education, vocational/technical education, and proprietary education. Some countries, for example, simply do not collect expenditure data for private "center-based" day care because they do not define this as "education." Indeed, in some countries, even public day care is not managed by education authorities; rather, it is the responsibility of human services departments.

The exact location of each "boundary" also varies from country to country and even within each country. In Canada, for example, vocational/technical students in Québec choose to enter vocational/technical college in the 12th grade, while in the other Canadian provinces with vocational/technical colleges, they enter in the 13th or 14th grade. Thus, vocational/technical students in the other provinces spend another year or two at the upper secondary level. The more time the average student spends in a level of education, the greater will be the expenditure at that level.

Even these three domains do not include all the possible comparability problems. There remain, for example, inconsistencies in how different countries treat public contributions to teacher retirement and fringe benefits, student financial aid, and university research and hospitals.

The National Center for Education Statistics (NCES) has sponsored two studies designed to examine the issue of the comparability of national figures on education expenditure. The studies,

entitled *The International Expenditure Comparability Study* and *Improving the Comparability of International Expenditure Data*, involve 10 countries and examine in detail the content of their education expenditures as they are reported to the OECD.

Thus far, participating education ministries have been receptive to the idea of improving comparability in the OECD data collection. Indeed, some countries had already modified their data submissions to the OECD for the 1991–92 school year, thus improving the comparability of education expenditures across countries for the data collected used for this report. These changes were motivated in part by preliminary findings from the NCES expenditure comparability studies.[3]

NOTES:

[1] For a further argument against using market exchange rates, see Edith M. Rasel and Lawrence Mishel, *Short-changing Education*, Economic Policy Institute, January 1990.

[2] PPP Indices for other aggregates such as private consumption expenditures are available. See Stephen M. Barro, *International Comparisons of Education Spending: Some Conceptual and Methodological Issues*, SMB Economic Research, Inc., April 1990, for a discussion of the strengths and weaknesses of using various indices.

[3] Stephen M. Barro. *Preliminary Findings from the Expenditure Comparability Study*. SMB Economic Research, Inc., June 1993.

Table 53-2 Percentage distribution of educational and general expenditures of institutions of higher education per full-time-equivalent (FTE) student across types of expenditure, by type of institution: Academic years ending 1977–93

Academic year ending	Total	Instruc-tion	Adminis-tration[1]	Student services	Research	Libraries	Public services	Operation and main-tenance of plant	Scholar-ships and fellowships	Manda-tory transfers
Private universities[2]										
1977	100.0	38.0	13.2	3.3	21.1	4.2	2.2	8.8	8.1	1.1
1978	100.0	37.9	13.4	3.4	20.8	4.2	2.1	8.7	8.4	1.1
1979	100.0	37.4	14.0	3.4	20.7	3.9	2.1	9.0	8.1	1.3
1980	100.0	37.9	14.2	3.4	20.5	3.7	2.3	8.9	7.9	1.3
1981	100.0	38.1	13.9	3.5	19.8	3.7	2.1	9.1	8.2	1.5
1982	100.0	39.1	13.8	3.6	18.9	3.7	2.0	9.5	8.2	1.2
1983	100.0	39.4	14.8	3.7	17.9	3.6	2.1	9.2	8.2	1.2
1984	100.0	38.6	15.2	3.7	17.7	3.8	2.0	9.1	8.8	1.2
1985	100.0	38.0	14.9	3.8	18.1	3.5	2.4	8.9	8.9	1.4
1986	100.0	37.8	15.0	3.8	18.5	3.5	2.4	8.6	9.1	1.3
1987	100.0	38.4	15.2	3.9	18.4	3.1	2.6	7.7	9.4	1.4
1988	100.0	37.5	15.2	3.8	18.7	3.5	2.5	7.7	9.6	1.5
1989	100.0	38.0	15.2	3.7	18.4	3.4	2.5	7.5	9.7	1.6
1990	100.0	37.8	14.7	3.7	18.6	3.4	2.5	7.5	9.9	1.8
1991	100.0	38.3	14.8	3.8	17.8	3.2	2.6	7.8	10.3	1.6
1992	100.0	38.2	14.8	3.7	17.4	3.2	2.5	7.5	11.1	1.6
1993	100.0	38.4	14.1	3.5	17.9	3.2	2.7	7.3	11.4	1.7
Public universities[2]										
1977	100.0	39.0	13.0	3.7	18.4	3.5	8.1	9.1	4.0	1.2
1978	100.0	39.2	13.2	3.8	18.6	3.4	7.9	9.2	3.8	1.0
1979	100.0	39.1	13.1	3.7	18.9	3.2	8.2	9.3	3.5	1.0
1980	100.0	38.8	12.5	3.8	19.5	3.7	8.1	9.2	3.5	1.0
1981	100.0	38.5	12.9	3.8	19.7	3.2	8.3	9.1	3.5	1.0
1982	100.0	38.8	13.1	3.8	19.3	3.2	8.1	9.4	3.5	0.9
1983	100.0	38.8	13.1	3.8	19.2	3.3	8.1	9.4	3.5	0.9
1984	100.0	38.6	13.1	3.7	19.1	3.3	8.0	9.4	3.6	1.0
1985	100.0	38.3	13.7	3.7	19.4	3.2	8.0	9.2	3.6	0.9
1986	100.0	37.7	13.9	3.7	19.7	3.2	8.0	8.8	3.8	1.2
1987	100.0	38.0	14.0	3.7	20.0	3.1	7.8	8.3	3.8	1.2
1988	100.0	37.3	13.9	3.7	20.6	3.2	7.8	8.1	4.0	1.4
1989	100.0	36.8	13.9	3.7	21.0	3.1	8.0	7.9	4.2	1.3
1990	100.0	36.6	13.8	3.7	21.4	3.1	8.1	7.8	4.3	1.4
1991	100.0	36.3	13.7	3.6	21.7	3.0	8.2	7.6	4.5	1.4
1992	100.0	36.0	13.3	3.7	22.0	3.0	8.3	7.4	4.9	1.5
1993	100.0	35.7	13.1	3.7	22.3	2.9	8.3	7.2	5.3	1.5
Private 4-year colleges										
1977	100.0	37.3	20.4	7.4	5.0	3.9	2.4	11.2	10.0	2.3
1978	100.0	37.5	20.6	7.6	4.8	3.9	2.2	11.3	9.8	2.3
1979	100.0	37.2	20.7	7.7	5.2	3.8	2.2	11.2	9.6	2.3
1980	100.0	36.7	20.8	7.8	5.3	3.7	2.2	11.4	9.8	2.4
1981	100.0	36.1	21.1	7.9	5.1	3.6	2.3	11.5	10.1	2.3
1982	100.0	36.1	21.4	8.0	4.6	3.6	2.5	11.4	10.1	2.2
1983	100.0	36.2	21.7	8.2	4.5	3.6	2.4	11.1	10.0	2.2
1984	100.0	36.0	21.6	8.2	4.4	3.6	2.4	10.9	10.6	2.2
1985	100.0	35.6	21.7	8.3	4.6	3.5	2.4	10.6	11.1	2.3
1986	100.0	35.1	21.7	8.3	4.8	3.5	2.6	10.2	11.5	2.3
1987	100.0	34.3	22.8	8.3	4.9	2.9	2.7	9.7	12.1	2.2
1988	100.0	34.1	22.1	8.4	5.0	3.2	3.0	9.5	12.8	2.0
1989	100.0	33.8	22.2	8.5	5.0	3.1	2.9	9.4	12.9	2.2
1990	100.0	33.5	21.9	8.5	4.9	3.1	3.1	9.1	13.6	2.2
1991	100.0	33.4	22.2	8.7	4.4	2.9	3.1	8.9	14.2	2.2
1992	100.0	33.1	21.4	8.7	4.3	3.0	3.2	8.6	15.7	2.1
1993	100.0	32.8	20.7	8.7	4.4	2.9	3.5	8.5	16.5	2.1

Table 53-2   Percentage distribution of educational and general expenditures of institutions of higher education per full-time-equivalent (FTE) student across types of expenditure, by type of institution: Academic years ending 1977–93—Continued

Academic year ending	Total	Instruc- tion	Adminis- tration[1]	Student services	Research	Libraries	Public services	Operation and main- tenance of plant	Scholar- ships and fellowships	Manda- tory transfers
Public 4-year colleges										
1977	100.0	46.4	16.7	5.8	7.0	3.9	2.9	11.5	3.9	2.0
1978	100.0	46.2	16.7	6.0	7.1	3.9	2.9	11.7	3.5	2.1
1979	100.0	45.6	17.1	6.2	7.5	3.8	2.9	11.6	3.2	2.0
1980	100.0	44.9	17.3	6.2	8.0	3.8	3.1	11.7	3.3	1.8
1981	100.0	44.8	17.2	6.1	7.9	3.9	3.1	11.9	3.1	1.8
1982	100.0	45.7	17.6	5.8	7.6	3.7	3.1	12.1	2.8	1.6
1983	100.0	45.7	17.4	5.9	7.5	3.7	3.1	12.2	2.9	1.7
1984	100.0	45.1	18.2	6.3	7.5	3.8	3.1	11.3	2.9	1.7
1985	100.0	44.8	18.4	6.2	7.7	3.7	3.3	11.7	2.7	1.6
1986	100.0	45.0	18.4	6.2	8.2	3.6	3.3	10.7	2.9	1.8
1987	100.0	44.7	18.7	6.1	8.6	3.2	3.6	10.4	3.1	1.6
1988	100.0	44.6	18.4	6.2	8.9	3.3	3.7	10.1	3.1	1.6
1989	100.0	44.6	18.2	6.1	9.4	3.3	3.8	9.9	3.1	1.6
1990	100.0	44.4	18.7	6.1	9.3	3.3	4.0	9.6	3.2	1.6
1991	100.0	44.4	18.6	6.2	9.5	3.1	4.0	9.4	3.3	1.5
1992	100.0	43.2	18.9	6.1	9.7	3.1	4.3	9.1	4.1	1.6
1993	100.0	42.0	19.4	6.5	9.8	3.0	4.4	8.9	4.4	1.6
Public 2-year colleges										
1977	100.0	51.1	18.1	8.4	0.3	3.5	2.0	11.2	2.9	2.4
1978	100.0	50.6	19.4	8.2	0.2	3.5	2.1	11.3	2.2	2.4
1979	100.0	50.2	19.5	8.4	0.4	3.4	1.9	11.3	2.2	2.6
1980	100.0	50.3	19.0	8.6	0.4	3.2	2.2	11.7	2.3	2.2
1981	100.0	50.6	19.1	8.7	0.4	3.1	2.2	12.0	2.3	1.7
1982	100.0	50.9	19.0	8.8	0.2	3.4	1.9	12.3	2.1	1.5
1983	100.0	50.9	19.5	8.9	0.2	3.0	1.5	12.3	2.1	1.6
1984	100.0	50.8	19.8	8.8	0.2	3.0	1.7	12.2	2.0	1.5
1985	100.0	50.3	20.2	8.8	0.2	2.9	2.0	12.1	2.2	1.4
1986	100.0	49.9	20.7	9.0	0.1	2.9	2.0	11.9	2.2	1.4
1987	100.0	49.6	21.8	9.4	0.1	2.3	2.2	11.5	2.2	0.8
1988	100.0	49.2	21.3	9.9	0.1	2.7	2.3	11.4	2.4	0.8
1989	100.0	49.6	21.5	9.5	0.1	2.6	2.5	11.2	2.4	0.7
1990	100.0	49.8	21.5	9.7	0.1	2.5	2.4	11.0	2.3	0.7
1991	100.0	49.9	21.6	9.9	0.1	2.5	2.4	10.7	2.4	0.6
1992	100.0	50.3	20.9	10.2	0.2	2.4	2.2	10.4	2.8	0.6
1993	100.0	50.1	20.9	10.4	0.2	2.3	2.3	10.1	3.1	0.6

[1] Includes institutional and academic support less libraries.

[2] Includes institutions with medical schools. Private doctoral institutions with a medical school have substantially higher instructional expenditures than those without a medical school.

NOTE: The Higher Education Price Index (HEPI) was used to calculate constant dollars, and the CPI was used to forecast the HEPI to July 1995. Data in this table may differ slightly from data appearing in other tables. Data for academic years 1976–77 through 1985–86 include only institutions that provided both enrollment and finance data. See the supplemental note to *Indicator 51* for resources on alternative approaches to adjusting cost and expenditures.

SOURCE: U.S. Department of Education, National Center for Education Statistics, *Digest of Education Statistics, 1995*, tables 335–339 (based on the IPEDS/HEGIS "Institutional Characteristics," "Financial Statistics," and "Fall Enrollment" surveys).

Table 54-1 Current fund revenues (in 1995 constant dollars) of institutions of higher education per full-time-equivalent (FTE) student, by type of revenue sources and institution: Academic years ending 1977–93

Academic year ending	Total	Tuition and fees[1]	Federal appro-priations	State and local appro-priations	Federal grants and contracts	State and local grants and contracts	Private gifts	Endow-ment	Sales and services of educational activities
				Private universities[2]					
1977	$22,206	$8,941	$487	$391	$6,156	$550	$2,875	$1,783	$1,023
1978	21,983	8,927	436	351	6,025	476	2,936	1,684	1,130
1979	22,087	9,017	436	339	6,043	476	2,859	1,808	1,090
1980	22,611	9,064	441	320	6,295	576	2,806	1,871	1,217
1981	22,775	9,292	408	345	6,247	460	2,905	1,918	1,182
1982	22,670	9,639	385	326	5,810	425	2,883	1,974	1,211
1983	22,890	10,306	413	326	5,315	475	2,956	1,773	1,307
1984	24,830	10,983	400	318	5,668	517	3,339	2,077	1,509
1985	25,625	11,377	396	317	5,843	525	3,458	2,239	1,450
1986	26,714	11,807	366	325	6,190	556	3,627	2,291	1,531
1987	28,817	12,618	331	319	6,892	769	3,830	2,374	1,654
1988	29,384	12,939	325	295	6,552	1,028	3,955	2,489	1,761
1989	29,966	13,176	335	280	6,575	1,073	3,957	2,590	1,938
1990	30,331	13,329	343	276	6,650	1,072	4,075	2,597	1,948
1991	30,627	13,772	289	244	6,496	934	4,167	2,596	2,093
1992	31,404	14,155	279	170	6,631	1,028	4,249	2,532	2,321
1993	32,350	14,491	257	137	6,830	1,047	4,524	2,606	2,416
				Public universities[2]					
1977	14,774	2,424	428	7,748	2,516	314	696	105	543
1978	15,049	2,456	452	7,905	2,507	323	730	148	528
1979	15,651	2,496	463	8,160	2,646	355	740	163	628
1980	15,549	2,469	397	8,059	2,700	334	773	175	642
1981	15,122	2,484	347	7,761	2,613	341	761	166	648
1982	14,793	2,598	314	7,610	2,336	320	791	169	655
1983	14,830	2,814	304	7,457	2,226	312	871	183	665
1984	15,332	2,934	304	7,762	2,277	291	884	203	678
1985	16,145	2,954	344	8,265	2,387	321	957	213	705
1986	16,825	3,135	346	8,490	2,490	340	1,044	239	742
1987	16,807	3,270	315	8,287	2,521	412	1,073	175	755
1988	17,251	3,423	258	8,409	2,659	422	1,141	171	768
1989	17,491	3,498	262	8,346	2,722	452	1,223	182	807
1990	17,644	3,589	246	8,262	2,747	506	1,296	185	813
1991	17,601	3,709	242	8,025	2,810	522	1,267	188	838
1992	17,457	3,874	236	7,486	2,947	476	1,321	217	898
1993	17,102	3,941	238	7,148	2,912	457	1,312	216	878
				Private 4-year colleges					
1977	10,975	6,770	102	229	1,187	223	1,714	642	107
1978	10,904	6,814	107	215	1,148	219	1,658	629	113
1979	11,029	6,857	112	208	1,214	219	1,623	681	116
1980	11,357	6,931	118	211	1,311	259	1,647	753	127
1981	11,316	6,973	122	212	1,210	257	1,623	786	134
1982	11,395	7,184	96	199	1,051	260	1,619	868	117
1983	11,607	7,504	71	201	895	273	1,676	869	119
1984	11,919	7,752	65	201	912	282	1,697	878	133
1985	12,356	8,012	66	197	946	309	1,766	930	129
1986	12,745	8,267	62	202	999	331	1,801	948	134
1987	13,480	8,787	74	218	991	392	1,895	976	145
1988	13,750	9,013	74	226	1,018	421	1,847	1,005	147
1989	13,873	9,156	59	188	988	503	1,798	1,034	147
1990	14,138	9,451	53	175	1,003	533	1,749	1,033	141
1991	14,313	9,743	53	163	971	504	1,722	1,021	137
1992	14,671	10,103	54	121	1,020	599	1,681	952	140
1993	14,845	10,281	39	106	1,046	563	1,677	910	223

Table 54-1 Current fund revenues (in 1995 constant dollars) of institutions of higher education per full-time-equivalent (FTE) student, by type of revenue sources and institution: Academic years ending 1977–93—Continued

Academic year ending	Total	Tuition and fees[1]	Federal appro-priations	State and local appro-priations	Federal grants and contracts	State and local grants and contracts	Private gifts	Endow-ment	Sales and services of educational activities
				Public 4-year colleges					
1977	11,098	1,818	545	6,733	1,289	230	263	35	184
1978	11,227	1,795	546	6,896	1,227	249	281	27	205
1979	11,586	1,763	570	7,143	1,296	269	287	33	225
1980	11,727	1,746	591	7,210	1,323	261	304	40	251
1981	11,508	1,767	613	7,002	1,259	256	307	45	259
1982	11,455	1,848	534	7,046	1,111	245	336	49	286
1983	11,156	1,900	533	6,830	967	240	361	45	280
1984	11,315	2,059	531	6,765	966	260	377	48	309
1985	12,037	2,120	553	7,307	996	258	412	49	342
1986	12,498	2,207	533	7,505	1,054	321	451	53	373
1987	12,255	2,205	529	7,201	1,026	366	462	59	406
1988	12,435	2,290	529	7,267	1,035	356	458	61	440
1989	12,209	2,343	344	7,088	1,049	366	501	68	450
1990	12,149	2,389	514	6,758	1,044	383	525	68	468
1991	11,622	2,403	445	6,256	1,037	397	556	39	488
1992	12,151	2,719	433	6,231	1,139	455	600	75	499
1993	12,971	3,102	421	6,238	1,353	521	669	98	570
				Public 2-year colleges					
1977	5,905	992	117	4,282	340	116	30	4	24
1978	5,923	954	105	4,343	327	136	29	4	24
1979	6,046	956	117	4,395	364	151	28	4	31
1980	5,970	962	80	4,332	377	155	28	5	31
1981	5,687	957	70	4,080	355	159	28	6	31
1982	5,623	1,011	61	4,032	294	161	30	7	28
1983	5,267	1,016	43	3,763	228	153	30	8	28
1984	5,406	1,055	46	3,841	237	159	32	8	28
1985	5,896	1,124	44	4,181	273	200	36	8	29
1986	6,167	1,146	38	4,400	276	225	39	8	35
1987	6,248	1,155	46	4,401	259	301	40	9	36
1988	6,088	1,139	44	4,292	247	284	43	6	32
1989	6,239	1,191	41	4,288	262	372	49	6	31
1990	6,088	1,193	40	4,121	256	385	52	6	33
1991	6,074	1,244	42	4,095	254	347	54	6	32
1992	5,922	1,309	49	3,859	268	341	57	5	32
1993	6,257	1,637	36	3,815	311	348	59	5	45

[1] Federally supported student aid received through students (e.g., Pell grants) is included under tuition and auxiliary enterprises.
[2] Includes institutions with medical schools. Private doctoral-granting institutions with a medical school have substantially different revenue income per FTE student than those without a medical school.

NOTE: The Higher Education Price Index (HEPI) was used to calculate constant dollars, and the Consumer Price Index (CPI) was used to forecast the HEPI to July 1995. Data in this table may differ slightly from data appearing in other tables. Data for academic years 1976–77 through 1985–86 include only institutions that provide both enrollment and finance data. Details may not add to totals because of rounding.

SOURCE: U.S. Department of Education, National Center for Education Statistics, Financial Statistics of Institutions of Higher Education Survey and Integrated Postsecondary Education Data System (IPEDS), "Finance" survey.

Table 54-2   Percentage distribution of current fund revenues of institutions of higher education per full-time-equivalent (FTE) student according to revenue source, by type of institution: Academic years ending 1977–93

Academic year ending	Total	Tuition and fees*	Federal appropriations	State and local appropriations	Federal grants and contracts	State and local grants and contracts	Private gifts	Endowment	Sales and services of educational activities
				Private universities					
1977	100.0	40.3	2.2	1.8	27.7	2.5	12.9	8.0	4.6
1978	100.0	40.6	2.0	1.6	27.4	2.2	13.4	7.7	5.1
1979	100.0	40.8	2.0	1.5	27.4	2.2	12.9	8.2	4.9
1980	100.0	40.1	1.9	1.4	27.8	2.5	12.4	8.3	5.4
1981	100.0	40.8	1.8	1.5	27.4	2.0	12.8	8.4	5.2
1982	100.0	42.5	1.7	1.4	25.6	1.9	12.7	8.7	5.3
1983	100.0	45.0	1.8	1.4	23.2	2.1	12.9	7.7	5.7
1984	100.0	44.2	1.6	1.3	22.8	2.1	13.4	8.4	6.1
1985	100.0	44.4	1.5	1.2	22.8	2.0	13.5	8.7	5.7
1986	100.0	44.2	1.4	1.2	23.2	2.1	13.6	8.6	5.7
1987	100.0	43.8	1.1	1.1	23.9	2.7	13.3	8.2	5.7
1988	100.0	44.0	1.1	1.0	22.3	3.5	13.5	8.5	6.0
1989	100.0	44.0	1.1	0.9	21.9	3.6	13.2	8.6	6.5
1990	100.0	43.9	1.1	0.9	21.9	3.5	13.4	8.6	6.4
1991	100.0	45.0	0.9	0.8	21.2	3.0	13.6	8.5	6.8
1992	100.0	45.1	0.9	0.5	21.1	3.3	13.5	8.1	7.4
1993	100.0	44.8	0.8	0.4	21.1	3.2	14.0	8.1	7.5
				Public universities					
1977	100.0	16.4	2.9	52.4	17.0	2.1	4.7	0.7	3.7
1978	100.0	16.3	3.0	52.5	16.7	2.1	4.8	1.0	3.5
1979	100.0	15.9	3.0	52.1	16.9	2.3	4.7	1.0	4.0
1980	100.0	15.9	2.6	51.8	17.4	2.1	5.0	1.1	4.1
1981	100.0	16.4	2.3	51.3	17.3	2.3	5.0	1.1	4.3
1982	100.0	17.6	2.1	51.4	15.8	2.2	5.3	1.1	4.4
1983	100.0	19.0	2.0	50.3	15.0	2.1	5.9	1.2	4.5
1984	100.0	19.1	2.0	50.6	14.9	1.9	5.8	1.3	4.4
1985	100.0	18.3	2.1	51.2	14.8	2.0	5.9	1.3	4.4
1986	100.0	18.6	2.1	50.5	14.8	2.0	6.2	1.4	4.4
1987	100.0	19.5	1.9	49.3	15.0	2.4	6.4	1.0	4.5
1988	100.0	19.8	1.5	48.7	15.4	2.4	6.6	1.0	4.5
1989	100.0	20.0	1.5	47.7	15.6	2.6	7.0	1.0	4.6
1990	100.0	20.3	1.4	46.8	15.6	2.9	7.3	1.0	4.6
1991	100.0	21.1	1.4	45.6	16.0	3.0	7.2	1.1	4.8
1992	100.0	22.2	1.4	42.9	16.9	2.7	7.6	1.2	5.1
1993	100.0	23.0	1.4	41.8	17.0	2.7	7.7	1.3	5.1
				Private 4-year colleges					
1977	100.0	61.7	0.9	2.1	10.8	2.0	15.6	5.8	1.0
1978	100.0	62.5	1.0	2.0	10.5	2.0	15.2	5.8	1.0
1979	100.0	62.2	1.0	1.9	11.0	2.0	14.7	6.2	1.0
1980	100.0	61.0	1.0	1.9	11.5	2.3	14.5	6.6	1.1
1981	100.0	61.6	1.1	1.9	10.7	2.3	14.3	6.9	1.2
1982	100.0	63.0	0.8	1.7	9.2	2.3	14.2	7.6	1.0
1983	100.0	64.6	0.6	1.7	7.7	2.4	14.4	7.5	1.0
1984	100.0	65.0	0.5	1.7	7.7	2.4	14.2	7.4	1.1
1985	100.0	64.8	0.5	1.6	7.7	2.5	14.3	7.5	1.0
1986	100.0	64.9	0.5	1.6	7.8	2.6	14.1	7.4	1.1
1987	100.0	65.2	0.6	1.6	7.4	2.9	14.1	7.2	1.1
1988	100.0	65.5	0.5	1.6	7.4	3.1	13.4	7.3	1.1
1989	100.0	66.0	0.4	1.4	7.1	3.6	13.0	7.5	1.1
1990	100.0	66.8	0.4	1.2	7.1	3.8	12.4	7.3	1.0
1991	100.0	68.1	0.4	1.1	6.8	3.5	12.0	7.1	1.0
1992	100.0	68.9	0.4	0.8	7.0	4.1	11.5	6.5	1.0
1993	100.0	69.3	0.3	0.7	7.0	3.8	11.3	6.1	1.5

Table 54-2   Percentage distribution of current fund revenues of institutions of higher education per full-time-equivalent (FTE) student according to revenue source, by type of institution: Academic years ending 1977–93—Continued

Academic year ending	Total	Tuition and fees*	Federal appro-priations	State and local appro-priations	Federal grants and contracts	State and local grants and contracts	Private gifts	Endow-ment	Sales and services of educational activities
Public 4-year colleges									
1977	100.0	16.4	4.9	60.7	11.6	2.1	2.4	0.3	1.7
1978	100.0	16.0	4.9	61.4	10.9	2.2	2.5	0.2	1.8
1979	100.0	15.2	4.9	61.6	11.2	2.3	2.5	0.3	1.9
1980	100.0	14.9	5.0	61.5	11.3	2.2	2.6	0.3	2.1
1981	100.0	15.4	5.3	60.8	10.9	2.2	2.7	0.4	2.3
1982	100.0	16.1	4.7	61.5	9.7	2.1	2.9	0.4	2.5
1983	100.0	17.0	4.8	61.2	8.7	2.1	3.2	0.4	2.5
1984	100.0	18.2	4.7	59.8	8.5	2.3	3.3	0.4	2.7
1985	100.0	17.6	4.6	60.7	8.3	2.1	3.4	0.4	2.8
1986	100.0	17.7	4.3	60.0	8.4	2.6	3.6	0.4	3.0
1987	100.0	18.0	4.3	58.8	8.4	3.0	3.8	0.5	3.3
1988	100.0	18.4	4.3	58.4	8.3	2.9	3.7	0.5	3.5
1989	100.0	19.2	2.8	58.1	8.6	3.0	4.1	0.6	3.7
1990	100.0	19.7	4.2	55.6	8.6	3.2	4.3	0.6	3.8
1991	100.0	20.7	3.8	53.8	8.9	3.4	4.8	0.3	4.2
1992	100.0	22.4	3.6	51.3	9.4	3.7	4.9	0.6	4.1
1993	100.0	23.9	3.2	48.1	10.4	4.0	5.2	0.8	4.4
Public 2-year colleges									
1977	100.0	16.8	2.0	72.5	5.8	2.0	0.5	0.1	0.4
1978	100.0	16.1	1.8	73.3	5.5	2.3	0.5	0.1	0.4
1979	100.0	15.8	1.9	72.7	6.0	2.5	0.5	0.1	0.5
1980	100.0	16.1	1.3	72.6	6.3	2.6	0.5	0.1	0.5
1981	100.0	16.8	1.2	71.7	6.3	2.8	0.5	0.1	0.6
1982	100.0	18.0	1.1	71.7	5.2	2.9	0.5	0.1	0.5
1983	100.0	19.3	0.8	71.4	4.3	2.9	0.6	0.1	0.5
1984	100.0	19.5	0.9	71.0	4.4	2.9	0.6	0.1	0.5
1985	100.0	19.1	0.7	70.9	4.6	3.4	0.6	0.1	0.5
1986	100.0	18.6	0.6	71.4	4.5	3.7	0.6	0.1	0.6
1987	100.0	18.5	0.7	70.4	4.1	4.8	0.6	0.1	0.6
1988	100.0	18.7	0.7	70.5	4.1	4.7	0.7	0.1	0.5
1989	100.0	19.1	0.7	68.7	4.2	6.0	0.8	0.1	0.5
1990	100.0	19.6	0.7	67.7	4.2	6.3	0.9	0.1	0.5
1991	100.0	20.5	0.7	67.4	4.2	5.7	0.9	0.1	0.5
1992	100.0	22.1	0.8	65.2	4.5	5.8	1.0	0.1	0.5
1993	100.0	26.2	0.6	61.0	5.0	5.6	1.0	0.1	0.7

* Federally supported student aid received through students (e.g., Pell grants) is included under tuition and auxiliary enterprises.

NOTE: The Higher Education Price Index (HEPI) was used to calculate constant dollars, and the CPI was used to forecast the HEPI to July 1995. Data in this table may differ slightly from data appearing in other tables. Data for academic years 1976–77 through 1985–86 include only institutions that provided both enrollment and finance data. See the supplemental note to *Indicator 51* for resources on alternative approaches to adjusting cost and expenditures.

SOURCE: U.S. Department of Education, National Center for Education Statistics, Financial Statistics of Institutions of Higher Education Survey and Integrated Postsecondary Education Data System (IPEDS), "Finance" survey.

Table 55-1   **Average annual salaries (in 1995 constant dollars) of public elementary and secondary teachers: Selected school years ending 1960–95**

School year ending	All teachers	Elementary teachers	Secondary teachers	Beginning teachers*
1960	$25,959	$25,023	$27,419	—
1962	28,018	27,128	29,338	—
1964	29,682	28,740	31,024	—
1966	31,035	30,049	32,356	—
1968	33,330	32,365	34,538	—
1970	34,869	34,004	35,940	—
1971	35,626	34,676	36,779	—
1972	36,014	34,971	37,223	$25,462
1973	36,292	35,290	37,480	—
1974	35,272	34,412	36,278	23,317
1975	34,321	33,417	35,380	—
1976	34,694	33,813	35,622	23,109
1977	34,743	33,793	35,841	—
1978	34,615	33,755	35,600	22,284
1979	33,509	32,727	34,441	—
1980	31,412	30,624	32,374	19,749
1981	31,102	30,373	31,980	—
1982	31,274	30,591	32,135	19,930
1983	32,197	31,468	33,124	—
1984	32,908	32,236	33,837	20,984
1985	34,072	33,495	34,920	—
1986	35,361	34,686	36,269	23,256
1987	36,473	35,771	37,400	—
1988	36,954	36,274	37,961	24,082
1989	37,250	36,567	38,074	—
1990	37,722	37,079	38,543	24,108
1991	37,725	37,048	38,651	—
1992	37,635	36,989	38,476	24,717
1993	37,529	36,788	38,442	24,626
1994	37,407	36,863	38,297	24,670
1995	37,436	36,874	38,249	24,463

— Not available.

* Salary for beginning teachers is for the calendar year.

SOURCE: U.S. Department of Education, National Center for Education Statistics, *Digest of Education Statistics, 1995*, table 76. American Federation of Teachers, *Survey and Analysis of Salary Trends 1995*, December 1995, table III-2.

Table 55-6 Percentage of public school districts and private schools with salary schedules, average scheduled salary (in current dollars) of full-time teachers, by highest degree earned and years of teaching experience, percentage of schools without salary schedules, and average lowest and highest schedules: School year 1993–94

School characteristics	Districts/schools with scheduled salary					Districts/schools without schedules		
	Percent with salary schedules	Bachelor's no experience	Master's no experience	Master's 20 years experience	Highest step on schedule	Percent without salary schedules	Salary range	
							Average Lowest	Average Highest
Public districts	**93.9**	**$21,923**	**$23,956**	**$37,213**	**$40,517**	**6.1**	**$20,179**	**$29,499**
Region								
Northeast	91.9	25,581	27,727	46,594	51,270	8.1	24,164	45,356
Midwest	91.4	20,879	23,013	35,718	38,415	8.6	18,155	22,695
South	99.5	20,407	21,714	30,955	33,848	0.5	—	—
West	94.5	21,913	24,505	37,800	41,318	5.5	—	—
District size								
Less than 1,000	89.6	20,817	22,777	34,360	36,491	10.4	19,575	26,416
1,000 to 4,999	98.2	22,821	24,900	39,687	43,785	1.8	23,741	48,640
5,000 to 9,999	98.8	23,624	25,856	41,349	46,470	1.2	—	—
10,000 or more	99.2	23,212	25,327	39,657	45,578	0.8	—	—
Minority enrollment								
Less than 20 percent	92.6	21,705	23,785	37,125	40,197	7.4	19,550	28,331
20 percent or more	97.2	22,432	24,356	37,404	41,253	2.8	24,179	36,765
Minority teachers								
Less than 20 percent	93.6	21,931	23,991	37,435	40,675	6.4	20,116	29,247
20 percent or more	98.5	21,823	23,523	34,443	38,552	1.5	—	—
Private schools	**63.4**	**16,239**	**17,621**	**25,189**	**27,274**	**36.6**	**13,249**	**21,831**
Region								
Northeast	63.8	16,465	17,694	26,122	28,363	36.2	12,656	24,590
Midwest	68.1	15,849	17,188	25,294	27,246	31.9	13,664	20,389
South	57.7	15,072	16,312	22,151	24,274	42.3	13,220	20,472
West	63.7	18,249	20,108	27,998	30,054	36.3	13,559	22,040
School size								
Less than 150	47.9	15,334	16,684	22,936	24,556	52.1	12,370	19,354
150 to 499	81.9	16,584	17,967	26,206	28,461	18.1	15,570	27,354
500 to 749	80.0	17,975	19,344	28,609	31,241	20.0	17,217	36,524
750 or more	80.3	19,424	21,248	32,261	36,783	19.7	17,066	41,028
Minority enrollment								
Less than 20 percent	63.3	15,930	17,280	24,913	26,990	36.7	12,210	20,941
20 percent or more	63.6	16,925	18,378	25,804	27,904	36.4	15,504	23,760
Minority teachers								
Less than 20 percent	63.3	16,137	17,494	25,231	27,327	36.7	12,978	21,910
20 percent or more	63.6	16,906	18,449	24,912	26,927	36.4	15,065	21,301

— Too few sample observations for a reliable estimate.

NOTE: Included in "total" and "other school composition" are other sources of income reported after excluding outside income. Data for this analysis were calculated from SASS School and Teacher Questionnaires; therefore, salaries shown here may not match other published figures. Excludes a small number of teachers whose schools did not respond to the questionnaire.

SOURCE: U.S. Department of Education, National Center for Education Statistics, Schools and Staffing Survey, 1993–94 (Private School and Teacher Demand and Shortage Questionnaires).

Table 57-2 **Percentage of public secondary students in selected subjects taught by teachers with selected qualifications, by percentage of students eligible for free or reduced-price lunch and class subject: School year 1993–94**

Class subject	Percentage of students eligible for free or reduced-price lunch			
	0–5	6–20	21–40	41–100
Majored in class subject				
English	82.5	76.6	73.6	71.2
Social sciences	89.0	86.7	84.1	80.5
Mathematics	73.3	71.6	65.3	60.1
Science*	83.7	82.0	82.0	73.8
Biology	74.8	66.0	70.2	57.4
Chemistry	57.5	52.7	50.2	54.6
Physics	36.3	33.0	26.2	26.7
Foreign languages	80.4	84.1	74.5	82.1
Visual and performing arts	89.7	87.9	81.5	85.1
Health and physical education	91.2	91.6	90.8	89.9
Vocational education	83.6		82.6	81.6	78.4
Majored or minored in class subject				
English	88.4	82.7	83.9	81.5
Social sciences	91.8	94.0	91.5	87.2
Mathematics	83.3	79.7	76.1	74.1
Science*	92.0	90.1	91.5	86.5
Biology	80.9	73.5	75.7	72.7
Chemistry	77.2	64.8	72.1	62.9
Physics	42.8	50.5	39.3	29.3
Foreign languages	89.4	91.2	86.3	88.0
Visual and performing arts	90.2	89.2	83.9	85.6
Health and physical education	93.9	92.7	93.4	92.7
Vocational education	85.5	84.2	82.3	80.6
Certified in class subject				
English	94.0	91.2	89.9	86.8
Social sciences	92.3	87.8	89.4	86.1
Mathematics	89.3	87.6	86.0	78.8
Science*	93.1	94.3	88.8	86.6
Biology	93.2	92.2	83.3	74.8
Chemistry	92.2	90.9	85.6	80.2
Physics	88.4	88.0	68.1	65.0
Foreign languages	87.2	90.9	87.4	83.4
Visual and performing arts	92.5	87.8	86.9	83.9
Health and physical education	93.5	91.2	91.5	89.6
Vocational education	90.5	89.1	86.8	87.0

* It is easier to have majored, minored, or become certified in "science" than in a specific discipline, such as biology, because a teacher from any scientific field may qualify in "science," whereas a discipline requires a specific match.

SOURCE: U.S. Department of Education, National Center for Education Statistics, Schools and Staffing Survey, 1993–94 (Teacher Questionnaire).

Note on definition of student percentages, certification in class subject, and major/minor in class subject

Indicator 57 reports the percentages of students taught by full-time teachers with different qualifications. These values were calculated from teacher survey information on the number of classes taught, number of students in each class, subject matter of each class, and teachers' education and certification. The information obtained from each teacher was weighted to properly represent national levels.

For example, we used the following procedure to calculate the percentage of mathematics students taught by certified mathematics teachers: First, for each full-time teacher who reported teaching a mathematics class, the weighted number of students in each class was summed to get an estimate of the total number of mathematics students taught by these teachers. Next, for each full-time teacher certified to teach mathematics, the weighted number of students in each mathematics class was summed to get an estimate of the number of mathematics students taught by certified teachers. The two estimates were then divided to obtain the estimated percentage of mathematics students taught by a full-time teacher certified in mathematics. The percentages reported in each of the tables in this analysis were calculated by limiting the selection to specific subjects and specific school and teacher characteristics.

There are many ways to match a major/minor field of study with class subjects. One method is to include both the general or specific field and the education major/minor parallel field as a match for a specific class subject. For example, a teacher who majored or minored in mathematics or mathematics education could be defined as having majored or minored in the subject of mathematics. A stricter definition would exclude the mathematics teachers who majored or minored in mathematics education. The more general definition is used for all the core subjects, including science, in all the tables in this analysis. The stricter definition is used for the specific science disciplines (biology, chemistry, and physics) in all tables.

Classes excluded from the text table and tables 57-1 through 57-5

Some classes are excluded because it was difficult to match each class subject matter to the appropriate major/minor, or because, in the case of computer science, a major in the field has existed for only a few years. The following subject matters were excluded from the tables in this analysis: computer science, driver education, religion, philosophy, and unspecified.

Certification in class subject

Certification, as defined here, includes advanced, standard, and probationary certification by a state or full certification by an accrediting body other than a state. Teachers with a temporary or emergency certification were classified as not certified in this analysis.

The table below shows teacher certifications classified by class subject. Teachers were classified as being certified in a class subject if they were certified in an assignment field (shown in the left-hand column) that corresponds to the subject matter listed in the right-hand column. Only certifications as defined above were considered as we matched subject matter.

Class subject(s)	**Certification in assignment field(s)**
English	English/language arts, reading, bilingual education, English as a second language
Social sciences	Social studies/social sciences (including history), American Indian/Native American studies
Mathematics	Mathematics
Natural sciences	Geology/earth science, space science education, physical science, general science and all other sciences

Biology/life science	Biology/life science
Chemistry	Chemistry
Physics	Physics
Foreign languages	French, German, Latin, Russian, Spanish, other foreign languages, English as a second language
Visual and performing arts	Art, dance, drama/theater, music
Health and physical education	Health, physical education
Vocational education	Accounting, agriculture, business, marketing, health occupations, industrial arts, trade and industry, technical, other vocational/technical education, home economics, journalism

Majored or minored in class subject

Teachers were classified as having majored or minored in the class subject if they majored or minored in a field (shown in the right-hand column) that corresponds to the class subject listed in the left-hand column. Both undergraduate and graduate level degrees were considered in determining if a match had occurred.

<u>Class subject(s)</u>	<u>Major/minor field(s)</u>
English	English, English education, reading education, humanities, English as a second language
Social sciences	Social studies/social sciences education, cross-cultural education, area and ethnic studies, psychology, public affairs, economics, history, political science and government, sociology, other social sciences
Mathematics	Mathematics, mathematics education, engineering, physics
Natural sciences	Geology/earth science, science education, other natural sciences and majors listed below
Biology/life science	Biology/life science
Chemistry	Chemistry
Physics	Physics
Foreign languages	French, German, Latin, Russian, Spanish, other foreign languages, foreign language education, bilingual education, English as a second language
Visual and performing arts	Art (fine and applied), art education, drama, theater, music, music education
Health, physical education	Health professions and occupations, physical education/health education
Vocational education	Agricultural education, home economics education, industrial arts, vocational and technical, trade and industrial education, agricultural and natural resources, business and management, business, commerce, and distributive education, communications and journalism

Table 59-1 Percentage of teachers who participated in a formal teacher induction or a master or mentor program, by years of teaching experience and control and level of school: 1994

Control and level of school	Participated in a formal teacher induction program during first year of teaching			Master or mentor program
	1 year	2–3 years	4 years or more	
Public	**59.9**	**54.8**	**23.3**	**11.3**
Elementary	59.4	54.5	23.8	11.4
Secondary	60.7	55.3	22.5	11.3
Private	**30.2**	**33.8**	**24.2**	**10.1**
Elementary	26.8	31.7	23.5	8.9
Secondary	42.7	39.5	26.0	13.7

NOTE: Excludes a small number of teachers whose schools did not respond to the questionnaire.

SOURCE: U.S. Department of Education, National Center for Education Statistics, Schools and Staffing Survey, 1993–94 (Teacher Questionnaire).

Table 59-2 Percentage of teachers who participated in professional development activities during the 1993–94 school year, by topic, type of support and activity, outcomes, and level, control and urbanicity of school

Topic, type of support and activity, and outcomes of professional development	Elementary teachers				Secondary teachers			
	Total	Central city	Urban fringe/ large town	Rural/ small town	Total	Central city	Urban fringe/ large town	Rural/ small town
Public								
In-service education or professional development topic								
Uses of educational technology for instruction	49.7	51.6	51.7	46.7	50.7	50.8	51.8	49.9
Methods of teaching in specific subject field	69.7	73.4	70.8	65.9	55.0	59.1	55.3	52.2
In-depth study in specific field	31.6	36.6	31.1	28.1	27.5	30.8	27.5	25.4
Student assessment	55.4	56.8	58.2	52.2	45.8	46.7	45.7	45.3
Cooperative learning in the classroom	52.7	56.6	50.7	51.4	49.2	52.1	49.0	47.5
Type of support received during 1993–94 school year for in-service education or professional development								
Released time from teaching	50.7	50.4	52.8	49.3	43.5	42.2	43.6	44.2
Scheduled time (built-in time)	43.6	47.1	42.5	41.9	35.4	37.9	34.1	35.0
Travel and/or per diem expenses	21.2	15.3	18.2	28.1	26.9	21.5	23.5	32.7
Tuition and/or fees	24.3	20.9	24.2	26.9	20.7	17.0	20.3	23.2
Professional growth credits	34.8	35.5	34.1	34.8	28.9	30.7	27.5	29.0
None of above	19.4	20.1	18.4	19.7	27.1	27.0	28.3	26.3
Type of professional development activity								
School district sponsored workshop or in-service	89.6	87.7	91.0	89.9	84.9	82.8	84.7	86.3
School sponsored workshop or in-service	83.7	86.4	83.2	82.1	79.1	81.5	78.7	78.0
University extension or adult education course	25.1	25.3	25.1	24.9	25.5	23.9	26.5	25.7
College course in specific subject field	26.1	26.5	25.1	26.6	24.3	22.6	23.8	25.7
Professional association sponsored workshop	50.5	49.2	52.0	50.3	51.9	51.3	53.1	51.5
Those who agreed with the following statements about their in-service education or professional development*								
Provided information that was new to me	85.4	85.3	86.4	84.8	83.0	81.2	83.4	83.7
Changed my views on teaching	44.0	45.4	41.4	44.9	38.6	38.7	38.8	38.4
Caused me to change my teaching practices	68.0	66.6	69.3	68.0	59.5	57.6	61.5	59.1
Caused me to seek further information or training	64.6	64.5	66.0	63.4	59.1	59.5	59.6	58.3
Were generally a waste of my time	9.1	9.7	8.0	9.6	13.8	15.9	13.1	13.2
Private								
In-service education or professional development topic								
Uses of educational technology for instruction	32.8	33.9	33.1	29.4	38.5	37.0	39.7	40.0
Methods of teaching in specific subject field	63.1	66.7	60.6	60.1	50.8	52.1	50.5	48.0
In-depth study in specific field	24.7	24.6	25.3	23.6	29.2	28.8	29.7	29.3
Student assessment	42.5	46.8	40.3	37.2	34.7	36.2	34.0	32.4
Cooperative learning in the classroom	45.5	49.7	44.2	38.5	38.5	40.8	37.0	35.3

Table 59-2 **Percentage of teachers who participated in professional development activities during the 1993–94 school year, by topic, type of support and activity, outcomes, and level, control and urbanicity of school—Continued**

Topic, type of support and activity, and outcomes of professional development	Elementary teachers				Secondary teachers			
	Total	Central city	Urban fringe/ large town	Rural/ small town	Total	Central city	Urban fringe/ large town	Rural/ small town
Type of support received during 1993–94 school year for in-service education or professional development								
Released time from teaching	42.6	41.4	42.6	45.4	39.2	38.2	38.9	42.7
Scheduled time (built-in time)	37.1	39.4	35.7	34.7	34.3	36.2	34.1	29.3
Travel and/or per diem expenses	19.8	18.2	17.2	29.6	24.6	21.8	22.7	36.4
Tuition and/or fees	36.0	32.3	38.5	39.3	33.3	28.6	35.9	40.7
Professional growth credits	27.7	28.7	25.3	30.6	21.3	21.0	21.9	20.9
None of above	25.1	25.4	25.3	24.0	28.4	30.0	26.8	27.6
Type of professional development activity								
School district sponsored workshop or in-service	78.9	78.7	78.2	80.9	68.9	71.0	67.9	65.3
School sponsored workshop or in-service	78.0	77.9	79.0	75.8	78.4	80.6	78.8	71.4
University extension or adult education course	24.8	26.6	21.3	28.0	23.6	24.7	22.8	22.4
College course in specific subject field	23.7	25.3	20.9	26.1	24.1	25.0	22.9	23.9
Professional association sponsored workshop	46.8	47.7	45.5	47.6	48.2	49.0	48.2	45.8
Those who agreed with the following statements about their in-service education or professional development*								
Provided information that was new to me	85.2	84.8	84.9	86.8	87.1	84.4	88.4	92.0
Changed my views on teaching	41.9	41.9	40.0	46.4	43.7	40.3	46.5	47.3
Caused me to change my teaching practices	65.0	63.9	64.1	70.0	62.8	61.0	65.8	61.6
Caused me to seek further information or training	61.2	60.6	60.6	64.1	62.5	60.6	64.5	63.5
Were generally a waste of my time	6.8	7.2	6.8	5.8	9.4	11.3	8.6	5.6

* Includes those who responded "strongly agree" or "agree."
NOTE: Excludes a small number of teachers whose schools did not respond to the questionnaire.
SOURCE: U.S. Department of Education, National Center for Education Statistics, Schools and Staffing Survey, 1993–94 (Teacher Questionnaire).

Table 60-1   Average salaries (in 1995 constant dollars) of full-time faculty in institutions of higher education, by academic rank and type and control of institution: Selected academic years ending 1972–94

Academic year ending	All institutions			Public institutions			Private institutions		
	Full professor	Associate professor	Assistant professor	Full professor	Associate professor	Assistant professor	Full professor	Associate professor	Assistant professor
All institutions									
1972	$65,453	$49,566	$40,970	$66,119	$50,445	$41,685	$64,143	$47,588	$39,305
1975	58,548	44,408	36,593	59,427	45,627	37,601	56,723	41,533	34,247
1976	58,825	44,297	36,336	59,710	45,528	37,327	57,056	41,420	34,127
1978	56,026	42,326	34,619	56,829	43,434	35,569	54,256	39,504	32,408
1980	50,042	37,813	30,787	50,743	38,853	31,705	48,416	35,220	28,738
1982	52,179	39,399	32,093	52,408	40,200	32,941	51,632	37,384	30,302
1985	55,771	42,021	34,616	55,459	42,597	35,300	56,524	40,644	33,210
1986	58,025	43,637	36,073	58,107	44,433	36,998	57,819	41,733	34,170
1988	59,277	44,392	36,677	59,340	45,353	37,617	59,190	42,392	34,580
1990	60,217	44,917	37,274	60,280	45,823	38,185	60,082	43,121	35,659
1991	61,364	45,757	38,045	61,177	46,516	38,821	61,774	44,175	36,588
1992	61,533	45,994	38,297	60,610	46,285	38,751	63,555	45,388	37,462
1993	61,402	45,899	38,253	60,092	45,951	38,512	64,274	45,791	37,779
1994	62,406	46,590	38,720	61,074	46,690	39,012	65,343	46,386	38,175
4-year institutions									
1972	65,903	49,600	40,934	66,696	50,483	41,658	64,401	47,760	39,415
1975	58,959	44,265	36,333	60,019	45,504	37,333	56,930	41,663	34,351
1976	59,263	44,278	36,257	60,308	45,590	37,317	57,316	41,553	34,233
1978	56,305	42,288	34,466	57,217	43,492	35,475	54,421	39,591	32,479
1980	50,394	37,845	30,692	51,238	39,014	31,679	48,575	35,303	28,820
1982	52,629	39,481	32,051	53,021	40,411	32,984	51,759	37,448	30,378
1985	56,480	42,226	34,705	56,377	42,933	35,485	56,705	40,764	33,338
1986	58,759	43,846	36,152	59,090	44,811	37,203	58,015	41,851	34,303
1988	60,051	44,602	36,803	60,375	45,702	37,846	59,378	42,509	35,081
1990	61,028	45,227	37,430	61,426	46,366	38,490	60,272	43,240	35,764
1991	62,408	46,195	38,291	62,610	47,224	39,245	62,012	44,329	36,720
1992	62,654	46,423	38,544	62,084	46,903	39,123	63,756	45,550	37,606
1993	62,655	46,287	38,511	61,692	46,478	38,883	64,480	45,950	37,919
1994	63,615	46,979	38,999	62,633	47,233	39,433	65,506	46,529	38,292
2-year institutions									
1972	52,671	49,081	41,364	54,280	50,060	41,902	36,798	36,541	33,106
1975	52,259	45,821	38,438	53,174	46,500	38,922	34,363	33,482	29,338
1976	51,437	44,489	36,941	52,695	45,101	37,384	32,264	32,823	28,861
1978	50,873	42,678	35,716	51,766	43,044	36,017	31,523	32,152	27,738
1980	44,247	37,533	31,495	44,926	37,852	31,836	29,181	28,525	23,947
1982	45,415	38,663	32,412	45,826	38,881	32,721	33,300	31,290	25,314
1985	47,007	40,274	33,926	47,437	40,606	34,342	33,090	29,998	25,877
1986	49,524	41,847	35,450	49,994	42,190	35,915	33,659	30,601	26,491
1988	49,341	42,622	35,619	49,700	42,724	35,935	33,761	30,507	26,973
1990	50,112	41,752	35,610	50,621	42,165	36,071	34,741	30,064	28,265
1991	49,626	41,598	35,635	50,173	42,041	36,099	32,615	29,116	27,165
1992	49,626	41,784	35,798	50,014	42,230	36,287	34,592	30,204	27,296
1993	50,098	42,514	35,830	50,433	42,921	36,256	35,258	30,248	28,118
1994	50,598	42,737	36,135	50,867	43,137	36,475	36,570	31,075	28,709

NOTE: Salaries are for full-time instructional faculty on 9- or 10-month contracts. Data for 1990–91 through 1993–94 include imputations for nonrespondent institutions. The Integrated Postsecondary Education Data System (IPEDS) is a universe survey of all institutions and may yield different faculty salaries than would a sample survey such as the National Survey of Postsecondary Faculty (NSOPF).

SOURCE: U.S. Department of Education, National Center for Education Statistics, *Digest of Education Statistics* (based on IPEDS/ HEGIS "Salaries of Full-time Instructional Faculty" surveys) various years.

Note on salaries of full-time postsecondary faculty

Sources of earned income

Basic faculty salary: Income received from the academic institution as indicated by the faculty respondent under a category called "basic salary."

Other income from the academic institution: Income including the estimated value of non-monetary compensation (e.g., food, housing, car) received for: administration, research, coaching, summer session teaching, or other activities not included in the basic salary.

Consulting income: Income received from sources other than the academic institution such as legal or medical services, psychological counseling, outside consulting, freelance work, professional performances or exhibitions, speaking fees, or honoraria.

Other outside income: Income received from sources other than the academic institution, including other academic institutions, self-owned businesses (other than consulting), royalties, commissions, non-monetary compensation from other sources, retirement income, grants or research income, or any other employment.

Total earned income: The sum of all of the above sources.

Types of institutions

Research university: Institution that is among the 100 leading universities receiving federal research funds. Each of these universities awards substantial numbers of doctorates across many fields.

Doctoral university: Institution that offers a full range of baccalaureate programs and PhD degrees in at least three disciplines, but tends to be less focused on research and receives fewer federal research dollars than the research universities.

Comprehensive institution: Institution that offers liberal arts and professional programs. The master's degree is the highest degree offered.

Liberal arts institution: Institution that is smaller and generally more selective than comprehensive colleges and universities. A liberal arts institution primarily offers bachelor's degrees, although some offer master's degrees.

2-year institution: Institution that offers certificate or degree programs through the Associate of Arts level and, with few exceptions, offers no baccalaureate degrees, although some offer master's degrees.

Note on the National Survey of Postsecondary Faculty (NSOPF)

In this analysis, medical institutions and their faculty, as well as medical faculty at other institutions, were excluded from the NSOPF portion of this analysis.

The NSOPF analysis includes full-time faculty who taught at least one class for credit. Teaching assistants and part-time faculty were not included in the estimates.

For more information on NSOPF, see the supplemental note to *Indicator 49*.

Standard Error Tables

General information about standard errors

The information presented in this report was obtained from many sources, including federal and state agencies, private research organizations, and professional associations. The data were collected using many research methods, including surveys of a universe (such as all school districts) or of a sample, compilations of administrative records, and statistical projections. Users of *The Condition of Education* should take particular care when comparing data from different sources. Differences in procedures, timing, phrasing of questions, interviewer training, and so forth mean that the results are not strictly comparable. Following the general discussion of data accuracy below, descriptions of the information sources and data collection methods are presented, grouped by sponsoring organization. More extensive documentation of procedures used in one survey as compared to another does not imply more problems with the data, only that more information is available.

Unless otherwise noted, all statements cited in the text were tested for statistical significance and are statistically significant at the .05 level. Several test procedures were used. Which procedure was used depended upon the type of data being interpreted and the nature of the statement being tested. The most commonly used test procedures were: 1) *t*-tests, 2) multiple *t*-tests with a Bonferroni adjustment to the significance level, 3) linear trend tests, and 4) sign tests. When a simple comparison between two sample estimates was made, for example, between the first and last years in a time series or between males and females, a *t*-test was used. When multiple comparisons between more than two groups were made, and even if only one comparison is cited in the text, a Bonferroni adjustment to the significance level was made to ensure the significance level for the tests as a group was at the .05 level. This procedure commonly arises when making comparisons between racial/ethnic groups and between the United States and other countries. A linear trend test was used when a statement describing a trend, such as the growth of enrollment rates over time, was made or when a statement describing a relationship, such as the relationship between a parent's educational attainment and a student's

reading proficiency, was made. A sign test was used when a statement describing a consistent pattern of differences over the years was made.

The accuracy of any statistic is determined by the joint effects of "sampling" and "nonsampling" errors. Estimates based on a sample will differ somewhat from the figures that would have been obtained if a complete census had been taken using the same survey instruments, instructions, and procedures. In addition to such sampling errors, all surveys, both universe and sample, are subject to design, reporting, and processing errors and errors due to nonresponse. To the extent possible, these nonsampling errors are kept to a minimum by methods built into the survey procedures; however, the effects of nonsampling errors are more difficult to gauge than those produced by sampling variability.

The estimated standard error of a statistic is a measure of the variation due to sampling and can be used to examine the precision obtained in a particular sample. The sample estimate and an estimate of its standard error permit the construction of interval estimates with prescribed confidence that the interval includes the average result of all possible samples. If all possible samples were selected, and each were surveyed under the same conditions, and an estimate and its standard error were calculated from each sample, then approximately 90 percent of the intervals from 1.6 standard errors below the estimate to 1.6 standard errors above the estimate would include the actual value; 95 percent of the intervals from two standard errors below the estimate to two standard errors above the estimate would include the actual value; and 99 percent of all intervals from 2.5 standard errors below the estimate to 2.5 standard errors above the estimate would include the actual value. These intervals are called 90 percent, 95 percent, and 99 percent confidence intervals, respectively.

To illustrate this further, consider the text table for *Indicator 1* and the standard error table S1 for estimates of standard errors from the Current Population Surveys (CPS). For the 1992 estimate of the percentage of 3-year-olds enrolled in school (27.7 percent), table S1 shows a standard error of 1.2. Therefore, we can construct a 95 percent confidence interval from 25.3 to 30.1 (27.7 ± 2 x 1.2). If this procedure were followed for every possible sample, about 95 percent of the intervals would include the actual percentage of 3-year-olds enrolled in school in 1992.

The estimated standard errors for two sample statistics can be used to estimate the precision of the difference between the two statistics and to avoid concluding that there is an actual difference when the difference in sample estimates may be due only to sampling error. The need to be aware of the precision of differences arises, for example, when comparing mean proficiency scores between groups or years in the National Assessment of Educational Progress (NAEP) or when comparing percentages between groups or years in the CPS. The standard error (se) of the difference between sample estimate A and sample estimate B (when A and B don't overlap) is:

$$se_{A-B} = \sqrt{se_A^2 + se_B^2}$$

When the ratio (called a *t*-statistic) of the difference between the two sample statistics and the standard error of the difference as calculated above is less than 2, one cannot be sure the difference is not due only to sampling error and caution should be taken in drawing any conclusions. In this report, for example, using the rationale above, we would not conclude that there is a difference between the two sample statistics. Some analysts, however, use the less restrictive criterion of 1.64, which corresponds to a 10 percent significance level.

To illustrate this further, consider the data on mathematics proficiency of Hispanic 17-year-olds in the 2nd text table for *Indicator 15* and the associated standard error table S15(b). The estimated average mathematics proficiency score for the sample of Hispanic 17-year-olds in 1990 was 284. For the (new) sample in 1992, the estimated average was 292. Is there enough evidence to conclude that the actual average score for all Hispanic 17-year-olds increased 8 points between 1990 and 1992? The standard errors for these two estimates are 2.9 and 2.6, respectively. Using the above formula, the standard error of the difference is calculated as 3.9. The ratio of the estimated difference of 8 to the standard error of the difference of 3.9 is 2.05. Using the table

below, we see that there is less than a 5 percent chance that the 8 point difference is due only to sampling error and one may conclude that the proficiency scores of Hispanic 17-year-olds grew between 1990 and 1992.

Percent chance that a difference is due only to sampling error:

t-statistic	1.00	1.64	1.96	2.57
Percent chance	32	10	5	1

It should be noted that most of the standard errors presented in this report and in the original documents are approximations. That is, to derive estimates of standard errors that would be applicable to a wide variety of items and that could be prepared at a moderate cost, a number of approximations were required. As a result, most of the standard errors presented provide a general order of magnitude rather than the exact standard error for any specific item.

The preceding discussion on sampling variability was directed toward a situation concerning one or two estimates. Determining the accuracy of statistical projections is more difficult. In general, the further away the projection date is from the date of the actual data being used for the projection, the greater the possible error in the projection. If, for instance, annual data from 1980 to 1994 are used to project enrollment in elementary and secondary education, the further beyond 1994 one projects, the more variability in the projection. The enrollment projection for the year 2001 will be less certain than the projection for 1996. A detailed discussion of the projections methodology is contained in *Projections of Education Statistics to 2006* (National Center for Education Statistics 1996).

Both universe and sample surveys are subject to nonsampling errors. Nonsampling errors can arise in various ways including: 1) from respondents or interviewers interpreting questions differently; 2) from respondents estimating the values that they provide; 3) from partial to total nonresponse; 4) from imputation or reweighting to adjust for nonresponse; 5) from inability or unwillingness on the part of respondents to provide correct information; 6) from recording and keying errors; or 7) from overcoverage or undercoverage of the target universe.

Sampling and nonsampling error combine to yield total survey error. Since estimating the magnitude of nonsampling errors would require special experiments or access to independent data, these magnitudes are seldom available. In almost all situations, the sampling error represents an underestimate of the total survey error, and thus an overestimate of the precision of the survey estimates.

To compensate for suspected nonrandom errors, adjustments of the sample estimates are often made. For example, adjustments are frequently made for nonresponse, both partial and total. An adjustment made for either type of nonresponse is often referred to as an imputation—substitution of the "average" questionnaire response for the nonresponse. Imputations are usually made separately within various groups of sample members, which have similar survey characteristics. Imputation for item nonresponse is usually made by substituting for a missing item the response to that item of a respondent having characteristics that are similar to those of the nonrespondent.

In editions prior to the 1992 edition of *The Condition of Education*, when reporting race-specific data from the CPS, Hispanics were usually included among whites and blacks (i.e., "Hispanics may be of any race"). Beginning with the 1992 edition of the report, racial/ethnic data from the CPS excludes Hispanics from whites and blacks (e.g., whites are non-Hispanic whites and blacks are non-Hispanic blacks).

Unless otherwise noted, all dollar values in this volume are expressed in 1995 constant dollars. The Consumer Price Index (CPI) is used to convert current dollars for earlier years to 1995 dollars. The CPI index for calendar year 1995 is 152.7. See table 37 in *the Digest of Education Statistics, 1995* (National Center for Education Statistics 1995) for CPI adjustments.

How to obtain standard errors for the supplemental tables

To obtain estimates of standard errors for the statistics in the supplemental tables, please complete the reply card located in this edition of *The Condition of Education*.

Table S1 (a)   Standard errors for the first text table in *Indicator 1*

October	Age															
	3	4	5	6	7	8	9	10	11	12	13	14	15	16	17	18
1970	0.9	1.1	1.0	0.3	0.1	0.1	0.1	0.1	0.1	0.1	0.1	0.2	0.3	0.5	0.8	1.2
1980	1.2	1.4	0.7	0.2	0.2	0.2	0.1	0.2	0.1	0.1	0.1	0.3	0.3	0.6	0.8	1.1
1990	—	—	0.7	0.1	0.2	0.1	0.2	0.2	0.2	0.2	0.2	0.2	0.3	0.5	0.8	1.3
1993	1.2	1.3	0.7	0.3	0.2	0.2	0.2	0.2	0.2	0.1	0.2	0.2	0.3	0.5	0.8	1.3
1994	—	—	0.6	0.3	0.2	0.3	0.2	0.2	0.2	0.2	0.2	0.3	0.3	0.5	0.7	1.3

October	Age															
	19	20	21	22	23	24	25	26	27	28	29	30	31	32	33	34
1970	1.2	1.3	1.2	1.0	0.9	1.0	0.9	0.8	0.8	0.7	0.8	0.7	0.8	0.7	0.7	0.7
1980	1.1	1.1	1.1	1.0	0.9	0.8	0.8	0.7	0.7	0.7	0.6	0.6	0.6	0.5	0.5	0.6
1990	1.3	1.3	1.3	1.2	1.1	1.0	0.8	0.8	0.7	0.7	0.6	0.6	0.6	0.5	0.5	0.5
1993	1.4	1.4	1.3	1.2	1.1	1.0	0.9	0.8	0.7	0.7	0.7	0.6	0.6	0.5	0.5	0.5
1994	1.3	1.4	1.3	1.3	1.1	1.0	0.9	0.9	0.8	0.7	0.6	0.7	0.6	0.6	0.6	0.6

Table S1(b)   Standard errors for the second text table in *Indicator 1*

October	Age													
	3	4	5	16	17	18	19	20	21	22	23	24	25
1970	0.9	1.1	1.0	0.5	0.8	1.2	1.2	1.3	1.2	1.0	0.9	1.0	0.9
1972	0.9	1.2	0.9	0.5	0.8	1.1	1.2	1.2	1.1	1.0	0.9	0.9	0.8
1974	1.0	1.2	0.8	0.5	0.8	1.1	1.1	1.1	1.1	1.0	0.9	0.9	0.9
1976	1.1	1.3	0.7	0.6	0.8	1.1	1.1	1.1	1.1	1.0	0.9	0.8	0.8
1978	1.2	1.4	0.8	0.5	0.8	1.1	1.1	1.1	1.1	1.0	0.9	0.8	0.8
1980	1.2	1.4	0.7	0.6	0.8	1.1	1.1	1.1	1.1	1.0	0.9	0.8	0.8
1982	1.2	1.4	0.8	0.6	0.8	1.2	1.2	1.2	1.1	1.0	0.9	0.8	0.7
1984	1.2	1.4	0.8	0.5	0.8	1.2	1.3	1.2	1.1	1.1	0.9	0.8	0.7
1986	1.2	1.3	0.7	0.5	0.8	1.2	1.3	1.2	1.1	1.1	1.0	0.9	0.8
1988	1.3	1.5	0.8	0.6	0.9	1.3	1.4	1.4	1.3	1.2	1.0	1.0	0.8
1990	—	—	0.7	0.6	0.9	1.3	1.3	1.3	1.3	1.2	1.1	1.0	0.9
1991	1.2	1.4	0.8	0.5	0.8	1.3	1.4	1.3	1.3	1.1	1.1	1.0	0.9
1992	1.2	1.4	0.7	0.5	0.7	1.3	1.4	1.4	1.3	1.2	1.1	1.0	0.9
1993	1.2	1.3	0.7	0.5	0.8	1.3	1.3	1.4	1.3	1.3	1.1	1.0	0.9
1994	—	—	0.6	0.5	0.7	1.3	1.3	1.4	1.3	1.3	1.1	1.0	0.9

— Not available.

SOURCE: U.S. Department of Commerce, Bureau of the Census, October Current Population Surveys.

Table S2   Standard errors for the text table in *Indicator 2*

	Enrollment rate								
	3-year-olds			4-year-olds			5-year-olds		
Student characteristics	Total	Center-based programs	Kinder-garten	Total	Center-based programs	Kinder-garten	Total	Center-based programs	Kinder-garten
Total	**1.5**	**1.5**	**0.2**	**1.5**	**1.5**	**0.3**	**0.8**	**1.0**	**1.3**
Race/ethnicity									
White	2.3	2.3	0.2	2.0	2.0	0.3	1.0	1.3	1.6
Black	4.2	4.2	0.7	4.3	4.1	0.9	2.4	2.5	3.5
Hispanic	2.5	2.6	0.8	2.9	3.1	1.5	1.7	2.3	2.5
Family income									
$10,000 or less	3.8	3.7	0.4	4.0	4.0	0.4	2.8	2.4	3.5
10,001–20,000	3.7	3.7	0.0	4.1	4.1	0.8	2.6	2.3	3.4
20,001–35,000	2.8	2.8	0.3	2.8	2.8	0.6	1.5	2.0	2.3
35,001–50,000	3.4	3.4	0.8	3.0	2.9	0.9	2.1	2.3	2.7
50,001 or more	3.0	3.0	0.1	2.3	2.1	0.6	1.6	1.9	2.2
Parents' highest education level									
Less than high school diploma	3.7	3.3	1.3	5.9	5.7	0.6	2.5	3.5	4.3
High school diploma or GED	2.5	2.5	0.4	2.7	2.6	0.5	1.6	1.6	2.1
Some college/vocational/ technical	2.6	2.6	0.3	2.8	3.0	0.6	1.7	2.2	2.5
Bachelor's degree	3.6	3.6	0.2	3.6	3.9	0.9	1.6	2.4	2.8
Graduate/professional school	5.0	4.5	0.4	3.1	3.3	0.9	2.9	3.1	3.6
Family structure									
Two biological or adoptive parents	1.8	1.8	0.3	1.7	1.6	0.4	1.0	1.2	1.4
One biological or adoptive parent	3.2	3.2	0.0	3.3	3.2	0.5	1.3	1.8	2.1
One biological and one step parent	8.8	7.8	2.7	6.6	6.6	1.8	4.7	3.4	4.7
Other relatives	7.3	7.3	0.0	10.2	10.2	0.0	7.8	8.5	10.1

SOURCE: U.S. Department of Education, National Center for Education Statistics, National Household Education Survey (NHES), 1995 (Early Childhood Program Participation File).

Table S3   Standard errors for the text table in *Indicator 3*

October	Total	Family income			Sex		Race/ethnicity		
		Low	Middle	High	Male	Female	White	Black	Hispanic
1972	0.8	3.1	1.0	1.6	1.2	1.1	0.9	2.5	3.6
1973	0.8	3.0	1.0	1.6	1.2	1.1	0.9	2.4	3.5
1974	0.8	—	—	—	1.2	1.1	0.9	2.1	3.2
1975	0.8	3.0	1.0	1.6	1.2	1.1	0.9	2.2	3.1
1976	0.8	2.7	0.9	1.5	1.2	1.0	0.9	2.2	3.1
1977	0.8	2.6	1.0	1.6	1.3	1.1	1.0	2.2	2.9
1978	0.9	2.8	1.1	1.7	1.4	1.2	1.0	2.4	3.5
1979	0.9	2.7	1.2	1.6	1.4	1.3	—	—	—
1980	1.0	2.9	1.2	2.0	1.5	1.3	1.1	2.6	3.4
1981	1.0	2.7	1.2	1.9	1.4	1.3	1.1	2.5	2.8
1982	1.1	2.6	1.3	2.4	1.5	1.4	1.2	2.8	3.4
1983	1.0	2.7	1.3	1.9	1.5	1.4	1.2	2.6	3.5
1984	1.1	2.7	1.4	1.8	1.5	1.4	1.2	2.9	3.5
1985	1.1	2.7	1.3	2.4	1.5	1.4	1.2	2.6	3.4
1986	1.1	2.6	1.4	2.1	1.6	1.4	1.3	2.7	3.3
1987	1.1	2.8	1.3	2.3	1.6	1.5	1.3	2.8	3.2
1988	1.2	2.8	1.5	2.5	1.7	1.6	1.4	2.7	3.8
1989	1.2	3.0	1.5	2.5	1.7	1.6	1.5	2.8	3.7
1990	1.1	2.8	1.5	2.3	1.6	1.6	1.4	2.8	3.4
1991	1.1	2.8	1.4	2.2	1.6	1.5	1.3	2.9	3.1
1992	1.1	2.6	1.4	2.2	1.5	1.5	1.3	2.8	3.1
1993	1.1	2.8	1.4	2.0	1.6	1.4	1.3	2.6	3.3
1994	1.1	2.6	1.4	2.2	1.6	1.5	1.3	2.7	3.2

— Not available.

SOURCE: U.S. Department of Commerce, Bureau of the Census, October Current Population Surveys.

Table S4   Standard errors for the text table in *Indicator 4*

Student characteristics	Chosen school			Assigned public school		
	Total	Public	Private	Total	Choice of residence influenced by school	Other
Total	**0.4**	**0.4**	**0.3**	**0.4**	**0.6**	**0.6**
Race/ethnicity						
White	0.6	0.5	0.4	0.6	0.8	0.7
Black	1.1	1.0	0.4	1.1	1.5	1.3
Hispanic	1.2	1.1	0.6	1.2	1.4	1.8
Urbanicity						
Inside urban area	0.6	0.4	0.4	0.6	0.7	0.7
Outside urban area	1.0	0.9	0.6	1.0	1.6	1.6
Rural	1.4	1.3	0.5	1.4	1.8	1.3
Parents' highest education level						
Less than high school diploma	1.3	1.3	0.5	1.3	2.4	2.6
High school diploma or GED	0.8	0.7	0.4	0.8	0.9	1.1
Some college/vocational/technical	0.9	0.8	0.5	0.9	0.9	0.9
Bachelor's degree	1.7	0.8	1.3	1.7	1.6	1.8
Graduate/professional school	1.1	0.8	1.0	1.1	1.2	1.2
Family income						
Less than $15,000	1.2	1.2	0.5	1.2	1.3	1.5
15,001–30,000	0.9	0.8	0.5	0.9	1.2	1.3
30,001–50,000	0.7	0.6	0.7	0.7	1.2	1.1
50,001 or more	0.8	0.5	0.7	0.8	0.9	0.7

SOURCE: U.S. Department of Education, National Center for Education Statistics, National Household Education Survey (NHES), 1993 (School Safety and Discipline File).

Table S5 **Standard errors for the text table in** *Indicator 5*

October	Total	Sex		Race/ethnicity			Family income		
		Male	Female	White	Black	Hispanic	Low	Middle	High
1972	0.2	0.3	0.3	0.2	0.9	1.5	1.1	0.3	0.3
1973	0.2	0.4	0.3	0.2	1.0	1.5	1.2	0.3	0.2
1974	0.2	0.4	0.3	0.3	1.0	1.4	—	—	—
1975	0.2	0.3	0.3	0.2	0.9	1.4	1.1	0.3	0.3
1976	0.2	0.3	0.3	0.3	0.8	1.1	1.1	0.3	0.2
1977	0.2	0.4	0.3	0.3	0.9	1.2	1.1	0.4	0.3
1978	0.3	0.4	0.3	0.3	1.0	1.5	1.2	0.4	0.3
1979	0.3	0.4	0.4	0.3	1.0	1.4	1.2	0.3	0.3
1980	0.2	0.4	0.3	0.3	0.9	1.4	1.1	0.3	0.3
1981	0.2	0.3	0.3	0.3	1.0	1.3	1.1	0.3	0.3
1982	0.3	0.4	0.4	0.3	1.0	1.6	1.3	0.4	0.3
1983	0.3	0.4	0.4	0.3	1.0	1.6	1.1	0.4	0.3
1984	0.3	0.4	0.4	0.3	0.9	1.7	1.2	0.4	0.3
1985	0.3	0.4	0.4	0.3	1.1	2.3	1.3	0.4	0.3
1986	0.3	0.4	0.4	0.3	0.9	2.4	1.1	0.4	0.3
1987	0.3	0.4	0.4	0.3	1.0	1.7	1.1	0.4	0.2
1988	0.4	0.6	0.6	0.4	1.3	4.6	1.8	0.5	0.4
1989	0.4	0.6	0.6	0.4	1.6	3.9	1.6	0.6	0.4
1990	0.3	0.5	0.5	0.4	1.1	2.3	1.4	0.4	0.3
1991	0.3	0.5	0.5	0.4	1.2	2.2	1.4	0.4	0.3
1992	0.4	0.5	0.5	0.4	1.1	2.2	1.4	0.5	0.4
1993	0.4	0.5	0.5	0.4	1.2	2.0	1.6	0.5	0.4
1994	0.4	0.5	0.5	0.4	1.2	2.2	1.6	0.5	0.4

— Not available.

SOURCE: U.S. Department of Education, National Center for Education Statistics, *Dropout Rates in the United States: 1994*, table A1 (based on the October Current Population Surveys).

Table S6   Standard errors for the text table in *Indicator 6*

Selected characteristics	Status in August following scheduled high school graduation			Status of August dropouts in the spring 2 years later				Total completed spring 2 years following scheduled graduation
	Completed high school	Still enrolled	Dropout	Graduated	Received alternative credential	Enrolled in high school	Dropout	
1990 Sophomore Cohort								
Total	**0.5**	**0.4**	**0.4**	**3.6**	**1.4**	**2.9**	**3.2**	**0.4**
Sex								
Male	0.8	0.6	0.5	4.0	1.9	3.4	4.4	0.7
Female	0.7	0.5	0.6	5.3	2.0	4.6	4.4	0.6
Race/ethnicity								
White	0.5	0.3	0.3	3.8	2.1	3.3	3.8	0.4
Black	2.2	2.0	1.2	10.6	2.2	7.5	7.1	1.9
Hispanic	1.8	1.3	1.4	3.2	1.7	8.1	7.5	1.7
Mathematics achievement in 10th grade								
Below lowest quartile	1.2	1.0	0.9	3.7	1.6	3.5	3.9	1.1
Above lowest quartile	0.4	0.3	0.3	6.8	2.8	5.0	5.3	0.3
1980 Sophomore Cohort								
Total	**0.6**	**0.4**	**0.4**	**1.2**	**1.2**	**1.7**	**2.1**	**0.5**
Sex								
Male	0.8	0.6	0.6	1.6	1.8	2.2	2.9	0.7
Female	0.7	0.5	0.5	2.0	1.6	2.6	3.1	0.6
Race/ethnicity								
White	0.6	0.4	0.5	1.6	1.6	2.2	2.7	0.5
Black	1.4	1.1	1.1	3.2	1.6	4.1	4.9	1.5
Hispanic	1.9	1.3	1.6	2.1	2.4	1.6	3.8	1.7
Mathematics achievement in 10th grade								
Below lowest quartile	1.0	0.7	0.9	1.5	1.3	2.2	2.6	1.0
Above lowest quartile	0.4	0.4	0.2	1.7	2.3	1.7	3.0	0.3

SOURCE: U.S. Department of Education, National Center for Education Statistics, High School and Beyond (HS&B) study, Sophomore Cohort, Base Year, First, and Second Follow-up Surveys; and National Education Longitudinal Study of 1988, First, Second, and Third Follow-up surveys.

Table S7   Standard errors for the text table in *Indicator 7*

October	Total	Type of college		Family income			Race/ethnicity		
		2-year	4-year	Low	Middle	High	White	Black	Hispanic
1972	1.3	—	—	3.4	1.7	2.2	1.4	4.6	9.8
1973	1.3	0.9	1.2	3.2	1.7	2.1	1.4	4.3	9.0
1975	1.3	1.0	1.2	3.6	1.7	2.1	1.4	4.7	8.5
1977	1.3	1.0	1.2	3.5	1.8	2.0	1.4	4.7	8.0
1979	1.3	1.0	1.2	3.8	1.7	2.0	1.4	4.7	7.9
1981	1.3	1.1	1.2	3.9	1.7	2.1	1.4	4.4	8.2
1983	1.4	1.1	1.3	4.0	1.9	2.2	1.6	4.4	9.0
1985	1.5	1.2	1.4	4.1	2.0	2.2	1.6	4.8	9.8
1987	1.5	1.2	1.4	3.9	2.1	2.2	1.7	4.8	8.3
1989	1.7	1.4	1.7	4.6	2.3	2.7	1.9	5.3	10.5
1990	1.6	1.3	1.6	4.8	2.1	2.5	1.8	5.1	10.8
1991	1.6	1.4	1.6	4.5	2.2	2.4	1.8	5.3	9.6
1992	1.6	1.4	1.6	4.4	2.2	2.3	1.8	4.9	8.5
1993	1.6	1.4	1.6	4.6	2.1	2.5	1.9	5.3	8.2
1994	1.5	1.3	1.6	4.4	2.1	2.4	1.7	5.2	9.5

— Not available.

SOURCE: U.S. Department of Commerce, Bureau of the Census, October Current Population Surveys.

Table S8   Standard errors for the text table in *Indicator 8*

October	Aged 18–24				Aged 25–34				Aged 35 or older			
	Total	White	Black	Hispanic	Total	White	Black	Hispanic	Total	White	Black	Hispanic
1972	0.5	0.5	1.7	3.3	0.3	0.3	1.1	2.0	—	—	—	—
1973	0.5	0.5	1.6	3.4	0.3	0.3	1.0	2.4	—	—	—	—
1974	0.5	0.5	1.6	3.2	0.3	0.3	1.1	2.2	—	—	—	—
1975	0.5	0.5	1.7	3.3	0.3	0.3	1.1	2.1	—	—	—	—
1976	0.5	0.5	1.7	3.2	0.3	0.3	1.1	2.0	0.1	0.1	0.6	1.2
1977	0.5	0.5	1.6	3.1	0.3	0.3	1.2	2.1	—	—	—	—
1978	0.4	0.5	1.6	2.9	0.2	0.3	1.0	1.8	0.1	0.1	0.6	1.2
1979	0.4	0.5	1.6	2.9	0.2	0.3	0.9	1.9	0.1	0.1	0.5	0.9
1980	0.4	0.5	1.5	2.8	0.2	0.3	0.9	1.6	0.1	0.1	0.5	0.9
1981	0.4	0.5	1.5	2.7	0.2	0.2	0.9	1.6	0.1	0.1	0.5	1.0
1982	0.5	0.5	1.5	2.8	0.2	0.3	0.9	1.6	0.1	0.1	0.5	0.9
1983	0.5	0.5	1.5	2.9	0.2	0.3	0.8	1.6	0.1	0.1	0.4	0.9
1984	0.5	0.5	1.5	2.8	0.2	0.3	0.8	1.6	0.1	0.1	0.4	0.6
1985	0.5	0.5	1.5	2.8	0.2	0.3	0.7	1.6	0.1	.0.1	0.4	0.9
1986	0.5	0.6	1.5	2.7	0.2	0.2	0.8	1.5	0.1	0.1	0.4	0.8
1987	0.5	0.6	1.5	2.6	0.2	0.2	0.7	1.4	0.1	0.1	0.4	0.7
1988	0.6	0.6	1.7	3.3	0.2	0.3	0.8	1.5	0.1	0.1	0.4	0.9
1989	0.6	0.7	1.7	3.1	0.2	0.3	0.7	1.5	0.1	0.1	0.3	0.9
1990	0.5	0.6	1.7	2.8	0.2	0.3	0.7	1.3	0.1	0.1	0.4	0.8
1991	0.6	0.6	1.7	2.9	0.2	0.3	0.8	1.4	0.1	0.1	0.4	0.7
1992	0.6	0.6	1.7	2.9	0.2	0.3	0.7	1.4	0.1	0.1	0.3	0.7
1993	0.6	0.6	1.7	2.8	0.2	0.3	0.8	1.4	0.1	0.1	0.4	0.7
1994	0.6	0.6	1.7	2.7	0.2	0.3	0.8	1.4	0.1	0.1	0.4	0.8

— Not available.

SOURCE: U.S. Department of Commerce, Bureau of the Census, October Current Population Surveys.

Table S9   Standard errors for the text table in *Indicator 9*

Selected characteristics	Attainment at first institution			1994 attainment at any institution									
				Attained						No degree			
					Certificate		Associate's				Enrolled		
	None	Certi-ficate	Asso-ciate's	Total	Not en-rolled at 4-year	En-rolled at 4-year	Not en-rolled at 4-year	En-rolled at 4-year	Bache-lor's	Total	Less-than-4-year	4-year	Not en-rolled
Total	1.7	1.0	1.6	1.9	1.3	0.3	1.5	0.7	1.0	1.5	1.3	0.9	2.0
Age as of 12/31/89													
18 years or younger	2.5	1.0	2.6	2.6	1.6	0.7	2.3	1.3	2.0	2.1	1.7	1.6	2.7
19 years	4.4	2.5	3.9	4.5	3.4	0.0	3.5	1.6	1.2	3.9	3.4	2.6	4.8
20–29 years	3.4	2.0	2.7	3.8	3.1	0.0	2.1	1.0	1.1	3.1	3.0	1.0	4.3
30 years or older	3.8	2.9	2.2	4.5	3.5	0.0	2.4	0.6	0.6	2.9	2.9	0.0	4.4
Enrollment status, first term													
Full-time	2.7	1.3	2.5	2.8	1.8	0.6	2.0	1.2	1.9	1.8	1.4	1.3	2.8
At least half, less than full-time	2.6	1.3	2.4	3.6	2.5	0.6	2.9	1.0	1.0	3.5	3.1	2.0	4.0
Less than half-time	2.9	2.3	2.2	3.5	3.0	0.0	2.3	0.9	1.3	2.9	2.6	1.8	4.6
First transfer													
Did not transfer	2.4	1.6	2.0	2.5	1.7	(*)	1.9	(*)	(*)	1.6	1.6	(*)	2.5
Transferred to less-than-4-year	2.2	1.5	1.8	4.9	4.2	0.0	3.2	0.0	0.6	3.8	3.8	0.0	4.5
Transferred to 4-year	3.7	0.6	3.6	4.0	0.6	1.4	2.7	3.1	3.8	3.2	1.7	3.0	2.9
Average number of months enrolled at first institution	0.5	2.1	1.2	0.9	1.1	—	1.6	1.6	1.2	1.3	1.9	2.3	0.5

— Not available.

* Not applicable.

SOURCE: U.S. Department of Education, National Center for Education Statistics, 1990 Beginning Postsecondary Students Longitudinal Study, Second Follow-up (BPS:90/94).

Table S10   Standard errors for the text table in *Indicator 10*

| Selected characteristics | Completed a degree | | | | Still enrolled for bach-elor's | No degree, no longer enrolled toward a bachelor's | | | | | | |
| | Highest degree completed | | | Total any de-gree | | Total no degree | Number of months enrolled | | | | | |
	Bach-elor's	Asso-ciate's	Certi-ficate				Less than 9	9–18	19–27	28–36	37–45	More than 45
Total	**1.4**	**0.9**	**0.5**	**1.3**	**1.0**	**1.2**	**0.5**	**0.8**	**0.6**	**0.7**	**0.5**	**0.4**
Level of first institution												
4-year	1.4	0.4	0.3	1.3	0.9	1.1	0.4	0.5	0.5	0.5	0.4	0.3
2-year	2.0	3.4	2.0	3.7	3.1	3.5	1.7	3.1	2.2	2.3	1.8	1.3
Age as of 12/31/89												
18 years or younger	1.5	0.9	0.6	1.5	1.1	1.3	0.4	0.7	0.8	0.7	0.5	0.5
19 years	2.9	1.3	1.1	3.1	2.9	3.1	1.4	2.5	0.9	1.6	1.1	0.9
20–29 years	3.6	3.9	3.4	4.9	4.5	5.8	3.0	3.9	2.3	1.3	4.0	0.6
30 years or older	3.3	4.5	1.8	5.9	7.0	8.6	7.1	9.7	2.6	6.7	0.6	0.0
Enrollment status, first term												
Full-time	1.4	0.6	0.4	1.3	1.0	1.2	0.4	0.7	0.6	0.7	0.4	0.4
At least half, less than full-time	3.1	4.5	2.5	4.8	4.1	4.9	2.5	4.4	1.8	1.5	3.2	1.5
Less than half-time	4.7	3.1	6.6	7.9	7.8	8.9	5.8	3.9	6.7	5.5	0.3	3.7
Received aid in 1989–1990												
No	2.0	1.6	0.9	2.1	1.6	1.8	0.8	1.3	1.1	1.0	0.8	0.6
Yes	1.6	0.6	0.4	1.5	0.9	1.4	0.6	0.8	0.6	0.8	0.6	0.5

SOURCE: U.S. Department of Education, National Center for Education Statistics, 1990 Beginning Postsecondary Students Longitudinal Study, Second Follow-up (BPS:90/94).

Table S11(a)   Standard errors for the first text table in *Indicator 11*

| Year of college graduation | Total | | | | Male | | | | Female | | | |
	4 years or less	5 years or less	6 years or less	More than 6 years	4 years or less	5 years or less	6 years or less	More than 6 years	4 years or less	5 years or less	6 years or less	More than 6 years
1977	1.5	1.4	1.3	1.3	1.6	1.5	1.4	1.4	1.7	1.5	1.4	1.4
1986	0.9	0.9	0.8	0.8	1.0	1.1	1.0	1.0	0.9	0.9	0.9	0.9
1990	0.8	1.0	1.0	1.0	1.0	1.1	1.0	1.0	0.9	1.1	1.1	1.1
1993	1.1	1.2	1.1	1.1	1.3	1.5	1.3	1.3	1.3	1.3	1.2	1.2

SOURCE: U.S. Department of Education, National Center for Education Statistics, Recent College Graduates Survey for 1977–90 graduates and 1993 Baccalaureate and Beyond Longitudinal Study, First Follow-up (B&B:93/94).

Table S11(b)   Standard errors for the second text table in *Indicator 11*

Student and institution characteristics	4 years or less	More than 4 up to 5 years	More than 5 up to 6 years	More than 6 years
Total	**1.2**	**0.8**	**0.5**	**1.0**
Years between high school graduation and beginning postsecondary education				
Less than 1 year	1.2	0.8	0.5	1.0
One year or more	1.1	1.6	1.3	2.1
First institution attended				
4-year	1.3	0.9	0.5	0.9
2-year	1.6	1.7	1.3	2.1
Institution granting bachelor's degree				
Public 4-year	1.3	0.9	0.6	1.1
Private 4-year	2.3	1.0	0.6	2.1

SOURCE: U.S. Department of Education, National Center for Education Statistics, 1993 Baccalaureate and Beyond Longitudinal Study, First Follow-up (B&B:93/94).

Table S13   Standard errors for the text table in *Indicator 13*

Type and control of institution and family income of dependent students	Tuition and fees	Total cost	Grant aid	Total aid	Net cost	Ratios	
						Grants to tuition and fees	Net cost to total cost
Public 4-year institutions							
Dependent, full-time students	$85	$105	$25	$47	$136	1	2
Low income	60	107	53	91	120	3	2
Lower middle	76	109	44	85	128	2	2
Upper middle	82	106	32	60	140	1	2
High income	107	122	26	41	150	1	2
Private, not-for-profit, 4-year							
Dependent, full-time students	403	407	111	171	434	2	3
Low income	781	786	424	690	403	8	4
Lower middle	387	395	229	301	362	3	2
Upper middle	303	310	211	273	349	2	2
High income	358	363	95	137	446	1	3
Public 2-year							
Dependent, full-time students	55	82	33	49	153	4	3
Low income	59	106	92	113	245	12	4
Lower middle	73	107	55	82	165	6	3
Upper middle	105	125	36	50	278	3	4
High income	129	142	26	43	210	2	4

SOURCE: U.S. Department of Education, National Center for Education Statistics, National Postsecondary Student Aid Study, 1993 (Data Analysis System).

Table S14   Standard errors for the text table in *Indicator 14*

Educational attainment and labor force status	1991 total	1995				
		Total	Type of adult education activity			
			Basic skills	Credential	Work-related	Personal
Total	**1.0**	**0.5**	**0.1**	**0.2**	**0.4**	**0.4**
Educational attainment						
Grade 8 or less	1.4	1.1	0.5	0.1	0.6	1.0
Grades 9–12	2.3	1.4	0.5	0.3	0.7	1.0
High school diploma	1.1	0.8	0.1	0.3	0.7	0.6
Vocational/technical school	3.8	2.1	0.3	0.9	1.7	1.9
Some college	1.6	0.9	0.1	0.6	0.7	1.0
Associate's degree	5.9	1.9	0.2	0.8	1.5	1.5
Bachelor's degree or higher	2.0	1.0	—	0.4	0.9	0.7
Labor force status						
Employed	1.0	0.5	0.1	0.2	0.5	0.6
Unemployed	3.1	1.9	0.7	0.8	1.2	2.3
Not in labor force	1.0	0.7	0.1	0.2	0.2	0.7

— Not applicable.

SOURCE: U.S. Department of Education, National Center for Education Statistics, National Household Education Survey (NHES), 1991 and 1995 (Adult Education Component).

Table S15(a) Standard errors for the first text table in *Indicator 15*

Year	Total			Male			Female		
	Age 9	Age 13	Age 17	Age 9	Age 13	Age 17	Age 9	Age 13	Age 17
1973	0.8	0.8	1.1	0.7	1.3	1.2	1.1	1.1	1.1
1978	0.8	1.1	1.0	0.7	1.3	1.0	1.0	1.1	1.0
1982	1.1	1.1	0.9	1.2	1.4	1.0	1.2	1.1	1.0
1986	1.0	1.2	0.9	1.1	1.1	1.2	1.2	1.5	1.0
1990	0.8	0.9	0.9	0.9	1.2	1.1	1.1	0.9	1.1
1992	0.8	0.9	0.9	1.0	1.1	1.1	1.0	1.0	1.1

Table S15(b) Standard errors for the second text table in *Indicator 15*

Year	White			Black			Hispanic		
	Age 9	Age 13	Age 17	Age 9	Age 13	Age 17	Age 9	Age 13	Age 17
1973	1.0	0.9	1.1	1.8	1.9	1.3	2.4	2.2	2.2
1978	0.9	0.8	0.9	1.1	1.9	1.3	2.2	2.0	2.3
1982	1.1	1.0	0.9	1.6	1.6	1.2	1.3	1.7	1.8
1986	1.1	1.3	1.0	1.6	2.3	2.1	2.1	2.9	2.9
1990	0.8	1.1	1.0	2.2	2.3	2.8	2.1	1.8	2.9
1992	0.8	0.9	0.8	2.0	1.9	2.2	2.3	1.8	2.6

SOURCE: U.S. Department of Education, National Center for Education Statistics, National Assessment of Educational Progress, *Trends in Academic Progress: Achievement of U.S. Students in Science, 1969 to 1992; Mathematics, 1973 to 1992; Reading, 1971 to 1992; and Writing, 1984 to 1992,* 1994.

Table S16(a) Standard errors for the first text table in *Indicator 16*

Year	Total			Male			Female		
	Age 9	Age 13	Age 17	Age 9	Age 13	Age 17	Age 9	Age 13	Age 17
1970	1.2	1.1	1.0	1.3	1.3	1.2	1.2	1.2	1.1
1973	1.2	1.1	1.0	1.3	1.3	1.2	1.2	1.2	1.1
1977	1.2	1.1	1.0	1.3	1.3	1.2	1.2	1.2	1.1
1982	1.8	1.3	1.2	2.3	1.5	1.4	2.0	1.3	1.3
1986	1.2	1.4	1.4	1.4	1.6	1.9	1.4	1.5	1.5
1990	0.8	0.9	1.1	1.1	1.1	1.3	1.0	1.1	1.6
1992	1.0	0.8	1.3	1.2	1.2	1.7	1.0	1.0	1.5

Table S16(b) Standard errors for the second text table in *Indicator 16*

Year	White			Black			Hispanic		
	Age 9	Age 13	Age 17	Age 9	Age 13	Age 17	Age 9	Age 13	Age 17
1970	0.9	0.8	0.8	1.9	2.4	1.5	—	—	—
1973	0.9	0.8	0.8	1.9	2.4	1.5	—	—	—
1977	0.9	0.8	0.7	1.8	2.4	1.5	2.7	1.9	2.2
1982	1.9	1.1	1.0	3.0	1.3	1.7	4.2	3.9	2.3
1986	1.2	1.4	1.7	1.9	2.5	2.9	3.1	3.1	3.8
1990	0.8	0.9	1.1	2.0	3.1	4.5	2.2	2.6	4.4
1992	1.0	1.0	1.3	2.7	2.7	3.2	2.8	2.6	5.6

— Not available.

SOURCE: U.S. Department of Education, National Center for Education Statistics, National Assessment of Educational Progress, *Trends in Academic Progress: Achievement of U.S. Students in Science, 1969 to 1992; Mathematics, 1973 to 1992; Reading, 1971 to 1992; and Writing, 1984 to 1992,* 1994.

Table S17   Standard errors for the text table in *Indicator 17*

Selected characteristics	Grade 4				Grade 8				Grade 12			
	1992		1994		1992		1994		1992		1994	
	Percent	Score	Percent	Score	Percent	Score	Percent	Score	Percent	Score	Percent	Score
Total	—	**0.9**	—	**1.0**	—	**0.9**	—	**0.8**	—	**0.6**	—	**0.7**
Number of different types of reading materials at home												
Four	0.9	1.3	0.8	1.1	0.8	0.9	0.8	0.9	0.7	0.6	0.7	0.9
Three	0.7	1.3	0.7	1.2	0.5	1.3	0.5	1.1	0.6	0.9	0.6	1.1
Two or fewer	0.8	0.9	0.9	1.4	0.7	1.2	0.6	1.3	0.4	1.1	0.5	1.1
Frequency of reading for fun on their own time												
Almost every day	0.9	1.2	0.7	1.2	0.5	1.1	0.7	1.4	0.6	0.9	0.5	1.1
Once or twice a week	0.8	1.2	0.7	1.1	0.6	1.0	0.5	1.1	0.7	0.7	0.6	1.0
Once or twice a month	0.4	1.6	0.5	2.1	0.5	1.2	0.5	0.8	0.5	0.9	0.5	1.0
Never or hardly ever	0.5	1.8	0.4	1.9	0.7	1.4	0.7	1.1	0.6	1.0	0.6	1.1
Amount read each day for school and homework												
11 or more pages	1.2	1.1	1.1	1.3	0.6	1.5	0.8	1.7	0.9	0.8	1.1	1.0
6 to 10 pages	0.7	1.3	0.7	1.3	0.4	1.3	0.5	1.6	0.4	0.9	0.6	1.1
5 or fewer pages	1.0	1.4	0.8	1.2	0.7	1.0	1.0	0.9	0.7	0.8	0.8	0.9
Time spent watching television each day												
6 hours or more	0.7	1.5	0.7	1.4	0.5	1.6	0.5	1.4	0.3	1.7	0.3	1.7
4 to 5 hours	0.8	1.3	0.7	1.7	0.5	1.2	0.6	1.0	0.4	0.9	0.6	1.1
2 to 3 hours	0.8	1.1	0.7	1.1	0.5	1.1	0.8	1.0	0.6	0.7	0.6	0.7
1 hour or less	0.8	1.6	0.7	1.9	0.5	1.5	0.4	1.7	0.8	1.0	0.5.	1.0

— Not applicable.

SOURCE: U.S. Department of Education, National Center for Education Statistics, National Assessment of Educational Progress, *1994 Reading Report Card for the Nation and the States,* 1996.

Table S18   Standard errors for the text table in *Indicator 18*

Sex and race/ethnicity	Grade 4		Grade 8		Grade 12	
	Percentage distribution	Average proficiency	Percentage distribution	Average proficiency	Percentage distribution	Average proficiency
Total	—	**1.0**	—	**0.6**	—	**0.8**
Sex						
Male	0.8	1.5	0.5	0.8	0.8	0.8
Female	0.8	1.1	0.5	0.7	0.8	0.9
Race/ethnicity						
White	0.3	0.2	0.2	0.8	0.4	0.8
Black	0.1	1.6	0.1	1.4	0.2	1.5
Hispanic	0.2	2.7	0.1	1.3	0.3	1.6
Asian	0.2	4.6	0.1	3.6	0.2	4.0
Pacific Islander	0.2	5.9	0.3	*7.1	0.2	3.9
American Indian	0.3	6.1	0.3	*3.7	0.2	*4.0

— Not applicable.

* Interpret with caution any comparisons involving this statistic. The nature of the sample does not allow for accurate determination of the variability of this value.

SOURCE: U.S. Department of Education, National Center for Education Statistics, National Assessment of Educational Progress, *1994 NAEP U.S. History Report Card,* 1996.

Table S19   Standard errors for the text table in *Indicator 19*

Selected characteristics	Grade 4 Percentage distribution	Grade 4 Average score	Grade 8 Percentage distribution	Grade 8 Average score	Grade 12 Percentage distribution	Grade 12 Average score
Total	—	**1.2**	—	**0.7**	—	**0.7**
Sex						
Male	1.0	1.4	0.7	0.9	1.0	0.8
Female	1.0	1.4	0.7	0.8	1.0	0.9
Race/ethnicity						
White	0.2	1.5	0.2	0.8	0.3	0.8
Black	0.1	2.5	0.1	1.7	0.4	1.4
Hispanic	0.2	2.5	0.1	1.9	0.2	1.5
Asian	0.2	5.0	0.1	2.7	0.2	3.2
Region						
Northeast	0.8	2.7	0.8	1.9	0.5	1.6
Southeast	1.0	2.5	1.0	1.6	0.8	1.1
Central	0.8	3.2	0.6	1.6	0.7	1.8
West	0.7	1.7	0.7	1.8	0.7	1.9
Parents' education level						
Did not finish high school	0.4	3.7	0.5	1.7	0.4	1.2
Graduated high school	0.6	2.5	0.9	1.2	0.8	1.1
Some education after high school	0.4	2.5	0.7	1.0	0.7	1.0
Graduated college	1.0	1.6	1.2	1.0	1.2	0.9

— Not applicable.

SOURCE: U.S. Department of Education, National Center for Education Statistics, National Assessment of Educational Progress, *1994 Geography Report Card for the Nation and the States*, 1996.

Table S20   Standard errors for the text table in *Indicator 20*

Larger countries	Average overall score Total	Male	Female	Average domain scale score Narrative	Expository	Documents	Non-school language spoken at home Percentage of students	Average score	School language spoken at home Percentage of students	Average score
Age 9										
United States	2.8	3.6	3.4	3.1	2.6	2.7	—	12.3	—	2.5
France	4.0	5.7	5.6	4.1	4.1	3.9	—	12.2	—	4.2
Italy	4.3	5.2	5.1	4.0	4.0	4.9	—	6.9	—	4.1
Spain	2.5	3.4	3.3	2.4	2.3	2.7	—	6.2	—	2.5
West Germany	3.0	3.9	3.8	2.8	2.9	3.2	—	8.1	—	2.9
Age 14										
France	4.3	5.0	4.2	4.2	4.3	4.2	—	16.1	—	3.3
United States	4.8	6.3	5.9	4.9	5.6	4.0	—	21.0	—	4.4
West Germany	4.4	4.4	4.4	4.9	4.5	3.9	—	10.7	—	3.2
Italy	3.4	4.0	3.9	3.6	3.2	3.3	—	5.1	—	3.3
Spain	2.5	3.3	3.1	3.0	2.6	2.0	—	6.8	—	2.4

— Not available.

SOURCE: International Association for the Evaluation of Educational Achievement, Study of Reading Literacy, *How in the World Do Students Read?*, 1992.

Table S23   Standard errors for the text table in *Indicator 23*

Larger countries	Average proficiency score			Percentile score						
	Total	Male	Female	1st	5th	10th	Median	90th	95th	99th
Age 9										
South Korea	1.8	2.0	2.4	7.5	6.8	1.9	1.4	1.8	3.5	2.5
Taiwan	2.2	2.4	2.7	5.7	4.4	3.3	1.8	4.8	3.1	1.1
Soviet Union	3.3	3.2	3.8	5.9	4.1	5.5	3.9	2.4	5.4	5.9
Spain	2.9	3.8	3.0	1.6	4.9	4.1	3.4	3.1	3.3	2.7
Canada	1.5	1.9	1.7	8.8	3.2	2.0	1.8	2.2	2.5	5.9
United States	3.2	3.6	3.7	4.5	2.9	5.7	2.9	5.0	5.7	1.5
Age 13										
Taiwan	2.0	3.1	2.5	9.9	7.3	4.9	1.7	3.5	9.0	2.4
South Korea	1.9	2.7	2.6	11.8	4.6	3.9	1.4	7.7	3.0	3.3
Soviet Union	2.2	2.8	1.9	5.5	4.5	3.5	2.0	1.5	3.6	5.0
France	1.8	2.1	2.1	4.0	2.4	1.8	0.8	3.8	4.1	8.3
Canada	1.4	1.8	1.6	12.9	3.8	1.9	1.4	2.1	2.8	3.2
Spain	1.8	2.5	1.9	18.4	2.0	1.9	3.0	2.9	1.9	4.2
United States	2.9	3.1	3.3	8.4	5.8	5.7	3.2	2.7	5.7	10.1

SOURCE: Educational Testing Service, International Assessment of Educational Progress, 1992.

Table S24   Standard errors for the text table in *Indicator 24*

Larger countries	Average proficiency score			Percentile score						
	Total	Male	Female	1st	5th	10th	Median	90th	95th	99th
Age 9										
South Korea	2.3	3.2	2.3	8.7	5.6	3.3	2.5	1.7	3.1	5.2
Taiwan	2.7	3.0	3.8	9.2	5.3	4.1	4.1	5.4	5.6	2.9
United States	4.6	6.2	4.2	2.3	9.8	6.1	2.9	2.7	3.2	6.0
Canada	1.9	2.3	2.3	3.5	5.5	1.8	1.9	1.0	4.0	1.3
Soviet Union	5.1	5.6	5.3	6.1	7.0	6.4	6.3	8.6	10.9	8.4
Spain	3.6	4.5	3.7	4.2	10.6	4.6	3.5	3.4	2.9	0.7
Age 13										
South Korea	2.3	3.0	3.2	16.5	8.1	5.1	2.7	3.9	2.6	4.7
Taiwan	1.9	2.8	2.5	11.4	3.3	3.3	2.4	2.7	2.9	6.5
Soviet Union	3.5	3.9	3.6	8.8	9.6	4.9	3.1	5.5	3.9	3.8
Canada	1.6	2.1	1.5	3.2	1.1	3.1	1.1	2.2	1.7	6.6
France	2.5	3.0	3.0	1.9	6.0	4.8	1.8	3.3	2.3	6.0
Spain	2.3	3.0	2.9	4.2	1.4	2.8	2.7	3.4	2.9	4.8
United States	4.4	5.6	3.6	8.4	6.5	7.5	4.0	4.9	3.9	8.0

SOURCE: Educational Testing Service, International Assessment of Educational Progress, 1992.

Table S25   Standard errors for the text table in *Indicator 25*

| | High school graduates | | | | High school graduates completing: | | | | | | | |
| | | | | | 1 or more years of college | | | | 4 or more years of college | | | |
March	Total	White	Black	Hispanic	Total	White	Black	Hispanic	Total	White	Black	Hispanic
1971	0.5	0.5	2.2	2.9	0.7	0.7	2.6	3.8	0.6	0.6	1.8	2.5
1973	0.5	0.5	2.0	2.6	0.6	0.7	2.5	3.3	0.5	0.6	1.8	2.2
1975	0.4	0.4	1.8	2.5	0.6	0.7	2.3	3.3	0.5	0.6	1.7	2.5
1977	0.4	0.4	1.7	2.5	0.6	0.6	2.2	3.3	0.5	0.6	1.7	2.1
1979	0.4	0.4	1.6	2.3	0.6	0.6	2.1	3.1	0.5	0.6	1.6	2.1
1981	0.4	0.3	1.5	2.1	0.6	0.6	2.0	2.7	0.5	0.5	1.4	1.8
1983	0.4	0.4	1.4	2.2	0.6	0.6	2.0	2.8	0.5	0.6	1.5	2.2
1985	0.4	0.4	1.4	2.1	0.6	0.6	1.9	2.8	0.5	0.6	1.4	2.1
1987	0.4	0.4	1.3	2.0	0.6	0.6	1.9	2.6	0.5	0.6	1.3	1.9
1989	0.4	0.4	1.4	2.2	0.6	0.7	2.0	2.9	0.5	0.6	1.5	2.2
1991	0.4	0.4	1.4	2.0	0.6	0.7	2.0	2.6	0.5	0.6	1.3	2.0
	Diploma or equivalency certificate				**Some college or more**				**Bachelor's degree or higher**			
1992	0.4	0.4	1.4	2.0	0.6	0.7	2.0	2.6	0.5	0.6	1.4	1.9
1993	0.4	0.4	1.4	1.9	0.6	0.7	2.0	2.5	0.5	0.6	1.5	1.7
1994	0.4	0.4	1.3	1.8	0.6	0.7	2.0	2.4	0.5	0.7	1.5	1.6
1995	0.4	0.4	1.2	1.8	0.6	0.7	2.0	2.4	0.6	0.7	1.5	1.8

SOURCE: U.S. Department of Commerce, Bureau of the Census, March Current Population Surveys.

Table S26(a)   Standard errors for the first text table in *Indicator 26*

| | Low test quartile | | | | Middle test quartiles | | | | High test quartile | | | |
Socioeconomic status	4-year	Public 2-year	Other	Never attended	4-year	Public 2-year	Other	Never attended	4-year	Public 2-year	Other	Never attended
Total	**0.8**	**1.1**	**1.0**	**1.4**	**0.8**	**0.9**	**0.7**	**0.9**	**1.2**	**1.0**	**0.7**	**0.7**
Low quartile	1.1	1.6	1.6	2.2	1.4	1.7	1.6	2.1	4.2	4.2	2.1	2.7
Middle quartiles	1.2	1.7	1.3	2.1	1.0	1.2	0.9	1.2	1.7	1.5	1.1	1.1
High quartile	3.2	3.8	3.6	5.0	2.0	2.0	1.2	1.4	1.7	1.4	0.8	0.6

Table S26(b)   Standard errors for the second text table in *Indicator 26*

| | Low test quartile | | | | Middle test quartiles | | | | High test quartile | | | |
Socioeconomic status	High school or less	Certificate/ assoc.	Bachelor's	Advanced	High school or less	Certificate/ assoc.	Bachelor's	Advanced	High school or less	Certificate/ assoc.	Bachelor's	Advanced
Total	**1.1**	**1.0**	**0.4**	**0.1**	**0.9**	**0.8**	**0.6**	**0.2**	**1.1**	**0.8**	**1.2**	**0.8**
Low quartile	1.7	1.5	0.6	0.3	1.9	1.7	0.9	0.3	3.9	3.7	3.4	1.9
Middle quartiles	1.7	1.5	0.8	0.2	1.2	1.1	0.8	0.3	1.7	1.3	1.8	1.0
High quartile	4.4	3.8	2.7	0.2	2.0	1.5	1.8	0.9	1.5	1.1	1.9	1.4

SOURCE: U.S. Department of Education, National Center for Education Statistics, High School and Beyond (HS&B) study 1980 Sophomore Cohort, Base Year, First, and Fourth Follow-up surveys.

Table S28   Standard errors for text table in *Indicator 28*

Characteristics	"New Basics" curriculum				Less restrictive curriculum			
	1982	1987	1990	1994	1982	1987	1990	1994
Total	**0.5**	**1.2**	**1.6**	**1.6**	**1.0**	**1.6**	**2.2**	**1.6**
Sex								
Male	0.8	1.4	1.8	1.6	1.3	1.9	2.3	1.7
Female	0.8	1.4	1.6	1.6	1.3	1.7	2.2	1.6
Race/ethnicity								
White	0.6	1.4	1.8	1.8	1.3	2.1	2.5	1.8
Black	1.2	3.1	3.8	2.5	2.5	3.2	3.4	2.4
Hispanic	0.6	2.2	2.7	2.9	1.5	2.3	3.2	3.0
Asian/Pacific Islander	2.8	4.1	3.1	2.2	3.0	4.2	3.9	3.3
American Indian/Alaskan Native	2.7	3.6	4.9	3.2	8.1	5.3	6.8	3.4
Student program								
Academic	1.1	1.6	1.8	1.6	1.4	1.7	1.9	1.5
Vocational	0.0	0.0	0.0	0.0	0.6	1.5	2.1	3.0
Both	1.3	1.6	2.5	2.0	1.9	2.0	2.0	1.6
Neither	0.0	0.0	0.0	0.0	0.9	1.7	1.8	2.1

SOURCE: U.S. Department of Education, National Center for Education Statistics, *The 1994 High School Transcript Study Tabulations: Comparative Data on Credits Earned and Demographics for 1994, 1990, 1987, and 1982 High School Graduates*, 1996.

Table S29   Standard errors for the text table in *Indicator 29*

Mathematics and science courses	Total				Male				Female			
	1982*	1987*	1990*	1994	1982*	1987*	1990*	1994	1982*	1987*	1990*	1994
Mathematics												
Algebra I	0.9	1.0	1.6	1.4	1.0	1.2	1.7	1.4	1.2	1.1	1.8	1.4
Geometry	0.8	1.0	1.3	1.4	0.8	1.2	1.6	1.5	1.2	1.0	1.3	1.4
Algebra II	0.9	1.2	1.1	1.3	1.1	1.4	1.3	1.3	1.0	1.2	1.1	1.4
Trigonometry	0.6	1.5	1.3	1.3	1.0	1.8	1.4	1.4	0.5	1.4	1.3	1.4
Analysis/pre-calculus	0.4	0.9	1.0	0.8	0.5	1.0	1.1	0.8	0.6	0.8	0.9	0.9
Calculus	0.4	0.4	0.5	0.5	0.5	0.5	0.6	0.6	0.4	0.4	0.4	0.6
Science												
Biology	0.8	1.0	1.0	1.0	1.0	1.2	1.1	1.1	1.1	0.8	0.9	0.9
Chemistry	0.8	1.1	1.2	1.0	1.1	1.3	1.4	1.0	0.7	1.2	1.3	1.2
Physics	0.5	0.9	0.8	0.8	1.0	1.0	0.9	1.0	0.4	0.9	0.8	0.9
Biology and chemistry	0.8	1.1	1.3	1.2	1.2	1.3	1.4	1.2	0.6	1.2	1.3	1.4
Biology, chemistry, and physics	0.5	0.7	0.7	0.8	0.8	0.8	0.8	0.8	0.4	0.7	0.8	0.9

* Revised from previously published figures.

SOURCE: U.S. Department of Education, National Center for Education Statistics, *The 1994 High School Transcript Study Tabulations: Comparative Data on Credits Earned and Demographics for 1994, 1990, 1987, and 1982 High School Graduates*, 1996.

Table S30   Standard errors for the text table in *Indicator 30*

October	Recent high school graduates not enrolled in college				Recent school dropouts			
	Total	White	Black	Hispanic	Total	White	Black	Hispanic
1972	1.7	1.7	5.4	—	2.7	3.2	6.1	—
1973	1.6	1.7	4.9	—	2.6	3.0	5.7	—
1974	1.6	1.7	5.5	—	2.6	3.1	5.4	—
1975	1.7	1.8	5.2	—	2.6	3.2	5.2	7.4
1976	1.7	1.7	5.5	—	2.6	3.1	5.2	—
1977	1.6	1.7	5.6	7.3	2.6	3.0	5.8	—
1978	1.6	1.6	5.3	7.0	2.6	3.1	4.8	—
1979	1.6	1.7	5.5	6.7	2.6	3.1	5.4	—
1980	1.7	1.7	4.9	—	2.7	3.3	5.2	7.2
1981	1.8	1.9	4.8	—	2.7	3.5	3.7	7.4
1982	1.9	2.0	4.5	7.1	2.9	3.7	5.1	—
1983	1.9	2.1	4.7	—	3.2	4.1	6.3	—
1984	2.0	2.2	4.7	7.0	3.1	3.9	6.6	7.5
1985	2.2	2.3	5.3	—	3.1	4.1	6.3	7.9
1986	2.0	2.2	4.9	7.7	3.2	4.3	8.1	7.0
1987	2.0	2.2	6.1	7.2	3.3	4.2	6.4	—
1988	2.2	2.4	5.8	10.4	3.5	4.4	6.5	9.2
1989	2.4	2.5	6.8	10.6	3.9	5.1	7.0	—
1990	2.4	2.6	6.0	—	3.9	5.0	8.2	—
1991	2.6	3.0	5.8	—	3.9	5.2	7.2	—
1992	2.5	2.8	5.7	8.6	3.8	5.0	—	8.1
1993	2.5	2.8	6.8	9.2	3.9	5.0	8.1	—
1994	2.4	2.7	6.3	9.0	3.5	4.7	7.7	7.5

— Not available.

SOURCE: U.S. Department of Commerce, Bureau of the Census, October Current Population Surveys.

Table S31   Standard errors for the text table in *Indicator 31*

Selected characteristics	Employment and enrollment status					Relatedness of job to education		
	Employed full time, not enrolled	Employed part time, not enrolled	In labor force, enrolled	Not in labor force, enrolled	Not employed, not enrolled	Job related to field of study	Job required college degree	Job had career potential
Total	**0.7**	**0.4**	**0.4**	**0.3**	**0.3**	**0.7**	**0.9**	**0.8**
Field of study								
Business and management	1.3	0.8	0.9	0.4	0.6	1.3	2.0	1.5
Education	1.7	1.4	1.1	0.7	0.7	1.7	1.8	1.6
Engineering	2.2	0.9	1.5	1.0	1.3	1.5	2.1	1.7
Health professions	2.1	1.0	1.7	0.8	1.1	1.2	2.6	1.9
Public affairs/social services	2.8	1.8	1.8	1.6	1.6	3.5	4.0	3.4
Biological sciences	2.8	1.1	2.1	2.1	2.1	3.6	4.0	3.7
Mathematics and science	2.5	1.9	1.5	1.5	1.3	2.1	3.0	2.3
Social sciences	1.7	0.8	1.3	0.8	0.9	2.2	2.7	2.0
History	4.2	2.5	3.5	1.7	1.3	6.2	6.3	6.7
Humanities	2.0	1.4	1.3	0.8	1.3	2.7	2.7	2.6
Psychology	3.2	1.4	2.7	1.8	2.3	4.1	4.1	4.2
Other	1.6	1.0	1.0	0.5	0.8	1.8	2.4	2.7
Sex								
Male	1.0	0.5	0.6	0.5	0.5	1.1	1.3	1.1
Female	0.9	0.5	0.6	0.3	0.4	0.9	1.1	1.0
College grade point average								
Less than 3.0	1.1	0.7	0.7	0.3	0.6	1.3	1.5	1.3
3.0 to 3.49	0.9	0.6	0.6	0.4	0.5	1.0	1.3	1.4
3.5 and higher	1.2	0.7	0.8	0.7	0.6	1.3	1.8	1.3

SOURCE: U.S. Department of Education, National Center for Education Statistics, 1993 Baccalaureate and Beyond Longitudinal Study, First Follow-up (B&B:93/94).

Table S32   Standard errors for the text table in *Indicator 32*

March	Male				Female			
	Grades 9–11	High school diploma	Some college	Bachelor's degree or higher	Grades 9–11	High school diploma	Some college	Bachelor's degree or higher
1971	1.1	0.5	1.0	0.8	1.4	0.9	1.6	1.7
1973	1.1	0.5	0.9	0.7	1.5	0.8	1.6	1.5
1975	1.5	0.6	0.9	0.6	1.4	0.8	1.4	1.3
1977	1.4	0.6	0.8	0.5	1.5	0.8	1.3	1.1
1979	1.5	0.5	0.7	0.5	1.6	0.8	1.1	1.1
1981	1.5	0.6	0.7	0.5	1.6	0.8	1.0	1.0
1983	1.7	0.7	0.9	0.6	1.6	0.8	1.1	0.9
1985	1.5	0.6	0.7	0.6	1.7	0.8	1.0	0.9
1987	1.4	0.6	0.7	0.6	1.7	0.7	1.0	0.8
1989	1.5	0.6	0.7	0.5	1.9	0.8	1.0	0.9
1991	1.6	0.6	0.8	0.6	1.7	0.8	1.0	0.8
1992	1.6	0.6	0.8	0.6	1.7	0.8	0.9	0.8
1993	1.6	0.7	0.7	0.6	1.8	0.9	0.9	0.9
1994	1.6	0.7	0.7	0.6	1.8	0.9	0.9	0.9
1995	1.6	0.6	0.7	0.6	1.9	0.9	0.9	0.8

SOURCE: U.S. Department of Commerce, Bureau of the Census, March Current Population Surveys.

Table S33   Standard errors for the text table in *Indicator 33*

Sex and educational attainment	Work status				Status involuntary		
	Year-round, primarily full-time worker	Primarily part-time worker	Part-year worker	Non-worker	Of part-time workers	Of part-year workers	Of non-workers
Total	**0.4**	**0.3**	**1.0**	**0.1**	**0.9**	**0.8**	**2.7**
Sex							
Male	0.5	0.3	2.1	0.1	1.8	1.2	3.2
Female	0.6	0.5	1.1	0.2	1.0	1.1	3.8
Educational attainment, by sex							
Male							
Less than high school completion	1.6	1.0	4.8	0.6	4.1	2.5	5.0
High school completion	0.9	0.5	4.0	0.3	3.6	1.7	4.3
Some college, no degree	1.1	0.8	4.2	0.3	3.9	3.0	—
Associate's degree	1.6	1.1	5.7	0.4	5.3	5.4	—
Bachelor's degree	1.0	0.6	4.7	0.2	4.2	3.3	—
Advanced degree	2.0	1.4	5.4	0.4	5.1	4.7	—
Female							
Less than high school completion	2.1	2.0	4.0	1.2	3.3	3.2	7.4
High school completion	1.1	0.9	1.9	0.4	1.6	2.0	5.8
Some college, no degree	1.3	1.2	2.0	0.4	1.9	2.3	9.8
Associate's degree	1.8	1.5	3.3	0.5	3.1	3.8	—
Bachelor's degree	1.3	1.0	2.1	0.3	2.0	2.4	—
Advanced degree	2.4	1.8	5.1	0.4	4.9	4.3	—

— Not available.
SOURCE: U.S. Department of Commerce, Bureau of the Census, March Current Population Surveys, 1995.

Table S34 Standard errors for the text table in *Indicator 34*

Year	Grades 9–11		Some college		Bachelor's degree or higher	
	Male	Female	Male	Female	Male	Female
1970	0.02	0.05	0.02	0.06	0.02	0.06
1972	0.02	0.03	0.02	0.05	0.02	0.05
1974	0.02	0.05	0.02	0.05	0.02	0.06
1976	0.02	0.04	0.02	0.05	0.02	0.05
1978	0.03	0.02	0.03	0.04	0.03	0.05
1980	0.02	0.04	0.02	0.04	0.02	0.04
1982	0.02	0.04	0.02	0.03	0.02	0.05
1984	0.03	0.04	0.04	0.03	0.05	0.04
1986	0.02	0.04	0.02	0.04	0.03	0.04
1988	0.03	0.03	0.02	0.04	0.04	0.03
1990	0.03	0.04	0.03	0.03	0.03	0.04
1991	0.03	0.05	0.03	0.03	0.02	0.04
1992	0.03	0.04	0.03	0.04	0.03	0.05
1993	0.03	0.03	0.02	0.04	0.03	0.05
1994	0.03	0.04	0.03	0.03	0.03	0.05

SOURCE: U.S. Department of Commerce, Bureau of the Census, March Current Population Surveys.

Table S35(a) Standard errors for the first text table in *Indicator 35*

Major field of study	Year of graduation					
	1977	1980	1984	1986	1990	1993
Humanities	3.4	1.9	2.4	1.5	2.4	2.2
Social and behavioral sciences	1.8	1.8	2.3	1.8	1.6	1.6
Natural sciences	3.1	4.1	3.1	2.2	3.1	2.3
Computer sciences and engineering	2.9	2.9	1.9	1.5	1.8	2.9
Education	1.3	1.2	1.8	1.2	1.6	1.6
Business and management	1.6	1.8	1.4	0.8	1.6	2.2
Other professional or technical	2.8	2.2	1.7	1.2	2.1	2.4

SOURCE: U.S. Department of Education, National Center for Education Statistics, Recent College Graduates Surveys (1977–90) and 1993 Baccalaureate and Beyond Longitudinal Study, First Follow-up (B&B:93/94).

Table S35(b) Standard errors for the second text table in *Indicator 35*

Major field of study	All graduates	Male		Female	
		Percent in field	Median salary	Percent in field	Median salary
Total	**$237**	—	**$371**	—	**$221**
Humanities	475	0.8	668	0.8	496
Social and behavioral sciences	333	0.8	663	0.8	422
Natural sciences	491	0.6	894	0.6	685
Computer sciences and engineering	605	1.2	629	0.4	1,559
Education	344	0.6	689	1.8	378
Business and management	512	1.6	638	1.2	553
Other professional and technical	552	1.2	959	1.1	726

— Not applicable.

SOURCE: U.S. Department of Education, National Center for Education Statistics, Recent College Graduates Surveys (1977–90) and 1993 Baccalaureate and Beyond Longitudinal Study, First Follow-up (B&B:93/94).

Table S36   Standard errors for the text table in *Indicator 36*

Year	All persons						White		Black		Hispanic	
	All levels	Less than 9 years	9–11 years	12 years	13–15 years	16 years or more	9–11 years	12 years	9–11 years	12 years	9–11 years	12 years
1972	0.2	0.9	0.6	0.2	0.3	0.1	0.6	0.2	2.2	1.4	2.9	1.4
1973	0.2	0.9	0.6	0.2	0.3	0.1	0.6	0.2	2.4	1.3	3.9	1.7
1974	0.2	1.0	0.7	0.2	0.2	0.1	0.7	0.2	2.4	1.2	3.5	1.5
1975	0.1	1.1	0.7	0.2	0.3	0.2	0.7	0.2	2.6	1.1	3.1	1.4
1976	0.2	1.0	0.7	0.2	0.2	0.1	0.7	0.2	2.4	1.2	3.4	1.6
1977	0.2	1.0	0.7	0.2	0.2	0.1	0.7	0.2	2.5	1.3	3.2	1.8
1978	0.1	1.0	0.8	0.2	0.2	0.1	0.8	0.2	2.4	1.2	3.5	1.8
1979	0.1	1.0	0.8	0.2	0.3	0.1	0.8	0.2	2.4	1.2	3.2	1.5
1980	0.2	1.1	0.8	0.2	0.2	0.1	0.8	0.2	2.4	1.2	3.3	1.4
1981	0.2	1.1	0.8	0.2	0.3	0.1	0.9	0.2	2.7	1.3	3.1	1.3
1982	0.1	1.1	0.8	0.2	0.3	0.1	0.9	0.2	2.5	1.2	3.1	1.4
1983	0.2	1.0	0.8	0.2	0.2	0.1	0.9	0.2	2.5	1.1	2.7	1.2
1984	0.2	1.1	0.9	0.2	0.3	0.1	0.9	0.2	2.6	1.1	2.1	1.1
1985	0.1	1.2	0.9	0.2	0.2	0.1	0.9	0.2	2.7	1.0	2.2	1.0
1986	0.1	1.1	0.8	0.2	0.2	0.1	0.9	0.2	2.4	1.0	2.0	1.1
1987	0.2	1.1	0.8	0.2	0.2	0.1	0.8	0.2	2.7	1.1	2.3	1.2
1988	0.1	1.3	0.8	0.2	0.3	0.1	0.9	0.2	2.6	1.0	2.2	1.0
1989	0.1	1.1	0.8	0.2	0.2	0.1	0.8	0.2	2.7	1.0	2.0	0.9
1990	0.2	1.0	0.8	0.2	0.2	0.1	0.9	0.2	2.6	1.1	1.9	1.0
1991	0.2	1.0	0.8	0.2	0.2	0.1	1.0	0.3	2.5	1.1	2.1	1.1
1992	0.2	1.2	0.9	0.3	0.3	0.1	1.1	0.3	3.2	1.3	2.4	1.3
1993	0.2	1.1	0.9	0.3	0.3	0.1	1.1	0.3	3.1	1.4	2.1	1.3
1994	0.2	1.1	0.9	0.3	0.3	0.1	1.1	0.3	3.2	1.3	1.8	1.1

SOURCE: U.S. Department of Commerce, Bureau of the Census, March Current Population Surveys.

Table S37   Standard errors for the text table in *Indicator 37*

Type of election and year	Total	1–3 years of high school	4 years of high school	1–3 years of college	4 or more years of college
			Voting rates		
Congressional election					
1974	0.34	0.80	0.54	0.85	0.77
1982	0.40	1.04	0.61	0.87	0.81
1990	0.30	0.80	0.46	0.65	0.60
1994	0.29	0.71	0.48	0.57	0.59
Presidential elections					
1964	0.70	1.30	0.90	1.40	1.20
1976	0.34	0.92	0.53	0.76	0.62
1984	0.40	1.33	0.69	0.93	0.80
1988	0.30	1.06	0.56	0.73	0.60
1992	0.30	0.93	0.52	0.55	0.49
		Ratio of voting rates to those of high school graduates			
Congressional election					
1974	—	0.02	—	0.03	0.03
1982	—	0.03	—	0.03	0.04
1990	—	0.02	—	0.03	0.03
1994	—	0.02	—	0.03	0.03
Presidential elections					
1964	—	0.02	—	0.02	0.02
1976	—	0.02	—	0.02	0.02
1984	—	0.03	—	0.02	0.02
1988	—	0.02	—	0.02	0.02
1992	—	0.02	—	0.02	0.02

— Not applicable.

SOURCE: U.S. Department of Commerce, Bureau of the Census, *Current Population Reports*, "Voting and Registration in the Election of November...," Series P-20, Nos. 143, 293, 322, 383, 440, 453, 466, and PPL-25.

Table S42 (a) Standard errors for the first text table in *Indicator 42*

Urbanicity	Total	Control		Public school level				Percentage of students eligible for free or reduced-price lunch in public high schools			
		Public	Private	Elementary	Middle	High	Combined	0–5	6–20	21–40	41–100
Total	**0.1**	**0.1**	**0.1**	**0.1**	**0.1**	**0.1**	**0.2**	**1.1**	**0.2**	**0.3**	**0.3**
Central city	0.1	0.1	0.1	0.1	0.3	0.3	0.7	0.3	0.4	0.4	0.5
Urban fringe/large town	0.1	0.1	0.2	0.2	0.2	0.3	0.6	0.6	0.5	0.9	1.0
Rural/small town	0.1	0.1	0.4	0.1	0.2	0.2	0.2	2.6	0.3	0.3	0.4

Table S42 (b) Standard errors for the second text table in *Indicator 42*

Urbanicity	Total	Control		Public school level				Percentage of students eligible for free or reduced-price lunch in public high schools			
		Public	Private	Elementary	Middle	High	Combined	0–5	6–20	21–40	41–100
							Absenteeism				
Total	**0.3**	**0.3**	**0.2**	**0.4**	**0.7**	**0.7**	**1.6**	**1.3**	**0.8**	**1.4**	**1.5**
Central city	0.5	0.6	0.2	1.0	1.6	1.4	3.9	3.1	2.5	3.1	2.0
Urban fringe/large town	0.4	0.5	0.3	0.7	0.9	1.4	2.0	1.9	1.7	2.1	3.6
Rural/small town	0.3	0.3	0.8	0.3	0.9	0.6	0.9	1.4	1.1	1.0	1.3
							Tardiness				
Total	**0.2**	**0.3**	**0.2**	**0.4**	**0.7**	**0.6**	**1.1**	**0.9**	**0.7**	**1.1**	**1.4**
Central city	0.5	0.6	0.3	0.9	1.9	1.4	2.6	3.0	1.8	2.5	2.3
Urban fringe/large town	0.4	0.5	0.5	0.9	0.8	0.9	1.5	1.2	1.1	1.8	2.3
Rural/small town	0.2	0.2	0.5	0.2	0.8	0.5	0.7	1.0	0.9	0.9	1.0

SOURCE: U.S. Department of Education, National Center for Education Statistics, Schools and Staffing Survey, 1993–94 (Teacher and School Questionnaires).

Table S44   Standard errors for the text table in *Indicator 44*

Year	Percent of children who live in poverty				Percent of children in poverty who live with a female householder			
	Total	White	Black	Hispanic	Total	White	Black	Hispanic
1960	0.4	0.4	1.4	—	0.8	1.0	1.7	—
1965	0.4	0.4	1.3	—	1.0	1.2	1.9	—
1970	0.4	0.3	1.3	—	1.3	1.6	2.0	—
1975	0.4	0.4	1.3	1.7	1.2	1.5	1.9	2.8
1980	0.4	0.4	1.3	1.7	1.2	1.5	1.8	2.8
1981	0.4	0.4	1.3	1.7	1.2	1.5	1.8	2.7
1982	0.4	0.4	1.3	1.7	—	—	—	—
1983	0.4	0.4	1.3	1.6	1.1	1.4	1.7	2.5
1984	0.4	0.4	1.3	1.6	1.1	1.4	1.7	2.5
1985	0.4	0.4	1.3	1.5	1.2	1.4	1.7	2.4
1986	0.4	0.4	1.3	1.5	1.2	1.5	1.6	2.4
1987	0.4	0.4	1.3	1.5	1.2	1.5	1.6	2.4
1988	0.4	0.4	1.3	1.5	1.2	1.5	1.6	2.3
1989	0.4	0.4	1.3	1.5	1.2	1.5	1.7	2.4
1990	0.4	0.4	1.3	1.4	1.1	1.5	1.5	2.3
1991	0.4	0.4	1.3	1.5	1.1	1.4	1.8	2.2
1992	0.4	0.4	1.3	1.4	1.1	1.4	1.6	2.2
1993	0.4	0.4	1.3	1.4	1.1	1.4	1.5	2.2
1994	0.4	0.4	1.3	1.4	1.1	1.4	1.5	2.2

— Not available.

SOURCE: U.S. Department of Commerce, Bureau of the Census, *Current Population Reports*, Series P-60, "Income, Poverty, and Valuation of Non-cash Benefits: 1994" (based on March Current Population Surveys).

Table S46   Standard errors for the text table in *Indicator 46*

School characteristics and achievement test quartile	Total	Strictly voluntary	Some or all of community service was:			
			Required			
			Total	For class	Court ordered	For other reasons
Total	**0.7**	**0.7**	**0.5**	**0.4**	**0.2**	**0.3**
Control of school						
Public	0.7	0.7	0.5	0.4	0.2	0.3
Catholic	2.8	3.4	3.6	3.4	0.6	2.9
Private, other	4.0	3.8	3.1	2.5	0.7	2.2
Percentage of students receiving free or reduced-price lunch						
0–5	1.6	1.5	1.2	1.0	0.3	0.8
6–20	1.2	1.1	1.0	0.8	0.3	0.6
21–40	1.3	1.3	0.8	0.6	0.2	0.6
41–100	1.6	1.5	1.2	0.7	0.6	1.0
Achievement test quartile						
First (low)	1.8	1.7	1.1	0.9	0.4	0.8
Second	1.4	1.4	0.8	0.6	0.2	0.5
Third	1.0	1.0	0.7	0.5	0.3	0.4
Fourth (high)	1.1	1.1	1.0	0.9	0.3	0.8

SOURCE: U.S. Department of Education, National Center for Education Statistics, National Education Longitudinal Study of 1988, Second Follow-up (1992).

Table S47   Standard errors for the text table in *Indicator 47*

Decisions	All schools	Public			Private		
		Total	Elementary	Secondary	Total	Elementary	Secondary
Percentage of teachers reporting that teachers had a good deal of influence in their school over:							
Setting discipline policy	0.4	0.4	0.7	0.3	0.8	0.9	1.1
Determining the content of in-service programs	0.4	0.4	0.7	0.4	0.6	0.8	1.0
Establishing curriculum	0.4	0.4	0.6	0.4	0.6	0.8	1.0
Percentage of teachers reporting a good deal of control in their classroom over:							
Selecting textbooks and other instructional materials	0.4	0.4	0.7	0.4	0.6	0.8	0.9
Selecting content, topics, and skills to be taught	0.4	0.4	0.7	0.4	0.5	0.9	0.8
Selecting teaching techniques	0.2	0.3	0.5	0.3	0.4	0.5	0.5
Evaluating and grading students	0.2	0.3	0.4	0.3	0.3	0.5	0.5
Disciplining students	0.4	0.4	0.7	0.5	0.4	0.6	0.7
Determining the amount of homework to be assigned	0.3	0.4	0.6	0.3	0.5	0.7	0.6
Percentage of principals reporting that teachers had a good deal of influence over:							
Setting discipline policy	0.5	0.6	0.7	1.0	1.3	1.5	2.5
Determining the content of in-service programs	0.6	0.7	0.9	0.7	1.3	1.6	3.0
Establishing curriculum	0.7	0.8	1.1	0.8	1.4	1.6	2.2

SOURCE: U.S. Department of Education, National Center for Education Statistics, Schools and Staffing Survey, 1993–94 (Teacher and Administrator Questionnaires).

Table S48   Standard errors for the text table in *Indicator 48*

| Control and level of school and teacher characteristics | Average hours worked per week | Average hours required at school | Average hours spent before and after school and on weekends | | | Average class size | Average number of classes taught per day |
			Total	Activities involving students	Other related activities		
Public	**0.1**	**0.1**	**0.1**	***0.0**	***0.0**	**0.1**	***0.0**
Level of school							
Elementary	0.1	0.1	0.1	0.1	0.1	0.4	0.1
Secondary	0.1	0.1	0.1	0.1	0.1	0.1	*0.0
Years of teaching experience							
Less than 4 years	0.3	0.3	0.2	0.1	0.2	0.2	0.1
4 years or more	0.1	0.1	0.1	*0.0	0.1	0.1	*0.0
Private	**0.2**	**0.1**	**0.1**	**0.1**	**0.1**	**0.2**	***0.0**
Level of school							
Elementary	0.3	0.2	0.2	0.1	0.1	0.4	0.2
Secondary	0.3	0.2	0.2	0.1	0.1	0.2	*0.0
Years of teaching experience							
Less than 4 years	0.3	0.2	0.3	0.2	0.2	0.3	0.1
4 years or more	0.2	0.2	0.1	0.1	0.1	0.2	0.1

* Standard errors less than 0.05 are rounded to 0.0.

SOURCE: U.S. Department of Education, National Center for Education Statistics, Schools and Staffing Survey, 1993–94 (Teacher Questionnaire).

Table S49   Standard errors for the text table in *Indicator 49*

| Activity | Total | Academic rank | | | | | Type of institution | | | | |
		Full professor	Associate professor	Assistant professor	Instructor	Lecturer	Research	Doctoral	Comprehensive	Liberal arts	2-year
				Fall 1992							
Teaching	0.4	0.7	0.7	0.6	0.8	2.4	0.7	0.8	0.5	0.8	0.7
Research/scholarship	0.4	0.6	0.6	0.6	0.4	1.3	0.8	0.8	0.4	0.6	0.2
Professional growth	0.1	0.1	0.2	0.1	0.2	0.6	0.2	0.2	0.1	0.2	0.2
Administration	0.2	0.4	0.4	0.3	0.5	1.8	0.5	0.6	0.4	0.6	0.7
Outside consulting/freelance work	0.1	0.1	0.2	0.1	0.2	0.4	0.2	0.2	0.1	0.2	0.2
Service and other	0.1	0.2	0.2	0.2	0.4	0.8	0.3	0.2	0.2	0.4	0.3
				Fall 1987							
Teaching	0.5	0.9	0.8	0.8	1.3	2.5	0.9	1.3	0.9	1.2	1.1
Research/scholarship	0.4	0.7	0.7	0.7	0.5	1.2	1.0	1.2	0.5	1.2	0.4
Professional growth	0.1	0.2	0.3	0.3	0.5	1.1	0.3	0.2	0.3	0.5	0.3
Administration	0.3	0.5	0.5	0.4	0.9	1.2	0.6	0.9	0.5	0.8	0.8
Outside consulting/freelance work	0.1	0.2	0.2	0.2	0.6	1.2	0.2	0.3	0.2	0.3	0.3
Service and other	0.1	0.2	0.3	0.2	0.4	1.4	0.3	0.2	0.2	0.3	0.4

SOURCE: U.S. Department of Education, National Center for Education Statistics, National Survey of Postsecondary Faculty, 1988 and 1993.

Table S50   Standard errors for the text table in *Indicator 50*

Academic rank	Fall 1987 Type of institution and course division					Fall 1992 Type of institution and course division				
	Total	Research	Doctoral	Compre-hensive	Liberal arts	Total	Research	Doctoral	Compre-hensive	Liberal arts
	Undergraduate, lower division courses					*Undergraduate, lower division courses*				
Full professor	2.3	6.5	5.2	2.6	4.5	1.4	4.6	2.3	1.7	2.4
Associate professor	2.7	8.1	4.9	2.2	3.0	1.4	4.2	2.5	1.2	2.3
Assistant professor	1.6	3.4	3.0	2.0	5.5	1.1	2.6	2.7	1.4	2.6
Instructor	1.3	1.2	3.5	2.0	2.8	1.2	2.8	2.4	1.8	2.3
Lecturer	1.4	3.8	1.5	2.0	1.8	0.9	3.2	1.6	0.9	1.3
Other	0.5	0.5	0.8	0.7	2.9	0.6	—	0.4	0.4	3.8
	Undergraduate, upper division courses					*Undergraduate, upper division courses*				
Full professor	2.9	6.9	5.5	3.7	7.0	1.4	3.2	2.3	2.0	3.1
Associate professor	2.8	7.5	4.8	3.6	8.1	1.1	2.6	2.3	1.6	2.1
Assistant professor	4.7	6.3	9.6	5.3	16.2	1.1	2.6	2.7	1.5	2.0
Instructor	1.6	0.8	4.9	2.3	2.0	0.7	1.1	1.7	1.1	1.7
Lecturer	1.0	2.5	3.7	1.3	*0.0	0.6	1.6	1.0	0.7	1.2
Other	0.3	*0.0	*0.0	0.3	1.9	0.5	—	0.9	1.0	1.5
	Graduate courses					*Graduate courses*				
Full professor	10.3	6.7	17.0	14.2	—	2.5	4.6	4.1	2.9	3.1
Associate professor	7.9	12.9	17.1	9.3	—	2.3	4.3	2.1	2.4	7.6
Assistant professor	6.6	11.8	12.6	8.7	—	1.7	2.0	4.8	2.3	3.8
Instructor	10.6	*0.0	0.9	14.8	—	2.1	3.4	1.2	4.2	11.5
Lecturer	*0.0	0.1	*0.0	0.1	—	0.6	0.8	—	1.3	—
Other	*0.0	0.1	*0.0	*0.0	—	0.7	—	—	0.7	—

— Not available.

* Standard errors less than 0.05 are rounded to 0.0.

SOURCE: U.S. Department of Education, National Center for Education Statistics, National Survey of Postsecondary Faculty, 1988 and 1993.

Table S55   Standard errors for the second text table in *Indicator 55*

| Percentage of minority students within urbanicity | School earnings | | | | Non-school compensation |
	Total school earnings	Base salary	Summer supplemental	Other school compensation	
Total	**$90**	**$92**	**$43**	**$27**	**$143**
Central city	169	171	95	59	240
Less than 20 percent	328	321	87	75	413
20 percent or more	193	196	133	84	293
Urban fringe/large town	236	228	64	66	354
Less than 20 percent	383	377	91	85	239
20 percent or more	322	317	91	99	748
Rural/small town	154	149	39	36	160
Less than 20 percent	210	206	49	43	213
20 percent or more	266	265	68	69	246

SOURCE: U.S. Department of Education, National Center for Education Statistics, Schools and Staffing Survey, 1993–94 (School, Administrator, and Teacher Questionnaires).

Table S56   Standard errors for the text table in *Indicator 56*

| Supply source and main activity in the previous year | Public schools | | | Private schools | | |
	1988	1991	1994	1988	1991	1994
First-time teachers	**1.0**	**1.3**	**1.2**	**1.4**	**1.8**	**1.4**
Transfers	**1.3**	**1.3**	**1.2**	**1.8**	**2.1**	**1.4**
Within state and sector	1.0	1.0	1.2	1.9	1.6	1.0
Across state	0.6	0.6	0.5	1.2	1.3	1.0
Across sector	0.8	0.9	0.5	1.3	1.2	0.7
Reentrants	**1.1**	**1.2**	**0.9**	**2.1**	**2.0**	**1.2**
Main previous year activity						
First-time teachers						
Work in education (non-teaching)	1.0	0.8	1.0	1.4	1.4	1.4
Work outside education	1.2	1.3	2.0	3.4	2.7	2.5
College	1.9	2.3	2.7	3.0	3.0	1.5
Homemaking/childrearing	0.8	0.9	1.8	3.5	1.6	2.5
Other	—	—	1.3	—	—	1.4
Substitute teaching	—	1.8	1.3	—	2.4	1.3
Reentrants						
Work in education (non-teaching)	1.0	3.3	1.6	2.2	1.9	2.3
Work outside education	1.2	1.7	1.0	2.8	3.7	1.7
College	1.8	1.6	1.6	3.0	1.3	2.0
Homemaking/childrearing	2.1	3.0	0.4	3.2	3.7	0.8
Other	—	—	2.4	—	—	1.8
Substitute teaching	—	2.7	2.4	—	2.5	1.8

— Not available.

SOURCE: U.S. Department of Education, National Center for Education Statistics, Schools and Staffing Survey, 1987–88, 1990–91, and 1993–94 (Teacher Questionnaire).

Table S57   Standard errors for the text table in *Indicator 57*

Control of school and class subject	Majored in class subject	Majored or minored in class subject	Graduate degree in class subject	Certified in class subject
Public				
English	0.8	0.6	0.7	0.5
Social sciences	0.7	0.5	0.9	0.7
Mathematics	0.9	1.0	0.7	0.8
Science	1.0	0.6	1.1	0.7
Biology	1.6	1.2	1.1	1.1
Chemistry	2.3	2.2	1.8	1.6
Physics	3.5	3.6	1.9	2.1
Foreign languages	1.3	0.9	1.6	0.9
Visual and performing arts	0.9	0.9	1.3	1.0
Health and physical education	0.8	0.7	1.3	0.9
Vocational education	0.9	0.9	0.9	0.6
Private				
English	2.3	2.2	2.7	2.9
Social sciences	2.1	2.0	3.0	3.0
Mathematics	2.6	2.5	1.8	2.6
Science	1.6	1.1	2.9	2.3
Biology	3.7	3.2	4.8	2.7
Chemistry	6.2	5.1	4.4	6.3
Physics	5.7	6.3	2.8	6.6
Foreign languages	3.5	3.5	3.0	4.3
Visual and performing arts	2.3	2.3	4.1	4.6
Health and physical education	3.2	2.7	3.8	3.8
Vocational education	6.6	6.5	4.1	7.1

SOURCE: U.S. Department of Education, National Center for Education Statistics, Schools and Staffing Survey, 1993–94 (Teacher Questionnaire).

Table S58   Standard errors for text table in *Indicator 58*

Selected occupations	Average prose literacy scores	Average annual earnings in 1991	Average weekly wage last week	Average weeks worked in 1991	Average age	Percentage with graduate degrees	Percentage female
All bachelor's degree recipients	**1.1**	**$881**	**$25**	**0.3**	**0.2**	**1.0**	**1.0**
Scientists	5.2	1,855	42	1.0	0.7	4.3	2.8
Lawyers and judges	6.8	7,139	555	1.2	1.0	3.6	5.6
Accountants and auditors	4.5	2,879	64	0.6	1.2	5.9	5.2
Private-sector executives and managers	2.9	2,481	46	0.3	0.5	2.7	2.9
Postsecondary teachers	7.2	8,190	153	1.2	1.3	3.9	5.6
Engineers	6.1	2,386	45	0.7	1.5	4.6	1.7
Physicians	10.2	14,685	325	1.3	2.2	0.0	6.0
Teachers	**2.8**	**1,126**	**20**	**0.8**	**0.6**	**2.9**	**2.8**
Writers and artists	7.6	3,266	73	2.1	1.2	7.5	8.0
Social workers	6.7	2,208	44	1.0	1.6	8.1	6.8
Sales representatives	4.9	2,323	79	1.1	1.1	2.9	3.7
Education administrators	8.6	4,995	103	0.9	1.6	5.0	9.2
Registered nurses	5.1	2,414	51	1.2	1.8	4.6	5.1
Sales supervisors and proprietors	6.2	4,694	109	0.6	1.6	5.5	5.3

SOURCE: U.S. Department of Education, National Center for Education Statistics, National Adult Literacy Survey, 1992.

Table S59   Standard errors for the text table in *Indicator 59*

Professional development topic and type of support received	Public			Private		
	Total	Elementary	Secondary	Total	Elementary	Secondary
In-service education or professional development topic						
Uses of educational technology for instruction	0.5	0.6	0.5	0.8	0.9	1.2
Methods of teaching in specific subject field	0.4	0.6	0.4	0.6	0.8	1.4
In-depth study in specific field	0.3	0.5	0.3	0.4	0.5	1.1
Student assessment	0.4	0.6	0.5	0.7	1.0	1.3
Cooperative learning in the classroom	0.4	0.6	0.5	1.0	1.0	1.5
Type of support received during the 1993–94 school year for in-service education or professional development						
Released time from teaching	0.4	0.7	0.4	0.9	1.1	1.0
Scheduled time	0.4	0.6	0.4	0.6	0.9	1.0
Travel and/or per diem expenses	0.4	0.6	0.3	0.6	0.8	1.1
Tuition and/or fees	0.3	0.5	0.3	0.8	0.9	1.4
Professional growth credits	0.4	0.5	0.3	0.6	0.7	0.9
None of the above	0.3	0.5	0.3	0.7	0.9	1.2

SOURCE: U.S. Department of Education, National Center for Education Statistics, Schools and Staffing Survey, 1993–94 (Teacher Questionnaire).

Table S60   Standard errors for the text table in *Indicator 60*

Control of institution, academic discipline, and academic rank	Percent of faculty with earnings in addition to basic faculty salary (BFS)	Mean basic faculty salary (BFS)	Mean total earned income (TEI)	BFS as a percentage of TEI (mean)
Total	**0.5**	**$470**	**$688**	**0.2**
Control of institution				
Public	0.6	542	799	0.3
Private	1.0	139	1,458	0.5
Academic discipline				
Agriculture	4.2	1,912	2,922	1.7
Business	1.4	1,805	2,444	0.8
Education	1.4	859	1,363	0.7
Engineering	2.2	1,787	2,354	1.0
Fine arts	1.6	2,098	2,480	0.7
Humanities	1.1	682	954	0.4
Natural sciences	1.2	891	1,158	0.5
Social sciences	1.1	722	1,264	0.6
Academic rank				
Full professor	0.9	758	1,259	0.4
Associate professor	1.0	1,089	1,244	0.5
Assistant professor	1.0	545	818	0.4
Instructor	1.3	796	1,070	0.6
Lecturer	4.9	2,054	2,881	1.5

SOURCE: U.S. Department of Education, National Center for Education Statistics, National Survey of Postsecondary Faculty, 1993.

Sources of Data

1. Federal Agency Sources
National Center for Education Statistics
U.S. Department of Education

Baccalaureate and Beyond Longitudinal Study

The Baccalaureate and Beyond Longitudinal Study (B&B) is based on the National Postsecondary Student Aid Study (NPSAS) and provides information concerning education and work experience after completing the bachelor's degree. B&B provides cross-sectional information 1 year after bachelor's degree completion (comparable to the Recent College Graduate Study), while at the same time provides longitudinal data concerning entry into and progress through graduate level education, and the work force. Also provides information on entry into, persistence and progress through, and completing of graduate level education information not available through followups involving high school cohorts or even college entry cohorts, both of which are restricted in the number who actually complete a bachelor's degree and continue their education.

B&B will follow NPSAS baccalaureate degree completers for a 12-year period after completion, beginning with NPSAS:93. About 11,000 students who completed their degree in the 1992–93 academic year were included in the first B&B (B&B:93/94). In addition to the student data, B&B will collect postsecondary transcripts covering the undergraduate period, providing complete information on progress and persistence at both the undergraduate and graduate levels. New B&B cohorts will alternate with BPS in using NPSAS as their base.

For additional information about B&B contact:

Paula R. Knepper
Postsecondary Education Statistics Division
National Center for Education Statistics
555 New Jersey Avenue NW
Washington, DC 20208-5652
Telephone: (202) 219-1914
e-mail: Paula_Knepper@ed.gov

Beginning Postsecondary Students Longitudinal Study

The Beginning Postsecondary Students Longitudinal Study (BPS) provides information on persistence, progress, and attainment of students from their initial time of entry into postsecondary education through their leaving school and entering the work force. BPS includes traditional and nontraditional (e.g., older) students and is representative of all beginning students in postsecondary education. BPS follows first-time, beginning students for at least 6 years at 2-year intervals, collecting student data, postsecondary transcripts, and financial aid reports. By starting with a cohort that has already entered postsecondary education (from the NPSAS:90), and following it for 6 years (with the first followup in spring 1992 and the second followup in spring 1994), BPS is able to determine to what extent, if any, students who start postsecondary education later differ in their progress, persistence, and attainment.

For additional information about BPS, contact:

Paula R. Knepper
Postsecondary Education Statistics Division
National Center for Education Statistics
555 New Jersey Avenue NW
Washington, DC 20208-5652
Telephone: (202) 219-1914
e-mail: Paula_Knepper@ed.gov

Common Core of Data

The Common Core of Data (CCD) survey provides the National Center for Education Statistics (NCES) with a way to acquire and maintain statistical data on the 50 states, the District of Columbia, and five outlying areas from the universe of state-level education agencies. Information about staff and students is collected annually at the school, local education agency or school district (LEA), and state levels. Information about revenues and expenditures also is collected at the state level, and NCES joins the Bureau of Census in collecting school district finance data. Data are collected for a particular school year (October 1 through September 30) via survey instruments sent to the states by October 15 of the subsequent school year. States have 1 year in which to modify the data originally submitted.

For additional information about CCD, contact:

John Sietsema
Elementary and Secondary Education
  Statistics Division
National Center for Education Statistics
555 New Jersey Avenue NW
Washington, DC 20208–5651
Telephone: (202) 219-1335
e-mail: John_Sietsema@ed.gov

High School and Beyond

High School and Beyond (HS&B) is a national longitudinal study of 1980 high school sophomores and seniors. The base-year survey was a probability sample of 1,015 high schools, with a target number of 36 sophomores and 36 seniors in each of the schools. A total of 58,270 students participated in the base-year survey. Substitutions were made for noncooperating schools—but not for students—in those strata where it was possible. Overall, 1,122 schools were selected in the original sample and 811 of these schools participated in the survey. An additional 204 schools were drawn in a replacement sample. Student refusals and student absences resulted in an 82 percent completion rate for the survey.

HS&B first followup activities were conducted in the spring of 1982. The sample design of the first followup survey called for the selection of approximately 30,000 individuals who were sophomores in 1980. The completion rate for sophomores eligible for on-campus survey administration was about 96 percent. About 89 percent of the students who left school between the base-year and first followup surveys (dropouts, transfer students, and early graduates) completed the first followup sophomore questionnaire.

The sample for the second followup, which took place in the spring of 1984, consisted of about 12,000 members of the senior cohort and about 15,000 members of the sophomore cohort. The completion rates were 91 and 92 percent, respectively.

HS&B third followup data collection activities were conducted in the spring of 1986. Both the sophomore and senior cohort samples for this round of data collection were the same as those used for the second followup survey. The completion rates for the sophomore and senior cohort samples were 91 percent and 88 percent, respectively.

For additional information about HS&B, contact:

Aurora M. D'Amico
Postsecondary Education Statistics Division
National Center for Education Statistics
555 New Jersey Avenue NW
Washington, DC 20208–5652
Telephone: (202) 219-1365
e-mail: Aurora_D'Amico@ed.gov

High School Transcript Studies

As part of the first followup survey of High School and Beyond (HS&B), transcripts were requested in fall 1982 for an 18,152-member subsample of the sophomore cohort. Of the 15,941 transcripts actually obtained, 1,969 were excluded because the students had dropped out of school before graduation; 799 were excluded because they were incomplete; and 1,057 were excluded because the students graduated before 1982 or the transcript indicated neither a dropout status nor graduation. Thus, 12,116 transcripts were used for an overall curriculum analysis.

Transcripts of 1987 high school graduates were compared to transcripts of 1982 graduates to describe changes in course-taking patterns across this 5-year period. The sample of schools for the 1987 High School Transcript Study consisted of a nationally representative sample of 497 secondary schools selected for the 1986 National Assessment of Educational Progress (NAEP) for students in grade 11 who were 17 years old, of which 433 schools participated. The 1987 study was restricted to students who were in grade 11 during school year 1985–86 equaling 27,732 graduates.

The 1990 High School Transcript Study was conducted using methodology and techniques nearly identical to those used in the 1987 study.

The analyses in the *Condition* focuses on high school graduates, so only those students who had graduated from high school were included from the 1990 study, the 1987 High School Transcript Study, and from HS&B. Because the methods used to identify and define disabled students were different for the later studies, and in order to make the samples as comparable as possible, it was necessary to restrict the samples to those students whose records indicated they had not participated in a special education program.

In the spring of 1991, transcripts were collected from 21,607 students who graduated from high school in 1990. These students attended 330 schools that had previously been sampled for the NAEP.

Between May and November of 1994, high school transcripts were collected from 25,573 students who graduated from high school in 1994. To be consistent with the 1982 study, students with an Individualized Education Program (IEP) were omitted. Also, students with incomplete transcripts were dropped, bringing the number of transcripts analyzed to 24,374. These students attended 340 schools that had previously been sample by NAEP.

For additional information about the HS&B Transcripts, contact:

> Steve Gorman
> Education Assessment Division
> National Center for Education Statistics
> 555 New Jersey Avenue NW
> Washington, DC 20208–5653
> Telephone: (202) 219-1937
> e-mail: Steve_Gorman@ed.gov

Integrated Postsecondary Education Data System

The Integrated Postsecondary Education Data System (IPEDS) surveys all postsecondary institutions, including universities and colleges, as well as institutions offering technical and vocational education beyond the high school level. This survey, which began in 1986, replaces and expands upon the Higher Education General Information Survey (HEGIS).

IPEDS consists of several integrated components that obtain information on where postsecondary education is available (institutions), who participates in it and completes it (students), which programs are offered and are completed, and which human and financial resources are involved in the provision of institutionally based postsecondary education. Specifically, these components include: fall enrollment in occupationally specific programs; salaries of full-time instructional faculty; completions (degrees awarded); finance; staff; institutional

characteristics, including institutional activity; fall enrollment, including age and residence; and academic libraries.

For additional information about IPEDS, contact:

> Roslyn A. Korb
> Postsecondary Education Statistics Division
> National Center for Education Statistics
> 555 New Jersey Avenue NW
> Washington, DC 20208–5652
> Telephone: (202) 219-1587
> e-mail: Roslyn_Korb@ed.gov

Fall Enrollment. This survey has been part of the IPEDS or HEGIS series since 1966. The enrollment survey response rate is relatively high; for example, the 1992 response rate was 86.9 percent.

Beginning in fall 1986, the survey system was redesigned with the introduction of IPEDS (see above). The new survey system comprises all postsecondary institutions, but also maintains comparability with earlier surveys by allowing HEGIS institutions to be tabulated separately. The new system also provides for preliminary and revised data releases. This allows NCES the flexibility to release early data sets while still maintaining a more accurate final database.

Salaries, Tenure, and Fringe Benefits of Full-time Instructional Faculty. This survey has been conducted for most years between 1966–67 and 1985–86, and in 1987–88 and 1989–90. Although the survey form was changed a number of times during those years, only comparable data are presented in this report. The data were collected from the individual colleges and universities.

Between 1966–67 and 1985–86 this survey differed from other HEGIS surveys in that imputations were not made for nonrespondents. Thus, there is some possibility that the salary averages presented in this report may differ from the results of a complete enumeration of all colleges and universities. Beginning with the surveys for 1987–88, the IPEDS data tabulation procedures included imputations for survey nonrespondents. The response rate for the 1993–94 survey was 90.1 percent.

Completions. This survey was always part of the HEGIS series. However, the degree classification taxonomy was revised in 1970 and again in 1980, with additional revisions in 1985 and 1990. Collection of degree data has been maintained through the IPEDS system.

Though information from survey years 1970–71 through 1981–82 is directly comparable, care must be taken if information before or after that period is included in any comparison. For example, degrees-conferred trend tables arranged by the 1982–83 classification were added to the *Digest of Education Statistics, 1992* to provide consistent data from 1970–71 to 1988–89. However, data on associate's degrees and other formal awards below the baccalaureate, by field of study after 1982–83, are not comparable with figures for earlier years. The nonresponse rate did not appear to be a significant source of nonsampling error for this survey. The return rate over the years was high, with a response rate for the 1992–93 survey of 88.2 percent. Because of the high return rate, nonsampling error caused by imputation was also minimal.

Financial Statistics. This survey was part of the HEGIS series and has been continued under the IPEDS system. Changes were made in the financial survey instruments in fiscal years (FY) 1976, 1982, and 1987. The FY 76 survey instrument contained numerous revisions to earlier survey forms and made direct comparisons of line items very difficult. Beginning in FY 82, Pell grant data were collected on federal restricted grants and contracts revenues and restricted scholarships and fellowships expenditures. The introduction of IPEDS in the FY 87 survey included several important changes to the survey instrument and data processing procedures. While these changes were significant, considerable effort has been made to present only comparable information on trends in this report and to note inconsistencies. Finance tables for this publication have been adjusted by subtracting the largely duplicative Pell Grant amounts from the later data to maintain comparability with pre-FY 82 data.

To reduce reporting error, NCES used national standards for reporting financial statistics. These standards are contained in *College and University Business Administration: Administrative Services* (1974 edition), published by the National Association of College and University Business Officers; *Audits of Colleges and Universities* (as

amended August 31, 1974), by the American Institute of Certified Public Accountants; and *HEGIS Financial Reporting Guide* (1980), by NCES. Wherever possible, definitions and formats in the survey form are consistent with those in these three accounting texts.

Fall Staff. The fall staff data presented in this publication were collected in cooperation with the U.S. Equal Employment Opportunity Commission (EEOC). In 1989, survey instruments were mailed to 6,669 in-scope postsecondary education institutions, including 2,576 4-year schools, 2,739 2-year schools, and 273 public less-than-2-year schools. The universe of 5,002 less-than-2-year private institutions were represented by a sample of 1,071 institutions.

The 3,589 institutions of higher education (in the 50 states and the District of Columbia) in operation in 1989 form a subset of the universe of postsecondary institutions in this report. These institutions are accredited at the college level by an agency recognized by the Secretary, U.S. Department of Education; these institutions were previously surveyed under HEGIS, which IPEDS supersedes. The EEO-6 1991 "Fall Staff" survey had an overall response rate of 84.9 percent.

Institutional Characteristics. This survey provided the basis for the universe of institutions presented in the *Education Directory, Colleges and Universities.* The universe comprised institutions that met certain accreditation criteria and offered at least a 1-year program of college-level studies leading toward a degree. All of these institutions were certified as eligible by the U.S. Department of Education's Division of Eligibility and Agency Evaluation. Each fall, institutions listed in the previous year's *Directory* were asked to update a computer printout of their information.

International Assessment of Educational Progress

In 1990–91, a total of 20 countries assessed the mathematics and science achievement of 13-year-old students in the International Assessment of Educational Progress (IAEP), and 14 of the 20 countries assessed 9-year-old students. Some countries assessed virtually all age-eligible children in the appropriate age group; others confined their samples to certain geographic regions, language groups, or grade levels. The definition of populations often followed the structure of school systems, political divisions, and cultural distinctions. In some countries, significant proportions of age-eligible children were not represented because they did not attend school. Also, in some countries, low rates of school or student participation mean results may be biased.

Typically, a random sample of 3,300 students from about 110 different schools was selected from each population at each age level; half were assessed in mathematics and half in science. A total of about 175,000 9- and 13-year-olds (those born in calendar years 1981 and 1977, respectively) were tested in 13 different languages in March 1991.

For further information about IAEP, contact:

> Maureen E. Treacy
> Education Assessment Division
> National Center for Education Statistics
> 555 New Jersey Avenue NW
> Washington, DC 20208–5653
> Telephone: (202) 219-1739
> e-mail: Maureen_Treacy@ed.gov

National Adult Literacy Survey

The National Adult Literacy Survey (NALS) was created as a new measure of literacy and funded by the U.S. Department of Education and by 12 states. It is the third, and largest assessment, of adult literacy funded by the federal government. The aim of the survey is to profile the English literacy of adults in the United States based on their performance across a wide array of tasks that reflect the types of materials and demands they encounter in their daily lives.

To gather the information on adults' literacy skills, trained staff interviewed nearly 13,600 individuals age 16 and older during the first 8 months of 1992. These participants had been randomly selected to represent the adult population in the country as a whole. In addition, some 1,100 inmates from 80 federal and state prisons were interviewed to gather information on the proficiencies of the prison population. In total, over 26,000 adults were surveyed.

For additional information about NALS, contact:

Andrew Kolstad
Education Assessment Division
National Center for Education Statistics
555 New Jersey Avenue NW
Washington, DC 20208-5653
Telephone: (202) 219-1773
e-mail: Andrew_Kolstad@ed.gov

National Assessment of Educational Progress

The National Assessment of Educational Progress (NAEP) is a congressionally mandated study funded by the Office of Educational Research and Improvement (OERI), U.S. Department of Education. The overall goal of the project is to determine the nation's progress in education. To accomplish this goal, a cross-sectional study was designed and initially implemented in 1969. Periodically, NAEP has gathered information about levels of educational achievement across the country. NAEP has surveyed the educational accomplishments of 9-, 13-, and 17-year-old students (and in recent years, students in grades 4, 8, and 12), and occasionally young adults, in 10 learning areas. Different learning areas were assessed annually and, as of 1980–81, biennially. Most areas have been periodically reassessed in order to measure possible changes in education achievement.

For additional information on NAEP, contact:

> Gary Phillips
> Education Assessment Division
> National Center for Education Statistics
> 555 New Jersey Avenue NW
> Washington, DC 20208–5653
> Telephone: (202) 219-1763
> e-mail: Gary_Phillips@ed.gov

National Education Longitudinal Study of 1988

The National Education Longitudinal Study of 1988 (NELS:88) is the third major longitudinal study sponsored by NCES. The two studies that preceded NELS:88, the National Longitudinal Study of the High School Class of 1972 (NLS–72) and HS&B surveyed high school seniors (and sophomores in HS&B) through high school, postsecondary education, and work and family formation experiences. Unlike its predecessors, NELS:88 began with a cohort of 8th-grade students.

NELS:88 is designed to provide trend data about critical transitions experienced by young people as they develop, attend school, and embark on their careers. It complements and strengthens state and local efforts by furnishing new information on how school policies, teacher practices, and family involvement affect student educational outcomes (i.e., academic achievement, persistence in school, and participation in postsecondary education). The base-year NELS:88 was a multifaceted study questionnaire with four cognitive tests, and questionnaires for students, teachers, parents, and the school.

Within the school sample, 26,000 8th-grade students were selected at random. The first and second followups revisited the same sample of students in 1990, 1992 and 1994, when the 1988 8th-graders were in the 10th and 12th grades and then 2 years after their scheduled high school graduation. A similar followup is being conducted in 1997.

For additional information about NELS, contact:

Jeffrey A. Owings
Elementary and Secondary Education Division
National Center for Education Statistics
555 New Jersey Avenue NW
Washington, DC 20208–5651
Telephone: (202) 219-1777
e-mail: Jeffrey_Owings@ed.gov

National Household Education Survey

The National Household Education Survey (NHES) is the first major attempt by NCES to go beyond its traditional, school-based data collection to a household survey. Historically, NCES has collected data from teachers, students, and schools through school-based surveys and from administrative records data through surveys of school districts and state education agencies. NHES has the potential to address many issues in education that have not been addressed previously by NCES data collection activities.

During the spring of 1991, NCES fielded a full-scale NHES on early education. Approximately 60,000 households were screened to identify a sample of children aged 3–8. The parents of these children were interviewed in order to collect information about their children's educational activities and the role of the family in children's learning. The NHES:93 is a subsequent survey conducted in the spring of 1993. It addressed readiness for school and safety and discipline in school. The NHES:93 early childhood component focused on readiness for school in a broad sense and examined several relevant issues. The School Safety and Discipline component of the NHES:93 addressed a new topic for the NHES. It focused on four areas: school environment, school safety, school discipline policy, and alcohol/other drug used and education. In the NHES:95 survey, the Early Childhood Program Participation component provides information on infants', toddlers' and preschoolers' participation in a variety of early care and education settings, including both home-based and center-based arrangements. The survey component also includes data on kindergarten and primary school history and experiences.

In NHES, an adult education supplement was also fielded. Adult household members were sampled and questioned about their participation in adult education. The adult education component was, for the most part, adapted from the previous Current Population Survey (CPS) adult education supplements. However, unlike the CPS, NHES collects information on both adult education participants and nonparticipants. The NHES:91 survey identified and screened more than 60,000 households. During the survey, a knowledgeable adult was asked a series of questions to screen all household members for adult education participation in a sample of about 20,000 of these 60,000 households, resulting in interviews with approximately 9,800 adult education participants. In the NHES:95 survey, of the 23,969 adults sampled for the adult education component, 80 percent (19,722) completed the interview.

For additional information about the child care and early education program participation component of NHES, contact:

Kathryn A. Chandler
Elementary and Secondary Education
  Statistics Division
National Center for Education Statistics
555 New Jersey Avenue NW
Washington, DC 20208–5651
Telephone: (202) 219-1767
e-mail: Kathryn_Chandler@ed.gov

For additional information on the adult education component of NHES, contact:

> Peter S. Stowe
> Elementary and Secondary Education
> Statistics Division
> National Center for Education Statistics
> 555 New Jersey Avenue NW
> Washington, DC 20208–5651
> Telephone: (202) 219-2099
> e-mail: Peter_Stowe@ed.gov

National Postsecondary Student Aid Study

NCES conducted the National Postsecondary Student Aid Study (NPSAS) for the first time during the 1986–87 school year. This survey established the first comprehensive student financial aid database. Data were gathered from 1,074 postsecondary institutions and approximately 60,000 students and 14,000 parents. These data provided information on the cost of postsecondary education, the distribution of financial aid, the characteristics of both aided and nonaided students and their families, and the nature of aid packages.

In response to the continuing need for these data, NCES conducted the second and third cycle of NPSAS in the 1989–90 and 1992–93 school years.

The 1990 in-school sample involved approximately 70,000 students selected from registrar lists of enrollees at 1,200 postsecondary institutions. The 1993 sample was taken from 77,000 students at 1,000 postsecondary institutions. The sample included both aided and non-aided students. Student information such as field of study, education level, and attendance status (part time or full time) was obtained from registrar records. Types and amounts of financial aid and family financial characteristics were abstracted from school financial aid records. Also, approximately 16,000 parents of students were sampled in 1990 and 12,500 parents were sampled in 1993. Data on family composition and parent financial characteristics also was compiled. Students enrolled in postsecondary education for the first time in 1990 will serve as the base for the longitudinal component of NPSAS.

For additional information about NPSAS, contact:

> Andrew G. Malizio
> Postsecondary Education Statistics Division
> National Center for Educational Statistics
> 555 New Jersey Avenue NW
> Washington, DC 20208–5652
> Telephone: (202) 219-1448
> e-mail: Andrew_Malizio@ed.gov

National Survey of Postsecondary Faculty

The National Survey of Postsecondary Faculty (NSOPF-88) was a comprehensive survey of higher education instructional faculty in the fall of 1987. It was the first such survey conducted since 1963, and it gathered information regarding the backgrounds, responsibilities, workloads, salaries, benefits, and attitudes of both full- and part-time instructional faculty in 2- and 4-year institutions under both public and private control. In addition, information was gathered from institutional and department-level respondents on such issues as faculty composition, new hires, departures and recruitment, retention, and tenure policies.

There were three major components of the study: a survey of institutional-level respondents at a stratified random sample of 480 U.S. colleges and universities; a survey of a stratified random sample of 3,029 eligible department chairpersons (or their equivalent) within the participating 4-year institutions; and a survey of a stratified random sample of 11,013 eligible faculty members within the participating institutions. Response rates for the three surveys were 88 percent, 80 percent, and 76 percent, respectively.

The universe of institutions from which the sample was selected was all accredited nonproprietary U.S. postsecondary institutions that grant a 2-year (associate's) or higher degree and whose accreditation at the higher education level is recognized by the U.S. Department of Education. This includes religious, medical, and other specialized postsecondary institutions as well as 2- and 4-year nonspecialized institutions. According to the 1987 IPEDS, this universe comprised 3,159 institutions. The universe does not include proprietary 2- and 4-year institutions or less-than-2-year postsecondary institutions.

The second cycle of NSOPF, conducted in 1992–93, was limited to surveys of faculty and institutions, but with a substantially expanded sample of 974 public and private nonproprietary higher education institutions and 31,354 faculty. Unlike NSOPF-88, which was limited to faculty whose regular assignment included instruction, the faculty universe for NSOPF-93 was expanded to include anyone who was designated as faculty, whether or not their responsibilities included instruction, and other (non faculty) personnel with instructional responsibilities. Under this definition, researchers and administrators and other institutional staff who hold faculty positions, but who do not teach, were included in the sample. The definition of the institution universe for NSOPF-93 was identical to the one used in NSOPF-88.

For additional information about NSOPF, contact:

Linda J. Zimbler
Postsecondary Education Statistics Division
National Center for Education Statistics
555 New Jersey Avenue NW
Washington, DC 20208–5652
Telephone: (202) 219-1834
e-mail: Linda_Zimbler@ed.gov

Projections of Education Statistics

Since 1964, NCES has published *Projections of Education Statistics*, a report that shows projections of key statistics for elementary and secondary schools and institutions of higher education. Data are included for enrollments, instructional staff, graduates, and earned degrees. *Projections* includes several alternative projection series and a methodology section describing the techniques and assumptions used to prepare them. Data in this edition of *The Condition of Education* reflect the intermediate projection series only.

For additional information about projection methodology and accuracy, contact:

Debra E. Gerald
Statistical Standards and Methodology
 Division
National Center for Education Statistics
555 New Jersey Avenue NW
Washington, DC 20208–5654
Telephone: (202) 219-1581
e-mail: Debra_Gerald@ed.gov

Recent College Graduates Study

NCES has conducted periodic surveys of individuals, about 1 year after graduation, to collect information on college outcomes. The Recent College Graduates (RCG) surveys have concentrated on those graduates entering the teaching profession. To obtain accurate results on this smaller subgroup, graduates who are newly qualified to teach have been oversampled in each of the surveys.

The 1976 survey of 1974–75 college graduates was the first and smallest in the series. The sample consisted of 209 schools, of which 200 (96 percent) responded. Of the 5,506 graduates in the sample, 4,350 responded, for a response rate of 79 percent.

The 1981 survey was larger, with 301 institutions and 15,852 graduates. Responses were obtained from 286 institutions, for an institutional response rate of 95 percent, and from 9,312 graduates (716 others were determined to be out of scope), for a response rate of 62 percent.

The 1985 survey requested data from 18,738 graduates from 404 colleges. Responses were obtained from 13,200 students, for a response rate of 74 percent (885 were out of scope). The response rate for the colleges was 98 percent.

The 1987 survey form was sent to 21,957 graduates. Responses were received from 16,878, for a response rate of 79.7 percent. The *1987 Transcript Study* collected transcripts for each student who was part of the 1987 sample.

The 1991 survey sampled 18,135 graduates and 400 institutions. The response rates were 95 percent for the institutions and 83 percent for the graduates.

For additional information about RCG, contact:

Peter S. Stowe
Postsecondary Education Statistics Division
National Center for Education Statistics
555 New Jersey Avenue NW
Washington, DC 20208–5652
Telephone: (202) 219-2099
e-mail: Peter_Stowe@ed.gov

Schools and Staffing Survey

The school work force and teacher supply and demand are fundamental features of America's public and private school landscape. Yet, until recently, there was a lack of data on the characteristics of our children's teachers and administrators and their workplace conditions. The Schools and Staffing Survey (SASS) was designed to meet this need. This survey is a comprehensive public and private, elementary/secondary education database that combines and expands 12 separate surveys that NCES has conducted in the past. These included surveys of teacher demand and shortage; public and private schools; public and private school teachers; public administrators; students; public and private library/media centers; and public and private librarians.

Schools were the primary sampling unit for SASS, and a sample of teachers was selected in each school; public school districts were included in the sample when one or more of their schools was selected. The 1990–91 SASS included approximately 12,800 schools (9,300 public and 3,500 private), 65,000 teachers (52,000 public and 13,000 private), and 5,600 public school districts. The 1993–94 SASS included approximately 11,352 schools (8,767 public and 2,585 private), 55,477 teachers (47,105 public and 8372 private) 4,993 public school districts, 6,233 students (5,032 public and 1,210 private), 96,874 libraries (77,573 public and 19,301 private), 76,668 librarians (67,832 public and 8,834 private), and 11,841 administrators (9,098 public and 2,743 private). The survey was conducted by mail and telephone.

Another component of SASS is the Teacher Followup Survey (TFS). The survey consists of a subsample of SASS, and is implemented 1 year after each SASS. The survey identifies and collects data from various groups of teachers who were interviewed the previous year: 1) those individuals who remain in the teaching profession, including those who remain in the same school, as well as those who have moved; and 2) those individuals who have left the teaching profession. These data are used to provide information about teacher attrition and retention in the public and private schools and to project teacher demand during the 1990s.

For additional information about SASS, contact:

> Dan Kasprzyk
> Elementary and Secondary Education
> Division
> National Center for Education Statistics
> 555 New Jersey Avenue NW
> Washington, DC 20208–5651
> Telephone: (202) 219-1588
> e-mail: Dan_Kasprzyk@ed.gov

Office of Special Education and Rehabilitative Services
U.S. Department of Education

Annual Report to Congress on the Implementation of the Individuals with Disabilities Education Act

The Individuals with Disabilities Education Act (IDEA), formerly the Education of the Handicapped Act (EHA), requires the Secretary of Education to annually transmit to Congress a report that describes our school systems progress in serving the nation's disabled children. The annual report contains information on such children served by the public schools under the provisions of Part B of the IDEA and on children served in state-operated programs (SOP) for the disabled under Chapter I of the Education Consolidation and Improvement Act (ECIA). Statistics on children who receive special education and related services in various settings and on school personnel who provide such services are reported in an annual submission of data to the Office of Special Education and Rehabilitative Services (OSERS) by the 50 states, the District of Columbia, and the outlying areas. The child count information is based on the number of disabled children who receive special education and related services on December 1 of each year for IDEA and October 1 for Chapter I of ECIA/SOP.

For more information about the *Annual Report to Congress* contact:

> Lou Danielson
> Office of Special Education and
> Rehabilitative Services
> Office of Special Education Programs
> Room 3523, Switzer Building
> 330 C Street SW
> Washington, DC 20202

The Condition of Education 1996
Reply Card

In order to save printing costs for this edition of *The Condition of Education*, some of the materials that have been included in past editions have been excluded from the printed document. For example, many of the supplemental tables (and their corresponding standard error tables) have not been included here. We will, however, make this information available to you. The supplemental information, as well as many other NCES products, are available on the NCES World Wide Web Site at **http://www.ed.gov/NCES/**.

If you would like to receive this information by mail, please check the line indicating the product and format you are interested in and return this card.

_____**CD-ROM** of EdSearch--A searchable database of tables from various NCES publications, including *The Condition of Education, The Digest of Education Statistics, Projections of Education Statistics, Youth Indicators, State Education Trends*, etc. in MS DOS format.

_____**3 1/2 inch disk** of EdSearch (description above)

_____**Printed copy** of the supplemental tables

_____Supplemental and standard error tables in Microsoft Excel 4.0 for Windows on a **3 1/2 inch disk**

Your name:_____

Position/Office:_____Company/Organization:_____

Street:_____

City:_____State:_____Zip Code:_____

User Survey

According to the Paperwork Reduction Act of 1995, no persons are required to respond to a collection of information unless it displays a valid OMB control number. The valid OMB control number of this information collection is 1880–0529. The time required to complete this information collection is estimated to average 15 minutes. If you have any questions concerning the accuracy of the time estimate or suggestions for improving this form, please write to U.S. Department of Education, Washington, DC 20202-4651. If you have comments or concerns regarding the status of your individual submission of this form, write to NCES, 555 New Jersey Ave, NW, Washington, DC 20208.

To help us improve future editions of *The Condition of Education*, we would greatly appreciate your comments. You can return this survey by mail to the address listed on the reverse side of this form or FAX it to 202-219-1575.

1. How often do you use *The Condition of Education*?
   □ Every day   □ Once a week   □ Once a month   □ Once a year   □ First time ever

2. Do you have access to the World Wide Web?   □ Yes   □ No   3. Do you have a CD-ROM drive?   □ Yes   □ No

4. Do you have any comments on the format or content of *The Condition of Education*?

5. How can we make *The Condition of Education* more useful to you?

6. Would you like to participate in a follow-up telephone survey about your uses of *The Condition of Education* and other NCES information?   □ Yes   □ No
      If yes, daytime phone number   (   )_____

NO POSTAGE
NECESSARY
IF MAILED
IN THE
UNITED
STATES

BUSINESS REPLY MAIL
FIRST CLASS PERMIT NO. 012935 WASHINGTON, DC

POSTAGE WILL BE PAID BY U.S. DEPARTMENT OF EDUCATION

**U.S. Department of Education
Mail Code: 5721
600 Independence Avenue, S.W.
Washington, D.C. 20277-2935**

Fold on line–TAPE CLOSED–DO NOT STAPLE

Bureau of the Census
U.S. Department of Commerce

Current Population Survey

Current estimates of school enrollment and social and economic characteristics of students are based on data collected in the Bureau of the Census' monthly household survey of about 60,000 households, known as the Current Population Survey (CPS). The CPS covers 729 sample areas consisting of 1,973 counties, independent cities, and minor civil divisions throughout the 50 states and the District of Columbia. Up to 1993, the sample was selected from 1980 census files and is periodically updated to reflect new housing construction. In 1994, the questionnaire for the CPS was redesigned, and the computer-assisted personal interviewing (CAPI) method was implemented. In addition, the 1990 census-based population controls with adjustments for the estimated population undercount were also introduced.

The primary function of the monthly CPS is to collect data on labor force participation of the civilian noninstitutional population. (It excludes military personnel and inmates of institutions.) In October of each year, questions on school enrollment by grade and other school characteristics are asked about each member of the household.

For additional information refer to the *Current Population Reports*, Series P-20, or contact:

> Education and Social Stratification Branch
> Population Division
> Bureau of the Census
> U.S. Department of Commerce
> Washington, DC 20233

School Enrollment. Each October, the CPS includes supplemental questions on the enrollment status of the population aged 3 and older. Annual reports documenting school enrollment of this population have been produced by the Bureau of the Census since 1946. The latest report is *Current Population Reports*, Series P-20, *School Enrollment— Social and Economic Characteristics of Students: October 1994.*

For additional information about the CPS school enrollment data, contact:

> Education and Social Stratification Branch
> Population Division
> Bureau of the Census
> U.S. Department of Commerce
> Washington, DC 20233

Educational Attainment. Data on years of school completed are derived from two questions on the CPS instrument. Biennial reports documenting educational attainment are produced by the Bureau of the Census using March CPS data. The latest report is *Current Population Reports*, Series P-20, No. 476 *Educational Attainment in the United States, March 1993 and 1992*.

Beginning with the data for March 1994, tabulations are controlled to the 1990 census. Estimates for earlier years were controlled to earlier censuses.

For additional information about educational attainment data, contact:

> Education and Social Stratification Branch
> Population Division
> Bureau of the Census
> U.S. Department of Commerce
> Washington, DC 20233

Voting and Registration. In November of election years, the CPS includes supplemental questions on voting and registration within the civilian noninstitutional population. CPS voting estimates exceed counts of the actual number of votes cast. On balance, the CPS overstates voting in Presidential elections by 10–20 percent of the total number of persons reported as having voted.

Data on voter participation by social and economic characteristics of the population of voting age have been published since 1964 in *Current Population Reports*, Series P-20. The latest report is "Voting and Registration in the Election of November 1994."

For additional information about voting and registration, contact:

> Jerry T. Jennings
> Population Division
> Bureau of the Census
> U.S. Department of Commerce
> Washington, DC 20233

2. Other Organization Sources

American College Testing Program

The American College Testing (ACT) Assessment is designed to measure educational development in the areas of English, mathematics, social studies, and natural sciences. The ACT Assessment is taken by college bound high school students, and the test results are used to predict how well students might perform in college.

Prior to the 1984–85 school year, national norms were based on a 10 percent sample of the students taking the test. Since then, national norms have been based on the test scores of all students taking the test. Moreover, beginning with 1984–85, these norms have been based on the most recent ACT scores available from students scheduled to graduate in the spring of the year in which they take the test. Duplicate test records are no longer used to produce national figures.

The 1990 ACT assessment is significantly different from previous years. Consequently, it is not possible to make direct comparisons between scores earned in 1990 and scores earned in previous years. To permit continuity in the tracking of score trends, ACT has established links between scores earned on ACT tests administered before October 1989 and scores on the new ACT.

For additional information about the ACT Assessment, contact:

> The American College Testing Program
> 2201 North Dodge Street
> P.O. Box 168
> Iowa City, IA 52243

American Federation of Teachers

The American Federation of Teachers (AFT) reports national and state average salaries and earnings of teachers, other school employees, government workers, and professional employees over the past 25 years. The AFT's survey of state departments of education obtains information on minimum salaries, experienced teachers reentering the classroom, and teacher age and experience. Most data from the survey are reported as received, although some data are confirmed by telephone. These data are available

in the AFT's annual report *Survey and Analysis of Salary Trends*. While serving as the primary vehicle for reporting the results of the AFT's annual survey of state departments of education, several other data sources are also used in this report.

For additional information about this survey, contact:

> American Federation of Teachers
> 555 New Jersey Avenue NW
> Washington, DC 20001

College Entrance Examination Board

The Admissions Testing Program of the College Board comprises a number of college admissions tests, including the Preliminary Scholastic Assessment Test (PSAT) and the Scholastic Assessment Test (SAT). High school students participate in the testing program as sophomores, juniors, or seniors—some more than once during these 3 years. If they have taken the tests more than once, only the most recent scores are tabulated. The PSAT and SAT report subscores in the areas of mathematics and verbal ability.

The SAT results are not representative of high school students or college bound students nationally since the sample is self-selected. Generally, tests are taken by students who need the results to attend a particular college or university. The state totals are greatly affected by the requirements of its state colleges. Public colleges in a number of states require ACT scores rather than SAT scores. Thus, the proportion of students taking the SAT in these states is very low and is inappropriate for any comparison. In recent years, about 1 million high school students have taken the examination annually.

For additional information about the SAT, contact:

> College Entrance Examination Board
> Educational Testing Service
> Princeton, NJ 08541

National Education Association

Estimates of School Statistics

The National Education Association (NEA) reports revenues and expenditure data in its annual publication, *Estimates of School Statistics*.

Each year NEA prepares regression-based estimates of financial and other education statistics and submits them to the states for verification. Generally, about 30 states adjust these estimates based on their own data. These preliminary data are published by NEA along with revised data from previous years. States are asked to revise previously submitted data as final figures become available. The most recent publication contains all changes reported to the NEA. Some tables in *The Condition of Education* use revised estimates of financial data prepared by the NEA because it is the most current source. Since expenditure data reported to NCES must be certified for use in the U.S. Department of Education formula grant programs (such as Chapter I of the ECIA), NCES data are not available as soon as NEA estimates.

For additional information about this data, contact:

National Education Association—Research
1201 16th Street NW
Washington, DC 20036

The International Association for the Evaluation of Educational Achievement

IEA Reading Literacy Study

In the period 1989–92, the International Association for the Evaluation of Educational Achievement (IEA) conducted a Reading Literacy Study in 32 systems of education. The study focused on two levels in each of these systems: 1) the grade level where most 9-year-olds were to be found; and 2) the grade level where most 14-year-olds were to be found.

To obtain comparable samples of students, multistage sampling was used in each country and schools or classes were typically drawn with a probability proportional to the size of the school or class.

Additional information is available in the IEA, report *How in the World Do Students Read?* by Warwick B. Elley.

Organization for Economic Co-operation and Development

The Organization for Economic Co-operation and Development (OECD) publishes analyses of national policies in education, training, and economics in 23 countries. The countries surveyed include: Australia, Austria, Belgium, Canada, Denmark, Finland, France, Germany, Ireland, Italy, Japan, Luxembourg, Netherlands, New Zealand, Norway, Portugal, Spain, Sweden, Switzerland, Turkey, United Kingdom, United States, and Yugoslavia.

Since only developed nations, mostly European, are included in OECD studies, the range of analysis is limited. However, OECD data allow for some detailed international comparisons of financial resources or other education variables to be made for this selected group of countries.

For additional information about OECD data, contact:

OECD
2, rue Andre-Pascal
75775 PARIS CEDEX 16, France

Sources by Indicator

Federal Agency Sources

1. **National Center for Education Statistics**   **Indicator Number**
    U.S. Department of Education

    A. Surveys

    Baccalaureate and Beyond Longitudinal Study
        First Follow-up (1994)   11, 31, 35

    Beginning Postsecondary Students Longitudinal Survey
        Base Year (1990)   9, 10
        Second Follow-up (1994)   9, 10

    Common Core of Data (CCD)   38, 40, 51

    Financial Statistics of Institutions of Higher Education Survey   53, 54

    High School and Beyond (HS&B)   6, 26

    International Assessment of Education Progress   23, 24

    Integrated Postsecondary Education Data System (IPEDS)
        Fall Enrollment Survey   12, 39, 45, 51
        Financial Statistics   53, 54
        Institutional Characteristics   12
        Degrees Conferred   40, 41

    National Adult Literacy Survey (NALS)   58

    National Assessment of Educational Progress (NAEP)   15, 16, 17, 19

    National Education Longitudinal Study of 1988 (NELS:88)
        Base Year (1988)   6
        First Follow-up (1990)   6
        Second Follow-up (1992)   6, 46
        Third Follow-up (1994)   6

    National Household Education Survey (NHES)
        Adult Education Component   14
        Early Childhood Program Participation   2
        School Safety and Discipline File   4

    National Postsecondary Student Aid Study (NPSAS)   13

    National Survey of Postsecondary Faculty (NSOPF)   49, 50, 59

    Recent College Graduates Survey (RCG)   11, 35

    Schools and Staffing Survey (SASS)   42, 47, 48, 55, 56, 57, 59

B. Publications

2. Office of Special Education and Rehabilitative Services
U.S. Department of Education

3. Bureau of the Census
U.S. Department of Commerce

4. Executive Office of the President

Other Organization Sources

Glossary

Academic support: (See Expenditures.)

Adult education: College, vocational, or occupational programs, continuing education or non-credit courses, correspondence courses and tutoring, as well as courses and other educational activities provided by employers, community groups, and other providers.

Advanced degree: Any formal degree attained after the bachelor's degree. Advanced degrees include master's degrees, doctoral degrees, and professional degrees.

Advantaged urban: Students in this group live in metropolitan statistical areas (MSAs) and attend schools where a high proportion of the students' parents are in professional or managerial positions. Schools were placed into this category on the basis of information about the type of community, the size of its population, and an occupational profile of residents provided by school principals participating in the National Assessment of Educational Progress (NAEP).

Appropriations (federal funds): Budget authority provided through the congressional appropriation process that permits federal agencies to incur obligations and to make payments.

Appropriations (institutional revenues): An amount (other than a grant or contract) received from or made available to an institution through an act of a legislative body.

Associate's degree: A degree granted for the successful completion of a sub-baccalaureate program of studies, usually requiring at least 2 years (or equivalent) of full-time college-level study. This includes degrees granted in a cooperative or work-study program.

Auxiliary enterprises: (See Revenues.)

Average daily attendance (ADA): The aggregate attendance of students in a school during a reporting period (normally a school year) divided by the number of days that school is in session during this period. Only days on which the students are under the guidance and direction of teachers should be considered days in session.

Average daily membership (ADM): The aggregate membership of a school during a reporting period (normally a school year) divided by the number of days that school is in session during this period. Only days on which the students are under the guidance and direction of teachers should be considered days in session. The average daily membership for groups of schools having varying lengths of terms is the average of the average daily memberships obtained for the individual schools.

Baccalaureate degree: (See Bachelor's degree.)

Bachelor's degree: A degree granted for the successful completion of a baccalaureate program of studies, usually requiring at least 4 years (or equivalent) of full-time college-level study. This includes degrees granted in a cooperative or work-study program.

Carnegie unit: A standard of measurement used for secondary education that represents the completion of a course that meets one period per day for 1 year.

Catholic school: (See Orientation.)

Cohort: A group of individuals who have a statistical factor in common, for example, year of birth.

Certificate: An award granted for the successful completion of a sub-baccalaureate program of studies, usually requiring less than 2 years of full-time postsecondary study.

College: A postsecondary school that offers general or liberal arts education, usually leading to an associate's, bachelor's, master's, doctor's, or first-professional degree. Junior colleges and community colleges are included under this terminology.

Combined elementary and secondary school: A school that encompasses instruction at both the elementary and secondary levels. Examples of combined elementary and secondary school grade spans would be grades 1–12 or grades 5–12.

Computer and information sciences: A group of instructional programs that describes computer and information sciences, including computer programming, data processing, and information systems.

Constant dollars: Dollar amounts that have been adjusted by means of price and cost indexes to eliminate inflationary factors and allow direct comparison across years.

Consumer price index (CPI): This price index measures the average change in the cost of a fixed-market basket of goods and services purchased by consumers.

Control of institutions: A classification of institutions of elementary/secondary or higher education by whether the institution is operated by publicly elected or appointed officials (public control) or by privately elected or appointed officials and derives its major source of funds from private sources (private control).

Core subjects: *A Nation at Risk* recommended that all students seeking a high school diploma be required to enroll in a core curriculum called "New Basics." The core subjects included in this plan are 4 units of English, 3 units each of science, social studies, and mathematics, and 0.5 units of computer science.

Cost of college attendance: Cost of living for students attending postsecondary institutions, including tuition and fees, books, room and board, child care, transportation, and other miscellaneous expenses.

Current dollars: Dollar amounts that have not been adjusted to compensate for inflation.

Current expenditures per pupil in enrollment: (See Expenditures.)

Current-fund expenditures: (See Expenditures.)

Current-fund revenues: (See Revenues.)

Dependent student: A student who under federal criteria is considered to be financially dependent on his or her parents or guardians. Most full-time students are considered dependent until they are 24 years old.

Disadvantaged urban: Students in this group live in metropolitan statistical areas (MSAs) and attend schools where a high proportion of the students' parents are on welfare or are not regularly employed. Schools were placed into this category on the basis of information about the type of community, the size of its population, and an occupational profile of residents provided by school principals participating in NAEP.

Doctor's degree: An earned degree carrying the title of Doctor. The Doctor of Philosophy degree (Ph.D.) is the highest academic degree and requires mastery within a field of knowledge and demonstrated ability to perform scholarly research. Other doctorates are awarded for fulfilling specialized requirements in professional fields, such as education (Ed.D.), musical arts (D.M.A.), business administration (D.B.A.), and engineering (D.Eng. or D.E.S.). Many doctor's degrees in both academic and professional fields require an earned master's degree as a prerequisite. First-professional degrees, such as M.D. and D.D.S., are not included under this heading. (See First-professional degree.)

Dropout: The term is used both to describe the event of leaving school before graduating and the status of an individual who is not in school and who is not a graduate. Transferring schools, for example, from a public to a private school, is not regarded as a dropout event. A person who drops out of school may later return and graduate. At the time the person left school initially, he or she is called a *dropout*. At the time the person returns to school, he or she is called a *stopout*. Measures to describe these often complicated behaviors include the event dropout rate (or the closely related school persistence rate), the status dropout rate, and the high school completion rate.

Educational and general expenditures: (See Expenditures.)

Educational attainment: The highest grade of regular school attended and completed.

Elementary school: A school classified as elementary by state and local practice and composed of any span of grades not above grade 8. Preschool or kindergarten is included under this heading only if it is an integral part of an elementary school or a regularly established school system.

Elementary/secondary school: As reported in this publication, includes only regular schools (i.e., schools that are part of state and local school systems, and also most not-for-profit private elementary/secondary schools, both religiously affiliated and nonsectarian). Schools not reported include subcollegiate departments of institutions of higher education, residential schools for exceptional children, federal schools for American Indians, and federal schools on military posts and other federal installations.

Employed: Includes civilian, non-institutionalized persons who 1) worked during any part of the survey week as paid employees; worked in their own businesses, professions, or farms; or worked 15 hours or more as unpaid workers in a family-owned enterprise; or 2) who were not working but had jobs or businesses from which they were temporarily absent due to illness, bad weather, vacation, labor-management dispute, or personal reasons, whether or not they were seeking another job.

Engineering and engineering technologies: Instructional programs that describe the mathematical and natural science knowledge gained by study, experience, and practice and applied with judgment to develop ways to economically use the materials and forces of nature for the benefit of humanity. Includes programs that prepare individuals to support and assist engineers and similar professionals.

English: A group of instructional programs that describes the English language arts, including composition, creative writing, and the study of literature.

Enrollment: The total number of students registered in a given school unit at a given time, generally in the fall of a year.

Expected family contribution (EFC): The amount that a family is expected to pay toward meeting costs of postsecondary attendance (both students and parents of dependent students are expected to make contributions). This amount is determined through an analysis of need (i.e., the Congressional Methodology) and is based on taxable and nontaxable income and assets as well as family size, the number of family members attending postsecondary institutions, extraordinary medical expenses, and so forth. For dependent students, the EFC consists of both a parental contribution and a separately calculated student contribution. The minimum student contribution in 1988–89 was $700 for freshmen and $900 for other undergraduates.

Expenditures: Charges incurred, whether paid or unpaid, which are presumed to benefit the current fiscal year. For elementary/secondary schools, these include all charges for current outlays plus capital outlays and interest on school debt. For institutions of higher education, these include current outlays plus capital outlays. For government, these include charges net of recoveries and other correcting transactions other than for retirement of debt, investment in securities, extension of credit, or as agency transaction. Also, government expenditures include only external transactions, such as the provision of prerequisites or other payments in kind. Aggregates for groups of governments exclude intergovernmental transactions among the governments.

Academic support: This category of college expenditures includes expenditures for support services that are an integral part of the institution's primary missions of instruction, research, or public service. Includes expenditures for libraries, galleries, audio/visual services, academic computing support, ancillary support, academic administration, personnel development, and course and curriculum development.

Current expenditures (elementary/secondary): The expenditures for operating local public schools, excluding capital outlay and interest on school debt. These expenditures include such items as salaries for school personnel, fixed charges, student transportation, school books and materials, and energy costs. Beginning in 1980–81, expenditures for state administration are excluded.

Current expenditures per pupil in enrollment: Current expenditures for the regular school term divided by the total number of students registered in a given school unit at a given time, generally in the fall of a year.

Current-fund expenditures (higher education): Money spent to meet current operating costs, including salaries, wages, utilities, student services, public services, research libraries, scholarships, fellowships, auxiliary enterprises, hospitals, and independent operations. Excludes loans, capital expenditures, and investments.

Educational and general expenditures: The sum of current-fund expenditures on instruction, research, public service, academic support, student services, institutional support, operation and maintenance of plant, and awards from restricted and unrestricted funds.

Instruction: This category includes expenditures of the colleges, schools, departments, and other instructional divisions of higher education institutions, and expenditures for departmental research and public service, which are not separately budgeted. Includes expenditures for both credit and non-credit activities. Excludes expenditures for academic administration where the primary function is administration (e.g., academic deans).

Scholarships and fellowships: This category of college expenditures applies only to money given in the form of outright grants and trainee stipends to individuals enrolled in formal course work, either for credit or not. Aid to students in the form of tuition or fee remissions is included. College work-study funds are excluded and are reported under the program in which the student is working. In the tabulations in this volume, Pell grants are not included in this expenditure category.

Expenditures per pupil: Charges incurred for a particular period of time divided by a student unit of measure, such as enrollment, average daily attendance, or average daily membership.

Family income: The combined income of all family members 14 years old and older living in the household for the period of 1 year. Income includes money income from jobs; net income from business, farm, or rent; pensions; dividends; interest; social security payments; and any other money income.

Federal aid: Student financial aid whose source is the federal government. This aid can either be provided by or administered by a federal agency. Federal agencies providing aid include the Department of Education, Department of Health and Human Services, Department of Defense, Veterans Administration, and the National Science Foundation. Federal aid can be in the form of grants, loans, and work-study aid.

Federal funds: Amounts collected and used by the federal government for the general purposes of the government. There are four types of federal fund accounts: the general fund, special

funds, public enterprise funds, and intragovernmental funds. The major federal fund is the general fund, which is derived from general taxes and borrowing. Federal funds also include certain earmarked collections, such as those generated by and used to finance a continuing cycle of business-type operations.

First-professional degree: A degree that signifies both completion of the academic requirements for beginning practice in a given profession and a level of professional skill beyond that normally required for a bachelor's degree. This degree is usually based on a program requiring at least 2 academic years of work prior to entrance and a total of at least 6 academic years of work to complete the degree program, including both prior-required college work and the professional program itself. By NCES definition, first-professional degrees are awarded in the fields of dentistry (D.D.S or D.M.D.), medicine (M.D.), optometry (O.D.), osteopathic medicine (D.O.), pharmacy (D.Phar.), podiatric medicine (D.P.M.), veterinary medicine (D.V.M.), chiropractic (D.C. or D.C.M.), law (J.D.), and theological professions (M.Div. or M.H.L.).

First-time teachers: Individuals who are teaching full time in the nation's school system this year for the first time. These teachers include recent college graduates, former substitute teachers, or individuals who had other jobs besides teaching either inside or outside the field of education.

Fiscal year: The yearly accounting period for the federal government, which begins on October 1 and ends on the following September 30. The fiscal year is designated by the calendar year in which it ends; for example, fiscal year 1992 begins on October 1, 1991, and ends on September 30, 1992. (From fiscal year 1844 to fiscal year 1976 the fiscal year began on July 1 and ended on the following June 30.)

Foreign languages: A group of instructional programs that describes the structure and use of language that is common or indigenous to individuals of the same community or nation, the same geographical area, or the same cultural traditions. Programs cover such features as sound, literature, syntax, phonology, semantics, sentences, prose, and verse, as well as the development of skills and attitudes used in communicating and evaluating thoughts and feelings through oral and written language.

Free lunch eligibles: The National School Lunch Program's assistance program for low income children. Families with school-aged children who fall below the poverty level and have no other significant assets are eligible to receive government assistance in the form of free or reduced-price school lunches.

Full-time enrollment: The number of students enrolled in higher education courses with a total credit load equal to at least 75 percent of the normal full-time course load.

Full-time-equivalent (FTE) enrollment: For institutions of higher education, enrollment of full-time students, plus the full-time equivalent of part-time students as reported by institutions. In the absence of an equivalent reported by an institution, the FTE enrollment is estimated by adding one-third of part-time enrollment to full-time enrollment.

Full-time instructional faculty: Those members of the instruction/research staff who are employed full-time as defined by the institution, including faculty with released time for research and faculty on sabbatical leave. Full-time counts exclude faculty who are employed to teach less than two semesters, three quarters, two trimesters, or two 4-month sessions; replacements for faculty on sabbatical leave or those on leave without pay; faculty for preclinical and clinical medicine; faculty who are donating their services; faculty who are members of military organizations and paid on a different pay scale from civilian employees; academic officers whose primary duties are administrative; and graduate students who assist in the instruction of courses.

Full-time worker: One who is employed for 35 or more hours per week, including paid leave for illness, vacation, and holidays. Hours may be reported either for a survey reference week, or for the previous calendar year, in which case they refer to the usual hours worked.

GED recipient: A person who has obtained certification of high school equivalency by meeting state requirements and passing an approved exam, which is intended to provide an appraisal of the person's achievement or performance in the broad subject matter areas

usually required for high school graduation. (See General Educational Development Test.)

General Educational Development (GED) Test: A test administered by the American Council on Education as the basis for awarding a high school equivalency certification.

Geographic region: 1) The four regions used by the Bureau of Economic Analysis of the U.S. Department of Commerce, the National Assessment of Educational Progress, and the National Education Association (NEA) are as follows (note that the NEA designated the Central region as the Middle region in its classification):

Northeast	*Southeast*
Connecticut	Alabama
Delaware	Arkansas
District of Columbia	Florida
Maine	Georgia
Maryland	Kentucky
Massachusetts	Louisiana
New Hampshire	Mississippi
New Jersey	North Carolina
New York	South Carolina
Pennsylvania	Tennessee
Rhode Island	Virginia
Vermont	West Virginia

Central (Middle)	*West*
Illinois	Alaska
Indiana	Arizona
Iowa	California
Kansas	Colorado
Michigan	Hawaii
Minnesota	Idaho
Missouri	Montana
Nebraska	Nevada
North Dakota	New Mexico
Ohio	Oklahoma
South Dakota	Oregon
Wisconsin	Texas
	Utah
	Washington
	Wyoming

2) The regions used by the Bureau of the Census in Current Population Survey (CPS) tabulations are as follows:

Northeast
(New England)
Maine
New Hampshire
Vermont
Massachusetts
Rhode Island
Connecticut

(Middle Atlantic)
New York
New Jersey
Pennsylvania

South
(South Atlantic)
Delaware
Maryland
District of Columbia
Virginia
West Virginia
North Carolina
South Carolina
Georgia
Florida

(East South Central)
Kentucky
Tennessee
Alabama
Mississippi

(West South Central)
Arkansas
Louisiana
Oklahoma
Texas

Midwest
(East North Central)
Ohio
Indiana
Illinois
Michigan
Wisconsin

(West North Central)
Minnesota
Iowa
Missouri
North Dakota
South Dakota
Nebraska
Kansas

West
(Mountain)
Montana
Idaho
Wyoming
Colorado
New Mexico
Arizona
Utah
Nevada

(Pacific)
Washington
Oregon
California
Alaska
Hawaii

Government appropriation: An amount (other than a grant or contract) received from or made available to an institution through an act of a legislative body.

Government grant or contract: Revenues from a government agency for a specific research project or other program.

Graduate: An individual who has received formal recognition for the successful completion of a prescribed program of studies.

Graduate Record Examination (GRE): Multiple-choice examinations administered by the Educational Testing Service (ETS) and taken by applicants who plan to attend certain graduate schools. Two generalized tests are offered, plus specialized tests in a variety of subject areas. Ordinarily, a student will take only the specialized test that applies to the intended field of study.

Grants: Also known as scholarships, these are funds for postsecondary education that do not have to be repaid.

Gross Domestic Product (GDP): Gross national product less net property income from abroad. Both gross national product and gross domestic product aggregate only the incomes of residents of a nation, corporate and individual, derived directly from the current production of goods and services. However, gross national product also includes net property from abroad. (See also Gross National Product.)

Gross National Product (GNP): A measure of the money value of the goods and services available to the nation from economic activity. GNP can be viewed in terms of expenditure categories, which include purchases of goods and services by consumers and government, gross private domestic investment, and net exports of goods and services. The goods and services included are largely those bought for final use (excluding illegal transactions) in the market economy. A number of inclusions, however, represent imputed values, the most important of which is rental value of owner-occupied housing. GNP, in this broad context, measures the output attributable to the factors of production, labor, and property supplied by U.S. residents.

Guidance counselor: (See Staff, elementary/secondary education.)

High school: A secondary school offering the final years of high school work necessary for graduation, usually including grades 10, 11, 12 (in a 6-3-3 plan) or grades 9, 10, 11, and 12 (in a 6-2-4 plan).

High school program: A program of studies designed to prepare students for their postsecondary education and occupation. Four types of programs are usually distinguished as academic, vocational, general, and personal use. An academic program is designed to prepare students for continued study at a college or university. A vocational program is designed to prepare students for employment in one or more semiskilled, skilled, or technical occupations. A general program is designed to provide students with the understanding and competence to function effectively in a free society, and usually represents a mixture of academic and vocational components. A personal use program provides a student with general skills in areas such as health, religion, and military science.

Higher education: Study beyond secondary school at an institution that offers programs terminating in an associate's, bachelor's, or higher degree.

Higher education institutions (general definition): Institutions providing education above the instructional level of the secondary schools, usually beginning with grade 13. Typically, these institutions include colleges, universities, graduate schools, professional schools, and other degree-granting institutions.

Higher education price index: A price index that measures average changes in the prices of goods and services purchased by colleges and universities through current-fund education and general expenditures (excluding expenditures for sponsored research and auxiliary enterprises).

Humanities: Instructional programs in the following fields: area and ethnic studies, foreign languages, letters, liberal/general studies, multi/interdisciplinary studies, philosophy and religion, theology, and the visual and performing arts.

Independent operations: A group of self-supporting activities under control of a college or university. For purposes of financial surveys conducted by the National Center for Education Statistics, this category is composed principally of federally funded research and development centers (FFRDC).

Inflation: An upward movement in general price levels that results in a decline of purchasing power.

Institutional support: The category of higher education expenditures that includes day-to-day operational support for colleges, excluding expenditures for physical plant operations. Examples of institutional support include general administrative services, executive direction and planning, legal and fiscal operations, and community relations.

Instruction: (See Expenditures.)

Instructional staff: Full-time-equivalent number of positions, not the number of different individuals occupying the positions during the school year. In local schools, includes all public elementary and secondary (junior and senior high) day-school positions that are in the nature of teaching or in the improvement of the teaching-learning situation. Includes consultants or supervisors of instruction, principals, teachers, guidance personnel, librarians, psychological personnel, and other instructional staff. Excludes administrative staff, attendance personnel, clerical personnel, and junior college staff.

Labor force: Individuals employed as civilians, unemployed, or in the armed services during the survey week. The "civilian labor force" is composed of all civilians classified as employed or unemployed. (See Employed and Unemployed.)

Life sciences: Life sciences are instructional programs that describe the systematic study of living organisms. Life sciences include biology, biochemistry, biophysics, and zoology.

Limited-English-proficient: A concept developed to assist in identifying those language-minority students (children from language backgrounds other than English) who need language assistance services, in their own language or in English, in the schools. The Bilingual Education Act, reauthorized in 1988 (P.L. 100-297), describes a limited-English-proficient (LEP) student as one who

1) meets one or more of the following conditions:
   a) a student who was born outside the United States or whose native language is not English;
   b) a student who comes from an environment where a language other than English is dominant; or

c) a student who is an American Indian or Alaskan Native and comes from an environment where a language other than English has had a significant impact on his/her level of English language proficiency; and

2) has sufficient difficulty speaking, reading, writing, or understanding the English language to deny him or her the opportunity to learn successfully in English-only classrooms.

In practice, many ways of making this determination about an individual student are being used by school systems across the United States. These include various combinations of home language surveys, informal teacher determination, formal interviews, and a number of types of assessment tests for classification, placement, and monitoring of progress.

Literacy: See supplemental note to *Indicator 31.*

Loan: Borrowed money that must be repaid.

Local education agency (LEA): (See School district.)

Master's degree: A degree awarded for successful completion of a program generally requiring 1 or 2 years of full-time college-level study beyond the bachelor's degree. One type of master's degree, including the Master of Arts degree, or M.A., and the Master of Science degree, or M.S., is awarded in the liberal arts and sciences for advanced scholarship in a subject field or discipline and demonstrated ability to perform scholarly research. A second type of master's degree is awarded for the completion of a professionally oriented program, for example, an M.Ed. in education, an M.B.A. in business administration, an M.F.A. in fine arts, an M.M. in music, an M.S.W. in social work, and an M.P.A. in public administration. A third type of master's degree is awarded in professional fields for study beyond the first-professional degree, for example, the Master of Laws (LL.M.) and Master of Science in various medical specializations.

Mathematics: A group of instructional programs that describes the science of logical symbolic language and its applications.

Metropolitan population: The population residing in metropolitan statistical areas (MSAs). (See Metropolitan Statistical Area.)

Metropolitan Statistical Area (MSA): A large population nucleus and the nearby communities that have a high degree of economic and social integration with that nucleus. Each MSA consists of one or more entire counties (or county equivalents) that meet specified standards pertaining to population, commuting ties, and metropolitan character. In New England, towns and cities, rather than counties, are the basic units. MSAs are designated by the Office of Management and Budget. An MSA includes a city and, generally, its entire urban area and the remainder of the county or counties in which the urban area is located. An MSA also includes such additional outlying counties that meet specified criteria relating to metropolitan character and level of commuting of workers into the central city or counties. Specified criteria governing the definition of MSAs recognized before 1980 are published in *Standard Metropolitan Statistical Areas: 1975,* issued by the Office of Management and Budget. New MSAs were designated when 1980 counts showed that they met one or both of the following criteria:

1) Included a city with a population of at least 50,000 within their corporate limits; or

2) Included a Census Bureau-defined urbanized area (which must have a population of at least 50,000) and a total MSA population of at least 100,000 (or, in New England, 75,000).

Minority: Any racial/ethnic group that is non-white is considered minority. (See Racial/ethnic group.)

Modal grade: The modal grade is the year of school in which the largest proportion of students of a given age are enrolled. Enrolled persons are classified according to their relative progress in school, that is, whether the grade or year in which they were enrolled was below, at, or above the modal (or typical) grade for persons of their age at the time of the survey.

A Nation at Risk: A report published by the U.S. Department of Education in 1983 highlighting deficiencies in knowledge of the nation's students and population as a whole in areas such as literacy, mathematics, geography, and basic science.

Natural sciences: A group of fields of study that includes the life sciences, physical sciences, and mathematics.

Nonmetropolitan residence group: The population residing outside metropolitan statistical areas. (See Metropolitan statistical area.)

Nonsupervisory instructional staff: Persons such as curriculum specialists, counselors, librarians, remedial specialists, and others possessing education certification but not responsible for day-to-day teaching of the same group of pupils.

Nursery school: (See Preprimary.)

Obligations: Amounts of orders placed, contracts awarded, services received, or similar legally binding commitments made by federal agencies during a given period that will require outlays during the same or some future period.

Orientation (private school): The group or groups, if any, with which a private elementary/secondary school is affiliated, or from which it derives subsidy or support. Such organizations include the following:

> **Catholic school:** A private school over which a Roman Catholic church group exercises some control or provides some form of subsidy. Catholic schools for the most part include those operated or supported by: a parish, a group of parishes, a diocese, or a Catholic religious order.

> **Other religious school:** A private school that is affiliated with an organized religion or denomination other than Roman Catholicism or that has a religious orientation other than Catholicism in its operation and curriculum.

> **Nonsectarian school:** A private school whose curriculum and operation are independent of religious orientation and influence in all but incidental ways.

Other technical/professional fields: A group of occupationally oriented fields, other than business, computer science, education, and engineering, which includes agriculture and agricultural sciences, architecture,

communications, communications technologies, home economics, law, library and archival sciences, military sciences, parks and recreation, protective services, and public affairs.

Outlays: The value of checks issued, interest accrued on the public debt, or other payments made, net of refunds and reimbursements.

Part-time enrollment: The number of students enrolled in higher education courses with a total credit load less than 75 percent of the normal full-time credit load.

Part-time worker: One who is employed for 1–34 hours a week, including paid leave for illness, vacation, and holidays. Hours may be reported either for a survey reference week, or for the previous calendar year, in which case they refer to the usual hours worked.

Part-year worker: One who was employed at least 1 week but fewer than 50 weeks during the previous calendar year, including paid leave for illness, vacation, or other reasons.

Percentile (score): A value on a scale of zero to 100 that indicates the percent of a distribution that is equal to or below it. A score in the 95th percentile is a score equal to or better than 95 percent of all other scores.

Personal income: Current income received by persons from all sources minus their personal contributions for social insurance. Classified as "persons" are individuals (including owners of unincorporated firms), nonprofit institutions serving individuals, private trust funds, and private non-insured welfare funds. Personal income includes transfers (payments not resulting from current production) from government and business such as social security benefits and military pensions, but excludes transfers among persons.

Physical sciences: Physical sciences are instructional programs that describe inanimate objects, processes, or matter, energy, and associated phenomena. Physical sciences include astronomy, astrophysics, atmospheric sciences, chemistry, geology, physics, planetary science, and science technologies.

Postsecondary education: The provision of formal instructional programs with a curriculum designed primarily for students who have completed the requirements for a high school diploma or equivalent. This includes programs of an academic, vocational, and continuing professional education purpose, and excludes vocational and adult basic education programs.

Poverty level: Poverty status is based on reports of family income on the March Current Population Survey. Families or individuals with gross incomes below the poverty threshold are classified as below the poverty level. Poverty thresholds in 1992 ranged from $7,143 for a person living alone to $28,745 for a family of four or more.

Prekindergarten: (See Preprimary.)

Preprimary: Elementary education programs for children who are too young for first grade. The year before first grade is called kindergarten; the year(s) before kindergarten is called preschool, nursery school, or prekindergarten. Not included in prekindergarten is essentially custodial care provided in private homes. Prekindergarten programs may be provided in regular elementary schools (with kindergarten, first-grade and higher grade programs) or in preschools (with only prekindergarten programs.)

Private school or institution: A school or institution that is controlled by an individual or agency other than a state, a subdivision of a state, or the federal government, which is usually not supported primarily by public funds, and is not operated by publicly elected or appointed officials.

Proprietary institution: An educational institution that is under private control but whose profits derive from revenues subject to taxation.

Purchasing power parity: A method of converting other countries' expenditures to U.S. dollars in order to compare expenditure rates. Purchasing power parity indices are calculated by comparing the cost of a fixed-market basket of goods in each country.

Racial/ethnic group: Classification indicating general racial or ethnic heritage based on self-identification, as in data collected by the Bureau of the Census, or on observer identification, as in data collected by the Office for Civil Rights. These categories are in accordance with the Office of Management and Budget standard classification scheme presented below:

American Indian/ Alaskan Native: A person having origins in any of the original peoples of North America and maintaining cultural identification through tribal affiliation or community recognition.

Asian/ Pacific Islander: A person having origins in any of the original peoples of the Far East, Southeast Asia, the Indian subcontinent, or the Pacific Islands. This area includes, for example, China, India, Japan, Korea, the Philippine Islands, and Samoa.

Black: A person having origins in any of the black racial groups in Africa. Normally excludes persons of Hispanic origin except for tabulations produced by the Bureau of the Census, which are noted accordingly.

Hispanic: A person of Mexican, Puerto Rican, Cuban, Central or South American, or other Spanish culture or origin, regardless of race.

White: A person having origins in any of the original peoples of Europe, North Africa, or the Middle East. Normally excludes persons of Hispanic origin except for tabulations produced by the Bureau of the Census, which are noted accordingly.

Reentrants: Teachers who left the school system for a period of time, and have now returned to classroom teaching.

Remedial education: Instruction for a student lacking the reading, writing, or mathematics skills necessary to perform college-level work at the level required by the attended institution.

Revenues: All funds received from external sources, net of refunds, and correcting transactions. Non-cash transactions such as receipt of services, commodities, or other receipts "in kind" are excluded as are funds received from the issuance of debt, liquidation of investments, and non-routine sale of property.

Auxiliary enterprises: This category includes those essentially self-supporting operations that exist to furnish a service to students, faculty, or staff, and that charge a fee that is directly related to, although not necessarily equal to, the cost of the service. Examples are residence halls, food services, college stores, and intercollegiate athletics.

Current-fund revenues (higher education): Money received during the current fiscal year from revenue that can be used to pay obligations currently due, and surpluses reappropriated for the current fiscal year.

Salary: The total amount regularly paid or stipulated to be paid to an individual, before deductions, for personal services rendered while on the payroll of a business or organization.

Salary workers: Any person who worked one or more days during the previous year and was paid on the basis of a yearly salary is considered a salary worker.

Scholarships and fellowships: (See Expenditures.)

Scholastic Assessment Test (SAT): An examination administered by the Educational Testing Service and used to predict the facility with which an individual will progress in learning college-level academic subjects.

School climate: The social system and culture of the school, including the organizational structure of the school and values and expectations within it.

School district: An education agency at the local level that exists primarily to operate public schools or to contract for public school services. Synonyms are "local basic administrative unit" and "local education agency."

School year: The 12-month period of time denoting the beginning and ending dates for school accounting purposes, usually from July 1 through June 30.

Science: The body of related courses concerned with knowledge of the physical and biological world and with the processes of discovering and validating this knowledge.

Secondary school: A school that has any span of grades beginning with the next grade following an elementary or middle-school (usually grade 7, 8, or 9) and ending with or below grade 12. Both junior high schools and senior high schools are included.

Social and behavioral sciences: A group of scientific fields of study that includes anthropology, archeology, criminology, demography, economics, geography, history, international relations, psychology, sociology, and urban studies.

Social studies: A group of instructional programs that describes the substantive portions of behavior, past and present activities, interactions, and organizations of people associated together for religious, benevolent, cultural, scientific, political, patriotic, or other purposes.

Socioeconomic status (SES): The SES quartile variable used for both High School and Beyond and the National Education Longitudinal Study of 1988 was built using parental education level, parental occupation, family income, and household items. Students were placed in quartiles based on their standardized composite score. By definition, one quarter of each cohort will reside in the bottom SES quartile, even if education levels, income, and the number of persons in more prestigious occupations increase. The terms high, middle, and low SES refer to the upper, middle two, and lower quartiles of the weighted SES composite index distribution.

Staff assignments, elementary and secondary school:

District administrative support staff: Personnel who are assigned to the staffs of the district administrators. They may be clerks, computer programmers, and others concerned with the functioning of the entire district.

District administrators: The chief executive officers of education agencies (such as superintendents and deputies) and all others with district-wide responsibility. Such positions may be business managers, administrative assistants, coordinators, and the like.

Guidance counselors: Professional staff whose activities involve counseling students and parents, consulting with other staff members on learning problems, evaluating the abilities of students, assisting students in personal and social development, providing referral assistance, and working with other staff members in planning and conducting guidance programs for students.

Instructional (teacher) aides: Those staff members assigned to assist a teacher with routine activities associated with teaching (i.e., those activities requiring minor decisions regarding students, such as monitoring, conducting rote exercises, operating equipment, and clerking). Volunteer aides are not included in this category.

Librarians: Staff members assigned to perform professional library service activities such as selecting, acquiring, preparing, cataloging, and circulating books and other printed materials; planning the use of the library by students, teachers, and other members of the instructional staff; and guiding individuals in their use of library books and materials that are maintained separately or as part of an instructional materials center.

Other support services staff: All staff not reported in other categories. This group includes media personnel, social workers, data processors, health maintenance workers, bus drivers, security, cafeteria workers, and other staff.

School administrators: Those staff members whose activities are concerned with directing and managing the operation of a particular school. They may be principals or assistant principals, including those who coordinate school instructional activities with those of the local education agency (LEA) and other appropriate units.

Stopout: (See Dropout.)

Tax expenditures: Losses of tax revenue attributable to provisions of the federal income tax laws that allow a special exclusion, exemption, or deduction from gross income or provide a special credit, preferential rate of tax, or a deferral of tax liability affecting individual or corporate income tax liabilities.

Technical/professional fields: A group of occupationally oriented fields of study, other than engineering and computer science, that includes agriculture and agricultural sciences, architecture, business and management, communications, education, health sciences, home economics, law, library and archival sciences, military sciences, parks and recreation, protective services, and public affairs.

Total expenditure per pupil in average daily attendance: Includes all expenditures allocable to per pupil costs divided by average daily attendance. These allocable expenditures include current expenditures for regular school programs, interest on school debt, and capital outlay. Beginning in 1980–81, expenditures for state administration are excluded and expenditures for other programs (summer schools, community colleges, and private schools) are included.

Tuition and fees: A payment or charge for instruction or compensation for services, privileges, or the use of equipment, books, or other goods.

Type of higher education institutions:

4-year institution: An institution legally authorized to offer and offering at least a 4-year program of college-level studies wholly or principally creditable toward a baccalaureate degree. In some tables a further division between universities and other 4-year institutions is made. A "university" is a postsecondary institution that typically comprises one or more graduate professional schools. (See also University.)

2-year institution: An institution legally authorized to offer and offering at least a 2-year program of college-level studies that terminates in an associate's degree or is principally creditable toward a baccalaureate degree.

Undergraduate students: Students registered at an institution of higher education in a program leading to a baccalaureate degree or other formal award below the baccalaureate such as an associate's degree.

Unemployed: Civilians who had no employment but were available for work and 1) had engaged in any specific job-seeking activity within the past 4 weeks, 2) were waiting to be called back to a job from which they had been laid off, or 3) were waiting to report to a new wage or salary job within 30 days.

University: An institution of higher education that consists of a liberal arts college, a diverse graduate program, and usually two or more professional schools or faculties, and is empowered to confer degrees in various fields of study.

Urbanicity:

1) In the Schools and Staffing Survey, school location is categorized based on the classification in both the Common Core of Data (CCD) and the Quality Education data (QED), as drawn from U.S. Census data and definition. The results are summarized in three variables:

> *Central city:* central city of an MSA (Metropolitan Statistical Area).
> *Urban fringe/large town:* area surrounding a central city but within a county constituting an MSA.
> *Rural/small town:* outside an MSA.

2) In the High School and Beyond Survey, urbanicity is classified based on the Curriculum Information Center code as follows:

> *Urban:* within a central city of an MSA.
> *Suburban:* within an MSA but outside the central city area.
> *Rural:* outside a designated MSA.

Vocational education: Organized educational programs, services, and activities that are directly related to the preparation of individuals for paid or unpaid employment, or for additional preparation for a career, requiring other than a baccalaureate or advanced degree.

Work-study: A generic term for programs designed to provide part-time employment as a source of funds to pay for postsecondary education as well as a federal program that is administered through postsecondary institutions.

Year-round worker: One who was employed at least 50 weeks during the previous calendar year, including paid leave for illness, vacation or other reasons.

SOURCES:

Handicapped Children, 34 Code of Federal Regulations S300.5, 1986.

The McGraw-Hill Dictionary of Modern Economics, New York: McGraw-Hill, 1975.

National Education Association, *Estimates of School Statistics, 1984–85,* Washington, D.C., 1985.

Pearce, David W., *The Dictionary of Modern Economics,* Cambridge, Massachusetts: The MIT Press, 1981.

Shryock, H.S., and Siegel, J.S., *The Methods and Materials of Demography,* Washington, D.C.: U.S. Government Printing Office, 1975.

U.S. Department of Commerce, Bureau of the Census, *Current Population Reports,* Series P-20 "School Enrollment-Social and Economic Characteristics of Students: October 1988 and 1987."

U.S. Department of Commerce, Bureau of the Census, *Current Population Reports,* Series P-60 "Poverty in the United States...various years."

U.S. Department of Education, National Center for Education Statistics, *A Classification of Instructional Programs,* Washington, D.C.: U.S. Government Printing Office, 1981.

U.S. Department of Education, National Center for Education Statistics, *Combined Glossary: Terms and Definitions From the Handbook of the State Educational Records and Reports Series,* Washington, D.C.: U.S. Government Printing Office, 1974.

U.S. Department of Education, National Center for Education Statistics, *High School and Beyond,* Base Year Student Survey, 1980.

U.S. Department of Education, Office for Civil Rights, Elementary and Secondary School Civil Rights Survey, *Individual School Report* (ED 102), 1984.

Index

Following each entry is the related indicator numbers (e.g., 29, 30), supplemental table numbers (e.g., 29-1), and, when not available in the current edition, the volume number, indicator number, and year in brackets when last published (e.g., 2:14 [1991]). Beginning in 1992, *The Condition of Education* was published as a single volume; references to the 1992 and following editions contain only the indicator number and the year in brackets (e.g., 26 [1992]). Indicators that are new to *The Condition of Education 1996* are referenced using an italicized typeface (e.g., *Community service performed by high school seniors*).

I

K

L

Selected Publications of the National Center for Education Statistics

Adult Literacy in America
GPO #065-000-00588-3, $12

Advanced Telecommunications in U.S. Public Schools, K-12
GPO #065-000-00743-6, $4.50

America's High School Sophomores: A 10-Year Comparison
GPO #065-000-00572-7, $7.50

America's Teachers: Profile of a Profession
GPO #065-000-00567-1, $13

Approaching Kindergarten: A Look at Preschoolers in the United States
GPO #065-000-00807-6, $3

Arts in Public Elementary and Secondary Schools
GPO #065-000-00811-4, $5.50

Characteristics of Students Who Borrow to Finance Their Postsecondary Education
GPO #065-000-00719-3, $7

The Condition of Education 1996
GPO #065-000-00871-8, $25

The Cost of Higher Education: Findings from the Condition of Education 1995
GPO #065–000–00861–1, $2

The Educational Progress of Hispanic Students: Findings from the Condition of Education 1995
GPO #065-000-00799-1, $2.25

The Educational Progress of Women: Findings from the Condition of Education 1995
GPO #065-000-00831-9, $1.25

The Educational Progress of Black Students: Findings from the Condition of Education 1994
GPO #065-000-00762-2, $2

High School Students Ten Years After "A Nation At Risk": Findings from the Condition of Education 1994
GPO #065-000-00761-4, $2

America's Teachers Ten Years After "A Nation At Risk": Findings from the Condition of Education 1994
GPO #065-000-00763-1, $2

Curricular Differentiation in Public High Schools
GPO #065-000-00723-1, $3.75

Digest of Education Statistics, 1995
GPO #065-000-00803-3, $35

Disparities in Public School Spending, 1989-90
GPO #065-000-00720-7, $13

Dropout Rates in the U.S., 1993
GPO #065-000-00684-7, $12

Education in the States and Nations
GPO #065-000-00621-9, $9

Historically Black Colleges and Universities, 1976-90
GPO #065-000-00511-5, $6.50

Literacy Behind Prison Walls
GPO #065-000-00716-9, $13

NAEP 1992 Trends in Academic Progress
GPO #065-000-00672-3, $41

1992 Mathematics Report Card for the Nation and the States
GPO #065-000-00559-0, $22

NAEP 1994 Reading Report Card for the Nation and the States
GPO #065-000-00845-9, $13

NAEP 1994 Geography: A First Look
GPO #065-000-00821-1, $5

NAEP 1994 History: A First Look
GPO #065-000-00824-6, $4.50

Profile of the American High School Sophomore, 1990
GPO #065-000-00726-6, $18

Understanding Racial-Ethnic Differences in Secondary School Science and Mathematics Achievement
GPO #065-000-00747-9, $6

Patterns of Teacher Compensation: Statistical Analysis
GPO #065-000-00835-1, $11

Private Schools in the U.S.: A Statistical Profile, 1990-91
GPO #0657000-00739-8, $14

Profile of Undergraduates in U.S. Postsecondary Education Institutions: 1992-93
GPO #065-000-00802-5, $12

Programs at Higher Education Institutions for Disadvantaged Precollege Students
GPO #065-000-00833-5, $6.50

Projections of Education Statistics to 2006
GPO #065-000-00853-0, $14

Public School Teacher Cost Differences Across the United States
GPO #065-000-00812-2, $9

Schools and Staffing Survey (SASS)—SASS by State
GPO #065-000-00655-3, $11

Undergraduates Who Work While Enrolled in Postsecondary Education: 1989-90
GPO #065-000-00678-2, $6

Vocational Education in the United States: The Early 1990's
GPO #065-000-00820-3, $21

Youth Indicators: 1993
GPO #065-000-00611-1, $11

—Free from OERI—

"At-Risk" Eighth-Graders Four Years Later
NCES #95-736

Changes in Math Proficiency Between 8th and 10th Grades
NCES #93-455

How Much Time Do Public and Private School Teachers Spend in Their Work?
NCES #94-709

Programs and Plans of the National Center for Education Statistics
NCES #95-133

Student Strategies To Avoid Harm at School
NCES #95-203

Student Victimization at School
NCES #95-204

Ordering Information

Additional copies of this publication, *The Condition of Education,* or of the other publications listed on the preceding page, are available for sale from the Government Printing Office. Please use the order form provided below.

Most NCES reports also are available via the Internet at gopher.ed.gov:10000 or http://www.ed.gov/NCES/

Single copies of OERI publications also are available by writing or calling U.S. Department of Education, Office of Educational Research and Improvement, National Library of Education, 555 New Jersey Avenue NW, Washington, D.C. 20208–5721 or 1–800–424–1616.

U.S. Department of Education
Online Library

Public Access via Internet
through the
National Library of Education's INet System

Individuals with access to the Internet can tap a rich collection of education related information at the U.S. Department of Education (ED), including:

- General Information about the Department's Mission, Organization, Key Staff, and Programs
- Information about Key Departmental Initiatives, such as GOALS 2000, Technology, Family Involvement, School-to-Work Programs, and Elementary and Secondary Schoolwide Projects
- Full-text Publications for Teachers, Parents, and Researchers
- Statistical Tables, Charts, and Data Sets
- Research Findings and Syntheses
- Directories of Effective Programs and Exemplary Schools
- Directories of Information Centers and Sources of Assistance
- Student Financial Aid Information
- Press Releases
- Status of Legislation and Budget
- Selected Speeches and Testimony by the Secretary of Education
- Grant Announcements and Applications
- Event Calendars
- Announcements of New Publications and Data Sets
- Searchable ED Staff Directory
- Links to Public Internet Resources at ERIC Clearinghouses, Regional Laboratories, R&D Centers, and other ED-Funded Institutions
- Links to other Education-Related Internet Resources

The Department's Internet Online Library is maintained by the National Library of Education (NLE) in the Office of Educational Research and Improvement (OERI) on its Institutional Communications Network (INet).

Latest Developments

The GOALS 2000 legislation reauthorized OERI and created the National Library of Education (NLE), which is responsible for assembling and providing access to a comprehensive collection of education information, as well as promoting resource sharing and cooperation among libraries and other providers of education information. INet and ERIC are core components of a distributed electronic repository which NLE plans to develop in close collaboration with the National Education Dissemination System (NEDS), which also was established in OERI's reauthorization.

Latest Developments (continued)

In response to customer demand we are making much more information available in hypertext markup language (HTML) format on our World Wide Web server. In September we unveiled a new, completely redesigned WWW home page which was very well-received. *Government Executive* (11/95) called it "among the classiest--and most useful--of all federal sites." Point Communications rates us among the top 5% of Web sites. In October we logged more than 1.3 million accesses from 75 countries.

Access via Internet

Although WWW is the access method of choice for 75% of our customers, we are committed to providing access to as much of our information as possible through Gopher, FTP, and E-Mail for those users who still depend on those methods. We are committed to providing text-only equivalents to all graphical features to accommodate visually impaired users.

Our **WWW Server** can be accessed at URL (uniform resource locator):
> **http://www.ed.gov/**

The **Gopher Server's** address is:
> **gopher.ed.gov**

> or select **North America-->USA-->General-->U.S. Department of Education** from the All/Other Gophers menu on your system

FTP users can access the information by ftping to:

> **ftp.ed.gov** (log on anonymous)

E-mail users can get our catalog and instructions on the usafe of our Mail server by sending e-mail to:
> **almanac@inet.ed.gov**
> in the body of the message type **send catalog**
> (avoid the use of signature blocks)

Please note that no public telnet access is available. You must either have an appropriate WWW, Gopher, or FTP client at your site or be able to telnet to a public access client elsewhere.

Questions and Comments

If you have any suggestions or questions about the contents of the WWW, Gopher, FTP, and Mail servers, please use one of the following addresses:

E-mail:	**inetmgr@inet.ed.gov**	Snail Mail:	**INet Project Manager**
	gopheradm@inet.ed.gov		**National Library of Education**
	webmaster@inet.ed.gov		**U.S. Department of Education/OERI**
Telephone:	**(202) 219-2266**		**555 New Jersey Ave., N.W., Rm. 214**
Fax:	**(202) 219-1817**		**Washington, D.C. 20208-5725**

ISBN 0-16-048679-3

90000

☆U.S. GOVERNMENT PRINTING OFFICE: 1996— 411-459